THE
MOVIE
TRAVELLER

A Film Fan's
Travel Guide to
the UK and Ireland

Allan Foster

Polygon

© Allan Foster, 2000

Polygon
An imprint of Edinburgh University Press Ltd
22 George Square, Edinburgh

Typeset in Gill Sans and Garamond
by the author, and printed and bound in
Great Britain by The Bath Press

A CIP Record for this book is available from
the British Library

ISBN 0 7486 6249 9 (paperback)

Picture Credits

The illustrations in this book consist mostly
of photographs taken by myself and stills
issued for publicity purposes by the
following organisations: The Tony Hillman
Collection, British Film Institute (Stills, Posters
and Designs), Scottish Film & Television
Archive, Imperial War Museum Film & Video
Archive, East Anglian Film Archive, Graphic
Photo Union, Dorking Museum, Dudley
Libraries, The Leys School, Elmbridge
Museum, The Nottingham Post, The Sutcliffe
Gallery, James Gillespie's School, Bluebell
RPS Archives, Glasgow City Council, East
Riding of Yorkshire Council, Anthony
MacMillan Photography, The Belfast
Telegraph and John Donat Photography. Film
companies are are acknowledged in the
photo captions. Although every effort has
been made to trace all other present
copyright owners, apologies are offered for
any unintentional omissions or neglect; we
will be happy to insert appropriate
acknowledgement to companies or
individuals in subsequent editions of the
book.

Maps by Crispin Sage
Icon design by Jack Foster

CONTENTS

Acknowledgements *VII*
Introduction *VIII*
Key to Symbols
& Abbreviations *IX*

Gazetteer of Counties
& Unitary Authorities:

ENGLAND
Barnsley 10
Bath & NE Somerset 11
Birmingham 12
Bolton 12
Bournemouth 14
Bradford 15
Brighton & Hove 22
Bristol 25
Buckinghamshire 29
Calderdale 37
Cambridgeshire 38
Cheshire 41
Cornwall 41
Cumbria 45
Darlington 51
Derby 51
Derbyshire 52
Devon 54
Dorset 60
Dudley 64
Durham 67
East Sussex 68
East Yorkshire 72
Essex 72
Gloucestershire 73
Hampshire 75
Herefordshire 79
Hertfordshire 79
Isle of Wight 82
Kent 83
Kingston-upon-Hull 90
Kingston-upon-Thames 91
Kirklees 92
Knowsley 93
Lancashire 94
Leeds 97

Leicestershire 99
Lincolnshire 100
Liverpool 102
Manchester 103
Newcastle-upon-Tyne 105
Norfolk 106
North Somerset 108
North Tyneside 108
North Yorkshire 108
Northumberland 113
Nottingham 115
Nottinghamshire 116
Oxfordshire 116
Peterborough 120
Poole 121
Portsmouth 121
Reading 122
Rochdale 122
Salford 123
Sandwell 124
Sefton 125
Sheffield 126
Somerset 128
Staffordshire 130
Stockport 131
Stockton-on-Tees 131
Suffolk 132
Surrey 133
Swindon 138
Trafford 138
Warrington 139
Warwickshire 140
West Sussex 140
Wigan 142
Wiltshire 143
Windsor & Maidenhead 145
Wirral 146
Wokingham 148
Worcestershire 149
York 149

LONDON
Barking & Dagenham 150
Barnet 150
Bexley 151

Brent 152
Camden 153
Croydon 157
Ealing 158
Enfield 159
Greenwich 160
Hackney 162
Hammersmith & Fulham 163
Haringey 163
Hillingdon 164
Hounslow 165
Islington 166
Kensington & Chelsea 167
Lambeth 171
Merton 182
Newham 183
Redbridge 184
Richmond-upon-Thames 185
Southwark 187
Tower Hamlets 190
Waltham Forest 191
Wandsworth 192
Westminster 193

SCOTLAND
Aberdeenshire 202
Angus 205
Argyll & Bute 206
Borders 210
Dumfries & Galloway 212
Dundee 216
East Dunbartonshire 216
Edinburgh 217
Falkirk 226
Fife 227
Glasgow 229
Highland 232
North Lanarkshire 236
Perth & Kinross 237
Renfrewshire 239
Shetland 242
Stirling 243
West Dunbartonshire 245
West Lothian 245
Western Isles 247

WALES
Blaenau Gwent 248
Bridgend 248
Carmarthenshire 249
Ceredigion 249
Flintshire 250
Gwynedd 250
Neath Port Talbot 253
Newport 254
Pembrokeshire 255
Powys 255
Rhondda Cynon Taff 257

NORTHERN IRELAND
Antrim 258
Ards 259
Ballymena 260
Belfast 260
County Down 262

REPUBLIC OF IRELAND
Clare 264
Cork 265
Dublin 265
Galway 276
Kerry 277
Limerick 278
Mayo 279
Meath 282
Roscommon 283
Sligo 284
Wexford 285
Wicklow 286

Appendix:
Film Festival Calendar 288
Sons of the Desert 290
Source Notes 292
Bibliography 292

Index 294

In memory of the seventy-one children
who lost their lives in the
Glen Cinema disaster,
Paisley, 31st December 1929.

Alexander Telfer	Caroline Brain	Francis Curran
Sarah McCafferty	John Bowes	Jane Stevenson
Elizabeth Hart	Robert McConnell	Thomas Howard
Thomas Renfrew	Margaret Morrow	George Scott
Agnes Coyle	Elizabeth Leonard	Mary Green
Robert Niven	William Fitch	Samuel McBlane
Thomas Kilkie	Janet Fitch	George Hammond
Helen Kilkie	James Gatherer	Margaret Gibson
Robert Wingate	Henry Green	Georgina Peacock
John Pinkerton	William Speirs	Daniel Corbett
William Pinkerton	William Rae	Helen McCran
Elizabeth Corrigan	George Elliott	Williamina McCran
Norman Gillies	George Kennedy	Julia Irvine
Thomas Perkins	John Goodwin	Robert McGirr
John Gielty	Leah Dixon	Annie Hamilton
James Gielty	Henry Elliott	William Irvine
Robert Craig	Robert Alexander	James Johnston
Denis McGarrity	Archibald Grogan	Robert Adams
Mary McWattie	John Bell	John Cairns
Jeanie McGrattan	Enso Fiori	Peter Houston
Hugh Blue	Margaret McEnhill	Thamas Jackson
Lily Buchanan	Edward McEnhill	William Black
Elizabeth Finlay	James McEnhill	David Boyd
Elizabeth Dempster	Mary Dolan	

ACKNOWLEDGEMENTS

(A good cast is worth repeating)

This book could not have been written without the help of those below. Thank you to you all.

I would like to extend special thanks to my wife, Chris, for her endless days of proofing and advice, to Thomas Hartman for sharing his computer hardware and expertise, and to Tony Hillman for allowing me to enter his Aladdin's Cave of movie memorabilia. Also Marjorie Blake and the staff of Kelso Library, the staff of Morpeth Library, Jack Foster, Philip Weller, Ian Rintoul, J.J. Tohill, Donald Sinden, Tony Merrick, Giles Semper and The Vauxhall Heritage Centre, Hazel and John Sant, The Sons of the Desert, Hamish MacInnes, South Bucks District Council, The Department of Tourism and Leisure Services at Scarborough Borough Council, Robin Crichton, R.J. Duckett, Ken Howe, Adam Unger, Ian Docherty and Radio Scotland, Kenny Eggo and The South West Scotland Screen Commission, Dawn and Richard Hooper, Anne Inglis, Irvine Taylor & Co., Margaret Gibson, Rosemary Moore, Arthur Jones, Jeremy Buck, Roger Smither and the Imperial War Museum, Linda Kirkwood, Tony Ashcroft, Margaret Marshall and Whitstable Tourist Information, Dave Miles, Pat McCann, Jim O'Neil, Ken Fosteskew, Ronald Grant, Sir Sydney Samuelson, Jim Bellamy, Rob Muskett, Helen Brown, Sam Whinfield, Linda Owen, Jo Taylor, Arthur Russel, Peter Menzies, Robert Menzies, John Land & Durham County Council Museums & Libraries, Gwen Bridges, Chloe Foster, Jenny Agutter, Kit Foster, Doug & Mal Smith, The Berwickshire News, Colin Saunders, Anthony Phillips, Peter Robinson, Stuart Reid and Scottish Roots, British Federation of Film Societies, Irish Film Institute, Irish Federation of Film Societies, British Film Institute, Chris Fletcher, William Stewart, Bruce Peter, Fred Clarke and The Arthur C. Clarke Foundation, Sam Wyper and Hollywood Nites, Lucy Foster, Dawn Dyer, Leslie Kipling and Huddersfield Library, Christopher Stacey, Dick Mungin, Jim Wilson, Noel Tom, Jason Patient, Trevor Jones, Jim Kneafsey, Peter Kendrick, Peter Delaney, Claire Baxter, The Basingstoke Gazette, Sybil Cavanagh, Dorothy Marlborough, Neil White, Bob Monks and The National Library of Ireland, Anna Cowan, Jonathan and Adam LeRoy, Doug Bannen, Robin Freeman, Bill Christie, Alice Blakeway, Ken Oultram, Geoff Houghton, Verna Hale-Gibbons, Bradford Film Office, Bradford Council's Countryside Service, Peter Weir, Brian Davenport, Eric Moir & JCB, Baden Gibson, Graham Mitchell and the Keighley & Worth Valley Railway Preservation Society, Tom Mason, Maureen Maciver, Jim Dempster, Ian Kerr, Mark Bauer, Neil Chue Hong, Scott Keir, Bob Beerman, London Film Commission, Elizabeth Hoy and the N.E. Education & Library Board, Francis Cassidy, Gail Ashurst, Michael Kirkland, John Donat, Laurence Payne, Noel Spence, Sarah Tobias, Maire McQueeney, Scottish Screen, Pat Berry, Eleanor Harris, John Stonebanks, Ian Platford, Paul Hill, Christine Boulby and The Northern Screen Commission, Janet McBain and The Scottish Film & Television Archive, Southern Screen Commission, Liverpool Film Office, South West Film Commission, The Cinema Theatre Association, The Mercia Cinema Society, Susie Cuthbertson and The Royal College of Surgeons of Edinburgh, and Jackie Jones and Ian Davidson of Edinburgh University Press.

INTRODUCTION

"Has anything escaped me?...
I trust there is nothing of consequence which I have overlooked?"
John H. Watson, M.D., *The Hound of the Baskervilles*

When I began researching the material for this book, I knew I was tackling a vast subject which could never be told in full. Cinema has spanned over a hundred years, and any attempt at a definitive guide to movie sites would have kept me occupied for the rest of my life. My approach, therefore, had to be selective, and this has resulted in a book which embraces a rich nucleus of the historical, the worthy, the cult, and the eccentric.

For an art form which has been a major influence on our culture for more than a century, film tourism remains surprisingly underdeveloped. While California has made an industry out of it, the rest of the world is still waking up to it. There are many reasons why film tourism is struggling to be born here; one them is class. The roots of this prejudice stem from the beginnings of cinema, which, because it developed from such working class arenas as the fairground and the music-hall, is still perceived by many to be low in prestige, beyond their perception of what constitutes an art form, and consequently not worthy of a place in the nation's heritage. Many establishments I contacted (mainly castles and stately homes) had difficulty grasping the concept, and where they did, it was not something with which they necessarily wished to be associated.

Also, few organisations I spoke to understood the power of film tourism, which, in a way, is closely related to movie merchandising - such as the soundtrack, the poster and the collectable - the revenue from which can be enormous. To date, film tourism has been mostly equated with movie locations, but film tourism need not be so limited, and may describe anything connected to cinema that is interesting to visit, whether it be the birthplace of Boris Karloff, the grave of Edgar Wallace who co-wrote *King Kong*, or the pub in which the young Charlie Chaplin last saw his father alive.

Having travelled the length and breadth of the country tracking down and photographing many of the sites featured in this book, I can highly recommend the experience. The pickings are rich, the destinations diverse and stimulating, and with over one hundred years' worth to choose from, it is a long adventurous journey - a film fan's odyssey - and you may never reach The End.

Allan Foster.

Any further information from readers on UK & Irish movie sites for future editions will be gratefully appreciated and acknowledged. I can be contacted via the publisher, or email: allanfoster@movietraveller.co.uk

KEY TO SYMBOLS
& ABBREVIATIONS

Birthplaces, Childhood & Former Homes - Where to locate the origins of those associated with moviemaking, including actors, directors, writers, film pioneers and historical characters portrayed on the screen.

Burial Places
Where to locate the last resting place of the above.

Movie Places
Where to unearth places with a movie connection - from the village where Walt Disney tried to trace his ancestors to the home of the original 'Mr. Chips'.

Movie Walks & Trails
Where to locate walks and trails incorporating a movie theme.

Movie Locations
Where to pinpoint locations - from the rural idyll of *The Quiet Man* to the urban nightmare of *A Clockwork Orange.*

Restaurants & Pubs
Where to locate premises with a movie connection or theme - from the Stan Laurel Inn to Peter Cushing's favourite tea-room.

Screens
Where to locate exceptional, unusual and historic venues.

Film Archives & Specialist Libraries
Where to locate organisations which provide an information service on film, video, sound material, photographs, books, posters, periodicals and scripts.

Museum Exhibits
Where to locate museums containing exhibits relating to the moving image.

Book & Memorabilia Stores
Where to locate books, magazines, posters, postcards, videos, stills, soundtracks, pressbooks and movie ephemera.

Credit Abbreviations
p (producer); d (director); w (writer); ph (cinematographer); ed (editor); m (music composer); prod d (production designer); art d (art director); fx (special effects); chor (choreographer); cos (costume designer); AA (Academy Award); AAN (Academy Award Nomination)

ENGLAND

Barnsley

BRASSED OFF
Grimethorpe

• 1996 103m c Comedy / Drama
Prominent Features / Film Four (UK)
• Pete Postlethwaite (Danny), Tara Fitzgerald
(Gloria), Ewan McGregor (Andy), Stephen
Tompkinson (Phil), Jim Carter (Harry), Philip
Jackson (Jim), Peter Martin (Ernie), Sue Johnston
(Vera), Mary Healey (Ida), Melanie Hill (Sandra)
• p, Steve Abbott; d & w, Mark Herman; ed,
Michael Ellis; ph, Andy Collind; prod d, Don
Taylor; m, The Grimethorpe Colliery Band

*Ewan McGregor and Tara Fitzgerald in **Brassed Off** (1996, Prominent Features/Film Four)*

Soon to be stripped of their livelihood
with the inevitable closure of their pit,
the only dignity and hope Grimley
miners have left is secured by their
brass band. Temporarily abandoning
their despair they channel their
energies into competing in the World
Brass Band Championships at London's
Albert Hall.

The closing credits of *Brassed Off*
begin with the statement, *"Since 1984
there have been 140 pit closures in
Great Britain at a cost of nearly a
quarter of a million jobs,"* which
resolutely reminds the audience that

although they have just watched an
excellent comedy drama, the film's
inspiration was born out of the savage
demise of Britain's coal-mining
communities.

The former pit village of Grimethorpe,
near Barnsley, and one-time home of
the Grimethorpe and Houghton Main
Colliery, took on the glamour of
tinseltown for six months in 1995 when
it became the production base for Mark
Herman's hit movie. The **Acorn
Community Resource & Business
Centre at 51 High Street** was the
production unit's H.Q. and a mock pit-

head exterior was built at the centre on
the **Cudworth View** side. This is also,
according to the Acorn Staff, where
Pete Postlethwaite learned to ride a
bicycle. Other locations included: the
old **Community Hall in the High
Street** which was used as the band's
practice hall; **The Grimethorpe Hotel**
(01226 716090), High Street (opp.
Acorn Centre) which doubled as the
Lantern Pub and digs of Tara
Fitzgerald, and **The Red Rum pub**
(01226 716334) which doubled as the
Collier's Arms and the site of the coach
pick-up point. The houses of the band
members were on Grimethorpe's **White**

City Estate and the chip shop, which never was a chip shop, is a derelict building on the High Street, near the Acorn Centre. At the time of writing the 'In Cod We Trust' sign is still in place. Scenes were also shot at the **Hatfield Colliery, Hatfield, near Doncaster**.

See also: *Little Voice*, Ewan McGregor

THE PUBLIC HALL DISASTER

In January, 1908, the World's Animated Picture Company had been presenting a 'cinematograph exhibition and variety entertainment' every night at Barnsley's Harvey Institute in **Eldon Street**. On the afternoon of Saturday, January 11th, they gave a special children's matinee performance when over a thousand children attended and the prices of admission were reduced to threepence, twopence and a penny. Those seeking admission to the penny gallery reached it by a separate stone staircase entrance in **Porter's Yard**. The gallery was soon filled and those still pouring up the stairs were told that if they went round to the main entrance they would be allowed to enter the stalls for the same charge. It was this simple redirection which led to tragedy. When the pressure of the children forcing their way back down the stairs met those coming up, children stumbled and fell, and a pile-up of bodies occurred on a small landing near the bottom of the stairs, which resulted in sixteen of the children being suffocated or trampled to death.

The Barnsley Chronicle reported the heartrending scenes: *"...Those who first went to the help of the young people at the foot of the staircase encountered a scene of inexpressible confusion and terror, which they could not speak of afterwards without deep emotion. A struggling, shrieking mass of little ones, piled one on top of the other, met their gaze. Some had just their heads peeping out at the bottom of the heap; some were merely showing hands, which clutched at the clothes of other children as they vainly tried to pull themselves free; some had only their legs free. Children on the stairs were still forcing their way down. Some were treading over the pile of agonised and dying children; some were falling into it, to be themselves pressed down by other unfortunates coming behind. It was a spectacle to almost paralyse the strongest, and the frantic appeals of the little ones, to 'Pull me out', were most heartrending. For the moment the rescuers hardly knew what to do. They saw those at the bottom of the heap were in the greatest danger, and began trying to get them out. But the weight above them was too great for that to be possible. Then, grasping the situation, they tried to stop the children from coming down the stairs. But their shouts could hardly be heard above the terrified screams of the children, and one of them had to force a way round the bend at the foot of the stairs and compel the children to keep back. He eventually succeeded... Telephone messages had been sent for medical and police assistance, and many helpers were quickly on the spot, tenderly lifting out the dead and injured into the yard... A number of lifeless bodies were gently laid aside upon a bed of straw... When the landing had been cleared it was found that fourteen were dead. Two others died on their way to hospital, making sixteen in all... Of the sixteen dead only one or two were in the least disfigured by cuts and abrasions, and their faces wore a peaceful expression..."*

Panic was averted in the main auditorium by the immediate screening of the first film, leaving the children unaware of the chaos on the gallery staircase. As in the similar Glen Cinema disaster in Paisley in 1929, better staffing and crowd control could have averted the tragedy.

After some design modifications the Public Hall continued as a cinema venue until 1940. In 1962, after major restoration work, it was renamed **Barnsley Civic Hall**, and in 1976 the Civic Hall auditorium was transformed into the **Civic Theatre**.

See also: Glen Cinema Disaster, Scala Picture House Tragedy

Bath & NE Somerset

THE REMAINS OF THE DAY
Dyrham

• 1993 Drama / Historical / Romance Merchant Ivory / Columbia (US)
• Anthony Hopkins (Stevens), Emma Thompson (Miss Kenton), James Fox (Lord Darlington), Christopher Reeve (Lewis)
• p, Mike Nichols, John Calley, Ismail Merchant; d, James Ivory; w, Ruth Prawer Jhabvala (from the novel by Kazuo Ishiguro)

"I can't say it's simple now, but it's taken years to distil my work to a more economic form. I suppose I'm pretty adept now at playing these rather still parts."
Anthony Hopkins

Anthony Hopkins and Emma Thompson in **The Remains of the Day** *(1993, Columbia)*

The film was adapted for the screen from Kazuo Ishiguro's Booker Prize-winning novel about the relationship between a dutiful butler and an efficacious housekeeper. Stevens' ingrained loyalty to his employer, Lord Darlington, overides his ardour for the housekeeper and he is unable to rise above his English reserve and sense of duty.

Dyrham Park, the former home of Lord Blathwayt, was used for the exterior of Darlington Hall, the seat of Stevens' Nazi sympathiser employer,

Lord Darlington, portrayed by James Fox. Other interior locations included **Corsham Court, near Chippenham, Wiltshire; Powderham Castle, near Exeter; Badminton House, near Thornbury, Gloucestershire** and various locations around **Weston-super-Mare**, including **The Highbury Hotel, Atlantic Road**, which doubled as Miss Kenton's guest house, the **Winter Gardens Pavilion** where they had tea, and the **Grand Pier** where they said their farewells.

See also: Anthony Hopkins

Further information: Dyrham Park is a National Trust property with a 265 acre deer park and is four miles north of Bath on the A46. Open April to October. Tel: 01225 891364.

Birmingham

BIRTHPLACE OF SAX ROHMER (1883-1959)
Birmingham

The Face of Fu Manchu (1965, Anglo-Amalgamated)

Arthur Henry Ward, better known as Sax Rohmer the author of the Fu Manchu mystery stories, was born at **28 Rann Street, Ladywood**, Birmingham on 15 February 1883, the only child of Irish immigrants, William Ward, an office clerk, and Margaret Furey. His mother, an alcoholic, claimed descent from Patrick Sarsfield, a 17th century Irish general, and in 1901 her son adopted this as his new middle name, christening himself Arthur Sarsfield

Ward. He suffered badly from somnambulism and on one occasion tried to strangle his father to death in his sleep. His father, an ex-amateur boxer, fortunately survived the experience. He more or less had the freedom to do as he pleased as a child and was nine years old before he attended school where he never excelled. During his last year at school in 1901 his mother died of a combination of alcoholism and tuberculosis.

On leaving school he became a bank clerk in Threadneedle Street, but was forced to leave after hypnotising a member of staff. At this time he lived with his father in lodgings in **Stockwell Road** and it was here he began writing and sending short stories to popular magazines. His efforts were unsuccessful and he covered an entire wall with his rejection slips. He worked for a short spell as a reporter, but that too failed.

It was his interest in orientalism and Egyptology which inspired him to write his first successful short story, *The Leopard Couch*, published by *Chamber's Journal* in 1904, and in 1913, after many dangerous forays into London's Chinatown he created the sinister oriental villain, Fu Manchu, in *The Mystery of Fu Manchu*. This was the first book to be written under the exotic pen name, Sax Rohmer ('sax' means 'blade' in Saxon and 'rohmer' equals 'roamer'). He wrote many thrillers, but it will be the Fu Manchu series for which he will be best remembered. Translated into twenty-five languages, the series was first adapted for the cinema in the 1920s. Swedish actor Warner Oland portrayed him in *The Mysterious Fu Manchu* (1929), Boris Karloff in *Mask of Fu Manchu* (1932), Henry Brandon in *Drums of Fu Manchu* (1941), Manuel Requena in *The Other Fu Manchu* (1945), Christopher Lee portrayed him five times, beginning with *The Face of Fu Manchu* (1965) and Peter Sellers in *The Fiendish Plot of Dr Fu Manchu* (1980).

As well as writing the Fu Manchu series over a period of forty years, Sax Rohmer wrote forty-one novels, eleven collections of short stories, two non-fiction books and dozens of short stories for magazines and newspapers. In 1905 he met Rose Elizabeth Knox whom he later married; they had no children. Rohmer died of a combination of pneumonia, arteriosclerosis and haemorrhaging at University College Hospital, London, in 1959.

See also: Fu Manchu, Christopher Lee, Boris Karloff

Bolton

BIRTHPLACE OF ROBERT SHAW (1927-78)
Westhoughton

Robert Shaw's father was a depressive alcoholic doctor who committed suicide by poisoning himself in his surgery when his son Robert was only eleven years old. It was an incident that would haunt Shaw for the rest of his life and may be seen as being partly responsible for his demanding personality, and, in later life, his chronic alcoholism.

He was born on 9 August 1927 at **51 King Street, Westhoughton,** near his father's surgery, the first child of Thomas Shaw M.D. and Doreen Avery. His parents originated from Cornwall and after his father's death in 1938 his mother returned there with her five children. Robert attended Truro School and in 1946 was accepted for RADA. His first professional appearance was in a performance of *Macbeth*, directed by Anthony Quayle. He made his film debut as Flight Sgt. Pulford in *The Dambusters* (1954) for which he was paid £500 for four weeks' work. Other roles have included those of the blond psychopath in *From Russia With Love* (1963), the despotic Henry VIII in *A Man For All Seasons* (1966), the menacing gangster, Doyle Lonnegan, in *The Sting* (1973) and Quint the shark specialist in *Jaws* (1975). Forced to live as a tax exile, he was married three times and had nine children. His drinking problems later led to his early death, aged fifty-one. A plaque commemorating his birthplace can be seen in **Westhoughton Town Hall.**

See also: *A Man For All Seasons, The Dambusters*

BIRTHPLACE OF LESLIE HALLIWELL (1929-89)
Great Lever

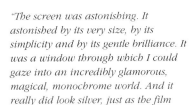

"The screen was astonishing. It astonished by its very size, by its simplicity and by its gentle brilliance. It was a window through which I could gaze into an incredibly glamorous, magical, monochrome world. And it really did look silver, just as the film magazines said."
Leslie Halliwell describing his first visit to The Queen's Cinema, Bolton.

Written with his trademark acidity and encyclopaedic mind, the cinema reference books of film historian and critic, Leslie Halliwell, have grown into a cinematic institution. He was born Robert James Leslie Halliwell on 23 February 1929, at **12 Parkfield Road, Great Lever**, Bolton, where his father worked as a cotton spinner. In 1934 the family moved to **166 Bradford Road.** Both his parents left school at the age of eleven to work in the mills, where his father remained until he was almost eighty years of age.

166 Bradford Road, childhood home of Leslie Halliwell

Leslie's curiosity about movies was first awakened by his elder sisters' gossip about their screen heart-throbs, but it was with his mother he was to experience the early joys of filmgoing: *"It all started at the Queen's, Bolton, when I saw my first film. I was about three or four, so it must have been about 1933. I remember to this day going down past Trinity Station in a tram. They had to make a right turn at the bottom of the hill and one always felt a bit alarmed. My mother always wanted to get off the tram in case it turned over when it rounded the corner. I remember we did get off on the day I went to the Queen's. The film I saw was Madame Butterfly with Sylvia Sidney and Cary Grant."*

The Tivoli Cinema in Derby Street was forbidden to young Leslie because the cotton spinners frequented it and left the seats sticky and smelly from their oiled clothing. At the age of nine he won a scholarship to Bolton School where he ran the school film society and at eighteen he left for Cambridge University. After graduating in 1952, then completing his national service in the Army, he began working as a journalist with 'Picturegoer' magazine. He joined the J. Arthur Rank Organisation where he met his wife, Ruth, with whom he had three children.

A prolific writer, his works include the play *Make Your Own Bed*, which was performed at Bolton's Hippodrome in the late fifties, and a novel called *Portion for Foxes*. In later years he worked with Granada Television where he commuted between Hollywood and London buying films for the independent television network.

In 1989 he died of stomach cancer. Afterwards his widow, Ruth said: *"The week before he died, Leslie touched his books and told me, 'I am leaving these behind anyway.'"*

BIRTHPLACE OF HYLDA BAKER (1909-86)
Farnworth

"No-one has ever dallied with my afflictions and I say that without fear of contraception."
Hylda Baker

Often described as 'Bolton's Marie Lloyd', diminutive comedienne Hylda Baker was born on 14 February 1905 at **23 Ashworth Street, Farnworth**, her grandmother's home near Bolton, but she spent most of her early years at her family's later home in **Plodder Lane**. The eldest of seven children, she followed her father, music-hall comedian Harold 'Chucky' Baker, on to the stage when she was only ten years old.

Best known for her stage routine with tall dumb Cynthia and her catchphrase, *"She knows, y'know'*, she became widely known in the early 1970s portraying pickle factory owner, Nellie Pledge, in the the TV sitcom *Nearest and Dearest*. Her feature film appearances were rare but memorable performances, such as those of Aunt Ada in *Saturday Night and Sunday Morning* (1960) and Mrs Sowerberry in *Oliver* (1968).

She led a flamboyant lifestyle with pet monkeys and American limousines, while at her home in Cleveleys, her private flag, emblazoned with *She Knows, Y'know* flew from a tall flagstaff when she was in residence. Suffering from senility after a life-long fear of mental illness she spent her final years in a home run by the Entertainment Artists Benevolent Fund. She died on May Day 1986 in hospital in Surrey. Her ashes were taken back to Bolton and scattered on her parents' grave. Comedian Roy Hudd recalls: *"As far as I can remember, there were only about seven of us at her funeral, which was so sad considering the great star she had been."*

See also: *Saturday Night and Sunday Morning*

Bournemouth

GRAVE OF MARY SHELLEY (1797-1851)

Bournemouth

"It was the secrets of heaven and earth that I desired to learn."
Victor Frankenstein

Mary Shelley the poet, and creator of cinema's most enduring mad scientist, *Victor Frankenstein*, is buried in the family tomb in **St Peter's Churchyard, Hinton Road**, together with a silver casket containing the heart of her husband, Percy Bysshe Shelley, who died in a drowning accident in Italy, aged thirty.

*Christopher Lee in **The Curse of Frankenstein** (1957, Warner/Hammer)*

Her achievements are often overshadowed by her husband Percy's reputation, but she was an extremely talented novelist in her own right and her gothic fantasy *Frankenstein* (1818) written when she was only eighteen years old - is a landmark in the history of literature and can claim to be the world's first science fiction novel.

The first film version was made by Thomas Edison's film company in 1910, but the definitive monster, who evoked both fear and compassion, was immortalised by Boris Karloff in Universal Studios' 1931 classic. The film was actually based on a play by Peggy Webling rather than on Mary Shelley's novel and it retains only the bare bones of the book.

Those who have portrayed Frankenstein's Monster over the years have included Lon Chaney, Jr. in *The Ghost of Frankenstein* (1942), Bela Lugosi in *Frankenstein Meets the Wolf Man* (1943), Christopher Lee in *The Curse of Frankenstein* (1957), Dave Prowse in *The Horror of Frankenstein* (1970) and Robert De Niro in *Mary Shelley's Frankenstein* (1994).

See also: Boris Karloff, James Whale, Peter Cushing, Christopher Lee, Hammer Studios

CHILDHOOD HOME OF TONY HANCOCK (1924-68)

Bournemouth

Although a success on radio and T.V., Tony Hancock's film career never really happened. Apart from a few lack-lustre

movies, he is probably best remembered for his portrayal of *The Punch and Judy Man* (1962). Born in Small Heath, Birmingham, his family moved to Bournemouth when he was six months old to the **Durlston Court Hotel, 47 Gervis Road** (plaque erected), where his father was a publican. His first engagement was at Bournemouth's **Sacred Heart Church hall, Richmond Hill**, entertaining troops. He gained popularity after appearing for two years in the radio series, *Educating Archie*, broadcasting his first *Hancock's Half Hour* in 1954 which transferred to television two years later and rocketed him to stardom. Other films included: *Orders are Orders* (1961), *The Rebel* (1961), *Those Magnificent Men in their Flying Machines* (1965) and *The Wrong Box* (1966).

The Punch and Judy Man (1962, Macconkey)

Discontented with his career and upset by his recent divorce, he was prone to bouts of depression and excessive drinking, ending his life with an overdose of sleeping pills in a Sydney flat in 1968.

See also: *The Punch and Judy Man*

CHILDHOOD HOME OF STEWART GRANGER (1913-93)

Bournemouth

James Lablanche Stewart was born on 6 May 1913 in a flat in the **Old**

Brompton Road, London, the second child of Frederica Lablanche and Major James Stewart. Educated at boarding schools, most of his boyhood was spent on the south coast where his family lived at **East Cliff Cottage in Grove Road**, Bournemouth.

He once recalled that Bournemouth was where he first fell in love at the age of fourteen: *"She was a professional dance hostess. I used to borrow a pound from my father and buy up all her dances. then I would sit and look at her but I never had the courage to ask her to dance."* He had ambitions to become a doctor, but was unable to attend university due to his father's financial situation. He left school at sixteen and a half and started work with the Bell Punch Company from which he was eventually sacked. After losing his virginity to a Parisian prostitute he registered with an agency as a film extra where he was classed as 'young upper-class playboy type'. He later joined the Webber Douglas Academy of Dramatic Art, reputedly because the female students vastly outnumbered the males.

He made his professional stage debut, aged twenty-two, with the Hull Repertory Theatre and later joined the prestigious Birmingham Repertory Theatre and the Old Vic. He changed his name to Stewart Granger to avoid confusion with Hollywood's Jimmy Stewart. In 1943 he rocketed to stardom in Gainsborough film studio's costume romp, *The Man In Grey*,

The Railway Children (1970, EMI) From the left: Iain Cuthbertson, Gary Warren, Jenny Agutter, Dinah Sheridan, Sally Thomsett

becoming one of British cinema's leading men of the forties, typecast as the romantic swashbuckler in films such as: *Fanny By Gaslight* (1943), *Madonna of the Seven Moons* (1946), *Caravan* (1946), *Blanche Fury* (1948) and *Saraband* (1948). He left for Hollywood in 1949 where he continued in romantic roles which included: *King Solomon's Mines* (1950), *The Prisoner of Zenda* (1952), *Scaramouche* (1952) and *Beau Brummel* (1954).

He appeared in television in the 1970s and 80s after his film career had waned, and died of cancer, aged eighty, at St. John's Hospital and Health Centre in Santa Monica. He was married to actress, Elspeth March, and later to actress Jean Simmons.

Bradford

THE RAILWAY CHILDREN WALK
Keighley & Worth Valley

• 1970 108m c Historical/Children's
EMI (UK)
• Dinah Sheridan (Mother), Bernard Cribbins (Perks), William Mervyn (Old Gentleman), Iain Cuthbertson (Father), Jenny Agutter (Bobbie), Sally Thomsett (Phyllis), Gary Warren (Peter). • p, Robert Lynn; d & w, Lionel Jeffries

(based on E. Nesbit's novel); ph, Arthur Ibbetson; ed, Teddy Darvas; m, Johnny Douglas.

"They were not railway children to begin with... They were just ordinary suburban children, and they lived with their father and mother in an ordinary red-bricked-fronted villa..."
Edith Nesbit's *The Railway Children*

Only the MGM masterpiece, *The Wizard of Oz*, prevents this film from attaining my personal accolade for the best children's film ever made. Set at the turn of the century the storyline centres on the false accusation for treason and the unjust imprisonment of a Foreign Office official. His family disgraced, they move from their refined metropolitan surroundings to a cottage on the Yorkshire moors, where the children discover a new world of exile, poverty and adventure.

Director, Lionel Jeffries, stumbled on the story by accident while returning from America. When his train was derailed in Chicago, all his books for the journey were lost, and desperate for reading matter he devoured his daughter's copy of *The Railway Chidren*, and fell in love with it. When he arrived in England he bought a six-month option on it for £300 and wrote the screenplay. MGM wouldn't touch it unless it was turned into a musical with Julie Andrews, but Bryan Forbes at

Bradford

Elstree decided to handle it, and persuaded Jeffries to direct it. Sally Thomsett was actually twenty one at the time of filming (four years older than Jenny Agutter) and portrayed a character meant to be eight, a fact the producers desperately tried to suppress. Gary Warren who portrayed Peter, now works as a furrier in Canada.

Filming took six weeks in the summer of 1970 on the Keighley & Worth Valley Railway which had then just recently been reopened in 1968. The K&WVR runs trains every weekend throughout the year as well as midweek during the summer, and is operated almost entirely by volunteer members.

The Railway Children Walk:
Length of walk: 6 miles (10km)
Time: Allow 3 hours

This waymarked route has been devised to enable the walker to visit various locations. Many are on private land; please help to respect the owner's privacy by keeping to the public rights of way from where all the points of interest can be seen and photographed. Being a circular walk there are several places from where the walk can start or finish.

From **1: Tourist Information Centre, the Butcher's Shop in the film**, walk down Main Street to see the shops where the children were seen collecting gifts for Perks birthday. 150 metres down on your right, Lodge Street can be found. The first house on the corner, number 2, was used as the **Ironmonger's / Cobbler's Shop** where the children were given a small hand shovel as a gift for Perks. Continue down Main Street until you come to the end of the shops on the left hand side. Here leave Main Street turning left down the narrow setted lane crossing over the main road. Continue down the setted lane, passing the school complex to take the next turning left along the short unmade road. Turn right at the end then bear left to a field gate to follow the surfaced footpath diagonally across the

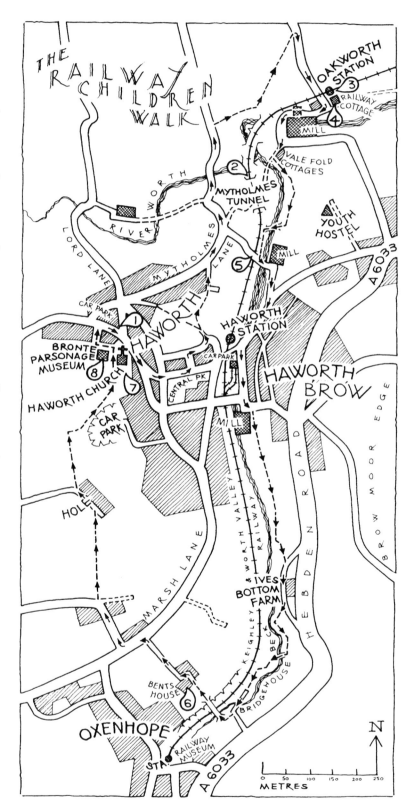

Shops on Haworth Main Street, **Church Street** *and* **Lodge Street***. Seen when the children are collecting birthday gifts for Perks.*

Oakworth Station *(The Railway Children's Station)*

Railway Cottage *(Mr Perks' home)*

Bents House *(The Three Chimneys).*

The Railway Children Engine, *still in use on the Keighley & Worth Valley Railway , steams out of Haworth Station*

fields and through a stone stile. Turn left along a short unmade road to join the main road, Mytholmes Lane. Turn right downhill for approximately half a mile (0.8km) to where Mytholmes Lane levels out and becomes Providence Lane. Continue on for a further 200 metres, passing a row of cottages on your left and the Hebble Garage on the right. Opposite the end of these cottages the route rejoins the footpath by turning right and ascending several stone steps. Walk along a short distance before stopping near the electricity pylon to look to your right to see **2: Mytholmes Railway Tunnel** where Jim the schoolboy injured his leg whilst running in a paper chase. Being only 82 metres long, the film makers had to build a scaffold and cover the other end of the tunnel with a tarpaulin to make the tunnel appear longer and much darker. The embankment on the left hand side of the tunnel mouth is where the landslide was filmed (best views from here are in winter when the trees have lost their foliage). Nearby on the railway line the girls used their red flannel petticoats as flags to warn the driver of the 11.29 train of the danger. Continue along the footpath as it bears left uphill to a kissing gate, go through the gate across the field to join Station Road, turn right down hill to **3: Oakworth Station**, the Railway Children's Station: Perks' station, Peter's coal mine, the presentation ceremony, the 'shabby Russian' and the homecoming of the children's father. Oakworth Station retained its original name for the film. The station, which has never had electricity and is still lit by gas, is kept as close as possible to its 1905-1914 condition by the K&WVR. A plaque was erected in 1996 commemorating the filming. Continue the walk by crossing over the level crossing, the first house on the left, **4: Railway Cottage**, was Mr. Perks' home. The stone-built extension next door is of recent origin and did not appear in the film. Follow the road passing under the mill building, taking care at the blind corner, continue along the road for 100 metres and turn right in front of **Vale Fold Cottages**, seen in

the film during the paper chase. The mill dam seen in front of these cottages has been drained and planted with trees. Just past these cottages look out for a stile on your left. Climb over the stile and follow the path over a second stile where the path runs next to Bridgehouse Beck, and parallel to the railway line. Continue along the path and look to the right after the footbridge to see the opposite end of Mytholmes Tunnel. Nearing the end of the path the road bridge in front of you is a concrete replacement of the **5: Metal bridge** seen at the end of the film under which on the embankment the cast were waving and where Roberta writes 'THE END' on a chalk board. At the end of the footpath turn left to follow the minor road (Ebor Lane), crossing the Mill Dam to go uphill to join the main Haworth road. Here turn right and walk down past the shops to Haworth Station.

From Haworth Station continue along Station Road passing the **Locomotive Depot** and car park. If the Railway Children Engine is not operating on the line it will probably be in the depot. 0-6-0 Pannier Tank Engine 5775 (formerly Great Western Railway), was painted in the fictitious orange livery and logo of the Great Northern & Southern Railway for the film, and has since been repainted BR dark green. Look carefully at the grab rails outside the cab where you can see the Railway Children orange exposed). Continue past the Fire Station, War Memorial and garage and turn left up Brow Road. After a short distance a footpath sign on the right directs you one and a half miles (2.4km) to Oxenhope. Follow this well trodden waymarked path across the fields, through farm yards, alongside Bridgehouse Beck and passing Oxenhope Water Treatment Works until you almost reach Oxenhope Railway Station.

Here the path divides. Our walk goes right, over a stone stile and across the railway line, bearing left uphill to another stile. Once over, a steep climb to the top of the fields brings you to

6: Bents House / the Three Chimneys, the Yorkshire home of the Railway Children. Much of the field in front of the house seen in the film covered in buttercups has been replaced by a much more formal garden. To the rear of the house can be seen the stone gap stile which Perks had difficulty negotiating whilst delivering to the Three Chimneys.

Do not go through this stile but continue up the track at the rear of Bents House onto a tarmac road, Marsh Lane, here turn left, cross over the road and turn right up Old Oxenhope Lane until you reach Old Oxenhope Farm. At the rear of the farm turn right and then left by the water trough and over a stile into the field, keeping the stone wall on your left, follow the footpath up the field. Keep straight on and the path will lead you to the Hamlet of Hole.

At Hole the path joins a track, follow this track uphill for a short distance looking out for the stile on the right (next to a street light). Go through into the field, then straight on until the path reaches the large house ahead. Here turn right down a doubled wall path, follow this path (grass at first then stone flagged), passing a car park and picnic area, through a metal kissing gate into **7: Haworth Churchyard**, seen when Peter runs to fetch Dr Forrester because his mother is unwell and also seen when Roberta fetches Dr Forrester to attend the 'shabby Russian'. Here take a left turn up three steps, in front of you can now be seen **8: Brontë Parsonage Museum, the Doctor's house** in the film.

Turning right at the top of the steps walk along the cobbled path through the church yard to a second metal gate. Turn right down Church Street, in front of you the shop at the top of the steps was the **Post Office and General Store** where the children were given a pram amongst other gifts for Mr. Perks.

Continue down Church Street passing the Kings Arms pub to emerge into

The Railway Children Engine: 0-6-0 Pannier Tank Engine 5775

Haworth Main Street by the Tourist Information Centre where the walk started.

See also: Edith Nesbit

Further information: Keighley & Worth Valley Railway Preservation Society, The Railway Station, Haworth, Keighley, West Yorkshire, BD22 8NJ. Tel: 01535 645214 / 24hr Information 01535 647777. Keighley is on the national rail network with direct trains to Carlisle, Lancaster, Leeds, Bradford and London Kings Cross. Through rail tickets to 'Oxenhope K&WVR' may be booked from any rail travel centre in the U.K. Haworth Tourist Information: 01535 642329.

I would like to thank Bradford Council's Countryside Service for help in compiling the above information.

BIRTHPLACE OF MICHAEL RENNIE (1909-71)
Bradford

Michael Rennie lived until the age of four at **Norman Bank, Idle Road**, before his family moved to Harrogate. After attending Oatlands Preparatory School, Harrogate and Leys College, Cambridge, he entered his father's business, W. M. Rennie and Co.,

worsted spinners, at Stanningley. After later working as a car salesman and steel rope manufacturer he decided to turn to the theatre, making his first stage appearance in *Pygmalion* in 1938 at Wakefield.

He entered films as an extra and one of his earliest appearances was a bit part in Hitchcock's *Secret Agent* in 1936. In WWII he joined the RAF and became a pilot-instructor. After the war he signed a contract with 20th Century Fox, and became an American citizen in 1960.

He made many films, including *The Wicked Lady* (1945), *King of The Khyber Rifles* (1953), *The Robe* (1953) and *The Lost World* (1960). He gained TV popularity for his portrayal of Harry Lime in the series *The Third Man*, but film fans will best remember him as the pacifist alien, Klaatu, with his robot

bodyguard, Gort (*"Klaatu barada nikto!"*), in *The Day the Earth Stood Still* (1951). He died in Harrogate while on a visit to his mother in 1971.

HOME & GRAVES OF EMILY BRONTË (1818-48) & CHARLOTTE BRONTË (1816-55)

Haworth

"Seated here, we were hidden from all the world, nothing appeared in view but miles and miles of moorland, a glorious sky and a brightening sun".
Emily Brontë

The Brontë Parsonage Museum

The Brontës were an outstanding literary family who arrived in Haworth in 1820. Their father, Reverend Patrick Brontë, was the new rector and with his wife brought their five daughters and one son to live at **Haworth Parsonage**. Maria and Elizabeth, the eldest girls, died in childhood shortly after the death of their mother. Charlotte, Emily, Anne and their brother Bramwell survived into adulthood where the surrounding Yorkshire moorlands inspired the three sisters to write some of the greatest novels in the English language.

Emily Brontë's memorable novel of metaphysical passion and obsessional love, *Wuthering Heights*, was published in 1847 to no great acclaim, a year before her death. The novel was first filmed in England in 1920 by A.V. Bramble, and other noteworthy versions were adapted by Luis Bunuel in 1953 and Robert Fuest in 1970, but it is William Wyler's 1939 production,

Laurence Olivier and Merle Oberon in
Wuthering Heights *(1939, Goldwyn)*

starring Merle Oberon and Laurence Olivier, which has evolved into a cinema classic.

It was filmed on a Hollywood set and in the Conejo hills north of Los Angeles where thousands of tumbleweeds were sprayed with purple sawdust to resemble the heather of the Yorkshire moors. A period mansion house was constructed, 1,000 real heather plants were used for close-up shots, and prop-man, Irving Sindler, ensured his immortality by inscribing a tombstone in the film *'I. Sindler. A Good Man.'* Charlotte's moving and mysterious love story *Jane Eyre* was published in the same year as *Wuthering Heights* and was an immediate best seller. It has been adapted for the screen many times, the most notable adaptation being Robert Stevenson's 1944 version with Joan Fontaine in the title role and Orson Welles as Rochester .

Bramwell, Emily and Anne all died of consumption and Charlotte, who was the eldest, died in the early stages of pregnancy, aged thirty-eight. With the exception of Anne, who is buried in Scarborough, they are all buried in the family tomb in **Haworth Church**.

See also: Laurence Olivier, Merle Oberon

Further information: The Brontë Parsonage Museum, Haworth, Keighley, BD22 8DR. Tel: 01535 642323.

NATIONAL MUSEUM OF PHOTOGRAPHY, FILM & TELEVISION

Bradford

Opened in 1983, the National Museum of Photography, Film and Television is the most visited British museum outside London averaging around 740,000 visitors per year. The museum is home to the first giant IMAX cinema in Britain. The national photographic collection is held by the Museum along with a substantial and important collection of artefacts relating to the history of cinema and television. In September 1998, the Museum closed its doors to embark upon a £15 million redevelopment project, and reopened in 1999 incorporating several new features and galleries which include: an upgraded IMAX cinema allowing both 3D and 2D films to be shown; the Digital Imaging Gallery: the first ever gallery dedicated to the new media; a major new exhibition space enabling the Museum to accommodate more and larger temporary exhibitions; increased education facilities, a larger lecture room and work rooms and improved dark room facilities; an updated news gallery; improved and refurbished TV galleries; an enlarged TV Heaven, allowing access to a library of TV classics; a major new research centre, offering improved access to those parts of the collection which are not on display, both on-line and direct; the Light and Magic gallery: a hands-on exploration of the principles behind image making for children of all ages; a new look and location for the Kodak Museum and a second cinema screen incorporating a multi-media theatre. In addition, facilities aimed at visitor comfort have been improved, with a new enlarged cafe and a more easily accessible shop, stocked with souvenirs, books and image making kits, as well as improved disabled access to all parts of the museum.

Further information: National Museum of Photography, Film and Television, Prince's View, Bradford. Tel: 01274 732277 / 727488

Bradford

PICTUREVILLE CINEMA
Bradford

Described by David Putnam as "the best cinema in Britain", Pictureville Cinema offers one of the best movie-going experiences . Opened in 1983, as part of the National Museum of Photography, Film and Television, Pictureville is home to the world's only publicly accessible Cinerama screen which opened in 1993.

The Cinerama format was created in the U.S.A. in the 1950s, and was a forerunner of the later giant cinema systems - such as IMAX which appeared twenty years later - in that it attempted to fill the field of vision of the audience and give as realistic an impression as possible of being involved in the action. The film is shot on one three lens camera, but is then exhibited through three projectors simultaneously to create a widescreen effect onto a curved screen.

There were a number of films made in this format, the most famous of which are *This is Cinerama*, which is shown on the first Saturday of each month at Pictureville, and *How the West Was Won*, which was pieced together from sections of film found in Germany and Belgium and exhibited at the 1996 Bradford Film Festival for the first time in decades. Due to its running costs (three projectionists rather than one for instance), Cinerama has not continued into the present day very widely.

Pictureville Cinema is also host to a continuous programme of events and special guest appearances, as well as being the host cinema to three film festivals: the Bradford Film Festival, the Bite the Mango Film Festival and the Bradford Animation Festival. Able to project everything from video, through 16mm, 35mm, 70mm up to Cinerama movies, Pictureville is a cinema-goers paradise, the luxury surroundings provide a comfortable experience, whilst the digital surround sound and up-to-the-minute projection equipment

provide the highest quality cinema experience for miles around.

See also: BFI London Imax

Further information: Pictureville Cinema, NMPFTV, Pictureville BD1 1NQ. Tel: 01274 732277.

BILLY LIAR
Bradford

• 1963 98m b/w Drama Vic Films Ltd. (UK)
• Tom Courtenay (Billy Fisher), Julie Christie (Liz), Wilfred Pickles (Geoffrey Fisher), Mona Washbourne (Alice fisher), Ethel Griffies (Florence), Finlay Currie (Duxbury), Rodney Bewes (Arthur Crabtree), Helen Fraser (Barbara), George Innes (Eric Stamp), Leonard Rossiter (Shadrack)
• p, Joseph Janni; d, John Schlesinger; w, Keith Waterhouse, Willis Hall (based on their play); ph, Denys Cooper; ed, Roger Cherrill; m, Richard Rodney Bennett; art d, Ray Simon

"... any healthy male who turns down an opportunity to run off to London with the young Julie Christie must be off his chump."
Ken Russell, 1993

Billy Fisher, like Walter Mitty before him, lives his life surrounded by unbelievable daydreams. A perpetual liar, he escapes his miserable home life and monotonous job as an undertaker's clerk, by retreating into a world of

Tom Courtenay in **Billy Liar** *(1963, Vic Films Ltd)*

make believe, dreaming of the day when he will leave his dreary northern town forever.

One of the key films of the sixties, John Schlesinger's urban comedy boosted the careers of Tom Courtenay and Julie Christie, and was later adapted for television and the stage. Filmed on location in the Bradford district including **Baildon** (on the hills overlooking Bradford and at **37 Hinchcliffe Avenue** - Billy's home), **Southgate, Victoria Hotel** (exteriors), **War Memorial, Victoria Square, Undercliffe Cemetery, Bolton Woods Quarries,** the **Mecca** on **Manningham Lane** and the **coffee bar** on **Great Horton Road.**

See also: Keith Waterhouse, Willis Hall, Finlay Currie, Portman & Pickles pub

QUEEN VICTORIA'S DIAMOND JUBILEE SCREENING
Bradford

Bradford cinema pioneer, Richard James Appleton, invented the little-known, but successful cinematograph device called the 'Cieroscope': a combined camera and projector; he also claimed to be the inventor of 'dissolving views' then used in magic lantern projection. R.J. Appleton and Co., Photographic and Lantern Outfitters, were situated in a corner shop at **58 Manningham Lane, Bradford**. Appleton will be best remembered, however, not for his inventions, but for filming Queen Victoria's Diamond Jubilee Celebrations on Tuesday 22 June 1897.

The *Bradford Argus* newspaper engaged Appleton to attempt to film the Jubilee procession in London, and within a few hours, screen the event in Bradford. *The Bradford Argus* described the event on 23 June 1897 thus: *"... Mr Appleton placed his cinematograph camera in a position where the State procession leaving St Paul's could be photographed. The event*

Simone Signoret and Laurence Harvey in **Room at the Top** *(1959, Romulus)*

recorded, he hurried to St Pancras' Station where the Midland Railway had equipped a special coach as a dark room. This was labelled 'The Bradford Argus Photo Laboratory', and when the huge milk can, full of water, was hoisted into the carriege to provide liquid for the 'baths', there was much speculation as to the capacity of two men who could 'drink all that'. The label was read with curiosity wherever the train stopped... This process of development was an exceedingly irksome part of the process, for the carriage had been made totally light-tight and practically air-tight as well... Telegrams were despatched from place to place to the head office of the Argus to keep the management there in full possession of the details of the work."

Appleton arrived at Bradford's Forster Square Station with the historic film and just before midnight it was screened to a waiting crowd from the second-floor window in the *Argus* Buildings onto a white sheet erected across **Watkins Alley**. The *Argus* described the events as: *"A triumph in Science"*, *a*nd repeated the screenings for the following three evenings, with the high point of the week on Saturday: *"On Saturday June 26 the lights of* **Forster Square** *were temporarily extinguished and a large sheet faced the Square. At 11pm it was estimated that some 10,000 people had assembled in the Square to witness the*

screening of the historic Animated Pictures. When the programme was concluded the National Anthem was played and the huge crowd dispersed in an orderly manner,"

ROOM AT THE TOP
Bradford

• 1959 115m b/w Drama Romulus (UK)
• Laurence Harvey (Joe Lampton), Simone Signoret (Alice Aisgill), Heather Sears (Susan Brown), Donald Wolfit (Mr Brown), Ambrosine Phillpotts (Mrs Brown), Donald Houston (Charles Soames)
• p, John Woolf, James Woolf; d, Jack Clayton; w, Neil Paterson (based on the novel by John Braine); ph, Freddie Francis; ed, Ralph Kemplen
• AA Best Actress: Simone Signoret; AA Best Adapted Screenplay: Neil Paterson

"A ruthless indictment of the British class system... a hallmark, seminal film in the social realist British 'kitchen sink' movement."
Baseline

Ambitious local government employee, Joe Lampton (Laurence Harvey), is desperate to shake free of his working-class origins. His quickest route to the top is to marry the daughter of a local wealthy industrialist. Mercilessly Joe executes his plan, which includes betraying his lover, Alice (Simone

Signoret),with fatal consequences. Based on local librarian John Braine's acclaimed novel, and set in the industrial north, *Room at the Top* was the first British film to portray sex as a pleasurable pursuit rather than one to be cast into hell for. Its reproach of the British class system and England at its provincial worst, make it one of the most memorable British films of the fifties.

Filmed on location in the Bradford district including **Bradford City Hall** (interior office scenes and Council Chamber), **Ivegate, Kirkgate, James Gate, Westgate** ('Boy and Barrel' pub), **Cartwright Memorial Hall** (interiors), **Bankfield Hotel, Bingley** (dance scene), **Gilstead Moor** and **Canal Road Mills.**

SCALA PICTURE HOUSE TRAGEDY
Bradford

On New Year's Day, 1916, storms were sweeping across the country and Bradford suffered more severely than did most inland towns. Fierce gales uprooted trees, windows were blown in and hoardings torn down. A tram was overturned and telephone, telegraph and tramway wires were broken. The one fatality happened around 6.30pm at the Scala Picture House, East Parade, where an audience was gathering for an early performance. On the roof of St Mary's Catholic Church next door, an ornamental stone cross was dislodged by wind or lightning causing it to come crashing through the cinema roof killing a twelve-year-old boy instantly. The *Bradford Daily Telegraph* reported: *"The cross weighed about three hundredweights, and when it fell through the roof with a deafening crash the people rushed out terrified. There were about a hundred people in the house at the time, so it was a wonder there were no more deaths. The victim of this disaster was a boy named Albert Edward Rawse, 12 years of age, upon whom the main mass of*

masonry fell. He was killed instantly, his skull being fractured and both legs broken. Other people in the immediate neighbourhood of the unfortunate lad also suffered injuries... A man named Jarge was sitting next to the deceased boy, and was reading an evening paper, when there came the startling crash on the roof. and the instantaneous death of the boy under the weight of the main mass which fell through. Jarge, who was himself cut about the hands and knocked about the shoulders by falling slate fragments, picked up the boy and carried him to the manager's office. He said to a 'Telegraph' man: "I did not see the hole in the roof or in fact anything. I was glad to get out and hoped to do something for the boy, but he never moved, and must have been dead at once,"

WORKSHOP OF WRAY & BAXTER
Bradford

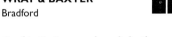

"In this Business we have led, others have followed"
Cecil Wray advertisement

Borough Mills, 76 Manchester Road, Bradford (near the present Mercury House and Central Library), was the site of the workshop of film pioneer, Cecil Wray, and his partner, Cecil William Baxter. An electrical engineer, Wray invented the B&W cinematograph, reputed to be the first cinematograph to be imported by Japan. In 1897 Baxter and Wray patented their 'Perfection' cinematograph, but by 1899 their partnership had ended.

CAPTAIN KETTLE FILM COMPANY
Bradford

Formed in 1913 by Henry Hibbert of Hibbert's Pictures and local adventure writer, Cuttliffe Hyne, mainly to film the exploits of Hyne's fictional seafaring character, *Captain Kettle*. Located at **Towers Hall, Manchester Road, off**

Newton Place, Bradford (opposite Tower Fisheries, 570 Manchester Road). A former skating rink, thirty films were shot there, including *The Costner's Holiday, A Modern Don Juan* and *Eggs is Eggs*. Only one film based on *Captain Kettle* was filmed before the studios were taken over by Pyramid Films in 1915. Their output included newsreels and feature films, such as *My Yorkshire Lass* (1916), a comedy drama about factory life in West Yorkshire. The Towers Hall Studios closed in 1916.

A PRIVATE FUNCTION
Bradford

Malcolm Mowbray's 1984 satire, set in post war Yorkshire, was filmed on location at **S.M Furniss Butcher's Shop, 116 Bolling Road; Ben Rhydding** (formerly Barraclough's Butcher Shop) and the former **Rosenthal's Butcher's Shop, Church Street, Ilkley**. BAFTA awards were won by Maggie Smith, Liz Smith, Denholm Elliott and Alan Bennett for his first screenplay.

See also: Maggie Smith

A BOY, A GIRL AND A BIKE & YANKS
Steeton

Gainsborough's 1947 drama about the life and loves of a Yorkshire cycling club, starring a very young Diana Dors, Anthony Newley and Honor Blackman, was filmed on location in **Steeton, Silsden** and in countryside outside **Addingham** and further north to **Bolton Abbey** (Barden Towers). **Steeton Ordinance Camp**, a disused army camp near Steeton Railway Station, was a key location for John Schlesinger's 1979 G.I. drama, *Yanks*, starring Richard Gere and Vanessa Redgrave. Other locations included **Cavendish Street, Keighley** and **Keighley Railway Station**.

Brighton & Hove

ASHES OF C. AUBREY SMITH (1863-1948)
Hove

"All you boys had to do was deal with 'Fuzzy Wuzzy', but The Crimea was different. War was war in those days - no room for weaklings - take Balaclava for instance..."
Gen. Burroughs (C. Aubrey Smith) *The Four Feathers* (1939)

A former member of England's cricket team, Charles Aubrey Smith did not appear on the stage until he was thirty, after which time he regularly appeared on both sides of the Atlantic before making his film debut, aged fifty-two, in 1915. He will be best remembered as a Hollywood character actor of the thirties and forties, whose tall military bearing and authoritarian tones frequently cast him as the quintessential old soldier, whose bark was worse than his bite. His films included: *Lives of a Bengal Lancer* (1935), *The Prisoner of Zenda* (1937), *The Four Feathers* (1939) and *Rebecca* (1940).

His ashes are interred in **St. Leonard's Churchyard, New Church Road, Aldrington**.

DUKE OF YORK'S CINEMA
Brighton

One of the oldest purpose-built cinemas in Britain, the Duke of York's cinema opened on 22 September 1910. Formerly the site of the Amber Ale Brewery, it was built by its owner, theatrical impresario, Violette Melnotte, who named it after her London theatre, The Duke of York. Always known to her staff as 'Madam', she was distinguished by snow-white hair, piercing eyes, elbow gloves, heavy make-up and large hats adorned with jewels.

When it first opened the cinema seated 800 people (present seating 330). Audiences declined in the 1970s, and it was forced to promote wrestling bouts and bingo. It was rescued in 1979 when it became the Brighton Film Theatre, presenting a varied programme of art and cult films. Its facade, in the style of Edwardian baroque, remains largely unaltered - although it was once topped by two small domes.

Further information: Duke of York's, Preston Circus. Tel: 01273 602503.

BRIGHTON ROCK
Brighton

- 1947 92m b/w Crime Boulting Bros (UK)
- Richard Attenborough (Pinkie Brown), Hermione Baddeley (Ida Arnold), William Hartnell (Dallow), Carol Marsh (Rose Brown), Nigel Stock (Cubitt), Wylie Watson (Spicer), Harcourt Williams (Prewitt), Alan Wheatley (Fred Hale)
- p, Roy Boulting; d, John Boulting; w, Graham Greene, Terence Rattigan (based on the novel by Graham Greene)

"Shots of the real Brighton - the streets, the promenade, the Pavilion, the Lanes - are skilfully cut into the fiction of murder; there is an acute feeling of actual place..."
Dilys Powell

Teenage thug and gang leader, Pinkie Brown (Richard Attenborough), marries a waitress (Carol Marsh) who witnesses a murder he has committed. Fearing she will eventually betray him, he resolves to kill her.

Adapted from Graham Greene's 1938 psychological thriller about the nature of evil, the film is set in the dark and shabby domains of the Brighton underworld. Richard Attenborough gave one of the finest performances of his career as the psychopathic gangster with a compulsion to break the law, and in so doing bequeathed to British cinema one of its most memorable villains.

Shot on location in Brighton and at Welwyn Studios and Borehamwood. Brighton locations included the **Palace Pier**, the **seafront**, the **Brighton Racecourse**, and Fred Hale's run of terror through **The Lanes** and **North Laine**.

Further information: Author and literary explorer, Maire McQueeney, has produced *The Brighton Rock Map*, a walker's guide to Graham Greene's Brighton, and *The Brighton Rock Picture Book*. She also organises walking tours of literary and movie sites in London, Brighton and the S.E. of England.
Tel: 01273 607910. Web: www3.mistral.co.uk/mcq20cwalk. Brighton Rock website: www.brighton.co.uk/brightonrock

THE GREAT CINEMA TOUR
Brighton

Sarah Tobias' illustrated walking tour around the sites of some of the many flea-pits and picture-palaces that form Brighton's rich cinematic history. Various early evenings and Sunday afternoons from April to September. Tel: 01273 672806.

A second walking tour also includes a look round the 1950s projection box at the Duke of York's cinema, complete with tea in the cinema and a selected screening. Sunday afternoons only, April to September. Tickets available from the Duke of York's box office. Tel: 01273 602503.

LOOT
Brighton

Director Silvio Narizzano's 1970 tame and processed version of Joe Orton's outrageous black comedy, was penned by Ray Galton and Alan Simpson, in which a crook conceals stolen money from a bank raid in his mother's coffin.

Locations included **Hartington Road** (near the top), the **Lewes Road Cemetery**, and the top of **Bear Road** (opposite Brighton Racecourse).

OH! WHAT A LOVELY WAR
Brighton

Richard Attenborough's 1962 anti-war musical about the follies of war was also his directing debut. The cast reads like a roll-call from a theatrical *Who's Who*, with John Mills, Laurence Olivier, Ralph Richardson, John Gielgud, Jack Hawkins and Dirk Bogarde.

Locations included the **West Pier, Brighton Station, Sheepcote Valley Amenity Site** and **Wilson Avenue**, site of battle.

Brighton & Hove

QUADROPHENIA
Brighton

- 1979 120m c Drama Who Films (UK)
- Phil Daniels (Jimmy Michael Cooper), Mark Wingett (Dave), Philip Davis (Chalky), Leslie Ash (Steph), Garry Cooper (Pete), Toyah Wilcox (Monkey), Sting (The Ace Face), Trevor Laird (Ferdy), Gary Shall (Spider), Kate Williams (Mrs. Cooper)
- p, Roy Baird, Bill Curbishley; d, Franc Roddam; w, Dave Humphries, Martin Stellman, Franc Roddam, Pete Townsend; ph, Brian Tufano; ed, Mike Taylor; m, The Who; prod d, Simon Holland; chor, Gillian Gregory

The Ace Face (Sting)

Inspired by The Who's *Quadrophenia* album (MCA/Track 1973) this powerful film is one of the best youth rebellion films ever made, which recounts the empty and aimless existence of Jimmy (Phil Daniels), a young Mod in 1964 London.

With a dead-end job and a miserable home life, he lives only for encounters with his Mod mates on his prized Lambretta scooter. The highlight of their year is the annual Bank Holiday trip to Brighton, where, after the customary riot with Rockers and police, he returns to London, only to lose his job, scooter and girlfriend. Looking for solace, he returns to Brighton, only to discover his Mod idol, Ace Face (Sting), is just a humble hotel bell-boy. Resentful and disillusioned he steals Ace Face's supreme machine and sends it hurtling over a cliff.

Much of the film was shot on location in Brighton. When the Mod scooter gang first saw their bank holiday Nirvana from the crest of a hill, they were not looking at Brighton, but **Eastbourne**. The Mods parked their scooters alongside the pillars on **Madeira Drive**. When Jimmy was drunk he tried to catch a train from **Waterloo Station** to Brighton (trains don't go to Brighton from Waterloo). In the finale, Jimmy sends Ace Face's scooter plummeting to oblivion over **Beachy Head**, near Eastbourne.

MAP KEY: -

1: East Street. Scene of the riot.
2: East Lane, which links East Street and Little East Street, was the alley where Jimmy did it standing up with Steph.
3: Sealife Centre. The exterior of the Aquarium at the bottom of the steps was the outside of the dance hall.
4: The Waterfront Cafe where the Mods had breakfast is off the map, along Madeira Drive.
5: The West Pier was where the Mods slept unknowingly beside a gang of Rockers.
6: The Grand Hotel was where Ace Face was employed as a bell-boy. The railings against which his flash scooter was parked are still there.
7: The Cafe that was charged and smashed up is on the corner of Kings Road and Ship Street, and is now a chip shop.

Further information: Brighton is still a popular haunt for Mods and **Jump the Gun, 36 Gardener Street, Brighton** (01273 626777), is the location of the only 'proper' Mod shop in Britain. Managed by local *Quadrophenia* authority, Doug Bannen, it stocks the original 'Ace Face' gear, including parkas, tonic suits, Ben Sherman shirts, Jam and bowling shoes, and a wide range of early 60s and 70s clothing. Regular 60s mod nights are also held at **The Joint, West Street, Brighton** (01273 321692), featuring the best live bands from the international Mod scene. Early arrival is advised, and don't forget... 'dress to impress'.

The Cafe

The Grand Hotel

Brighton Sea-Life Centre

East Street

Doug Bannen: Brighton's Ace Face

Phil Daniels and Lambretta in **Quadrophenia** *(1979, Who Films)*

THE SOUTH EAST FILM & VIDEO ARCHIVE
Brighton

SEFVA is the recognised regional moving image archive for the South East of England and locates, collects, preserves and promotes significant films and videotapes made in the region. Its collection includes documentaries, newsreels, advertisements, features, television programmes, artists' films and 'home movies'. The SEFVA Conservation Centre is found within the West Sussex Record Office at Chichester and its office is located at the University of Brighton.

Further information: South East Film & Video Archive, University of Brighton, 68 Grand Parade, Brighton BN2 2JY.

Bristol

BIRTHPLACE OF WILLIAM FRIESE-GREENE (1855-1921)

Frequently referred to as the man who made moving pictures possible, and subject of the misleading biopic, *The Magic Box* (1951), William Friese-Greene's contribution to motion picture history was nothing if not prolific. He was born William Edward Green the son of metal craftsman, James Green, at **96 College Street** (since demolished), Bristol, on 7 September, 1855. The youngest of seven children,

Bristol

he attended **Queen Elizabeth's Hospital School** (plaque erected in QEII Theatre) on the slopes of **Brandon Hill** as a foundation scholar when he was eleven. He left school in 1869 and went to work as an apprentice photographer with Maurice Guttenberg at **29 Queen's Road**, Bristol. Photography was still in its infancy and only thirty years had passed since Louis Daguerre invented his single image process, the daguerreotype. Here William learned the principles of Victorian photography and also the art of how to make the sulky child smile and the plain feel beautiful.

On 24 March 1874, he married Helena Friese, the sister of a Swiss friend, at the **Parish Church of St. George, Brandon Hill**, Bristol. Shortly after his marriage he quarrelled with Guttenberg and left his employ, eventually setting up his own studio at **34 Gay Street, Bath.** It was here that their daughter Ethel was born in 1876 and after a struggle to get established, which often meant pawning equipment and photographic plates to buy food and fuel, his 'Photographic Institute' started building a reputation for quality portraits. Now that he was a successful photographer he felt his name lacked the distinctive sound of the 'professional' and added his wife's maiden name to his own, plus an 'e' to Green. Thereafter he was known as Friese-Greene. He later opened a further two studios in Bristol (one at

109 **Queen's Road** near Guttenberg's studio), and one in Plymouth. In 1880 he became intrigued by the work of Bath instrument maker, J.A.R. Rudge, whose magic lantern attachments were capable of creating the illusion of movement, and began working with him.

In 1885 he became a partner in several photographic studios in London and prospered as a successful portrait photographer. His real interest lay in trying to develop moving pictures, and in 1889 he invented a sequence camera with engineer Mortimer Evans capable of shooting five photographs a second. There is no record, however, of the film being successfully projected. The subsequent neglect of his portrait business led to his bankruptcy in 1891. Undeterred by poverty, considerable hardship, and the eventual collapse of his marriage, Friese-Greene continued his research. He registered many patents including a camera/projector in 1893, but by this time other film pioneers were leading the field. He later began experimenting with colour photography in 1898 which occupied him for most of his life. Although a disastrous businessman, who was eventually imprisoned as a consequence of his bankruptcy, Friese-Greene was a creative and fruitful inventor who registered over seventy patents, including ones for phototypesetting and rapid photographic printing.

Almost forgotten today, Friese-Greene died virtually penniless when he collapsed at a film industry meeting at London's Connaught Rooms. On his body they found the sum of one and tenpence, exactly the price of a cinema seat. He is buried in Highgate Cemetery.

See also: William Friese-Greene (Camden)

Further information: Kingston Museum, Kingston-on-Thames (0181 546 5386), have on display two incomplete projectors of William Friese

Green which were rescued from the factory of Lege & Co., in north London when it was demolished in the sixties. The projectors are thought to date from the late 1890s.

BIRTHPLACE OF J. LEE THOMPSON (1914-)

Director and screenwriter, John Lee Thompson, whose biggest box-office success was *The Guns of Navarone* (1961), was born on 1 August 1914 at **3 Westbury Road, Bristol** (plaque erected). He joined the Nottingham Repertory Theatre, aged seventeen, and two years later wrote his first stage play, *Double Error*. In 1934 he worked as assistant to David Lean and became a dialogue director with Hitchcock and Charles Laughton. He also acted in films and played a small part in Carol Reed's *Midshipman Easy* (1935). During WWII he served as an RAF radar operator during which time he continued to write plays and screenplays, including *Murder Without a Crime*. Its subsequent London and Broadway success led to his selling the film rights, but only on condition he direct the film. He once remarked, *"It was not so much that I wanted to direct movies but I wanted to get money so that I could continue writing plays... while directing it, I got the feeling that I wanted to be a movie director. Suddenly I thought there was so much one could do with a camera."* *

His best films include: *Yield to the Night* (1956), *The Good Companions* (1957), *Ice Cold in Alex* (1958), *Tiger Bay* (1959) and *Cape Fear* (1962).

3 Westbury Road, Bristol - birthplace of J. Lee Thompson

ST. GEORGE'S HALL PUB

Formerly the St. George's Hall Picture House, it opened as a pub in 1998. The exterior is unchanged and the old seating still exists in the balcony. Movie stills and posters decorate its walls, including photos and information on the old Picture House, Cary Grant, and a brief history of Bristol cinemas.

Further Information: St. George's Hall, 203-207 Church Road, Redford, Bristol. Tel: 0117 955 1488.

BIRTHPLACE OF BLACKBEARD THE PIRATE (d.1718)

Edward Teach, better known as Blackbeard, was a real-life pirate who was born in Bristol's Redcliffe district, reputedly the illegitimate son of a nobleman and a barmaid. Little is known of his life in Bristol, but he served his apprenticeship privateering, a form of legalised 18th century piracy, against the French. There is no doubt he had a talent for the trade, for he became one of the most feared sea dogs in history. Married fourteen times, his stamping ground was the Caribbean. A fearsome sight, he plaited his beard with coloured ribbons and

inserted slow burning matches into his hat brim whenever he went into action. He died while fighting with a cutlass and six pistols strapped to his chest, after being shot five times and receiving twenty stab wounds, at the hands of His Majesty's Navy, who returned to port with his head impaled on their bowsprit.

Much fiercer than anything Hollywood could invent, sanitised Blackbeards have been portrayed on screen by Louis Bacigalupi in *Double Crossbones* (1950), Thomas Gomez in *Anne of the Indies* (1951), Robert Newton in *Blackbeard the Pirate* (1952), Murvyn Vye in *The Boy and the Pirates* (1960) and Peter Ustinov in *Blackbeard's Ghost* (1967).

BIRTHPLACE OF CARY GRANT (1904-86)

"Everybody wants to be Cary Grant. Even I want to be Cary Grant."
Cary Grant

Described by film critic David Thomson as *"the best and most important actor in the history of the cinema"*, Cary Grant was the embodiment of the Hollywood 'star': handsome, elegant, charming, irresistible to women, and a great actor to boot.

Archibald Alexander Leach was born on Sunday 18 January 1904, at **15 Hughenden Rd., Horfield** (plaque

erected), and was baptised into the Episcopal faith on February 8, 1904, at **Horfield Parish Church, Kellaway Avenue.** He was an only child. *"We weren't poor. We lived a typical lower, middle-class life. But we weren't rich either,"* he once said. His father, Elias Leach, was a tailor's presser by trade, and for most of his life he worked for **Todd's Clothing Factory off Portland Square** (now part of Eagle Insurance). His mother, Elsie, originated from a family of ship's carpenters, laundresses and brewery workers. Archie started at **Bishop Road Junior School** when he was four and a half years old; when he was nine years old he returned from school one day to find that his mother had left home. It was many years before he discovered she had suffered a breakdown and had been committed to Bristol's Fishpond's Mental Hospital. She remained at this institution for twenty years. Archie and his father went to live at his paternal grandmother's house in **Picton Street, Montpelier**. In 1915 he won a scholarship and attended nearby **Fairfield Grammar School in Fairfield Road**. During WWI he served as a junior air raid warden and was a member of the 1st Bristol Scout Group. After school he helped the electricians backstage at Bristol's Hippodrome and Empire Theatres which stimulated his interest in showbusiness.

In 1917, while still at school, he ran off to join a troupe of acrobatic dancers and stilt-walkers known as Bob Pender's Knockabout Comedians. His father eventually tracked him down in Ipswich and brought him home, vowing he could only return when he had finished his schooling. This was to be sooner rather than later, for on 13 March 1918 he was expelled from school for reasons unknown. During the school assembly he was denounced as *"inattentive... irresponsible and incorrigible... a discredit to the school."* There are various expulsion theories, including being caught stealing, investigating the girls' lavatories, and being discovered in the girls' playground. More than likely it was

Bristol

engineered by Archie to enable him to rejoin Bob Pender's troupe, which he did three days later.

After two years of touring English theatres and music halls, the Pender troupe was engaged to play in New York, and on 21 July 1920, Archie left for the United States. When the two year tour ended he stayed behind in New York and worked at various jobs, including those of Coney Island lifeguard, stilt-walking placard carrier, society escort, song and dance man, and singer in light operettas. He toured in Vaudeville for many years, until eventually, in 1931, he arrived in Los Angeles for a screen test with Paramount. He was offered a five year contract, and on 7 December 1931, Archie Leach vanished. Taking the name Cary from one of the characters he'd played, and Grant from Paramount's list of suitable surnames, he constructed his image piece by piece until his reincarnation was complete, describing it as *"a combination of Jack Buchanan, Noel Coward and Rex Harrison. I pretended to be somebody I wanted to be, and, finally, I became that person. Or he became me."*

One of his earliest roles was opposite Mae West in *She Done Him Wrong* (1933); she reputedly commented when she spotted him on the Paramount lot: *"If this one can talk, I'll take him."*

During his career he appeared in over seventy films, and became particularly adept at screwball comedies such as *Topper* (1937), *The Awful Truth* (1937), *Bringing Up Baby* (1938), *His Girl Friday* (1940), *My Favourite Wife* (1940) and *The Philadelphia Story* (1940). In his later work with Alfred Hitchcock he almost parodied his screen personae in films such as *Suspicion* (1941), *Notorious* (1946), *To Catch a Thief* (1955), *North By Northwest* (1959) and Stanley Donen's Hitchcock-esque *Charade* (1963).

In 1934, he married his first wife, the English actress, Virginia Cherrill. They

divorced in 1935. In 1942, he married Woolworth heiress, Barbara Hutton. They separated three years later. He married his third wife, actress Betsy Drake in 1949. They divorced in 1962. In 1965, he married his fourth wife, actress Dyan Cannon, mother of his only child, Jennifer. They separated after a couple of years, and he married his fifth wife, Barbara Harris, in 1981.

His mother refused to join him in America; he returned regularly to Bristol to visit her, but was always fearful of getting her involved with the press, who hovered around her house in **Coldharbour Road** whenever his visits were imminent. He eventually offered the press a deal which they readily accepted: in return for their promise never to approach his mother he agreed to alert them whenever he was coming to Bristol. The remaining days of her life were spent in Chesterfield Nursing Home, where her son would often pick her up in a Rolls Royce and take her on a trip to the Downs. She died in 1973, a few days before her ninety-sixth birthday. Details of her funeral were kept secret from the press to avoid publicity. His father died of alcoholism in the mid-thirties.

In 1968 he became an executive and front man for the cosmetic company, Fabergé. Throughout his life he repelled rumours that he was homosexual and in 1980 filed a $10m suit for slander against the comedian Chevy Chase, after he made the accusation on television.

He died from a massive stroke on 29 November 1986, at home in Davenport, Iowa, where his ashes are scattered.

A favourite Cary Grant story concerns a magazine editor who was trying to determine his age, and telegraphed the question, *"How old Cary Grant?"* To this was sent the reply, *"Old Cary Grant fine, how you?"*

See also: Bob Pender

15 Hughenden Rd., Horfield. **Birthplace of Archibald Leach**

Horfield Parish Church, Kellaway Avenue. Where Archie was baptised

Bishop Road Junior School

Fairfield Grammar School, Fairfield Road

Further information: The next time you watch *North By Northwest*, look closely at the scene in the Mount Rushmore Restaurant, where Eve Kendall (Eva Marie Saint) pulls a gun out of her handbag and pretends to shoot Roger Thornhill (Cary Grant). In the background there are two extras, a mother and son, sitting at a table. The little boy has obviously sat through the scene several times as he can be clearly seen sticking his fingers in his ears.

Buckinghamshire

GRAVE OF G.K. CHESTERTON (1874-1936)
Beaconsfield

Gilbert Keith Chesterton, creator of the *Father Brown* stories, was born at **32 Sheffield Terrace, Campden Hill, London**. He trained to be a book-illustrator and later became a cartoonist. In the early 1900s he made a name for himself as a poet, critic, novelist and short story writer. In 1922 he was received into the Roman Catholic Church at the age of forty-eight by his friend Father J. O'Connor, the inspiration for the priestly detective, *Father Brown*.

Chesterton wrote the first *Father Brown* story in 1910, the eponymous hero of which was first portrayed on the screen by Walter Connolly in 1935. No further films appeared until the 1950s when Alec Guinness played the title role in *Father Brown* (1954). Mervyn Johns and Kenneth More have portrayed him on TV, but only one subsequent film, *Father Brown, Detective* (1979) (US title, *The Girl in the Park*) has been produced, casting the sleuth as a clerical jogger.

He is buried in the Catholic Cemetery, Candlemas Lane. The monument was designed by Eric Gill.

GRAVE OF MARGARET RUTHERFORD (1892-1972)
Gerrard's Cross

Dame Margaret Rutherford was an eccentric character actress usually portrayed in comic roles such as the cycling spiritualist, Madame Arcati in David Lean's *Blithe Spirit* (1945) and Agatha Christie's tweeded sleuth, Miss Marples. She is buried beside her husband, Stringer Davis, in **St. James's churchyard** under a blue Colorado spruce tree at the north side of the island site in the churchyard extension, where her headstone is inscribed with the words, 'A Blithe Spirit'.

See also: Margaret Rutherford (Wandsworth)

WENT THE DAY WELL?
Turville

- 1942 92m b/w War Drama Ealing Studios (UK)
- Leslie Banks (Oliver Wilsford), Elizabeth Allan (Peggy Fry), Frank Lawton (Tom Sturry), Basil Sydney (Major Ortier), Valerie Taylor (Nora Ashton), Mervyn Johns (Charles Sims), Thora Hird (Ivy)
- p, Michael Balcon; d, Alberto Cavalcanti; ph, Wilkie Cooper; m, William Walton; ed, Sydney Cole; w, John Dighton, Diana Morgan, Angus McPhail (based on a story by Graham Greene)

"Went the day well?
We died and never knew.
But, well or ill,
Freedom, we died for you."

St. Mary the Virgin, Turville

The antithesis of the Ealing laughter factory, this unique and unsentimental film was made by Ealing during WWII when things looked pretty bleak for Britain and people were preparing themselves for an inevitable invasion. It almost resembles a dramatised Ministry of Information film about 'The Enemy Within' showing how a rural community is capable of mustering as much courage and tactics as does a crack commando unit.

Based on a Graham Greene story called *The Lieutenant Died Last*, it tells the story of the invasion of an isolated English village by German paratroopers disguised as Royal Engineers (a ruse which the locals soon rumble), and their bloody battle with the villagers. After 'The Battle of Bramley End' the village returns to its rural idyll and the only evidence of the incident for future generations is a small war memorial in the village churchyard recording the German dead.

Originally entitled, *They Came in Khaki*, the film took three months to shoot and went into production on 26 March 1942 with a budget of £56,000. Location filming was done in **Turville** and in the local church and churchyard of **St. Mary the Virgin**. Being wartime, strict rationing was still in place and the village pub, 'The Bull and Butcher', only received a certain quota of beer for its locals - which the film crew soon drank. Later, village criticism of landlord Lacey Becket's mismanagement of beer supplies was said to have contributed to his death. After shooting his wife and dog he walked into the garden and shot himself under an apple tree. His ghost is reputed to haunt the pub.

See also: Ealing Studios

GRAVE OF EDGAR WALLACE (1875-1932)
Little Marlow

Often dismissed as a pulp crime writer, Edgar Wallace wrote over 170 books in a 28 year writing career. Born in Greenwich, he was found abandoned by a Billingsgate fish-porter when he was a just a few days old. He left school at the age of twelve, and worked at various jobs, including those of printer's boy, newsboy, shoe shop employee, milkman, trawlerman and builder's labourer. At eighteen he joined the army and was posted to South Africa where he later wrote newspaper articles and became correspondent for *Reuters* , the *Daily Mail*. and eventually editor of the *Rand Daily Mail* in 1902. His newspaper training taught him to write quickly and simply, often dictating to a secretary or a dictaphone: this resulted in a prolific literary deluge of novels and plays.

Much of his work was adapted for the screen, including *The Case of the Frightened Lady* (1930,40), *The Calendar* (1932,48), *The Crimson Circle* ((1930, 37, 61), *The Terror* (1928, 39), *Sanders of the River* (1935), *The Four Just Men* (1939) and *The Ringer* (1932, 52). He also co-wrote the original story of *King Kong* (1933) with the film's co-director and co-producer, Merian C. Cooper.

In the 1920s he bought **'Chalklands' (now the Ramakrishna Vedanta Centre), off Blind Lane, in nearby Bourne End**, as a country retreat where his study has been kept exactly

Grave of Edgar Wallace, Little Marlow Cemetery

as it was. His two marriages produced four children. He died in Hollywood on 10 February 1932 while writing *King Kong* and is buried in **Little Marlow Cemetery**.

GOLDFINGER
Stoke Poges

In this third Bond film, 007 played billionaire Auric Goldfinger (Gert Frobe) for a shilling a hole on **Stoke**

Poges Golf Course. Posing as a dubious gold dealer, Bond humiliates Goldfinger after he discovers him cheating. Goldfinger cautions Bond not to mess with him, and to demonstrate his power, he orders his mute Korean manservant, Oddjob, to decapitate one of the club's statues with his razor-edged bowler hat.

Shot on the 16th, 17th, and 18th holes, Stoke Poges Golf Club remains more or less unchanged today. The club is open to non-members and all Bond fans are invited to sample the 'Bond Bar' which is decorated with Bond memorabilia.

See also: Ian Fleming, Sean Connery, Roger Moore, Desmond Llewelyn

Further information: Stoke Poges Golf Club, Stoke Park, Park Road, Stoke Poges, Bucks. Tel: 01753 717172.

THE BLUE MAX MOVIE AIRCRAFT COLLECTION
Booker

The Blue Max Museum was officially opened at Wycombe Air Park, Booker on June 20 1993 and was the brainchild of mother and son team, Edna and Tony Bianchi of Personal Plane Services (PPS). Over the years, Bianchi Aviation Film Services, an offshoot of PPS, have been involved in over a hundred feature films.

The aircraft in the museum include rare collectors' aircraft and replicas used in the movies. All are in airworthy condition and fly regularly. Fifteen aircraft are currently on display, including the eccentric professor Waxflatter's flying machine in *Young Sherlock Holmes* (1985); Spitfire AR213, restored to airworthy condition for *Battle of Britain*; Type NG-AWBU used in *The Thirty Nine Steps* (1978); a Stampe SV-4C G-AZTR and Pilatus P.2 G-BLKZ, both used in *Indiana Jones and the Last Crusade* (1989); a Sopwith Camel replica used in *The Great Waldo Pepper* (1975), and a

*Oddjob (Harold Sakata) and Goldfinger (Gert Frobe) at **Stoke Poges Golf Club**, Goldfinger (1964, UA/Eon)*

Morane 230 G-AVEB, which was the reserve aircraft for *The Blue Max* (1966).

The walls of the museum's hangar are adorned with relics and memorabilia from film work, such as: radio controlled models, dummy guns and fuselages, camera mounts, a large scale model of a Heinkel 111 bomber, clapper boards and 'front of house' posters. The museum shop also sells everything from flying jackets to postcards.

Tony Bianchi, who was chief pilot in *Indiana Jones and the Last Crusade*, hopes to start a museum club membership and social club. He also wants to expand the hangar and is looking for volunteers to help with the museum.

See also: The Old Flying Machine Company

Further information: The Blue Max Movie Aircraft Collection, Wycombe Air Park, Clay Lane, Booker, Nr. Marlow, Bucks., SL7 3DP. Tel: 01494 529432.

Open March to November, 7 days a week, 10am - 5pm. Sited on an active airfield with restaurant facilities.

GENEVIEVE
Farnham Common

- 1953 86m c comedy Sirius (UK)
- John Gregson (Alan McKim), Dinah Sheridan (Wendy McKim), Kenneth More (Ambrose Claverhouse), Kay Kendall (Rosalind Peters), Geoffrey Keen (1st Traffic Policeman), Harold Siddons (2nd Traffic Policeman), Reginald Beckwith (J.C. Callahan), Arthur Wontner (Elderly Gentleman), Joyce Grenfell (Hotel Proprietress), Leslie Mitchell (Himself)

- p, Henry Cornelius; d, Henry Cornelius; w, William Rose; ph, Christopher Challis; ed, Clive Donner; m, Larry Adler; chor, Eric Rogers
- AAN Best Original Screenplay, AAN Best Score

One of the great post-war road movies which is so English you can hear the tea cups chink. Two couples challenge each other to a race in their vintage cars in the annual London to Brighton car rally. After a series of hilarious pitfalls, pursued by Larry Adler's harmonica theme tune, they eventually cross the finish line on Westminster Bridge.

Filming took place between the months of October and February 1952-3, however, as the film was actually set in the summertime, powerful lighting had to be used to give the effect of a bright summer's day. **Collins Wood Road**, Farnham Common, doubled as the London to Brighton Road and the **Yew Tree Pub** can be seen in the background. **The One Pin Pub** (01753 643035), One Pin Lane, Farnham Common, was where the couple stopped for a drink. The pub's wall displays stills from the film and the bar-billiards room was used as a dressing room during filming.

See also: Kay Kendall

CLASSIC LOCATION: THE BURNHAM BEECHES WALK
Farnham Common

Within easy reach of Pinewood, Denham and Beaconsfield Studios, the ancient woodlands of Burnham Beeches have provided locations for many films. The trees themselves are hundreds of years old and the depth of the woods means that film crews don't have to worry about buildings appearing in the background or noisy traffic, whilst there is still easy access for them and their vehicles.

Buckinghamshire

The walk takes around one and a half hours, during which time you will pass many film locations in this atmospheric woodland. Burnham Beeches is a National Nature Reserve and visitors are asked to take special care of its fragile ecology and respect the bye laws. Your walk begins at the crossroads of **Victory Cross**, where there is plenty of free parking space.

The first location on your walk is on Lord Mayor's Drive, just below Victory Cross, and the film in which it featured was **The Company of Wolves** (1984). The film is a mixture of modern fairy tale and childhood fantasy and tells the story of a young girl, Rosaleen, growing up in a world where men whose eyebrows meet in the middle are to be avoided at all costs. The majority of the magical outdoor scenes depicted in the film were in fact sets built at Pinewood Studios, but this was one of the few real locations that were used.

Leave the Victory Cross crossroads by turning left on to Sir Henry Peeks Drive. At 50m down on the right is a path, walk along it keeping the wire fence on your left and Lord Mayor's Drive on your right. Follow the fence round to the left, down towards the pond. This was one of the settings used in **Lost** (1955), in which police go on the trail of a kidnapped girl. The path is the one that she walked down, as she made her journey home through the dark and lonely woodland. When you reach the pond turn right and follow the path towards the far end. This area later featured in **Agatha** (1978). This path was lined with gas lights to recreate a gloomy 1920s England. This pond was the lake which police trawled, in search of Agatha Christie's body. The same area at the end of the pond also doubled as Ireland in **Circle of Friends** (1995). The trees all around this pond were the first part of Burnham Beeches to be used as Sherwood Forest, when Walt Disney came to England to make **The Story of Robin Hood and His Merrie**

The Company of Wolves (1984, Palace)

Men (1952). This film was one of the first to be shot at Burnham Beeches, but was sadly the last ever to be made at Denham Studios before it closed.

Do not continue around the pond, but instead walk straight on ahead and take the path in front of you up through the trees. After walking 80m you will come to a large dead tree, about 10 feet high, after which the path forks. Take the right hand fork. About 60m ahead of you is a 'pollarded beech tree' (a large beech tree with a mass of thick branches growing straight upwards from about 10 feet up the trunk) on the edge of a holly thicket. **A Town Like Alice** (1956) used this unlikely area as the location for Malaya. Virginia McKenna and her fellow prisoners were forced to watch as the Japanese crucified Australian soldier, Peter Finch, on this beech tree for stealing chickens.

Carry on along the path, soon you will see another pond on your left. Walk alongside the pond and you will see a bench in front of you. 20m before the bench turn right and you will see a wide path leading through the trees. Follow this path and walk up through the trees, towards Lord Mayors Drive. Cross over Lord Mayor's Drive.

These are the trees through which IRA soldier Fergus (Stephen Rea) chased his English squaddie hostage Jody (Forest Whitaker) in **The Crying Game** (1992). Moments later, Jody escapes and runs onto Lord Mayor's Drive where you have just crossed, and is killed under the wheels of a British Army truck.

Ahead of you, about 50m from the road is a wooden fence. Go through the kissing gate, straight ahead you will see a large pollarded beech tree, with a hollow trunk. In front of the hollow pollard was where the burial scene of Duncan, squire to Lord Loxley, in **Robin Hood Prince of Thieves** (1991) took place. Walk past the hollow pollard and turn left out of the kissing gate. Follow the path down alongside the fence. After about 125m the path forks, take the right hand fork for about 150m. Again at the next fork take the right hand path and walk down the hill. At the crossroads, turn left (onto Victoria Drive). After 16m there is a

The Crying Game (1992, Palace Pictures)

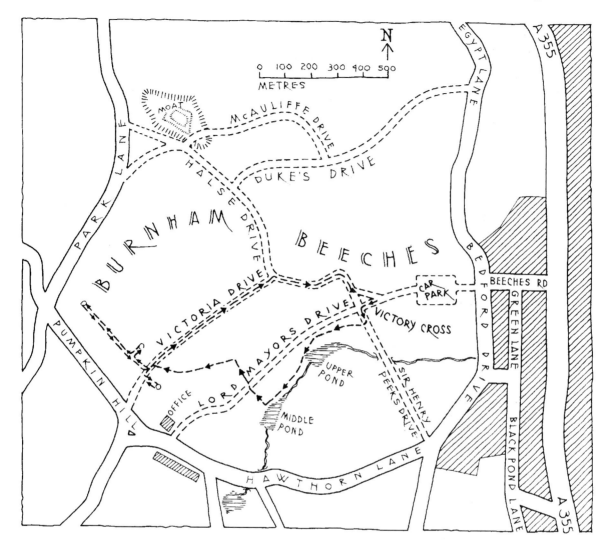

tiny path on your left. Follow it up to the bank and look down towards the big hollow in the ground. This was the site of Robin Hood's camp in **Robin Hood, Prince of Thieves**. Production designer Peter Young, whose previous work included *Batman*, went to great lengths to make this scene of 13th century England historically accurate. The structure of the camp included tree houses, rope bridges and ladders, all fixed to the ancient beech trees without using a single nail, so as not to damage them. This same site was used for another 'Thieves Camp' in **The Princess Bride** (1987). About 20m to your right is a very steep bank, dropping down. This is where Toad crashed his car in **The Wind in the**

Willows (1996), leaving it jack-knifed around the tree at the bottom of the slope.

Retrace your steps back to the crossroads. Take the left turning, about 150m up you will see a tiny path on your left. Follow it into the clearing. On your left, in the clearing, are three large pollarded beech trees, one of which has fallen down. This was the clearing used in **The Princess Bride**. The film was based on a fairy story by William Goldman in which Buttercup (Robin Wright) pines for her missing lover Westley (Cary Elwes), who has been taken prisoner by the evil Prince Humperdinck (Chris Sarandon). For the film, this clearing had four pollards.

The fourth one was false and contained the doorway to the 'Pit of Despair' where the unhappy Westley is incarcerated. If you look behind the fallen beech pollard you can see a slight dent in the forest floor, about a metre across, which is all that remains of the false tree.

Go back to the main path, and carry on walking in the same direction that you were. Just ahead of you, you can see a tree with just two branches, one of which twists out over the path, about 2m above the ground. In **The Wind in the Willows**, this tree had a third, 'soft' branch attached, which knocked the long-suffering Ratty (Eric Idle) flying off the top of Toad's (Terry Jones) car. If you walk straight past this tree, after about 30m, you can see another large pollarded beech tree. This was the site of one of the love scenes between Lancelot (Richard Gere) and Guinevere (Julia Ormond) in **First Knight** (1995). If you look closely at the base of the tree where the roots are, you can see traces of plaster of Paris. This is where designers altered the shape of the tree to make a comfortable 'natural' love seat for the couple to sit on, and is the only trace left of any of the filming which has taken place in Burnham Beeches over the years. Retrace your steps back to Victoria Drive and turn left along the path towards Halse Drive.

This is the driveway where Guinevere's coach is attacked in **First Knight**. The gallant Lancelot rushes to her rescue, but when he later tries to get a kiss in exchange for his troubles, he receives a slap across the face. This scene was shot in the woods just to the left of the drive and was one that Julia Ormond performed with so much energy that director Jerry Zucker had to ask her to "go easy on the punch" to protect his male lead during many retakes. Just a few yards further on was the location for a more romantic scene, that of the wedding of Robin Hood and Maid Marion in **Robin Hood, Prince of Thieves**. The cast and crew spent a total of three months shooting at Burnham Beeches, one of the longest film shoots at the Beeches.
Carry on to the end of Victoria Drive and walk up the road right onto Halse Drive. Just before you get to Victory Cross, the road bends sharply to the right. This corner is the first part of Burnham Beeches ever to have been used for a film location. The film was **London Belongs To Me** (1948) and starred Richard Attenborough as a young man who borrows a car from the garage in which he works, to impress his girlfriend. Just as they are driving up towards this corner his girlfriend realises the car has been stolen and a fight breaks out. In the commotion she falls out of the car and is killed under the wheels and her boyfriend is later accused of murdering

her. This same corner was later used for the famous Aston Martin chase in **Goldfinger** (1964). James Bond is trying desperately to escape from Goldfinger's henchmen, and just as he hurtles round this corner he releases an oil-slick in the path of his pursuers Continue along this road, back to Victory Cross, where the walk ends. As you set off home, with your car bumping over the speed control humps, think that during the filming of **First Knight** all the humps on Morton Drive and McAuliffe Drive were flattened for just one day of shooting and then put back in again at a cost of £8,000. If your journey home takes you down Hawthorn Lane, pause at the driveway up to Juniper Cottages. This is the path up which Sid James and Bernard Bresslaw wandered, desperately hoping to find a Nudist Camp in **Carry on Camping** (1969).

Further information: Burnham Beeches, Hawthorn Lane, Farnham Common, South Bucks. SL2 3TE. Tel: 01753 647358.

CLASSIC LOCATION: BLACK PARK COUNTRY PARK WALK
Wexham

Situated right next to Pinewood Studios, Black Park's dense pine forest, grassy plains, large lake and ease of access for film crews have made it one of England's most popular and convenient movie locations. Over the years the area has seen Dracula's horse and carriage galloping through the forests of 'Transylvania', prisoners freezing in bitter 'Siberian' nights and Supergirl 'flying' through the sky in a

bid to save the planet. The walk will take about one and a half hours and can be tackled by all age groups. The Country Park itself is fairly flat and the numerous paths are quite smooth.

The walk starts at the car park, just off Black Park Road. If you look to the left hand side of the car park, you will see a wooden signpost pointing to the picnic area. This is where the beginning of **Octopussy** (1983) was shot. In this scene the knife thrower from the Octopussy circus chases agent 009, who is disguised as a clown, through the woodlands. Later, 009 staggers, fatally wounded, into the 'British Embassy' in 'East Germany' and James Bond's mission begins. The woodland paths surrounding this end of the car park were also featured in the musical gangster spoof, **Bugsy Malone** (1976). Set in 1920s New York, the all child cast (including a young Jodie Foster as Tallulah) hurtled around this area in specially made pedal-powered cars and shot each other with ice-cream firing 'splurge guns'.

Walk up to the far end of the car park and follow the path on the right down towards the lake. Right in front of you was where Lancelot (Richard Gere) rescued damsel-in-distress Guinevere (Julie Ormond) who was stranded on

the lake in **First Knight** (1995). The crane used for these shots tipped over during filming and if you look to the right of the bench, by the lake, you can see a tree with a two foot scar down it, marking the spot.

Turn left and walk along the bank. Almost immediately you will see an island on the lake. The path in front of you is where Supergirl touched down on dry land after 'walking on water' across the lake, in **Supergirl** (1983). On the bank next to the island is a bench, and just to the left (as you look at the lake) are the trees from behind which the wounded Violette Szabo (Virginia McKenna) machine-gunned German troops, while her companion (played by Paul Scofield) escaped across the lake, in **Carve Her Name with Pride** (1958). Violette Szabo was a real life French Resistance fighter who was executed by the Nazis. The the film tells the story of this remarkable woman who was posthumously awarded the Victoria Cross.

After the island, ignore the right hand fork down towards the lake and instead follow the path down which Dracula's henchman drove his carriage, pulled by black horses, in Hammer Studios' classic version of **Dracula** (1958) starring Christopher Lee as the Count.

Carry on walking, keeping the wooden fence on your right. At the crossroads go straight over onto Queens Drive (marked with a Map Board). The clearing on your right was used for the site of the Summer Camp in **Please Sir** (1971), a spin-off from the popular television series, starring John Alderton.

Carry on walking up Queen's Drive. This is the path that the all-girl army charged up in Morecambe and Wise's, **The Magnificent Two** (1966).

Carry on walking, you will reach a junction with six points. The fort which the all-girl army is planning to attack, was built straight across the path in front of you. At this junction, take the right turning slightly downhill. When

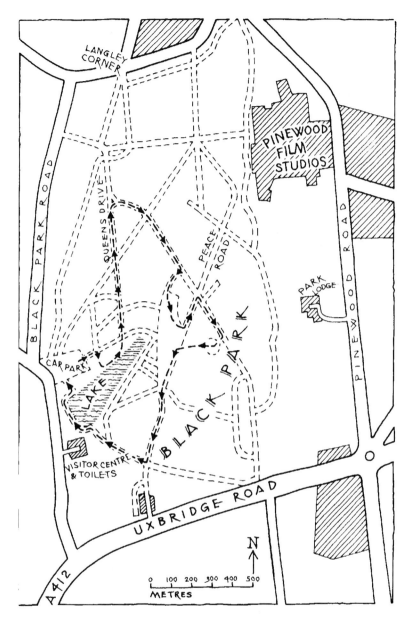

you reach the crossroads at the bottom, take the path to the right. You will cross over a tiny stream. Turn left at the junction just after it.

In the woodlands just to your right is another location from **Please Sir**, this time the gypsy camp. Carry on walking up the path then bear right diagonally towards the grassy open space.

This particular area has been home to numerous, lavish film and television

sets over the years. All the grass was replaced by earth to create the Indian c camp in **Carry On Cowboy** (1965). Later it was sprayed with artificial snow and covered in huge shed like buildings to portray a Siberian labour camp in **One Day in the Life of Ivan Denisovich** (1971), starring Tom Courtenay. Another campsite was built here for **The Charge of the Light Brigade** (1968) - the most accurate version to date about the famous Crimean War blunder. In Terence

Black Beauty (1994, Warner Bros.)

Fisher's **Island of Terror** (1966), a village hall was built here in which terrified villagers took refuge from a plague of bone-eating 'silicates', which had been created by a mad scientist. The bottom half only of an airship (because no-one saw the top half on film) was constructed here for **The Assassination Bureau** (1968), starring Diana Rigg. Later a torch lit horse procession passed through in the elaborate special effects extravaganza **Krull** (1983), which took two years to make. One of the few times the green grass was left untouched was when it doubled as Wimbledon Common in **Wombling Free** (1977).

Carry on walking across the open space to the main path ahead. This is Peace Road. Bearing to the left you will reach a crossroads which has an information board on your left. At this crossroads turn right. You will see a gate in the distance. The path you are walking along was the one down which Reuben Smith (Alun Armstrong) rode in the 1994 remake of **Black Beauty.**

Walk about 200 metres up to the gate. At the gate turn right and walk down the path until you reach a small grass clearing. This area was home to another two Hammer films, **The Devil Rides Out** (1967) and **Twins of Evil**

(1971). In **The Devil Rides Out**, this clearing was packed with Satanists, who gathered together in their long white robes to worship the devil and make human sacrifices. They are interrupted by the Duc de Richleau (Christopher Lee), who arrives just in time to save the lives of his friends. **Twins of Evil** tells the story of identical twins, who fall under the spell of a vampire Baron whilst in the care of their Puritan uncle, Peter Cushing. The uncle and Baron are arch enemies and must eventually fight it out in an eerie graveyard, which the production designers built entirely from plaster of Paris on the land where you are standing.

Turn right, back towards Peace Road. At Peace Road turn left, and walk down the path keeping the open space on your right. This is the path down which the unicorn wandered in one of the flashback sequences in Ken Russell's **Mahler** (1974). The hawk featured in this scene was tied by its feet to a branch of one of the trees on the left, to make sure it flapped its wings at the correct moment but didn't fly away.

When you reach a small junction bear left keeping to the main path passing a

picnic bench on your right. Carry on walking down to Ron Owen's crossroads and then take the turning on the right. The area just on your right in the trees, became the woodland of 19th century Bavaria in Hammer's **Blood Will Have Blood** (1971). The film featured a crazed Baron who tries to drive his children insane, following their mother's suicide, and this is the site where the milkmaid's cottage was built.

Carry on walking down towards Centenary Lodge. The area just before the gate is another one of the locations used in **The Magnificent Two**, this time as the training ground where Morecambe and Wise put the girl-army through their paces. At the gate bear right with the Centenary Lodge on your left. After Centenary Lodge, follow the path around to the left, past the lake and up to the car park, where the walk ends.

The scene where Robert De Niro first makes contact with the Indians whilst hauling his armour through the jungle in Roland Joffe's, **The Mission** (1986), was filmed at Black Park. Although filmed on location in South America, this scene was considered wanting and reshot.

The Mission (1985, Warner Bros.)

The Devil Rides Out (1967, Hammer Films)

Further information: Country Parks Office, Black Park Country Park, Black Park Road, Wexham, South Bucks. SL3 6DR. Anyone who has mobility difficulties can borrow an electric wheelchair from the country park office. The wheelchairs are available free of charge, but must be booked in advance. Please contact the office on 01753 511060.

I would like to thank South Bucks District Council for their help in compiling the Burnham Beeches and Black Park walk information.

FOUR WEDDINGS AND A FUNERAL
Amersham

• 1994 116m c Romance/Comedy Working Title/Channel Four (UK)
• Hugh Grant (Charles), James Fleet (Tom), Simon Callow (Gareth), John Hannah (Matthew), Kristin Scott Thomas (Fiona), David Bower (David), Charlotte Coleman (Scarlett), Andie MacDowell (Carrie), Timothy Walker (Angus the Groom), Sara Crowe (Laura the Bride)
• p, Duncan Kenworthy; d, Mike Newell; w, Richard Curtis; ph, Michael Coulter; ed, Jon Gregory; m, Richard Rodney Bennett
• AAN Best Picture; AAN Best Original Screenplay

Mike Newell's romantic comedy was the surprise hit of 1994, grossing over $200 million in its first six months of release. It established Hugh Grant as an unlikely matinee idol and gave countless young couples an appetite for sex in a four-poster bed. The plot revolves around Charles, who is in search of the perfect relationship, and eventually finds it with Carrie while attending other people's weddings and a funeral.

Although there were numerous locations used in the film, the one which has proved the most popular with fans has been the four-poster bedroom at the **Crown Hotel, Amersham**, where Charles and Carrie jump into bed together. The room is now booked regularly by couples for

Charles (Hugh Grant) meets Carrie (Andie MacDowell), at the first wedding.
Four Weddings and a Funeral *(1994, Working Title/Channel Four)*

romantic liaisons, and has witnessed at least three proposals of marriage. Dating back to the early 16th century, with beamed ceilings, inglenook fireplaces, wall paintings and an Elizabethan interior, the Crown is now owned by the Forte group.

The first wedding was shot at **St. Michael's, in the village of Betchworth**, just off the A25 in Surrey, and the reception was held at Goldington's manor house (not open to the public), near Sarrat, in Hertfordshire. The inn where Charles and Carrie met later was a combination of the exterior of the **King's Arms** and the interior of the **Crown Hotel**, both in **Amersham**. The second wedding was shot in the **Royal Naval College Chapel at Greenwich**, and the reception was held at **Luton Hoo, Luton, in Bedfordshire**. Carrie went in search of her wedding gown at **Albrissi, in London's Sloane Square**, and afterwards relaxed at **The Dome, Wellington Street**. Carrie and Hamish's wedding location was at **Albury Park, near Guildford, in Surrey**, and the reception was nearby at **Rotherfield Park, East Tisted**. Gareth's funeral service was held at **St. Clement's Church at West Thurrock, near the Dartford Tunnel, London**, and the reading was W.H. Auden's *Funeral Blues*. The last wedding was shot at the **Priory Church of St Bartholomew the Great, opposite St Bart's Hospital in Little Britain, Holborn, London**.

Further information: The Crown Hotel, 16 High St., Old Amersham, Bucks., HP7 ODH. Tel: 01494 721541.

Calderdale

PORTMAN & PICKLES PUB
Halifax

Named after local actor Eric Portman (*49th Parallel, Millions Like Us*) and radio star and character actor, Wilfred

Pickles (*Billy Liar, The Family Way*) who used to drink in the pub. Part of the Carlsberg-Tetley Group, its walls are strewn with Portman and Pickles memorabilia, serving good real ales in a friendly atmosphere to its student, biker and thespian locals.

See also: *Billy Liar*

Further information: Portman & Pickles, 18 Market Street, Halifax.

Cambridgeshire

FULL METAL JACKET
Bassingbourne

Gunnery Sgt. Hartman (Lee Ermey) spouts obscenities at Pvt. Joker (Matthew Modine). **Full Metal Jacket** *(1987, Natant)*

Stanley Kubrick recreated the Parris Island assault course and the base at Da Nang for his harrowing Vietnam war film at **Bassingbourne Air Base**. Kubrick wanted his actors to be drilled for real, and ex-Marine sergeant, Lee Ermey, former technical adviser on *Apocalypse Now* and the *Boys in Company 'C'* was hired for the task. During Ermey's audition he managed to spout obscenities for fifteen minutes without repeating himself while having tennis balls and oranges thrown at him. He was so convincing that Kubrick cast him in the movie as the terrifying Gunnery Sgt. Hartman, who dehumanizes his recruits into cold-blooded fighting machines.

See also: *Full Metal Jacket* (Newham).

THE OLD FLYING MACHINE COMPANY
Duxford

EXHIBIT

A former R.A.F. fighter airfield and US fighter base, the Imperial War Museum at Duxford is now the leading aviation museum in Europe with an exceptional collection of over 150 historic aircraft. Also based at Duxford is The Old Flying Machine Company, formed in 1981 by Ray and Mark Hanna with the intention of preserving and maintaining rare vintage aircraft in airworthy condition. In addition to air displays, OFMC specializes in film work, flying in the majority of European based aviation productions since 1987, including *Empire of the Sun* (1987), *Memphis Belle* (1990), *Hope & Glory* (1987), *Air America* (1990) and numerous Bond movies. Aircraft used in film-making ranges from Mustangs and Spitfires to B17 bombers.

See also: The Blue Max Movie Aircraft Collection

Further Information: Imperial War Museum Duxford, Cambridge CB2 4QR. 01223 835000. http://www.iwm.org.uk OFMC aircraft can be seen in Hangar 3.

HOME & SCHOOL OF W.H. BALGARNIE: THE 'ORIGINAL' MR. CHIPS
Cambridge

"I thought I heard you say it was a pity, pity, I'd never had any children, but you're wrong. I have. Thousands of them. Thousands of them, and all boys...."
The deathbed farewell of Mr. Chipping (Robert Donat) in *Goodbye Mr. Chips* (1939).

So inseparable was Robert Donat from the role of the schoolmaster, Mr. Chipping, that when he died in 1958 the headlines of one national newspaper simply read *Goodbye, Mr Chips* . Written by James Hilton in four days during 1934, and adapted for the

screen in 1939 and 1969, the novel tells the story of a schoolmaster who devotes his life to his school and its pupils. The book and the 1939 film are now recognised classics, but few are aware of the relationship between Hilton and his own schoolmaster, W.H. Balgarnie, of The Leys School, Cambridge, the inspiration behind the legend.

William Balgarnie was born in London in 1869 to the Rev. Robert and Isabella Balgarnie at **Gloucester House, Upper Whitworth Road, Plumstead, Woolwich**. The family remained in Woolwich from 1869 to 1879, and at Gravesend from 1879 to 1886, where his father was minister of St. Andrew's Presbyterian Church. Young William attended the Roan School in Greenwich and later Elmfield School, York, where he studied for the London University B.A. He later taught at Fowey Grammar School in Cornwall and at the School for the Sons of Missionaries at Blackheath, in south-east London (now Eltham College). In 1894, Balgarnie was awarded a sizarship at Trinity College, Cambridge, from which he graduated in 1897. Having been associated with three universities before he was thirty

Robert Donat *as Mr. Chipping in Goodbye Mr. Chips (1939. MGM)*

(he obtained Master of Arts degrees from Cambridge and London and spent a year or two as assistant professor of Greek at Glasgow University) he took up his appointment at **The Leys School, Cambridge,** in January 1900, where he would spend the next fifty years of his life.

During his years at The Leys, he taught Latin and Greek as Senior Classics Master, and became endeared to many generations of boys. Three boys he influenced and encouraged were Joseph Arthur Rank, Malcolm Lowry and James Hilton. When comparing the fictional Mr Chipping with the real-life Mr Balgarnie, there are many similarities to be found. Balgarnie did have problems with class discipline in his early days at The Leys, as did Mr Chipping. On one occasion Balgarnie was tied up by pupils and placed under his desk. He also had the same love of dry puns and humour, but unlike Chips, he never married. Like the fictional character, he was brought out of retirement during WWII.

In 1951 Hilton recalled a very old master who had taught him as possibly being the inspiration of the name 'Mr Chips'. He was T.P.I. Walker who sported mutton-chop whiskers and had the nickname 'Chops'. Many claim Hilton based the fictional Herr Staefcl, Brookfield's German master, on his own teacher of French and German, Dr Marseille, who was psychologically tortured by the futility of WW1 and committed suicide in 1918.

In 1929 Balgarnie retired at the age of sixty and lived across the road from the School at **No. 6 Brookside**. He remained very much in contact with the school and it was here that he was visited by his old pupil, James Hilton, who was inspired to write in *Goodbye, Mr Chips* : *"Across the road, behind a rampart of ancient elms was Brookfield, russet under its autumn mantle of creeper."* Sadly, the trees have since disappeared, victims of Dutch Elm disease.

William Balgarnie

No. 6 Brookside

T.P.I. Walker ('Chops')

James Hilton

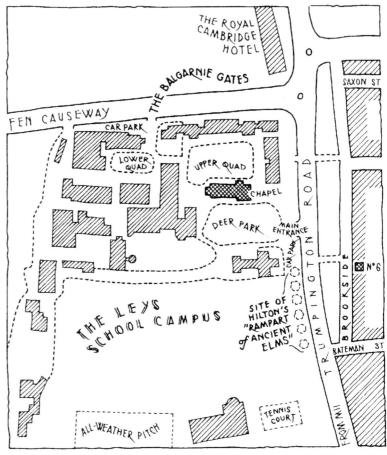

The Leys School

In May 1939 the stage version of *Goodbye, Mr Chips* ran at the Golders Green Hippodrome. Hilton invited Balgarnie to the performance, but he did not welcome the limelight, and later commented: *"It was a lowly sort of fame just to be mistaken for half of the original of a character in fiction."*

William Balgarnie died while spending his summer holidays with his sisters in Wales on 15th July 1951, aged eighty-two. He is buried in Porthmadog, and is commemorated at The Leys by a plaque erected on what is known as the 'Balgarnie Gates' opening onto **Fen Causeway by North 'A' House**.

In 1954 James Hilton wrote to the headmaster, following the death of Balgarnie.

235 Argonne,
Long Beach,
California.
November 24, 1951.

Dear Dr. Humphrey,
I have been sent a copy of the Cambridge Daily News containing a report of the Memorial Service for W.H. Balgarnie. I was touched and gratified by your quotation from "Goodbye Mr. Chips". Balgarnie was, I suppose, the chief model for my story, so far as I had one; certainly in my school life his was a personality I have never forgotten.

When I read so many other stories about public school life I am struck with the fact that I myself suffered no such purgatory as their authors apparently did, and much of this miracle (if indeed it was one) was due to W.H.B. He not only realised that I was not a typical schoolboy, but I suspect he had discovered the deeper truth that no such animal exists...

I remember too that during the first term I was at The Leys (the summer of 1915) there was a very old master called "Chops" Walker who must have been born a century ago - after that summer he retired. I had little to do with him, but I have often thought that subconsciously his nickname may have in its own way contributed to my story.

May I add my personal good wishes to you and The Leys.

*Yours sincerely,
James Hilton*

See also: James Hilton, Robert Donat, Greer Garson, Repton School, Sherborne School

Further information: The Leys School, Cambridge, CB2 2AD. Those wishing to visit the school should contact Geoff Houghton on 01223 508900.

Cheshire

OLDEST BUILDING TO SCREEN FILMS
Chester

The Music Hall, on **St Werburgh and Northgate Streets**, is thought to be the oldest building in Britain in which films have been shown. It was originally the ancient Chapel of St Nicholas, built in 1280 by Abbot Simon. In 1777 it became the Theatre Royal and it was converted into the Music Hall in 1854. Charles Dickens gave a talk here in 1867 and it was also a venue for many famous music hall artists. Films were shown regularly from 1915 up until April 29th 1961 when the theatre screened its final film, *Never on a Sunday*. Currently it is a retail shop.

*Marooned on the River Fal - **Treasure Island** (1950, Walt Disney)*

Cornwall

TREASURE ISLAND
Falmouth

• 1950 96m c Adventure Walt Disney (US)
• Bobby Driscoll (Jim Hawkins), Robert Newton (Long John Silver), Basil Sydney (Capt Smollett), Walter Fitzgerald (Squire Trelawney), Finlay Currie (Capt Bones), John Laurie (Pew), Geoff Wilkinson (Ben Gunn)
• p, Perce Pearce; d, Byron Haskin; ph, Freddie Young; w, Lawrence Watkin, based on the novel by Robert Louis Stevenson; ed, Alan Jaggs; m, Clifton Parker

Disney's first live action feature film and probably the best version of Stevenson's novel was filmed in Falmouth and at locations in **Carrick Roads** and up the **River Fal**, mostly using the entrance to the River Fal at **Turnaware Bar** opposite **Feock**, and the area further up river close to the **King Harry Ferry**. The trading schooner, *Ryland*, was converted into the pirate ship *Hispaniola* at Bideford, and had inboard engines installed for greater manoeuvrability at sea. 'Glass shots' were used to create the special

effects of castles and tropical vegetation.

Robert Newton went on to appear in the TV series *Long John Silver* in 1955. He died the following year, aged fifty-one. Bobby Driscoll, who portrayed Jim Hawkins and was also the voice of Disney's *Peter Pan* , died a heroin addict, aged thirty-one.

See also: Robert Louis Stevenson, Finlay Currie

BIRTH OF THE WICKER MAN
Padstow

A chance and disquieting encounter with Padstow's Obby Oss festival inspired Anthony Shaffer (*Sleuth, Frenzy*) to write the screenplay for the cult horror film *The Wicker Man* (1973), a tale of clashing religions and pagan sacrifice. The Obby Oss festival is reputed to be the oldest dance festival in the country, possibly even in Europe, and is believed to have its origins in an ancient rite in which the horse was worshipped as a fertility god. The festival marks the arrival of summer and the town and its maypole are decked with flowers. At 10 am a stable door is opened and the 'Oss' appears, a black canvas-skirted monster, six feet in diameter, with a witch-doctor's mask...

Further information: Festivities take place each year on 1 May, except when it falls on a Sunday, when celebrations take place on 2 May. Padstow Tourist Information: 01841 533449

See also: *The Wicker Man Trail*

THE OLD FERRY INN
Bodinnick-by-Fowey

In January 1945, David Lean and Ronald Neame came here to write the bulk of the screenplay for *Great Expectations* (1946). Nestling close to the banks of the Fowey River where there has been a ferry crossing since the 13th century, this family-run inn has been here for four hundred years.

See also: *Great Expectations*, David Lean

Further information: The Old Ferry Inn, Bodinnick-by-Fowey, South Cornwall, PL23 1LX. Tel: 01726 870237.

THE THIEF OF BAGHDAD
Sennen

• 1940 106m c Fantasy London films (UK)
• Conrad Veidt (Jaffar), Sabu (Abu), June Duprez (Princess), John Justin (Ahmad), Rex Ingram (Djinni), Miles Malleson (Sultan), Morton Selten (King)
• p, Alexander Korda; d, Ludwig Berger, Michael Powell, Tim Whelan, Zoltan Korda, William Cameron Menzies, Alexander Korda; w, Lajos Biro, Miles Malleson; ph, Georges Perinal, Osmond Borradaile; ed, William Hornbeck, Charles Crichton; m, Miklos Rozsa; prod d, Vincent Korda; fx, Lawrence Butler, Tom Howard, John Mills
• AA Best Cinematography: Georges Perinal; AA Best Visual Effects: Lawrence Butler, Jack Whitney

Often said to be the best fantasy film ever made, this spectacular adaptation of *Arabian Nights* required six directors to stitch it together, but it is impossible to see joins. The outbreak of WWII made shooting in the intended Middle East locations impossible. The project, weighed down with production difficulties, took two years to complete in Denham Studios and Hollywood, using locations in the Grand Canyon and the Painted Desert. The beach scenes where Abu (Sabu) encounters the Djinni (Rex Ingram) of the bottle were filmed on the Pembrokeshire coast in Wales and at **Sennen Cove near Land's End.**

See also: Michael Powell, William Cameron Menzies

BIRTHPLACE OF HERMAN 'SAPPER' McNEILE (1888-1937)
Bodmin

Bodmin was the birthplace of the creator of Bulldog Drummond, the tough, no-nonsense Englishman who fought clean and tackled villains with a square blow to the jaw accompanied by the phrases, *"you vile hound"*, *"blackguard"*, and *"conceited ass"*.

His creator was Herman Cyril McNeile who was born at **Bodmin Jail, Berrycombe Road**, where his father was Governor of the Naval Prison. Educated at Cheltenham College and at the Royal Military Academy in Woolwich, McNeile joined the Royal Engineers (the origin of his nickname 'Sapper') in 1907, retiring in 1919 with the Military Cross and the rank of Lieut-Colonel.

His best known works were the Bulldog Drummond novels, which he began writing in 1920 - the first of which was subtitled *The Adventures of a Demobilised Officer Who Found Peace Dull*. He first appeared on the screen in silent films and was still being portrayed in the cinema - though somewhat less cleanly - in the late

sixties. Ronald Colman played the definitive hero and Claud Allister his trusty sidekick Algy, in *Bulldog Drummond* (1929) and *Bulldog Drummond Strikes Back* (1934). Others who have portrayed him over the years include: Jack Buchanan, Ralph Richardson, John Howard, Ray Milland, John Lodge, Walter Pidgeon, Ron Randall and Tom Conway.

Hugh Drummond (Richard Johnson) and Brenda (Virginia North) in Deadlier Than The Male (1967, Rank)

The antithesis of James Bond, this dashing, sexless hero seems amusingly simplistic today, but gained a wide audience in its day. In 1914 'Sapper' married Violet Baird and they had two sons. He died at West Chiltington, near Pulborough, West Sussex. Bodmin Jail is open to the public all year.

See also: Ronald Colman

DRACULA
Tintagel

• 1979 Horror 109m c (UK)
• Frank Langella (Dracula), Laurence Olivier (Van Helsing), Donald Pleasence (Seward), Kate Nelligan (Lucy)
• P, Walter Mirisch; D, John Badham; w, W.D. Richter

This version of Bram Stoker's oft filmed vampire novel by director John Badham (*Saturday Night Fever*), obviously benefitted from Frank Langella's lengthy Broadway stage run as the Count, whose portrayal is closer to the original literary counterpart than most.

The lunatic asylum which imprisoned Renfield with his insatiable appetite for flies, spiders and sparrows was **King Arthur's Castle Hotel**, which occupies a magnificent position overlooking the sea and the ruins of Tintagel Castle. It stands on the spot where Tennyson received his inspiration for the *'Idylls of the King'* and was also used as a location for *Knights of the Round Table* (1953), starring Robert Taylor and Ava Gardner. **St. Michael's Mount**, a National Trust property on an island near Penzance, doubled as Dracula's Transylvanian castle and is reachable at low tide. The Count's attempted departure for home was filmed in the fishing village of **Mevagissey** and the shipwreck scenes were shot nearby at **Crinnis Beach** in **Carlyon Bay**.

See also: Bram Stoker, The Dracula Trail, Birthplace of *Dracula*

Further information: King Arthur's Castle Hotel, Tintagel, North Cornwall. Tel: 01840 770202. Penzance T.I.: 01736 362207.

THE REBECCA TRAIL
Fowey

"Last night I dreamt of Manderley again..." , the first line of dialogue hauntingly spoken by Joan Fontaine in Alfred Hitchcock's 1940 classic, *Rebecca*, is one of the most memorable openings in the movies. *Rebecca* and *The Birds* were both based on stories by the English writer of suspense classics, Daphne du Maurier (1907-89). Born in London, she was the daughter of the actor-manager, Sir Gerald du Maurier. After frequent holidaying in Cornwall, her family eventually moved there in 1926, where the wild and romantic landscape was to inspire many of her stories.

Their house was **Ferryside** at **Bodinnick**, where she wrote *Jamaica Inn* (1936), *Rebecca* (1938) and

Frenchman's Creek (1942). Nearby **Menabilly**, west of Fowey (not open to the public), was her original inspiration for 'Manderley', the home of Max de Winter and the sinister Mrs. Danvers in *Rebecca*. Daphne du Maurier later moved there with her husband, Major Frederick Browning, in 1943. Near Menabilly is the cove at **Polridmouth**, the location of Rebecca's boat house and death. du Maurier's short story, *The Birds*, published in *The Apple Tree* (1952), was set in the fields around **Menabilly Barton Farm** before being transposed to California's Bodega Bay by Hitchcock in 1963. The location of her novel *Frenchman's Creek*, filmed in 1944 by Mitchell Leisen, was inspired by a smugglers' inlet on the south bank of the Helford River (OS Ref: 748258), near Helford, after a sailing trip with her husband in 1932. Her 1951 novel, *My Cousin Rachel*, was filmed by Henry Koster in 1952.

See also: *Jamaica Inn*, Alfred Hitchcock, Laurence Olivier, Gladys Cooper, C. Aubrey Smith

Further information: 'The Rebecca Trail' is app. 5mls. long. Lunch and refreshments can be bought at the pub in Polkerris. Fowey Tourist Information: 01726 833616. Cornish Riviera Guides

Nigel Bruce, Laurence Olivier, Gladys Cooper and Joan Fontaine on the steps of Manderley. **Rebecca** *(1940 Selznick)*

Mrs. Danvers (Judith Anderson) taunts Mrs. de Winter (Joan Fontaine). **Rebecca** *(1940, Selznick)*

do several guided du Maurier walks. Tel: 01726 813463. 'The Daphne du Maurier Festival of Arts and Literature' is held annually every May in Fowey and St. Austell Bay. Tel: 01726 77477.

JAMAICA INN
Bolventor

Daphne du Maurier's historical romance was filmed by Alfred Hitchcock in 1939 and is probably best forgotten. Starring Charles Laughton and Maureen O'Hara, it was described by Graham Greene as *"reminiscent of the nosier characters in Shakespeare acted at a girls' school."* A remake was made in 1996 starring Patrick McGoohan.

Legend has it that Daphne du Maurier and Foy Quiller-Couch (daughter of Sir Arthur Quiller-Couch) became lost in the mist while riding on the Moor and stumbled upon Jamaica Inn, which later became the inspiration for her best-selling smuggling yarn. The inn was built in the mid-eighteenth century to serve travellers using the new turnpike road between Launceston and Bodmin. Originally known as 'The New Inn', but when a member of the local Rodd family returned from Jamaica in the 1800s, it was renamed 'Jamaica Inn'. A memorial room to Daphne du Maurier has been created at the inn and includes her Sheraton writing desk and a dish of Glacier Mints, her favourite sweeties.

Further information: Jamaica Inn, Bolventor, Launceston, Cornwall, PL15 7TS. Tel: 01566 86250.

STRAW DOGS
St Buryan

"In the same year that Man first flew to the Moon and the last American soldier left Vietnam there were still corners of England where lived men and women who had never travelled more than fifteen miles from their own homes."
The Siege of Trencher's Farm

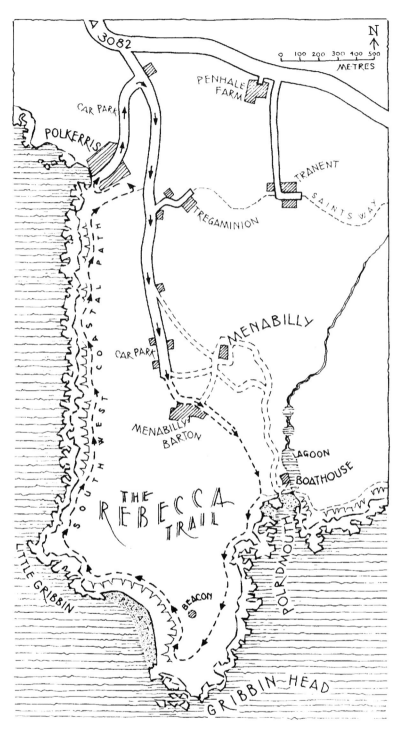

Described as *"Home Alone for psychopaths"* by critic Christopher Tookey, *Straw Dogs* was based on the novel *The Siege of Trencher's Farm* (1969) by Gordon M.Williams, and adapted for the screen by Sam Peckinpah and David Zelag in 1971. Peckinpah's most controversial film, it is the story of a couple (Dustin Hoffman and Susan George) who move to a small Cornish village and encounter local antagonism, which leads to one of the most violent finales ever to appear on screen. Strongly criticised on its release, particularly for its graphic rape scene, *Straw Dogs* is a memorable portrayal of man's confrontation with, and defeat of, the savage.

Location shooting was done in the village of **St Buryan**, four miles south west of Penzance, on the B3283. The village inn was a converted empty shop near the village centre.

*Dustin Hoffman and Susan George in **Straw Dogs** (1971, ABC/Amerbroco/Talent Ass.)*

FALMOUTH ARTS CENTRE
Falmouth

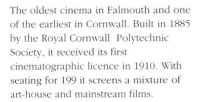

The oldest cinema in Falmouth and one of the earliest in Cornwall. Built in 1885 by the Royal Cornwall Polytechnic Society, it received its first cinematographic licence in 1910. With seating for 199 it screens a mixture of art-house and mainstream films.

Further information: Church St., Falmouth, Cornwall, TR11 3EG. Tel: 01326 314566.

CLASSIC LOCATION: CHARLESTOWN HARBOUR
Charlestown

This picturesque and unspoilt Cornish seaport, built in 1791 for the export of china-clay, appears regularly in feature films and television. It is also the home of Square Sail, who have gained a world-wide reputation for film location work with their fleet of square-rigged sailing ships. The company has created a working environment, where vessels are designed and built to suit virtually any period, along with the remodelling and dressing of existing ships. Square Sail marine co-ordinated the D-Day landings for Steven Spielberg's *Saving Private Ryan* (1998), including the supply and refurbishment of all the landing craft. Other films their ships have starred in include *Cutthroat Island, Princess Caraboo, 1492 Conquest of Paradise, Mansfield Park* and *Amy Foster*. Tours of the harbour and fleet (depending on whether or not filming is in progress), which includes a display of Square Sail's film location work, are every half hour from May to September.

See also: *Saving Private Ryan*

Further information: Square Sail, Charlestown Harbour, St. Austell, Cornwall, PL25 3NJ. Tel: 01726 67526 / 70241.

Cumbria

LAUREL & HARDY MUSEUM
Ulverston

"Those two fellows we created, they were nice, very nice people. They never get anywhere because they are both so dumb, but they don't know they're dumb. One of the reasons why people like us, I guess, is because they feel superior to us."
Oliver Hardy

The Laurel and Hardy museum is the only museum in the world devoted to the memory of Stan Laurel and Oliver Hardy and is housed in a former childhood home of Stan Laurel. The museum's collection contains photographs, letters, books, memorabilia, and a small cinema screening the duo's films. The museum's late founder, Bill Cubin, became fascinated with Laurel and Hardy as a child, when he started collecting everything he could find connected with them. A former Town Councillor and Mayor of Ulverston, Bill devoted his life to his two favourite comedians. In 1974, he opened his museum on premises where he once repaired washing machines for a living. Unsophisticated, and run on a shoe-string, the museum is a jumble of Laurel and Hardy folklore guaranteed to make you laugh.

See also: Stan Laurel, Laurel and Hardy, Fred Karno

Further information: Laurel & Hardy Museum, 4c, Upper Brook St., Ulverston, Cumbria, LA12 7BQ. Tel: 01229 582292.

BIRTHPLACE OF STAN LAUREL
Ulverston

"We were doing a very simple thing, giving some people some laughs, and that's all we were trying to do."
Stan Laurel

In the 1880's actor impresario, Arthur Jefferson, managed a small theatre called **Spencer's Gaff** (since demolished) opposite **Foundry Cottages (renamed Argyll Street)**. George and Sarah Metcalfe lived at Foundry Cottages and Arthur fell in love with their daughter Madge, marrying her on 19 March 1884. Madge became an actress, working with Arthur acting and managing halls around the country. When she was pregnant with her second child (she had five in all) they were working and living in Bishop

The Laurel and Hardy Museum - *gateway
to laughter.*

The Stan Laurel Inn, *The Ellers*

Foundry Cottages / Argyll Street - **birthplace of
Stan Laurel**

Auckland. Madge returned to her parents in Ulverston for the birth, and on 16 June 1890, Arthur Stanley Jefferson (always known as Stan) was born at Foundry Cottages. His birth was a difficult one and as he was not expected to survive, was hastily christened at home. Stan stayed with his maternal grandparents until he was six, when he left to attend school in Bishop Auckland.

Stan made his stage debut aged sixteen in a Glasgow theatre. In 1910 he joined the famous Fred Karno company and became Charlie Chaplin's understudy during the troupe's first American tour. In 1917 he made the first of his many film appearances until eventually teaming with Oliver Hardy in 1927. Stan was the creative half, while Olly

usually headed for the golf course. On screen the pair portrayed clumsy, genteel misfits who turned minor problems into major disasters. They brought joy to millions with films such as *Putting Pants on Philip* (1927), *The Music Box* (1932), *Sons of the Desert* (1934), *Babes in Toyland* (1934), *Bonnie Scotland* (1935) and *Way Out West* (1937).

Laurel and Hardy last visited Ulverston in 1947; Stan died in 1965. **The Stan Laurel Inn** (01229 582814), nearby in **The Ellers**, is a favourite watering hole for Laurel and Hardy fans, with L&H pictures and prints displayed on its walls.

See also: Laurel & Hardy Museum, Pickard's Museum, Fred Karno, The Stan Laurel Walk,

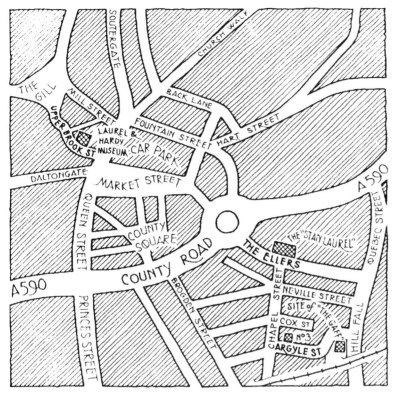

Ulverston

BIRTHPLACE OF FLETCHER CHRISTIAN (1764-c.94)
Cockermouth

"When you're back in England with the fleet again, you'll hear the hue and cry against me. From now on they'll spell mutiny with my name." Clark Gable

Although most movies based on the mutiny on the Bounty have provided excellent cinema, all of them have been economical with the truth. The mutiny has fascinated filmmakers over the years, especially the seemingly black and white relationship between the 'sadistic' Captain Bligh and that 'romantic and heroic leader of men', Fletcher Christian, portrayed on screen by various heart throbs, including Marlon Brando, Mel Gibson and Clark Gable, who in 1935 commented, *"... I'll be damned if I'll shave off my moustache just because the British Navy didn't allow them. This moustache has*

been damned lucky for me." Interpretations of the legend to date include *In the Wake of the Bounty* (1933), *Mutiny On The Bounty* (1916, 1935 & 1962) and *The Bounty* (1984).

Fletcher Christian was born on September 25, 1764, the sixth of seven sons of Ann Dixon and Charles Christian, a local coroner, at **Moorland Close** (plaque erected), a farmhouse still standing about two miles from **Cockermouth** on the right of the A5086 towards Egremont. Local legend

Mutiny on the Bounty *(1935, MGM)*

has it that he was actually born in the nearby **Summerhouse**, once the **Old Gatehouse** to the main house, and that his boyhood footprint can be seen in its lead gutter. He attended school at **Brigham** dame school (now **Eller Cottage**) and the Cockermouth Free Grammar School (demolished 1896 and now the site of **All Saints Parish Rooms** (plaque erected), off Kirkgate, Cockermouth). It is not clear when he actually joined the navy, but he was probably quite young when he enlisted. During 1786-7 he made two voyages with Captain Bligh as a Midshipman to the West Indies in the *Britannia.* A friendship was formed, and he often visited Bligh's home. Edward Lamb, chief mate on the *Britannia's* first voyage, commented that Bligh *"was blind to his faults... he went about every point of his duty with a degree of indifference that was truly unpleasant."*

His last trip with Bligh was as first mate on the Bounty's ill-fated bread-fruit collecting expedition to Tahiti, where the crew's five month sojourn on this south sea paradise, in the arms of sexually obliging native girls, slowly eroded their discipline. Many of the crew, including Christian, contracted venereal diseases and covering their bodies in Tahitian tattoos, turned 'native'. Twelve of the forty-three crew mutinied during the return voyage on the night of April 27, 1789, following Bligh's harsh attempts to harness discipline. Although Christian was the ringleader, he had previously tried to jump ship on a makeshift raft, but was persuaded by the others to mutiny instead, making him an unlikely inciter of the mutiny. Bligh and eighteen crew, plus supplies, were set adrift in an open launch, sentenced to what appeared a certain death. After a voyage of 3,600 miles, Bligh's exceptional seamanship and navigational skills landed them in Timor.

The mutineers, together with their native women and a few men, eventually settled on the uncharted island of Pitcairn, where their descendants live today. No one knows the real fate of Christian, but he was more than likely murdered by natives, together with three other mutineers. No grave has ever been found. One story tells of his return to Cumberland and another that he settled in Scotland and took up smuggling, but whatever Christian's fate was, his name will be forever synonymous with mutiny.

See also: Captain Bligh, Charles Laughton

THE ONE THAT GOT AWAY
Grizedale Forest Park

This film is based on the true story of a Luftwaffe pilot, Franz von Werra, who was shot down over Kent during the Battle of Britain in 1940. He was recaptured twice before he finally reached freedom in the United States after jumping from a moving train in Canada becoming the only Nazi prisoner to escape from British hands. Von Werra's first escape attempt was from a P.O.W. camp at **Grizedale Hall,** between **Windermere** and **Coniston Water**. The resulting search for Von Werra by soldiers, the Home Guard and police took place in October 1940, over the **Furness Fells** and around **Broughton Mills** to the **Duddon Valley**.

Director Roy Ward Baker used the original Grizedale Hall in his 1958 film, starring Hardy Kruger as Von Werra.

Scenes were also shot in and around the village of **Ulpha** where the Workington Fire Brigade sprayed daily downpours of rain for the film crew. Three coach loads of troops were transported from Catterick each day to provide the search party. The two bloodhounds used in the film refused to walk through any rainy patches and had to be dragged by their handlers. Eventually they trailed a pork chop and a farm cat to make them strain at the leash, both to no avail!

Further information: Grizedale Hall was demolished in the fifties and a 'Camping and Caravanning Club' is now on the original site.
Tel: 01229 860257.
Grizedale Forest Park Visitor Centre -
Tel: 01229 860010

CARS OF THE STARS MOTOR MUSEUM
Keswick

Started by local dentist, Peter Nelson in 1989, this museum features solely TV and film vehicles from his own private collection. Vehicles featured include: Chitty Chitty Bang Bang, Herbie the Love -Bug, and James Bond's Aston Martin. Also on display are recreations of the Batmobile, James Dean's Porsche, the DeLorean from *Back to the Future* and many other famous vehicles and motorcycles.

Further information: Cars of the Stars Motor Museum, Standish St., Town Centre, Keswick. Tel: 017687 73757. Open 7 days 10am to 5pm, Easter to New Year & February half term. Weekends only in December.

HOME OF BEATRIX POTTER (1866-1943)
Sawrey

Members of the Royal Ballet depicted Beatrix Potter's characters in *Tales of Beatrix Potter* (1971), choreographed by Frederick Ashton, who also portrayed Mrs. Tiggy-Winkle. In life-like masks and costumes, other members of the cast including Wayne Sleep, brought to life, amongst others, Jemima Puddle-Duck, Jeremy Fisher, Squirrel Nutkin and Peter Rabbit.

The young Beatrix Potter had her first taste of the countryside during family holidays to the Lake District and Scotland. It was here she studied flora and fauna and began to draw the animal characters that would later make her famous. Initially, no publisher was

Frederick Ashton as Mrs. Tiggywinkle in **Tales of Beatrix Potter** *(1971)*

interested in *Peter Rabbit* and in 1900 she printed the book privately. Shortly afterwards she began an association with Frederick Warne & Co. which lasted the rest of her life.

With her earnings she bought **Hill Top** farm at Sawey and in 1913 married William Heelis, a solicitor from Ambleside. She devoted the rest of her life to farming and when she died in 1943 her ashes were scattered by her shepherd in a secret location close to Hill Top.

Further information: Hill Top Farm, Nr. Sawrey, Ambleside, Cumbria, LA22 OLF. Tel: 015394 36269. Hill Top was bequeathed to the National Trust and is open to the public.

CLASSIC LOCATION: LAKESIDE & HAVERTHWAITE RAILWAY
Haverthwaite

Originally this Furness Railway branch line carried passengers and freight from Ulverston to Lakeside, but now the only part remaining is the three and a half mile section from Haverthwaite through Newby Bridge to the terminus at Lakeside.

Feature films shot on the line include *Swallows and the Amazons* (1973) starring Virginia McKenna, *Wagner* (1983) and *Testimony* (1987), Tony Palmer's biopics of composers Richard Wagner and Dmitri Shostakovich, starring Ben Kingsley and Richard Burton respectively, and the Sherlock Holmes farce, *Without a Clue* (1988), starring Michael Caine.

Further information: Lakeside & Haverthwaite Railway Co. Ltd., Haverthwaite Station, Nr. Ulverston, Cumbria, LA12 8AL. Tel: 015395 31594.

RANDOM HARVEST
Lake District

*Greer Garson and Ronald Colman in **Random Harvest** (1942, MGM)*

"One of the truly fine motion pictures of this or any year... an emotional experience of rare quality."
Hollywood Reporter

When WWI amnesiac, Charles Rainier, wanders off from hospital during the armistice celebrations he is befriended by Paula (Greer Garson), a music hall artist. They fall in love, have a baby, and settle down to an idyllic rural life, but when Charles is hit by a taxi in Liverpool the memory of his previous life returns to him, and his wife and child are forgotten.

Mervyn LeRoy's 1942 drama, based on a James Hilton story, is often disregarded as sentimental slush, but it remains a memorable entertainment and deserves its place alongside the MGM greats. Location filming was done in **Borrowdale**, between **Keswick** and **Grange**, in the Lake District.

See also: Ronald Colman, Greer Garson, Henry Travers, James Hilton

THE PARADINE CASE
Ambleside

Alfred Hitchcock's 1948 courtroom thriller, in which barrister Anthony Keane (Gregory Peck) falls in love with Maddalena Paradine (Alida Valli), the woman he is defending on a murder charge, was shot on location in the Lake District. Settings included **The Langdale Chase Hotel** (between Windermere and Ambleside on the A591. Tel: 015394) and **The Drunken Duck Inn** (between Ambleside and Hawkshead. Tel: 01539 436347).

See also: Alfred Hitchcock

THE STARS LOOK DOWN
Workington

Based on A.J. Cronin's novel, Carol Reed's 1939 film dramatically portrays the struggles of a small mining community in Northern England. Unlike John Ford's romanticised *How Green Was My Valley* (1941), seen through the rose-tinted spectacles of Hollywood, *The Stars Look Down* is much more in touch with the real-life plight of the miner. Michael Redgrave portrays the young idealist who dedicates his life to improving conditions for miners, and Margaret Lockwood plays his flighty wife.

Shot on location at **Workington coal mine and railway station**, and **Clifton Village**, near Penrith.
See also: A.J. Cronin, Carol Reed

ZEFFIRELLI'S
Ambleside

Formerly Ambleside's Assembly Rooms and cinema, Zeffirelli's incorporates a wholefood Pizzeria with two cinemas, shopping arcade and Garden Room Cafe. Launched in 1979 by Derek Hook, it was named after film director, Franco Zeffirelli, and is reputedly Ken Russell's favourite cinema. A former Blackpool butcher's boy, Derek came up with the then novel idea of having a bottle of wine, a pizza, and a movie, all under the same roof.

The cinema has hosted the premieres of three of George Harrison's Hand-made Film Productions - *Withnail and I, Bellman and True* and *Pow Wow Highway*, and has also premiered Ken Russell's *Gothic*.

See also: *Withnail and I*

Further information: Zeffirelli's, Compston Road, Ambleside, Cumbria LA22 9AD. Tel: 015394 31771 / 33845. Seats may only be reserved for the combined dinner and cinema 'Double Feature'. Situated in the centre of Ambleside, on the left hand side of Compston Road (coming in from the south, on the one way system) at the junction with Millans Park.

Cumbria

WITHNAIL & I
Shap

• 1987 108m c comedy drama
Handmade (UK)
• Richard E. Grant (Withnail), Paul McGann
(Marwood), Richard Griffiths (Monty), Ralph
Brown (Danny), Michael Elphick (Jake)
• p, Paul M. Heller; d, Bruce Robinson; w,
Bruce Robinson (based on his novel); ph,
Peter Hannan; ed, Alan Strachan; m, David
Dundas

*"They're selling hippy wigs in
Woolworths man. The greatest decade
in the history of mankind is over, and
as Presuming Ed here has so
consistently pointed out - we have failed
to paint it black."*
Danny

Paul McGann (Marwood) and Richard E. Grant (Withnail) in **Withnail & I** *(1987, Handmade)*

Set in 1969, this cult comedy is a side-
splitting testament to the last days of
the sixties. In a life devoid of any
evidence of peace and love, out-of-
work thespians Withnail and Marwood
exist only in misery and squalor.
Cracking under the strain of their
revolting city life, they decide to have a
holiday away from it all. Withnail's gay
uncle Monty lets them have Crow
Cragg, his isolated cottage in the Lake
District, but rather than the rural idyll
they had imagined, it turns out to be a
freezing, mud and rain-sodden bothy.
Things pick up, though, when Uncle
Monty unexpectedly arrives with food,
wine, and designs on Marwood's body.

Director and writer Bruce Robinson
based the character of Withnail on
Vivian MacKerrell (now deceased), one
of the many flat-mates he shared a
house with in Camden's **Albert Street**
during the sixties. Robinson described
MacKerrell as *"[Having] the pomposity
of the thespian. He was a very smart
guy, very bright, but he was sad too,
because he was jack of all and master
of none. He always used to say to me,
"'If I wrote I'd write a fuck sight better
than you ever would, or if I painted I'd
paint a fuck sight better than you ever
would... but the fact is he never did
anything. All he ever did was booze.'"*

Various views of **Sleddale Hall** *(Crow Cragg) in the Wet Sleddale Valley (photos Noel Tom)*

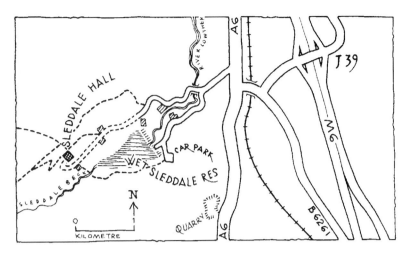

Richard E. Grant, incidentally, is allergic to alcohol, and is a life-long teetotaller.

Crow Cragg was an isolated 18th century cottage called **Sleddale Hall, near Shap village**, off the A6, in the **Wet Sleddale Valley**. Fans of the movie, including Noel Gallagher of Oasis, have pilgrimaged here from all over the world.

The cottage lay derelict for many years, and in 1998 its owner, North West Water, applied for planning permission to rebuild it and convert two outbuildings into holiday homes. Following objections from planners that it might change the character of the valley, the scheme was withdrawn. At the time of writing the property lies empty.

The view from nearby **Mardale Common overlooking Haweswater Reservoir** was used as the view from Crow Cragg, and the phone box from which Withnail calls his agent is in **Helton**.

The London locations were shot in **Camden Town** and included **Camden Street, Albany Street** and **Regents Park**. The film's premiere was at Zeffirelli's, Compston Road, Ambleside.

See also: Zeffirelli's

Darlington

BIRTHPLACE OF ANTHONY HAVELOCK-ALLAN (1903-)

Anthony Havelock-Allan, prolific film producer and screenwriter, was born at **Blackwell Manor** (now demolished and replaced by a church and terraced houses). A BFI plaque commemorating his contribution to the cinema was erected in 1997, close to his birth site, outside number **63 Blackwell**.

His first job was in the jewellery trade and in 1933 he managed the Brunswick gramophone company which brought him into contact with showbusiness personalities, signing up, amongst

others, Gracie Fields, Jessie Matthews and Leslie Hutchinson. He started in the film industry as a casting director and was soon directing low budget feature films. In the early forties he formed the film company, Cineguild, with David Lean and Ronald Neame, which produced some of the great classics of the British cinema, including *This Happy Breed* (1944, produced & co-written), *Blithe Spirit* (1945, co-written), *Brief Encounter* (1945, co-written), *Geat Expectations* (1946, co-written) and *Oliver Twist* (1948, produced & co-written).

He also produced Zeffirelli's *Romeo and Juliet* in 1968 and finally, *Ryan's Daughter* in 1970. He was married three times; his first wife was actress, Valerie Hobson.

See also: David Lean, Noel Coward, *Brief Encounter, Great Expectations, Ryan's Daughter,* Valerie Hobson

Derby

BIRTHPLACE OF ALAN BATES (1934-)
Allestree

"It is not that Alan Bates is a difficult man, merely one who has seen and done too much to be interested in selling himself."
Lesley White, Sunday Times

Alan Bates is an actor who likes his privacy and has never courted showbiz glitz. A stage actor at heart, he once commented, *"What films teach you is to trust in your own personality, but if you stay in them too long you lose the pace and rhythm of the live theatre."*

He was born on 17 February 1934 at **3 Derwent Avenue** (plaque erected), Allestree, Derby, the eldest of three brothers. He decided on an acting career when he was eleven. His middle-class parents, both professional musicians, always encouraged him in his acting pursuits, which included hiring a voice coach and introducing him to the local drama group. One of his earliest performances was in a school production of *The Importance of Being Earnest* in Belper. He attended RADA with O'Toole, Finney and Courtenay, and later joined the new English Stage Company at the Royal Court. In 1956 he portrayed Cliff in the original 1956 production of *Look Back in Anger* which led to his first major film role in John Osborne's *The Entertainer* (1960). Many of his later films were also based on stage plays,

including *The Caretaker* (1964), *Three Sisters* (1970), *A Day in the Death of Joe Egg* (1972), *Butley* (1974) and *In Celebration* (1975). He made cinema history in 1969 when he became the first full-frontal male nude to appear in a British film in Ken Russell's *Women in Love*. Other memorable roles have included the escaped convict mistaken for Jesus Christ in *Whistle Down the Wind* (1961), young Northerner Vic Brown in *A Kind of Loving* (1962), Basil the intellectual Englishman in *Zorba the Greek* (1965), Gabriel Oak in *Far From the Madding Crowd* (1967), Yakov Bok in *The Fixer* (1968) and farmer Ted Burgess in *The Go-Between* (1971).

Tragedy entered Alan Bates' life in 1990 when his nineteen year old son Tristan, one of identical twins, died from an asthma attack (not - as reported by some of the press - from a drug overdose, but after taking a drug for his asthma) while working as a model in Tokyo. In 1992 Bates' wife, Victoria,

also died. He now lives next door to his son in St. John's Wood.

See also: *Whistle Down the Wind, Far From the Madding Crowd, The Go-Between*

Derbyshire

THE DAMBUSTERS
Derwent Valley

• 1954 124m bw War Associated British Pictures (UK)
• Richard Todd (Guy Gibson), Michael Redgrave (Barnes Wallis), Ursula Jeans (Mrs Wallis) Basil Sydney (Sir Arthur Harris)
• p, Robert Clark; d, Michael Anderson; ph, Erwin Hillier; sfx, Gilbert Taylor; ed, Richard Best; w, R.C. Sheriff (based on the book by Paul Brickhill); m, Eric Coates

In March 1943, under the command of Wing Commander Guy Gibson, aircrews were handpicked to form a special squadron whose mission was to breach the German dams in the Ruhr valley. Following six weeks of low-level training in the Derwent Valley, 19 Lancasters took off on the night of 16/17th May, carrying Dr Barnes Wallis' bouncing mine. The Mohne and Eder dams were successfully breached, but 53 men were lost, 3 taken prisoner and 8 aircraft went missing. The operation earned 617 Squadron 33 decorations, including one for Guy Gibson, and the squadron passed into legend as 'The Dambusters'.

The locations used in the film were for the most part the real locations used by 617 Squadron. **Scampton RAF Station** in Lincolnshire was used for shooting ground scenes (617 Squadron moved from Scampton via Conningsby to Woodhall Spa in 1943 where they remained for the rest of the war) and the **Derwent Valley Reservoir and Dam** were chosen for the aerial sequences because of their resemblance to their German counterparts. Filming in the Derwent

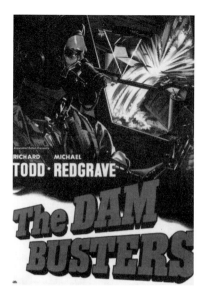

Valley took two weeks in August, 1954, using one Lancaster and two Shackletons from RAF Waddington in Lincolnshire and took place in daylight - the film being over-exposed to create the effect of night-flying. The bomb dropping trial sequences were shot on **Skegness Beach** and the studio scenes were done at **Elstree**.

See also: Dambusters' Memorial, Richard Todd

Further information: Derwent Valley Visitors' Centre 01433 650953.

GRAVE OF LITTLE JOHN
Hathersage

Robin Hood's titan side-kick is allegedly buried in the village churchyard under an extra-large hummock.

See also: *Robin Hood: Prince of Thieves,* Robin Hood

GRAVE OF EDITH MAUDE HULL (1880-1947)
Hazelwood

In Hazelwood Churchyard lies the grave of Edith Maude Hull, whose

desert romance, *The Sheik* (1919) was instrumental in creating the legend of Rudolph Valentino. Her novel recounts the tale of English aristocratic heroine, Diana Mayo, who is kidnapped by a barbarous sheik and spirited off to a land of sandstorms, brigands, sunsets, desert daring and ultimately rape: *"She had fought until the unequal struggle had left her exhausted and helpless in his arms, until her whole body was one agonised ache from the brutal hands that forced her to compliance, until her courageous spirit was crushed by the realisation of her own powerlessness."*

The book's eroticism caused a moral outrage on publication and the Literary Review claimed that the novel was 'poisonously salacious', with its apparent depiction of the heroine enjoying her sexual assault by a mysterious Arab. The sado-masochistic Sheik, however, is ultimately revealed as a European in disguise; presumably this revelation was intended to render the man's offence acceptable, and certainly, amid prevalent contemporary attitudes towards colonialism, this seems to have been the case.

The 1921 film adapted from the novel was a box-office hit; hysterical women fainted in their seats and Valentino's reputation as the world's heart-throb was secured. A sequel, adapted from Edith Hull's novel, *Son of the Sheik*, was made in 1926 and its success restored Valentino's waning popularity before he died the same year from peritonitis, aged thirty-one.

Edith Maude Hull was the daughter of James Henderson of Liverpool. She married a Derbyshire pig farmer and lived much of her life in Hazelwood at **'The Knowle'**, home of the Hull family for four generations. They had one daughter named Cecil (so-named because they had wanted a boy).

Edith Hull first visited Algeria as a child and throughout her life she travelled extensively, including four visits to the Sahara. Her books commanded a wide public, especially in the U.S.A. and

Rudolph Valentino

Grave of Edith Maude Hull, *Hazelwood Churchyard*

Europe, where *The Sheik* was translated into fourteen languages. Her other works include: *The Shadow of the East* (1921), *Desert Healer* (1923), *Sons of the Sheik* (1926) and a travel book, *Camping in the Sahara* (1927).

The ghost of Edith Maude Hull, wearing eastern robes and gold bracelets is said to haunt the **Garden House** at The Knowle. Her grave can be found in **Hazelwood Churchyard** to the right of the church doorway. She is buried beside her husband beneath a large marble cross.

THE SCALA
Ilkeston

The first purpose-built cinema in Ilkeston was constructed over the graveyard of Burns Street Independent Chapel and gave its first screening on September 4th, 1913, consisting of *A Fair Saint, A Way Women Have, Ruins of Pompeii* and *The Shunter's Daughter*. Designed by Bulwell architects Parson & Sons, it cost £5,000 to build and originally seated 1,000 patrons. Today it seats only half that audience, but its ornate plaster work, oak carvings on the balcony and impressive domed entrance still remain. It has been in continuous use since 1913 and became a listed building in 1986.

Further information: The Scala, Market Place, Ilkeston. Tel: 0115 932 4612.

GOODBYE MR CHIPS
Repton

- 1939 114m bw Drama MGM (UK)
- Robert Donat (Charles Chipping), Greer Garson (Katherine Ellis), Terry Kilburn (John/Peter Colley), John Mills (Peter Colley as a young man), Paul Henreid (Max Staefel), Judith Furse (Flora), Lyn Harding (Dr, Wetherby), Milton Rosmer (Charteris)
- p, Victor Saville; d, Sam Wood; w, R.C.

Sheriff, Claudine West, Eric Maschwitz, Sidney Franklin (based on the novella by James Hilton); ph, Freddie Young; ed, Charles Frend, m, Richard Addinsell; art d, Alfred Junge; cos, Julie Harris
• AA Best Actor: Robert Donat

"If, in fact, we must have a sentimental film about the English public school system, this is probably the film to have."
Dilys Powell

Robert Donat gave the performance of his life in this screen adaptation of James Hilton's story of the shy and unpretentious schoolmaster, Mr. Chipping, who devotes his life to Brookfield School for Boys. From his early days as a fledgling schoolmaster, to his final years as a venerable academic and school institution, the film charts his unassuming life. Donat's portrayal won him a Best Actor Oscar (against the formidable competition of Clark Gable in *Gone With The Wind*), and his name became synonymous with 'Chips' for the rest of his life.

Location filming was done at **Repton School** where extras who took part in the film still live in the village. The village church of **St Wystan's** can be seen in the opening scenes. The School **Arch** and **Causeway** (used in the registration scenes) appear in the film, and the **Common Room** was used as the location for Mr Chips' lodgings.

Established on the site of a twelfth century Augustinian Priory, Repton School was founded in 1557 by local landowner, Sir John Port. Repton and the Priory were once the centre of Christianity in the Midlands, and at times the capital of Mercia. The majority of the school buildings are grouped around the ancient buildings of the Old Priory, consisting of classrooms, libraries, laboratories, a theatre and a hall. Repton's old boys include Basil Rathbone (plaque erected) who attended the school from 1906 to 1910, Roald Dahl, film director John Paddy Carstairs, and Olympic athlete Harold Abrahams, portrayed by

The Priory and Pears School, *Repton*

Ben Cross in *Chariots of Fire* (1981). The BBC version of *Goodbye Mr Chips* was also shot on location here, and a plaque commemorating the 1939 film was erected at the school in 1996.

See also: James Hilton, Robert Donat, Greer Garson, W.H. Balgarnie, Sherborne School

Further information: Repton School, Repton, Derby DE65 6FH. Anyone wishing to visit should contact John Plowright, on 01283 559200 / Email: boss@repton.org.uk

Devon

THE HOUND OF
THE BASKERVILLES
Dartmoor

Twelve film versions have been made to date of Sir Arthur Conan Doyle's gripping mystery novel, *The Hound of the Baskervilles*, considered by many to be the finest detective story in the English language. Nearly all of them were studio productions, many of

Doctor Watson (André Morell) and Sir Henry Baskerville (Christopher Lee) survey the moor in Hammer's 1959 version of **The Hound of the Baskervilles.**

which tried to faithfully recreate the threatening atmosphere of the moor. It first appeared on screen in a 1917 German production. The earliest British talkie version was in 1931, and starred Robert Rendel; locations included **Lustleigh Railway Station**, which became Baskerville, and **Moretonhampstead Hotel**, which doubled for Baskerville Hall. The most memorable version, however, was director Sidney Lanfield's 1939 production, starring Basil Rathbone, whose lean stature and hawkish looks created cinema's definitive Sherlock Holmes. The set which 20th Century Fox built for Grimpen Mire was then the largest in the world, and Richard Greene once got lost in it.

Conan Doyle first heard of the Dartmoor hound legends from his friend Fletcher Robinson during a holiday at Cromer, on the Norfolk coast, and both agreed to collaborate on a book about them. There are many hound legends in West Country folklore, and one which Conan Doyle may have woven into his plot was that of the iniquitous 17th century squire, Richard Cabell, on whose death a pack of hounds are alleged to have gathered and howled around his house. His tomb can be seen in a small sepulchre near the remains of **Holy Trinity Church, Buckfast Leigh**, where he was buried in 1672. Fearing that he might rise from the grave, anxious locals supposedly drove an iron stake through his heart and covered his tomb with a large granite slab. Until recently, the stonemason's guiding marks for cutting the name on the tomb were visible, and these showed that the proposed cutting of his surname was never completed, implying that something happened to unnerve the stonemason.

Fletcher Robinson lived near Dartmoor at **Park Hill House**, about four miles from **Newton Abbot**, and it was here that Conan Doyle stayed in early 1901 to research and write at least part of the book. Using the house as a base, they explored the surrounding

countryside for locations in the company of Robinson's young carriage driver, William Henry Baskerville, known as Harry, who always claimed he donated his name to the story. Harry lived in the small lodge house called **Park Lodge** on the corner of **Park Hill Crossroads**, and it was here that the Robinson family carriage was kept for excursions on the Moor. The Rowe's 'Duchy Hotel, now **The High Moorland Visitor Centre in Princetown**, was where Conan Doyle

stayed in 1901 whilst writing part of the book. He also used it as a base to explore parts of the moor unreachable by carriage.

The Hound of the Baskervilles was never intended to be a Sherlock Holmes story as Conan Doyle had plunged Holmes and Moriarty to their supposed deaths at the Reichenbach Falls in 1891, ten years previously. He got round the problem by predating it to before Holmes' demise and so

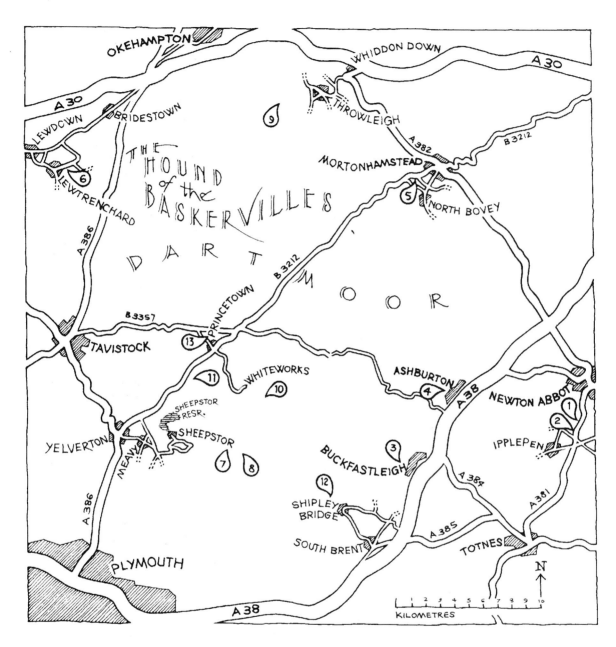

Sherlock Holmes made a spectacular comeback.

Many Holmesian scholars have attempted to determine the whereabouts of all the real-life locations in the *The Hound of the Baskervilles*, and to date, all have failed. The main reasons for this failure can be attributed to Conan Doyle's atmospheric merging of fact with fiction, for example by increasing and

decreasing distances and by combining the components of various locations into one, making it almost impossible to identify them, even though the area has changed very little since the time of Conan Doyle's visit. Originally he used many of the real names of places on the moor, but subsequently he changed some of these, thus making the search for the exact spot of many of the locations difficult to identify. Some of the most important sites, arrived at by

the calculated guesswork of Holmesian scholars, are detailed on the map.

When venturing onto the moor, make sure someone knows your itinerary and your estimated return time. Take great care if deviating from the beaten track, and always take warm and waterproof clothing with you, as the weather can change dramatically within a matter of minutes. Large areas are used as artillery firing ranges. Do not pick up anything that looks suspicious. When in use these ranges have red flags flying on their boundaries. By far the best map for locational exploration is the Ordnance Survey - Outdoor Leisure Map - Sheet No 28 - Dartmoor - 1: 25000 scale.

MAP KEY:

1. Fletcher Robinson's House: Park Hill is the large house slightly up the hill from the Harry Baskerville lodge (see below) in the direction of Newton Abbot.

2. Harry Baskerville's House: This small lodge house, called 'Park Lodge' is located on the corner of the Park Hill crossroads, the junction between the Newton Abbot to Totnes main road and the lane leading to Ipplepen. It is a private residence, but it can be seen from the main road.

3. The Cabell Sepulchre: The tomb of Richard Cabell (1622? -1672), who, it is claimed, was the original Hugo Baskerville, is located in a sepulchre in the churchyard of The Church of the Holy Trinity on the hill overlooking Buckfastleigh.

4. Harry Baskerville's Grave: Buried in the upper section of the churchyard of the parish church of St. Andrew in Ashburton, under his formal name of Henry Baskerville.

5. Manor House Hotel / Baskerville Hall: Near Moretonhampstead, this hotel was used in the 1931 Gainsborough Pictures version, starring Robert Rendel, who was born in Lustleigh on Dartmoor, where the 'Baskerville' railway scenes were filmed. Unfortunately the building was not built until 1907, so it could not have been used by Doyle as a location, who completed his book in 1902.

6. Lewtrenchard / Baskerville Hall: This location was strongly recommended by one of the greatest-ever Holmesian scholars, William S Baring-Gould, but then this was his

family's ancestral home. It is now a hotel.

7. Giant's Basin (MR:595670) & 8. Deadman's Bottom (MR:608668) / Hugo's Death Site: Hugo chased the young maiden across the moor before meeting the hound of death. His death took place in a goyal, or deep dip, and there are two standing stones shaped like fangs nearby. The two candidates for this site can be reached on a 7-mile circuit around Higher Hartor Tor, but this route should only be followed by experienced Moor navigators.

9. Raybarrow Pool (MR:640902) & 10. Fox Tor Mires (MR:618707) / Grimpen Mire: These are the only two realistic candidates for the location where Stapleton kept the hound. A mire is an area of swampy ground, but it is usually taken to indicate an area where a person or creature can actually sink beneath the surface. Even in these two areas it would be extremely difficult for a person to become fully submerged, as depths of these mires have decreased greatly with drier weather conditions and the introduction of drainage systems on the moor. Care is still needed, however, in the area of the mire.

11. Black Tor (Meavy) (MR573718) & 12. Black Tor (Avon) (MR681635) / Black Tor: This is the tor upon which Holmes was seen when Watson and Sir Henry chased Selden, and Watson later walks to it in the rain. There are four Black Tors on the moor, but only these two are candidates because they are within reasonable distances of candidates for Baskerville Hall.

13. Princetown Prison: There is no doubt about Doyle's prison location. It has been where it is now since the Napoleonic Wars, and there is no other major prison on the Moor. The main gate of the prison can be seen from the road, but be warned that photography is not permitted in this area. There are graves of French and American prisoners of war in the Princetown cemetery.

See also: Sir Arthur Conan Doyle, Joseph Bell, Peter Cushing, Hammer Studios, Sherlock Holmes Festival, Frensham Common

Further information: The Franco-Midland Hardware Company and The Baskerville Hounds, 6 Bramham Moor, Hill Head, Fareham, Hampshire, PO14 3RU. Tel: 01329 667325. The FMHC is an international Sherlock Holmes correspondence study group and the TBH specialises in studies of Dartmoor and *The Hound of the Baskervilles*. The High Moorland Visitor Centre, Princetown. Open daily, except Christmas Day. Easter to 31 October: 10am-5pm. Winter opening 10am-4pm. Admission free.

I would like to thank Holmesian scholar, Phillip Weller, who helped with the compilation of this information. Those who require a more in-depth exploration are advised to read his detailed monograph: *The Dartmoor Locations of The Hound of the Baskervilles* available from the FMHC.

BRITISH PHOTOGRAPHIC MUSEUM
Totnes

Housed in a historic Tudor and Queen Anne house, the BPM has a vast collection of photographic bygones, including many vintage and classic cinematography exhibits. Oldie film shows are screened daily at 1pm.

Further information: British Photographic Museum, Bowden House, Totnes, TQ9 7PW. Tel: 01803 863664. Open: 25th March to 31st October. Monday to Thursday. Noon to 5.30pm.

THE CRUEL SEA
Devonport

- 1953 120m bw War Ealing (U.K.).
- Jack Hawkins (Capt. Ericson), Donald Sinden (Lockhart), John Stratton (Ferraby), Denholm Elliott (Morrell), Stanley Baker

Devon

(Bennett), Virginia McKenna (Julie Hallam).
- p, Leslie Norman; d, Charles Frend; W, Eric Ambler; ph, Gordon Dines; ed, Peter Tanner; m, Alan Rawsthorne.
- AAN Best Original Screenplay: Eric Ambler.

Shot in documentary style, *The Cruel Sea* was based on Nicholas Monsarrat's best-selling novel which recounts the hazardous duties of the small but plucky Corvette Class convoy escorts during WWII and the crews who served on them.

Devonport doubled for Liverpool as the home port of *HMS Compass Rose*, a dilapidated Greek Navy hulk which was on its way to be broken up at Sunderland. Its demise was postponed by Ealing who made it ship-shape and ready for filming in only two weeks.

Donald Sinden, who made his screen debut in the film, recalls an incident which occurred while steaming into harbour and trying to pull up alongside a destroyer already moored at the quayside. Jack Hawkins appeared to be in command on the bridge, but the real skipper was kneeling down off camera peering through two peepholes specially bored in the bulkhead: *"I noticed the sea was rushing past us...suddenly the whole ship heaved, as our anchor, protruding from the side of the bows, tore a hole nine feet long and ten inches wide in the side of Her Majesty's destroyer! And there was Jack Hawkins in full view on the bridge. From the wheelhouse of the destroyer emerged an officer, who, with perfect RN understatement, surveyed the damage and said, 'Who the flipping hell's driving your boat - Errol Flynn?'* *

See also: Jack Hawkins, Stanley Baker, Ealing Studios

BIRTHPLACE OF FRED KARNO (1866-1941)
Exeter

We are Fred Karno's army
A ragtime infantry
We cannot fight, we cannot shoot
What earthly use are we?
And when we get to Berlin
The Kaiser he will say
Hoch! Hoch! Mein Gott
What a bloody fine lot
Are the ragtime infantry
Fred Karno's 'Army' song, sung to the tune of 'The Church's One Foundation'

Fred Karno was a music hall comedian who became the most successful showman in England, but he is probably best remembered today for the famous names his company gave a start to, than for his own brand of comedy and showmanship.

Born Frederick John Westcott on the 26th of March 1866 at **Waterbeer Street**, the eldest of seven children of John Westcott, cabinet-maker and French polisher, and his wife Emily Bowden. He started his working life in the 1880s with the 'Karno Trio' as an

Fred Karno

acrobat and gymnast from which he took his own stage name. For ten years, Fred ran Exeter's Hippodrome Theatre, which stood on the **London Inn Square site**, now occupied by Boots the Chemist. In the 1890's he had established **'Karno's Fun Factory' in Brixton (top of Harbour Road, off Coldharbour Lane)** from where teams of comedians were despatched to perform set-shows on music-hall bills.

His travelling troupe of comedians became known as 'Fred Karno's Army' which included Charlie Chaplin, Stan Laurel, Will Hay, Max Miller, Sandy Powell and Wee Georgie Wood. Charlie

'Karno's Fun Factory', Brixton

Chaplin and Stan Laurel both toured America with 'Fred Karno's Army' which was instrumental in launching their Hollywood careers.

After having made his fortune he bought Tagg's Island on the Thames in 1913. Here he built 'The Karsino', a resort with a hotel, restaurant, golf course and tennis courts. Unfortunately it rained all through the summer season and because business was consequently so disastrous, he was ruined by his overheads and ended his days running an off-licence in Poole.

See also: Charlie Chaplin, Stan Laurel, Will Hay.

THE BILL DOUGLAS CENTRE FOR THE HISTORY OF CINEMA & POPULAR CULTURE

Exeter

"Bill Douglas shot far less footage than many other film-makers. But everything he made showed passionate feeling, as well as a beautiful developing artistry. He was one of the very few. He always will be."
Lindsay Anderson

When Bill Douglas died in 1991 the British cinema lost one of its most original artists, whose autobiographical trilogy *My Childhood* (1972), *My Ain Folk* (1973) and *My Way Home* (1978) is acknowledged to be among the masterpieces of poetic cinema.

He grew up in the impoverished Scottish mining village of **Newcraighall**, outside Edinburgh. He rose above the unbending poverty of his childhood to become an actor and later a film-maker, graduating from the London Film School in 1970. He died of cancer on 18 June 1991, aged fifty-seven, and is buried in **Bishop Tawton Churchyard**.

Over a period of more than thirty years, he and his companion Peter Jewell built up an amazing collection of

Bill Douglas

artefacts, books, prints and other material on the technical and cultural history and prehistory of the cinema. Peter Jewell has now donated the collection to the Exeter University Foundation, in order that it may be established as a memorial to Bill Douglas.

The collection encompasses the development of popular entertainment from the the late 18th century to classical Hollywood and the present day. It includes examples of equipment used for 'optical recreations' in the 19th century; early cinema equipment including a Lumière Cinematographe (only 400 were ever made, and perhaps 50 survive); posters and silent cinema programmes; cigarette cards; Charlie Chaplin toby jugs; "movie star eyelashes" for 1950s teenagers; Snow White crockery and first editions of the most important books in the history of cinematography. The collection's estimated 18,000 books and periodicals constitutes the largest university library collection on cinema in the country; a library comparable only with that of the British Film Institute.

The University has converted part of its Old Library building to house the Bill Douglas Centre in a purpose-designed space of 4,400 sq. ft., which allows for exhibition of many of the collection's

artefacts in a public museum. The Centre's display areas are open to the public free of charge, and the remainder of the material is held in a research collection available to students and private researchers.

See also: *Comrades*

Further information: The Bill Douglas Centre, The Old Library, University of Exeter (off Prince of Wales Rd.) Opening times: Monday to Friday, 10:00 am to 4:00 pm during university term. Tel: 01392 264321) Web site: http://www.ex.ac.uk/bill.douglas/

LAST PUBLIC APPEARANCE OF LAUREL & HARDY IN BRITAIN

Plymouth

On their fourth and last tour in 1954, Laurel and Hardy unknowingly gave their last performance in the U.K. at the **Palace Theatre** (now disused, previously The Academy nightclub)**, Union St.**, Plymouth on Monday 17 May. It was intended to be the penultimate week of the tour, which was scheduled to finish in Swansea, but Ollie developed flu and suffered a mild heart attack and the remainder of the tour was cancelled. Stan refused to appear without Ollie, and in an interview with the *Western Independent* he explained: *"I would not attempt it. I know it would have been disappointing. I am completely lost without Hardy. We do comedy sketches - situations. I am not a gag man."* On 30 May they departed from Hull for Los Angeles on the merchant ship, the *Manchuria*.

See also: Laurel and Hardy, Stan Laurel

TORBAY CINEMA

Paignton

Reputedly the oldest purpose-built cinema in the country. There appears to be some doubt over the precise age of the Torbay Cinema, with some sources quoting 1907, and others 1910. Originally named the Byoscopic Exhibition Hall, it opened as the Torbay Picture House in 1914. Now a listed building, it still retains many of its original fittings, including its art nouveau light fittings and ticket booth. Its regulars over the years have included Isadora Duncan, Edgar Wallace and Agatha Christie, whose favourite seat was number 11 in the circle. The cinema featured in the 1984 screen adaptation of her book, *Ordeal by Innocence*, starring Donald Sutherland, and has also appeared in numerous Hammer productions.

The ghost of Farrant Gilly, a former managing director from the 30s to the 60s, is said to haunt the cinema. John Mann, the present manager explained, *"Mr Gilly was a man of distinction. He always wore a trilby and smoked a Havana cigar. He died in the late sixties, aged eighty, and I can still smell his cigar smoke in the cinema. Occasionally customers have complained of an illicit cigar smoker. He is, however, a friendly spirit, and brings us good luck."*

In 1910 when trams passed by they sent a reverse charge through the power system which would speed up films. Recently, a wall was demolished in the cinema revealing parcelled documents dating back many years, including receipts from Gaumont News for footage of the sinking of the Lusitania, a letter from a violinist in the cinema's orchestra complaining he was unable to keep up with westerns because the projectionist was running

them too fast, and a weekly wage bill for the 21-piece orchestra from 1910 amounting to £16.16s.0d.

Further information: Torbay Cinema, Torbay Road, Paignton. Tel: 01803 559544. Seats: 484

A MATTER OF LIFE AND DEATH
Saunton

• 1946 104m c/bw Fantasy/Romance Archers/Independent Producers (U.K.)
• David Niven (Squadron Leader Peter D. Carter), Kim Hunter (June), Roger Livesey (Dr. Reeves), Robert Coote (Bob Trubshawe), Marius Goring (Conductor 71), Raymond Massey (Abraham Farlan), Kathleen Byron (An Angel)
• p, Michael Powell, Emeric Pressburger; d, Michael Powell, Emeric Pressburger; w, Michael Powell, Emeric Pressburger; ph, Jack Cardiff; ed, Reginald Mills; prod d, Alfred Junge

"Where are you? Where are you? Request your position! Request your position! Come in Lancaster... come in Lancaster..."

Death seems a certainty for WWII bomber pilot Peter Carter (David Niven). His crew have baled out, his instruments have gone and his undercarriage is shot away. In the last moments before his inevitable death he talks over the radio to June, an American girl on the airfield where he is unable to land, and their love story begins. He is washed ashore on an isolated beach but is unable to decide whether he is alive, or hallucinating. Conductor 71 (Marius Goring) is sent to collect and transport him Heavenwards, but discovers someone has blundered when he finds Carter very much alive and in love with June. Peter subsequently battles to remain on earth and fights his case with Doctor Frank Reeves in the boundless High Court in the Other World.

A Matter of Life and Death (aka Stairway to Heaven) was made at the

*David Niven and Kim Hunter in **A Matter of Life and Death** (1946, Archers)*

request of the Ministry of Information who wanted Powell and Pressburger to make a film which advocated goodwill between Britain and America. The result was a masterpeice of British cinema, whose fusing of fantasy and reality has never been equalled. Studio scenes were shot at Denham. For the 'Stairway to Heaven' set, a giant escalator was constructed consisting of 106 stairs, twenty feet wide, driven by a two-gear 12 h.p. engine. The distant effect of the escalator was created by hanging models. All the location filming was done at **Saunton Sands**, about ten miles down the coast from Ilfracombe, where, unknown to the film crew (until pointed out by the army), a stretch of sand they were using was part of the largest belt of unexploded mines on the British coast.

See also: Michael Powell, Emeric Pressburger, David Niven

Dorset

THE LAWRENCE OF ARABIA TRAIL
Wareham, Moreton, Bovington, & Turnerspuddle

"My rare visits to the cinema always deepen in me a sense of their superficial falsity... The camera seems wholly in place as journalism; but when it tries to recreate, it boobs and sets my teeth on

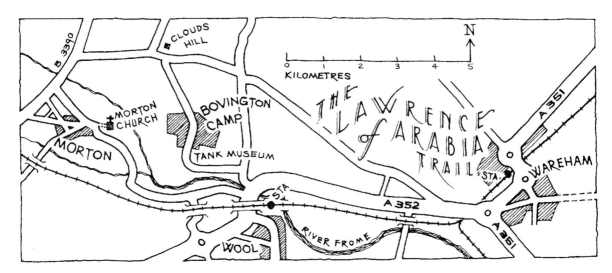

edge. So there won't be a film of me."
T.E. Lawrence writing to Robert Graves, 1935.

David Lean was not the first film maker to envisage Lawrence's life on film. Director Rex Ingram approached Lawrence in 1927 with a view to adapting his memoirs for the screen, but his offer was turned down. In 1934, film producer Alexander Korda secured the film rights to T.E. Lawrence's book, *Revolt in the Desert* (an abridged version of *The Seven Pillars of Wisdom*), and for four years he struggled to get the movie off the ground in the face of opposition, both from T.E. Lawrence and the British government who were under pressure from the Turkish government to veto the project. Leslie Howard was to portray Lawrence and Lewis Milestone was to direct. Due to a combination of censorship, artistic and financial problems the production was abandoned. J. Arthur Rank attempted the project in the mid fifties, with a script by Terence Rattigan, casting Dirk Bogarde as Lawrence, but it was cancelled due to its escalating budget. Finally in 1962, Peter O'Toole gave us cinema's definitive Lawrence and the one whom most people associate with the legend.

Adventurer, soldier, writer, recluse and mystic, Thomas Edward Lawrence was a complex and enigmatic man. With his

knowledge of Arabic and Middle East travels, he was made an Intelligence Officer in the Arab Bureau in Egypt at the beginning of WWI, where his military and diplomatic skills united the Arab tribes against the occupying Turkish army. He proved himself to be a brilliant guerrilla leader in daring raids against the Turks which led to their defeat. When Britain and her allies did not keep their agreement with the Arabs over the creation of independent Arab states, he resigned and enlisted in the R.A.F. His friends called him simply 'T.E.' because he changed his name so many times in his quest for anonymity. He joined the Tank Corps in 1923 under the name of T.E. Shaw, which brought him to Bovington and Clouds Hill.

The Lawrence of Arabia Trail:

The small Saxon church of **St. Martin in North St., Wareham**, houses an effigy of Lawrence sculpted by his friend Eric Kennington which was placed in the church in September 1939. It depicts Lawrence in Arab dress gripping an Arabian dagger with his head resting on a camel saddle beside three books which travelled with him in Arabia: *The Oxford Book of Verse*, Mallory's *Morte d'Arthur* and a Greek anthology. **Wareham's Museum in East St.** has a display of Lawrence memorabilia and the **Angelbury Coffee House, North St.**, has a corner

seat with a small brass plate saying that Lawrence sat there. **Bovington Tank Museum** has a small display of items connected with Lawrence's life in the desert and **Clouds Hill**, the cottage where he lived from 1923 (and where he wrote *Seven Pillars of Wisdom*) up until his death is open to the public.

On 13th May 1935 while returning from the post office at Bovington Camp on his motorcycle he swerved to avoid hitting two boy cyclists and was thrown from his bike. He was taken to **Bovington Camp** hospital and lay in a coma for six days with severe brain damage before he died on 19th May. If he had lived he would have been paralysed for life and his memory

*Peter O'Toole in the title role of **Lawrence of Arabia** (1962, Horizon)*

erased. He was buried in the cemetery of **St. Nicholas Church, Moreton**, where the mourners included Siegfried Sassoon, Augustus John, Winston Churchill, Lady Astor and Mrs Thomas Hardy.

See also: David Lean, Peter O'Toole Robert Bolt

Further information: Wareham Tourist Information: Tel: 01929 552740, Wareham Museum: Tel: 01929 553448 / Easter to October. Visitors to St. Martin's Church out of season can obtain a key from: A.F. Joy, Men's Outfitters, 35 North St., Wareham. Clouds Hill, Turnerspuddle (01929 405616). T.E. Lawrence Society, 24 Martleaves Close, Weymouth, Dorset, DT4 9UT.

SLEUTH
Athelhampton

• 1972 138m c Mystery Palomar (UK)
• Laurence Olivier (Andrew Wyke), Michael Caine (Milo Tindle), Alec Cawthorne (Inspector Doppler), Margo Channing (Marguerite), John Matthews (Detective Sgt. Tarrant), Teddy Martin (Police Constable Higgs)
• p, Morton Gottlieb; d, Joseph L. Mankiewicz; w, Anthony Shaffer (based on his play); ph, Oswald Morris; ed, Richard Marden; m, John Addison; • AAN Best Actor: Michael Caine, Laurence Olivier; AAN Best Director: Joseph L. Mankiewicz; AAN Best Score: John Addison

"With Olivier, I can't lose."
Michael Caine

Whodunnit crime writer, Andrew Wyke (Laurence Olivier), invites his estranged wife's lover, Milo Tindle (Michael Caine) to his stately home and suggests a plan that will benefit them both financially. Tindle will dress up as a clown and steal his wife's jewels, while Wyke claims the insurance money and Tindle uses the profits to support his lover's expensive tastes: a seemingly simple plot which evolves into a deadly game of intrigue and suspense.

Exterior shooting was done at **Athelhampton House** and gardens, near Puddletown, one of the finest 15th century houses in England, and the house interiors were reconstructed at Pinewood. A maze was erected by the film makers in the sunken part of the Great Court and statues were added to the front drive. During filming Olivier and Caine were given dressing rooms in the servants quarters' in the north wing. Milo Tindle's MGB Roadster, used in the opening sequence, is now a resident here.

The Great Hall at Athelhampton was built by Sir William Martyn in 1485. In the Elizabethan West Wing are the Great Chamber, Wine Cellar and Library. The East Wing includes the Dining room, Green Parlour and State Bedroom. The gardens date from 1891 and the walled gardens include topiary pyramids and two garden pavilions designed by Inigo Thomas.

See also: Laurence Olivier, Michael Caine

Further information: Athelhampton House, Athelhampton, Dorchester, Dorset, DT2 7LG. Tel: 01305 848363 http://www.athelhampton.co.uk

Alan Bates and Julie Christie in **Far From The Madding Crowd** *(1967, MGM)*

FAR FROM THE MADDING CROWD
Shaftesbury

• 1967 168m c Drama MGM (UK)
• Julie Christie (Bathsheba Everdene), Terence Stamp (Sgt. Troy), Peter Finch (William Boldwood), Alan Bates (Gabriel Oak), Prunella Ransome (Fanny Robin), Fiona Walker (Liddy), Paul Dawkins (Henry Fray), Andrew Robertson (Andrew Randle), John Barrett (Joseph Poorgrass), Julian Somers (Jan Coggan)
• p, Joseph Janni; d, John Schlesinger; w, Frederic Raphael (adapted from the novel by Thomas Hardy); ph, Nicolas Roeg; ed, Malcolm Cooke; m, Richard Rodney Benett; art d, Roy Forge Smith; cos, Alan Barrett
• ANN Best Score: Richard Rodney Bennett

Best remembered for Nicolas Roeg's spectacular cinematography, John Schlesinger's film is a very literary adaptation of Hardy's Wessex tale about Bathsheba Everdene (Christie) and the consequences of her selfish behaviour towards her lovers.

Over twenty different locations were used across Dorset: Shaftesbury's **Gold Hill** (also used in Hovis ads) was the location for Gabriel Oak's arrival in Casterbridge and pregnant Fanny's path to the poorhouse; **Waddon House** at Portesham was the home of William Boldwood; the 120ft folly, **Horton Tower**, between Verwood and Wimborne, was the location for the cock-fighting scene; **Thornhill House** near Sturminster Newton was the venue for the party at which Boldwood shoots Sgt. Troy and **Maiden Castle** near Dorchester was where Bathsheba and Troy have their mock swordfight. Other locations included **Eggardon Hill** near Powerstock, **Sydling St Nicholas Church** doubled as Weatherbury Church, the **Golden Bowl** at Encombe, the **Tithe Barn** at Abbotsbury, **Bloxworth House** near Bere Regis and the coastline near **Durdle Door**.

See also: Alan Bates

COMRADES
Lulworth

In 1834 six Dorset farm labourers from Tolpuddle, near Dorchester, were transported to Australia for forming a trade union. Following a national outcry they were released two years later. Scottish film maker, Bill Douglas, became inspired with the idea of making a film about the Tolpuddle Martyrs after reading a pamphlet on them during a visit to Dorset in the late 1970s. It took him a year to write the script and after visiting 130 villages in search of a suitable location, he settled on **Tyneham**, a deserted village in the middle of the army firing range at Lulworth. Shooting began in September 1985, and included in the cast were Robin Soans, Alex Norton, Robert Stephens, Freddie Jones, Vanessa Redgrave, Michael Hordern and James Fox. *Comrades* was released in August 1987, but despite good reviews, the public showed little interest and today it is rarely seen in the cinema.

See also: The Bill Douglas Centre

CLASSIC LOCATION SHERBORNE SCHOOL
Sherborne

A popular location for public school dramas, Sherborne School hosted the 1951 original and the 1994 remake of Terence Rattigan's, *The Browning Version*, about a middle-aged school-master's feeling of inadequacy, portrayed by Michael Redgrave and Albert Finney respectively. **Milton Abbey School, near Milton Abbas** was used for exterior shots in the 1994 version. The school was also used for the location of the 1969 musical remake of *Goodbye, Mr Chips*, starring Peter O'Toole and Petula Clark. Richard Attenborough also starred in another school drama here in 1948 called *The Guinea Pig*.

Sherborne School exudes history and with Gothic gargoyles breathing down on one from the Courts one might think the school was really old, but although the origins of the school go back to 705 A.D., the present buildings are only just over a hundred years old. Former pupils of the school include Jeremy Irons, Richard Eyre and David Cornwall (John Le Carre).

See also: *Goodbye Mr Chips*, Terence Rattigan

Further information: Sherborne School, Abbey Road, Sherborne, Dorset, DT9 3AP. Tours of the school are by appointment only and are arranged through the Sherborne Tourist Office (01935 815341) or contact Richard Gould at the school on 01935 815253.

THE FRENCH LIEUTENANT'S WOMAN
Lyme Regis

"There is no way you can film the book. You can tell the same story in a movie, of course, but not in the same way. And how Fowles tells his story is what makes the book so good."
John Frankenheimer

Frankenheimer may have thought the book unfilmable, but screenwriter Harold Pinter and director Karel Reisz proved him wrong, succeeding where previous attempts by Fred Zinnemann, Richard Lester and Mike Nichols, had failed. The most popular of all John Fowle's novels, this 1981 film tells the story of two doomed lovers, Sarah/Anna (Meryl Streep) and Charles/Mike (Jeremy Irons), set in Victorian and contemporary England.

Locations included the area called the **Undercliff**, between Lyme Regis and Seaton, and Lyme's harbour wall, known as the **Cobb**, both of which were the original locations in the book. The main street location in Lyme was **Broad Street**. **Kingswear Station** in Devon doubled for Exeter Station, and the nearby **Steampacket Inn** (01803 752208) doubled as Endicott's Family Hotel. Filming was also done at

Meryl Streep in **The French Lieutenant's Woman** *(1981, UA)*

Windermere in the Lake District, and included **Crag Wood, Crag Wood Country House Hotel, Brockhole Visitors' Centre** and **Voysey House** (now HQ of Windermere Motor Boat Club). Various London locations were also used and studio scenes were shot at Twickenham Studios.

John Fowles was born in Leigh-on-Sea, Essex, in 1926. A former schoolteacher, his first novel was *The Collector* (1963, filmed by William Wyler in 1965), but it was *The Magus* (1965, filmed by Guy Green in 1968) which established his reputation. He still lives and works in Lyme Regis.

Further information: The six mile 'Undercliffe coastal walk' starts at Holmbush car park, Pound Street, Lyme Regis. Lyme Regis Tourist Information 01297 442138.

THE SMALL BACK ROOM
Abbotsbury

"The [bomb-defusing] sequence ran about seventeen minutes - the same length, more or less, as the Ballet of the Red Shoes. Seventeen minutes must be the longest time that an audience can hold its breath."
Michael Powell

The life of bomb-disposal expert, Sammy Rice (David Farrar), who lost a foot in a bomb blast, is slowly disintegrating. A sense of inferiority and constant quarrels with his girlfriend Sue (Kathleen Byron) force him to retreat into drunkenness. Summoned to defuse a new Nazi anti-personnel bomb which no one has yet mastered, he tries to redeem himself.

Michael Powell's 1949 screen adaptation of Nigel Balchin's story of a tormented WWII bomb-disposal expert was filmed at various locations in England and Wales. The gripping scene where Sammy Rice dismantles the bomb on the beach was shot at **Chesil Bank**, and **St. Catherine's Chapel**, which overlooks Chesil Bank, was where he met officer in charge Colonel Strang (Anthony Bushell).

The film was a success with the critics, but the public, who had had a bellyfull of war and war films by the late forties, spurned it.

See also: Michael Powell, Emeric Pressburger

BIRTHPLACE OF MAURICE EVANS (1901-89)
Dorchester

It is ironic that this great Shakespearian actor will be best remembered in the cinema as the grumpy old chief ape in the science fiction classic, *Planet of the Apes* (1968). Born in **Icen Way, off High East Street**, Dorchester, he was the son of an apothecary and was educated at the town's Grocers' Company School. He began his stage career taking part in his father's amateur productions of Thomas Hardy's plays. After leaving school he became clerk to a music publisher, then ran a garment cleaning and dyeing company before making his professional stage debut in 1926.

He came to prominence as Lieutenant Raleigh in R.C. Sherriff's *Journey's End* in 1928. He joined the Old Vic company in 1934 and became an American citizen in 1941 where he was recognised as one of New York's leading classical actors for more than thirty years.

*Maurice Evans as Dr. Zaius in **Planet of the Apes** (1968, Apjac)*

Primarily a stage actor, he appeared sporadically in films from 1930, including, *Scrooge* (1935), *Macbeth* (1960), *The War Lord* (1965), *Rosemary's Baby* (1968), *Beneath the Planet of the Apes* (1970) and *The Jerk* (1979).

SHAFTESBURY ARTS CENTRE FILM SOCIETY
Shaftesbury

*Alan Parker presents the Roebuck Cup to **Paul Schilling** of SACFS for services to the Film Society movement in 1998.*

Formerly housed in an old school building, it moved in March 1983 to the Shaftesbury Arts Centre, changing its name in the process. Benefitting greatly from its new location, particularly in terms of facilities, it now boasts a separate projection room and theatre accommodation for its members. Winner of the 'Best Film Society of the

Year' award in 1999, the SACFS is one of the most successful film societies in the country.

Further information: The Secretary, Shaftesbury Arts Centre, Bell Street, Shaftesbury, Dorset SP7 8AR. Tel: 01747 854321

Dudley

BIRTHPLACE OF JAMES WHALE (1889-1957)

"To a new world of Gods and monsters."
Dr. Pretorious' toast,
The Bride of Frankenstein

When director James Whale cast Boris Karloff in *Frankenstein* (1931) he unknowingly created one of cinema's most enduring images. His talent, however, never achieved the success it deserved, and after a short Hollywood career, he abandoned film-making, ending his life in a tragic suicide, aged sixty seven.

Born on 22 July 1889 at **41 Brewery Street, Kates Hill, Dudley** (now demolished and redeveloped), James was the sixth of seven children of Sarah and Will Whale, a blast furnaceman. With no prospect of furthering his education at university he left school and went to work first as a cobbler's assistant and then as a pattern maker in a brass fender factory. A talented artist, he had aspirations to become an art teacher and enrolled as a student at Dudley Art School's evening classes.

He was commissioned as a second lieutenant during WWI and fought in France and Belgium. Captured by the Germans during a night attack on a German pill-box in 1917, he spent the rest of his military service as a prisoner of war. It was during his internment that he became involved in drama productions and after the war he decided to pursue acting as a career.

He joined the Birmingham Rep and later London's Savoy Theatre Company, acting, producing and set-designing. In 1929 he produced R.C. Sheriff's play *Journey's End*. The play's success led to his staging an American production which resulted in his being invited to work in Hollywood. He began as a dialogue director on Paramount's *The Love Doctor* (1929) and Howard Hughes' *Hell's Angels* (1930). He directed his first feature, *Journey's End* in 1930, and joined Carl Laemmle snr. and jnr. at Universal the same year.

In 1931 he directed *Frankenstein*. The film seems tame today because it has been so often copied and parodied, but when it opened in Los Angeles in 1932, it caused a sensation. It was based on a play by Peggy Webling and retained only the bare bones of Mary Shelley's gothic fantasy novel. Whale pencil-sketched the original image of the monster which inspired make-up artist Jack Pierce's memorable mutant, and launched the career of Boris Karloff.

Between 1930 and 1936, he directed the films he will be mostly remembered for, including *The Old Dark House* (1932), *The Invisible Man* (1933), *The Bride of Frankenstein* (1935), *Remember Last Night?* (1935) and *Showboat* (1936).

The Laemmles sold Universal in 1936 after which time Whale's career went into decline; he made his last film in 1941, aged fifty-two. He later commented, *"I got up to £1,500 a week, but they wanted a Michaelangelo every time...so I gave it up just to be free."*

Most of his final years were spent visiting galleries abroad and painting in his studio. He was homosexual, and in 1957, suffering from depression and illness, he dived into the shallow end of his swimming pool, knocked himself unconscious, and drowned. An extract from his suicide note reads, *"The future is just old age and pain...Goodbye all*

*Ian McKellen and Brendan Fraser in **Gods and Monsters** (1998)*

and thank you for all your love. I must have peace and this is the only way."

James Whale is only generally remembered today as the director of *Frankenstein* and *The Bride of Frankenstein*, but he was a master film-maker and a multifaceted artist. In 1998 Ian McKellen portrayed James Whale during the last days of his life in the award-winning *Gods and Monsters*, based on the novel *Father of Frankenstein* by Christopher Bram.

See also: Boris Karloff, Mary Shelley, Peter Cushing, Claude Rains

LIMELIGHT CINEMA
Dudley

The Limelight Cinema was built by John Revill in 1917 on land he owned adjacent to his house which was

situated behind numbers **49 and 51 Vine Street, Harts Hill.** A Cinematography Licence, granted in 1921, describes it as being thirty feet by fifteen feet, with a seating capacity for 103. Access to the Limelight was via a pair of wooden gates and down a back alley to the pay box where Mrs. Revill sold the tuppence ha'penny and fivepenny tickets from a wooden pay booth. Seating consisted of simple wooden benches, and a wind up gramophone provided musical accompaniment to the silent films.

It closed in 1929, unable to compete with the new 'talkie' cinemas; henceforth John used the auditorium for storing his collection of tropical fish. He died in 1965 and in the late 1970s the property was acquired by a haulage company who offered the cinema building to the Black Country Museum's open air site in Dudley. The museum considered it important to

Dudley

save the Limelight because it was a rare surviving example of an early 'fleapit' cinema. In 1993 the building was carefully dismantled by an experienced building team and rebuilt in the middle of the museum's village. It has now been successfully restored to its former glory where it entertains a new generation of cinema-goers.

Further information: The Black Country Museum, Tipton Road, Dudley. 0121 557 9643

BIRTHPLACE OF CEDRIC HARDWICKE (1893-1964)
Lye

Lye Cross, Dudley, 1910

Distinguished Hollywood actor, Cedric Hardwicke did not recall his birthplace at the turn of the century with particular fondness, recalling it as an unlovely spot, characterised by squalor, filth, dreary slums, poverty and ignorance. He was born on 19 February 1893, in a cold, damp Queen Anne house at **Lye Cross** (now demolished), the only son of three children to Jessie Masterson and Edwin Webster Hardwicke, a doctor. His father was a dour man, but a dedicated doctor to the poverty-stricken industrial workers, many of whom were unable to pay his fee. Cedric was educated at Stourbridge Grammar School and became interested in drama after becoming a patron of the Alhambra Theatre, the last wooden playhouse in Britain, which stood on the site at the rear of the Post Office in

Stourbridge High Street. He staged his first amateur performance at **The Temperance Hall**, Lye, in a production of *The Merchant of Venice*. The play was well received and the profits were divided amongst the elderly in the audience, each receiving 1/6d. He followed his success with three performances of *Hamlet* at the Alhambra. His father, who disapproved of his thespian aspirations, packed him off to boarding school at Bridgnorth Grammar School. Dr. Hardwicke hoped his son would follow in his footsteps and take up a career in medicine, but Cedric failed to fulfil the academic requirements. When he was seventeen he auditioned for Sir Herbert Beerbohm Tree and was accepted as a student at RADA in London.

He made his first professional appearance at the Lyceum in *The Monk and the Woman* and later joined the F.R. Benson Shakespearian Company with which he toured South Africa. Commissioned into the army during WWI, he served in France. After the war he toured with the Birmingham Repertory Theatre and went on to lead a successful stage career.

He appeared in his first film in 1911, but his film career really began when he was cast in the title role of *Nelson*

in 1926. He departed for Hollywood in the mid-thirties and will be chiefly remembered for his scholarly and authoritarian roles such as Allan Quartermain in *King Solomon's Mines* (1937), David Livingstone in *Stanley and Livingstone* (1939), Dr Arnold in *Tom Brown's Schooldays* (1940), Ralph Nickleby in *Nicholas Nickleby* (1947) and Arthur Winslow in *The Winslow Boy* (1948).

He was knighted in 1934 by King George V, who, on account of his deafness allegedly dubbed him Sir Samuel Pickwick. He was married twice and had two sons. After a life of big spending and extravagance he died virtually penniless in a New York hospital after a long respiratory illness in August 1964.

See also: Rider Haggard, *Tom Brown's Schooldays*, Terence Rattigan

THE CLIFTON PUB
Sedgley

Formerly the Clifton Cinema which closed in 1974, it opened as a pub in 1998. The frontage is basically unaltered and the balcony seating is still intact with its three original projectors still in place. The bar is

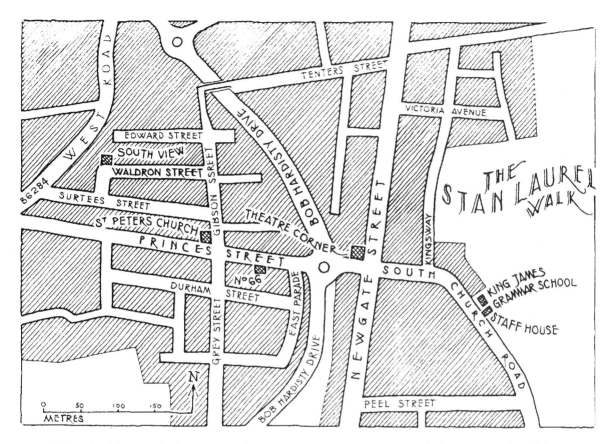

situated below the old screen which displays a projected image from a West Rex projector. Movie stills, posters and pictures of the old cinema decorate its walls.

Further information: The Clifton, The Bullring, Sedgley, West Midlands. Tel: 01902 677448.

Durham

THE STAN LAUREL WALK
Bishop Auckland

Stan Laurel (born Arthur Stanley Jefferson) was the son of Arthur and Madge Jefferson, who came to Bishop Auckland in 1889 to take over the town's Theatre Royal. Arthur was an actor, playwright and impresario. Madge was an actress and a talented

stage designer. Her stage name was Madge Metcalfe. In 1890, Madge returned to her home town of Ulverston to have a baby, and on June 16th, a boy was born called Arthur Stanley. Stan was a sickly child and was left with his grandparents in Ulverston to be looked after while Madge returned to her busy theatre life in Bishop Auckland. When Stan was fourteen months old, he was brought to Bishop Auckland to be baptised at St. Peter's Church in Princes Street - just up the hill from the Jefferson's theatre.

On display in '**The Laurel Room**', a cafe / bar and 'Sons of the Desert' meeting place at **Bishop Auckland Town Hall in Market Place** are a few items of Laurel and Hardy memorabilia, including a signed photo of Laurel and Hardy, Arthur Jefferson's account book and some Eden Theatre and Hippodrome programmes. Laurel and Hardy film stills decorate the walls, and a motto above the bar reads: *"Duae*

tabulae rasae in quibus nihil scriptum est." (Two minds without a single thought), the official motto of the Laurel and Hardy appreciation society.

The Stan Laurel Walk:

Leave the **Town Hall** and cross Market Place to Newgate Street (the main shopping street). Walk through the

King James Grammar School

pedestrianised area to the first street on the right (Tenters Street). Turn right and follow this street, passing the main Post Office to the foot bridge. Cross the foot-bridge and bear to the left.

Take the second road on the right up the hill (Waldron Street). The houses in this street were theatrical boarding houses at the time Stan Laurel's father ran the theatre. At the top, the last house on the right corner - Number 220 is **South View**. Stan's sister, Beatrice Olga was born in this house on 16th December 1894. Stan stayed for Christmas and attended her baptism.

Leave South View behind you and walk to the next junction. Turn left and walk down the hill; turn right to **St. Peter's Church** on the corner. Turn right for the main door. Stan was baptised in this church and a plaque to mark the occasion is to be found on the wall to the left of the font.

With the church on your left, move down the hill. On the opposite side of the road below the butcher's shop is number **66 Princes Street**. This was the home of the Jeffersons in 1891. It was from this house that Stan was taken to be baptised. A plaque marks the house. Continue down the hill to the roundabout (take care!) - cross over the junction on the left-hand side towards the traffic lights to Theatre Corner. Theatre Royal - later **Eden Theatre**. You are now passing over the site of Stan's father's theatre which he managed twice - 1889 to 1896 and again from 1922 to 1925. This was the

home of his touring melodrama companies who performed the plays Arthur wrote and which were thought to be used by Stan as the plots for his early films. The site of the theatre is marked by a plaque on the wall. Cross the main street. Take the road facing Princes Street to the next set of traffic lights (again, take care), cross over the road toward the building with the small spire passing the Cricket Club on your left, to the building with the iron railings - **King James Grammar School** - where Stan was a boarder in 1903. At that time, the school catered for the sons of middle-class gentlemen. The Jeffersons lived in North Shields. On the right of Stan's school facing the playing fields, stands a double-fronted house. **Staff House** - It was here that Stan gave his first performances in the staff room. He neglected his school work and was sent to Gainford Academy near Barnard Castle. Return to the traffic lights, turn right past the football grounds to the first street on the left which leads you back onto the main street. Turn right for the Market Place and Town Hall.

I would like to thank John Land and Durham County Council Museums & Libraries for their help in compiling the above information.

See also: Stan Laurel (Cumbria, North Tyneside, Glasgow), Laurel & Hardy

East Sussex

GRAVE OF EDITH BAGNOLD (1889-1981)
Rottingdean

Edith Bagnold was the creator of the famous children's novel, *National Velvet* (1935), about a girl who wins a horse in a raffle and rides to victory in the Grand National. Bagnold's childhood was spent in Jamaica, but she later came to Europe where she became a painter, journalist and lively socialite,

National Velvet (1944, MGM)

mixing with the celebrated social and political figures of her day. She is buried in Rottingdean churchyard.

MGM's 1944 adaptation of *National Velvet*, directed by Clarence Brown, was responsible for propelling Elizabeth Taylor on the road to stardom. Remade as *International Velvet*, with Tatum O'Neal and Christopher Plummer in 1978.

See also: Elizabeth Taylor

HOME OF RUDYARD KIPLING (1865-1936)
Burwash

Many of Kipling's stories and poems have been adapted for the screen, including at least four versions of *The Light That Failed*, the earliest being in 1914; Victor Fleming directed *Captains Courageous* with Spencer Tracy in 1937 and John Ford's *Wee Willie Winkie*, starring Shirley Temple, appeared in the same year; George Stevens' *Gunga Din* was inspired by a Kipling poem in 1939; MGM made *Kim* in 1950 with Errol Flynn, and *Soldiers Three* in 1951, with Stewart Granger, David Niven and Walter Pidgeon; United Artists cast Indian child actor,

Sabu, in two productions - *Elephant Boy* (1936, based on the story 'Toomai of the Elephants') and *The Jungle Book* (1942) of which Disney made a version in 1967; John Huston's *The Man Who Would Be King* was an adaptation of a short story which cast Christopher Plummer as Kipling;, and Lindsay Anderson's *If* (1968) borrows the title of Kipling's poem.

The Kiplings were beginning to turn into a tourist attraction at their home at **The Grange, Rottingdean** and so in 1902 they moved to the seclusion of the seventeenth century house called **Bateman's near Burwash**, where Kipling lived until his death in 1936. *Puck of Pook's Hill* and *Rewards and Fairies*, which included the poem *If*, were written here. Kipling's ashes are interred in **Poets Corner, Westminster Abbey**. After the death of Kipling's widow in 1939, Bateman's was left to the National Trust.

Further information: Bateman's, Burwash, Etchingham. Tel: 01435 882302. Open April to October, closed Thursdays and Fridays. The Grange, Rottingdean (above library, opposite Plough Inn) is open all year round except Sundays. Tel: 01273 301004. The Kipling Society, 2 Brownleaf Rd., Brighton, East Sussex, BN2 6LB. Tel: 01273 303719.

See also: *If*

*Sabu and Rosemary DeCamp in **The Jungle Book** (1942, UA)*

THE SHERLOCK HOLMES FESTIVAL
Crowborough

The first festival celebrating cinema's greatest detectective was in 1996 and for a brief weekend in July the town now annually becomes a centre of crime and mystery, six decades after the death of its most famous resident, Sir Arthur Conan Doyle. Past festivals have included guided walks around Conan Doyle's haunts, screenings of Sherlock Holmes movies, mystery writers' workshops featuring top writers, The Hound of the Baskerville Dog Show, a Victorian Street Fair, a Sherlock Holmes cricket and golf tournament, classical concerts playing the music Holmes might have listened to and even a church service at All Saints Church looking at the Gospels from the perspective of Sherlock Holmes.

It was a visit to friends which first brought the widower Sir Arthur Conan Doyle to Crowborough where he fell in love with their daughter, Jean Leckie. They married in 1907 and bought a local property, **Windlesham Manor** (now a home for the elderly). It was here that Conan Doyle wrote many of the Sherlock Holmes Stories, including *The Valley of Fear, His Last Bow* and *The Casebook of Sherlock Holmes.*. He died following a heart attack on 7 July 1930 and was buried in the garden where his wife joined him in 1940. When the house was sold their bodies were exhumed and reburied in **Minstead Churchyard**, in the **New Forest**.

See also: Sir Arthur Conan Doyle, Peter Cushing, Hammer Studios, The Sherlock Holmes Collection, Frensham Common, *The Hound of the Baskervilles*.

Further information: Sherlock Holmes Festival, The Town Hall, Crowborough, East Sussex, TN6 1DA. Tel: 01892 665464.

BIRTHPLACE OF RUMER GODDEN (1907-98)
Eastbourne

"I think nuns are irresistibly dramatic. Theirs is the greatest love story on earth."
Rumer Godden

Prolific novelist, playwright and poet, Rumer Godden will be best remembered in the cinema for Michael Powell's adaptation of her 1938 bestseller, *Black Narcissus*, which she was inspired to write while on a picnic in Assam where she saw the grave of a nun who had died at the same age as she then was. She hated the film, commenting, *"I saw it only once but never again. It is an absolute travesty of the book, I cannot bear it. Micky Powell said he saw it as a fairy tale, whereas for me it was true. The whole thing was an abomination."*

Born at **Tanglin**, the house of her uncle, local solicitor Alfred Hingley, at **30 Milnthorpe Road, Meads, Eastbourne** (now converted into two flats), she spent her childhood in Narayanganj, India (now Bangladesh) where her father controlled the traffic on the town's inland waterways. The second eldest of four daughters, she was sent to England after WWI to be educated and did not return to India until she was seventeen.

She published her first novel, a children's book, when she was twenty-eight. After WWII she returned to England where she wrote a successful series of novels and children's books. Jean Renoir adapted her autobiographical novel, *The River*, about her Indian childhood for the screen in 1951, and *The Greengage Summer* (aka *Loss of Innocence*) was filmed by Lewis Gilbert in 1961.

She was twice married and had two daughters. She died at her home in Dumfries on November 8, 1998.

See also: *Black Narcissus.*

East Sussex

CLASSIC LOCATION
BLUEBELL RAILWAY
Haywards Heath

Opened in 1960, the Bluebell Railway is run mainly by volunteers. Its nine miles of track runs from Victorian Sheffield Park Station, through 1930s Horsted Keynes Station, to 1950s Kinscote Station. Its headquarters, which includes a museum, restaurant / bar and locomotive collection are housed at Sheffield Park.

It was first used for feature film locations in *The Innocents* (1961) with Deborah Kerr and Michael Redgrave, and *The Waltz of the Toreadors* (1962) with Peter Sellers. The troop train sequences for Spike Milligan's *Adolf Hitler - My Part in His Downfall* (1972) were filmed at Horsted Keynes, which also featured the opening troop train scenes in John Boorman's *Hope and Glory* (1987). The Bluebell was a favourite location of Ken Russell and features in *Savage Messiah* (1972), *Mahler* (1974), *Tommy* (1975) and *Lisztomania* (1975). Other films shot on the line include *Khartoum* (1966)

featuring Horsted Keynes Station, and *A Room With A View* (1985).

Further information: Bluebell Railway, Sheffield Park Station, TN22 3QL. Tel: 01825 723777. It is planned to link the line from Kingscote to East Grinstead by 2001; meanwhile a bus service is in operation.

CHILDHOOD IDYLL
OF DIRK BOGARDE
(1921-99)
Lullington

"... and that's the altar where the murder was." She [Elizabeth] was speaking in a rather whispery way, not because of the murder but because you do whisper in church... even if it is very small.
Dirk Bogarde, *A Postillion Struck by Lightning* *

Actor, writer and artist, Derek Niven Van den Bogaerde was born on 28 March 1921 in a London taxi, the eldest of three children to a Scottish mother and a Dutch father. His mother was

Margaret Niven, a frustrated actress who descended into alcoholism, and his father was Ulrich Van den Bogaerde, art editor of *The Times*.

As a child his summers were spent at **The Rectory** in **Lullington**, Sussex, which he lovingly evokes in his first volume of autobiography, *A Postillion Struck by Lightning* (1977), in which he recalls the lost world of his childhood and make-believe adventures in the countryside, accompanied by his younger sister Elizabeth. He also reminisces about his beloved nanny, Lally, and shopping trips to nearby **Seaford**, which included visits to the **Martello Tearooms**.

Once a month they attended services at **Lullington Church**, the smallest church in England. In *Postillion* Bogarde recounts the legend of a murder that happened there long ago: the vicar allegedly caught his wife kissing another man, whereupon he took a candlestick from the altar and bludgeoned him to death; he then set fire to the building, which is reputedly why the church is so small today. Bogarde described the church in *Postillion* : *"There was a little wooden fence all round the church, with a squeaky iron gate and inside the gate was the churchyard. All the tombs and gravestones were squinty, like people standing on a ship in a storm."* *

He made his first stage appearance while still at school in a local production of *Alf's Button*. His father, however, was intent on his cultivating a career in art, and sent him to the Allan Glen's School, a local technical college in Glasgow, which he hated, and later to a commercial art course at Chelsea Polytechnic, where his teachers were Henry Moore and Graham Sutherland. Dirk, however, had his heart set on an acting career, and associated himself as much as he could with amateur theatre, where he was once mistakenly billed as 'Birt Gocart'.

In 1939 he was an extra in George Formby's comedy, *Come On, George,*

*Deborah Kerr on location with the Bluebell Railway shooting scenes for **The Innocents** (1961. 20th Century Fox/Achilles).*

and the same year he made his professional stage debut at the Q Theatre, near Kew Bridge, in J.B. Priestley's, *When We Are Married*. A few months later his West End debut was in Priestley's *Cornelius*, and *The Stage* applauded his role of the *"sulky true-to-life office boy."*

He was engaged briefly to the actress Annie Deans, but at Amersham Rep he met Anthony Forwood, who was to become his companion and manager for the next fifty years. In 1940 he joined the Signal Corps and worked with ENSA. He was later attached to Army Intelligence and took part in the D-Day invasion and the liberation of the Bergen-Belsen concentration camp. Shortly after his demob in Singapore he officially anglicised his name.

In 1947 he was offered a contract by the Rank Organisation after his performance in *Esther Waters* (1947), but it was his portrayal of murderer Tom Riley in *The Blue Lamp* (1949) which launched his career, and within a decade he became a major British star. He left Rank in 1961, devoting the remainder of his career to films which would secure his reputation as an actor unafraid of the unorthodox and the controversial, whether it was exposing the dangers of illegal homosexuality in *Victim* (1961) or exhibiting a compulsion for expressing sado-masochism in *The Night Porter* (1974). Other films included *Doctor in the House* (1953), *The Servant* (1963), *King and Country* (1964), *Darling* (1965), *Accident* (1967) and *Death in Venice* (1970).

In 1974 he went to live at Le Haut Clermont, a farmhouse near Grasse in the South of France, and in 1977 he wrote his first volume of memoirs, which was the beginning of a prolific writing career. After Tony Forwood's death in 1988, he spent the remainder of his life at his Chelsea flat where he died of a heart attack on 8 May 1999. His ashes were scattered in France.

See also: *The Blue Lamp, The Servant*

Lullington Church

Dirk Bogarde

Further information: The Martello Tower Tearoom is now Seaford Museum, at the eastern end of the Esplanade. Open: Easter to mid-October. Tel: 01323 898222.

CARRINGTON
Hartfield

• 1995 122m c Biography/Hist/Romance UK/France

• Emma Thompson (Dora Carrington), Jonathan Pryce (Lytton Strachey), Steven Waddington (Ralph Partridge), Samuel West (Gerald Brenan)

• p, Ronald Shedlo, John McGrath; d, Christopher Hampton; w, Christopher Hampton (based on the book *Lytton Strachey* by Michael Holroyd); ph, Denis Lenoir

"A diagram of their love affairs would look like an underground system where every train stopped at every station." Roger Ebert on the Bloomsbury Group

Christopher Hampton's 1995 biopic of the strange and tormented platonic love affair between English painter, Dora Carrington (Emma Thompson) and the epigram-spouting homosexual writer Lytton Strachey (Jonathan Pryce), is a fascinating insight into the relationships of the Bloomsbury Group. Carrington's will to live ended with the death of Strachey, when she took her own life with a shotgun at Ham Spray House.

Bolebroke Mill in Hartfield, now an award-winning guest house (strictly non-smoking) doubled as Tidmarsh Mill, the idyllic country house they shared where Carrington painted her beautiful murals. It was first recorded in the Domesday Book in 1086 AD, and continued as a working corn-mill until 1948. Today, corn is no longer ground, but all the internal machinery remains. One of the Carrington-style wall paintings used in the film can still be seen in the Mill's lounge, and is autographed by Emma Thompson and Jonathan Pryce.

Norney Grange (not open to the public) in **Godalming, Surrey**, doubled for Ham Spray, and **Turville Lodge in Henley-on-Thames** was used as the home of Vanessa and Clive Bell. The coast around **Robin Hood's Bay, near Scarborough**, represented the Sussex Downs and the Welsh coast.

Bolebroke Mill

Further information: Bolebroke Mill, Perry Hill, Edenbridge Road, Hartfield, E. Sussex TN7 4JP. Tel: 01892 770425.

East Yorkshire

BIRTHPLACE OF KAY KENDALL (1926-59) & KAY KENDALL MEMORIAL MUSEUM
Withernsea

Leading lady and comedy actress of the 1950's, Kay Kendall was born Justine McCarthy at **Stanley House, Hull Road, Withernsea**. Her parents were professional dancers, and as a child she toured with her sister as part of a variety act.

Her early film appearances were in British musicals such as *Champagne Charlie* (1944) and *London Town* (1946). She will, however, be best remembered for her role as the trumpet playing Rosalind, in Henry Cornelius' classic comedy, *Genevieve* (1953). Her other films include: *Doctor in The House* (1954), *The Constant Husband* (1955), *Quentin Durward* (1955) and her last film, *Once More With Feeling* (1960).

She married Rex Harrison in 1957 and died of leukaemia, aged thirty-three.

She is buried in the south-east corner of the extension of **St. John's churchyard, Hampstead, London**. **Withernsea Lighthouse** was opened in 1989 by Kim Campbell, as a memorial museum to her sister Kay Kendall, featuring memorabilia and video excerpts from her films.

See also: Rex Harrison, *Genevieve*

Further information: Withernsea Lighthouse Museum, Hull Road, Withernsea, E.R. Yorks, HU19 2DY, Tel: 01964 614834.

THE PLAYHOUSE CINEMA
Beverley

On January 18th, 1897, the first moving picture show in Beverley is believed to have been screened by film pioneer, Birt Acres, at the Assembly Rooms (corner of Norwood & Manor Rd., now demolished) in Beverley. On February 20th, 1911, the first cinema was opened by local portrait photographer, Ernest Symmons, at the Corn Exchange. The opening programme included: a coloured Pathe film entitled *A Drama of 200 Years Ago, The Opening of Parliament by King George V* and *Bird Nesting on Flamboro' Head*.

In September 1911, after its summer break, it reopened as The Picture Playhouse. Symmons also obtained his own motion picture camera to record local events and the public subsequently flocked to see themselves on the Playhouse screen. The

Playhouse remained under the control of the Symmons family until 1981, when new management took over. It continues today both as a cinema and a venue for live shows.

Further information: The Playhouse Cinema, Saturday Market, Beverley. Tel: 01482 881315.

Essex

APOCALYPSE NOW
Stanford Le-Hope

"I love the smell of napalm in the morning. It smells like... victory," - Lt. Col. Kilgore (Robert Duvall) in **Apocalypse Now** (1979, UA)

Born in Poland as Theodor Korzeniowski, Joseph Conrad started out in life as a sailor and then became a novelist. He lived in Stanford from 1896 to 1898, with his wife, Jessie, where they rented a house (now demolished) in what is now **Victoria Road** (called New Road until the 1897 Jubilee) - the number has not been established. Whilst here, he wrote *Heart of Darkness*, a tale told from the deck of a cruising yacht anchored off Gravesend, which was the inspiration for Francis Coppola's controversial Vietnam epic, *Apocalypse Now.* (1979).

ELECTRIC PALACE CINEMA
Harwich

Gloucestershire

BIRTHPLACE OF RALPH RICHARDSON (1902-83)
Cheltenham

"Harwich's future is as a modern port, not a museum of olde tea-shoppes." Harwich mayor, Alderman Jack Thorn, commenting on the conservation of the Electric Palace. Sunday Times, 10.12.72.

One of the oldest surviving purpose-built cinemas in England, the Electric Palace was designed by Charles Thurston and opened on 29th November 1911. It was built for Charles Thurston, a well known travelling showman who had toured the country before the turn of the century with his tent cinema, 'Thurston's Royal Travelling Picture Show.' Resembling a large stone tent, its architectural style retains much of the fairground's atmosphere. It survived both world wars and an aerial torpedo which landed in a nearby churchyard in 1917, but didn't explode. One member of staff remembers spraying the audience during the show with a disinfectant perfume, *"to kill the smell of smoke and the great unwashed fishermen down front."*

It closed without warning in 1956 due to financial difficulties, and remained cocooned with its projectors and tickets in the pay box until 1972, when Harwich Council applied for planning permission to demolish it in order to build a car park. Fortunately, local conservationists defeated the Council's plans and secured a Department of the Environment statutory listing for the building.

In April 1975 a trust was set up to restore the fabric and function of the building and it now stands as a magnificent example of an original, purpose-built, 'silent cinema', screening classic films and the latest releases, with seating for 204.

Further information: Electric Palace, King's Quay Street, Harwich. Tel: 01255 553333.

Ralph David Richardson was born on 19 December 1902 at **'Langsyne', Tivoli Road, Cheltenham** (plaque erected), the third son of Lydia Russell and Arthur Richardson, a senior art master at Cheltenham Ladies' College. His parents separated in 1906 and his mother took young Ralph to live in two converted railway carriages on the beach at Shoreham-by-Sea in Sussex. He would not see his father again until he was eighteen. He attended Catholic schools in Shoreham, Norwood and in Brighton, living with his mother in a succession of flats, boarding houses and hotels. In 1919 he left school and took a job as an office-boy in a Brighton insurance office at ten shillings a week. He left his job when his grandmother bequeathed him £500 in her will whereupon he attended Brighton School of Art. He soon discovered his preference for acting over painting and so joined a Brighton company called 'The St. Nicholas

Ralph Richardson as Alexei Karenin in Anna Karenina (1947, Korda/London Films)

Players' with which he made his first stage appearance as a gendarme in Balzac's *The Bishop's Candlesticks*. He later worked with many theatre companies establishing himself as a formidable stage actor, including The Birmingham Repertory Company and The Old Vic Company.

He made over sixty films, making his screen debut as a parson in *The Ghoul* (1933), with Boris Karloff in the title role. His future in films was secured beyond dispute when he portrayed the fascist leader, 'The Boss' in *Things To Come* (1936) in a masterly display of primitive menace. His other film roles included: Doctor Denny in *The Citadel* (1938), Major Hammond in *Q-Planes* (1939), Captain Durrance in *The Four Feathers* (1939), Baines the butler in *The Fallen Idol* (1948), James Tyrone in *Long Day's Journey into Night* (1962) and in his final film role as Earl of Greystoke, Tarzan's grandfather in *Greystoke* (1983).

His first wife of eighteen years, actress Muriel (Kit) Hewitt, died in 1942 and two years later he married actress Meriel Forbes with whom he had one son, Charles. He served with the RNVR as a pilot during WWII and was knighted in 1947. He died, aged eighty, after a series of strokes in 1983 and is buried in **Highgate Eastern Cemetery.**

See also: Ralph Richardson (Camden), *Greystoke*, *The Citadel*, A.E.W. Mason

IF
Cheltenham

• 1968 110m c/bw Drama Memorial (UK)
• Malcolm McDowell (Mick Travers), David Wood (Johnny), Richard Warwick (Wallace), Christine Noonan (the Girl), Rupert Webster (Bobby Philips), Robert Swan (Roundtree), Hugh Thomas (Denison), Peter Jeffrey (Headmaster),
• p, Michael Medwin, Lindsay Anderson; d, Lindsay Anderson; w, David Sherwin (based on a script by Sherwin, John Howlett,

entitled *The Crusaders*); ph, Miroslav Ondricek; ed, David Gladwell; m, Marc Wilkinson; prod d, Jocelyn Herbert; art d, Brian Eatwell

"One man can change the world with a bullet in the right place."

Mick (Malcolm McDowell) and his three schoolfriends imprisoned within their privileged school walls relieve their miserable existence with clandestine trips into town, drinking binges and sexual fantasies until the day arrives when they can suffer it no longer and declare war. In a bloody finale they set fire to the school on Founder's Day and destroy anything that moves...

A kind of *Tom Brown's Schooldays* with guns and grenades, Lindsay Anderson's groundbreaking film is about class, homoeroticism, sexual repression and violent revolution in an English public school. Shifting continually from institutionalized hell to bizarre surrealism, many parallels can be seen with Jean Vigo's *Zero de Conduite* (1933) and was much applauded by the sixties counter-culture.

Lindsay Anderson used his old boarding school at **Cheltenham College, Bath Road**, near Cheltenham town centre for the location, a place he has happy and idyllic memories of. Cheltenham College, however, is still recovering from the blow.

See also: Rudyard Kipling, *A Clockwork Orange*

GRAVE OF P.C. WREN (1875-1941)
Amberley

Percy Wren will be best remembered in the cinema for his series of books depicting the romance and adventure of the French Foreign Legion, most notably in his best known work, *Beau Geste* (1924), a haunting tale which

Robert Preston, Gary Cooper and Ray Milland in ***Beau Geste*** *(1939, Paramount).*

captivated movie audiences and inspired a succession of Hollywood desert dramas. *Beau Geste* was filmed three times, in 1926, 1939 and 1966. The most memorable version was William Wellman's 1939 production filmed in the Arizona desert, starring Gary Cooper, Ray Milland and Robert Preston as the honourable brothers 'Beau', John and Digby Geste. Brian Donlevy, who portrayed the sadistic Sergeant Markoff received an AAN for Best Supporting Actor. Wren's two other Foreign Legion novels, *Beau Sabreur* (1926) and *Beau Ideal* (1928), were also filmed in 1928 and 1931.

Born Percival Wren on 1 November 1875 in Deptford to Ellen Sasbury, and John Wilkins Wren, a schoolteacher, he was educated at West Kent School and St. Catherine's College, Oxford, and began his working life as a schoolteacher. In 1903 he joined the Indian Educational Service as headmaster of Karachi High School which was the beginning of a succession of posts in India.

Between 1910 and 1912 he wrote four educational textbooks and his first novel, *Dew and Mildew*, set in India, was published in 1912. His first Foreign Legion novel was *The Wages of Virtue* (1916). During his lifetime he wrote over thirty novels, adding the middle name of Christopher when he found success as an author.

He is buried in the graveyard opposite **Holy Trinity Church**, Amberley.

See also: Ray Milland, Ronald Coleman

THE REGAL PUB
Gloucester

The Regal Pub is located in the former Regal Cinema which closed as a cinema in the mid 1980s. The original stage and balcony, now draped with a twelve foot King Kong and Manhattan skyline, are still intact. Photos of the cinema in its heyday and assorted movie stars adorn its walls, together with stills of the Beatles who played here in the sixties.

Further information: The Regal, 32A St. Aldate Street, King's Square, Gloucester GL1 1RP. Tel: 01452 332344.

GRAVE OF MICHAEL POWELL (1905-90)
Avening

"He will be remembered as a man who defied the critics but lived his life without bitterness."
David Puttnam

Director, screenwriter and producer, Michael Powell was one of the great maverick film makers, who, together with Emeric Pressburger produced some of the best cinema to come out of England, including *I know Where I'm Going* (1945), *A Matter of Life and Death* (1946), *Black Narcissus* (1946) and *The Red Shoes* (1948). His career never recovered from the critics' savage reception of his controversial *Peeping Tom* (1960), and he worked only sporadically afterwards. He emigrated to Australia and spent much of his later life in the U.S.A. where he married film editor Thelma Schoonmaker in 1984.

Suffering from cancer, he insisted on flying from the United States so that he could be buried in his beloved Cotswolds, where he died on 19 February 1990 at **Lee Cottages**, in Avening. Director Martin Scorsese and David Puttnam were among the mourners at his funeral at the tiny village church of **Holy Cross**, where he is buried in the **southwest corner** of the churchyard.

See also: Michael Powell (Kent), *The Edge of the World, The Thief of Baghdad, A Canterbury Tale, I Know Where I'm Going, A Matter of Life and Death, Black Narcissus, The Small Back Room, Peeping Tom*

CHELTENHAM FILM SOCIETY
Cheltenham

The proposal to form a film society in Cheltenham was first mooted at a meeting of interested people on 6 March 1945. A committee was set up to examine the proposal and draw up a draft constitution. This was accepted at a public meeting held in the School of Art on 1 May 1945 and the Cheltenham Film Society was born. The opening screeening was held at the Daffodil Cinema (now a restaurant) during July 1945, where Eisenstein's *Alexander Nevsky* was shown to an audience of about 450. With one exception in the mid-1980s it has shown films every season since: in total over 780 full length feature films and 2,000 shorts. With David Puttnam as its president, it is now one of the longest running film societies in the UK, and in 1999 it won the national award for 'Best Film Society of the Year'.

Further information: Cheltenham Film Society, A. Thompson, 29 Maidenhall, Highnam, Glos GL2 8DJ.

Hampshire

OH, MR. PORTER!
Cliddesden

• 1937 85m b/w Comedy Gainsborough Pictures (UK)
• Will Hay (William Porter), Moore Marriott (Harbottle), Graham Moffat (Albert), Dennis Wyndham (Grogan), Dave O'Toole (Postman)

Station master Porter (Will Hay) and Harbottle (Moore Marriott) being reprimanded by a guard for stopping his train at their 'dirty little halt' in **Oh Mr. Porter!** (1939, Gainsborough).

• p, Edward Black; d, Marcel Varnel; ph, Arthur Crabtree; ed, R.E. Dearing & Alfred Roome; w, J. Orton, Val Guest & Marriott Edgar (from an original story by Frank Launder)

"The next train's gone!"
Harbottle

Oh, Mr Porter! is a masterpiece of pre-war British cinema. The humour is timeless and the setting has the magical allure of a vanished era, in which that bungling trio of idiots, Will Hay, Moore Marriott and 'fat boy' Graham Moffat endeavour to run a railway station.

Filmed on the Basingstoke-Alton Light Railway, Gainsborough was given only six weeks to make the film as the line had recently closed and track was being lifted as they were filming. The station used was **Cliddesden**, which was renamed 'Buggleskelly' for the film. The station's old corrugated buildings were sheathed with wood and a signal box was built near the level crossing. A tunnel was constructed in a cutting on the Basingstoke side and the houses next to the station were hidden by haystacks.

'Gladstone', the engine, whose real name was 'Northiam', was a Hawthorn Leslie 2-4-0 tank, built in 1899, loaned from the Rother Valley Railway in Kent. Its tall, spiked chimney was added by the props department to give it a

Site of **Cliddesden Station** today. A line of trees marks where the platform once stood - sections of which are just visible through the undergrowth.

vintage appearance. Unfortunately it was scrapped in 1941.

Local farmer, Richard Hooper, recalls that his father loaned a cow for a milking scene with Graham Moffatt, who had never milked a cow in his life. His father had to rig up a bucket filled with chalky water and stirrup-pump it through a tube behind the cow's udder which gave the appearance of milking. Continual re-shooting of the scene worried the cow so much that she died and a substitute had to be found.

The underwear strung across the line belonged to Wilfred Bone who lived in the house next to the station and who also taught Graham Moffat in the proper use of red and green flags. As his underwear was virtually ruined, the production donated the wooden buildings to Wilfred, which he afterwards converted into a garage.

No stunt man was used in the scene where Albert (Graham Moffat) is on the roof of the moving carriage trying to prevent the gun-runners from escaping with his shovel. His foot was merely tied to a ventilator when he leaned over the side. The final scene where 'Gladstone' blows up was shot at **Basingstoke**.

During filming, Moore Marriott stayed at the **Red Lion** (01256 328525) in Basingstoke and drove through the town in full make-up. Will Hay stayed at the **Swan Hotel** (01420 83777), Alton.

See also: Will Hay

GRAVE OF LORD CARNARVON (1866-1923)
Highclere

"They who enter this sacred tomb shall swift be visited by wings of death."
One of many fabricated curses from Tutankhamen's tomb

*Christopher Lee and Peter Cushing in **The Mummy** (1959. Hammer)*

Here lies the man whose death was the inspiration for a multitude of mummy movies and their obligatory curse. The list is endless, but the definitive version starred Boris Karloff in Universal's *The Mummy* in 1932, which inspired many mediocre sequels.

In 1922 Howard Carter and the Earl of Carnarvon discovered the tomb of Tutankhamen in the Valley of the Kings near Luxor. While the tomb was still being excavated the Earl died. At the precise moment of his death all the lights of Cairo blacked out for no apparent reason and his pet dog howled in torment before dropping dead. Newspapers immediately attributed his death to a 'Pharaoh's curse' from the tomb. On further investigation the press uncovered other people who had died after contact with the tomb: a tourist who had entered the tomb was hit by a taxi in Cairo, a member of staff died labelling objects in the British Museum and Prince Ali Fahmy Bey was murdered by his wife in the Savoy Hotel in London. Some articles suggested there was a deadly bacteria in the tomb and many newspapers published lists of people who had died, who had been connected with the tomb. The stories panicked people who owned Egyptian artifacts and hundreds sent them to the British Museum for disposal.

No curse was ever found in the tomb and most of the hysteria was, in fact, fuelled by newspaper fabrications;

however, when the current Lord Carnarvon was asked on NBC television in 1977 if he believed in the curse, he answered that he *"neither believed it nor disbelieved it and would not accept a million pounds to enter the tomb of Tutankhamun in the Valley of the Kings."*

George Edward Stanhope Molyneux Herbert, Fifth Earl of Carnarvon is buried at the top of **Beacon Hill**, overlooking **Highclere Castle**, his family home.

See also: Boris Karloff, Christopher Lee, Peter Cushing, Hammer Studios

Further information: Highclere Castle has a small permanent Egyptian exhibition, and is situated 4 miles south of Newbury, off the A34 and A343. Tel: 01635 253210

THE WRECKER
Lasham

• 1928 b/w Gainsborough Pictures (UK)
• Carlyle Blackwell, Benita Hume, Pauline Johnson
• p, Michael Balcon; d, G.M. Bolvary

In August 1928 a spectacular train crash was shot on the Basingstoke-Alton Light Railway at Salter's Ash crossing, Lasham. The film was Michael Balcon's *The Wrecker* and the scene was so successful it was used again in *Seven Sinners* (1930). A thirty-man breakdown crew was required using two steam cranes to clear the wreckage and repair the track, which was operational the following day.

The Basingstoke Gazette, 25 August 1928, printed an eye-witness account: *A special train from Waterloo consisting of corridor and dining saloon arrived at Salter's Ash crossing at 6.30 a.m. on Sunday. The chief operator and his assistants arrived by motor-car at a large marquee erected at Hill Farm, Lasham. For several days a large number of workmen had been engaged digging trenches and carting hundreds* of sandbags to the corn field and dummy haystacks where five batteries of film photographers with 22 cameras were to be entrenched for their safety. As well as cameras concealed in the haystack there were three stands packed with cameramen and masked by greenery to resemble trees.

The Southern Railway Co. had sold to the producers a six-coach bogie set train and an express engine of the South Eastern type painted grey and having 'United coast Lines' on the tender. The approach to Lasham Hill Farm for the general public was through the village of Lasham, all other roads being blocked except to those provided with permits. A large number of police were present to keep the public out of danger and to ensure the safety of those carrying out the operation.

After rehearsing for several hours up and down the track with the train and across the private crossing with the steam Foden wagon, everything was ready for the final masterpiece. The Foden wagon was placed across the track... At about 1.10 p.m. the Director gave the signal to the linesman - "Let her come". An electric camera was placed on the front of the engine, and two dummies placed in their proper positions. The regulator was opened with full steam ahead. The driver shouted to his fireman to jump and then himself left the footplate. In 65 seconds it was all over. Rushing down the incline on a gradient of about 1 in 50 the train reached the point of impact at 45 m.p.h. There was a terrible explosion, which could be heard a mile away. Smoke and sparks shot 15 ft. into the air. After ploughing up the track for 120 yards the engine fell on its side - a perfect wreck. The electric camera on the front of the engine was found with the camera glass broken and a 30 ft. rail had pierced through the tender into the guard's van. The whole of the train had left the track with the exception of the last pair of wheels.

At 3 p.m. the Director and his cameramen were ready to play the grim

scene of rescuing passengers from the wrecked train. At 4 p.m. a large van loaded with petrol arrived. Petrol was quickly poured on the train which was then set on fire, presenting a very interesting but pitiful picture... The cost of the day's work was estimated to be between £6,000 and £7,000.

CLASSIC LOCATION: LONGMOOR MILITARY RAILWAY
Woolmer Forest

Originally called the Woolmer Instructional Railway, (popularly known as the Will It Move Railway (WIMR) because of the steep gradients of the forest and heath) it was built at the turn of the century to link Longmoor and Borden army camps.

The railway and its surrounding **Woolmer Forest** became a popular location for film makers in the late 1930s. Some of the first location shooting done here was for Hitchcock's *The Lady Vanishes* (1938). The

The Lady Vanishes (1938, Gaumont)

skidmarks from the car used in the train chase scene could be seen for a long time on the **Liphook Road at Whitehill**. The tanned troops of the 10th Railway Squadron, who had recently returned from Suez, were used as extras on the line during the filming of George Cukor's *Bhowani Junction* (1956), starring Ava Gardner, when the **Hollywater loop** was turned into a post-war Indian landscape. A Chinese railway station set was built at **Liss**

Forest Road in 1958 for *The Inn of the Sixth Happiness*, starring Ingrid Bergman and Curt Jurgens. The line closed in 1970, but two years later **Weavers Down** to **Liss** was transformed into a South African landscape to shoot scenes for Richard Attenborough's, *Young Winston* (1972). Other films shot here over the years include *The Interrupted Journey* (1949), *The Happiest Days of Your Life* (1950), *Melba* (1953), *Sons and Lovers* (1960) and *The Great St. Trinian's Train Robbery* (1966).

See also: Gainsborough Studios, *The Inn of the Sixth Happiness, St Trinians*

ASHES OF ALICE LIDDELL (1852-1934)
Lyndhurst

"'What is the use of a book', thought Alice, 'without pictures or conversations?'"
Alice's Adventures in Wonderland

Oxford don, Charles Lutwidge Dodgson, aka 'Lewis Carroll', was inspired to write the acclaimed children's books *Alice in Wonderland* (1865) and *Through the Looking Glass* (1861) after a boating trip on the Thames on 4 July 1862 with H.G. Liddell's (Dean of Christ Church College, Oxford) three daughters, Alice, Lorinn and Erith. In 1880, Alice married Reginald Hargreaves, whose name her ashes are buried under in **Lyndhurst Churchyard** in the **New Forest**.

All film versions of *Alice in Wonderland* to date have been little more than awkward costume romps, failing to capture the atmosphere of the books. The earliest sound version was adapted for the screen in 1931 with Ruth Gilbert playing Alice. Other portrayals of Alice have included Charlotte Henry (1933), Carol Marsh (1950) and Fiona Fullerton (1972). Kathryn Beaumont was the voice of Alice in Disney's 1951 animated version, and Coral Browne portrayed a grown-up Alice in *Dreamchild* (1985) in which she travels to the U.S.A. in 1932 as an old lady to attend a Lewis Carroll centenary celebration.

GRAVE OF F.L. GREEN (1902-53)
Havant

Laurie Green is largely forgotten today, but his most famous novel, *Odd Man Out*, about an IRA fugitive was filmed by Carol Reed in 1947. James Mason's portrayal of the dying fugitive is one of the most memorable scenes in post-war cinema. Although he shares a script credit with R.C. Sheriff, most of the screenplay was written by Green.

Known as 'the Irish Dostoyevsky', he was actually born in Portsmouth, one of six children of George Green, a headmaster. Plagued by ill health, tuberculosis resulted in his leg being amputated at the knee when he was twenty. He became an accountant after leaving school and in 1929 he married Meg Edwards. In 1934 they moved to Belfast where he wrote his first novel, *Julius Penton*. He wrote fourteen novels during his lifetime, including *The Sound of Winter* (1940), *On the Edge of the Sea* (1944) and *Clouds in the Wind* (1950). In the early fifties he moved to Bristol where he died from a brain haemorrhage in 1953, aged fifty-one. He is buried in the family plot at **Havant cemetery, at Eastern Road and New Lane**, where his tombstone inscription reads, *"Through his work shall he be remembered"*.

See also: *Odd Man Out*

GRAVE OF MERLE OBERON'S MOTHER
Micheldever

Throughout her life Merle Oberon denied her Eurasian origins. Listed in most film indexes as born in Hobart, Tasmania, she was actually born in Bombay to a Eurasian mother and an English father. Her real name was Estelle Merle O'Brien Thompson. When she became a prolific actress, she passed her mother off as her Indian servant. After her death in 1937, Oberon had her mother's 'portrait' painted: it depicted a white skinned woman with blue eyes and brown hair. Her mother is buried in an unmarked grave at Micheldever.

See also: Merle Oberon

CLASSIC LOCATION: BLACKBUSHE AIRPORT
Camberley

"Great little airfield you got here." Frank Sinatra's comment while on location at nearby Minley Manor. Film unknown.

Repeatedly used for filming and as a location for countless 'B' movies. Scenes from *No Highway in the Sky* (1951, aka *No Highway*) a drama about the discovery of aircraft metal-

fatigue was shot here, starring James Stewart and Marlene Dietrich; also *Girl on a Motorcycle* (1968) with Marianne Faithful, *Hanover Street* (1979) with Harrison Ford and *Eye of the Needle* (1981) with Donald Sutherland.

On one occasion during film-making, a passing motorist swerved into a ditch and had to be taken to the terminal building to calm down after he saw a 'body' and thousands of banknotes being thrown from a low-flying airliner.

Blackbushe is still a working airport and is also the site of a huge Sunday market. It is just off the A30, between Hartley Wintney and Camberley.

CLASSIC LOCATION: THE WATERCRESS LINE
Alresford

BR closed the line between Alton and Winchester in 1973, but a group of enthusiasts purchased the section between Alresford and Alton. Four years later the Watercress Line steam railway (so called because watercress has always been grown locally) was re-opened between Alresford and Ropley, and extended to Alton by 1985 - a total distance of ten miles. There are four stations on the line and their headquarters at Arlesford represents a typical Southern Railways station, circa 1923-1947. Used frequently for location filming, feature films shot here include the 1981 WWII drama, *The Eye of the Needle*, starring Donald Sutherland and Kate Nelligan and Michael Winner's *Bullseye* (1989) with Michael Caine and Roger Moore.

Further information: The Watercress Line, The Railway Station, Alresford, Hampshire, SO24 9JG. Tel: 01962 733810. Website http://www.itoeye.co.uk

GRAVE OF SIR ARTHUR CONAN DOYLE (1859-1930)
Minstead

"Matilda Briggs... was a ship which is associated with the giant rat of Sumatra, a story for which the world is not yet prepared."
'The Sussex Vampire', *The Case-Book of Sherlock Holmes* (1927) '

The creator of the most filmed fictional character in the history of the cinema, Sherlock Holmes, is buried beneath an oak tree at the south-east end of **All Saint's churchyard, Minstead** beside his wife Jean, where his headstone inscription reads *Steel true, blade straight.*. Conan Doyle and his wife were actually buried twice; their first place of burial was the grounds of

Nigel Bruce, Basil Rathbone and Mary Gordon in
The Hound of the Baskervilles *(1939, Fox)*

Windlesham, their house at **Crowborough in East Sussex,** but when the house was sold in 1955, their remains were moved to Minstead (reputedly in a laundry van to avoid publicity) where they had owned a house at **Bignell Wood.**

Born in Edinburgh, Conan Doyle was educated at Stonyhurst and studied medicine at Edinburgh University. He began writing as a struggling practitioner, serializing his Sherlock Holmes stories in the *Strand Magazine.* When he later tried to kill off his hero, public outrage was so great that he was forced to resurrect him. His historical romances were considered to have greater literary merit, but it is for his detective fiction he will be best remembered.

Sherlock Holmes appeared in over 60 silent films, but it was not until 1939 that cinema's definitive Holmes arrived, portrayed by Basil Rathbone in 20th Century-Fox's *The Hound of the Baskervilles.* With bumbling sidekick Nigel Bruce as Dr. Watson, Rathbone appeared in many successful productions, where his aquiline features and cunning demeanour made him forever synonymous with Holmes. Most of his films, however, such as *Sherlock Holmes and the Voice of Terror* (1942), where Holmes battles with Nazis, and *Sherlock Holmes in Washington* (1943), were set in contemporary, rather than Victorian England. Other portrayals of Holmes over the years include those of Clive

Brook, Arthur Wotner, Raymond Massey, Robert Rendal, Peter Cushing, Christopher Lee, Peter Cook and Nicholas Rowe.

See also: *The Hound of the Baskervilles,* Peter Cushing, Joseph Bell, Hammer Studios, Sherlock Holmes Festival, The Sherlock Holmes Collection

Herefordshire

SHADOWLANDS
Whitchurch

• 1993 130m c Biography/Drama/Romance
Shadowlands Productions/Price Entertainment (UK)
• Anthony Hopkins (Jack Lewis), Debra Winger (Joy Gresham), John Wood (Christopher Riley), Edward Hardwicke (Warnie Lewis), Robert Flemyng (Claude Bird), Joseph Mazzello (Douglas Gresham), • p, Richard Attenborough, Brian Eastman; d, Richard Attenborough; w, William Nicholson (from his play); ph, Roger Pratt; ed, Lesley Walker; m, George Fenton; prod d, Stuart Craig; art d, Michael Lamont;

"What do you do when you go to bed?"
"I put on my pyjamas and say my prayers and get under the covers."
"Well, then, that's what I want you to do right now, except that when you get under the covers, I'll be there."

Based on the stage play by William Nicholson, *Shadowlands* is the true story of the romance between

Anthony Hopkins and director Richard Attenborough on the set of **Shadowlands**

celebrated children's writer C.S. Lewis and American divorcee Joy Gresham. Lewis lives a contented, but unfulfilled bachelor's existence with his brother Warnie, surrounded by books, teaching, and brilliant, sexist academics. When plain-speaking Joy bursts into his cloistered world his life is rejuvenated and he falls in love.

Tragically Joy contracts cancer and her harrowing and painful death tests his Christian beliefs to their limit. During a remission in her illness, Jack decides to take Joy on a visit to the **Golden Valley,** a place he knows only through a painting which has been in his family since childhood.

The film makers discovered that the real Golden Valley between Vowchurch and Dorstone on the B4348 was nothing like the Arcadian paradise depicted in Lewis's painting and decided instead to use **Symond's Yat Rock,** off the A40 near Whitchurch, in the **Wye Valley** as the spot where Jack and Joy get their first glimpse of their Garden of Eden. Jack and Joy stayed in the **Pengethley Manor Hotel** (01989 730211), Pengethley Park, near Ross-on-Wye, during their trip, and **Bicknor Court Farm,** near Symond's Yat Rock, was used for the final scene when Jack and Douglas return to the valley after Joy's death.

See also: *Shadowlands* (Oxford), Anthony Hopkins, C.S. Lewis

Hertfordshire

NIGHT OF THE DEMON
Bricket Wood

• aka Curse of the Demon
• 1957 82m b/w Horror / Thriller Sabre (UK)
• Dana Andrews (John Holden), Peggy Cummins (Joanna Harrington), Niall MacGinnis (Doctor Karswell), Maurice Denham (Prof Harrington), Athene Sayler (Mrs Karswell)

Hertfordshire

• p, Frank Bevis; d, Jacques Tourneur; ph, Ted Scaife; w, Charles Bennet & Hal E. Chester; m, Clifton Parker

"...I make films about the supernatural because I believe in it. I believe in the power of the dead, witches. I even met a few when I was preparing Night of the Demon. I had a long conversation with the oldest witch in England about the spirit world, the power of cats. I also visited haunted houses. I happen to possess some powers myself... I also know that there are universes parallel to ours".
Jacques Tourneur *

Based on the short story, *Casting the Runes* , by M.R. James, *Night of the Demon* is the chilling tale of sceptical scientist, John Holden (Dana Andrews), whose disbelief in black magic is gradually undermined when his life is threatened by a mysterious black magician, Doctor Karswell (Niall MacGinnis).

Holden's metamorphosis from fearless cynic to terror-stricken believer is skilfully directed by Tourneur using virtually no special effects. The producer, however, thought the film was lacking and added the appearance of a demon in the final scene without Tourneur's permission. Intended as a terrifying climax, the scene only makes one titter in disbelief at the ruin of a small masterpiece.

The final scenes at the station and on the railway track where Doctor Karswell is killed by the demon were filmed at night on the St. Albans to Watford line at **Bricket Wood Station**. Studio scenes were shot at Elstree.

ASHES OF ERIC MORECAMBE (1926-84)
Harpenden

John Eric Bartholomew, better known as Eric Morecambe, lived in Harpenden from 1961 until his death from a heart attack in 1984. Born Eric Bartholomew,

he started his career in comedy in the early 1940s and with his partner, Ernie Wise, achieved TV stardom in the sixties. The duo made three films at the height of their success which are now possibly best consigned to oblivion: *The Intelligence Men* (1964), *That Riviera Touch* (1966) and *The Magnificent Two* (1967). His ashes are buried in the **Garden of Remembrance at St. Nicholas's Church**.

ARTHUR MELBOURNE-COOPER & THE ALPHA PICTURE PALACE
St. Albans

Film pioneer Arthur Melbourne-Cooper was born at **1, Osborne Terrace, London Road**, in 1874. His father was a photographer, and as a child Arthur became interested in photography through helping him in his studio. In 1892 Arthur started work with Birt Acres, the first person in England to successfully project 35mm film onto a screen. As his assistant, Arthur began to see the potential of films as entertainment. In 1901, he formed his own company (Alpha Cinematograph Co.) and film studio at **Belford Park** and later at **14 Alma Road** where a 'Cinema 100 Plaque' commemorates the site. He made literally hundreds of films including *Dreams of Toyland* (one of the first animated puppet films), *Matches Appeal* (an advertisement appeal on behalf of Bryant & May for matches during the Boer War) and many slapstick comedies.

He opened his 'Alpha Picture Palace' on 27 July 1908 (seating capacity 800) in the old polytechnic building in **London Road**. It was the first cinema to have a sloping floor and an enclosed room for the projection equipment, with usherettes, chocolate boys, commissionaire, and free parking space for bicycles. Beside the paybox were phials of perfume (Pivor of Paris) from which the ladies could spray their

handkerchiefs. Tip-up seats were provided (except in 'the tuppennys'), and people were bussed in from the surrounding villages in a special bus known locally as 'The Flying Fornicator'! The cinema burned down in 1927 and another was built on the site in 1931. It closed in 1995 and is still disused.

After the war, Melbourne-Cooper moved to Blackpool where he worked for a company which made advertisements. He died in Cambridgeshire in 1961.

See also: Birt Acres

BIRTHPLACE OF MICHAEL HORDERN (1911-95)
Berkhamsted

Distinguished character actor, Michael Murray Hordern was born on 3 October 1911 at **The Poplars, Holiday Street, Berkhamsted,** the youngest of three sons of Margaret Murray - daughter of the inventor of Milk of Magnesia - and Ned Hordern, a lieutenant in the Royal Indian Marines. In 1916 when his mother sailed for India to visit his father, he was sent to join his brothers at Windlesham prep. school in Sussex. His mother's return was prevented by the war and he did not see her again until 1918. She surprised everyone when she arrived home with an adopted daughter whose mother had died in childbirth. Nicknamed Doody, she duly became one of the family. When he was eight his father retired from the Indian Marines on a £40 a month pension, suitably bolstered by the family Milk of Magnesia revenue. About this time the family moved to a flat in Brighton then later to a house in Haywards Heath. He remained at Windlesham School until he was fourteen when he joined his brothers at Brighton College. In 1925 the family left the comforts of suburbia for Dartmoor and bought **Jordan Manor House** near **Poundsgate.**

His first job on leaving school was as a schoolmaster in Beaconsfield and he later sold educational equipment to schools. His involvement with numerous amateur dramatic societies, however, encouraged him to turn professional and in 1937 he became Assistant Stage Manager at the Savoy Theatre in a play called *Night Sky.* He later joined the Rapier Players in Bristol doing weekly rep where he met his future wife, Eve Mortimer.

He made his film debut in 1939 as a junior counsel in Carol Reed's *The Girl in the News.* He was often portrayed as an anxious official but will be best remembered in the cinema for his roles as Inspector Bashford in *Passport to Pimlico* (1949), Jacob Marley in *Scrooge* (1951), Harrington Brande in *The Spanish Gardener* (1956) and as the spy chief Ashe in *The Spy Who Came in from the Cold* (1965).

He made over 100 films and was knighted in 1983. He died in Oxford on May 2 1995.

See also: *Passport to Pimlico, The Spy Who Came in from the Cold*

THE ORIGINAL PETER PAN & THE LOST BOYS
Berkhamsted

Between 1904 - 1907, J.M. Barrie was a frequent visitor to Egerton House on the High Street, the home of his friends, Arthur and Sylvia Llewelyn Davies. Their five sons (George, Jack, Peter, Michael and Nicholas) were reputedly a formative influence in the creation of *Peter Pan* (1904). When their parents died young, they were literally the 'Lost Boys' and J.M. Barrie became their guardian. One of them, Michael, photographed by Barrie in 1906, was the original inspiration for the *Peter Pan* statue in Kensington Gardens, London. Egerton House has since been demolished and at the time of writing it is a derelict site which includes the disused Rex Cinema where a plaque commemorating the link to *Peter Pan* is erected.

See also: J.M. Barrie

SAVING PRIVATE RYAN
Hatfield

"We miss them actually, they were very good customers."
Liz Potter, co-owner of Hatfield DIY who supplied the production company.

In the summer of 1997 a disused British Aerospace airfield on the edge of Hatfield was transformed by Steven Spielberg's production company into a ruined French village during the Normandy invasion. It was here that Tom Hanks and his heavily outnumbered squad fought a column of German Tiger Tanks, desperately trying to prevent them reaching the stone bridge and crossing the river. The set designers created everything from wrecked bridges to shell-damaged churches; even the river was created by excavating a huge ditch. Over 3,500 people worked on the location, including the extras. The site has now been reinstated and long term plans for it include housing, an industrial and a university complex. It is situated across the road from a shopping complex called the **Galleria Outlet Centre, Comet Way (on the A1M just of J3) on the north side of Hatfield**, but it is not accessible to the public.

Tom Hanks and Steven Spielberg on the set of **Saving Private Ryan**

A preview screening of the film at Hatfield UCI raised over £6000 for local charities.

See also: *Saving Private Ryan* (Wexford & Highland)

GRAVE OF STANLEY KUBRICK (1928-99)
St. Albans

"... If it can be written or thought, it can be filmed."
Stanley Kubrick

A doctor's son from the Bronx, Stanley Kubrick was one of the world's visionary and most mysterious film makers. When he was twelve his father gave him a Graflex camera which inspired him to take up photography. He later sold his work to the media

and was employed by *Look* magazine. He went on to make low-budget documentaries and in 1953 he made his first feature film, *Fear and Desire*, funded by prize money won in a local chess competition. Hollywood was impressed and gave him a contract which led to his first major film, *The Killing* (1958).

A passionate perfectionist and an autocrat, he worked only sporadically throughout his career, unyielding to the demands of Hollywood commercialism. In later life he became a virtual recluse and shunned the media.

Other films include *Paths of Glory* (1957), *Spartacus* (1958), *Lolita* (1962), *Dr Strangelove* (1964), *2001: A Space Odyssey* (1968), *A Clockwork Orange* (1971), *Barry Lyndon* (1975), *The Shining* (1980) and *Full Metal Jacket* (1985). His last film, *Eyes Wide Shut* (1999), was his first film for twelve years, and was completed only days before his death.

Kubrick moved to England in 1961 and had lived at **Childwickbury Manor** (pronounced Chillickbury) since 1977, where he is buried in the grounds of the estate. His funeral was conducted in secrecy and the identitiy of the 200 mourners was not revealed, but his cortege did include Steven Spielberg, David Putnam, Tom Cruise and Nicole Kidman. Kubrick was married three times and had three daughters. Childwickbury Manor is situated two miles north west of St. Albans, off the A1081. The red-bricked gate house of the estate can be seen from the main road but it is not open to the public.

See also: Arthur C. Clarke, *Full Metal Jacket, A Clockwork Orange*, Knebworth House

CLASSIC LOCATION: KNEBWORTH HOUSE
Stevenage

More famous for its contribution to rock culture than film culture,

Knebworth House

Knebworth has been home to many open air rock and jazz concerts since 1974, featuring legends such as Pink Floyd, The Rolling Stones, Led Zeppelin, Oasis, Ella Fitzgerald and Ray Charles.

It doubled for Wayne Manor in the first Batman movie in 1989, providing a tranquil bolt-hole for the caped crusader after the crime-ridden streets of Gotham. Stanley Kubrick spent a considerable amount of time and money preparing the library at Knebworth House for a scene in Eyes Wide Shut (1999), but after rehearsing for a day with Tom Cruise, he pulled out at the last moment before any filming began.

Other films shot here include *The Big Sleep* (1978), *Sir Henry at Rawlinson End* (1980), *The Great Muppet Caper* (1981), *Monty Python's the Meaning of Life* (1983), *The Shooting Party* (1984), *The Lair of the White Worm* (1988), *Wilde* (1996) and *The Wings of the Dove* (1997).

Originally a Tudor manor house, Knebworth was transformed to its present Gothic glory in 1843 with the addition of turrets and gargoyles. The Lytton family have lived there for five hundred years, and today it is home to David Lytton Cobbold, 2nd Lord Cobbold of Knebworth. Sites worth visiting are Knebworth Gardens, the house with its magnificent Jacobean Banqueting Hall and the 250 acre park.

Further information: Knebworth House, Knebworth, Stevenage, Herts. SG3 6PY. Tel: 01438 812661. Opening times vary between April and September. Contact house for details. Open all year round for pre-booked groups.

Isle of Wight

MRS BROWN
East Cowes

- 1997 103m c Historical Drama
- Judi Dench (Queen Victoria), Billy Connolly (John Brown), Geoffrey Palmer (Henry Ponsonby), Antony Sher (Disraeli), Gerard Butler (Archie Brown), Richard Pasco (Doctor Jenner), David Westhead (Bertie - Prince of Wales)
- p, Sarah Curtis; d, John Madden; w, Jeremy Brock (from an idea by George Rosie); ph. Richard Greatrex; ed, Robin Sales
- AAN Best Actress: Judi Dench; AAN Best Makeup

Judi Dench and Billy Connolly in **Mrs. Brown** *(1997)*

After Prince Albert's death in 1861, Victoria (Judi Dench) goes into seclusion for many years, shutting herself off from the world at large and ignoring affairs of state. Dissolution of the monarchy is whispered and the republican movement thrives. Into this melancholy scene bursts Her Majesty's Highland Servant, John Brown (Billy Connolly), like a cat among the royal pigeons. In fact, despite Brown's influence on the Queen being instrumental in bringing her out of mourning, court and government alike were fearful that this Scots hardman was getting too close to the Queen - perhaps even intimately - thereby influencing the destiny of the Empire. This sense is poignantly conveyed in *Mrs Brown*. Undeniably the best film about Queen Victoria ever made, even republicans will be amused.

Duns Castle in the Scottish Borders doubled for Balmoral, and **Wilton House**, near Salisbury stood in for Winsdor Castle, but the main location was **Osborne House**, an Italianate hideaway overlooking the Solent, built by Victoria and Albert in 1851. Their 'modest' country retreat, designed by Thomas Cubitt, was used as a holiday home for themselves and their nine children. It was also where Victoria first bathed in the sea and built Swiss Cottage, a special house for her children to play in. Still mourning for her beloved Albert, she died in the Queen's Bedroom on 22 January 1901. In 1954 the Queen gave permission for the royal suite to be opened to the public.

See also: Judi Dench, Billy Connolly

Further information: Osborne House is 1m SE of East Cowes. Tel: 01983 200022. Open: 22 March - 30 September daily. Duns Castle is not open to the public, but you can stay there as a paying guest. Tel: 01361 883211. Wilton House Tel: 01722 746729.

Kent

GRAVE OF EDITH NESBIT (1858-1924)
St. Mary's in the Marsh

E. Nesbit, one of the greatest children's writers of the century, whose story *The Railway Children* was brilliantly adapted for the screen, died at her home near the village of St Mary's in

Grave of Edith Nesbit, St. Mary's in the Marsh Churchyard.

the Marsh on 4 May 1924. She had moved there in 1921 with her second husband, marine engineer Thomas Tucker, known as 'Skipper', where they converted two WWI brick Air Force huts off **Jefferstone Lane** (now demolished) into a house. A heavy smoker, she suffered from chronic bronchial troubles for most of her life eventually dying of lung cancer aged sixty-five.

Her children's stories include *The Story of the Treasure Seekers* (1899), *The Would-be-Goods* (1901), *Five Children and It* (1902) and *The Enchanted Castle* (1907).

She was buried beneath an elm tree at the south end of the village churchyard. At her request, no memorial stone was erected, but the grave is marked by two wooden pillars linked by a carved crossbar made by 'Skipper', inscribed with her name, the words 'poet and author' and her clover leaf sign which was how she always wrote her initials.

See also: *The Railway Children*

Further information: E. Nesbit was born at 38 Lower Kennington Lane, London (now demolished). 'The Railway Children' map is available from Romney Resource Centre

(01797 367934) and local tourist offices which links local walks to sites connected with E. Nesbit.

GRAVE OF POCAHONTAS
Gravesend

Walt Disney's 1995 animated musical romance of the Pocahontas legend is typical of the studio's sugar-coated bunkum, where visual style frequently tramples historical fact. The real story of Princess Pocahontas remains shrouded in mystery.

She was born in 1595 in Gloucester, Virginia. Her real name was Princess Matoaka (her nickname was Pocahontas 'the playful one') and it is claimed that at the age of twelve she saved the life of Captain John Smith by saving him from execution at the hand of her father, Chief Powhatan. She converted to Christianity and was baptised in the name of Rebecca. In 1614 she married John Rolfe, Secretary and Recorder of the Colony and two years later they sailed to England with their son, where she was received at the court of King James.

After spending a year in England she became ill and it was decided she should return to Virginia but she died on board ship at Gravesend. No one knows what she died of, but plague was suspected as she was buried hurriedly. Her grave was unmarked and her final resting place cannot be identified, but it is generally recognised as being **St. George's Church**. In 1958 a bronze statue of Pocahontas was unveiled by the Governor of Virginia in the St. George's Church gardens.

Further information: St. George's Church is open on Wednesdays and Sundays and other times by appointment. Tel: 01474 566451 or call at the Rectory (next to church).

Gravesend Library, Windmill St., has a large collection of material about her life and some artifacts from Virginia may be seen in the Chantry Heritage Centre, Fort Gardens. Captain John Smith's grave can be visited at St. Sepulchre without Newgate, Holborn Viaduct, London.

BIRTHPLACE OF TREVOR HOWARD (1916-88)
Margate

Trevor Howard had no real roots. He was born on 28 September 1916 to Arthur Howard-Smith, an employee of Lloyd's of London and Canadian nurse, Mabel Wallace. No trace of the Howard-Smith family can be found in local records but it can be confirmed that Trevor Howard was born in the **Cliftonville** area although the precise address is unknown. Because of the nature of his father's job the family was always on the move and Margate was only one of many transient addresses. While Trevor was an infant the family moved to Ceylon where his sister Merla was born. He was boarded at **Clifton College** in **Bristol** when he was eight years old where he excelled at cricket and considered turning professional.

He joined RADA after leaving school and had been acting in the theatre for about ten years before he made his film debut in Carol Reed's 1944 wartime drama, *The Way Ahead*. After seeing him in his second film, *The Way To The Stars* (1945), producer Anthony Havelock-Allan suggested him for the male lead in *Brief Encounter* (1945) to David Lean. His fee for the film was £500 while Celia Johnston, an established actress, received £1,000.

He was again cast by Carol Reed in *The Third Man* (1949) as Vienna's British Military Police Chief, Colonel Calloway. While filming in Vienna he was arrested for impersonating an officer and discovered busker, Anton Karas, playing in a tavern, who later composed the film's memorable theme tune. In 1962 he portrayed Captain Bligh in MGM's disastrous remake of *Mutiny on the Bounty*, with an aloof

and sulky Marlon Brando, whom he disliked. He made seventy-four films, including: *Green For Danger* (1946), *The Heart of the Matter* (1953), *Sons and Lovers* (1960) and *Ryan's Daughter* (1970).

He had a reputation as a 'hellraiser' and a hard drinker, often disappearing on binges for days on end. One of the great British film actors he will be best remembered for his portrayal of the stiff upper-lipped Doctor Alec Harvey in *Brief Encounter*. He died of bronchitis complicated by jaundice on 7 January 1988, at Bushey Hospital in Hertfordshire.

See also: *Brief Encounter, Ryan's Daughter*, Captain Bligh

DR SYN, ALIAS THE SCARECROW
Romney Marsh

• 1962 98m Historical / Adventure Walt Disney
• Patrick McGoohan (Dr. Syn), George Cole (Mr. Mipps), Tony Britton (Bates), Michael Horden (Squire), Geoffrey Keen (Gen. Pugh)
• p, Walt Disney, Bill Anderson; d, James Neilson;; ph, Paul Beeson

The character Dr. Syn was created by Russell Thorndike who wrote the first book in 1915 in a lifeboat cottage on

Dymchurch sea wall (now demolished). The stories were set on the Romney Marsh in the late eighteenth century about a local clergyman who leads a double life as a smuggler and a pirate.

First filmed in 1937 with George Arliss and Margaret Lockwood, it was remade twice in 1962 as *Captain Clegg*, with Peter Cushing (original U.S. title: *Night Creatures*) and Disney's *Dr. Syn, Alias The Scarecrow*. For the latter the surrounding **Romney Marsh** and **St. Clements Church** in **Old Romney**, which closely resembled the church described in the novels, were used for locations. Every other year (on even years) on August Bank Holiday Monday the 'Day of Syn' festival is held in Dymchurch celebrating the characters in the stories.

See also: Peter Cushing

Further information: New Romney Tourist Information 01797 364194

DREAMLAND CINEMA
Margate

The Dreamland Cinema was designed by J.B. Iles, Leathart & Granger in 1935 and built on the site of the original 1912 cinema, the Hall-by-the-Sea. It is the first example of a cinema built in England in the style based on the *Titania Palast* of Berlin, 1924, a style used by the Odeon company from 1936 onwards. The auditorium originally seated 2,050 with public and saloon bars on the ground floor (now an entertainment centre), a restaurant seating 500 in the basement and a cafe (now play centre) seating 300 on the first floor, overlooking the sea. The auditorium retains its proscenium arch with gilt reliefs of Greek Gods but has been partitioned: a bingo hall occupies the former stalls and two cinemas the former circle. It still retains its original Compton Noterman theatre organ, installed in 1935.

Further information: Dreamland Cinema, Marine Terrace, Margate. Tel: 01843 227822.

CUSHING'S VIEW
Whitstable

Peter Cushing was born on 26 May, 1913, in the then small village of **Kenley** in Surrey and for many years lived at **32 St. James Road, Purley**, with his parents. After being educated at **Shoreham Grammar School** and **Purley County School,** he worked in the surveyor's department at Purley Council offices. Much of his spare time was spent working with amateur drama productions and for two years he wrote continuously to the Worthing repertory company imploring them to give him a job. In 1934 the Connaught Theatre in Worthing eventually sent for him and offered him a small walk-on part in J.B. Priestley's *Cornelius.*

In 1939 he left Britain to seek his fortune in Hollywood and landed a small part in James Whale's *The Man in the Iron Mask.* His first substantial role was in *Vigil in the Night* (1939) and he also appeared with Laurel and Hardy in *A Chump at Oxford* (1940).

In 1942 he met his future wife, Helen Beck, at ENSA's (Every Night Something Awful) headquarters at the Theatre Royal in Drury Lane. They were married the following year.

Cushing achieved world-wide fame when he was cast in the title role of Hammer Films' gothic horror movie,

Cushing's View.

The Curse of Frankenstein (1956). This was his first appearance with Christopher Lee and the beginning of his long association with Hammer Films for which he portrayed Baron Victor Frankenstein six times and Dracula's arch-enemy, Van Helsing five times. His other films include: *Hound of the Baskervilles* (1959), *Dr Who and the Daleks* (1965), *Star Wars* (1977, as the evil Grand Moff Tarkin) and *Biggles* (1985).

He made Whitstable his home for more than thirty years, affectionately referring to the town as 'the village'. When his wife died in 1971 from emphysema he was devastated and became a virtual recluse in his home at **Wavecrest** (on the sea side of Island Wall) for twelve years. He could often be seen at the **Tudor Tea Rooms**, his favourite

restaurant, in **Harbour Street**, which has a plaque dedicated to his memory, and some of his poems and photos are displayed on the walls. In June 1992, Peter Cushing donated a wooden bench with an inscribed plaque at **Cushing's View, Keam's Yard,** one of his favourite spots.

He died aged eighty-one on 11 August, 1994, at Pilgrims Hospice, London Road, Canterbury, after a long battle against cancer. He was cremated at **Barham** Crematorium. On the day of his funeral, thousands of people lined the streets of Whitstable and the town's shops closed in tribute.

See also: Hammer Studios, James Whale, *The Hound of the Baskervilles*

Further information: Whitstable Museum (01277 276998) in Oxford Street has some of Peter Cushing's effects, including a watercolour landscape painted by him, the suit worn by him in the role of Sherlock Holmes and his desk and chair.

GREAT EXPECTATIONS
St. Mary's Marshes

- 1946 118m b/w Drama Cineguild (UK)
- John Mills (Pip Pirrip), Valerie Hobson (Estella/Her Mother), Bernard Miles (Joe Gargery), Francis L. Sullivan (Jaggers), Martita Hunt (Miss Haversham). Finlay Currie (Abel Magwitch), Anthony Wagner (Pip as Child), Jean Simmons (Estella as Child), Alec Guinness (Herbert Pocket), Ivor Barnard (Wemmick)
- p, Ronald Neame; d, David Lean; w, David Lean, Ronald Neame, Anthony Havelock-Allan, Cecil McGivern, Kay Walsh (from the novel by Charles Dickens); ph, Guy Green; ed, Jack Harris; m, Walter Goehr; prod d, John Bryan; art d, Wilfred Shingleton; cos, Sophia Harris

"Ours was the marsh country, down by the river, within, as the river wound, twenty miles of the sea... the dark flat wilderness beyond the churchyard, intersected with dykes and mounds and

gates, with scattered cattle feeding on it,
was the marshes... the low leaden line
beyond, was the river,... the distant
savage lair from which the wind was
rushing, was the sea..."
Charles Dickens, *Great Expectations*

Inspired to make the film after seeing
Alec Guinness and Martita Hunt in a
stage production, David Lean's stylised
translation of Dickens' novel to the
screen must rank among his finest
work. The memorable churchyard
scene where Pip has his chilling
encounter with Magwitch was actually a
studio set with eerily fashioned trees
below a superimposed sky and a
church that was only ten feet high to
create the illusion of distance.

Location filming was done on **St.
Mary's Marshes** in the Thames
estuary, the original location which had
inspired Dickens. The production was
based in Rochester at the **Royal
Victoria and Bull Hotel**, on which
Dickens based the Blue Boar in his
novel. Dickens also based Joe Gargery's
house on the forge in the nearby
Chalk where he often stopped for a
chat, and a replica was built on St.
Mary's Marshes for the film. River
scenes were shot on the nearby River
Medway. *The Empress* steam ship used
in the film was scrapped in 1955.

See also: David Lean, The Old Ferry
Inn

Further Information: Dickens wrote
Great Expectations at Gads Hill Place,
the house where he lived from 1856
until his death in 1870. Situated in the
nearby hamlet of Gads Hill, it is now a
private girls' school. The 'Ship and
Lobster' pub, Denton, is reputed to be
'The Ship' in the novel. There are many
Dickens sites to visit in surrounding
Gravesham, including the Charles
Dickens Centre, Eastgate House, High
Street, Rochester (01634 844176), which
recreates many scenes from his books.
Gravesend Tourist Information: 01474
337600.

*Miss Havisham (Martita Hunt) and Pip (Anthony Wager) in **Great Expectations** (1946, Cineguild)*

ASHES OF H.E. BATES (1905-74)
Charing

Herbert Ernest Bates, novelist, short
story writer and creator of the Larkin
family, was born at **Rushden,
Northamptonshire** on 16 May 1905.
He lived in **Grove Road** in a terraced
house next to a shoe factory and
attended Newton Road School in
Rushden and Kettering Grammar school
where in 1919 he met English teacher,
Edmund Kirby, who inspired him to
become a writer.

He left school at sixteen and began
working as a junior reporter with the
Northampton Chronicle and later
became a clerk in a leather warehouse
where he spent much of his time
writing stories during work time until
he was sacked. After nine rejections
from previous publishers his
manuscript of *The Two Sisters* was
published by Jonathan Cape in 1925.

By 1941 he had published over 200
short stories when he was

commissioned into the R.A.F. as a flight
lieutenant. His job was to write stories
and propaganda, which he did under
the pseudonym, 'Flying Officer X'. He
was posted to the Far East and in 1944
wrote his best-selling novel, *Fair Stood
the Wind For France*. His 1947 novel,
The Purple Plain, was filmed in 1954
starring Gregory Peck as a disturbed
pilot and in 1958 MGM bought the film
rights of the first of the Larkin family
novels, *The Darling Buds of May*,
filmed as the *Mating Game* with
Debbie Reynolds. In 1973 Glenda
Jackson and Oliver Reed starred in
Triple Echo, based on his 1970 novella
about an army deserter in WWII.

Known to his friends as 'Aitchee', he
was married with four children and had
lived since 1931 in a converted granary
in the village of **Little Chart**. When he
died in a Canterbury hospital in 1974
he had written 21 novels and over 300
short stories. His ashes are buried at
nearby **Charing Crematorium** and are
marked by a pedestal urn memorial.

See also: Oliver Reed, Glenda Jackson

THE ORIGINAL SECRET GARDEN
Rolvenden

The 18 acres of grounds surrounding **Great Maytham Hall** contains the walled garden which inspired children's writer, Frances Hodgson Burnett, to write *The Secret Garden* (1911), her story of an orphan girl who returns from India to live with her uncle at the gloomy, Misselthwaite Manor, where she discovers a magical garden.

It was first filmed in 1948 with Margaret O'Brien and Herbert Marshall, and remade in 1987. Polish director, Agnieszka Holland (*Danton, Olivier Olivier, Europa Europa*), made a memorable version in 1993 featuring Kate Maberly as the orphan, Mary Lennox, and Maggie Smith as stern housekeeper, Mrs. Medlock. Locations for the 1993 version included **Allerton Park**, near Knaresborough, and **Luton Hoo**, near Luton.

Further information: Great Maytham Hall is open to the public on Wednesday and Thursday afternoons from May to September. Tel: 01580 241346.

ANNE OF THE THOUSAND DAYS
Hever

• 1969 145m c Historical Universal (UK)
• Richard Burton (King Henry VIII), Genevieve Bujold (Anne Boleyn), Irene Papas (Queen Katherine), Anthony Quayle (Wolsey), John Colicos (Cromwell), Michael Horden (Thomas Boleyn), Katherine Blake (Elizabeth), Peter Jeffrey (Norfolk)• p, Hal B. Wallis; d, Charles Jarrott; w, Bridget Boland, John Hale (adapted by Richard Sokolove, based on the play by Maxwell Anderson); ph, Arthur Ibbetson; ed, Richard Marden; m, Georges Delerue
• AA Best Costume Design: Margaret Furse

Anne of the Thousand Days tells the story of Henry VIII's courtship and subsequent marriage to Anne Boleyn with great pomp and pageantry. In 1529 the Pope refused to grant Henry a divorce from his first wife, Catherine of Aragon, which would have allowed him a clear field to marry Anne. Not one to admit defeat easily, Henry, assisted by Thomas Cromwell, renounced the papal supremacy, and with parliament's approval proclaimed himself head of the Church. Henry and Anne were married in 1533 and in the same year she gave birth to the future Queen Elizabeth. Anne failed to produce a male heir to the throne and was eventually found guilty of high treason for adultery and incest with her half-brother and was beheaded on Tower Green in 1536.

Filming took place at **Hever Castle, near Edenbridge**, the original home of the Boleyn family. Henry acquired the castle from his deceased wife's family, but made little further use of it except to grant it in 1540 to Anne of Cleves, his recently divorced fourth wife. The castle was bought at the turn of the century by the Astor family, who restored much of the castle and gardens to their former glory. The estate, which is open to the public and features a Tudor village, offers frequent special events - such as merrie England weekends, jousting tournaments, costume exhibitions and Longbow displays. Nearby **Penshurst Place, Penhurst**, doubled for Henry's Greenwich Palace and is also open to the public.

See also: Anne Boleyn, Richard Burton, Anthony Quayle

Further information: Hever Castle 01732 865224, Penshurst Place 01892 870307

KIND HEARTS AND CORONETS
Maidstone

• 1949 105m bw Comedy Ealing (UK)
• Dennis Price (Louis Mazzini), Alec Guinness (The Duke, The Banker, The Canon, The General, The Admiral, Young Ascoyne D'Ascoyne, Young Henry, Lady

*Valerie Hobson as Edith D'Ascoyne in **Kind Hearts and Coronets** (1949, Ealing)*

Agatha), Valerie Hobson (Edith D'Ascoyne), Joan Greenwood (Sibella), Audrey Fildes (Mama), Miles Malleson (The Hangman), Clive Morton (Prison Governor), John Penrose (Lionel)
• p, Michael Balcon; d, Robert Hamer; w, Robert Hamer, John Dighton (based on the novel Israel Rank by Roy Horniman); ph, Douglas Slocombe; ed, Peter Tanner; m, Wolfgang Amadeus Mozart; art d, William Kellner

"I always say that my west window has all the exuberance of Chaucer, without, happily, any of the concomitant crudities of his period."
Canon D'Ascoyne (Alec Guinness)

This is one of the classic Ealing black comedies and the film that made Alec Guinness a star. Louis Mazzini is the son of a Duke's daughter. In the eyes of her family she had married beneath herself, forfeiting her inheritance and privileges. When his mother is refused a burial in the family tomb Louis swears an oath to dispose of the members of the D'Ascoyne family who stand between him and the dukedom. Murdering the D'Ascoynes in swift succession, the dukedom finally becomes his. Ironically, he is eventually arrested for a murder he didn't commit; however, following the discovery of a suicide note he is freed at the eleventh hour, but inadvertently leaves his incriminating memoirs in his cell, and his fate is inconclusive at the end of the film. The ambiguous ending of the British version, however, rattled the American Production Code in which crime could not be seen to pay, and an additional scene had to be stitched on to the end showing Louis's memoirs in the hands of the prison staff.

Leeds Castle, near Maidstone, was used as the location for the family seat of the Duke of Chalfont. A Norman stronghold, the castle became a Royal palace and was for 300 years the home of Kings and Queens of England. Restored to its current glory by Lady Baillie, the last private owner, Leeds Castle and its 500 acres of parkland has been open to the public since 1975. Visitor attractions include a unique Dog Collar Museum, a yew tree maze with underground grotto and a vineyard first listed in the Domesday Book.

See also: Ealing Studios, Valerie Hobson

Further information: Leeds Castle is 4 miles east of Maidstone, close to Junction 8 on the M20.
Tel: 01622 765400

GRAVE OF DEREK JARMAN (1942-94)
Old Romney

'He approached film as a painter rather than a story teller and his films are perhaps best watched with an eye for the magic of image and composition.'
Tony Rayns

Painter, writer, designer, and avant-garde film maker, Derek Jarman was born on 31 January 1942 at the **Royal Victoria Nursing Home, Northwood, Middlesex**, to Elizabeth Puttock and Lancelot Jarman. His father, an RAF officer from New Zealand, met his mother, an assistant to royal couturier Norman Hartnell, at an RAF Northolt dance in 1939. They married at Holy

Grave of Derek Jarman - St. Clement's Churchyard, Old Romney.

Trinity church, Northwood, in 1940. After postings around the world, the family returned in the 1950s to live in Northwood, where his aunts and grandmother also lived. He attended Hordle House School at Milford on Sea and showed an early interest in drama. In 1955 he attended Canford School in Dorset where his artistic talents were encouraged and in 1960 he began a BA at King's College, London, in English, History and History of Art. In 1963 he studied painting and stage design at the Slade School of Art, achieving a Diploma in Fine Art. He exhibited in many prestigious exhibitions and in 1968 Frederick Ashton chose him to design his new ballet, *Jazz Calendar.*

He continued working as a painter and stage designer and made his first 8mm film, *Studio Bankside*, in 1970. After a chance meeting on a train, Ken Russell asked him to design the set for *The Devils* (1971). By 1977 he had made over a dozen notable Super 8 films and written a series of film scripts. His first full-length feature film, *Sebastiane*, was released in 1976 and tells the story of the martyrdom of St. Sebastiane in Latin with English subtitles. In the late seventies he concentrated more and more on film making, producing *Jubilee*

(1978), *The Tempest* (1979), *War Requiem* (1988), *Caravaggio* (1986), *Edward II* (1991) and *Wittgenstein* (1993).

On 22 December 1986 Jarman was diagnosed HIV positive and the following year he bought Prospect Cottage, a wooden fisherman's cottage at Dungeness on the Kent coast. Despite his deteriorating health, which included the gradual loss of his sight due to medication side-effects, he continued to work prolifically. During his final years he championed gay rights and continued to experiment with film, culminating in his final work, *Blue* (1993), which consists solely of a blue screen with a text and music sound-track.

He died on 19 February, age fifty-two, from AIDS-related illnesses and is buried in **St. Clement's Churchyard, Old Romney**, beneath a favourite yew tree.

A CANTERBURY TALE
Wickhambreaux

- 1944 124m b/w UK
- Eric Portman, Sheila Sim, Dennis Price, John Swett, Charles Hawtrey
- p, Michael Powell, Emeric Pressburger; d, Michael Powell; w, Michael Powell, Emeric Pressburger; ph, Erwin Hillier; ed, John Seabourne; m, Allan Gray; art d, Alfred Junge

"...essentially the film is a morality play in which three modern pilgrims to Canterbury receive their blessings".
Michael Powell

Three modern day pilgrims to Canterbury: a land girl, a British tank sergeant and an American army sergeant all arrive on the same train in the Kent village of Chillingbourne. A mysterious 'glue man' pours glue on the hair of the girl and other unsuspecting female victims late at night. The trio decide to get to the bottom of this bizarre phenomenon, and their investigations lead them to the local squire who is trying to preserve England's heritage by preventing local girls from fraternising with American GIs.

Filmed in the familiar Kent countryside of Powell's childhood and captured by Erwin Hillier's stunning photography, this is one of Powell and Pressburger's oddest films, but also one of their most magical, in which they try to explain the spiritual values and traditions Britain was fighting for during the war.

Wickhambreaux Court (now converted into private residences) was used for the exterior shots of the squire's house and the interiors were shot at Denham. The fictional village of Chillingbourne was an amalgam of Kent locations, including the old smithy at **Shottenden**; the **Red Lion Pub**, **Wingham**; **Selling** railway station and **Fordwich Town Hall**, the venue for the squire's lectures. Wartime bombing precautions meant that much of Canterbury Cathedral's windows were boarded up and its stained glass windows had been removed, together with the organ, making it unsuitable for filming. The scene in the nave of the Cathedral was shot at Denham Studios and the organ music was pre-recorded at St. Albans. Miniature replicas of the bells in Canterbury's Bell Harry Tower were constructed out of fibreglass at the studio and a team of expert bell-ringers synchronised their movement to a recording of the originals.

See also: Michael Powell, Emeric Pressburger

BIRTHPLACE OF MICHAEL POWELL (1905-90)
Bekesbourne

"As the years went by, whenever I saw the logo of The Archers appear on the screen, I knew I was in for something unique, a very special kind of experience."
Martin Scorsese

*Howlett's Farm - birthplace of **Michael Powell***

Michael Powell was born on 30 September 1905 at **Howlett's Farm, near Bekesbourne**, in a cottage in **Bekesbourne Lane** (plaque erected) near the farm entrance. He was born on the day after the Feast of St Michael (after whom he was named), the second son of Mabel Corbett and Thomas Powell, a hop farmer. His elder brother, and only sibling, John, died from peritonitis in his teens. In 1910 his family moved to the much larger four hundred acre **Hoath Farm, near Chislet**. He attended **King's School, Canterbury**, and later **Dulwich College** in S.E. London.

His father fought in France during WWI, and following the Armistice in 1918, he decided to remain in France and become a hotelier, where he bought the lease of a hotel at Cap Ferrat. Michael's mother was in two minds about the venture, but his father, a compulsive gambler and womaniser, was determined. The new life didn't suit his mother and she divorced her

husband, moving to **Ringwood in Hampshire** in 1921, where seventeen-year-old Michael began his working life as a junior clerk at the National Provincial Bank.

Around this time he became interested in the art of film-making through reading articles in *Picturegoer*, commenting in his 1986 autobiography: *"I was fascinated. Somehow the journalist had succeeded in conveying the camaraderie of a film company, the complete absence of class or wealth distinction, the combined enthusiasm towards a common end."* From that moment on he devoured anything to do with the cinema and was determined to become a director.

He acquired his first job in films through his father, who engineered an introduction to the Victorine Studios in Nice, where he was taken on as a grip by Rex Ingram's film unit who were shooting *Mare Nostrum*. By the late 1920s he was working at Elstree, first as a reader, and later as a stills photographer for Alfred Hitchcock. His first film as a director was *Two Crowded Hours* (1931), the first of a succession of low budget quota-quickies. In 1938 he made *The Edge of the World*, about a remote island community in Scotland, which became the turning point of his career. He was offered a contract by Alexander Korda at Denham Studios, where he was introduced to scriptwriter and Hungarian immigrant, Emeric Pressburger.

The first film they collaborated on was *The Spy in Black* (1939). Powell made the children's classic, *The Thief of Baghdad*, on his own in 1939, and made a further three films with Pressburger, before forming their own production company in 1943. The Archers became one of the greatest creative collaborations in the history of the British cinema, producing fifteen films over thirteen years, including *The Life and Death of Colonel Blimp* (1943, which Winston Churchill tried to suppress), *A Canterbury Tale* (1944), *I*

Know Where I'm Going! (1945), *A Matter of Life and Death* (1946), *The Red Shoes* (1948), *The Small Back Room* (1949), *Black Narcissus* (1951) and *The Tales of Hoffman* (1951).

Powell and Pressburger ended their partnership in 1956. In 1960 Powell made the controversial *Peeping Tom*, a film about a serial killer, which shocked and reviled audiences and critics alike, effectively ruining his career. Nothing of consequence followed, apart from *The Queen's Guards* (1961), his last British feature film and some TV work. In the mid-sixties he emigrated to Australia and spent his later life in the U.S.A. In the 1970s Powell was championed by Francis Coppola and Martin Scorsese who helped finance the re-release and subsequent redemption of *Peeping Tom* in 1979. He died of cancer on 19 February 1990 and is buried in **Avening, Gloucestershire**.

See also: Michael Powell (Gloucestershire), Emeric Pressburger, *A Matter of Life and Death, Peeping Tom, The Small Back Room, A Canterbury Tale, I Know Where I'm Going!, Black Narcissus, The Thief of Baghdad, The Edge of the World,* Hepworth Studios

A ROOM WITH A VIEW
Chiddingstone

• 1985 115m c Comedy/Drama Cinecom (UK)
• Maggie Smith (Charlotte Bartlett), Helena Bonham Carter (Lucy Honeychurch), Denholm Elliott (Mr. Emerson), Julian Sands (George Emerson), Daniel Day Lewis (Cecil Vyse), Simon Callow (Rev. Beebe), Judi Dench (Miss Lavish)
• p, Ismail Merchant; d, James Ivory; w, Ruth Prawer Jhabvala (based on the novel by E.M. Forster); ph, Tony Pierce-Roberts; ed, Humphrey Dixon; m, Richard Robbins
• AA Best Adapted Screenplay: Ruth Prawer Jhabvala; AA Best Art Direction: Gianni Quaranta, Brian Ackland-Snow, Brian Savegar, Elio Altramura; AA Best Costume Design: Jenny Beavan, John Bright

Lucy Honeychurch, a beautiful young English woman travelling in Italy with her cousin and chaperone, Miss Bartlett, finds her life altered forever when she meets passionate suitor, George Emerson. Whisked back to England after she is observed kissing him, she reconciles herself to a loveless relationship with her betrothed ninny, Cecil. When her young suitor and his father move into the area, her cloistered world is thrown into disarray.

E.M. Forster's tender satire of English culture was adapted for the screen in 1985 by Ruth Prawer Jhabvala. Stunningly filmed in England and Florence, the film became one of Merchant Ivory's greatest successes.

The local village in the film was the National Trust's single street village of **Chiddingstone, near Edenbridge**, which was used for both interior and exterior filming. The Rev. Beebe's thirteenth-century church can also be seen in the village. Nearby **Emmets Garden**, in the hamlet of **Ide Hill, near Sevenoaks**, was the location of the garden party. **Foxwold**, near Brasted, doubled for Windy Corner, the Honeychurch home. It is not open to the public.

See also: Maggie Smith, Daniel Day Lewis, Judi Dench

Kingston-upon-Hull

BIRTHPLACE OF J. ARTHUR RANK (1888-1972)

"The Rank Organisation did not interest him that much; he was far more interested in flour."
Fred Packard, grandson of J. Arthur Rank.

'The man behind the gong' was born on 22 December 1888 at **Willersley**

House, Pearson Park, Hull, to Emily Voase and Joseph Rank. The house has since been demolished and is now the site of new housing at **The Parade** which backs onto **Pearson Park**. He was the youngest son of seven children - three sons and four daughters. His father, Joseph, had made a fortune in the flour milling business and was a passionate Methodist. He donated much of his fortune to the Methodist movement and passed his religious fervour on to his children. On Sundays the family worshipped at the **Methodist Church, Queens Road, Hull** , where Arthur later taught at Sunday School. He attended The Leys Methodist School in Cambridge and began his working life at seventeen in his father's mills.

Like his father, he started at the bottom sweeping floors and worked his way up until he was familiar with every job in the milling business. The family moved to **Bushey Down, Tooting** in London in the early 1900s, and during WWI he became an ambulance driver in France.

In 1917 he married Laura Ellen Marshall. Two years later his father gave him £1 million, stating *'there won't be any more when I'm gone'*. After a disastrous period with a company called Peterkin's Self Raising Flour, he returned to the family business.

It was through his religious faith and his desire to spread the gospel that he discovered the communicatory powers of film. He first screened films to his Sunday School class and soon became convinced it was the way to promote the Christian message.

He therefore began by producing religious films; his first film made to appeal to the cinema-going public being *Turn of the Tide* (1935). Within a few years of these meagre beginnings he was to control most of the British film industry, entering into production, distribution and exhibition. His acquisitions included Denham, Pinewood and Islington studios and the Gaumont-British and Odeon cinema circuits. The Rank Organisation sustained the production companies of the Archers, Two Cities and Cineguild and the actors and directors associated with Rank made up almost the entire cast of British cinema, including David Lean, Powell and Pressburger, Laurence Olivier, John Mills, Margaret Lockwood, Launder and Gilliat and Ronald Neame.

As Rank's business empire grew so did his philanthropy. It is estimated that he gave away £100 million during his lifetime. One of the great British entrepreneurs, he loved his flour mills more than any film studio. Never greatly interested in film making or mixing with the movie glitterati, he led the life of a landowner and countryman at **Sutton Manor, in Sutton Scotney, Hampshire**, where he bred gun dogs. *"I named all the dogs after generals and the bitches after movie stars."*

J. Arthur Rank died First Baron Rank of Sutton Scotney (peerage created 1957) on 29 March 1972, aged eighty-three. The funeral took place at Sutton Scotney Methodist Church and was attended only by members of his family and estate employees. His ashes were buried under the sun-dial in the garden of Sutton Manor. After the sale of Sutton Manor (now a nursing home) his ashes were removed to another location. Lord Rank left no male heir; he is survived by two daughters.

See also: W.H. Balgarnie, *The Great Escape*

GRAVE OF ARTHUR LUCAN (1887-1954)
Hull

Comedian Arthur Lucan (real name Arthur Towle), who portrayed Irish washerwoman Old Mother Riley on stage and screen, is buried in the **Eastern Cemetery, Hedon Road**, Hull. He died in the wings waiting to go on stage prior to a performance of 'Old Mother Riley in Paris' on 17th May, 1954, at the old Tivoli Variety Theatre in **Paragon Street.** Lucan, who filed for bankruptcy shortly before his death, died penniless, and his son, Donald, a Harley Street specialist, paid for the funeral.

Old Mother Riley's daughter was portrayed on screen by Lucan's wife, Kitty McShane, who died of chronic alcoholism ten years after his death.

Skelton's Cafe was built on the site of the old Tivoli and its walls are decorated with Old Mother Riley memorabilia, including photographs, programmes, an original garter, and a bust of Lucan which was unveiled by Danny La Rue. The bust is reputedly located near the spot in the theatre wings where Lucan died.

See also: Arthur Lucan (Lincs)

Kingston-upon-Thames

BIRTHPLACE OF EADWEARD MUYBRIDGE (1830-1904)
Kingston

Eadweard Muybridge, whose sequence photography was instrumental in the development of cinematography, was born Edward James Muggeridge, on 9 April 1830, at **30 High Street**, to Susanna and John Muggeridge, a merchant trader. He was baptised at **All Saints Church, Kingston**, later changing his name to Muybridge, and adopting the Anglo-Saxon spelling of his Christian name: Eadweard.

In the 1850s he emigrated to America where he worked as a bookbinder's agent in New York. In 1856 he moved to California, where he became a bookseller and a publisher's agent. Following a six-year visit to Europe, Muybridge returned to America in 1866, from which time he took up professional photography, recording the landscapes of the West in a horse-drawn dark room. He soon became a notable photographer, selling his work, which included stereoscopic views and panoramas, to San Francisco's elite. He was commissioned by Leland Stanford, the former Governor of California, to settle the age old controversy of whether a trotting horse has all four feet off the ground at any one point in its stride. At his second attempt in 1873, Muybridge proved conclusively that it does.

He married Flora Stone in 1872, who gave birth to a son by her lover, Harry Larkyns, in 1874. When the boy was six months old Muybridge discovered the truth and shot Larkyns dead. In February 1875 he went on trial for murder, but was acquitted on the

grounds of justifiable homicide, and departed on an expedition to Central America.

In 1877-79 he set up a camera shed on Leland Stanford's stud farm at Palo Alto, using first twelve, and later twenty-four cameras, each with shutters attached to threads. When a horse broke a thread as it passed in front of the camera, an exposure was taken, and in half a second, twelve photographs revealed the cycle of movement. The results were later published in scientific and photographic journals to great acclaim, and Muybridge embarked on a series of animal and human studies.

In the 1880s he toured the USA and Europe giving lectures of his work using his Zoopraxiscope moving image projector. The University of Pennsylvania awarded him a grant of $40,000 to continue his research, and he later produced over 1,000,000 sequence photographs, many of which appeared in his book, *Animal Locomotion* (1887).

He retired to Kingston in 1894, residing at **2 Liverpool Road** (plaque erected), where he published two further books, *Animals in Motion* (1899) and *The Human Figure in Motion* (1901). He died on 8 May 1904 and was cremated at Woking.

Further information: On display at Kingston Museum can be seen the original Zoopraxiscope, Muybridge's binunial lantern with which he delivered his famous lecture tours on the Attitudes of Animals in Motion, a rare panorama of San Francisco (1878) and assorted packing crates and ephemera. The local history research library in the North Kingston Centre on Richmond Road (0181 547 6738) holds a reserve collection (viewable by appointment) of Muybridge's lantern slides, Zoopraxiscope discs, prints and a newspaper cutting book which Muybridge kept of his career and achievements.
Kingston Museum, Wheatfield Way, Kingston, KT1 2PS. Tel: 0181 546 5386.

Open 10am-5pm. Closed Sundays & Wednesdays.
http://www2.kingston.gov.uk/museum

Kirklees

GRAVE OF ROBIN HOOD (c1250)
Huddersfield

Kirklees Priory, Cooper's Bridge, Huddersfield, where he supposedly met his death at the hands of the vengeful nun, Elizabeth de Staynton, is generally recognised as the traditional burial place of the legendary outlaw, Robin Hood, According to the ancient *Sloane* manuscript he became *"distempered with could and age, he had great payne in his lymbes, his bloud being corrupted; therefore to be eased of his payne by letting of bloud, he repayred to the priores of Krkesley, which some say was his aunt, a woman very skylful in physique and surgery; who perceyving him to be Robyn Hood, and waying howe fel an enimy he was to religious persons, tok reveng of him for her owne house and all others, by letting him bleed to death; she buryed him under a greate stone, by the hywaye's syde."*

His body was buried about 650 yards from the priory gatehouse in unconsecrated ground marked by an elaborate grave slab, but most historians dismiss his tomb's epitaph as spurious and not older than the early 18th century. In recent years his tomb has become the haunt of vampire societies researching what they assume to be an unsolved case of medieval vampirism. Elizabeth de Staynton is also buried at Kirklees.

A figure from folklore of dubious genealogy, Robin Hood, along with Sherlock Holmes, is among cinema's most filmed characters and has been portrayed on screen by many. None, however, can touch Errol Flynn's

definitive 1938 version, *The Adventures of Robin Hood*, with Basil Rathbone as the unforgettable villain, Sir Guy of Gisbourne. Other portrayals included: Douglas Fairbanks Snr (*Robin Hood*, 1922), Richard Todd (*The Story of Robin Hood and His Merrie Men*, 1952), Richard Greene (*Sword of Sherwood*, 1960), Sean Connery (*Robin and Marian*, 1976), Kevin Costner (*Robin Hood: Prince of Thieves*, 1991) and Cary Elwes (*Robin Hood: Men in Tights*, 1993).

See also: *Robin Hood: Prince of Thieves*, Little John

Further information: At the time of writing Kirklees is not open to the public. This may change as the property was recently sold for housing development. Contact Kirklees Countryside Unit for further information on 01484 223200.

BIRTHPLACE OF JAMES MASON (1909-84)
Huddersfield

"If James Mason is in front of the cameras - just leave them rolling. He never makes a mistake!"
George Cukor

James Mason's film career spanned almost fifty years, during which time his good looks and magnetic sex appeal made him adept at portraying mean, moody and romantic villains. He was born on May 15, 1909, the youngest of three sons of wool merchant John Mason and Mabel Gaunt at their rambling Victorian mansion, **Croft House** in **Croft House Lane**,

Marsh (now demolished and the site of **Arncliffe Court** housing). He enjoyed a privileged upbringing and was educated at Marlborough and Peterhouse College, Cambridge, where he studied architecture. He became interested in acting at Cambridge where he met director Tyrone Guthrie and decided to pursue a stage career. He joined the Hull Repertory Theatre for a season in 1933 and later auditioned for Guthrie's new company at the Old Vic where his fellow actors included Charles Laughton, Alec Guinness and John Geilgud.

After a season with the Gate Theatre Company in Dublin he met American film director, Albert Parker, at a cocktail party in 1935 and was offered a screen test at the **Fox British Film Studio**, Wembley, where he made his first quota-quickie film, *Late Extra.* Nineteen films later, in 1943, the costume drama *The Man In Grey* shot him to stardom

and turned him into Britain's top box-office draw. At the height of his career his fan mail was averaging 5,000 letters a week. He will be best remembered for his roles as: the IRA leader, Johnny McQueen in *Odd Man Out* (1947); the alcoholic has-been, Norman Maine in *A Star Is Born* (1954); the mysterious Captain Nemo in *20,000 Leagues Under the Sea* (1954); the debonair villain, Phillip Vandamm in *North by Northwest*

(1959) and the voyeuristic Humbert

Humbert in *Lolita* (1962). He received his third Oscar nomination in 1982 for his role in *The Verdict.* and made his last film, *The Shooting Party,* in 1984.

Twice married, he had two children - a daughter Portland and son Morgan who was a presidential aide to Ronald Reagan. He died in 1984 and was buried in Switzerland, where he had lived for twenty-two years. A plaque was unveiled to his memory outside **Huddersfield Library, Princess Alexandra Walk**, by Sheridan Morley in 1996.

See also: *The Odd Man Out*

BIRTHPLACE OF ROY CASTLE (1932-94)
Scholes

Better known as a song and dance man, Roy Castle made a few sporadic films which are possibly better left unseen, including: *Doctor Terror's House of Horrors* (1966), *Dr Who and the Daleks* (1966), *Carry on Up the Khyber* (1971) and *Legend of the Werewolf* (1975).

The son of an insurance agent, he was born on 31 August 1932 and brought up at his parents' house at **5 Lee Terrace**, Scholes, near Holmfirth. He gave his first professional stage performance at the age of six, when he sang *Does A Lamp Post Catch Bronchitis In The Winter* at Huddersfield Palace Theatre in 1938. In a musical comedy career which spanned five decades he became a popular entertainer in clubs, pantomime, stage musicals and television.

He battled for ten years to overcome a heavy drinking habit and was diagnosed as having lung cancer in 1992. In the short period before his death in 1994, he turned his illness into a crusade, raising millions of pounds to found a cancer centre in Liverpool.

Knowsley

BIRTHPLACE OF REX HARRISON (1908-1990)
Huyton

"I am now at the age where I've got to prove that I'm just as good as I never was."
Rex Harrison, 1980

***Rex Harrison** in The Yellow Rolls-Royce (1965, MGM)*

Reginald Carey Harrison was born on Thursday 5 March 1908, the third child of William Harrison, a mechanical engineer and Edith Carey at their home, **Derry House** in **Tarbock Road**. When WWI was over the family moved to a small house at **5, Lancaster Avenue** in **Sefton Park, Liverpool**. At an early age he dropped 'Reginald' in favour of 'Rex' which he claimed he adopted after hearing someone calling a dog. He made his first dramatic appearance in a Liverpool College production of *A Midsummer Night's Dream*, in 1922, aged fourteen. Unable to afford drama school fees he joined the **Liverpool Playhouse, Williamson Square** in 1925 as a student with the Liverpool Rep. and made his first professional appearance here in a play entitled *Thirty Minutes in a Street.*.

He made his film debut in 1930 in Maurice Elvey's, *The School for Scandal* and appeared on the London stage the same year. His other films include: *Night Train to Munich* (1940), *Blithe Spirit* (1945), *The Ghost and Mrs. Muir* (1947), *Cleopatra* (1963) and *Doctor Doolittle* (1967). Married six times, his refined charm and elegance earned him the nickname 'Sexy Rexy'. He was knighted in 1989 and will be best remembered for his Oscar-winning portrayal of Professor Henry Higgins in *My Fair Lady* (1964).

See also: *Doctor Dolittle*, Kay Kendall

Lancashire

BRIEF ENCOUNTER
Carnforth

• 1945 86m bw Romance Cineguild/Eagle-Lion (U.K.)
• Celia Johnson (Laura Jesson), Trevor Howard (Alec Harvey), Cyril Raymond (Fred Jesson), Stanley Holloway (Albert Godby),
• p, Noel Coward; d, David Lean; w, Noel Coward, David Lean, Anthony Havelock-Allan (based on Noel Coward's play "Still Life"); ph, Robert Krasker; ed, Jack Harris; m, Sergei Rachmaninoff
• AAN Best Actress: Celia Johnson; AAN Best Director: David Lean; AAN Best Original Screenplay: Anthony Havelock-Allan, David Lean, Ronald Neame

"They know jolly well this chap's borrowed a flat, they know exactly why she's coming back to him, why doesn't he fuck her? All this talk about the wood being damp and that sort of stuff."
Trevor Howard *

Two happily married strangers - Celia Johnson and Trevor Howard, in **Brief Encounter**.

Few films over the years have equalled the compassion and realism of this great screen classic which tells the simple story of two happily married strangers who meet by chance in a station buffet, and as their casual friendship grows, they fall helplessly in love. Based on Noel Coward's play, *Still Life*, and set in the late thirties, this peculiarly English film is still as compelling today as it was fifty years ago. Despite its English reserve, middle-class mannerisms, cut-glass accents, repressed ardour and sexless sex scenes, it remains one of the great classics of British cinema.

London was the first choice for the station location, but due to the danger of air-raids it was decided to locate the station in the safer surroundings of Lancashire. Carnforth Station doubled for Milford Junction, once a bustling station and a thriving stopping-off point on the Euston to Glasgow mainline. It was here that trains changed engines and took on coal and water to 'shove up Shap' for the steep climb up to Shap Fell in Cumbria. Filming took place at night for two weeks during the bitter winter of 1945, and the film's portrayal of the golden age of steam has never been equalled in the cinema.

Studio scenes were filmed at **Denham Studios** in Buckinghamshire, including the interior shots of the Station Refreshment Room which was closely modelled on that of Carnforth. Other exterior locations were at

Beaconsfield, and the boating scene was shot at **Regent's Park, London**. The opening train scenes were shot at **Watford Junction** on the LMS line.

Today Carnforth Station is little used. Express trains speed through without stopping and the station stands derelict and vandalised, but the clock, the underpass, and the refreshment room, which appeared in the film, can still be seen. In 1998, Carnforth was chosen as the winner of *The Independent's* 'Worst Station Award'. Susan Howard, who nominated the station, described it as looking like *"the station from Hell - cold and unwelcoming. Tourists come expecting to see a little bit of nostalgia and all they get is a scene out of Mad Max."* With broken glass littering the platform, windows boarded up, and the subway a drug users haunt, the Station is a shadow of its former self.

Following considerable local concern, the 'Carnforth Station and Railway Trust Limited' was formed in 1996 to try to rescue the station buildings from decay. The Trust's proposals, for which planning permission has been obtained, are for the station buildings to be reinstated and converted to a mix of uses. These will include the provision of a Visitors' Centre celebrating Carnforth's link with *Brief Encounter* and its railway history, retail shops, and exhibition space for community use. The station will be refurbished in a style which will recapture its former glory, and will include the reinstatement of a replica 1940s Refreshment Room. The total project costs will be between £1 - £1.5 million.

MAP KEY:

1: Where Albert (Stanley Holloway) comes out of the ticket collector's hut and crosses the line at the start of the film.
2: Where they meet under the clock.
3: Where they kissed.
4: Where Laura (Celia Johnson) contemplates suicide.

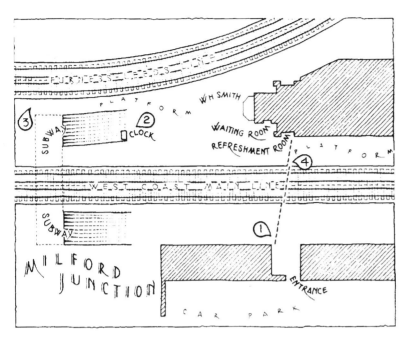

The subway under the clock.

The Waiting Room and Refreshment Room

"The station from Hell."

See also: Celia Johnson, Trevor Howard, Noel Coward, David Lean, Anthony Havelock-Allan, Stanley Holloway

Further information: Those interested in becoming involved in restoring Carnforth to its former glory or contributing to the appeal fund, should contact the 'Friends of Carnforth Station', c/o Ratcliffe and Bibby, 3-11 New Street, Carnforth, Lancashire LA5 9BU. email: carnforthstation@irvinetaylor.co.uk Further details of the project can be found on www.irvinetaylor.co.uk Carnforth is situated off the M6 at junction 35. The nearest mainline station is Lancaster, which has local connections to Carnforth.

GRAVE OF WALLACE HARTLEY (1879-1912)
Colne

A recurring scene in 'Titanic' movies is one in which the ship's orchestra plays as she slowly sinks. The leader of the *Titanic's* orchestra was Wallace Hartley who courageously played with his eight piece orchestra until the last moment, creating an island of calm amid the spiralling panic. The last piece they were heard to play was the hymn, *'Nearer, my God, to Thee'*. None of the musicians survived. Hartley's body was recovered from the sea and taken to the U.S.A. for embalming before being shipped back to England for burial, where 40,000 people lined the streets of Colne for its return.

Born in Dewsbury, he became a bank clerk before taking up music as a career and he played on the Lusitania and the Mauretania before joining the Titanic at short notice. His grave is in **Colne Cemetery, Keighley Road**, marked by a headstone of an open hymnbook and a violin.

See also: William Murdoch, *A Night To Remember*

Lancashire

WHISTLE DOWN THE WIND
Worston

- 1961 98m b/w Drama Beaver/Allied Film Makers (UK)
- Hayley Mills (Kathy Bostock), Bernard Lee (Mr. Bostock), Alan Bates (Arthur Blakely), Diane Holgate (Nan Bostock), Alan Barnes (Charles Bostock), Norman Bird (Eddie)
- p, Richard Attenborough; d, Bryan Forbes; w, Keith Waterhouse, Willis Hall (based on the novel by Mary Hayley Bell); ph, Arthur Ibbetson; ed, Max Benedict; m, Malcolm Arnold; art d, Ray Simm

Set on a bleak Lancashire hill farm in the shadow of Pendle Hill, three motherless children stumble across a desperate fugitive (Alan Bates) hiding in a barn and are convinced he's Jesus Christ.

*Hayley Mills and Alan Bates in the barn at Worsaw Hill Farm in **Whistle Down the Wind** (1961, Beaver/Allied)*

The film was Bryan Forbes' directorial debut; the original story was written by Mary Hayley Bell, wife of John Mills, and it starred their fourteen-year-old daughter Hayley who was already a rising star. The film's most outstanding performance was given by eight-year-old Alan Barnes (Charles Bostock), who was chosen from among local

*The farmhouse, **Worsaw Hill Farm.***

Chatburn schoolchildren. With no previous acting experience his complete naturalness and cheek made for the most memorable performance in the film.

Shooting began in mid-February, 1961, and the farm location was **Worsaw Hill Farm, near Worston**, where exterior and interior scenes in the barn were shot, but the farmhouse interior was a studio set. Other locations were in nearby **Downham** village where the local school was used and a house at the bottom of the village was made to resemble a shop. A plaque commemorating the film can be seen in the village information centre. The Sunday School scenes were shot in **St. Margaret's Church Hall, Burnley**. The film's charity premiere was held at the Burnley Odeon, where Hayley Mills was presented with a pair of Lancashire clogs.

Further information: Ian and Carol Hanson of Worsaw Hill Farm have fond memories of the film and members of their family appeared in it. Visitors are welcome. To reach the farm leave the A59 at the junction for Worston (near Clitheroe). Drive straight through the village for a mile or so until you reach

Angram Green Farm Camping and Caravan Site on your right. Worsaw Hill Farm is the first left after Angram Green. A 'public footpath:' signpost stands at the entrance.

CENTRAL HALL CINEMA
Colne

Local printer and kinetoscope proprietor, Joshua Duckworth, built what is reputed to be Britain's first purpose-built cinema in **Colne Lane** (first right after The Shepherd's Arms pub, going up Church St.) in 1907. A devout Methodist, he never screened

anything 'improper' and was partial to educational and travel subjects. The building continued as a cinema until 1924. It was a spiritualist chapel for many years and currently it is occupied by a local joinery company. Its original 1907 exterior remains intact.

Leeds

A SCENE FROM LEEDS BRIDGE (c.1889)

The fate of French inventor and film pioneer Louis Aimé Augustin Le Prince remains one of the greatest mysteries in the history of the moving image. In September 1890, prior to demonstrating his motion picture camera and projector to the world, he disappeared. After an exhaustive search by his family and the French police, no trace of him or his camera was ever found. The reason for his disappearance is still unexplained.

He was born in Metz on 28 August 1841, and studied chemistry in Leipzig, specialising in the painting and firing of pottery. In 1866 he met and became friendly with Yorkshireman, John Whitley, in Paris, and was invited to Leeds to meet his family, who ran an engineering company. In 1869 he married John's sister, Lizzie Whitley, and settled in Leeds, where they founded a school of applied art in **Park Square**. In 1881 he left for New York where he became involved with the Panorama: a fashionable entertainment of the day on which scenes were painted and revolved before an audience. This created his interest in the moving image and shortly afterwards he began experimenting with the possibilities of projecting motion pictures.

In 1886 he applied for an American patent for a machine using one or more lenses, and in Europe applied for patents for a one-lensed version. He

Leeds Bridge

Louis Le Prince in his twenties

rented a workshop at **160 Woodhouse Lane** (demolished in the sixties) and by 1888 he had built two single lens cameras equipped with paper negative rolls wound onto spools which moved intermittently. He conducted early trials in his father-in-law's garden at **Oakwood Grange, Roundhay** (since demolished) and later filmed traffic crossing **Leeds Bridge**. He shot this film at between twelve and twenty frames per second, from a window above Hick's the Ironmongers, in a building which still stands on the south-east corner of the bridge. Only twenty frames survive today.

Le Prince's family had remained in New York while he tried to perfect his machine, and were eagerly awaiting his return when he would demonstrate his invention to the world. In August 1890, prior to sailing for New York, he visited his brother in Dijon to sort out a family matter. On his departure his brother accompanied him to the station and watched him board the Paris train. He was never seen again.

Various speculative explanations have been put forward to account for his disappearance. One is that he was plagued by debt and assumed a new identity to avoid his creditors; another, more sinister theory, is that he was murdered by agents of Thomas Edison. Had he lived, and had his invention been a commercial success, Louis Aimé Augustin Le Prince would no doubt have won a deserved place in history and become a household name. He is, however, little known, and his achievements virtually unrecognised. In 1908 Thomas Edison was acknowledged to be the inventor of moving pictures.

See also: Armley Palace Picture Hall

Further information: BBC Studios were built on the site of Le Prince's workshop at Woodhouse Lane. Two plaques commemorate Le Prince inside the building. One was transferred from the wall of the original workshop, and the other was unveiled by Richard Attenborough on 13 October 1988, when the Leeds International Film Festival re-enacted Le Prince's filming of Leeds Bridge, one hundred years after the event. His American grandson, William Le Prince Huettel, unveiled a plaque on the bridge, where there is also a plaque which was unveiled by Le Prince's daughter, Marie, in 1930 commemorating his achievement. Two of Le Prince's projectors survived in Leeds Museum until 1941, when at least one was destroyed by bombing. As all records were destroyed the museum cannot be certain that the one that survived is an original built by Le Prince.

ARMLEY PALACE PICTURE HALL

Armley Mills Industrial Museum houses the city's industrial past which includes the 'Armley Palace Picture Hall', a reconstruction of a 1912 cinema. The official opening took place in 1982 when George Groves (son of the late Albert Groves, a Leeds cinema pioneer)

operated the projectors. The short films screened were: *Leeds Street Scenes of 1901, Turn-out the Leeds Fire Brigade, 1902* and *Scenes at Blackpool, 1900.* Authentic seating arrangements can accommodate thirty children on wooden forms at the front and twenty-six seats behind, with an upright piano beneath the screen.

Leed's association with moving pictures goes back to 1888, when Louis Le Prince (1842 - c1890) filmed traffic crossing Leeds Bridge. Replicas of both Le Prince's single and multi-lens cameras can be seen in the museum's projector collection. Kershaws, a local optical and scientific instrument manufacturer, produced the 'Kalee' projector in the 1920s which can be seen in the projection room.

See also: *A Scene From Leeds Bridge*

Further information: Armley Mills, The Leeds Industrial Museum, Canal Rd., Leeds, LS12 2QF. Tel: 0113 637861.

CHILDHOOD HOME OF PETER O'TOOLE

"If you're a Catholic, you aren't a sinner as long as you can drop in at what they call the "short twelve" - 12 o'clock Mass. It's there for actors, writers, painters and other drunks, and it's short because the priest needs a drink like everybody else."
Peter O'Toole

His guise of the wild 'Irishman' often precedes, and frequently clouds his stature as a great actor, but his time on Irish soil was brief. The son of a bookmaker known as the 'Captain', Peter Seamus O'Toole was born in Connemara, on August 2, 1932. His family moved to the **Hunslet** area of Leeds shortly after his birth, where they lived in a back-to-back terraced house in **Burton Street.** He was taught by nuns at St. Anne's, the local Catholic school. In 1972 he commented to the New York Times, *"Their whole denial of*

womanhood, the black dresses, the shaving of the hair, was so horrible, so terrifying." The family moved house frequently and in 1940 they lived at 15 Peartree Lane, Hunsbeck (now demolished), described by O'Toole as a 'rat's nest.' When he left school he wrapped parcels at a local warehouse, but later joined the Yorkshire Evening Post as a copyboy with aspirations of becoming a journalist.

***Peter O'Toole** in Creator (1985, Universal)*

He became involved in local theatre and made his first stage appearance in 1949 at the **Civic Theatre in Cookridge Street**. After being discharged from national service in the Navy for being 'temperamentally unsuited' he was awarded a scholarship to RADA. He later joined the Bristol Old Vic and the Royal Shakespeare Company. In 1959 he earned the Best Actor of the year award for his portrayal of Private Bamforth in Willis Hall's *The Long and the Short and the Tall.* He rocketed to stardom in 1962 following his starring role in David Lean's *Lawrence of Arabia* (a role turned down by both Marlon Brando and Albert Finney). Other notable screen performances include, King Henry II in *Becket* (1964), *Lord Jim* (title role, 1965), Jack, 14th Earl of Gurney in *The Ruling Class* (1972) and Scottish tutor, Reginald Johnston in *The Last Emperor* (1987).

See also: The Lawrence of Arabia Trail

SIEGE OF QUEEN'S HOTEL

In August, 1932, the **Queen's Hotel, City Square** (0113 2431323) was besieged by thousands of fans of Stan Laurel and Oliver Hardy who stayed here during their U.K. 'Holiday Tour'. Stan Laurel spent many holidays as a child with relatives in Dewsbury and his grandparents, Grandma and Grandad Metcalfe, are buried in the local cemetery. Media attention made it difficult for him to visit his relatives, who were invited to the Queen's Hotel to spend some time with him and Olly.

See also: Laurel and Hardy, Stan Laurel

BIRTHPLACE OF KEITH WATERHOUSE & WILLIS HALL

"I write to please myself."
Keith Waterhouse

"With regard to my early life, I've no idea how much or how little you need to know, but I'm sure we can solve it together."
Willis Hall *

The successful collaboration of playwrights and scriptwriters, Keith Waterhouse and Willis Hall, produced three outstanding films of the sixties - *Whistle Down the Wind* (1961), *A Kind of Loving* (1962) and *Billy Liar* (1963). Prolific writers, Waterhouse and Hall's offerings to the theatre and cinema have been exceptional.

Keith Spencer Waterhouse was born at **17 Low Road, Hunslet** (now demolished), on 6th February 1929, the youngest of five children. His father sold fruit, veg and unskinned rabbits from a horse and cart and kept a donkey in their walled garden. *"It had evidently been a seaside donkey since it would give us rides to the bottom of the garden, but not back again."* Due to a road-widening scheme, the family was forced to move **41 Middleton Park Grove** in the early thirties, and later to the **Halton Moor Estate** where he attended the John Blenkinsop Middle School at the age of ten. His first job was at J.T. Buckton and Sons, estate agents and undertakers, in **New Station Street**, an experience which provided the setting for daydreamer Billy Fisher's workplace in *Billy Liar*. In 1948 he became a journalist on the Yorkshire Evening Post for four years before moving to London. A copious novelist and playwright, his first successful work was the humorous novel, *Billy Liar* (1959). His other works include the novels *Jubb* (1963), *Office Life* (1978), *Unsweet Charity* (1992), and the plays *Saturday, Sunday, Monday* (1973) and *Filumena* (1977), both co-written with Willis Hall, and *Jeffrey Bernard is Unwell.* (1989).

Willis Hall was born on 6th April 1929 in one of the terraced houses known as the **'Addingtons' off Dewsbury Road** and attended the local Cockburn School. He left school at fourteen and became an apprentice deck-hand on a trawler. He later worked for a 'Yorkshire Relish' company and the Yorkshire Evening News before joining the army, where he learned the craft of script-writing following his posting to forces radio in the Far East. His first successful play was *The Long and the Short and the Tall* (1958) which he adapted for the screen with Wolf Mankowitz in 1961. His other plays include, *Last Day in Dreamland* and *A Glimpse of the Sea* (both 1959).

See also: *Whistle down the Wind, A Kind of Loving, Billy Liar*

Leicestershire

THE BULL INN
Bottesford

On 13 April 1952, during their third British tour, Laurel and Hardy visited Stan's sister Olga and brother-in-law Bill Healey who were landlords of the

*Stan and Olly enjoying a pint in the fireplace corner of **The Bull Inn***

The Bull Inn, Bottesford. They arrived around 2pm after the locals had gone home and stayed for the afternoon until the pub reopened in the evening when they departed for the **County Hotel, Nottingham**. Olga's friend, Ethel Challands, recalled her sometimes unrestrained behaviour: *"She was a strict landlady, but fair. Despite her tender years, she was always doing eccentric things to show us how athletic she was. At times, she would swing her leg high in the air and cock it on top of the bar. Other times, she would stand on her head in the corner. Anything for a laugh!"* *

Photographs and press clippings from Stan and Olly's British tours are displayed on the walls of the Bull Inn, and the fireplace corner featured in the photograph is unchanged. They toured Britain four time: in 1932, 1947, 1952 and 1953/4. Stan made a point of visiting his family and friends whenever his schedule permitted, while Olly headed for the nearest golf course.

See also: Stan Laurel, Laurel and Hardy

The Bull Inn

Further information: The Bull Inn, Market St., Bottesford.
Tel: 01949 842288.

CLASSIC LOCATION GT. CENTRAL RAILWAY
Loughborough

In 1969 a preservation group was formed to save as much of the Leicester - Nottingham section of the Great Central Railway as possible on which to run large steam locomotives. It ran its first public train in 1973 from Loughborough to Quorn and after

various phases the line now extends to Leicester, a distance of eight miles.

Feature films shot on the line include: the trackside scenes of the Great Train Robbery filmed at Swithland for *Buster* (1988) with Phil Collins, Richard Attenborough's *Shadowlands* (1993) in which Loughborough Central doubled for Oxford, and *The Secret Agent* (1997).

Debra Winger and Anthony Hopkins on location for Shadowlands on the GCR.

See also: *Shadowlands*

Further information: Great Central Railway PLC, Great Central Road, Loughborough, Leicestershire, LE11 1RW. Tel: 01509 230726.

Lincolnshire

THE DAMBUSTERS' MEMORIAL
Woodhall Spa

On the corner of **Station Road** and **Tattershall Road** stands the memorial to those of 617 Squadron who gave their lives during WWII. The erecting of the memorial was due to the efforts of the late Flight Lieutenant Chan Chandler, D.F.C. (1921-1995), who flew a remarkable 98 missions during WWII, 28 of them with the legendary

Dambuster Squadron. On one occasion he ditched his aircraft in the sea and was adrift with his crew for nine days. Chan attempted to auction his medals at Sotheby's in 1986 to contribute to the cost of a memorial. His gesture was spotted by John Paul Getty Jnr. who offered to pay for the memorial and return Chan's medals. Mr. Getty said, *"This man has earned his medals and therefore should be able to keep them. Consider this gesture my Red Poppy for this year: a truly great man."*

The **Petwood Hotel**, Woodhall Spa, was requisitioned by the R.A.F. during WWII and became the officer's mess for a number of squadrons, including 617 Squadron: 'The Dambusters'. Many notable characters became regulars at the Petwood, among them Group Captain Leonard Cheshire VC and Guy Gibson VC. There is a room of donated memorabilia dedicated to 617 Squadron containing photos, paintings and artifacts, and the 'Squadron Bar' has a branch placed across the bar which went through the cockpit of a plane forced to crash land when taking off for the 'Tirpitz raids'. In the car park at the front of the hotel there is a prototype of one of Barnes Wallis's famous bouncing bombs. Today the privately owned Petwood, standing in a 30 acre estate, still welcomes many WWII veterans.

See also: *The Dambusters*, Richard Todd

Further information: Petwood Hotel, Stixwold Road, Woodhall Spa, LN10 6QF. Tel: 01526 352411.

MEMPHIS BELLE
Binbrook

• 1991 103m c War / Drama Warner Brothers (US)
• Matthew Modine, Billy Zane, Eric Stoltz, Tate Donovan, DB Sweeney, John Lithgow, Harry Connick Jr., Sean Austin.
• p, David Putnam, Catherine Wyler; d, Michael Caton-Jones; ph, David Watkin; ed, Jim Clark; w, Monte Merrick; m, Geo. Fenton

Matthew Modine driving the crew of the **Memphis Belle.**

Memphis Belle tells the story of the first USAAF B17 Flying Fortress to fly twenty-five missions during WWII. Three weeks were spent filming at a former R.A.F. base in Binbrook which was chosen for its existing period hangars and nissen huts. About half of the film - which used 800 local extras - was actually shot here. Wooden replicas of Flying Fortresses were built which were simply flat pieces of wood, shaped and painted. The control tower was given a facelift and a church tower was positioned on the horizon.

Only five airworthy bombers were used, although special effects made them look like eighty. Two were from the U.S.A. and France and one from England. The air-to-air sequences, which also included three Messerschmits and eight Mustangs, were filmed at Duxford in Cambridgeshire. During filming at Binbrook one of the French B17's crashed into a cornfield and burst into flames. Miraculously, all ten people on board escaped with their lives.

The surviving veterans of the real *Memphis Belle* visited the set to pass on their experiences to the producers and to meet the actors portraying them. A special reception was held for them at the Cleethorpes R.A.F. Association.

See also: The Old Flying Machine Company

Further information: William Wyler made a documentary of the same name when he was stationed in England in charge of an air force combat camera crew in 1943. His daughter, Catherine, was co-producer for the 1991 feature film. The British airworthy B-17 Flying Fortress used in the film, 'Sally-B', is based at Duxford with 'The B-17 Preservation Society'.

WALT DISNEY'S SEARCH
Norton Disney

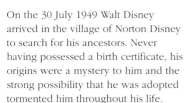

On the 30 July 1949 Walt Disney arrived in the village of Norton Disney to search for his ancestors. Never having possessed a birth certificate, his origins were a mystery to him and the strong possibility that he was adopted tormented him throughout his life.

St. Peter's, Norton Disney

The Disneys landed in England as Norman mercenaries with William the Conqueror from the village of Isigny, near Bayeaux in Normandy, and the name Disney is an anglicisation of d'Isigny (of Isigny). They settled in Lincolnshire, but in the 1600's they joined a failed rebellion against the King and were compelled to flee for their lives, hastily dispersing to Ireland, America and back to France.

The local pub, the **St. Vincent Arms**, displays press-cuttings on its wall commemorating Walt's visit, including a photograph of him playing darts in the bar. The village hall displays some drawings which he donated to the village, but not, alas, drawn by him.

The local church of **St. Peter's** contains five Disney monuments, and an entry in the visitors' book dated 15 September 1996 reads - *"Matthew Disney, Cambridge - direct descendant of William and Richard Disney"*.

Walt Disney failed to track down his roots in England and later discovered he was adopted.

CHILDHOOD HOME OF ARTHUR LUCAN (1887-1954)
Boston

Music-hall comedian Arthur Lucan, immortalised on screen as the Irish washer woman, Old Mother Riley, was born in the village of **Sibsey**, six miles from Boston. His real name was Arthur Towle, born 16 September 1885 to Lucy Ann Mawer, daughter of the village wheelwright and Thomas Towle, a groom on the Drax Estate. They had five children and lived in one of the tied cottages (now demolished) within the Workhouse Yard owned by the Manor House. **Lucan Close** on Sibsey's **Chartdale Estate** (off Station Road), was named in memory of Arthur Lucan.

The Towles moved to Boston when Arthur was five, where his father was employed as head groom at the

Kitty McShane and **Arthur Lucan**

Peacock and Royal Hotel (now Boot's the Chemist) in **Market Place**, and the family resided at **10 Craythorne Lane**. Mrs Towle also worked as a cleaner at the hotel and took in washing. One of Arthur's after school jobs was that of programme seller at **Shodfriars Hall, South Street** (now a Snooker Centre), near the hotel. It was here he made his first public appearance in 1895 after a measle epidemic wiped out many in the cast of a production of *Robinson Crusoe*, enabling Arthur to be cast as a native at short notice. As a teenager his first professional engagement was at the newly opened music hall, the **New Theatre, Market Place** (since demolished: now site of Marks & Spencer) playing an Irish comedian. He soon turned his back on Boston and left for Llandudno where he joined a travelling group called the Musical Cliftons, an act he toured with for the next seven years. During a tour of Ireland he met his future stage partner and wife, sixteen year-old Kitty McShane, whom he married in 1913.

He changed his name to Lucan after spotting a milkfloat in Dublin belonging to 'Lucan Dairies', and soon Lucan and McShane became a popular variety act. Lucan first portrayed the Irish washerwoman when he played the dame in pantomime at the Queen's Theatre, Dublin, and later created sketches based around the washerwoman and her daughter, Mrs. O'Flynn and daughter Bridget. The act was a huge success and led to lucrative film contracts and radio appearances and it was with the popularity of their comedy films, made between 1937 and 1952, that they decided to change their act name to Old Mother Riley and Daughter Kitty.

Success, however, seemed only to bring them misery. Their marriage deteriorated under the stress, Kitty had an affair, and she began drinking heavily. Her ruthless management tactics and tempestuous relationship with Arthur resulted in the BBC refusing them further radio work and film companies ruled they could not appear on the set together and must shoot scenes on different days. They separated in 1951 when Kitty began touring with Roy Rolland, an Old Mother Riley lookalike. Kitty had spent most of their fortune on various failed businesses, including hair salons which lost her £40,000, but even after their separation Arthur still sent her three-quarters of his income.

Arthur collapsed and died in the wings of the old Tivoli Variety Theatre in Hull while waiting to go on stage prior to a performance of 'Old Mother Riley in Paris' on 17th May, 1954. Shortly before his death he filed for bankruptcy which disclosed £14,000 owing to the Inland Revenue. Kitty tried to make a comeback with Roy Rolland, but with her reputation as a malcontent nobody wanted to work with her. She died of chronic alcoholism ten years later.

See also: Arthur Lucan (Kingston-upon-Hull)

KINEMA IN THE WOODS
Woodhall Spa

Originally built as a cricket pavilion for Petwood House, it was converted into the Pavilion Cinema by Captain Cole Allport in 1922, and it is believed to be the only cinema using rear projection in the U.K. in which films are projected on to a special silver surfaced mirror and then on to a translucent screen. During WWII regular visitors included 617 Squadron, The Dambusters, when it was nicknamed 'the flicks in the sticks'. In 1987 a Compton Kinestra organ was installed, which rises from

the pit during the interval. The walls are decorated by Canadian artist, Murray Hubick, using the trompe l'oeil technique, where the eye is tricked into believing it is seeing three dimensional images. A second screen was constructed in 1994. Located in woodland off the northside of the Broadway, Kinema in the Woods is unique and creates an atmosphere long vanished from today's cinemas.

Further information: Kinema in the Woods, Coronation Road, Woodhall Spa, Lincs. Tel: 01526 352166.

THE RITZ PUB
Lincoln

Previously the Ritz Theatre and Cinema it opened as a pub in 1998. The old stage is still intact and the frontage, which is brightly lit with green and pink neon, remains unchanged.

Further information: The Ritz, High Street, Lincoln. Tel: 01522 512103.

Liverpool

BACKBEAT

• 1994 100m c
Musical/Drama/Biography
Polygram/Scala Productions (U.K.)
• Sheryl Lee (Astrid Kirchherr), Stephen Dorff (Stuart Sutcliffe), Ian Hart (John Lennon), Gary Bakewell (Paul McCartney), Chris O'Neill (George Harrison), Scot Williams (Pete Best), Kai Wiesinger (Klaus Voormann), Jennifer Ehle (Cynthia Powell)
• p, Finola Dwyer, Stephen Wolley; d, Iain

Talacre Beach and *Point of Ayr Lighthouse*

Softley; w, Stephen Ward, Iain Softley, Michael Thomas; ph, Ian Wilson; ed, Martin Walsh

This above average biopic by first time director, Iain Softley, tells the story of Stuart Sutcliffe, 'fifth Beatle', who left the band before they rocketed to stardom and died of a brain haemorrhage aged twenty-one. The film explores Sutcliffe's obsession with Astrid Kirchherr, his relationship with John Lennon and their early experiences in the clubs of Liverpool and Hamburg.

Lennon and Sutcliffe's original 1960 flat was at **3 Gambier Terrace** but was considered unsuitable for filming and the location was moved a few houses along the street with a view of the Anglican Cathedral. The tower blocks at **Aigburth Drive** provided the location for their conversation about the future and their Hamburg departure was filmed at the **Victoria Dock, Birkenhead**. The beach scenes where Astrid (Sheryl Lee) declares her love for Sutcliffe to Lennon were shot at **Talacre Beach and Point of Ayr Lighthouse, near Prestatyn**.

WOOLTON PICTURE HOUSE

In **Mason Street** near Woolton village shopping centre stands the Woolton Picture House. Built in 1927 and partly rebuilt in 1958 after a fire, the cinema was taken over by David Wood in 1992. Behind its unremarkable exterior it retains many of its original features

and is well known as a friendly family venue. With photographs of Liverpool's picture palaces adorning the foyer and chandeliers hanging from the walls, the auditorium seats 256 and is divided into smoking and non-smoking areas. Every performance begins with the opening sequence of Richard Strauss' *Thus Spake Zarathustra* and the cinema is reputed to be haunted by the ghost of a former manager. David Wood's grandfather, John F. Wood, opened Liverpool's first purpose-built cinema, the Bedford Hall, Walton, in 1908 which led to a chain of forty Bedford cinemas.

Further information: The Woolton Picture House, Mason Street, Woolton, Liverpool, L25 5JH. Tel: 0151 428 1919.

LION: THE TITFIELD THUNDERBOLT

In 1952, Ealing Studios requested the loan of the locomotive, Lion, from the Mersey Engineering Society to star in T.E.B. Clarke's new comedy, *The Titfield Thunderbolt* (1953). This Ealing classic about a village's attempt to run its own railway line in competition with the local bus company, was filmed on the Limpley Stoke-Hallatrow line, near Bath, and was the first Ealing comedy to be made in colour. Lion amazingly arrived at the location under her own steam and operated reliably throughout filming. Her two other film appearances were in Herbert Wilcox's *Victoria the Great* (1937) and *The Lady With A Lamp* (1951).

In the 1830s she was delivered with her sister loco, Tiger, to the Liverpool & Manchester Railway Company by Todd, Kitson & Laird of Leeds. Lion is now one of the most important preserved locomotives in the U.K. and is reputed to be the oldest working locomotive in the world that still runs under her own steam. Lion can be seen at the Liverpool Museum.

See also: *The Titfield Thunderbolt*

*Trial steaming of **LION,** prior to completion at the works of Ruston Diesels Ltd., 1980.*

Further information: Liverpool Museum, William Brown Street, Liverpool, L3 8EN. Tel: 0151 4784399.

Manchester

NORTH WEST FILM ARCHIVE

The North West Film Archive is Britain's largest public film collection outside London. The archive was set up in 1977 and is the professionally recognised home for moving images made in or about Greater Manchester, Lancashire and Cheshire. The Archive cares for over 22,000 items dating from the pioneer days of film in the mid 1890s to modern video productions.

The work of both the amateur and the professional is collected, which includes cinema newsreels, documentaries, advertising and promotional material, educational and travel films, home movies, corporate videos and regional television programmes. Complementary collections of photographs, taped interviews and original documentation (totalling 12,500 items) have also been established.

The Archive offers a variety of access services to users in the public, academic and commercial sectors. New visitor facilities include a public viewing room and a database search station. All

interested parties must contact the Archive's access staff prior to their visit to arrange a viewing appointment.

Further information: North West Film Archive, The Manchester Metropolitan University, Minshull House, 47-49 Chorlton St., Manchester M1 3EU. Tel: 0161 247 3097 Fax: 0161 247 3098 e-mail: n.w.film archive@mmu.ac.uk URL: http://www.mmu.ac.uk/services/library/west.htm

THE MOON UNDER THE WATER PUB

Formerly the ABC cinema which closed in 1989, The Moon has a display on the upper floor of archive photos, which includes the old ABC, its staff and the last frame of film screened on the day the cinema closed, together with a general history of cinema in the North West. A mock seating area with wax dummies faces the site of the old screen.

Further information: The Moon Under The Water, 68-74 Deansgate, Manchester. Tel: 0161 834 5882.

BIRTHPLACE OF ROBERT DONAT (1905-58)

"Once he actually tried to be a film star - just once. He bought an outrageously flashy Sunbeam roadster... he offered Marlene Dietrich a lift from the studios. 'But Robert', purred Marlene, 'I LOVE little cars.'"
John Donat, Robert Donat's son

Frederick Robert Donat, one of the great British screen actors of the 1930s, was born on 18 March 1905 in **Albert Road (renamed Everett Road) Withington**, the youngest of four sons of Rose Green and Ernst Donat, a Polish immigrant and civil engineer. When he was five the family moved to

Manchester

20 St Paul's Road. He was a tall, lean boy, with a pronounced stammer whose name was often mispronounced 'doughnut'. He attended **Ducie Avenue Central School in Ardwick** and in 1916, aged eleven, he moved to the **Central High School for Boys, Whitworth Street**.

His family had no tradition of the theatre, but he became stage-struck after creating his own theatre in his garden toolshed. He was cured of his stammer by elocutionist and actor, James Bernard. When Robert left school at fifteen, with no qualifications, Bernard took him under his wing and encouraged him to take up acting as a career. In 1921 he was engaged by actor Henry Baynton at Birmingham's Prince of Wales Theatre and from 1924 to 1928 he toured with Sir Frank Benson's company.

He made his film debut in 1932, after accepting a contract from Alexander Korda, when he portrayed an Oxford undergraduate in London Films', *Men of Tomorrow*. It was his portrayal of Thomas Culpepper in *The Private Life of Henry VIII* (1933) which launched his screen career, and the following year he was lured to Hollywood to play the title role in *The Count of Monte Cristo*. Discontented with Hollywood and the 'star' system, he returned to England where he soon established himself as a popular leading man in films such as *The 39 Steps* (1935), *The Ghost Goes West* (1936), *The Citadel* (1938), *Goodbye Mr Chips* (1939, AA Best Actor), *The Young Mr Pitt* (1942), *The Winslow Boy* (1950) and *The Magic Box* (1951).

Plagued by asthma and ill-health in later life, he never fully achieved his expectations on the screen, refusing many roles because of his own perfectionism and self-doubt. His last film was *The Inn of the Sixth Happiness* (1958), based on the life of the missionary, Gladys Aylward. At this time he lived alone in a flat at **7, Brymon Court, Montagu Square, behind Baker Street**, having separated

Robert Donat *as a child*

from his second wife, actress Renee Asherson. The studio wanted to test him to see if he could portray an elderly Chinaman, but director Mark Robson intervened saying, *"You don't ask Donat to test. Just pin a thin goatee on a photograph."* Tormented by asthma he was driven to Elstree Studios daily, where he had a portable dressing room with an air-purifying plant, extra high ceiling and a nurse ready with oxygen. Towards the end of the film his speech was slurred and thick, and

when he uttered his poignant last line: *"We shall not meet each other again, I think. Farewell, Jen-Ai,"* - it was obvious he was approaching death.

He was admitted to the West End Hospital in Dean Street, Soho, where he died on 9 June 1958, from a stroke. Cerebral thrombosis was certified as the primary cause of death. A memorial service was held at St Martin-in-the-Fields, where Laurence Olivier read the lesson. He was cremated at **St**

Robert Donat as Sir Robert Morton in **The Winslow Boy** *(1948, Lon. Films/Eagle Lion)*

Marylebone Crematorium, East End Road, Finchley, and his ashes were scattered in the **Garden of Remembrance**. He was twice married with three children.

Although his asthma could wear him down physically and mentally, he always held on to his sense of humour; as his son John relates in J.C. Trewin's 1968 biography: *"One day... he was in very low spirits, wheezing uncontrollably, gasping for breath and feeling thoroughly sorry for himself... Suddenly, my sister Joanna appeared at the sitting-room door, took in the pathetic scene at a glance and announced without hesitation: 'I think you should stuff a rocket up your arse - and light it...' The effect of this unorthodox prescription on Robert was miraculous; his mouth fell open, the wheezing stopped, his eyes lit up, and he dissolved into uncontrollable boots of laughter which sustained him for the rest of the day. He kept murmuring to himself... 'And light it... don't forget to light it...'"*

See also: *The Inn of the Sixth Happiness*, *Goodbye Mr Chips*, *The Citadel*, W.H. Balgarnie, James Hilton, William Friese-Greene, Madeleine Carroll, Forth Bridge

Further information: 'The Robert Donat Archive' can be viewed by appointment at The John Rylands University Library, University of Manchester, 150 Deansgate, Manchester, M3 3EH. Tel: 0161 834 5343. Fax: 0161 834 5574.

Newcastle upon Tyne

TYNESIDE CINEMA

This beautifully refurbished 1930s Art Deco News Theatre in Newcastle's city centre has two auditoria: Cinema One seats 296 with access for people with disabilities and includes an induction loop; Cinema Two has seating for 122. There is also a Coffee Room and a Cinema Shop stocking movie books, posters, stills, videos, magazines and movie memorabilia. Since its launch as a Regional Film theatre in 1976 it has screened over 20,000 films and hosted sixteen international Film Festivals, including two Deaf Film Festivals. It also has an ongoing commitment to promote the international moving image, which includes running courses and workshops, and working with schools, colleges and young children.

Further information: Tyneside Cinema, Pilgrim Street, Newcastle upon Tyne, NE1 6QG. Tel: 0191 232 8289. Cinema Shop: 0191 232 5592. E-mail: staff@tynecine.org website: http://www.tynecine.org

GET CARTER

• 1971 112m c crime / drama UK
• Michael Caine (Jack Carter), Ian Hendry (Eric Paice), Britt Ekland (Anna Fletcher), John Osborne (Cyril Kinnear), Tony Beckley (Peter), George Sewell (McCarty), Geraldine Moffatt (Glenda), Rosemarie Dunham (Edna the Landlady), Bryan Mosley (Cliff Brumby)

• p, Michael Klinger; d, Mike Hodges; w, Mike Hodges (based on the novel *Jack's Return Home*, by Ted Lewis); ed, John Trumper; ph, Wolfgang Suschitzky

"It was too realistic for these people who had become used to the choreographed nonsense you usually saw in those days."
Michael Caine

When London gangster, Jack Carter (Michael Caine), arrives in Newcastle to investigate his brother's death, he upsets the local mafia, uncovers a porno movie scam, and seeks brutal revenge.

A powerful and memorable crime drama, *Get Carter* is one of those rare films that manipulates and weaves the surrounding landscape skilfully into the plot. Michael Caine recalls the grim settings used in the film in his 1992 autobiography, *What's It All About?* : *"By now I had seen poverty in different parts of the world that had made my own childhood look quite privileged, but I had never witnessed misery like this in my own country...* Way ahead of its time, it was severely criticised by the seventies' media for excessive violence. It was the feature film debut of TV director, Mike Hodges, and to date, he has not equalled it.

Newcastle locations included **Frank Street**, Benwell, home to Jack's brother and the starting point for the funeral cortege; the **Crematorium** in **West Road**; **Newcastle Race Course**; the **Quayside** between **Tyne Bridge** and **Swingbridge** and the **High Level Bridge** - where Carter and Margaret meet (a scene which was repeated in *Stormy Monday*, 1988). The dance hall was at the **Oxford Galleries** and **Newcastle Station** appears briefly at the beginning of the film, but the pub with the long bar Carter enters across the street is no longer there.

Gateshead locations included **Coburg Street** - where Jack takes lodgings, and site of the jazz band scene, and the **multi-storey car park on the corner**

*Michael Caine and Ian Hendry on **Blackhall Beach***

*The **car park** on the corner of West and Ellison Streets.*

Dunston Staithes

of **West Street** and **Ellison Street** from which Cliff Brumby was thrown. The scrapyard scene in which Jack examines his brother's car was shot a little up river from the **King Edward Railway Bridge**; Jack meets Paice at **Dunston Staithes** and chases him on foot to **Blackhall Beach**, near Peterlee.

Durham locations included **Milburn House**, Belmont, which doubled as Bryan Moseley's house; **Dryerdale Hall**, near Hamsterly, was Kinnear's house; **Hardwick Hall Park** was used for the grounds of Kinnear's house and road scenes and phone box were shot around **Hamsterly**.

See also: Michael Caine

Norfolk

GRAVE OF HENRY RIDER HAGGARD (1856-1925)
Ditchingham

Writer of the gripping yarns, *King Solomon's Mines* (1885) and *She* (1887), which has entertained generations of schoolboys, Rider Haggard's books were filled with the essential ingredients of romantic adventure: virtuous heroes and heroines, noble black servants, secret tribes and lost civilizations. His story of the immortal priestess, Ayesha ('She Who Must Be Obeyed'), in *She* was adapted for the screen many times, notably in 1935 with Randolph Scott and Helen Gahagan and in 1965 with Peter Cushing and Ursula Andress. His classic Victorian hero in *King Solomon's Mines*, Allan Quartermain, predated Indiana Jones by a century and was filmed in 1937 (with Paul Robeson as 'Umbopa'), 1950, 1977 and 1985.

Rider Haggard was born at **West Bradenham Hall, Norfolk**. He joined the colonial service in 1875 and was posted to South Africa. On his return to England in 1880 he married local heiress Mariana Margitson and settled down to the life of a gentleman farmer and writer, publishing his first work in 1882. He is buried in **Ditchingham Church**, where his grave is marked by a marble slab in the chancel.

*Deborah Kerr, Richard Carlson and Stewart Granger in **King Solomon's Mines** (1950, MGM).*

See also: Peter Cushing, Cedric Hardwicke, Stewart Granger

CHILDHOOD HOME OF EDITH CAVELL (1865-1915)
Swardeston

Edith Louisa Cavell was born in Swardeston where her father was vicar from 1864 to 1910. The village has changed very little since Edith's day and her birthplace is still known as the **Cavell House**. Her father built a new vicarage after her birth (now known as **'the Old Vicarage'**) and it was here she spent her childhood with her two sisters and brother. She left school at nineteen and became a governess, but in April 1896 she began nursing training at The London Hospital, Tooting. During the Great War she became matron of a Red Cross hospital in Brussels where she worked with the Belgian underground smuggling retreating British soldiers across the Dutch frontier, managing to save two hundred men before she was eventually arrested. She was imprisoned in St Gilles Prison in Brussels and ordered to be executed at the Tir National Rifle Range on October 12th 1915. One soldier who refused to carry out the execution order was also shot and buried beside her. Many in the firing squad fired wide.

After the war her remains were returned to England and buried outside **Norwich Cathedral** at **Life's Green**. A flower festival is held every October in Swardeston in her memory and in **St. Mary's Church** a portrait of her with her dogs Don and Jack and a section of a wooden cross returned from Brussels can be seen. The East Window is the Edith Cavell memorial window installed in 1917. Her dog Jack lived until 1923 when he was stuffed and presented to the Imperial War Museum.

She was first portrayed on the screen by silent actress, Cora Lee, in *Nurse and Martyr* (1915). Sybil Thorndike portrayed her in Herbert Wilcox's

Dawn (1928) and Anna Neagle in Wilcox's *Nurse Edith Cavell* (1939).

See also: Anna Neagle

STAGE DEBUT OF MICHAEL CAINE
North Runcton

Ten-year-old Maurice Joseph Micklewhite, better known as Michael Caine, was evacuated to the village of North Runcton during WWII and recalls his stay here as the happiest of his life. He lived with his family and two other families in the village schoolhouse (Church Farm). It was here he made his first ever stage appearance during Christmas, 1943, at the village hall (a new hall and sports complex was built on the site of the old hall in the mid-sixties) portraying the father of the Ugly Sisters, Baron Fitznoodle, in *Cinderella* - *"I went on and got a load of laughs and the local MP gave me five shillings as the best act of the evening. When I came off I found my flies were undone. Ever since then, just before I make my entrance I check that my flies aren't undone."* *

See also: Michael Caine, *Zulu, Sleuth, Little Voice, Get Carter, Educating Rita,* Metamorphosis of Maurice Micklewhite

THE GO-BETWEEN
Melton Constable

• 1970 118m c Drama MGM/EMI (UK)
• Julie Christie (Marian Maudsley), Alan Bates (Ted Burgess), Dominic Guard (Leo Colston), Margaret Leighton (Mrs. Maudsley), Michael Redgrave (The Older Leo), Michael Gough (Mr. Maudsley), Edward Fox (Hugh Trimingham),
• p, John Heyman, Norman Priggen; d, Joseph Losey; w, Harold Pinter (based on the novel by L.P. Hartley); ph, Gerry Fisher; ed, Reginald Beck; m, Michel Legrand; art d, Carmen Dillon; cos, John Furniss

Based on L.P. Hartley's 1953 novel about an old man who thinks back to a summer holiday in 1900 in which a

Dominic Guard and Julie Christie in **The Go-Between** *(1970)*

love affair observed by him influences the rest of his life. As a young boy he is employed as a go-between for the tragic love-affair between Marian Maudsley (Julie Christie) and coarse, uncultured farmer, Ted Burgess (Alan Bates). Like Ted, he too falls in love with Marian and remains devoted to her for the rest of his life, never marrying.

Filmed on location at the then vacant and neglected seventeenth-century **Melton Constable Hall**. Director Joseph Losey completely refurbished the house and the yellowing lawns were sprayed with green dye. The cricket match where farmer Ted proves more than a match for the aristocratic Hugh Trimingham was shot on the village green at nearby Thornage.

See also: Alan Bates, Joseph Losey

GRAVE OF ANNA SEWELL (1820-78)
Lamas

Anna Sewell was the writer of the children's story, *Black Beauty* (1877) about a black horse which suffers at the hands of various owners. She died soon after its publication, unaware she had written a children's classic. The book has been filmed several times, none of them memorable. She is buried beside her mother, Mary Sewell, in the **Quaker burial ground** at the meeting house in Lamas.

Mark Lester in **Black Beauty** *(197i)*

EAST ANGLIAN FILM ARCHIVE
Norwich

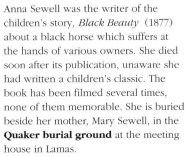

The East Anglian Film Archive in the Centre of East Anglian Studies at the University of East Anglia, was formed in the spring of 1976, and was the first regional film archive to be established in the U.K. The aim of the archive is to search out and preserve moving pictures, either on film or videotape, which show life and work in the counties of Norfolk, Suffolk, Cambridgeshire and Essex.

Films on all gauges and videos on all formats are acquired and kept for the future, as a record of East Anglia and its film makers. Material collected includes cinema films, newsreels, advertisements, publicity and instructional films, television programmes and family records, ranging from the professional and commercial to the amateur and personal. Amateur films account for about 50% of the collection with 2,500 titles in the main catalogue. A price list and catalogue is available on request. The archive's volunteer presenters, equipped with projector and screen and a varied programme of films, give presentations at the invitation of local organisations across the region. To

Eastern Sunshine (1933) - a publicity film for Gt. Yarmouth.

organise a film show phone 01603 592664. The archive has also produced a series of video compilations of archive film for sale. Access to the archive is available to all visitors interested in the collections.

Further information: University of East Anglia, Norwich, NR4 7TJ. Tel: 01603 458553. E-mail: p.russell@uea.ac.uk http://www.lib.uea.ac.uk/libinfo/archives/eafawelc/eafawelc.htm

North Somerset

THE ODEON
Weston-super-Mare

Designed by architect, Cecil Howitt, and described at the time as "modernity at its best", the grand opening night of the Weston Odeon on May 25th, 1935, was the largest social gathering in the town's history. An audience of 1,800 paid a shilling each to watch a preview of Jack Buchanan in *Brewster's Millions* and all the proceeds went to help the district's unemployed. A *"mighty Compton organ with its wonderful illuminated console"* was installed in 1935 and in 1989 a series of regular concerts were started featuring the original restored organ. In 1973 it was converted into a three-screen cinema.

Further information: Odeon, The Centre, Weston S.M. Tel: 01934 641251.

North Tyneside

CHILDHOOD HOME OF STAN LAUREL
North Shields

"It is a place for sentiment with me. I belong to Dockwray Square."
Stan Laurel

In October 1897, seven-year-old Arthur Stanley Jefferson and his family moved to **Gordon House, 8 Dockwray Square, North Shields** (plaque erected), where his father managed the town's *Theatre Royal*. Stan often described his time in North Shields as the happiest days of his life and vividly recalled celebrating the 'Relief of Mafeking' with hundreds of other locals in Dockwray Square. His father, Arthur Jefferson, commented in 1932: *"In our home in Shields in the old days I could see he had something in him. Always being funny, he was. So I made him a little theatre in the attic. Spent the day there, he and his sister Olga. Well what I say is, what's bred in the bone..."* * Stan's brothers, Sydney and Edward (Teddy) were born at Dockwray Square. Sydney died aged only five months and is buried in **Preston Cemetery, North Shields**. In 1902 the family moved to **Ayton House, Ayres Terrace, North Shields**, until 1905 when they moved to Glasgow.

When Laurel and Hardy arrived for a British tour in 1932, Stan tried to visit his old home in Dockwray Square but couldn't reach it due to the vast crowds which had turned out to see him. Instead, he was driven by a police escort to Ayton House, where the awaiting crowd was much smaller. Stan and Ollie also attended a Civic reception at the Town Hall and lunched at the nearby Albion Rooms. They returned again during their 1952 tour, for a guest appearance at Gaumont Cinema, North Shields.

Dockwray Square was once a prestigious area of North Shields and home to wealthy ship owners and

professionals. Over the years it fell into decline, but recently it has been transformed into a £10m housing development called Laurel Court, and a statue of Stan Laurel was erected in 1992 as its centrepiece. The statue, depicting Stan's famous head-scratching pose was made of concrete with a bronze finish, and was the work of local artist and sculptor, Bob Olley.

See also: Stan Laurel (Cumbria, Durham, Glasgow), Laurel and Hardy

North Yorkshire

BIRTHPLACE OF CHARLES LAUGHTON (1899-1962)
Scarborough

Charles Laughton, one of the great character actors of the thirties, was born on 1 July 1899 at **The Victoria Hotel (opp. railway station), Westborough**, the eldest of three sons of Elizabeth Conlon and Robert Laughton, a hotelier. His childhood was an unhappy one and staunchly Catholic. Bisexual, and exasperated by a glandular condition which made him overweight from infancy, his childhood was one of constant misery. He knew from the age of eight that he wanted to be an actor, frequently staging performances for the benefit of hotel staff, much to the annoyance of his parents, who were vehemently opposed to his thespian ambitions. In 1908 the Laughtons took over the nearby and much grander **Pavilion Hotel** (now site of Tourist Information & Halifax Building Society). He attended prep. school at a French convent in Filey and later attended Stonyhurst, which he left in 1915. He was sent to Claridge's in 1917 to learn the hotel trade, but by the end of the year he had joined The Royal Huntingdonshire Rifles and was posted to the trenches of Vimy ridge where he was badly gassed during the last week of WWI.

He returned to his Scarborough hotel duties in 1919 and in 1925 he enrolled at RADA where he won the gold medal. His stage career prospered and he made his film debut in 1928 in a

*Charles Laughton as in the title role of **The Private Life of Henry VIII** (1933, London Films)*

The Victoria Hotel - *birthplace of Charles Laughton*

twenty minute silent, based on an H.G. Wells story, called *Blue Bottles*, directed by Ivor Montagu. In 1931 he made his Broadway debut in *Payment Deferred* which took New York by storm. This resulted in an offer from Paramount who cast him in his first Hollywood movie, *The Old Dark House* (1932), directed by James Whale and starring Boris Karloff. His film career as a character actor prospered in both the U.K. and Hollywood with films such as,

*Charles Laughton in **Captain Kidd** (1945)*

The Private Life of Henry VIII (AA) (1933), *The Barretts of Wimpole Street* (1934), *Ruggles of Red Gap* (1935), *Mutiny on the Bounty* (1935), *Rembrandt* (1936), *The Hunchback of Notre Dame* (1939) and *Hobson's Choice* (1954). In 1955 he directed his only film, *Night of the Hunter*, which flopped. Recent reappraisal, however, now rates it as a flawed masterpiece. In 1929 he married the actress Elsa Lanchester. They had no children. He died in Hollywood on 15 December 1962.

See also: *The Barretts of Wimpole Street*, James Whale

THE DRACULA TRAIL
Whitby

The majority of *Dracula* films were studio productions and were never shot in Whitby, but Stoker's original Whitby locations have inspired many film-

makers, and the town should be visited by all Dracula fans and vampire enthusiasts.

Bram Stoker began taking notes for his novel *Dracula* (1897) during a three week holiday in the picturesque seaside town of Whitby in August, 1890. He arrived from London after an eight-hour train journey with his wife Florence and their eleven-year-old son Noel, and booked rooms with a sea view at **6 Royal Crescent**. During his visit he enjoyed long walks by the shore and along the cliff paths, mixing with the locals and listening to their tales of shipwrecks and superstition. He took notes on dialect and recorded the tombstone epitaphs of drowned mariners. During his research in **Whitby Public Library, Pier Road** (now The Harbour Diner), he first came across the name *Dracula* in *An Account of the Principalities of Wallachia and Moldavia*, by William Wilkinson, which read: *"Dracula in the Wallachian language means Devil. Wallachians were accustomed to give a surname to any person who rendered himself conspicuous by courage, cruel actions or cunning."* He learned from the local coast guard and the Whitby *Gazette* about the Russian brigantine, the *Dmitry*, from the port of Narva which ran aground on Tate Hill Sands in 1885 and weaved the story into his tale. He would also have seen local photographer, Frank Sutcliffe's picture of the wreck hanging in the library. In the novel, Count Dracula leaps off the *Demeter*, a Russian ship from Varna, in the shape of a dog.

The Dracula Trail:
Start from the **Bram Stoker Memorial Seat** at the south end of Spion Kop, West Cliff (from Khyber Pass go up steps/ramp, above tunnel turn right and it's the second bench on the right with cast iron legs). This Victorian-style seat was erected jointly by Scarborough Borough Council and the Dracula Society in April 1980 to commemorate the link between the author and the town, and the inspiration he derived from it while writing Chapters 6 - 8 of *Dracula*. The seat looks directly across the harbour to East Cliff - both cliffs provide settings for episodes in the story - and from it you can see every feature of the town mentioned in the novel.

Behind the seat and to the right is **East Crescent** (originally called *The Crescent* when this neighbourhood was built in the 1850s to house summer visitors). In one of the nine small houses in *The Crescent* the heroines of the story, Mina and her friend Lucy, are spending their summer holidays. Also, at No. 7, lives the lawyer engaged by Count Dracula to handle the import of his strange cargo from Transylvania - *fifty cases of common earth.*

Cross the top of Khyber Pass and take the steps leading to East Crescent, then follow the pavement along to the junction with North Terrace, by the **Royal Hotel**. At this end of the cliff, above the West Pier, Mina pauses one night in her search for the sleep-walking Lucy and gazes across towards the churchyard on East Cliff. In a shaft of moonlight she glimpses a familiar white figure with *what looked like something dark bending over it.*

Take the path which leads down below the flagstaff to the top of the flight of steps leading up from the Pier. A couple of days after their nocturnal adventure the girls pause after climbing the steps on their way home to tea to admire the sunset over Kettleness from the cliff-edge vantage point nearby. In the opposite direction they see what looks like a dark figure sitting on their favourite churchyard seat, and two glowing red points of light, which Mina imagines might be reflections from the sinking sun in the windows of the north transept of St. Mary's Church. Lucy, however, utters as if in a dream the strange words - *'His red eyes again'.* Follow the steps down to the bottom of Khyber Pass where it curves to join Pier Road. Having glimpsed Lucy in the moonlight, Mina races down these steps and along the quay in a desperate bid to reach her. Her route takes her past The Fish Market (since rebuilt and enlarged) and along St. Ann's Staith to the Bridge.

From this point a short detour along the waterside into New Quay Road will bring you to **Whitby Railway Station**, formerly the terminus of the old North Eastern Railway line from York and erected in 1847. Between the station and the harbour there used to be extensive goods sidings, and it is from here that Count Dracula leaves Whitby

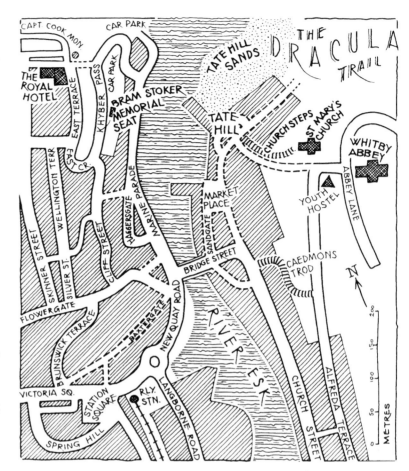

East Crescent

Whitby Abbey

St. Mary's Parish Church

for London (after a stay of ten days) in one of his fifty boxes, by the 9.30 goods train to King's Cross.

Retrace your steps and cross the harbour by **The Bridge**. This is referred to as *The Drawbridge* in the book, the name still used by Victorians after the old wooden lifting-bridge was demolished in 1835. It was actually an iron swing-bridge, somewhat narrower in span but otherwise very similar in design to the present one which replaced it in 1908. Mina has to run across it to the east side of the harbour in order to reach the churchyard.

Turn left at the top of Bridge Street into Church Street. This was the main street of the Old Town, and looks very much today as it did at the period of *Dracula*, with quaint yards and passages leading off between the houses and down to the water's edge. To reach the churchyard Mina has to run the length of the dark, silent street, past the Market Place and the Old Town Hall to the cluster of houses and narrow lanes below the cliff known as Tate Hill.

Fork left down Tate Hill to Tate Hill Pier, a long stone jetty projecting into the Lower Harbour and flanked by the curve of **Tate Hill Sands**. It is here, on the night of the mysterious and sudden storm, that the Russian schooner *Demeter* (chartered by Count Dracula) crashes into the pier after being driven through the harbour entrance in the teeth of the gale. (Bram Stoker based this episode on a real-life incident involving a Russian schooner which occurred in 1885). The Captain is found to be dead, the crew missing. The only sign of life aboard is an animal looking like an *immense dog*, which leaps from the bows on to the jetty as the ship strikes and disappears in the darkness among the alleys below the cliff *where churchyard hangs over the laneway to the East Pier*. This is the present Henrietta Street, and there is a link here with the thost-dog (a variant of the famous Yorkshire *Barguest*) which was once believed to haunt Haggerlythe, as the lane was formerly called.

Retrace your steps to where Church Street joins Henrietta Street at the foot of **Church Stairs**. There are 199 of

*The wreck of the Russian Schooner '**Dmitry**' on Tate Hill Sands, 31 October 1885 (Frank Sutcliffe)*

*Christopher Lee in **Dracula - Prince of Darkness** (1958, Hammer)*

these stone steps, with landings at intervals, and, in her frantic dash to rescue Lucy, Mina has torn up every one of them. Alongside the stairs is the precipitous stepped road known as Church Lane which leads to Abbey Plain. Mina also mentions this in her diary under its old nickname *The Donkey Road*.

From the top step of Church Stairs you can see the south side of the picturesque and unique parish church of **St. Mary's**. Looking past the tower you can also see a section of the cliff side path and graveyard - though not very far because of the dip of the ground. It is from this point that Mina catches sight of Lucy, still on their favourite seat, apparently asleep - though not alone, for there is *something, long and black* beside her. Mina's view, however, is cut off for some moments as she continues to run up the path, and by the time she reaches the seat Lucy is alone.

Continue up the path, then turn left along the main cliff-path, *or bier-baulk*, that runs the length of the graveyard. Note how your view of the section visible from the steps is cut off until you pass the corner of the church tower. Here, just off the path and in front of the tall Regency Gothic windows of the north transept, must have been the site of the girl's favourite seat, in an angle sheltered from the prevailing west winds and looking across the harbour to their lodgings in *The Crescent*. It was virtually on top of a flat tomb or *thruff-steean* belonging to one George Cannon - a suicide, though buried as an *accidental death*. No trace of such a grave survives today, but countless graves have disintegrated with weathering and subsidence in St. Mary's Churchyard over the years. Mina does not feel quite the same about their favourite seat after the night on which she finds Lucy there and takes her home - even less so when she recalls that early that morning their friend, the old sailor Mr. Swales, who lectured them so cynically on local hypocrisy and superstition, had been found dead with his neck broken on that very seat. Later it transpires that Count Dracula, apart from assuming the shape of a wolf or bat, as well as human form, had taken refuge for part of his stay in Whitby in

the unhallowed grave of the suicide. As for the seat itself, it must have been one of those comfortable timber and wrought iron affairs, such as Bram Stoker knew. Very similar, in fact, to the seat which has been erected on West Cliff to the memory of the man who created one of the world's great immortal characters and who, in doing so, helped to immortalise the town of Whitby.

See also: *Dracula*, Bram Stoker, Christopher Lee, Hammer Studios, Peter Cushing

Further information: 'In Search of Dracula Walking Tour': Harry Collett, Ashford Guest House, 8 Royal Crescent, Whitby YO21 3EJ. Tel: 01947 602138. email: fcoll@globalnet.co.uk web: www.whitbywalks.com 'The Dracula Experience', 9 Marine Parade, Whitby - old-fashioned museum of horrors which contains one of Christopher Lee's cloaks from *Dracula, Prince of Darkness* (1966). A large selection of the work of Frank Sutcliffe', who photographed the shipwrecked *Dmitry*, can be seen at The Sutcliffe Gallery, 1 Flowergate, Whitby. Tel: 01947 602239. Whitby Tourist Information - Tel: 01947 602674. Whitby Literary & Philosophical Society Library, Pannett Park, have a small Stoker archive. Tel: 01947 602908. A portrait of Stoker hangs in the foyer of The Royal Hotel, East Terrace.

I would like to thank Bernard Davies of the Dracula Society and the Department of Tourism and Leisure Services at Scarborough Borough Council, who helped with the compilation of *The Dracula Trail..*

LITTLE VOICE
Scarborough

"Singing live is a very rare thing in film, but the audience had to absolutely believe Little Voice is doing it. And if for a second they think that it's not really happening, you've lost the whole piece." Jane Horrocks

Little Voice is the nickname of Laura Hoff (Jane Horrocks), a shy, sensitive young girl who lives with her loud-mouthed mother Mari (Brenda Blethyn). Laura rarely leaves her

bedroom where she endlessly plays her late father's classic collection of great entertainers, which includes Garland, Sinatra, Bassey and Marilyn Monroe. One day she is heard impersonating one of them by her mother's current boyfriend, cheap talent promoter, Ray Say (Michael Caine) who sees her as his last chance to break into the big time.

Mark Herman's 1998 film, based on Jim Cartwright's hit play, *The Rise and Fall of Little Voice*, is a wonderfully inspired piece of film-making with stunning musical performances from Jane Horrocks; the decision to shoot her singing live instead of recording it makes the whole film glow.

Hoff's Record shop and home of Laura and her mother was on the corner of **Barwick Terrace** and **Barwick Street**, behind Scarborough Police Station in Northway. The white amphitheatre structure that Laura said she visited with her father and where she later met Billy, the telephone repairman, was the

Jane Horrocks as Little Voice

Spa Suncourt, which is part of the Victorian multi-functional **Spa complex in South Bay**.

Boo's Nightclub was the former Club Rendezvous which was once part of Wallace's Holiday Camp, but is now a disused building in the **Haven Holidays** complex at **Clayton Bay**, four miles south of Scarborough.

See also: Michael Caine

THE GREET ESCAPE
THE GREAT ESCAPE
Robin Hood's Bay

The character of 'The Scrounger', portrayed by James Garner in John Sturges' classic POW escape movie, *The Great Escape* (1963), was inspired by the exploits of Marcel Zillessen, a young pilot with No 6 Squadron in North Africa. On 6 April 1943 his Hurricane, used in low-level 'tank-busting' raids, was shot down at Wadi Akarit in Tunisia. He was captured and eventually taken to Stalag Luft 3 in Sagen, Germany. Zillessen spoke fluent German having studied in Germany before the war and soon gained the trust of the guards. They frequently asked him to write love letters to their wives and girlfriends and supplied him with writing materials. Any excess paper, pens and ink he filtered to the camp 'forgers' who created documents and passports essential for survival after an escape.

A tunnel was dug and on the night of 23 March 1944, 200 Allied officers prepared themselves for one of the largest mass breakouts of WWII. Seventy-six managed to escape before the alarm was raised. Zillessen, one of the last in line, was left behind. Only three men eventually reached freedom, the rest were re-captured and fifty were executed.

Zillessen, who was never consulted by the filmmakers, lost six stone in Stalag Luft 3 and always thought James Garner "a little bulky" for the part. He spent most of his time translating 19th-century German poetry into English at the camp which was liberated by British troops in May, 1945.

After the war he joined the family textile business and later established a chain of take-away food stores in the North-East. In semi-retirement he ran a guest house with his wife Lyn at **Lyndhurst, Mount Pleasant North** in Robin Hood's Bay. He died in January, 1999.

Further information: Robin Hood's Bay was also the childhood home of Leo Walmsley (1892-1966), who wrote *Three Fever*, about the life of fishermen in the Bay at the turn of the century. It was adapted for the screen

*James Garner (right) as 'The Scrounger' in **The Great Escape** (1963, UA)*

by J. Arthur Rank under the title *Turn of the Tide* in 1935, and shot on location in the Bay and the surrounding coast.

Northumberland

THE FILM COLLECTION
Morpeth

'The Film Collection', housed in Morpeth Library, contains around 3,000 movie books on film, including a range of back numbers of specialist movie periodicals, a selection of movie reference books and the Film Index International on CD-ROM. Anyone can borrow books from Morpeth's Film Collection and the membership rules of the County Library do not preclude anyone from outside the county joining in order to use it.

Further information: Morpeth Library, Gas House Lane, Morpeth, Northumberland. Tel: 01670 534518

CHILDHOOD HOME OF HENRY TRAVERS (1874 - 1965)
Berwick-Upon-Tweed

Born in Ireland, Henry Travers Heagerty was one of the great character actors of the golden age of Hollywood, usually portraying bumbling, venerable old gentlemen with hearts of gold. He will be best remembered as Clarence Oddbody, angel second-class, who eventually earns his wings saving the life of the suicidal George Bailey (James Stewart) in Frank Capra's 1946 classic, *It's A Wonderful Life*.

He arrived in Berwick in the late 1880s when his father, Dr. Daniel Heagerty settled at **6 Main Street, Tweedmouth** (now part of a nursing home). Educated at Berwick Grammar School, 'Travie' became involved with local drama groups and joined the 'Tweedside Minstrels' who performed locally in amateur shows. He took up acting professionally and began touring in the U.K. and abroad, and was working on the American stage at the turn of the century.

Henry Travers in Hitchcock's Shadow of a Doubt (1943, Universal)

Childhood home of Henry Travers - 6 Main St., Tweedmouth

He made his first films for Hollywood in the early thirties, where he eventually settled under the name of Henry Travers. His character portrayals include: Dr. Cranley in *The Invisible Man* (1933), Dr. Irving in *Dodge City* (1939), Pa Leslie in *High Sierra* (1941), Dr. Sims in *Random Harvest* (1942), Mayor Orden in *The Moon is Down* (1943), Joseph Newton in *Shadow of a ·Doubt* (1943) and Mr. Ballard the rose-growing station-master in *Mrs. Miniver* (1942) for which he received an Oscar-nomination for Best Supporting Actor.

CLASSIC LOCATION: BAMBURGH CASTLE

Situated on a rocky outcrop overlooking the North Sea, Bamburgh Castle dominates the Northumbrian coastline. A Norman stronghold that has survived many battles, it became the first castle in England to surrender to gunfire from the cannons of Edward IV. The castle's restoration and refurbishment was begun in the 1890s by the 1st Baron Armstrong and today it is the home of Lady Armstrong. A period film maker's dream setting, Bamburgh looks like the original template for Hollywood's interpretation of what a medieval English castle should really look like.

Films shot on location here include *Hunting Tower* (1927) with Harry Lauder, *Becket* (1964), Ken Russell's *The Devils* (1970), *Mary Queen of Scots* (1971), Roman Polanski's *Macbeth* (1972) and *Elizabeth* (1998).

Further information: Bamburgh Castle, Bamburgh, Northumberland, NE69 7DF. Tel: 01668 214515. Open: April - October, 11.00am - 5.00pm.

ROBIN HOOD: PRINCE OF THIEVES
Sycamore Gap

"Where's Errol Flynn when we need him?"
Jami Bernard, New York Post

Warner Brothers' rickety 1991 interpretation of the Robin Hood legend, with Kevin Costner in the title role, was shot at Shepperton Studios and at various locations around England. One of the more picturesque locations was at **Sycamore Gap, Hadrian's Wall, near Housesteads** (3 miles north of Bardon Mill on B6318). This was the location of Robin and Azeem's (Morgan Freeman) encounter with the Sheriff of Nottingham's soldiers, shortly after they came ashore in England. Sycamore Gap can be seen from the B6318 and can be reached by walking westwards about one and a half miles along the wall from the car park at Housesteads Roman Fort and Museum (01434 344363).

Other locations used in the film include **Seven Sisters Cliffs**, Eastbourne, where they came ashore; **Old Wardour Castle**, near Tisbury in Wiltshire, doubled as Locksley Castle and has on display Kevin Costner's sword; **Hulne Priory**, Alnwick (not open to the public) was Maid Marion's home; the **Priory Church of St. Bartholomew**

the Great at Smithfield in London doubled as Nottingham Cathedral; **Mark Ash** in the New Forest was the site of the medieval village and **Burnham Beeches** in Buckinghamshire was where the outlaw's camp was built. The walled French medieval city of Carcassonne doubled for exterior shots of Nottingham and the town square where the outlaws are destined to be hanged was built at Shepperton.

See also: Burnham Beeches, Robin Hood, Little John

ALIEN 3
Blyth

When Ripley's (Sigourney Weaver) escape pod lands on galactic penal colony, Fiorina 161, even the company of murderers and rapists is preferrable to the acid-blooded Alien who arrived with her. No doubt inspired by Howard Hawk's *The Thing* (1951), David Fincher's 1992 film of subterranean tunnels and ventilation shafts was shot at Pinewood and on location at **Dawdon Colliery** and **beach**, and **Blyth Power Station**.

CLASSIC LOCATION: ALNWICK CASTLE

Described by the Victorians as the 'Windsor of the North', the border stronghold of Alnwick Castle is the main seat of the Duke of Northumberland, whose family, The Percys, have lived here since 1309. Furnished in palatial Renaissance style and housing the paintings of Van Dyck, Canaletto and Titian, it is also the home of the Regimental Museum of the Royal Northumberland Fusiliers. Unchanged since the Middle Ages it is the perfect setting for mediaval jousting epics.

Feature films shot here include, *Becket* (1964), *Mary Queen of Scots* (1971), *The Spaceman and King Arthur* (1979), *Robin Hood: Prince of Thieves* (1991), *A Knight in Camelot* (1999) and *Elizabeth* (1998), the latter involving the lifting of two and a half thousand square metres of lawn to accomodate the opening scene of the burning of the martyrs.

John Le Mesurier and Kenneth More on location at Alnwick Castle shooting **The Spaceman and King Arthur** (1979, Walt Disney Productions)

Further information: Alnwick Castle, Alnwick, Northumberland, NE66 1NQ. Tel: 01665 510777. Open: Daily (except Fridays) Easter to end of September, including Bank Holidays and Good Friday. 11am-5pm. House only 12noon.

Nottingham

SATURDAY NIGHT AND SUNDAY MORNING

• 1960 90m bw Drama Woodfall (UK)
• Albert Finney (Arthur Seaton), Shirley Ann Field (Doreen Gretton), Rachel Roberts (Brenda), Hylda Baker (Aunt Ada), Norman Rossington (Bert), Bryan Pringle (Jack), Robert Cawdron (Robboe), Edna Morris (Mrs. Bull), Elsie Wagstaffe (Mrs. Seaton), Frank Petitt (Mr. Seaton)
• p, Tony Richardson; d, Karel Reisz; w, Alan Sillitoe (based on his novel); ph, Freddie Francis; ed, Seth Holt; m, John Dankworth;

"All I want is a good time. The rest is propaganda."
Arthur Seaton

Lathe operator, Arthur Seaton, detests the monotony and hopelessness of his factory job, and spends much of his wage packet on boozing and time on chatting up girls. Young and contemptuous, his horizons stretch no further than the weekend binge. Inevitably he gets a local girl pregnant and his future seems sealed.

Saturday Night and Sunday Morning was twenty-three year old Albert

Finney's first major feature film and one of the typical, but superior Angry Young Man dramas of the period, which also included *Look Back in Anger* (1958) and *Room at the Top* (1959). The screenplay was adapted from the bestselling book by its author, Alan Sillitoe, who based much of the story on his own experiences.

Filming took place in the **Radford** area of Nottingham (where Sillitoe was brought up) which was then extensively back-to-back terraced housing. The opening pub scene where Arthur Seaton gets plastered after a drinking competition, falls down the stairs and throws up over a couple of regulars was shot at the **White Horse Inn (0115 9703806), 313 Ilkeston Road, Radford**. Some of the extras in the film are still regulars at the pub and the staircase Albert Finney fell down can still be seen. The **Raleigh bicycle factory**, where Alan Sillitoe himself once operated a lathe, **between Lenton Boulevard and Faraday Road** (now demolished), was the location used for Arthur Seaton's workplace.

See also: Albert Finney, Alan Sillitoe, Hylda Baker

BIRTHPLACE OF ALAN SILLITOE (1928-)

Alan Sillitoe made his name with the publication of his first novel, *Saturday Night and Sunday Morning* (1958), a gritty story of working-class life in post-war Nottingham. Born at **38 Manton Crescent, Radford**, he left school at fourteen to work at the Raleigh factory in Nottingham. At ninteen he joined the RAF and spent two years on active service in Malaya as a wireless operator. He began writing at twenty while he was in hospital in Malaya with TB. He was later invalided out of the RAF with a full pension which enabled him to live in Spain where he wrote his first novel, *Saturday Night and Sunday Morning*. He published his second novel, *The Loneliness of the Long Distance Runner*, the following year. Both were made into films. He has since written more than thirty novels, five children's books, eight poetry books and two plays. He married the American poet Ruth Fainlight and they have two children.

See also: *Saturday Night and Sunday Morning*

The White Horse Inn, Radford

Nottinghamshire

BIRTHPLACE OF D.H. LAWRENCE (1885-1930)
Eastwood

"Don't you find it a beautiful clean thought, a world empty of people, just uninterrupted grass, and a hare sitting up?"
Women in Love

Lawrence's notoriety as a writer of 'dirty books' and advocate of 'the free spirit' often overshadows his real talent as a novelist, playwright, poet and artist. To date his works have not been convincingly adapted for the screen, although Ken Russell's impressive 1969 version of *Women in Love* comes close.

He was born at **8A Victoria Street, Eastwood**, on 11 September 1885, the fourth child of Lydia Beardsall and John Lawrence, a miner. Known to his family as 'Bert', he was a delicate child, prone to TB, which spared him the traditional calling of life down the pit. At the age of thirteen he won a scholarship to Nottingham High School and later became a pupil teacher at the British School in Eastwood. He attended Nottingham University College, and taught at the Davidson Road School, Croydon.

After the publication, in 1911, of his first novel, *The White Peacock*, he decided to try to write for a living. It was the court case surrounding his novel, *Lady Chatterley's Lover* (1928) which assured him a world-wide scandalous reputation. Needless to say, it is the most filmed of his novels, with the 1981 version starring *Emmanuelle* star, Sylvia Kristel. A writer of great compassion and descriptive powers, he travelled widely for most of his life.

Aldous Huxley and Lawrence's wife Frieda were at his bedside when he died from tuberculosis in 1930 in Vence, France. He was buried in the cemetery there, but his body was exhumed five years later and cremated in Marseilles. His ashes were taken to the University of New Mexico where

Gerald (Oliver Reed) parted the curtain and Gudrun (Glenda Jackson) saw him... **Women in Love** *(1969, UA).*

they were mixed with concrete, to avoid theft, and housed in a shrine close to Frieda's grave. The couple had a ranch nearby in San Cristobal and the university owns several of his paintings.

Other screen adaptations of his works include: *Sons and Lovers* (1960), *The Fox* (1968), *Women in Love* (1969), *The Virgin and the Gypsy* (1970) and *The Rainbow* (1989). Ian McKellen portrayed Lawrence in his final years in *Priest of Love* (1981)

See also: Oliver Reed, Alan Bates, Glenda Jackson, Trevor Howard

Further information: The D.H. Lawrence Museum, 8A Victoria Street, Eastwood, is open daily and has been restored and refurbished to reflect his early childhood. Tel: 01773 717353.

The nearby Eastwood Library has an extensive collection of books about Lawrence, including the headstone from his grave in Vence. Local maps are available linking Lawrence-related sites.

GRAVE OF LORD BYRON (1788-1824)
Hucknall

"I am sure my bones would not rest in an English grave, or my clay mix with the earth of that country. I believe the thought would drive me mad on my deathbed, could I suppose that any of

my friends would be base enough to convey my carcass back to your soil."

The wild and excessive life of English poet and 6th Baron, George Gordon Byron has been well documented on screen. Born with a club foot to Captain 'Mad Jack' Byron and Catherine Gordon, his poetry and extravagant life-style endeared and repelled early nineteenth century society. Film makers have made much of his 'mad, bad and dangerous to know' image, concentrating on his love affair with Lady Caroline Lamb, his friendship with the Shelleys and his life of travel, adventure and immoral indulgence.

He was first portrayed on the silent screen by Howard Gaye in *A Prince of Lovers* (1922) and André de Béranger in *Beau Brummell* (1924). Gavin Gordon played Byron discoursing with the Shelleys in the prologue of *The Bride of Frankenstein* (1935) and other portrayals have included, Malcolm Graham in *The Last Rose of Summer* (1937), Dennis Price in *The Bad Lord Byron* (1949), Noel William in *Beau Brummell* (1954), Richard Chamberlain in *Lady Caroline Lamb* (1972), Gabriel Byrne in *Gothic* (1986), Eric Stoltz in *The Haunted Summer* (1988) and Hugh Grant in *Rowing in the Wind* (1988).

Byron died of marsh fever at Missolonghi after joining the Greek rebels who had risen against the Turks. Contrary to his wishes his body was returned to England for burial in the family vault at **Hucknall Church**, near the family seat at Newstead Abbey.

Oxfordshire

GRAVE OF CELIA JOHNSON (1908-82)
Nettlebed

Celia Johnson died of a stroke whilst playing bridge at Merrimoles, her home in Nettlebed where she had lived since 1935 after her marriage to writer and explorer, Peter Fleming, brother of Ian Fleming. They had three children. She was born in **Richmond, Surrey**, the daughter of a doctor and trained at RADA where she made her first professional appearance in Shaw's *Major Barbara* at Huddersfield in 1928. During WWII she joined the Women's Auxiliary Police Corps and did regular duties in Henley Police Station.

She made her film debut in 1942 portraying the naval wife of Captain Kinross (Noel Coward) in *In Which We Serve*. Usually cast in demure, middle-class roles, she will be best remembered for her portrayal of suburban housewife Laura Jesson, in David Lean's *Brief Encounter* (1945). Other films include: *Dear Octopus* (1942), *This Happy Breed* (1944), *The Holly and the Ivy* (1954), *The Good Companions* (1957) and *The Prime of Miss Jean Brodie* (1969). She was awarded the CBE in 1958 and became a Dame in 1981. She is buried in **St. Bartholomew's Churchyard** beside her husband. There is a memorial window in the church to Peter Fleming, who died in 1971.

See also: Celia Johnson (Surrey), *Brief Encounter, The Prime of Miss Jean Brodie*

HEAVEN'S GATE
Oxford

"I give you the end of a golden string; Only wind it into a ball, It will lead you in at Heaven's gate, Built in Jerusalem's wall."
William Blake, *Jerusalem* (1820)

Often cited as the biggest turkey of all time, Michael Cimino's 1980 epic western, *Heaven's Gate* became a watershed for the American film industry and brought its studio, United Artists, to its knees, triggering its purchase by MGM. Initially budgeted at $7.5 million, it rocketed to $36 million and included ridiculous excesses like having complete trains rebuilt and installing an irrigation system for an entire turfed battlefield. The American critics annihilated the film, but in Europe the film is still, in some circles, considered a masterpiece. The prologue for the film is set in Harvard

*Celia Johnson and Alec Guinness in **Captain's Paradise** (1953)*

***Grave of Celia Johnson**, St. Bartholomew's Churchyard, Nettlebed*

College, Massachusetts, but Harvard refused to allow filming on the campus because of previous problems with film crews and the scenes were eventually located in Oxford. The opening shots were of the **Tom Tower and Great Gate at Christ Church College**. Kris Kristofferson pursued a procession at **Hertford College Bridge** -which crosses **New College Lane**, the graduates listened to the Reverend Doctor (Joseph Cotton) at the **Sheldonian Theatre**, and they all celebrated on the quad of **Mansfield College**.

GRAVE OF C.S. LEWIS (1898-1963)
Oxford

"We have trained them [men] to think of the Future as a promised land which favoured heroes attain - not as something which everyone reaches at the rate of sixty minutes an hour, whatever he does, whoever he is."
The Screwtape Letters (1942)

Oxford lecturer, writer and creator of the Narnia Stories, Clive Staples Lewis and his brother Warnie are both buried in the graveyard of **Holy Trinity Church, Headington Quarry**, which has an etched window depicting characters from the Narnia stories. In 1993 Richard Attenborough co-produced and directed *Shadowlands*, the story of his romance with American woman, Joy Gresham.

See also: *Shadowlands*

GRAVE OF J.R.R. TOLKIEN (1892-1973)
Oxford

"One Ring to rule them all, One Ring to find them One Ring to bring them all and in the darkness bind them."
The Lord of the Rings

Only one film maker to date, American animator Ralph Bakshi (*Fritz the Cat*), has succeeded in transcribing Tolkien's colossal trilogy of Middle Earth, *The Lord of the Rings*, to the screen. His 1978 version covered only the first two volumes, but was a bold stab at an extremely complex subject.

John Ronald Reuel Tolkien is buried beside his wife, Edith, in **Wolvercote Cemetery, Bambury Road** (outside the ring-road). The tombstone inscription, 'Lúthien' and 'Beren', alludes to his poem, the 'Lay of Beren and Lúthien'.

GRAVE OF GEORGE ORWELL (1903-50)
Sutton Courtenay

Novelist, critic and journalist, Eric Blair, who wrote under the pseudonym of George Orwell is buried in a simple grave in the local churchyard. He will be best remembered for his two political allegories *Animal Farm* (1945) and *1984* (1949). Educated at Eton, he was a writer of political satire who also examined and chronicled the effects of poverty and social injustice.

His vision of a totalitarian state governed by 'Big Brother' in *1984*, was adapted for the screen in 1956 starring Edmond O'Brien and Michael Redgrave, and again in 1984 with John Hurt and Richard Burton. Both films were only moderately successful. John Halas and Joy Batchelor made an animated version of *Animal Farm* in 1955 and Richard E. Grant starred in a lack-lustre version of *Keep the Aspidistra Flying* in 1997.

See also: Richard Burton

ASHES OF JOHN BUCHAN (1875-1940)
Elsfield

Lord Tweedsmuir, better known as John Buchan, creator of the gentleman hero Richard Hannay in *The Thirty Nine Steps*, died after slipping and injuring his head on the side of his bath in Canada. His ashes were returned to Britain on board HMS *Orion* and are buried under a gravestone surrounded by cypress trees in **St. Thomas of Canterbury Churchyard, Elsfield.** The Buchan family had lived in nearby Elsfield manor-house since 1919.

See also: Birthplace of John Buchan (Perth & Kinross), Forth Bridge

BIRTHPLACE OF THOMAS HUGHES (1822-96)
Uffington

Thomas Hughes, author of *Tom Brown's Schooldays* (1857) - based on his own schooling at Rugby - was born at **Uffington Vicarage** (the original building has been demolished). His memory is marked by a brass tablet in the north transept of the church and by

Tom Brown's School Museum which contains details of his life and works.

Adapted for the screen in 1916, 1940 and 1951 with Freddie Bartholomew and John Howard Davies respectively in the latter two title roles, both films accurately depict the lonely and often brutal life of an English public school-boy in the late 19th century.

See also: Cedric Hardwicke, Rugby School

Further information: Tom Brown's School Museum (01367 820402) Open Easter - Oct. Weekends and BH only 2pm - 5pm, or by prior arrangement. Closed August BH.

HOWARDS END
Rotherfield Peppard

"Is this how the British cinema will end? Not with a bang, but a genteel whimper in full period costume."
Ken Russell

• 1992 Drama / Historical Merchant Ivory / Nippon Herald Films / Channel Four (UK)
• Anthony Hopkins (Henry Wilcox), Emma Thompson (Margaret Schlegel), Vanessa Redgrave (Ruth Wilcox), Helena Bonham Carter (Helen Schlegel), Sam West (Leonard Bast), Prunella Scales (Aunt Juley)
• p, Ismail Merchant; d, James Ivory; w, Ruth Prawer Jhabvala (based on the novel by E.M. Forster); ph, Tony Pierce-Roberts; ed, Andrew Marcus
• AA Best Actress: Emma Thompson; AA Best Adapted Screenplay: Ruth Prawer Jhabvala; AA Best Art Direction: Luciana Arrighi, Ian Whittaker

Terminally ill Ruth Wilcox bequeaths her country house, Howards End, in an unofficial will to her emancipated friend Margaret Schlegel. Because she is seen by the Wilcox family as a woman who has no means of support and who is considered a social inferior, they destroy the paper the will is written on. Ruth's widowed husband, industrialist Henry Wilcox, becomes attracted to Margaret and proposes marriage. Both return to live at Howards End where their opposing family values lie uneasily together.

Merchant Ivory's adaptation of E.M. Forster's 1910 novel was executed with

Sam West and Helena Bonham Carter in **Howards End**

their usual elegance and style. The house used to portray Howards End in the film was **Peppard Cottage in Rotherfield Peppard, near Henley-on-Thames**. Lady Ottoline Morrell, who owned the house at the turn of the century, was a friend of E.M. Forster, and the house is believed to have been the inspiration for Howards End. The house is not open to the public, but it can be seen from **Peppard Common** which is crossed by the B481.

The film used numerous locations, including **Dorchester-on-Thames, Oxfordshire**, as the local village; Helen Schlegel and Leonard Bast attended their musical lecture at **Oxford Town Hall;** the location of the Schlegel family home was in **Victoria Square, off Buckingham Palace Road, London**; Leonard Bast's residence was in **Park Street, Southwark, London**; the London residence of the Wilcoxes was the **St. James Court Hotel, Buckingham Gate** and the bank where Leonard worked was the **Baltic Exchange, St. Mary Axe, near Liverpool Street Station, London**. Other London locations include **St. Pancras Station, Admiralty Arch, Chiswick Mall and Simpson's-in-the-Strand.** The railway scenes were shot at **Bewdley Station in Worcestershire.**

See also: Anthony Hopkins, The Severn Valley Railway

SHADOWLANDS
Oxford

Richard Attenborough's 1993 film recounting the 1950s love affair between writer C.S. Lewis (Anthony Hopkins) and the brash American poet, Joy Gresham (Debra Winger), had numerous Oxford locations, including: **Magdalen College Chapel and dining hall, The Sheldonian Theatre, Radcliffe Camera, Christ Church Meadow and Duke Humphrey's Library.** The meeting place at which Lewis and his brother Warnie meet Joy for the first time is the **Fellows' Lounge** at the **Randolph Hotel** in Beaumont Street.

See also: *Shadowlands* (Herefordshire), C.S. Lewis

Further information: Oxford Tourist Information 01865 726871

A MAN FOR ALL SEASONS
Horton-cum-Studley

• 1966 120m c Drama Highland (UK)
• Paul Scofield (Sir Thomas More), Wendy Hiller (Alice More), Leo McKern (Thomas Cromwell), Robert Shaw (King Henry VIII), Orson Welles (Cardinal Wolsey), Susannah York (Margaret More)
• p, Fred Zinnemann; d, Fred Zinnemann; w, Robert Bolt, Constance Willis (based on the play by Robert Bolt); ph, Ted Moore; ed, Ralph Kemplen; m, Georges Delerue; prod d, John Box; art d, Terence Marsh; cos, Elizabeth Haffenden, Joan Bridge
• AA Best Picture; AA Best Actor: Paul Scofield; AA Best Director: Fred Zinnemann; AA Best Adapted Screenplay: Robert Bolt; AA Best Cinematography: Ted Moore; AA Best Costume Design: Elizabeth Haffenden, Joan Bridge

"...and Orson Welles appearing briefly as Cardinal Wolsey, a puckered, cantankerous clever face drooping over red robes like a deep imprint in sealing wax."
Observer

Following the arrest of Cardinal Wolsey on charges of high treason, Sir Thomas More becomes Lord Chancellor in 1529. After Wolsey has failed to persuade the Pope to grant the King a divorce from the barren Catherine of Aragon, Henry renounces papal supremacy, declares himself Head of the Church and marries Anne Boleyn whom he hopes will give him an heir. A devout Catholic, Sir Thomas More refuses to take the oath of supremacy to Henry VIII as head of the English Church and

is charged with high treason, imprisoned and beheaded.

Studley Priory, seven miles from Oxford, doubled as the home of Thomas More for the film. Situated in thirteen acres of wooded grounds the Priory was a Benedictine nunnery founded in the twelfth century. At the dissolution of the monasteries under Henry VIII the estate was purchased by the Croke family and remained in their hands for 335 years. Little change has been made to the exterior of the house since the days of Queen Elizabeth I and in 1961 it was converted into a hotel. Photographs taken during the shooting of the film can be seen in the hotel.

Henry VIII's Royal Barge did not sail up the Thames to Thomas More's home as shown in the film, because Studley Priory is not on the river. The **River Beaulieu** doubled as the Thames on **Lord Montagu's estate at Beaulieu in Hampshire** and the Hampton Court scenes were all studio sets constructed at Pinewood.

See also: Robert Shaw

Further information: Studley Priory Hotel, Horton-cum-Studley, Oxford, OX33 1AZ. Tel: 01865 351203. E-mail Res@studley-priory.co.uk http://www.hatton-hotels.co.uk

SHAKESPEARE IN LOVE
Banbury

• 1998 122m c Romance/Comedy (USA/UK)
• Joseph Fiennes (Will Shakespeare), Gwyneth Paltrow (Viola De Lessep), Judi Dench (Queen Elizabeth), Ben Affleck (Ned Alleyn), Colin Firth (Lord Wessex), Simon Callow (Tilney, Master of the Revels), Martin Clunes (Richard Burbage), Rupert Everett (Christopher Marlowe)
• p, Linda Bruce; d, John Madden; w, Tom Stoppard, Marc Norman; ph, Richard Greatrex; ed, David Gamble; art d, Steve Lawrence; cos, Sandy Powell; prod d, Martin Childs; m, Stephen Warbeck

"For never was a story of more woe Than this of Juliet and her Romeo."

Co-written by Tom Stoppard and Marc Norman, *Shakespeare in Love* tells the story of young Will Shakespeare's

*Susannah York, Robert Shaw and John Hurt relaxing at Studley Priory during the shooting of **A Man for all Seasons**.*

*Robert Shaw and Paul Scofield on location in the grounds of Studley Priory in **A Man For All Seasons***

doomed love affair with Viola De Lessep. Mirroring the plot of Romeo and Juliet and using Shakespeare's own practice of mistaken identity and gender, the film wonderfully portrays Shakespeare as a mere mortal suffering from the same stresses and temptations as the next man.

Some of the key locations included, **Broughton Castle**, near Banbury, which doubled as the De Lesseps' home. It is open from mid-May to mid-September on Wednesdays and Sundays; Thursdays in July and August; and Bank Holiday Sundays and Mondays. Tel: 01295 276070.

The London riverside locations were filmed near **Barnes Bridge**, and other river scenes by the De Lesseps' family home at **Marble Hill House in Twickenham, Middlesex**. Marble Hill House is open all Year. Tel: 0181 892 5115.

The church locations were the exterior of **Eton College Chapel** in Windsor and the interior of **St Bartholomew the Great** (0171 6065171) in **West Smithfield, London**. Eton College is open to the public from April to September. Visitors' Centre: 01753 671177.

The **Holkam Estate** on the Norfolk coast, about ten miles north of Fakenham, off the A149, was the location of the meadow scene where Viola declares her love for Will and of the final beach scene. Studio scenes were shot at Shepperton.

DIDCOT RAILWAY CENTRE
Didcot

Didcot Railway Centre boasts one of the finest collections of Great Western Railway steam locomotives, carriages and wagons in the country. The 16 acre centre is based around the original engine shed built in 1927 and displays many aspects of GWR history. The centre has been used for numerous films, TV and photo sessions.

Feature films shot here include scenes from Richard Attenborough's *Young Winston* (1972), Terence Davies' *Distant Voices, Still Lives* (1988) and *Fairytale* (1997) based on the story of the Cottingley Fairies.

Further information: Didcot Railway Centre, Didcot, Oxfordshire, OX11 7NJ. Tel: 01235 817200. Didcot Railway Centre is behind Didcot Parkway Main Line Station. Access is via the Station subway and up a short flight of steps.

ULTIMATE PICTURE PALACE
Oxford

One of Oxford's oldest cinemas, the Picture Palace, opened in 1911, and confidently proclaimed: *"People's Popular Palace Portrays Perfect Pictures, Produces Packed Performances."* Its confidence, however, was built on shaky ground. By 1920 it had closed and the premises became a furniture warehouse. Over fifty year later, in 1976, the cinema was brought back from the dead by William Heine and Pablo Butcher, and renamed the Penultimate Picture Palace. Painted Gothic black, with a large fibre-glass sculpture of Al Jolson above the doorway, and toilets named Pearl and Dean, the PPP gained a remarkable popularity. Screening a mix of classic, arthouse and the controversial, it once tried to screen Stanley Kubrick's withdrawn movie, *A Clockwork Orange*, until Kubrick's lawyers arrived and served an injunction minutes before the screening. The building was listed in 1994 and the PPP closed the same year. It was taken over by squatters for a short period and was renamed the Section 6 Cinema. In 1996, restored and refurbished, it was reopened by former

PPP employee, Saied Marham, as the Ultimate Picture Palace.

Further information: Ultimate Picture Palace, Jeune Street, Oxford. Tel: 01865 245288. Seats: 185

ABC MAGDALEN STREET
Oxford

The Oxford Cinematograph Theatre Company opened its second cinema in Magdalen Street in 1924 with a screening of Rex Ingram's, *The Four Horsemen of The Apocalypse*, complete with backstage sound effects created by young boys exploding detonators in dustbins! Originally called The Oxford 'Super' Cinema, it later became known as 'The Super'. It was designed by architects Frank Matcham and J.C. Leed, with a marbled entrance, stucco walls and a main lounge in the style of the French Renaissance. In 1930 it screened Oxford's first talkie, *Broadway Melody*, and remarkably, in 1965 the original Spurdon Rutt cinema organ was found intact in a concrete chamber behind the screen. In 1971 the cinema was leased to Associated British Cinemas and renamed the ABC Magdalen Street.

Further information: ABC Magdalen Street. Tel: 01865 243067. Seats: 864

Peterborough

CLASSIC LOCATION: NENE VALLEY RAILWAY
Peterborough

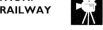

Over one hundred films, commercials and episodes for television have been made with the help of scenes shot on the Nene Valley Railway. The most ambitious project was the filming of some spectacular railway sequences for the James Bond film *Octopussy* in 1982. What ended up as a few minutes of the finished film took weeks to shoot. It involved a fight on the roof of a moving train, a Mercedes saloon on rail wheels having a head-on collision with a steam train at speed, and a car being catapulted up in the air and landing in the river. Four locomotives

were used, rather thinly disguised as East German engines. James Bond returned in April 1995 to the NVR to shoot scenes for *Goldeneye* which involved stunts and special effects using a disguised Class 20 diesel which hauled two specially adapted Mk. 1 coaches.

The Nene Valley Railway lends itself naturally to filming by having a number of features such as a Victorian station building, a tunnel over six hundred yards long, a manually operated level crossing controlled by a 60-lever signal-box, and seven and a half miles of track running alongside rural and urban settings. The locomotives and rolling stock are both British and foreign.

The present Nene Valley Railway is part of what was once the main line from East Anglia to the Midlands which was closed to through traffic by British Railways in 1966. A Peterborough clergyman, the Rev. Richard Paten bought one of the last BR steam locomotives working in the Manchester area, a BR Standard class '5' 4-6-0 No. 73050 for its scrap value of £3,000. It arrived in Peterborough under its own steam in September 1968 and a small group of enthusiasts began to restore it. In 1972 the Nene Valley Railway was formally launched. It supported the establishment of a standard gauge steam railway through the two thousand acre Nene Park and the Nene Valley Railway reopened as a preserved steam railway in 1977.

See also: Roger Moore, Black Park

Further information: Nene Valley Railway, Wansford Station, Stibbington, Peterborough, PE8 6LR. Tel: 01780 784444. Services operate at weekends from March to October. Visitor facilities

include a giftshop, bar, refreshments, museum and model railway.

Poole

THE HEROES OF THE TELEMARK

Poole doubled for Nazi occupied Norway when the **Quay and New Quay Road** were bedecked with Nazi flags, machine gun posts and barbed wire for the WWII thriller, *The Heroes of the Telemark* (1965). Directed by Anthony Mann (*Winchester 73, El Cid*), the film tells the true story of a resistance attack on a Nazi heavy water plant, starring Kirk Douglas and Richard Harris. Filming in Poole lasted three weeks and the RNLI boathouse can be easily spotted in the film. Most of the film was shot on location in Norway. John Huston's 1951 classic, *The African Queen*, features second unit footage shot in **Poole Harbour.**

Portsmouth

BIRTHPLACE OF PETER SELLERS (1925-80)
Southsea

"[Peter] was always searching for a bloody heart attack as if it were a letter that he knew had been posted and hadn't arrived."
Spike Milligan *

Comedian Peter Sellers was born on 8 September 1925 in a flat above a shop known as 'Postcard Corner' (now The Mayfair Restaurant) in **Castle Road**, Southsea, the only child of vaudeville entertainers, Peg and Bill Sellers. He began performing on stage from the age of three, when his mother put him in a white top hat and tails, and taught him the rudiments of stage-craft.

The family moved to a house near Regent's Park, London, where, to augment their income, his parents opened an antique shop in Highgate.

He attended school at St Mark's kindergarten, near Regent's Park and **St Aloysius College**, a Catholic school in **Hornsey Lane** (a choice he never understood as his mother was Jewish and his father Protestant).

During WWII he was evacuated to Ilfracombe in Devon where he worked at various jobs in his uncle's theatre. After being inspired by the drumming of Joe Daniels of 'The Hotshots' he decided to take up drumming lessons and later became an accomplished drummer, playing for Oscar Rabin, Henry Hall, and Waldini and his Gypsy Orchestra. He joined the RAF when he was eighteen and was posted to India where he entertained the troops in Squadron Leader Ralph Reader's RAF Gang Show. After his demob he became a fairground barker in Norwich, moving to Jersey where he became entertainments manager of a holiday camp. He was soon touring as a mimic and stand-up comedian, which included a stint at London's Windmill Theatre.

His first BBC broadcast was on *Showtime,* which established him as a successful radio comedian and led to appearances on shows such as *Variety Bandbox* and *Ray's a Laugh*, hosted by Ted Ray. Together with Michael Bentine, Spike Milligan and Harry Secombe he turned English humour on its head with the unconventional and anti-establishment radio programme, the *Goon Show.* He made his film debut in *Penny Points to Paradise*

Birthplace of Peter Sellers above the Mayfair Restaurant in Castle Road.

(1951) and subsequently appeared throughout the fifties and sixties in films such as *The Ladykillers* (1955), *The Smallest Show on Earth* (1957), *The Mouse That Roared* (1959), *I'm Alright Jack* (1959), *Only Two Can Play* (1962) and *I Love You Alice B. Toklas* (1968). He made two films with Stanley Kubrick: *Lolita* (1962) and *Dr Strangelove* (1963), but he will be best remembered on screen as the incompetent French policeman, Inspector Clouseau, in *The Pink Panther* (1963) and its resulting sequels.

A complex and difficult man, who claimed not to know his real self, he was married four times, the second time to Britt Ekland. He had a chronic heart condition and after a series of heart attacks he collapsed into a coma at London's Dorchester Hotel and died a few days later on 24 July 1980 at the Middlesex Hospital. He was cremated at Golders Green, where, at his own request, Glenn Miller's *In The Mood* was played to the mourners.

See also: *The Ladykillers*

Reading

DOUGLAS BADER'S CRASH
Woodley

The 1956 film, *Reach for The Sky*, based on Paul Brickhill's biography of Douglas Bader, immortalised the story of this legless airman whose courage overcame all odds.

On 14 December 1931, aged twenty-one, Bader flew to Woodley Aerodrome, Reading, with two other pilots. Over a coffee in the clubhouse of the flying club he was goaded into doing some aerobatics which were strictly against RAF regulations. Foolishly he responded to the challenge and flying just a few feet above Woodley Field he did a slow roll and crashed into the middle of the airfield. Still conscious, he felt no pain in his legs, but the rudder bar had gone through his right knee and the leg was almost severed. His left leg was broken between the ankle and the knee. Luckily the plane landed upright and did not burst into flames. He was taken to the Royal Berkshire Hospital at Reading where his right leg was amputated. His left leg was later also amputated following an infection. He was invalided out of the RAF following his accident, but because of a desperate shortage of pilots he was recalled to active duties during WWII where he fought in the Battle of Britain and was later shot down and imprisoned in Colditz. His wartime exploits became legendary and his personal courage and determination gave hope to many disabled people.

The part of Bader in *Reach for the Sky* had been promised to Richard Burton, but in the end it went to Kenneth More who felt the role ideal for himself.

Kenneth More portraying Douglas Bader in **Reach for the Sky** *(1956)*

More worried that he might just look like an actor playing a legless man, so he decided to visit a Roehampton Hospital which specialised in the rehabilitation of limbless patients. Here, a device was constructed for him which locked the joints in his feet and knees and gave him the rocking gait which made his performance so convincing. After the film's success he received hundreds of letters from people who had lost one or both legs explaining how Bader's example had been an immense help in restoring their faith and confidence. Douglas Bader died in 1982.

All that remains of Woodley Airfield - once the centre of the thriving Miles and Handley Page aircraft industry - is The Museum of Berkshire Aviation. Run as a charitable trust, the museum exhibits range from a Handley Page Herald, Miles Magister and Fairy Gyrodyne, to the wind tunnel model for the first ever supersonic aircraft. It also contains memorabilia relating to Douglas Bader.

Further information: The Museum of Berkshire Aviation, Mohawk Way, (off Bader Way), Woodley, Nr. Reading, Berkshire. Tel: 0118 934 0712.

Rochdale

BIRTHPLACE OF GRACIE FIELDS (1898-1979)
Rochdale

Known to millions as 'Our Gracie' she was born above her grandmother's fish and chip shop at **9 Molesworth Street** on 9 January 1898. A commemorative plaque marks the site which is now a Car Wash. Christened Grace Stansfield she was the eldest of four children of Fred Stansfield, an engineer, and his wife Sarah Jane Bamford. Her mother, who had always dreamed of becoming a performer, nurtured hopes that her ambition would be realised through her children and so Gracie's stage career began (and education neglected) with an endless round of talent shows, singing competitions and music hall appearances.

Her talent for singing, dancing, acting and improvisation was soon fully exploited and her fame began to spread. In 1911 Gracie got 35 shillings for a week at the Rochdale Hippodrome. In 1928 she received £600 for a week at London's Café Royal. By 1933 she had sold 4 million records: more than any other individual in the history of recording.

Her film career began in 1931 with *Sally In Our Alley*, which also gave her the signature tune that would be associated with her for the rest of her life. Initially she turned down the song and only accepted it after the songwriters had reworked it. After the film's success fan letters were often addressed to her as simply, 'Sally, London, England'. By the late 1930s she was the world's highest paid film star. She never liked filming and missed the atmosphere of a live audience. All of her fifteen films, including: *Sing As We Go* (1934), *Shipyard Sally* (1939) and *Holy Matrimony* (1943) were made in England.

She fell out of favour with her public and the press during WWII when she married Italian film director, Monty Bank (Mario Bianchi) and left for America to avoid his possible internment. Despite recovering from cancer, and among a barrage of bad press, Gracie raised many hundreds of

thousands of pounds for the war effort.

After the war she settled in Capri. She was married three times and had no children. Her third husband was Boris Alperovici, a local radio engineer. Gracie Fields was appointed CBE in 1938 and DBE in 1979. In July, 1979 she was taken ill with pneumonia and on 27 September she died at her home on Capri, aged eighty-one. She is buried in a cemetery near her home at Anacapri.

Further information: Gracie Fields' memorabilia, which includes her portrait and bust, are on display and for sale at the Town Hall, The Esplanade, Rochdale. The ABC Cinema, Sandbrook Park, has a Gracie Fields Art Deco bar. Rochdale Museum Services has a Gracie Fields collection which can be viewed by prior appointment (01706 641 1085).
Gracie Fields Website
http://www.rochdale.gov.uk/gracie

THE REGAL MOON PUB

Formerly the Regal Cinema which closed in the early 1990s. The frontage remains virtually unchanged, and the old balcony (which is still intact), may be viewed by appointment. Movie stills adorn its walls, including those of Gracie Fields who was born in Rochdale, and a full-size mock-up of an old cinema organ, complete with organist, hangs behind the bar.

Further information: The Regal Moon, The Butts (opposite Town Hall), Rochdale. Tel: 01706 657434.

Salford

CHILDHOOD HOME OF MIKE LEIGH (1943-)
Salford

Jewish art student, Mayer Liebermann (Mike Leigh's paternal grandfather), fled Russia in 1902 to avoid being conscripted into the army. Intending to

visit New York, he landed in Hull but missed his train to the port of Liverpool and ended up living in Manchester where he worked as a portrait miniaturist. He married Russian exile, Leah Blain with whom he had four children. The family grew up in **Cheetham Hill Road** and at the outbreak of WWII his two sons changed their Germanic sounding name to Leigh. Both sons became doctors, the second son, Abe, marrying health visitor and midwife, Phyliss Cousin, in 1941. Their first child, Michael David Leigh, was born on 20 February 1943 in the palatial surroundings of **Brocket Hall in Welwyn, Hertfordshire**, the wartime home of the City of London Maternity Hospital. When his father returned from army service in 1946 the family, now including their second child, Ruth, lived above Abe's surgery at **398 Great Cheetham Street**. Mike Leigh attended **North Grecian Street County Primary School** and **Salford Grammar** (now Buile Hill High School). When his grandparents died in the mid 1950s the family moved into their home at **125 Cavendish Street**.

In 1960 he won a scholarship to RADA, later working in a Birmingham arts centre and with a Manchester youth theatre. He also worked as an actor in bit parts in films and was an assistant director at the Royal Shakespeare Company. His first feature film, *Bleak Moments* (1971), was followed by a lengthy period working solely in stage and television where he made many notable films, including *Abigail's Party*

398 Great Cheetham Street - childhood home of **Mike Leigh**

and *Nuts in May.* He did not return to film making until 1988 when he made the critically acclaimed *High Hopes.* His other films include *Life is Sweet* (1991), *Naked* (1993) and *Secrets and Lies* (1995).

BIRTHPLACE OF ALBERT FINNEY (1936-)
Salford

"...a smouldering young Spencer Tracy... an actor who will soon disturb the dreams of Messrs Burton and Scofield".
Kenneth Tynan

Albert Finney, the glowering working class hero of the British stage and screen, was born on 9 May 1936 at **53 Romney Street, Pendleton**, the third child and only son of Alice Hobson and Albert Finney, a bookmaker. In 1941 they were forced to leave their 'two-up, two-down' terraced house because of bomb damage, and moved to a more salubrious semi-detached at **5 Gore Crescent, Weaste**. He attended his first school nearby at Tootal Drive Primary, and later Salford Grammar School at Leaf Square (now part of Salford College of Technology). At Grammar School he joined the Dramatic Society, where he made his stage debut as a pipe-smoking nightwatchman in *Clipper Ships*, the first of many notable school performances. His academic record,

however, was not as memorable: he acquired only one O level pass in Geography.

In 1953 he won a scholarship to RADA, where his fellow students included Peter O'Toole, Frank Finlay and Alan Bates. After two years he left RADA, and, turning his back on film offers, he joined the Birmingham Rep where he made his stage debut in *Julius Caesar* in 1956. In 1958 he made his West End debut in *The Party*, directed by Charles Laughton, and appeared at Stratford in 1959.

His film debut was in *The Entertainer* (1960), but it was his portrayal of the working-class anti-hero, Arthur Seaton, in *Saturday Night and Sunday Morning* (1960) which launched his film career and made him a star. Shortly afterwards he rejected the title role in David Lean's *Lawrence of Arabia* and the offer of a five year contract from producer Sam Spiegel, arguing that he did not want to become just a 'property'. He played the title role and displayed his skill at comedy in *Tom Jones* (1963), for which he received an AA nomination. A stage actor at heart, Finney chose his film roles carefully, the most memorable of which include *Two For The Road* (1967), *Charlie Bubbles* (1968, also prod. & d.), *Gumshoe* (1971, also prod.), *The Dresser* (1983), *Shoot the Moon* (1982), *Under the Volcano* (1984), *Miller's Crossing* (1990) and *The Browning Version* (1994). In 1965 he founded Memorial Enterprises Productions with Michael Medwin, whose productions have

Albert Finney as the bingo-caller turned sleuth, Eddie Ginley, in **Gumshoe** *(1971, Memorial)*

included Lindsay Anderson's *If* (1968) and *O Lucky Man* (1973). Often criticised, like Burton before him, for lacking direction and wasting his career, Finney still ranks among the greats.

See also: *Saturday Night and Sunday Morning, Tom Jones, If*

Sandwell

BIRTHPLACE OF MADELEINE CARROLL (1906-87)
West Bromwich

Edith Madeleine Carroll, leading lady of the thirties and forties, was born on 26 February 1906 at **32 Herbert Street**, West Bromwich, to a French mother, Helene Tuaillon and John Carroll, a schoolteacher. Her sister, Marguerite, was born nearby at **44 Herbert Street** in 1907 (both 32 & 44 are still standing). About 1911 they moved a short distance to a more upmarket address at **7 Jesson Street**. The family lived there until John Carroll retired after thirty five years at **Lodge Road Schools** in 1937. Madeleine and Marguerite attended the school where their father taught French and both were fluent speakers. Part of the school still exists as part of **West Bromwich College, Lodge Road**, near the junction with the High Street.

During her schooldays Madeleine was a regular user of the **Carnegie Library** on the **High Street** and in the foyer of the library her sister Marguerite's name appears on the War Dead Role of Honour: during WWII she had worked for British Intelligence and was captured and murdered by the Gestapo.

Madeleine attended Birmingham University from 1923 during which time, while taking a degree in French, she revealed her acting talents in a student production of *Salma*. After graduating in 1926 she briefly became a French mistress at a school in Hove, but decided to pursue a career on the stage.

They actually spent all day handcuffed together as Hitchcock wanted them to get acquainted and disappeared with the key! Her other films include: *The General Died at Dawn* (1936), *The Secret Agent* (1936) *The Prisoner of Zenda* (1937), *Northwest Mounted Police* (1940), *My Favourite Blonde* (1942) and her last film, Otto Preminger's *The Fan* (1949).

In the early thirties Madeleine Carroll departed for Hollywood and during WWII she worked for the Red Cross and was decorated by the French and American governments for her efforts. She had four failed marriages, one of which was to actor Sterling Hayden. Following her final divorce in 1965 she lived quietly in France then later Spain, where after the death of her only daughter she ended her days as a recluse. She died in 1987, aged eighty-one and is buried in Marbella, Spain.

See also: Alfred Hitchcock, Robert Donat, Gainsborough Studios, Forth Bridge

Further information: Nearly all publications give her name as Marie Madeleine Bernadette O'Carroll. A new copy of her birth certificate, however, reveals that her name was in fact Edith Madeleine Carroll. *

*32 Herbert Street - birthplace of **Madeleine Carroll***

Her first prominent role was in the 1927 west end play, *Mr. What's His Name* and she made her screen debut the same year in *The Guns of Loos*, a silent film about WWI munitions shortages. In 1932 she became the highest paid female star in Britain when she accepted £12,000 a year to make three pictures over two years.

In 1935 she starred in the film for which she will be best remembered: Alfred Hitchcock's *The Thirty-nine Steps*. The scenes in which she is handcuffed to fugitive Richard Hannay (Robert Donat) are among the most enduring images of the British cinema.

Sefton

BIRTHPLACE OF ANTHONY QUAYLE (1913-)
Ainsdale

Anthony Quayle was born on 7 September 1913 in a bungalow at **2 Delamere Road, Ainsdale**, the only child of Esther Overton and Arthur Quayle, a magistrate's clerk. In 1915, to be closer to the father's place of work at the courts, the Quayle family moved to **5 York Road, Birkdale, Southport**.

He was educated at Rugby but didn't follow its trodden path in Law, the Army, the Church and the Indian Civil Service. Instead he joined RADA and later got his first taste of showbusiness touring the music halls as a feed to comedian, Naylor Grimson (*The*

Meanest Man On Earth). He joined the Old Vic when he was nineteen and devoted his life to the theatre, becoming an actor, director and manager; much of his work was with the Royal Shakespeare Company.

Although primarily a stage actor he did make several films. One of his earliest appearances was in Powell & Pressburger's, *Battle of the River Plate* (1956) but he will be chiefly remembered as the German spy in *Ice Cold in Alex* (1958), the Greek patriot, Colonel Stavros in *The Guns of Navarone* 1961) and Col. Harry Brighton in *Lawrence of Arabia* (1962).

BIRTHPLACE OF G.B. SAMUELSON (1889-1947)
Southport

"My father, G.B. Samuelson, was one of the earliest pioneers of the British film industry. He was born in Southport, Lancashire, and it was there that he set up a cinema show in a local hall. He acquired a projector and purchased a programme of films - a drama, a comedy and sundry other items. Once he had rented it enough times for there to be no further interest on the part of the people of Southport, he purchased a new programme. This went on several times until, eventually, he came up with a revolutionary idea. Instead of selling the films that were no longer of interest (usually to the operator of a kinema show in a smaller town) he decided to

*41 Nevill Street, Southport - birthplace of **G.B. Samuelson***

rent programmes, a week at a time, to all the 'cinemas' he could identify in the Lancashire area. The great benefit of this system was that operators, including himself, could offer patrons a different programme every week, and the bonus was that my father employed a local person - with a rewinder and film joining fluid - to inspect each film between it being returned from one exhibitor and rented to another. The business was such a success it was soon decided to move to the geographical centre of our nation in order to expand the customer catchment area. So, in 1912, premises were taken in Corporation Street, Birmingham and it was from here that the business underwent a further period of expansion.

The next G.B. Samuelson career move was to make films for himself and the first one, A Study in Scarlet, based on Sir Arthur Conan Doyle's famous Sherlock Holmes yarn, was shot in 1914 on **Southport Sands**. One sequence in the story concerned the Mormon trek to Utah and this was brilliantly reproduced on the coast not far from Southport itself. Sadly, not one copy of this landmark British film has survived.

As part of the Centenary of Cinema, on April 24th 1996, a plaque in honour of my father's great contribution to our industry was unveiled at the shop (now an amusement arcade) above which he was born in **Nevill Street, Southport.** My grandmother was my father's partner in his earliest days, they were the first two generations in British cinema, and three further generations have been, or are, involved in the

industry, making a total of five Samuelson generations spanning 88 years. We believe this might be a record for continuous involvement in British film production and exhibition."
Sir Sydney Samuelson.

Sheffield

THE FULL MONTY

• 1997 90m c Comedy
Redwave Films / Fox Searchlight (UK)
• Robert Carlyle (Gaz), Tom Wilkinson (Gerald), Mark Addy (Dave), Paul Barber (Horse), Steve Huison (Lomper), Hugo Speer (Guy), Emily Woof (Mandy), Leslie Sharp (Jean), William Snape (Nathan), Deirdre Costello (Linda)
• p, Uberto Pasolini; d, Peter Cattaneo; w, Simon Beaufoy; ph, John de Borman; ed, Nick Moore, David Freeman; m, Anne Dudley; prod d, Max Gottlieb; art d, Chris Roope; fx, Ian Rowley; cos, Jill Taylor
• AA Best Original Musical or Comedy Score: Anne Dudley

"The Full Monty does not merely use Sheffield as a stage set. The city's depression, grime, jokes and despair are the film's essence."
Simon Jenkins, London Evening Standard

"He [Simon Jenkins] has taken a film which paints a caricature of life in

Sheffield and tried to make a link with real life... It is patronising to describe people in Sheffield as laughing their way through desperation."
Richard Allan MP

The Full Monty may have put Sheffield on the world tourist map, but not everyone was happy about its depiction of the town. The film, about six unemployed steelworkers who become male strippers, was accused of portraying the North as a world of pigeon fanciers and pea suppers as depicted in films such as *Room at the Top* and *This Sporting Life*.

The Sheffield Telegraph commented: *" If it had been a film about unemployed women, critics would have been quick to point out the degradation of stripping to earn money. The Full Monty is, on the face of it, a good-humoured little film about triumph in adversity and the hilarity of role-reversal. But it's a glib fantasy. The sadness for Sheffield is that it's set in an all-too-credible reality."*

Whatever your views on it are, this unassuming film, made for only £2.2 million, became one of the most successful British films of all time, taking over £20 million at the British box office alone. 'Montyland' is even reputed to be side-tracking Japanese travellers from their traditional tourist haunts in their quest to track down the locations of *Za Furu Monchi*.

*Shiregreen Working Men's Club - scene of the final strip in **The Full Monty***

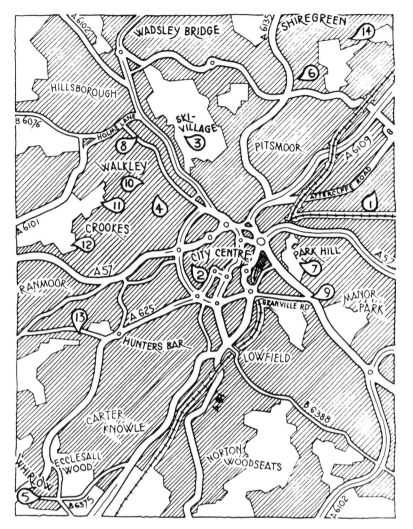

buys up all the newspapers revealing the strippers' identities), **The Blake Pub, Blake Street, Walkley** (where they converse about stripping), **Ruskin Park** (where they attempt to cheer up Gerald after his failed job interview), **Crookes Cemetery** (site of the burial scene for Lomper's mum), **66 Peveril Road** (home of Lomper's mum) and **Shiregreen Working Men's Club** (where the final strip scenes were filmed).

BIRTHPLACE OF MICHAEL PALIN (1943-)
Sheffield

"It flares up, very intensely and brilliantly for a very short period. If it lasted any longer, it would never have been as brilliant in the first place."
Michael Palin on *Monty Python*

Actor, writer and globetrotter, Michael Edward Palin was born on 5 May 1943 at **26 Whitworth Road** in the middle class suburb of **Ranmoor**, Sheffield, the second child of Mary and Ted Palin, manager of a local toilet paper factory. He was educated at **Birkdale**, a local prep school, and **Shrewsbury** public school. On leaving school he obtained a temporary job in the publicity department of **Edgar Allen & Co.**, a local steelworks where his father then worked as an export manager. Around this time he joined a local amateur theatre group called the Brightside and Carbrook Players.

In 1962 he was accepted for Brasenose College, Oxford. His parents wanted him to pursue a career in advertising, but university awakened in him a desire to write and act. While at Brasenose he immersed himself in college drama societies and began writing comedy and appearing on the Oxford cabaret circuit. In his second year he met and became friendly with fellow student and future Python, Terry Jones.

He left university in 1965 with a second class degree and the following year he married Helen Gibbins, a farmer's daughter from Cambridgeshire with whom he lived at Gospel Oak, North London.

(Left to right) William Snape, Mark Addy, Robert Carlyle, Steve Huison, and Tom Wilkinson. (photo Tom Hilton)

Locations include **1: Bacon Lane, off Effingham Road** (where Colin, Gaz and Nathan are trying to cross the canal using a car and a plank of wood as a bridge), **2: West Street Job Centre** (where they played cards and teased Gerald about his job-searching), **3: Sheffield Ski Village** (not in the film, but the side road which was the location for Lomper's failed suicide attempt is opposite it), **4: Burton Street School** (Gerald had his job interview here when the garden gnome went past the window. Gaz collected Nathan from school here and played football outside), **5: Whirlow Park Road, Whirlow** (Gerald's house and scene of their early practise strips), **6: Old Roxy Cinema, Page Hall** (used for the working men's club exteriors), **7: Sky Edge Playing Fields, Sky Edge Road** (location of the fitness training scenes), **8: Langsett Road filling station** (where Nathan tries to talk his dad out of doing the strip), **9: Corner of Granville Road and City Road** (site of the newspaper shop where Gerald

*Michael Palin as **The Missionary** (1982, photo David Farrell)*

*Brian Aherne portraying King Arthur in **Lancelot and Guinevere** (1962, Emblem)*

His first job was presenting an ITV pop programme called, *NOW!*, which sank without trace after a few months. An application to the BBC for a traineeship was turned down, but he soon began writing gags with Terry Jones who by this time was working for the BBC. David Frost spotted them doing cabaret and recruited them for a new BBC series called *The Frost Report* which began in March 1966. Other writers for the series included John Cleese, Graham Chapman and Eric Idle.

The Frost Report led to *Do Not Adjust Your Set*, and eventually to the birth of *Monty Python's Flying Circus* on 5 October 1969. The series, which consisted of 45 episodes over four years, and which Palin originally wanted to call *Gwen Dibley's Flying Circus*, became a launch pad for his career.

His TV work has included *Ripping Yarns* (1976-80), *G.B.H.* (1991) and the globe trotting documentaries *Around the World in 80 Days* (1989) and *Pole to Pole* (1992). Other films include *Monty Python and the Holy Grail* (1975), *Life of Brian* (1979), *A Private Function* (1984), *A Fish Called Wanda* (1988), *American Friends* (1991) and *Fierce Creatures* (1996).

See also: *Monty Python and the Holy Grail, A Private Function*

Somerset

GRAVE OF KING ARTHUR
Glastonbury

Myth or fact, Arthur, legendary sixth-century king of Britain is one of cinema's most enduring heroes who over the years has been portrayed by many, including Arthur Askey (*King Arthur Was a Gentleman*, 1942); Cedric Hardwicke (*A Connecticut Yankee in King Arthur's Court*, 1949); Mel Ferrer (*Knights of the Round Table*, 1953); Graham Chapman (*Monty Python and the Holy Grail*, 1975); Nigel Terry (*Excalibur*, 1981) and Ed Harris (*Knightriders*, 1981).

History, romantic literature, poetry and movies have all embellished the Arthurian legend, most of which was simply invented. The historian's most trustworthy source is Nenniu's *Historia Britonum*, written in the eighth century, but after that, much of his bibliography is suspect. The legendary birthplace of Arthur is at Tintagel Castle, Cornwall, but he is allegedly buried alongside Guinevere at **Glastonbury Abbey**, where 12th century monks reportedly dug up a stone slab inscribed: HIC IACET SEPULTUS INCLITUS REX ARTURIUS IN INSULA AVALON (Here lies buried

the renowned King Arthur in the Isle of Avalon), although many chroniclers claim he never died, but lies sleeping with his knights beneath the earth awaiting resurrection at various sites around Britain.

See also: Merlin

THE TITFIELD THUNDERBOLT
Monkton Combe

• 1953 84m c Comedy Ealing Studios (UK)
• Stanley Holloway (Valentine), George Relph (Rev. Weech), Naunton Wayne (Blakeworth), John Gregson (Gordon), Godfrey Tearle (The Bishop), Hugh Griffith (Dan), Gabrielle Brune (Joan), Sidney James (Hawkins), Reginald Beckwith (Coggett)
• P, Michael Truman; D, Charles Crichton; w, T.E.B. Clarke; ed, Seth Holt; ph, Douglas Slocombe; m, Georges Auric; art d, C.P. Norman

Not one of the great Ealing comedies but still memorable, especially for railway enthusiasts. This was the first Ealing comedy in Technicolour, written by studio stalwart, 'Tibby' Clarke (*Hue and Cry, Passport to Pimlico, The Lavender Hill Mob*) about a small community, battling against officialdom for the survival of their local railway line, who decide to run it themselves. The local bus company, which of course stands to profit by its closure, does all it can to sabotage the villagers' plans. When the regular engine is wrecked by the bus company the villagers 'borrow' a relic from the local museum to keep the line operational.

Location filming took six weeks on the Limpley Stoke-Camerton goods branch line of the Great Western Railway. Monkton Combe doubled for Titfield Station but has long been buried under the playing fields of Monkton Combe School. **Brassknocker Hill**, which the locals hurried down towards the station is still intact and the viaduct over which the express steams over the local train in the film, still stands nearby at **Midford**.

This engine was a genuine 1838 locomotive called Lion, loaned by Liverpool Museum and still in full working order. Re-named 'Titfield Thunderbolt', it successfully hauls the

*Stanley Holloway in **The Titfield Thunderbolt** (1953, Ealing)*

train on schedule to Mallingford Station (**Bristol Temple Meads**) and saves the line from closure.

One of the reasons for the film's failure to achieve the greatness of the classic Ealing comedies is perhaps explained by Hugh Sampson in *Picturegoer* : *'Odd point about this railway location: not a single railway enthusiast to be found in the whole crew. T.E.B. 'Tibby' Clarke, writer of the script, loathes trains. Producer Michael Truman can't get out of them quick enough. And director Crichton - well, you won't find him taking engine numbers at Paddington Station.' *

See also: Stanley Holloway, The Lion, Ealing Studios

CLASSIC LOCATION: WEST SOMERSET RAILWAY
Minehead

Recreating the era of a Great Western Railway country branch line, the West Somerset Railway runs from Bishops Lydeard (near Taunton) past the Quantock Hills northwards to the Bristol Channel coast at Minehead. The WSR has been in operation since 1976 and the line is now 20 miles in length passing through ten restored stations.

Location filming here has included scenes from the Beatles movie, *A Hard Day's Night* (1964) which was filmed in and around **Crowcombe Heathfield Station** when B.R. operated the line. *The Belstone Fox* (1973) with Eric Porter and Rachel Roberts, and *Land Girls* (1998), which involved Crowcombe Heathfield station being dressed in WWII guise, was also shot on the line.

Further information: West Somerset Railway, The Station, Minehead, ,Somerset, TA24 5BG. Tel: 01643 704996. Talking timetable (24hrs): 01643 707650.

TOM JONES
Williton

- 1963 131m c Comedy Woodfall (UK)
- Albert Finney (Tom Jones), Susannah York (Sophie Western), Hugh Griffith (Squire Western), Edith Evans (Miss Western), Joan Greenwood (Lady Bellaston), Diane Cilento (Molly Seagrim), George Devine (Squire Allworthy), David Tomlinson (Lord Fellamar), Joyce Redman (Mrs Waters / Jenny Jones), George A. Cooper (Fitzpatrick), Wilfred Lawson (Black George)
- p, Tony Richardson; d, Tony Richardson; w, John Osborne (based on the novel by Henry Fielding); ph, Walter Lassally; ed, Anthony Gibbs; m, John Addison; prod d, Ralph Brinton; art d, Ted Marshall; cos, John McCorry
- AA Best Picture; AA Best Director: Tony Richardson; AA Best Adapted Screenplay: John Osborne; AA Best Score: John Addison

"Tom Jones won prizes and finally Oscars. I didn't go to the awards - not to strike an attitude but because I had never understood their importance in the eyes of the industry and they were never important to me."
Tony Richardson

Tony Richardson's 1963 version of Henry Fielding's 1749 comic picaresque novel owed much of its phenomenal success to swinging sixties culture which embraced its colourful characters and their bawdy cheek. Albert Finney, who was initially reluctant to take on the role, gave one of his greatest performances in the title role.

The primary location was **Nettlecombe Court**, a seventeenth-century manor house near the village of Williton. Various interior and exterior sets were built here, including the great hall and

*Albert Finney and Susannah York in **Tom Jones** (1963, Woodfall)*

bedroom No. 23. A girls' school at the time of shooting, Nettlecombe's then eccentric owner imagined he was a bird and lived in a tree. Once a day he would descend to feed off the crumbs left for him by his butler. His eccentric artist son lived in the derelict stables. The film's cast also had its share of eccentrics, including Wilfred Lawson, who portrayed Black George, the gamekeeper. Usually blind drunk, his antics during filming included crashing his Rolls into a ditch, passing out drunk amid a flock of sheep and firing a shotgun through the roof of Tony Richardson's Thunderbird car.
Other locations included **Cranborne Manor House, Cranborne, Dorset; Castle Street in Bridgewater, Somerset** and **Exmoor.**

See also: Albert Finney

Further information: Nettlecombe is now an environmental education centre, but is open to the public all year, except Christmas, when it is closed for two weeks.
Nettlecombe Court, Williton, near Taunton. Tel: 01984 640320.

BIRTHPLACE OF ARTHUR C. CLARKE (1917-)
Minehead

"Arthur somehow manages to capture the hopeless but admirable human desire to know things that can really never be known."
Stanley Kubrick

Twentieth century visionary and bestselling science fiction writer, Arthur

*One of the startling special effect sequences from **2001: A Space Odyssey** (1968/Hawk/MGM)*

*4 Blenheim Road (now no. 13), Minehead, - birthplace of **Arthur C. Clarke***

Charles Clarke, achieved global fame in 1968 following the release of the classic sci-fi film *2001: A Space Odyssey*. A respected scientist, his research has since played a major part in the development of satellite technology and global communications.

He was born at his grandmother's house at **4 Blenheim Road**, Minehead (later **runumbered 13** due to a road extension; plaque erected) to Mary Nora Willis and Charles Clarke on 16 December 1917, the eldest of four children. He attended nursery in nearby **Irnham Road** and went to **Llanberis School in Blenheim Road**. His parents had both worked for the post

office, but after WW1 his father decided to take up farming. After a disastrous start they settled down to a smallholding at **Ballifants, near Bishops Lydeard**, Somerset, in 1924. Arthur and his brother Fred still lived at Blenheim Road at weekends and during school holidays.

It was at the house of his friend, Larry Kille, who lived in the same road, that Arthur read his first science fiction magazine, the November 1928 issue of *Amazing Stories*. Throughout his childhood Arthur was fascinated by astronomy and built telescopes, rockets and communication equipment using anything he could lay his hands on, from Meccano to bicycle bits.

He attended **elementary school in Bishop Lydeard** and later secondary school at **Huish Grammar School in Taunton** where his lunchtime consisted of searching out sci-fi magazines in Woolworths. When he was twelve he came across a book in Minehead Library which would inspire and influence his adult writing: W. Olaf Stapledon's *Last and First Men*. He later recalled: *"No book before or since ever had such an impact on my imagination."* *

A committed 'space cadet', Arthur left school in 1936 and took up a civil service post in London auditing accounts for the Board of Education in **King Charles Street**, near Downing Street, where he resided in a flat at **88 Gray's Inn Road**. He volunteered for the RAF during WWII and in 1946

enrolled at King's College where he gained a degree in physics and maths.

He was twenty-nine years old when he wrote his first book, *Prelude to Space* (1951), written in twenty days in 1947, and has followed it over the years with some of the greatest stories of the genre, including: *The Star, Childhood's End, The City and the Stars, Rendezvous with Rama* and *The Fountains of Paradise*.

Kubrick's remark when someone suggested he should work with Arthur on his new movie project was, *"But I understand he's a recluse, a nut who lives in a tree in India some place."* * Arthur climbed down from his tree and first met Kubrick on 22 April 1964 at Trader Vic's in the Plaza Hotel, New York, where they discussed making a movie about Man's relation to the universe. Both the novel and the screenplay were later written simultaneously and the title, *2001: A Space Odyssey*, was Kubrick's idea.

Filmed at Shepperton, the most expensive set was the centrifuge, which weighed forty tons and took six months to build at a cost of $300,000. The black monolith was a three-ton block of black painted lucite which could only be moved by crane. The film's lack of dialogue and mysterious imagery confused many audiences, but as Stanley Kubrick explained: *"I don't like to talk about 2001 much, because it's essentially a non-verbal experience. It attempts to communicate more to the subconscious and to feelings than it does to the intellect."* * Arthur C. Clarke emigrated to Sri Lanka in the fifties, where he still lives and writes.

See also: Stanley Kubrick

Staffordshire

THE PICTURE HOUSE PUB
Stafford

The Picture House Cinema opened on 23 February 1914 with a screening of *The House of Temperley*, where its 'Old

English' facade, ornamental verandah and tasteful interiors made it Stafford's first 'modern' cinema.

It began its new life as a pub in 1997 after a £1.5 million restoration. A listed building, it still retains much of its previous decor. The frontage is still intact and the original ticket kiosk can be seen, complete with a dummy which bears an amazing resemblance to Leslie Howard. The old screen is situated behind the bar and the entire auditorium is dominated by the cinema's magnificently decorative ceiling. Cinema stills, star portraits and movie posters decorate the walls. The Picture House is highly recommended. All movie fans should pilgrimage here.

Further information: The Picture House, 20 Bridge Street, Stafford. Tel: 01785 222941.

THE PLAZA PUB
Rugeley

The Plaza Pub was previously the Plaza cinema which closed its doors in 1997. Pictures of the old cinema are displayed on the walls and the frontage remains unchanged.

Further information: The Plaza, Horsefair, Rugeley. Tel: 0188 9586831.

Stockport

BIRTHPLACE OF SIDNEY GILLIAT (1908-94)

Sidney Gilliat will be best remembered for his partnership with scriptwriter

Frank Launder which produced a string of box office successes, including, *The Lady Vanishes* (1938), *Night Train To Munich* (1940), *Millions Like Us* (1943), *Green For Danger* (1946), and *The Belles of St. Trinians* (1954).

He was born at **Carmichael Street, Edgeley**, Stockport, on 15 February 1908, the son of a Manchester journalist who became editor of the London Evening Standard. Educated in London, Sidney went on to read English and History at university, and afterwards briefly joined the Evening Standard.

In 1927 the Standard's film critic, Walter Mycroft, became 'scenario chief' at British International Pictures and persuaded Sidney to become an assistant composing dialogue intertitles for silent films. He progressed to 'gag' writer for slapstick comedies and by the early thirties he had begun writing film scripts. Together with Frank Launder he later ran the production and distribution company, British Lion, ultimately becoming chairman of Shepperton Studios.

He died of leukaemia at his home in Pewsey Vale, Wiltshire, on 31 May, 1994.

See also: St. Trinians, Gainsborough Studios, Jamaica Inn

ELVIS'S PALACE

Not strictly a destination for the movie fan, but as this Chinese restaurant is a shrine to Elvis, who made many movies, it deserves a listing.

It is run by Michael and James Wong who entertain their guests with Elvis impersonations while serving up dishes which include "Love Me Tender Fillet Steak Cantonese Style", "King Creole Prawn Cracker" and "Blue Suede Spring Rolls".

Elvis cabarets take place on Friday and Saturday evenings.

Further information: Elvis's Palace, 116 London Road, Hazelgrove, Stockport. Tel: 0161 4199831.

Stockton-on-Tees

BIRTHPLACE OF WILL HAY (1888-1949)
Stockton-on-Tees

William Thomson Hay was born on 6 December 1888, in a two-up and two-down terraced house at **23 Durham Street** (since demolished, now site of Wellington St. car park) to Elizabeth Ebden, a fish merchant's daughter, and William Robert Hay, an engine fitter and inventor. Durham Street was only one of the family's many short-lived homes around the country, the length of time they spent in one place being dependent on the demand for William's work. They finally ended up in Manchester where William started his own engineering business.

Will Hay junior was the third of six children, a bright child with a photographic memory who became an engineering apprentice at the age of fifteen. Three years later he married sixteen year old Gladys Perkins and was by now becoming popular as an amateur stand-up comedian at local concerts.

He eventually turned professional when The Empire, Hull, offered him thirty-five shillings a week. Unable to

Wellington Street Car Park, Stockton-on-Tees - site of Will Hay's birthplace

join up during WWI because of haemorrhoids, he joined Fred Karno's Army and toured the music-halls.

He launched his film career in 1934 with the now virtually forgotten *Those Were The Days*, but it was American director, William Beaudine, who first teamed him with Graham Moffatt and Moore Marriott in *Windbag The Sailor* (1936). The inspired casting of these three produced some of cinema's great comedy classics, including: *Oh, Mr. Porter!* (1937), *Convict 99* (1938) and *Ask a Policeman* (1939).

In his private life Will Hay was erudite and reclusive. A member of BBC's Brain Trust, he had a scientific mind and was a noted astronomer. In 1933 he made national headlines when he discovered a white spot on Saturn. He died from a stroke at his Chelsea Embankment flat on Easter Sunday, 1949, aged sixty-one.

See also: Will Hay (Merton), Fred Karno, *Oh, Mr. Porter!*

Suffolk

GRAVE OF HAMMOND INNES (1913-98)
Kersey

Adventure writer and compulsive traveller, Ralph Hammond Innes was born in Horsham, Sussex. Leaving school at the age of eighteen he worked in publishing, teaching and in 1934 he became a journalist on the *Financial News*. He wrote his first

thriller in 1936 and later established a reputation for personally experiencing the backgrounds for his books. For *Maddon's Rock* (1948) he sailed in the Fastnet Race; for *Air Bridge* (1951) he flew with the RAF into blockaded Berlin, and for *The Angry Mountain* (1950) he was in San Sebastiano when Vesuvius erupted.

In 1954 *The White South* was adapted for the screen as *Hell Below Zero*, with Alan Ladd and Stanley Baker. His great love of the ocean resulted in one of his most popular stories, *The Wreck of the Mary Deare*, which was filmed in 1959, starring Gary Cooper.

With his ex-actress wife, Dorothy Laing, he cruised the coasts of Europe and Asia Minor for fifteen years searching for inspiration for his stories - six months travelling, six months writing - in his 42ft yacht, *Mary Deare*. He died at his home in Kersey on 10 June 1998 and is buried in **St. Mary's Churchyard.**

FILMS ON ART
Ipswich

The largest collection of documentaries on the arts in Great Britain is held by the Arts Council. Their film and video collection, which was established in 1981 and embodies twenty years of Arts Council commitment to arts programmes includes: British Art, European Art, American Art, Art & Society, Performance & Video Art, Artist's Film & Video, Photography, Architecture, Music, Dance, Poetry & Literature and Cultural Diversity.

Further information: Concord Video & Film Council Ltd., 201 Felixstowe Road, Ipswich, Suffolk, IP3 9BJ. Tel: 01473 726012

BIRTHPLACE OF HUMPHREY JENNINGS (1907-50)
Walberswick

" The only real poet the British cinema has yet produced."
Lindsay Anderson

Humphrey Jennings, who made many outstanding documentary films about

Britain's struggle on the Home Front during WWII, was born on 19 August 1907, at **The Gazebo**, Walberswick, near Southwold. In 1916 he started at Perse School, Cambridge. In 1926 he won a scholarship to Pembroke College, Cambridge, where he became involved in amateur dramatics and set design.

He joined the GPO Film Unit in 1934 and worked under Alberto Cavalcanti, directing films which demonstrated Britain's ability to stand alone after Dunkirk and during the Blitz, including *Spring Offensive* (1940), *Welfare of the Workers* (1940) and *London Can Take It* (1940). His other work includes: *Words for Battle* (1941), *Listen to Britain* (1941) and *Fires Were Started* (1942) about the recently formed National Fire Service.

After the war his work was less prolific and Lindsay Anderson commented that his *"traditionalist spirit was unable to adjust itself to the changed circumstances of Britain after the war."* Jennings died in a fall location hunting in the Greek Islands in 1950.

See also: John Grierson

GRAVE OF EMERIC PRESSBURGER (1902-88)
Aspall

Born in Miskolc, Hungary, he began his career as a journalist and scriptwriter in France and Germany, where he became one of the highest paid screenwriters at the UFA company at Neuebabelsberg Studios in Berlin. Escaping Nazi Germany he arrived in England in 1936.
He began working with director Michael Powell in 1939 when they made the WWI thriller, *The Spy in Black*. In 1942 they formed the Archers production company and collaborated on fourteen films between 1942 and 1957, including *The Life and Death of Colonel Blimp* (1943), *I Know Where I'm Going* (1945), *A Matter of Life and Death* (1946), *Black Narcissus* (1946) and *The Red Shoes* (1948). Following the demise of the Archers, he made *Twice Upon a Time* (1952, which he also produced and directed), *Operation Crossbow* (1965, as Richard Imrie) and

The Boy Who Turned Yellow (1972, his last collaboration with Michael Powell)

He spent the last twenty years of his life at **Shoemaker's Cottage**, Aspall, and died on 5 February 1988. He is buried in the village churchyard of **St. Mary of Grace** where lines from Sir Walter Scott are engraved upon his tombstone: *"Love rules the court, the camp, the grove, And men below, and saints above, For love is heaven, and heaven is love."*

See also: Michael Powell

Surrey

WAR OF THE WORLDS SCULPTURE
Woking

In Crown Passage, near Woking town centre, stands the Borough's largest sculpture. Commissioned by Woking Borough Council and created by talented young sculptor Michael Condron, "The Martian" rises over seven metres above the townscape and has been made from chrome electropolished steel. It is situated on the aliens' route through Woking, following their landing on nearby **Horsell Common**, as described in H.G. Wells' *The War Of The Worlds*, the 1898 novel he wrote while living in the town. The surrounding area makes up part of the work of art and features planters containing "red Martian weed", an alien pod ploughing into the ground, UFO style lighting and metal designs in the ground representing the bacteria that defeated the aliens. Paramount's 1953 screen adaptation of the novel, starring Gene Barry and directed by Byron Haskin, probably foresaw a special-effects nightmare in

trying to reproduce Wells' stilted Martians and opted for a simpler hovering saucer instead. The film was updated to 1950s California and won an Oscar for its visual effects.

See also: H.G. Wells.

CARRY ON SERGEANT
Stoughton

- 1959 88m Comedy (UK)
- William Hartnell, Bob Monkhouse, Shirley Eaton, Eric Barker, Dora Bryan, Bill Owen, Kenneth Williams, Kenneth Connor, Charles Hawtrey
- p, Peter Rogers; d, Gerald Thomas

Celluloid equivalent of the saucy seaside postcard, the *Carry On* series has been one of Pinewood Studios' great success stories, where its predictable cycle of tits, bums, sexual innuendo and corny jokes spawned one of cinema's longest-running series. The first, and probably the least bawdy, was *Carry On Sergeant.*

The army locations were shot in April, 1958 at the **Queen's Barracks, Grange Rd., Stoughton, near Guildford.** The barracks are now empty, with a future housing development being proposed for the site. Although disused the barracks are still owned by the military and are not open to the public.

The Carry On team had no qualms about using the same location again and again in different films. The corner

of **Sheet Street** and **Park Street, Windsor**, was the site of 'The Helping Hands Agency' in *Carry On Regardless;* it was also 'The Wedded Bliss Agency' in *Carry On Loving* and also appears in *Carry On Again Doctor.* **Maidenhead Town Hall** doubled as the hospital in *Carry On Doctor* and *Carry On Again Doctor* and also appeared in *Carry On Behind.* Because of their close proximity to Pinewood, **Black Park** and **Burnham Beeches** in **Buckinghamshire** were used in numerous films. Other locations have included **Camber Sands, East Sussex**, which doubled for the Sahara in *Carry On Follow that Camel* and **Heathfield Hospital, Ascot**, used in *Carry On Matron.*

See also: Kenneth Williams, Black Park, Burnham Beeches, Frensham Common

ASHES OF BORIS KARLOFF (1887-1969)
Guildford

"I dislike the word 'horror' yet it is a word that has been tagged to me all my life... My films even prompted the British censor to introduce a certificate in the early thirties known as 'H'... for horror."

Born William Henry Pratt on 23 November 1887, at **36 Forest Hill Road, East Dulwich** (plaque erected), the youngest of nine children of Eliza Millard and Edward Pratt, a civil servant in the Foreign Service. In his youth he abandoned a prospective vocation in the Consular Service and left for Canada to pursue a career on the stage. He worked in repertory across Canada and when acting jobs were difficult to find he worked on farms, circuses and travelling fairgrounds.

When he was twenty-four he adopted his old family name of Karloff and called himself Boris. In 1917 he started a tour in Chicago with the play, *The Virginian*, which ended in Hollywood where he found work as an extra. He wallowed in obscure roles for many years, making over 40 silent films, until director James Whale, after observing the exceptional shape of his head, cast him as the monster in *Frankenstein* (1931). The role, which was turned

Boris Karloff in Curse of the Crimson Altar (1968, Tigon/AIP)

*Ashes of **Boris Karloff** - The Garden of Remembrance, Mount Cemetery, Guildford*

down by Bela Lugosi, projected him to stardom and created one of the most famous icons of the cinema. Frankenstein's monster was to indelibly typecast him in the roles of demented monsters and unhinged scientists for the remainder of his career, appearing in films such as *The Mummy* (1932), *The Ghoul* (1933) and *The Body Snatcher* (1945).

He was married three times and his ashes are buried in the **Garden of Remembrance, Mount Cemetery, Wayside Road, Guildford.** Tel: 01483 561927.

See also: James Whale, Mary Shelley, Earl of Carnarvon, The Tudor Cinema

BIRTHPLACE OF CELIA JOHNSON (1908-82)
Richmond

Celia Johnson was born on 18 December 1908, at **3 Ellerker Gate** (since renumbered and renamed 46 Richmond Hill), the family home and surgery of her father, Robert Johnson M.D. The second of three children, one of her earliest performances was with her sister Pamela when they staged *King Cophetula and the Beggar Maid* for friends and successfully raised 22s 6d for the Red Cross during WWI. In the early twenties her father moved his surgery and family to nearby **Marshgate House** in **Sheen Road.** She was educated by a private tutor until she was eleven when she attended St. Paul's School in Hammersmith where her acting potential began to be recognised.

See also: Celia Johnson (Oxfordshire), *Brief Encounter*, Christina Kay

CLASSIC LOCATION: FRENSHAM COMMON

The lowland heath and ponds of Frensham Common, near Farnham, has provided a convenient location for nearby film studios for many years. It doubled for Dartmoor in Hammer's 1958 production of *The Hound of the Baskervilles*, starring Christopher Lee and Peter Cushing. The 'Moor' location shots were filmed on the ridge above Great Frensham Pond, on the eastern side of the A287 between Farnham and Hindhead, just a few miles from Conan Doyle's home in 1902, where he completed the writing of *The Hound of the Baskervilles* (1902). Other films shot here include *The Wicked Lady* (1945) with Margaret Lockwood and James Mason, *The Lady with a Lamp* (1951) with Anna Neagle and Michael Wilding, *The Last Valley* (1970) with Michael Caine and Omar Sharif, and numerous *Carry On* films.

See also: *Hound of the Baskervilles, Carry On Sergeant*

Further information: Frensham Common Rangers Office 01252 792416/792483.

GRAVE OF ANTHONY HOPE (1863-1933)
Leatherhead

*Deborah Kerr and Stewart Granger in **The Prisoner of Zenda** (1952, MGM)*

Anthony Hope was the pen-name of Sir Anthony Hope Hawkins, who, in 1894 created the mythical kingdom of Ruritania in his romantic adventure novel, *The Prisoner of Zenda*. It has since been adapted for the screen four times, but the most memorable version was directed by John Cromwell in 1937, with outstanding performances from Ronald Coleman, Madeleine Carroll, Douglas Fairbanks, Jnr., David Niven and C. Aubrey Smith.

Anthony Hope, who was the cousin of Kenneth Grahame, was educated at Marlborough and Baliol College, Oxford, before being called to the bar in 1887. In 1898 he wrote a successor to his 1894 bestseller, *Rupert of Hentzau*. He is buried in the parish churchyard.

THE REGENT PUB
Walton-on-Thames

Previously the Regent Cinema, it was converted to a pub in 1995. The building still has its original frontage and central staircase leading to the balcony. Movie stills and posters decorate the walls together with life-size statues of Laurel and Hardy.

Further information: The Regent, 19 Church Street, Walton-on-Thames. Tel: 01932 243980.

INSTITUTE OF AMATEUR CINEMATOGRAPHERS
Epsom

The IAC Film & Video Library in Epsom is the largest and most comprehensive collection in the world of amateur films dating back to 1932. The IAC is a non-commercial and non profit-making organisation devoted exclusively to amateurs, and films and videos may be hired by individuals or clubs. The IAC International Film & Video Festival is held annually in the spring and an autumn convention is held in a different part of Britain each year, in October / November.

Further information: IAC, 24c West Street, Epsom, Surrey, KT18 7RJ. Tel: 01372 739672. email: iacfilmvideo@compuserve.com

GRAVE OF HENRY MORTON STANLEY (1840-1904)
Pirbright

Spencer Tracy portraying a virtuous Stanley in **Stanley and Livingstone** *(1939, Fox).*

Born in Wales, Stanley made four expeditions to Africa and was sent by the New York Herald to search for Livingstone whom he found at Ujiji in 1871. Spencer Tracy portrayed him as a benign, almost saintly character in Henry King's *Stanley and Livingstone* (1939), when in fact he was denied a burial in Westminster Abbey on the grounds that he was a womaniser who maltreated his African servants. He is buried in St. Michael's churchyard under his own name and his African one, 'Bula Matari'.

See also: Henry Travers, Cedric Hardwicke

THE CORONATION HALL PUB
Surbiton

The Coronation Hall was a cinema from 1911 and opened as a pub themed around cinema in 1997. Supposedly haunted by a former projectionist who committed suicide on the premises, its decor includes movie stills, mock projectors, directors' chairs, etc.

Further information: The Coronation Hall, St. Mark's Hill, Surbiton, Surrey. Tel: 0181 3906164.

BIRTHPLACE OF PETULA CLARK (1932-)
Ewell

Actress and singer, Petula Clark appeared in over thirty films, but will be best remembered for her performances as a child star of the 1940s. Born Sally Clark on 15 November 1932, to Doris Phillips and Leslie Clark, a male nurse, her first home was at **20 Salmon's Road, Ewell**. Her father claimed that her nickname, Petula, was derived from two of his old girlfriends, Pet and Ula.

Her first professional engagement was in the restaurant at Bentalls department store, Kingston, aged eight, singing with its resident band. Film director, Maurice Elvey, spotted her at a concert which led to her film debut in *Medal for the General* (1944).

Her other films included *I Know Where I'm Going* (1945), *London Town* (1946), *Here Come the Huggetts* (1948) and *Vice Versa* (1948). Like many child actors her adult film career failed to make any impact, the most memorable being the 1969 remake of *Goodbye Mr Chips*. Her parallel career as a singer was more successful, particularly in France.

ELMBRIDGE FILM HERITAGE CENTRE
Weybridge

The Elmbridge Film Heritage Centre at Elmbridge Museum has collected material reflecting the work of the film studios at Walton-on-Thames started by Cecil Hepworth in 1900 and of the Esher playwright and screenwriter, R.C. Sherriff (*The Invisible Man, Goodbye Mr Chips, Mrs Miniver, The Dambusters*). They also hold information relating to Clifford Spain, a local cinema manager in the Walton area who filmed local events in the 1930s.

Further information: Elmbridge Museum, Church Street, Weybridge, Surrey, KT13 8DE. Tel: 01932 843573. Website: www.surrey-online.co.uk/elm-mus Closed: Thursday, Sunday and Bank Holidays.

AN AMERICAN WEREWOLF IN LONDON
Ockham

The Black Swan, *Ockham*

No stranger to film crews over the years, **The Black Swan** in Ockham doubled as The Slaughtered Lamb in John Landis' black sci-fi comedy, *An American Werewolf in London* (1981) and provided a threatening haven for two American hikers who are warned by the locals not to stray onto the moors (**Windsor Great Park** and the **Brecon Beacons** in Wales doubled for the Yorkshire Moors) during the full moon. Advice which they of course ignore to their peril.

In real life The Black Swan is a friendly family pub with 28 pumps and 14 real ales, set in four acres of grounds. It also has on offer a function room, camping facilities, children's playground, clay pigeon shooting, paint

balling and quad bikes, with food
served all day until 9.30pm.

See also: *An American Werewolf in
London* (Westminster)

Further information: The Black
Swan, Old Lane, Ockham (off junction
10 / M25). Tel: 01932 862364.

BIRTHPLACE OF LAURENCE OLIVIER (1907-89)
Dorking

*"Acting is a masochistic form of
exhibitionism. It is not quite the
occupation of an adult."*
Laurence Olivier, Time, 3 July 1978

Distinguished stage and screen actor,
Laurence Kerr Olivier, was born on
May 22 1907 at **26 Wathen Road**,
Dorking, the youngest of three children
of Agnes Crookenden and Gerard
Olivier, a former schoolmaster turned
clergyman. His father preached at **St.
Martin's Church, High Street,
Dorking.** In 1910 the family moved to
a new parish in Notting Hill, before
settling in 1912 in Pimlico at **22 Lupus
Street** where his father preached at
nearby **St. Saviour's Church, St.
George's Square.** Here the family
remained for the next six years.

In 1916 his father enrolled him at All
Saints, a Church of England boarding
school near Oxford Circus, where he
made his first appearance on stage as
Brutus in a school performance of
Julius Caesar and later in a celebrated
production of *The Taming of the Shrew*.

In his fourth year at All Saints his
mother died suddenly from a brain
tumour at the age of forty-eight. On her
death bed she pleaded with her son to
become a great actor, contrary to his
father's wishes. When he was fourteen
his father enrolled him at St. Edward's
School in Oxford having given him
strict instructions to forget about acting
and to concentrate on becoming an
Anglican priest. Shortly after his
mother's death his father remarried.
Fortunately, his new stepmother
recognised that Laurence was a natural
actor and persuaded his father to allow
him to pursue a career on the stage.

26 Wathen Road, Dorking - birthplace of
Laurence Olivier

Laurence Olivier as vaudevillian Archie Rice in **The Entertainer** *(1960, Woodfall)*

In 1924 he enrolled at the Central School of Speech Training and Dramatic Art and later joined the Birmingham Repertory Company where he secured his first leading role, in *Harold*, in 1927. His stage career soon blossomed and included many West End successes. In 1930 he married actress, Jill Esmond, and the following year while appearing on Broadway in *Private Lives*, they both made screen tests for Hollywood.

They were signed up by RKO and Olivier made his Hollywood screen debut in 1931 in a romantic adventure movie set in India called *Friends and Lovers*. Unaccustomed to film acting, his performance was a disaster and RKO immediately loaned him out to Fox studios for his second film, Raoul Walsh's *The Yellow Ticket* (1931). His next film for RKO was *Westward Passage* (1932), a box-office failure which convinced the studio there was no future in Olivier as a film actor, deciding never to use him again. Likewise, other studios showed no interest in hiring him and in fact they were more interested in Jill Esmond, whose film career was taking off. Disillusioned with Hollywood he returned to England with his wife in 1932. He was later hired to play opposite Greta Garbo in *Queen Christina* (1933) but was passed over in favour of John Gilbert.

His first notable film was *Wuthering Heights* (1939), the success of which led to romantic roles in *Rebecca* (1940), *Pride and Prejudice* (1940) and *That Hamilton Woman* (1941). After WWII he became more involved with the theatre and directed and starred in the Shakespearian films, *Henry V* (1945), *Hamlet* (1948) and *Richard III* (1955). In his later years he evolved into a character actor with roles such as vaudevillian Archie Rice in *The Entertainer* (1960), the Madhi in *Khartoum* (1966), the detective novelist in *Sleuth* (1972) and the Nazi dentist, Szell in *Marathon Man* (1976).

He was married to his second wife, Vivien Leigh, from 1940 to 1960 and in 1961 he married actress Joan Plowright. He was awarded a knighthood in 1947 and is buried in **Westminster Abbey**.

See also: Vivien Leigh, *Sleuth, Henry v*

HEPWORTH STUDIOS
Walton-on-Thames

"Come if fine."
Letter of engagement to Alma Taylor from Cecil Hepworth

Lambeth-born film pioneer, Cecil Hepworth (1874-1953), set up his studios at **Hurst Grove** (since demolished), Walton in 1899. He became interested in photography through his father, T.C. Hepworth, a magic lanternist lecturer, and in 1897 he wrote one of the first books on the cinema: *Animated Photography; or The ABC of the Cinematograph.*

He worked for the Charles Urban Company before setting up his own studio and company with his cousin Monty Wicks, called Hepwix at Walton. His first films were mostly 50ft films of short news items recording events such as the funeral of Queen Victoria and troops returning from the Boer War. *Alice in Wonderland* (1903) was his first lengthy feature, running to 800ft.

His first major success was *Rescued By Rover* (1905), which starred Hepworth himself, his wife, his baby daughter, Elizabeth, and the family dog, Blair, who portrayed Rover. The production costs were only £7, but more than 400 copies of the original negative had to be made to cope with the demand. The success of *Rover* enabled him to expand his studio and form the Hepworth Picture Players, a stock company of actors which included some of Britain's first film stars, notably Chrissie White, Alma Taylor, Henry Edwards and Ronald Colman.

Over 2,000 silent films were made at the Hepworth Film Studios between 1899 and 1924. Many films were shot on location in and around Walton, where **Hurst Grove, Manor Road** and **Bridge Street** proved particularly suitable settings, and passing villagers were pounced on at random to participate as extras. By the early twenties the post-war growth of the film industry had ended and Hepworth's films were being overshadowed by Hollywood. In 1924 his business folded and the studios were sold off.

Cecil Hepworth

Two of Britain's first film stars. **Chrissie White** and **Henry Edwards,** *principal actors in the Hepworth Players at Walton Studios.*

Film crew at the **Nettlefold Studios**, Walton on Thames c. 1929, with Walter Forde, film director, on the left.

In 1926 the studios were purchased by Arthur Nettlefold and became Nettlefold Studios. Michael Powell shot many quota quickies here, including his first film as director, *Two Crowded Hours* in 1931. Nettlefold closed down in 1961, and the studios were demolished shortly afterwards to make way for **Hepworth Way**, a new road connecting Bridge Street with Church Street. The power block, where the generators were located, was the only building left standing, and is now the **Playhouse Theatre**. A commemorative plaque was unveiled to Hepworth at the Playhouse in 1996.

Hepworth later lectured on the cinema and produced trailers and advertising shorts. He was made Honorary Fellow of the Royal Photographic Society and of the British Kinematograph Society in recognition of his services to the industry during its formative years. He died in Greenford, Middlesex.

See also: Ronald Colman,

Swindon

BIRTHPLACE OF DIANA DORS (1931-84)

"I am going to be a film star, with a swimming pool and a cream telephone." An excerpt from Diana Fluck's school essay, aged nine.

Diana Mary Fluck was born on 23 October 1931 in a semi-detached house built by her father at **210 Marlborough Road, Old Town, Swindon,** the only child of Winifred Payne and Bert Fluck, a railway clerk.

She joined the London Academy of Dramatic Art when she was fifteen and the same year made her film debut in *The Shop at Sly Corner.* She was offered a ten-year contract by the Rank Organisation and changed her unfortunate surname to that of her maternal grandmother. Billed as Britain's answer to Marilyn Monroe by the studio publicity machine, her reputation and 'blonde bombshell' image always exceeded her slender acting achievements. Her films are mostly forgettable, but she did show potential as a serious acress in *Oliver Twist* (1948), *A Boy a Girl and a Bike* (1949) and *Yield to the Night* (1956).

In later years she became a TV agony aunt and slimming personality when weight problems wiped out her 'bombshell' image. Diana Dors always enjoyed a love-hate relationship with her home town and declared in 1958, at the height of her fame, that Swindon

could *"go and jump in its own railway yard".* She was married three times and had three sons. She died of cancer, aged fifty-two.

See also: Diana Dors (Windsor & Maidenhead)

Further information: Diana Dors is honoured in the town with a bust at the Wyvern Theatre, Theatre Sq., and a statue outside the cinema at Shaw Ridge Leisure Park.

Trafford

BIRTHPLACE OF ROBERT BOLT (1924-95)
Sale

"What's interesting about Bob is not so much what he wrote but that he was a product of the times. He was a working class boy who made good and was destroyed by market forces. He loved money, much more than I did. I mean, he really loved it. It was a measure of his status."
Peter Hall *

Playwright and screenwriter Robert Oxton Bolt is best known in the cinema for his collaborations with David Lean and his marriage to actress Sarah Miles. A brilliant wordsmith, it was his self-confessed weakness for money that lured him into writing for the movies, which many considered was a squandering of his talent. From 1962 to 1985 only seven of his screenplays were realized on the screen, but without these movies, which include *Lawrence of Arabia* and *A Man For All Seasons,* the cinema would be a shallower place.

He was born, the second son of Leah Binyon and Ralph Bolt, on 15 August 1924 at **13 Northenden Road** (now a hairdressers), Sale, where his parents had a house above their furniture, glass and china shop. When he was four the family moved nearby to 68 School Road (now demolished) where his father built a furniture shop over the garden. Robert and his elder brother Sydney were educated at Sale

*Peter O'Toole and Omar Sharif in **Lawrence of Arabia** (1962, Columbia/Horizon)*

His other work included *A Man For All Seasons* (1966, AA), *Lady Caroline Lamb* (1972, also directed), *The Bounty* (1984) and *The Mission* (1986).

He was married four times and had four children, including a son to Sarah Miles. He died on 20 February1995, and is buried in the grounds of Chithurst Manor, his home near Petersfield, where his headstone reads: Robert Bolt, A Man for All Seasons.

See also: David Lean, The Lawrence of Arabia Trail, *Ryan's Daughter, A Man For All Seasons*

Warrington

GRAVE OF GEORGE FORMBY (1904-61)
Warrington

"We don't become stars. You people make us stars. We couldn't be anything without you. And any of our present stars today, if they ever believe anything different, they're crazy."
George Formby *

The Wigan lad whose films broke box-office records, but who never got to kiss a girl on screen, is buried in the **Catholic Cemetery in Manchester Road**. He lies beside his father, who was a successful music hall comedian known as 'The Wigan Nightingale'.

Young George was born blind on 26 May 1904 until a coughing fit a few weeks later freed the caul which was obscuring his sight. He became an apprentice jockey when he was seven, but left after his father's death, choosing to pursue a career in showbusiness.

He made his first professional appearance in April 1921 at the Hippodrome in Earlestown. Three years later he was appearing at the Alhambra, in London's West End, where his catchphrase, *"It's turned out nice again, hasn't it."* was first uttered. He later bought a banjulele, *"For a lark"*, and accompanied himself on

Come on George (1939, ATP/Ealing)

stage singing *"Going back to Tennessee"*. His performance sent the audience wild, and soon his shy personality, sexual innuendo, and *"daft little songs"* were pulling in the crowds.

He married Beryl, one half of a clog dancing act called 'The Two Violets', in 1923. She sharpened his image, polished his act, and dominated the rest of his life. He made his film debut with her in *Boots! Boots!* (1934) for a fee of £200, shot at a tiny studio above a garage in Albany Street, near Regent's Park, London. He was soon commanding in excess of £35,000 a picture, receiving 90,000 fan letters a year, and breaking box office records around the world. His films were simple, low-budget, predictable and unpretentious, and the public couldn't get enough of them.

His best included *No Limit* (1936), *Keep Your Seats Please* (1936), *Keep Fit* (1937), *It's in the Air* (1938) and *Let George Do It* (1940). He died from a coronary condition on 6 March 1961.

Further information: The motorcycle George rode in *No Limit* (1936), can be seen at the National Motorcycle Museum, Coventry Road, Bickenhill, Solihull.

Preparatory School and later at Sale High School and Manchester Grammar School. Never a model pupil, he left school and worked in an insurance office, but after private tutoring he was able to gain entrance to Manchester University. In 1943 the war interrupted his studies and he was enlisted in the RAF. He resumed his studies in 1946, and in 1948 he married art student Jo Roberts who gave birth to their daughter, Sally, the following year. After teacher-training in Exeter he took up his first full-time teaching post at **Bishopsteignton** village primary school in Devon. He worked at various teaching posts, including **Millfield Public School, near Glastonbury**, and wrote a number of BBC radio plays throughout the 1950s.

It was after the success of his stage plays, including *The Flowering Cherry* (1957) and *A Man for All Seasons* (1960), that producer Sam Speigel asked him to work on the screenplay of *Lawrence of Arabia*. He accepted, and his decision changed the course of his life, opening up a world of untold wealth. *Lawrence of Arabia* was his first collaboratiion with director David Lean, followed by *Doctor Zhivago* (1966, AA) and *Ryan's Daughter* (1970). He liked and respected Lean, but once commented: *"The bugger of writing for a brilliant film director is that while you are certainly writing for a superior skill you may be writing for an inferior mind."*

Warwickshire

PICTURE HOUSE
Stratford-on-Avon

In the summer of 1995 locals petitioned for a downtown cinema, starting with a donation of £25. City Screens took over the project, and, with Arts Council funding, the end product was no average cinema. It includes features at the cutting edge of modern design, such as a foyer on the first floor accessed by a talking lift, a bar at roof level which opens out on to a terrace, and metalwork fish door handles on the children's lavatories.

Further information: Picture House, Windsor Street, Stratford-on-Avon. Tel: 01789 41550 / 415511.
Seats: 1: 249, 2: 82

TOM BROWN'S SCHOOLDAYS
Rugby

"Now, you spotty and unpleasant denizens of pond life, we will apply ourselves to Caesar's Gallic Wars."
Wilkes (Michael Horden)

Thomas Hughes' story of a Victorian schoolboy was set in Rugby, one of the 'great' English public schools. He wrote the novel thirty years after leaving Rugby, where he experienced abuse

Flashman (John Forrest) and his beastly thugs threaten young Tom (John Howard Davies) in **Tom Brown's Schooldays** *(1951)*

Location shooting at Rugby School for **Tom Brown's Schooldays**.

and bullying. Director Gordon Parry's 1951 film, starring John Howard Davies in the title role, was shot on location at Rugby School, and vividly recreates the privileged but harsh world of a Victorian public school.

The screenplay was written by Noel Langley (who co-wrote *The Wizard of Oz*) and Robert Newton played the humane headmaster, Dr Arnold. It was, however, John Forrest's chilling portrayal of the bullying bounder, Flashman, which made the film memorable. A sadistic coward, he tours the school with his thugs terrorising the weak, until he meets his match in Brown. Flashman appeared on the screen again in 1975, portrayed by Malcolm McDowell, in Richard Lester's *Royal Flash*. Previous versions of Tom Brown's Schooldays were filmed in 1916 and 1940, with Laurie Leslie and Billy Halop as Flashman.

See also: Thomas Hughes

Further information: For details of school tours contact: Rugby School, Tour Administrator's Office, The Temple Reading Room, Barby Road, Rugby CV22 5DW. Tel: 01788 556227.

West Sussex

GRAVE OF STANLEY HOLLOWAY (1890-1982)
East Preston

Actor, singer and comedian, Stanley Holloway appeared in over sixty films

usually portraying comic working class, 'man next door' types and will be chiefly remembered as the philosophic cockney dustman, Alfred Doolittle, in *My Fair Lady* (1964).

Contrary to his screen personae, he came from an affluent background and was born 1 October 1890 in Manor Park, London, the youngest child of Florence Bell and George Holloway, a law clerk. A boy soprano, he pursued his singing career as an adult and studied in Milan. His varied career encompassed musical comedy, pantomime, revue, variety theatre and in 1921 he made his film debut in A.V. Bramble's *The Rotters*. He was cast in low-budget films until 1940 when he started to appear in more noteworthy films such as: *Major Barbara* (1941), *This Happy Breed* (1944), *Brief Encounter* (1945), *The Lavender Hill Mob* (1951) and *The Titfield Thunderbolt* (1952).

He was twice married and had five children. He died at Littlehampton on 30 January 1982 and is buried in **St. Mary's Churchyard, East Preston.**

See also: *Brief Encounter, The Titfield Thunderbolt*

BLACK NARCISSUS
Lower Beeding

- 1946 100m c Drama Archers (U.K.)
- Deborah Kerr (Sister Clodagh), Sabu (Dilip Rai), David Farrar (Mr. Dean), Flora Robson (Sister Philippa), Jean Simmons (Kanchi), Kathleen Byron (Sister Ruth)

• p, Michael Powell, Emeric Pressburger; d, Michael Powell, Emeric Pressburger; w, Michael Powell, Emeric Pressburger (based on the novel by Rumer Godden); ph, Jack Cardiff; ed, Reginald Mills; m, Brian Easdale • AA Best Cinematography: Jack Cardiff; AA Best Art Direction: Alfred Junge

Powell and Pressburger's haunting and erotic film portrays a group of Anglican nuns battling against loneliness, illness, sexual repression and the extreme climate in a remote mountain convent. Kathleen Byron gives the performance of her life as the randy Sister Ruth who lusts after handsome government agent, David Farrar, while Indian-born Sabu was cast in his last major role.

The set was built at Pinewood and glass shots were used to create the rugged mountain scenery. The location shooting was beautifully photographed by Jack Cardiff, not in the Himalayas, but in the steamy and exotic gardens of **Leonardslee House, Lower Beeding**. Developed by the Loder family for several generations the woodland gardens are in a tranquil valley extending for some 240 acres with a spectacular collection of rhododendrons, azaleas, choice trees and shrubs which could easily be mistaken for the foothills of the

Himalayas. Shooting took place mostly in the early summer when the gardens were in full bloom. One scene, however, had to be re-shot after the rhododendrons had finished flowering and red crepe paper was used as a substitute. At the foot of the valley flows a small stream, spreading out at intervals into a series of lakes; wallabies and deer are allowed to roam semi-wild over parts of the grounds.

See also: Rumer Godden, Michael Powell, Emeric Pressburger, Deborah Kerr

Further information: Leonardslee Gardens, Lower Beeding, near Horsham, RH13 6PP. Tel: 01403 891212. Opening Times: April - October, 9.30am - 6pm.

THE PUNCH AND JUDY MAN
Bognor Regis

Although never able to repeat his radio and T.V. success on film, *The Punch and Judy Man* (1962) is probably Tony Hancock's most memorable screen performance. Filmed on **Bognor Regis**

seafront, and starring Sylvie Sims, John Le Mesurier and Hugh Lloyd, it tells the story of a seaside entertainer's struggle for recognition in his home town.

See also: Tony Hancock

PLANET HOLLYWOOD
Gatwick Airport

Themed around movies and American cuisine this 120 seat restaurant and cocktail bar is situated in the South Terminal Village. Movie memorabilia on display includes a life-size model of Arnold Schwarzenegger as *The Terminator*, a model of Sylvester Stallone frozen in a Cryo-Pack as seen in *Demolition Man*, and a model of Tom Cruise's aircraft in *Top Gun*.

See also: Planet Hollywood Westminster & Dublin

Further information: Opening hours 6am - 10pm. Planet Hollywood, South Terminal Village, Gatwick Airport, Crawley, West Sussex RH6 NPP. Tel: 01293 579325.

WISH YOU WERE HERE
Worthing

"Do you fancy me?"
"Not half as much as you fancy yourself."

Set in the fifties, David Leland's 1987 debut film was based on the early life of brothel madam, Cynthia Payne. Sixteen year-old Lynda (Emily Lloyd) is a free-spirited adolescent who is drowning in the stifling morality of a seaside suburbia. Brazen, guiltless, and totally devoid of any understanding of the status quo, her rebellious behaviour involves flashing her legs and knickers and shouting *"Up yer bum!"* to townspeople wherever she goes. After a disastrous sexual encounter with a young bus conductor she has an affair with a middle-aged cinema projectionist who *"smells of booze and fags"*.

The cinema and bus station used in the film were the **Dome Cinema** and the

*Sister Ruth (Kathleen Byron) descends into madness amid the lush vegetation of Leonardslee in **Black Narcissus** (1946, The Archers)*

*Emily Lloyd and Tom Bell in **Wish you Were Here** (1987, Zenith/Film Four)*

Stagecoach Coastline bus depot ('Southdown' in the film), both on **Marine Parade.** The seafronts of both Worthing and Bognor Regis appear in the film and the dance location was at the **Village Hall, Woodland Avenue, Rustington**.

See also: Dome Cinema

DOME CINEMA
Worthing

"One of the warmest theatres on the South Coast."
An early Dome advertising slogan

A rare surviving example of a Kursaal or multi-purpose hall, it was renamed the Dome in 1914, and was converted into the Dome Cinema in 1921, replacing the smaller upstairs Electric Theatre. Its opening night featured

Mary Pickford in *Pollyanna*, accompanied by a six-piece orchestra.

With a striking facade overlooking the sea, the Dome is of exceptional architectural and historical interest. Its interior has survived remarkably intact, with a patterned terrazzo floor covering the entrance arcade, and with glazed green tile dado and decorative plasterwork. The main foyer is dominated by a rare 1921 polygonal paybox and the main auditorium has seating for 600.

It came to the notice of national cinema audiences when it was used as a location for *Wish You Were Here* in 1987. Interiors and exteriors were used and the room inside the dome (formerly a billiards room) was the setting for the lecherous projectionist's dingy lodging.

See also: *Wish you Were Here*

Further information: Dome Cinema, Marine Parade, Worthing. Tel: 01903 200461.

Wigan

BIRTHPLACE OF JAMES HILTON (1900-54)
Leigh

"...fame and fortune had come to him in a rush while young... but I felt the place [Hollywood] had destroyed him with its emotional strain."
Cecil Roberts, *The Pleasant Years,*

Creator of Shangri-la and one of cinema's most memorable characters, 'Mr Chips', adaptations of James Hilton's novels have produced some of the great classics of the golden age of cinema, including: *Lost Horizon* (1937), *Goodbye Mr. Chips* (1939), *Random Harvest* (1942) and *Mrs. Miniver* (1942).

He was born on 9 September 1900 at **26 Wilkinson Street** (between Twist Lane and Railway Road), the only child of schoolteachers John Hilton and Elizabeth Burch. His education began

*26 Wilkinson Street, Leigh - birthplace of **James Hilton***

in North London until 1915, after which time he attended The Leys School, Cambridge, where he met W.H. Balgarnie, the schoolmaster who was the inspiration for *Goodbye Mr Chips*.

Hilton wrote his first novel, *Catherine Herself* (1920) while still an undergraduate at Cambridge. The Manchester Guardian accepted his first journalistic writing and he also

*Teresa Wright, Walter Pidgeon, Greer Garson and Richard Ney in **Mrs. Miniver** (1942, MGM)*

Wiltshire

GRAVE OF CECIL BEATON (1904-80)
Broad Chalke

Artist, writer, illustrator, costume designer, diarist, aesthete, socialite, conversationalist, portrait and fashion photographer, Cecil Beaton was often accused of being a mere dabbler in the arts, but although he cast his net wide, the end product was usually unforgettable. Nowhere can this be seen more clearly than in his many design achievements in the cinema, including the set designs for *Gigi* (1958), which won him his first Oscar, and costume designs for *My Fair Lady* (1964). He photographed many of cinema's icons, including Marlene Dietrich and Gloria Swanson. He never married, although he proposed to Greta Garbo. He is buried in **All Saints' Churchyard**.

See also: Rex Harrison

DOCTOR DOLITTLE
Castle Combe

'*...a huge stillborn, dinosaur in quicksand..*'
Virgin Film Guide

• 1967 152m c Musical Fox (U.S.)
Rex Harrison (Dr. John Dolittle),
• Anthony Newley (Mathew Mugg), Peter Bull (Gen. Bellowes), William Dix (Tommy Stubbins), Portia Nelson (Sarah Dolittle), Samantha Eggar (Emma Fairfax), Richard Attenborough (Albert Blossom)
• p, Arthur P. Jacobs; d, Richard Fleischer; w, Leslie Bricusse (based on stories by Hugh Lofting); ph, Robert Surtess; ed, Samuel E. Beetley, Marjorie Fowler; prod d, Mario Chiari; art d, Jack Martin Smith, Ed Graves
• AAN Best Picture; AAN Best Cinematography; AAN Best Editing; AAN Best Score; AA Best Song; AAN Best Art Direction

Doctor Dolittle is based on Hugh Lofting's stories written for his own children in the trenches during the First World War about the exploits of a doctor who can talk to animals. Excellent stories, but a pity about the film, which was a total catastrophe for

reviewed books for the Daily Telegraph. A quiet, unassuming man, he struggled to make a living as a writer for eleven years before gaining success with *And Now Goodbye,* in 1932. His 1933 novel of Utopian Shangri-La, *Lost Horizon,* was written in only six weeks and became a world-wide success, becoming adapted for the screen by Robert Riskin in 1937 with a budget of $2.5 million. For this, director Frank Capra built the largest set ever constructed in Hollywood, a 1,000-foot-long, 500-foot-wide lamasery. Hilton followed this success in 1934 with another: *Goodbye Mr Chips,* the story of retired schoolmaster, Mr Chipping, which he wrote in four days to meet a magazine deadline. The novel has since been published in over twenty-two English language editions, and translated into more than twenty other languages, including a Japanese version. Two films, a play and a musical production have all been based on the book.

In the late thirties Hilton was invited to Hollywood where he became a highly paid scriptwriter, his imagination and style winning him an Oscar for the

script of *Mrs Miniver* in 1942. Married three times, he remained in America for the rest of his life, where he died of cancer at Long Beach, California, 20 December 1954, aged fifty-four.

See also: *Goodbye Mr Chips, Random Harvest,* W.H. Balgarnie

WIGAN PIER
Wigan

The Wigan Pier Experience focuses on the late Victorian period in Wigan and S.E. Lancashire. The Palace of Varieties Music Hall runs a magic lantern show throughout the day, presenting a series of comic and melodramatic scenes on 35mm slide taken from hand painted glass originals, circa 1900. The slides are taken from the collection of the Rev William Wickham, a Victorian vicar who photographed Wigan life at the end of the 19th century.

Further information: Wigan Pier, Wallgate, Wigan, WN3 4EU. Tel: 01942 323 666.

Wiltshire

Fox and one of the most harrowing experiences of Rex Harrison's career.

Working with animals is difficult for actors at the best of times, but working with more than 1,500 would push most people over the edge. When the film was finally completed he commented: *"To work in close proximity with all those animals for a year wasn't the most pleasant experience of my life...They would all be doing their business quite naturally, so we would then have to clear the set, sweep it up, air it, come back and start again."*

During the two months on location in Castle Combe various village locations were used, including seventeenth-century **Dower House** as Doctor Dolittle's home. It rained nearly every day and when the production crew dammed a local stream to create a waterfront, relations with the already sensitive villagers deteriorated rapidly. So much so, that they connived a plot to blow up the waterfront.

Rex Harrison's private life was also under great stress during this period as his wife, Rachel Roberts, was drinking heavily and prone to suicide attempts. The production moved in the end to Hollywood and the West Indies taking a year in all to complete.

See also: Rex Harrison

WEDDING OF DAVID NIVEN
Huish

In 1939 David Niven abandoned a promising Hollywood career to join the war effort as a soldier in the British army. In 1940 he fell in love with a young WAAF called 'Primmie', and after only ten days of courtship they were married in the tiny **Norman church of Huish**.

David Niven recalls in his 1971 autobiography, *The Moon's a Balloon* : *"Friends from far and near came by train, by bicycle or by blowing their petrol rations for a month... Primmie looked like a porcelain figure in a simple pale blue dress. The Battle of Britain on that cloudless September day, was raging in the skies above - it was no time for veil and orange blossom.*

After the war they went to live in California. In 1945, the year of their arrival in America, Primmie fell down the cellar stairs in their house and was taken to hospital with severe concussion. A few days later she died. She was only twenty five.

See also: David Niven (Angus)

GRAVE OF IAN FLEMING (1908-64)
Sevenhampton

Ian Fleming's cult hero, James Bond 007, the cinema's most famous secret agent, was born on the morning of 15 January 1952 when Fleming began writing his first novel, *Casino Royale*. The public's appetite for this cold, ruthless, sophisticated womanising Englishman proved insatiable and the Bond stories appeared annually until 1966. His other notable contribution to the cinema was the 1968 film adaptation of his chidren's story, *Chitty Chitty Bang Bang*.

Chitty Chitty Bang Bang (1968, UA/Warfield)

Ian Fleming was born on 28 May 1908 at **27 Green Street, off Park Lane, London**, the second of four sons of Evelyn Beatrice Ste. Croix and Valentine Fleming. His father was Conservative MP for South Oxfordshire in 1910 and was killed in action during WWI. Educated at Eton, Sandhurst, and privately in Europe, Fleming tried unsuccessfully to enter the Foreign Office before starting as journalist with Reuters News Agency in 1931. He later worked as a banker and a stockbroker in the City. During WWII he worked in

Naval Intelligence and rose to the rank of Commander.

In 1952 he married Ann O'Neill in Jamaica. He died in Canterbury on 12 August 1964 and is buried in an unmarked grave beside his wife and son in **St. Andrew's Churchyard**, close to where he lived at **Warneford Place**.

See also: Ian Fleming (Westminster), Sean Connery, *Goldfinger*

Further information: The Ian Fleming Foundation www.ianfleming.org

ODEON
Salisbury

The Odeon opened on 7 September 1931 as the Gaumont Palace and was designed by W.E. Trent, a prolific and extremely talented architect. The Salisbury Odeon was Trent's *tour de force*. The cinema was erected at the rear of the Hall of John Halle, a Victorian restoration of a medieval merchant's house, which is now the cinema foyer. The internal decoration of the cinema was designed in Tudor Gothic style to stay in keeping with the foyer, using framed canvas murals and oak panelling. A bizarre treat for the cinemagoer.

Further information: Odeon, New Canal, Salisbury, Wilts. Tel: 01722 335924.

CLASSIC LOCATION: WILTON HOUSE
Wilton

A former 9th century nunnery and home of the present 17th Earl of Pembroke, Wilton house is situated in 21 acres of landscaped parkland, and has been used extensively for locations of aristocratic and imposing grandeur. Its Double Cube Room, designed by Indigo Jones, was where the ballroom scene in Ang Lee's gentle satire, *Sense and Sensibility* (1995) was filmed. It also stood in for Windsor Castle in *Mrs Brown* (1997) and appeared in *Barry Lyndon* (1975), *Bounty* (1984), *Scandal* (1989), *Portrait of a Lady* (1996) and *The Madness of King George* (1994).

Further information: Wilton House is open to the public from March to October. Tel: 01722 746729.
The National Trust's **Mompesson House** in Salisbury doubled for the London home of Mrs Jennings in *Sense and Sensibility*, and **Cathedral Close** was transformed into a London Square.

Windsor & Maidenhead

HAMMER STUDIOS
Bray & Water
Oakley

The origins of Hammer go back to William Hinds (1887-1957), who was born into the family which created Britain's largest family jewellers in 1856. His various careers included those of music publisher, bicycle salesman, building society chairman, theatre manager and music hall comedian. He named his music hall comedy double-act, 'Hammer and Smith', because he and his partner lived in Hammersmith.

In 1934, Will Hammer, as he became known, ventured into film-making and formed Hammer Productions. The first Hammer film was a parody of Alexander Korda's *The Private Life of Henry VIII* (1933), entitled, *The Public Life of Henry the Ninth* (1934) and was shot in two weeks. The Hammer logo, featuring boxer Bombardier Billy Wells (the first Rank 'man with a gong') was shot during a lunch hour. In 1935 Will Hammer went into partnership with Enrique Carreras and formed the distribution company, Exclusive Films.

Rather than hire expensive purpose-built studios, Hammer began filming in large furnished period houses, known as 'house studios'. The first 'house studio' they used was Cookham Dean in Maidenhead, but in the early fifties, **Down Place** in Bray became the permanent home of Exclusive/Hammer for sixteen years. Due to restricted space, Bray Studios could only produce one film at a time, but its small family atmosphere was one of the reasons it could create original and quality

*Valerie Gaunt in the arms of Christopher Lee in **Dracula** (1958, Hammer)*

Down Place

productions. Next door to Down Place is **Oakley Court**, which was Exclusive/Hammer's second 'house studio'. Built in 1859, it was used as a location for many Hammer movies in the sixties. As the studios grew, new buildings and a sound stage were added.

The success of *The Quatermass Experiment* (1955) began to attract major distributors, but in 1957 Hammer produced the first British gothic horror movie, *The Curse of Frankenstein*, directed by Terence Fisher, and redefined the entire horror genre.

Oakley Court

Never before had so much spurting blood been seen on the screen.

Audiences loved it and the film grossed over seventy times its production costs. In 1958 Hammer released *Dracula*, starring Christopher Lee and Peter Cushing, which was shot at Bray in only twenty-five days, and became another huge success.

Other Hammer films shot at Bray include: *The Revenge of Frankenstein* (1958), *The Hound of the Baskervilles* (1959), *The Mummy* (1959), *The Brides of Dracula* (1960), *The Curse of the Werewolf* (1961) and the last Hammer film shot there, *The Mummy's Shroud* (1967).

Peter Cushing had fond memories of the studio and recalled, *"When I used to live in Kensington it took only forty-five minutes to get there and we had the road to ourselves...you used to arrive at what was a large country house by the river and this was Bray Studios. In the very first picture we did there, there was a bedroom scene and we literally went up to the bedroom of the house and used the bedroom. For the dining room scenes we went down to the dining-room..."* *

Hammer eventually outgrew Bray in the late sixties and moved to Elstree Studios. Bray is still a working studio which produces features, TV series, commercials and promos. Unfortunately it is not open to the public.

See also: Christopher Lee, Peter Cushing, *The Hound of the Baskervilles*, *Dracula*, *St Trinians*

Further information: Oakley Court is now a country house hotel. After its Hammer period it was used as a location by Southern Pictures, from the mid-sixties to the late seventies, for films such as: *The Rocky Horror Picture Show* (1975), the *St. Trinians* series, *Half a Sixpence* (1967) and *Murder by Death* (1976). It was also used as a location in many of Hammer's *Dracula* films. Oakley Court, Windsor Road, Water Oakley, Windsor, Berkshire SL4 5UR. Tel: 01753 609988. Email: oakleyct@atlas.co.uk Hampden House in Great Hampden, Buckinghamshire, was converted for use as a studio, location and production base for the *Hammer House of Horror* TV series in 1980.

GRAVE OF DIANA DORS (1931-84)
Sunningdale

Diana Dors was diagnosed as having cancer in 1982, and died two years later on 4 May 1984 in hospital at Windsor, aged fifty-two. A celebrity up until the end, she was buried wearing a gold lamé evening dress with matching cape and is buried with her third husband, Alan Lake, beneath a sycamore tree at the far end of **Sunningdale Cemetery.** Alan Lake never recovered from her death and committed suicide on 10 October 1984, the sixteenth anniversary of their first meeting.

See also: Diana Dors (Swindon)

CLASSIC LOCATION: ETON COLLEGE
Windsor

Founded in 1440 by Henry VI, Eton College is one of the oldest and most elite schools in the country. Situated on the north bank of the Thames, opposite Windsor, this bastion of privilege has produced many eminent old Etonians, including the Duke of Wellington, King George III, Gladstone, Lord Avon, Harold Macmillan, Sir Alec Douglas-Home, and film director Hugh Hudson who returned to Eton in 1980 to shoot scenes for *Chariots of Fire*. He was

denied permission to film scenes at Cambridge University because of the film's accusations of anti-semitism therefore Eton College was used instead. Scenes filmed at Eton include the race between Lord Andrew Lindsay (Nigel Havers) and Harold Abrahams (Ben Cross) around Trinity courtyard while the clock is chiming twelve. Other films shot here include *The Jokers* (1967), *Young Sherlock Holmes* (1985), *The Madness of King George* (1994), *The Secret Garden* (1993) and *Shakespeare in Love* (1999).

See also: *Chariots of Fire, Shakespeare in Love*

Further information: Casual visitors are welcome at the school and guided tours are available. Groups of ten or more must be by appointment. College closes October to April. For details contact The Visits Manager, Eton college, Windsor, Berkshire SL4 6DW. Tel: 01753 671177.

Wirral

BIRTHPLACE OF GLENDA JACKSON (1937-)
Birkenhead

*Glenda Jackson in **A Touch of Class** (1973)*

*Lake Place, Birkenhead - **birthplace of Glenda Jackson***

Holy Trinity C of E School

"When you're a brickie and you have a daughter like our Glenda, it's a nice feeling. You know she's the best, but you don't go round bragging about it, do you? Not round here you don't."
Harry ('Micky') Jackson *

Glenda Jackson was born on 9 May 1936 in her grandmother's house at **Lake Place** the eldest of four daughters of Joan Jackson, a daily help and Harry Jackson, a bricklayer. Her mother named her after Hollywood actress, Glenda Farrell, whose name she'd remembered from a movie magazine. In 1939 the family moved to a place of their own at **3 Evans Road, Hoylake**, six miles west of Birkenhead where Glenda attended **Hoylake Church School** (now Holy Trinity C of E School) in **Market Street** and **Church Lane**, and later West Kirby Grammar School for Girls in Graham Road. She left school in 1952, aged sixteen, with three 'O'levels having detested most of her secondary education. Her first jobs were as counter assistants in Woolworth's and the **West Kirby branch of Boot's the Chemist**.

She became interested in drama after joining an amateur theatrical group called the YMCA players in Hoylake and in 1954 she won a scholarship to

Clive Garner

RADA. Her first professional stage appearance was as a walk-on nurse in a production of *Doctor in the House* with the Worthing Repertory Theatre in 1957 followed by her West End debut in *All Kinds of Men* at the Arts Theatre.

Her first film role was a bit part in Lindsay Anderson's *This Sporting Life* (1963) and in 1964 she joined the Royal Shakespeare Company. It was Ken Russell's *Women in Love* (1969) which rocketed her to fame with her Oscar-winning portrayal of Gudrun Brangwen.

Her other films include: *The Music Lovers* (1970), *Sunday, Bloody Sunday* (1971), *Mary Queen of Scots* (1971), *The Triple Echo* (1972), *A Touch of Class* (1972) and *Stevie* (1978).

Further information: In 1983 she opened The Glenda Jackson Theatre, Borough Road, Birkenhead, named in her honour. She has since abandoned her movie career and is now a Labour politician.

CLIVE GARNER VINTAGE RECORDS, FILMS & HOME CINEMA
Wallasey

Clive Garner's film collection started in the 1960s as an adjunct to a large collection of 78 r.p.m. gramophone records (over 50,000). His films cover the same period as his records from the late 1920s to the early 1950s. Emphasis is on films that would form part of a 'full supporting programme' during the golden age of cinema. Included are trailers, special cinema advertising shorts, organ interlude films, cinema 'Day Titles', ice cream trailers, special interest and documentary films, and over 4,000 cinema organ song slides. The archive also has a large collection of local films showing scenes on Merseyside from 1929 through to the early 1960s.

In 1973 Clive built a small cinema (18' x 8') in his back garden where he screens films fortnightly for anyone wishing to attend. There are eleven seats (plus one for the usherette) with six sets of electronically-controlled curtains lit by eight changing colours. It was not until Clive retired from the Gas and Electricity Boards in 1972 that he could fully indulge in his passion for the classic cinema. 'Modern' films put him to sleep.

Further information: Clive Garner, 39 Mosslands Drive, Wallasey, Merseyside, L45 8PE. Tel: 0151 638 4711. Please phone prior to attending screenings.

CHARIOTS OF FIRE
Bebington

The small period sports ground of the
Bebington Oval in **Old Chester Road** was chosen by the film makers to double as the venue for the 1924 Paris Olympics in Hugh Hudsons 1981 Oscar-winning film. Edinburgh's Murrayfield had been considered but Bebington was opted for in the end, one reason possibly being its size. A large stadium with thousands of extras can be an expensive outlay for a limited budget.

See also: *Chariots of Fire* (Fife), Ian Charleson

Wokingham

ASHES OF ROBERT MORLEY (1908-92)
Wargrave

"Anyone who works is a fool. I don't work: I merely inflict myself on the public."
Robert Morley

Robert Morley, who starred in nearly a hundred films, and will be remembered as one of the great British character actors, was born on 26 May 1908 in **Semley, Wiltshire**, the second child of Gertrude Emily Fass and Major Robert Morley. His family never stayed long in one place and during his childhood he moved regularly between London and Folkestone. He attended eleven different preparatory schools until he was accepted for Wellington, which he loathed. He was withdrawn in 1924 due

*Robert Morley in **Law and Disorder** (1958, British Lion/Hotspur)*

to his father's financial difficulties and the separation of his parents.

His first appearance on stage was in the annual Folkestone mystery play, aged five. He joined RADA when he was eighteen and made his first professional stage appearance in 1926 as a pirate extra in Arthur Bourchier's production of *Treasure Island* at the Strand. His debut as an actor was in *Dr Syn* at the Margate Hippodrome in 1928 and he toured with various companies before playing the celebrated title role in *Oscar Wilde* (the first Wilde on stage and screen) at the Gate Theatre, Charing Cross, in 1936 and on Broadway in 1938.

He was Oscar-nominated for his first screen performance as Louis XVI in MGM's *Marie Antoinette* (1938) but will be best remembered for his screen character roles such as: the Rev. Samuel Sayer in *The African Queen* (1951), the desperate Peterson in *Beat the Devil* (1953), the electronic genius Cedric Page in *Topkapi* (1964) and Sir Ambrose Abercromby in *The Loved One* (1965).

Married with three children, Morley died at Dunedin Hospital, Reading, after a massive stroke on 3 June 1992, aged eighty-four.

His ashes are buried in Wargrave beneath a plaque bearing his name on the wall of **St Mary's Church, Mill Green**, near the hamlet of Crazies Hill, where he had lived since the 1960s.

See also: Oscar Wilde

Worcestershire

CLASSIC LOCATION: SEVERN VALLEY RAILWAY
Bewdley

The Severn Valley line operated from 1862 until its closure in 1963, and linked Hartlebury, near Droitwich, with Shrewsbury, covering a distance of forty miles. It re-opened in 1970 after a group of railway enthusiasts restored part of the line which is now sixteen miles long. It is a full-size standard gauge line running regular steam-hauled passenger trains, largely run by unpaid volunteers, for tourists and enthusiasts between Kidderminster and Bridgnorth. The highlight of the route, which passes through many picturesque villages and stations, is the crossing of the River Severn, via the 200ft single span Victoria Bridge.

Feature films shot on the line include, *The Seven Percent Solution* (1976),

Judi Dench as Queen Elizabeth I in **Shakespeare in Love** *(1998, photo: Laurie Sparham)*

Disney's *Candleshoe* (1977), Merchant Ivory's *Howards End* (1992) and *The Thirty-Nine Steps* (1978) with Robert Powell, in which the Victoria Bridge substituted for the Forth Rail Bridge.

See also: Forth Rail Bridge, *Howards End*

Further information: The Railway Station, Bewdley, Worcestershire, DY12 1BG. Tel: 01299 403816. 24-hour talking timetable and information: 01299 401001.

York

BIRTHPLACE OF JOHN BARRY (1933 -)
York

Oscar winning film music composer, John Barry, was born in a semi at **167 Hull Road** (plaque erected), and lived there from 1933 until 1947 with his show business family, the theatre-owning Prendergasts, before moving to **Fulford** to what is now **The Pavilion Hotel.**

A former rock'n'roll musician he founded and performed with The John Barry Seven and The John Barry Orchestra. He is probably best known for his 'James Bond' scores and has won five Oscars for Original Music Scores. He has written the music for over fifty films, including: *Born Free, The Lion in Winter, Goldfinger, Zulu, Midnight Cowboy, Walkabout, Out of Africa* and *Dances With Wolves.* He now lives on Long Island, New York.

See also: *Goldfinger, Zulu*

BIRTHPLACE OF JUDI DENCH (1934 -)
York

Born on 9 December 1934, at the Holgate Nursing Home (now **Holgate Hotel**) in **Holgate Road**, she was the youngest of three children of Doctor Reginald Dench and Olave Jones. She grew up in number **54 Heworth Green**, a Victorian terraced house on three floors, with her father's surgery and waiting room on the ground level. Judi's and the maid's bedrooms were in the attic.

From early dramatic beginnings portraying a snail, aged five, she gained a place at the Central School of Speech and Drama in London in 1953 and made her professional acting debut with the Old Vic in 1957, as Ophelia in Hamlet. She began her life-long relationship with The Royal Shakespeare Company in 1961 when she was cast as Anya, in *The Cherry Orchard*, a production which also included Peggy Ashcroft and John Geilgud.

She has remained essentially a stage actress but has recently made her mark in feature films, notably as M in *GoldenEye* (1995) and for her Oscar nominated performance as Queen Victoria in the acclaimed historical drama, *Mrs Brown* (1997). Other films include: *A Room With A View* (1985), *84 Charing Cross Road* (1987), *Henry V* (1989) and *Shakespeare in Love* (AA, 1999).

See also: *Mrs Brown, A Room With A View, Shakespeare in Love*

LONDON

Barking & Dagenham

BIRTHPLACE OF
DUDLEY MOORE
(1935 -)

Dagenham

Named after an obscure bishop, Dudley Moore was born at Charing Cross Hospital on 19 April 1935 to Ada Hughes and John Moore, a British Railways electrician. Born with a clubfoot, he was brought up on the working class **Beacontree Estate** at **14 Monmouth Road**. Nicknamed 'Hopalong' at school and frequently ridiculed, he underwent over a period of seven years as a child, but his foot never properly healed. 'Bombed out' during the war the family moved to **146 Barron Road** where his parents lived out the rest of their days.

In 1954 he won an organ scholarship to Magdalen College, Oxford, where as well as his music studies he composed scores and played in jazz clubs. After university he joined the Vic Lewis Band and the Johnny Dankworth Band, eventually forming the Dudley Moore Trio in 1959. Professional comedy entered his life when together with Peter Cook, Jonathan Miller and Alan Bennett they formed a ground-breaking late-night revue at the 1959 Edinburgh Festival called *Beyond the Fringe*, which was the beginning of his partnership with Peter Cook.

He launched his film career in 1966 with *The Wrong Box* which was followed by equally mediocre duds until Blake Edwards' *10* (1979) with Bo Derek and Julie Andrews, rocketed him to Hollywood stardom where he has remained (surprisingly) ever since. Other films include *Arthur* (1981), *Micki and Maude* (1984), *Santa Claus: The Movie* (1985) and *Blame It on the Bellboy* (1992).

After a life-long obsession with sex and countless love affairs he became a father again in 1995, aged sixty.

Barnet

BIRTHPLACE OF
ELIZABETH TAYLOR
(1932-)

Hampstead

Elizabeth Rosemond Taylor was born on 27 February 1932 at **8 Wildwood Road, Hampstead Heath**, the second child of affluent American parents, Sara Warmbrodt, a former actress, and Francis Taylor, an art dealer who worked for the London branch of his American uncle's gallery business in Bond Street. She attended Byron House School in Highgate for two years before her family departed

8 Wildwood Road - birthplace of **Elizabeth Taylor**

Elizabeth Taylor in **Cat on a Hot Tin Roof** *(1958, MGM)*

Her career has mirrored the predictable consequences of stardom: untold riches, flamboyant behaviour, drug and alcohol abuse, love affairs and nine marriages, but despite it all, she still remains a star.

See also: Richard Burton, Enid Bagnold

Bexley

BIRTHPLACE OF A.E.W. MASON (1865-1948)
West Heath

"...we are too ready to forget such figures as A.E.W. Mason, Stanley Weyman and Rider Haggard, perhaps the greatest of all who enchanted us when we were young."
Graham Greene *

Classic adventure writer, Alfred Edward Woodley Mason, will be chiefly remembered for his bestseller, *The Four Feathers* (1902), about a man accused of cowardice who embarks on a perilous quest in Kitchener's 1898 Sudan campaign to regain his reputation and redeem himself. Originally serialised in the *Cornhill* magazine, nearly a million copies of the book were sold during its first forty years. It is the only book which has been read both at the North and South Poles by explorer Roald Amundsen, who claimed that it was his bible, and that he "wouldn't be without it anywhere!" It was adapted for the screen five times, most notably by Zoltan and Alexander Korda in 1939, starring John Clements, Ralph Richardson and C. Aubrey Smith. Other novels adapted for the screen include, *Fire Over England* (1937) and *The Drum* (1938).

for California prior to the outbreak of WWII.

By this time her ambitious and assertive mother was desperately trying to persuade her daughter to follow in her own footsteps and take up a career in acting. In 1941 she negotiated a six-month contract for Elizabeth with Universal Pictures at $100 a week with whom she was cast in the forgettable *There's One Born Every Minute*. After six months had elapsed the contract was not renewed. The following year MGM started production on *Lassie Come Home,* but the female lead was considered too tall. Elizabeth auditioned, got the small part and began life as an

MGM contract player. In 1942 she was loaned to 20th Century Fox who cast her as one of the schoolgirls in *Jane Eyre*. It was not, however, until her first leading role in *National Velvet* in 1944, at the age of twelve, that she was rocketed to stardom.

Her first adult role was in Vincente Minneli's comedy, *Father of the Bride* (1950) whose release was timed to coincide with her first marriage to hotelier, Conrad Hilton Jnr. Her other films included: *A Place in the Sun* (1951), *Giant* (1956), *Cat on a Hot Tin Roof* (1958), *Cleopatra* (1962) and *Who's Afraid of Virginia Woolf?* (1966, AA).

*Captain John Durrance (Ralph Richardson) he has lost his sight in the Sudan in **The Four Feathers** (1939, Korda/London Films)*

Alfred Mason was born on 7 May 1865 at **Enfield Villa, Upper Grove Lane, West Heath**, to Elizabeth Gaines and William Mason, a chartered accountant. He entered Trinity College Oxford in 1884 and later became a touring actor, journalist, playwright and novelist. Inspiration for his adventure stories was gleaned from his own daring life and extensive travels in Sudan, Morocco, South America, Africa, India, Burma and Australia. He was an experienced mountaineer, a former M.P. and a secret agent in Spain and Mexico during WWI. In one of the last articles he wrote, on his friend J.M. Barrie, he quoted one of his own lines: *"To die will be an awfully big adventure!"*.

See also: Ralph Richardson, C. Aubrey Smith, *The Drum*

Brent

GRAVE OF LEW GRADE (1906-98)
Willesden

"The only good thing to come out of this is the thought that the world

shortage in Cuban cigars may now be at an end."
Part of Michael Grade's funeral address for his favourite uncle.

Legendary impresario, Lew Grade, did not move into film production until he was in his seventies, but he was a leading figure in British show business for over seventy years.

He was born Louis Winogradsky in the Ukranian town of Tokmak near the Black Sea, on Christmas Day 1906, the eldest of three sons to Isaac and Olga Winogradsky. When he was five his family emigrated to the East End of London where his father worked in the garment trade. Russian was his first language until he was eight and although a bright child, he left school at fourteen to work with his father. He became a professional dancer in the twenties after winning the World Charleston Championships at the Royal Albert Hall. When dancing damaged his knees he set up his own theatrical agency with his brother Bernard where he developed his taste for outsize cigars.

In 1956 he became deputy managing director of ATV (he became managing director in 1962 and chairman in 1973) where his production arm ITC dominated

ITV's schedules with programmes such as *Robin Hood* (165 episodes), *The Saint* (146 episodes), *Thunderbirds* and *The Prisoner*. In 1977 he retired from the chairmanship of ATV and began a career as a film producer, but had left it too late to make any great impact on the movie industry. Among his successes were *On Golden Pond* (1981), *The Pink Panther* series, *The Muppet Movie* (1979), and *Sophie's Choice* (1982). His greatest turkey was *Raise the Titanic* (1980) which was such an expensive flop he commented, *"It would have been cheaper to lower the Atlantic Ocean"*. Clive Kussler, on whose book the film was based, claimed to have retched at the film's premiere.

In 1942 he married dancer, Kathleen Moody with whom he adopted a son. Created a Baron in 1976, he died of a heart attack just twelve days before his ninety-second birthday and is buried at the **Liberal Jewish Cemetery** in **Willesden**, north London.

THE COLISEUM PUB
Harlesden

Formerly the Coliseum Cinema, it was converted to a pub in the early 1990s. It is decorated with movie stills, posters and has a large silhouette of Clark Gable and Vivien Leigh over the screen area.

Further information: The Coliseum, 26 Manor Park Road, Harlesden, London, NW10. Tel: 0181 961 6570.

CLASSIC LOCATION: SYON PARK
Brentford

Situated halfway between central London and Heathrow Airport, Syon Park, the London home of the Duke of Northumberland, is a

popular location with studios because of its proximity to London, and can lay claim to being the closest stately home to the city centre. Its 200 acre estate includes Syon House, built on the site of a medieval abbey, with interiors by Robert Adam and garden landscapes designed by Capability Brown.

Henry VIII dissolved the abbey in 1539, and in 1547 his coffin rested at Syon on its journey to Windsor for burial. During the night dogs were found licking up his remains which had seeped through the coffin from his swollen corpse. Feature films shot here include: *Bullshot* (1983), *King Ralph* (1991), *The Madness of King George* (1994), *Richard III* (1995), *The Wings of the Dove* (1997) and *The Avengers* (1998).

Further information: Syon Park, Brentford, Middlesex, TW8 8JF. Tel: 0181 560 0881. House open 17 March to 30 October, Wednesday, Thursday, Sunday & Bank Holiday Monday / Good Friday. 11am to 5pm. Gardens open daily.

Camden

CHILDHOOD HOME OF KENNETH WILLIAMS (1926-1988)
St. Pancras

"A melancholic, depressed man shot through with moments of delight." Miriam Margoyles

Kenneth Williams, the camp, nostril-flaring comedian and star of the *Carry On* films, was born on the 22nd February 1926 at **Bingfield Street**, off the Caledonian Road to Louisa and Charlie Williams, a hairdresser. The family moved a few years later to

57 Marchmont Street - childhood home of **Kenneth Williams**

premises above Charlie's shop at **57 Marchmont Street.** Very early in his life Williams became tormented by his homosexuality, growing up with an overbearing, homophobic father and a mother who doted on him. Throughout his life he was to have a very close and bizarre relationship with his mother. In 1940 he began training as a litho draughtsman before being conscripted into the Royal

Engineers' Survey Section, in Ceylon. Here he transferred to the newly formed Combined Services Entertainments (CSE) based in Singapore where he entertained the troops until the end of the war.

After his de-mob he returned briefly to working as a draughtsman before joining the Newquay Players theatre company which launched his career in post-war repertory. His first film role was as an innkeeper's pot-boy in *The Beggar's Opera* (1952) with Laurence Olivier, but he will be best remembered for his fifties radio cameos on *Hancock's Half Hour, Beyond Our Ken, Round the Horne* and for his hilarious camp roles in the predictable *Carry On* films, some of whose scripts he thought were appalling.

Throughout his life he suppressed his sexuality and shunned close relationships. He desperately wanted to be taken seriously as an actor, but his comic persona would always rise to the fore, almost as a form of self protection. In later life, his career flagging, he worked on the cabaret circuit. On April 14th 1988 he died from an overdose of barbiturates in his London flat.

See also: *Carry On Sergeant*

CLASSIC LOCATION: CHENEY ROAD
King's Cross

Cheney Road, at the rear of **Kings Cross Station** is frequently used by film makers to recreate London's East End. Its winding cobbled street and the backdrop of its now listed and preserved gasometers has been used as a location for countless films over the years, including the security van ambush scene filmed outside the German Gymnasium in *The Ladykillers* (1955), *Chaplin* (1992), *Richard III* (1995), *The Missionary* (1983), *The Secret*

Garden (1993), *Nuns on the Run* (1990) and *Shirley Valentine* (1989).

Cheney Road

See also: *The Ladykillers*

GRAVE OF GLADYS COOPER (1888-1971)
Hampstead

Gladys Constance Cooper was born in Lewisham on 18 December 1888, the eldest of three children of Charles Cooper, a journalist and editor, and Mabel Barnett. A child photographic model from the age of seven, she made her first stage appearance in the title role of Seymour Hicks' *Bluebell in Fairyland* in 1905, aged seventeen, and she performed almost continually on the British stage until the late thirties.

In the autumn of 1939, she left Britain for Hollywood when Alfred Hitchcock offered her the small role of Maxim de Winter's (Laurence Olivier) astute sister, Beatrice Lacey, in *Rebecca* (1940). She enjoyed California so much she remained there for thirty years. Contracted to MGM she made thirty films between 1940 and 1967,

usually in roles which required a distinguished bearing, including *Now Voyager* (1943), *The Bishop's Wife* (1947), *Separate Tables* (1958) and *My Fair Lady* (1964).

In 1967 she was appointed DBE. Married three times, she had three children and died at home in Henley, aged eighty-three. She is buried in **Hampstead Cemetery, Fortune Green Road.**

See also: The Rebecca Trail, Alfred Hitchcock

GRAVE OF WILLIAM FRIESE-GREENE (1855-1921)
Highgate

Film pioneer, William Friese-Greene, collapsed and died at a public meeting in London's Connaught Rooms. He died penniless and is buried in **Highgate Cemetery, Swains Lane**, where his headstone was erected by public subscription with the inscription: *William Friese-Greene. The inventor of kinematography.*

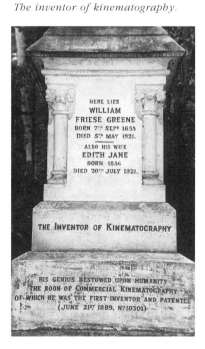

His genius bestowed upon humanity the boon of commercial kinematography, of which he was the first inventor and patentee. At his funeral a huge floral projector was mounted on the roof of the hearse projecting onto a cinema screen of white orchids. His life is chronicled in John Boulting's biopic, *The Magic Box* (1951), which stars Robert Donat as Friese-Greene.

See also: William Friese-Green (Bristol, Somerset)

GRAVE OF RALPH RICHARDSON (1902-83)
Highgate

Distinguished actor and thespian legend, Ralph Richardson made over sixty films during his long career. He died, aged eighty, after a series of strokes in 1983 and is buried in **Highgate Eastern Cemetery.**

See also: Ralph Richardson (Gloucestershire)

*Professor Marcus (Alec Guinness) and One-Round (Danny Green) dispose of a gang member over the Copenhagen Tunnel in **The Ladykillers** (1955, Ealing).*

THE LADYKILLERS
King's Cross

• 1955 96m c Comedy/Crime Ealing (UK)
• Alec Guinness (Professor Marcus), Cecil Parker (The Mayor), Herbert Lom (Louis), Peter Sellers (Harry), Danny Green (One-Round), Jack Warner (Police Superintendent), Katie Johnson (Mrs. Wilberforce), Edie Martin (Lettice), Philip Stainton (Police Sergeant), Frankie Howard (Barrow Boy)
• p, Seth Holt; d, Alexander Mackendrick; w, William Rose (based on his story); ph, Otto Heller; ed, Jack Harris; • AAN Best Original Screenplay: William Rose; BAA Best Actress: Katie Johnson

Passing themselves off as classical musicians, a gang of criminals led by Professor Marcus (Alec Guinness) rent rooms at the house of the eccentric Mrs. Wilberforce (Katie Johnson) and secretly plan a robbery at Kings Cross Station.

When Mrs. Wilberforce stumbles on the truth and thwarts their plans, the gang decides to do away with her. Unable to decide who should bump her off, the gang uproariously kill each other, one by one.

The ambush of the security van took place in **Cheney Road**, behind **Kings Cross Station**, where the stolen loot was temporarily deposited in a trunk. Mrs. Wilberforce's house was specially built by Ealing at the end of **Frederica Street**, off the **Caledonian Road**, and has since been substantially redeveloped to the point where it is now virtually unrecognizable. **St. Pancras Station** appeared to be at the bottom of Frederica Street in the film, but is in fact about a mile away at the end of Caledonian Road. The tunnel was the **Copenhagen Tunnel**, used frequently by goods trains, and a replica of the tunnel entrance was

constructed at Ealing. When filming was finished, Ealing studios held a street party for the residents of Frederica Street which was hosted by the cast and crew.

The Ladykillers was one of the last films produced at Ealing Studios before they were sold to the BBC in 1955 and it remains one of the great comic masterpieces of British cinema.

See also: Peter Sellers, Cheney Road, Ealing Studios

LONDON VIDEO ART ARCHIVE
Camden Town

London Electronic Arts' collection of Video Art is the most extensive in the U.K. Established in 1976, the collection houses over 1,000 tapes by British and international artists. Catalogue and price list available on request.

Further information: London Electronic Arts, 5-7 Buck St., London, NW1 8NJ. Tel: 0171 284 4588. E-mail: lea@easynet.co.uk

WORKSHOP OF ROBERT PAUL
Holborn

Film pioneer, Robert William Paul, was born on 3 October 1869 at **3 Albion Place**, off Liverpool Road, Highbury, North London. He attended the City and Guilds Technical College, Finsbury, and later worked as an electrical engineer and instrument maker at **44 Hatton Garden, Holborn** (plaque erected).

In 1894, two Greek entrepreneurs and Kinetoscope parlour operators approached Paul to manufacture copies of the Kinetoscope. The device, invented by Thomas Edison, was a peepshow machine for viewing moving pictures - a pursuit which was extremely popular in Victorian Britain. Paul discovered that Edison, normally an astute and ruthless businessman, had failed to register a patent for the Kinetoscope in Britain and he began to manufacture replicas.

To ensure a supply of films Paul joined forces with photographer, Birt Acres, and they constructed Britain's first moving picture camera between February and March 1895. Their first short film of a man leaving a house was shot outside Acres' house at **Clovelly Cottage, Park Road, Barnet** (plaque erected), and the following day they filmed the Oxford and Cambridge Boat Race. Within three months they had produced a string of films, including: *Carpenter's Shop, The Arrest of a Pickpocket, The Comic Shoeblack, The Boxing Kangaroo* and *The Derby* which can all lay claim to being Britain's first movies. These films were first seen at the Empire of India Exhibition, Earl's Court in 1895. Due to conflicting personalities which led to bitter disputes, Paul and Acres' partnership eventually collapsed.

See also: First Edison Kinetoscope Parlour

OFFSTAGE THEATRE & FILM BOOKSHOP
Camden Town

Founded in 1982 the OTF bookshop specialises in cinema and theatre literature, including books, screenplays, scripts, technical manuals and magazines.

Further information: OTF Bookshop, 37 Chalk Farm Road, London, NW1 8AJ. Tel: 0171 485 4996. Open 7 days a week.

THE CINEMA BOOKSHOP
Bloomsbury

Fred Zentner

Run by Fred Zentner as an extension to his collector's passion for books on film, this small shop is Europe's first bookshop dedicated to the cinema. Established over thirty years ago its speciality is out of print books, but it also stocks a comprehensive range of new and second-hand books, posters, pressbooks and stills.

Run on a shoe-string and tightly staffed, with no mod cons and no website, The Cinema Bookshop is the archetypal dusty old bookshop where many a gem is waiting to be unearthed.

Further information: The Cinema Bookshop, 13-14 Great Russell Street, London, WC1B 3NH. Tel: 0171 637 0206. Open: 10.30-5.30 Mon-Sat. Mail order service available.

RARE DISCS
Bloomsbury

Philip (or is it Martin?) **Masheter**

Rare Discs is jointly owned by twins Philip and Martin Masheter who specialize in film soundtracks, mainly on vinyl, with a sprinkling of show and theatre recordings. Catering very much for the specialist collector they also stock a range of original movie memorabilia, including posters, stills, autographs, postcards, books and magazines.

Past visitors to the shop in search of that 'rare disc' have included Jerry Goldsmith, John Barry, Elmer Bernstein, Terence Young, Jane Powell and Margaret O'Brien.

Further information: Rare Discs, 18 Bloomsbury Street, off New Oxford Street, London WC1. Tel: 0171 580 3516.

BRITISH FILM INSTITUTE
Fitzrovia

The world's largest collection of documentation on film and television is held by BFI Library and Information Services, and includes books, periodicals, press cuttings, scripts and publicity materials. Special collections include the private papers of Carol Reed, Michael Balcon and Emeric Pressburger. Library and Information Services answers over 30,000 telephone and 2,500 written enquiries each year, and the collection can be consulted by visitors in the reading room. There is an entry charge, which is discounted for BFI members.

The National Film and Television Archive is the largest of its kind in the world, with 275,000 film and TV titles dating from 1895. Preservation and restoration work is carried out at the J Paul Getty Jnr Conservation Centre in Berkhamsted, Hertfordshire, and its collection can be viewed at the BFI. The NFTVA also preserves and makes accessible stills, transparencies, posters, set and costume designs, storyboards, sketches and programmes through the BFI Stills, Posters and Designs department.

Further information: The British Film Institute, 21 Stephen Street, London W1P 1PL. Tel: 0171 255 1444.

Croydon

BEANOS
Croydon

Beanos' main business is collectable records, but it is also a sound-track specialist and has a large second-hand video collection.

It also has a sixties style cafe serving frothy coffee which you can drink in their tiny cinema. Established in 1975, it now occupies three floors of a converted 19th century printing works.

Further information: Beanos, Middle St., Croydon, CRO 1RE, London. Tel: 0181 680 1202. Beanos@easynet.co.uk

BIRTHPLACE OF DAVID LEAN (1908-91)
South Croydon

"Lean became the prisoner of big pictures, a great eye striving to show off a large mind. I challenge anyone to see Oliver Twist and Dr. Zhivago and not admit the loss."
David Thomson

From teaboy to director, David Lean's career spanned over fifty years, during which time his films have made a massive contribution to British cinema. He was born on 25 March 1908 at **38 Blenheim Crescent, South Croydon**, the eldest of two sons of Quakers, Helena Tangye and Frank Lean, a chartered accountant. *"My parents must have been very poor,"* Lean once commented, *"because it was a miserable little place. A small street in South Croydon - awfully simple and plain,"* * Shortly after he was born, his family moved to the village of **Mertsham**, between Redhill and Reigate, to a house (opposite the church) called '**The Fryennes**' where his younger brother Edward was born in 1911. The local Church of England school, however, refused to accept Quaker children and in 1915 the family moved back to Croydon where his father bought Wareham

*Anthony Havelock-Allan and **David Lean** on the set of Ryan's Daughter*

38 Blenheim Crescent - birthplace of
David Lean *(photo Jason Patient)*

Mount at 3 Wareham Road (now demolished). David attended kindergarten at a Miss Clayton's, **60 Park Lane**, East Croydon, and prep school at **The Limes in Melville Avenue**. He later boarded at Leighton Park, a Quaker school near Reading, where his school report read, *"either not very bright or incorrigibly lazy."*

His family's Quaker beliefs forbade him from attending the cinema; consequently he was seventeen before he saw his first film, *The Hound of the Baskervilles* (1922). While his 'brighter' younger brother was sent to Oxford, David joined the office of his father's accountancy firm, which he hated. Also around this time his parents separated, compounding his misery. It was his Aunt Edith, who, after seeing his enormous collection of film magazines, suggested he try a career in the film industry, something that had never occurred to him before.

After initially rejecting his son's pleas, his father was instrumental in securing him a job with Gaumont British's Lime Grove Studios in Shepherd's Bush. It was here he discovered his vocation in

life, and began to learn the many trades of film making, starting as a runner-cum-teaboy.

After working on various films, including Maurice Elvey's *Quinneys* (1927), and *Balaclava* (1928) where he was in charge of the uniforms, he ended up in the cutting room. He was soon editing the sound news, which included writing the commentaries and speaking them. In the early thirties he moved to the Briish-Dominion Studios at Elstree where he became a successful feature film editor, cutting quality films like *Pygmalion* (1938) and Michael Powell's, *49th Parallel* (1941). He turned down offers to direct several quota-quickies, fearing their cheap production techniques could damage his career, and it was not until Noel Coward asked him to direct the action scenes in *In Which We Serve* (1942) that he began his directing career.

His early films became noted for their strong narrative and his later work for the lengthy and breathtaking epic, and included *This Happy Breed* (1945), *Brief Encounter* (1946), definitive adaptations of Dickens' *Great Expectations* (1946) and *Oliver Twist* (1948), *The Sound Barrier* (1954), *Hobson's Choice* (1955), and his later epics *The Bridge on the River Kwai* (1957), *Lawrence of Arabia* (1962), *Dr. Zhivago* (1970), *Ryan's Daughter* (1984) and *A Passage to India* (1984).

He was married six times and was knighted in 1984. His second and third wives were the actresses, Kay Walsh and Ann Todd. He died on 16 April 1991 after developing pneumonia and his funeral was held at **Putney Vale Crematorium**.

See also: *Brief Encounter, Great Expectations,* The Lawrence of Arabia Trail, *Ryan's Daughter,* Robert Bolt

Ealing

EALING STUDIOS
Ealing Green

Britain's most famous film studio and home of the classic Ealing Comedies of the late 1940s and early 1950s was founded in the London suburbs by Will Barber in 1902. The site was extended by Basil Dean's production company, Associated Talking Pictures in 1931, and the studio produced over sixty feature films during the thirties with stars such as George Formby and Gracie Fields.

In 1938 Sir Michael Balcon became the studio's production head and shortly afterwards acquired control of the company. It was under his leadership that many of the Ealing classics were created using directors and writers such as Alberto Cavalcanti, T.E.B. Clarke, Alexander Mackendrick and Charles Crichton to create some of the best British films, including *Went The Day Well?* (1942), *Hue And Cry* (1947), *Whisky Galore* (1948), *The Blue Lamp* (1949), *Passport to Pimlico* (1949), *Kind Hearts and Coronets* (1949), *The Lavender Hill Mob* (1951), *The Man in the White Suit* (1951), *The Cruel Sea* (1953), *The Titfield Thunderbolt* (1953), *The Maggie* (1954) and *The Ladykillers* (1955).

It was the studio's comedies which became the Ealing hallmark, often featuring down-to-earth folk, with a generous sprinkling of eccentrics, reacting against oppression. Although virtually devoid of sex, gratuitous violence and any reference to a world beyond Britain, they must now be ranked among the greatest comedies ever made.

Ealing Studios were sold to the BBC in 1955, but the company

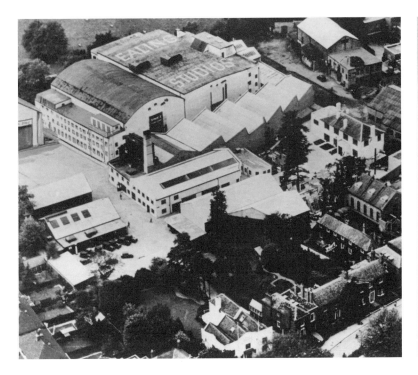

Ealing Studios

*Ingrid Bergman portraying **Gladys Aylward** in The Inn of the Sixth Happiness (1958, TCF)*

transferred production to Pinewood Studios, before eventually winding up in 1959. For nearly forty years the BBC maintained Ealing as a production centre, but following the BBC's vacation of the premises in the early nineties, the studios have been under the ownership of the National Film and Television School who are, at the time of writing, planning to sell off the site for development. As none of the buildings are listed as places of significant historical interest, the site, including Balcon's famous White House, could quite legitimately be flattened to make way for a hypermarket or a housing estate. A vigorous campaign is under way to save the studios which hopes to create a new funding body to operate the studios and create a visitor centre with a museum and behind the scenes tours.

See also: *Went The Day Well?, Hue and Cry, Whisky Galore, The Blue*

Lamp, Passport to Pimlico, Kind Hearts and Coronets, The Cruel Sea, The Titfield Thunderbolt, The Maggie, The Ladykillers.

Further information: Those wishing to be involved in the 'Save Ealing Studios Campaign' should contact the campaign office at Forever Ealing, PO Box 24443, Ealing, London W5 5WU. Tel/Fax: 0181 567 4550.
foreverealing@netscape.net
www.foreverealing.freeserve.co.uk

Enfield

FORMER HOME OF GLADYS AYLWARD (1902-70)
Lower Edmonton

Gladys Aylward's life in China was virtually unknown until her story was fictionalized by BBC writer, Alan Burgess in his bestseller, *The*

Small Woman (1957) and later in the film based on the book, *The Inn of The Sixth Happiness* (1958). Gladys Aylward loathed the film; she accused it of shamefully glamourizing her life and was outraged at the fabricated love-affair with a Eurasian Colonel (Kurt Jurgens) and Ingrid Bergman (Aylward), a divorcee.

She was born 24 February 1902 in Edmonton, Middlesex, the eldest of three children of Rosina Whiskin and Thomas Aylward, a postman. After leaving school at fourteen she worked as shop assistant, nanny and parlourmaid, before leaving for China to become a missionary in 1932. Known as Ai Weh-te, 'the virtuous one', her best-known achievement was during the Sino-Japanese war in 1940 when she led a hundred children across mountains to safety. She became a Chinese citizen in 1936 and is buried in a marble tomb at Christ's College, Tamshui, Taiwan. Her former childhood home is at **67 Cheddington Road, Edmonton**, and is marked by a plaque.

See also: *The Inn of The Sixth Happiness*

Greenwich

BIRTHPLACE OF BOB HOPE (1903-)
Eltham.

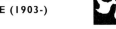

"... I left England when I was four because I found out I could never be King."

Born Leslie Towns Hope on 30 May 1903 at **44 Craighton Road.** His father, Harry Hope, was a stonemason who had married fifteen-year-old Avis Towns in Cardiff in 1891. They had seven children and moved house several times during Harry's search for employment before emigrating to Cleveland, Ohio in 1908.

Young Leslie never stayed in one job too long and tried his hand at such diverse occupations as selling newspapers, pool hustling, prizefighting, assisting in a butcher's shop and dancing. He toured in vaudeville as a comic dancer for many years before entering radio in the 1930s and making a name for himself on NBC's 'Pepsodent' show. Bing Crosby also broadcast a show sponsored by Kraft Foods and it was during this period that the famous feuding banter between the two began. Failing a screen test in 1930 was no deterrent; he eventually became a Paramount contract player where he made his first feature film, *The Big Broadcast of 1938.*

Bob Hope will probably be best remembered for the 'Road' films

*44 Craighton Road - birthplace of **Bob Hope***

with Dorothy Lamour and Bing Crosby. The first was *Road to Singapore* (1940) which was a box-office success and set the the mould for a further six, ending with *Road to Hong Kong* (1962). Hope and Crosby never stuck to the script, often to the annoyance of the scriptwriters: they ad-libbed their way through every film. Don Hartman, scriptwriter on three 'Road' films recalls: *"You take a piece of used chewing gum and flip it at a map. Wherever it lands you*

can lay a Road picture so long as there are jokers who cook and eat strangers..."

Other films included: *Thanks for the Memory* (1938), *The Cat and the Canary* (1939), *The Paleface* (1948), *Call Me Bwana* (1963).

THE KRAYS
Greenwich

- 1990 119m c Crime (UK)
- Billie Whitelaw (Violet Kray), Gary Kemp (Ronald Kray), Martin Kemp (Reginald Kray), Susan Fleetwood (Rose), Charlotte Cornwell (May), Jimmy Jewel (Cannonball Lee)
- P, Dominic Anciano, Ray Burdis; d, Peter Medak; w, Philip Ridley; ed, Martin Walsh; ph, Alex Thomson

The slums of the East End, once ruled over with an iron fist by Ronnie and Reggie Kray may have all but disappeared, but the fearsome memory of the Krays lingers on. Portrayed compellingly by Spandau Ballet twins, Gary and Martin Kemp, the film retraces their humble origins from local thugs to professional mobsters, who never stray too far from their doting mum (Billie Whitelaw).

East End redevelopment forced the film makers south of the river to **Caradoc Street** in Greenwich for the location of the Krays' childhood home, where the two-up and two-down terraced housing accurately recreated the East End of the 1930's.

The twins were sentenced to life imprisonment in 1969 for murdering hoodlums, George Cornell and Jack 'The Hat' McVitie, with a recommendation from the judge that they serve at least thirty years. **Bethnal Green** was the Krays' territory, now the heart of London's Bangladeshi community. In **Cheshire Street, near St. Matthew's Row**, is the **Carpenters**

Arms pub, once owned by the Krays and the pub in which Reggie had been drinking the night he murdered Jack 'The Hat' McVitie. The corner of **Cheshire Street and Hereford Street** was the location of the **Repton Boxing Club**, where the young twins learned to become accomplished boxers. Cheshire Street runs into **Vallance Road** where number **178** was the Krays' childhood home, and later the headquarters of their East End empire until it was demolished in 1966. The meeting which failed in its attempt to broker peace between the Krays and the Richardsons, a South London gang, took place at the **Grave Maurice pub, 269 Whitechapel Road**. One of the Richardsons' associates, George Cornell, signed his death warrant when he called Ronnie Kray a "fat poof". He was later shot dead by Ronnie while drinking at the bar in the **Blind Beggar pub, 337 Whitechapel Road**. Jack 'The Hat' was lured to a basement flat at **97 Evering Road, Stoke Newington**, on the pretext of a party, where he was stabbed in the face with a knife by Reggie.

Ronnie died of a heart attack in Broadmoor and Reggie discovered religion and married while still in prison. Ronnie's funeral service was held at **St. Matthew's Church, St. Matthew's Row**, in 1995, where Frank Sinatra's *My Way* was played to the mourners.

SPREAD EAGLE BOOKSHOP
Greenwich

Large selection of second-hand books on the cinema. Also stocks memorabilia, ephemera, posters, magazines and stills.

Further information: Spread Eagle Bookshop, 9 Nevada St., London, SE10 9JL.
Tel: 0181 305 1666.

CHILDHOOD HOME OF DANIEL DAY-LEWIS (1958-)
Greenwich

"Anyone can learn to paint with their left foot. But not everyone has to learn to paint with their left foot."
Daniel Day-Lewis

Daniel Day-Lewis as Newland Archer in The Age of Innocence (1993, Columbia/Cappa/De Fina)

6 Croom's Hill - childhood home of Daniel Day-Lewis

Daniel Michael Blake Day-Lewis was born at **96 Campden Hill Road, Kensington**, on 29 April 1957, the second child of Jill Balcon (daughter of Sir Michael Balcon) and the Poet Laureate, Cecil Day-Lewis. Shortly afterwards the family moved to **6 Croom's Hill, Greenwich**, opposite the Greenwich Theatre, where they remained for the next fifteen years. His illustrious father, Cecil, was fifty-three when Daniel was born, and is remembered as a remote figure who spent most of his time working in his study. Daniel and his older sister, Tamasin, were looked after by nannies, and led a very 'upstairs downstairs' existence.

A solitary and sheltered child, he was enrolled at the local state school in **Invicta Road**, in 1962. When he was seven he was transferred to its sister school, **Sherington Junior**, and in 1968 he became a weekly boarder at **Sevenoaks** public school in Kent, which he hated. In 1970 he made his film debut by pure chance. John Schlesinger was shooting a sequence for *Sunday, Bloody Sunday* (1971) in Greenwich, and needed some roguish street kids. The local greengrocer recommended Daniel and his mates, and they each earned £5 for their day's effort. The same year he enrolled at **Bedales**, his sister's co-educational school in Petersfield, Hampshire, where he blossomed, and became involved in the school drama group.

When he left school he joined the Bristol Old Vic Theatre School, and after three years was accepted by the Bristol Old Vic Company. He secured small parts in *Gandhi* (1982) and *Bounty* (1984), but established himself on the screen portraying a homosexual punk in Stephen Frear's *My Beautiful Laundrette* (1985) and the fastidious ninny, Cecil, in *A Room With A View* (1985). His first

*Thomas (David Hemmings) shoots a recumbent model in **Blow-Up** (1966, Bridge Films)*

Antonioni, Tonino Guerra, Edward Bond (based on a story by Julio Cortazar); ph, Carlo Di Palma; ed, Frank Clarke; m, Herbie Hancock, The Yardbirds; cos, Jocelyn Rickards
• AAN Best Director, AAN Best Original Screenplay

When trendy photographer, David Hemmings' blow-ups of snapshots in a public park reveal a corpse in the background, he returns to investigate, only to discover the body has disappeared...

Blow-Up burst upon a receptive swinging sixties with its abstract imagery, groovy sounds and full-frontal nudity to become one of the most lucrative art films ever made, and has since grown into a cult classic. The park location used was **Maryon Park**, off the **Woolwich Road**.

Hackney

THE LUX CENTRE
Hoxton

The Lux was established in September 1997 with a £4.5m Arts Council and National Lottery grant as a state-of-the-art cinema and cut-price centre for experimental film-makers. In the evening, its two-way projector can screen images indoors onto the screen and outdoors into the square simultaneously. The auditorium has removable seats for multimedia events, and if natural light is required, wall panels rotate and expose frosted glass windows. Video 'pits' on the foyer floor screen films by local multimedia artists. Editing suites and equipment are available for low-cost hire.

Further information: The Lux Centre, 2-4 Hoxton Sq., London N1. Tel: 0171 684 0201

leading role was in *The Unbearable Lightness of Being* (1988), but it was his moving portrayal of cerebral palsy sufferer, Christy Brown, in *My Left Foot* (1989) which brought him world acclaim and a Best Actor Oscar. Renowned for his detailed researching of roles, he studied the life of cerebral palsy sufferers for two months at the Sandymount School and Clinic in Dublin. On the film set he never came out of character and was fed and supported by the film crew.

His other films include *The Last of the Mohicans* (1992), *The Age of Innocence* (1994), *In the Name of the Father* (1994) and *The Crucible* (1996).

See also: Christy Brown, *My Left Foot*

BLOW-UP
Woolwich

• 1966 110m c Drama Bridge (U.K.)
• David Hemmings (Thomas), Vanessa Redgrave (Jane), Sarah Miles (Patricia), Jane Birkin, Gillian Hills (Teenagers),
• p, Pierre Rouve, Carlo Ponti; d, Michelangelo Antonioni; w, Michelangelo

GAINSBOROUGH FILM STUDIOS
Hoxton

In 1919 the American company, Famous Players-Lasky converted the former railway power station in **Poole Street, Islington,** into a film studio. They made many silent films here, until an industry recession forced them to pull out of British film production in 1924 when Michael Balcon bought the studios and founded Gainsborough Pictures. The studios were destroyed by fire in 1930 in a suspected arson attack and a sound engineer narrowly escaped with his life by jumping down a lift shaft. His thumb, however, remained behind; trapped in the shaft, where staff reputedly stared at it for many a year.

Gainsborough's first film was *The Passionate Adventure*, directed by Graham Cutts, with a screenplay written by twenty-five year old Alfred Hitchcock. Hitch began his film career at Islington Studios designing title cards for Famous Players-Lasky in 1919, eventually being given the opportunity to direct his first film in 1923: *Mrs Peabody*, which was never completed or released. In 1938 he made the classic thriller *The Lady Vanishes* here for MGM. Former music-hall comedian, Will Hay, also made two of his most successful films here in 1937 - *Oh, Mr Porter* and *Good-Morning Boys*. Other films shot here include: The Crazy Gang's *O-Kay For Sound* (1937), Carol Reed's *The Girl Must Live* (1938), Gracie Fields' *Shipyard Sally* (1939) and Margaret Lockwood's *The Wicked Lady* (1945).

After WWII the Rank Organisation took over the studios until the downfall of the Rank Film Empire forced the closure of the studio in 1949. The building has since been used as a carpet warehouse and a bottling plant. Developers recently announced conversion plans for the property which will include flats, a restaurant, work units, and new film-making facilities.

Gainsborough Film Studios

See also: J. Arthur Rank, Alfred Hitchcock, *Oh Mr Porter*.

Hammersmith & Fulham

GRAVE OF TERENCE RATTIGAN (1911-1977)
Kensal Green

Terence Mervyn Rattigan, playwright and screenwriter, was born in **Cornwall Gardens, Kensington**, in 1911, the second child of William Rattigan of the Diplomatic Service and Vera Houston. He attended Sandroyd Preparatory School near Cobham, Surrey, and won scholarships to Harrow and Trinity College, Oxford. He became a celebrated playwright in 1936 with the success of his early comedy, *French Without Tears.*

He will be best remembered in the cinema for his two moving screenplays adapted from his plays: *The Winslow Boy* (1950), starring Robert Donat, in which a father defends his naval-cadet son who is accused of petty theft and *The Browning Version* (1951) which cast Michael Redgrave as a failed public school master. Other original screenplays included: *The Sound Barrier* (1952), *The Deep Blue Sea* (1955), *The Prince and The Showgirl* (1957), *Separate Tables* (1958), *The V.I.P.s* (1963) and *Goodbye Mr. Chips* (1969).

His popularity declined in the 1950s and his middle-brow appeal was criticised by the emerging 'angry young men' playwrights. He was cremated in Bermuda and his remains are buried in the family tomb at **Kensal Green Cemetery, Harrow Road.** He was knighted in 1971.

See also: Sherborne School, *Goodbye Mr. Chips*

Haringey

BIRTHPLACE OF JACK HAWKINS (1910-73)
Wood Green

John Edward Hawkins was born on 14 September 1910, the youngest of four children, at **Lyndhurst Road, Wood Green**. In 1918 he was accepted for the choir of **St.**

Michael's Parish Church in Bounds Green Road and two years later he faced his first audience in a performance of Gilbert and Sullivan's *Patience*.

He enrolled at the Italia Conti School of Acting in 1922 and following a gruelling audition with Sybil Thorndike, Lewis Casson and George Bernard Shaw, he secured the part of the page-boy in Shaw's new play, *St. Joan*. He stayed with the company for three years where his boy-actor companions included Laurence Olivier and Carol Reed.

In 1929 he sailed to New York where he portrayed Lt. Hibbert in director James Welch's production of *Journey's End*. It was during the stage production of *Autumn Crocus* in 1931 that he first met actress Jessica Tandy. They were married the following year at **St. Paul's Church, Winchmore Hill (London N21)** but were to divorce seven years later.

His first notable film part was in Hitchcock's *The Lodger* (1932) for which he received £8 a day for a month's work. During WWII he joined the Royal Welsh Fusiliers and was involved in running ENSA in India and the Far East. After the war he was offered a three-year contract from Alexander Korda which launched his post-war film career.

In 1953 his career took off when he portrayed the headmaster of a school for the profoundly deaf in *Mandy* and in 1954 he was voted Britain's number one box office draw. He was often cast in authorative roles and will be best remembered as Capt. Ericson in *The Cruel Sea* (1953), Maj. Warden in *Bridge on the River Kwai* (1957), Quintus Arrius in *Ben Hur* (1959), Hyde in the *League of Gentlemen* (1960) and Gen. Allenby in *Lawrence of Arabia* (1962).

In 1966 he was diagnosed as having cancer of the throat. An operation successfully removed the growth and he learned to speak again through a hole in his throat. For seven years he struggled with his career and his voice was dubbed by other actors. After complications he died after repeated haemorrhaging in St. Stephen's Hospital, Fulham, in 1973.

See also: *The Cruel Sea*

ODEON
Muswell Hill

Opened on 9 September 1936 and designed by George Coles, the Odeon represents the best of 1930s Art Deco style and elegance. Fearing a view of lewd movie posters, garish neon and general immorality, the outraged congregation of neighbouring St. James' Church, on the opposite side of the road, made the stipulation that the entrance foyer would have to be built further up Fortis Green Road where the shops and trees would obscure it.

The fifty seventh cinema in Oscar Deutsch's Odeon chain, its opening film was Max Miller's *Educated Evans* and was attended by various celebrities, including Basil Rathbone and Joan Gardner. The auditorium design is said to be a symbolic portrayal of film, with ceiling lights resembling film strips, columns imitating film reels and a proscenium arch representing a camera shutter. It was converted to three screens in 1974, but its original features were retained.

Further information: Odeon, Fortis Green Road, London N10. Tel: 0181 315 4216.

Hillingdon

A NIGHT TO REMEMBER
Ruislip

- 1958 123m bw Rank (UK)
- Kenneth More (Second Officer Charles Lightoller), Ronald Allen (Clarke), Robert Ayres (Peuchen), Honor Blackman (Mrs. Lucas), Anthony Bushell (Captain Rostron), John Cairney (Murphy)
- p, William McQuitty; d, Roy Ward Baker; w, Eric Ambler (based on the book by Walter Lord); ph, Geoffrey Unsworth; ed, Sidney Hayers; m, William Alwyn; art d, Alex Vetchinsky;

This film never became a box-office success and today is somewhat lost and forgotten in the wake of James Cameron's 1997 blockbuster, *Titanic*. Made over forty years ago on a budget laughable in comparison to 20th Century Fox's epic, it nonetheless remains one of the best accounts of the disaster ever filmed.

In a field close to Pinewood Studios, three hundred feet of hull and superstructure were built. These were so heavy that four acres of concrete were needed as a base to support the tremendous weight. The actors worked mostly at night in freezing conditions because their breath had to be visible.

Pinewood didn't have a tank large enough to film the scenes of survivors trying to reach lifeboats in the sea, so **Ruislip Lido, Reservoir Road,** substituted for the icy North Atlantic instead. Today, the water level in Ruislip Lido is much lower than it was in the fifties. The original buildings have since been demolished and **The Water's Edge pub** now stands on the site.

See also: William Murdoch.

A CLOCKWORK ORANGE
Uxbridge

• 1971 137m c Science Fiction Warner Bros. (UK)
• Malcolm McDowell (Alex), Patrick Magee (Mr. Alexander), Michael Bates (Chief Guard), Warren Clarke (Dim), John Clive (Stage Actor), Adrienne Corri (Mrs. Alexander), Carl Duering (Dr. Brodsky), Paul Farrel (Hobo), Clive Francis (Lodger)
• p, Stanley Kubrick; d, Stanley Kubrick; w, Stanley Kubrick (based on the novel by Anthony Burgess); ph, John Alcott; ed, Bill Butler; m, Walter Carlos; prod d, John Barry; art d, Russell Hagg, Peter Shields; cos, Milena Canonero
• AAN Best Picture; AAN Best Director: Stanley Kubrick; AAN Best Adapted Screenplay: Stanley Kubrick; AAN Best Editing: Bill Butler

As queer as a clockwork orange
Cockney slang

Stanley Kubrick read Anthony Burgess's 1962 novel in the late

Being the adventures of a young man whose principal interests are rape, ultra-violence and Beethoven.

STANLEY KUBRICK'S CLOCKWORK ORANGE

sixties and was deeply impressed. Set in a violent Britain of the near future where language is debased and dapper gangs roam bleak landscapes, robbing, murdering and raping, Alex, a gang leader and Beethoven lover, brutally attacks a middle-aged couple. When Alex's violent behaviour is corrected by aversion therapy at the government's Ludovico Medical Facility, he becomes nauseous whenever he feels like getting nasty. Let loose on the streets without any defences, Alex is violently persecuted by the world to which he once belonged.

Kubrick and the film's designer, John Barry, trawled through ten years worth of architectural magazines searching for suitable building designs that could create the book's desolate suburb of Thamesmead. The suitably stark exteriors of the then newly built, **Brunel University, between Kingston Lane and Cleveland Lane, Uxbridge, Hillingdon** doubled as the Ludovico Medical Facility and the **American Drug Store in Kings Road, Chelsea** (now defunct) became the modish shopping complex where Alex encounters the opposite sex. Other

locations included Greenwich's **Binsey Walk, Tavy Bridge and Southmere Lake**.

It was the film's misfortune to be released shortly after the furore caused over the sex and violence in Peckinpah's *Straw Dogs*, and although received favourably by the critics, it was blamed by the tabloid press for every juvenile crime committed on the streets. In August 1973, having endured death-threats to his family, and being no doubt sick and tired of all the hysteria, Kubrick withdrew the U.K. distribution rights.

At the time of writing, however, the Kubrick family have begun discussions with the distributors, Warner Brothers, with a view to ending their boycott of the film.

See also: Stanley Kubrick, *Full Metal Jacket*

Hounslow

GRAVE OF CAROL REED (1906-1976)
Gunnersbury

Often pigeon-holed as a 'literary director', Carol Reed was a masterly storyteller who made some of the great masterpieces of the British cinema. Best known for his post-war thriller, *The Third Man* (1949), he reached his peak in the late forties, but today his genius is often overlooked.

He was born in Putney, one of six illegitimate children of the famous actor and stage manager, Sir Herbert Beerbohm Tree and May Pinney. Following his education at King's School, Canterbury, he went to the U.S.A. in 1922 to study chicken farming, but returned disillusioned within the year. He decided to try a career in drama and joined a theatre company run by Sybil Thorndike with which he made his London debut in 1924 in the play *Heraclius*. He later worked with a company formed by thriller writer Edgar Wallace and appeared in three West End plays.

Frequently doubling as stage manager, he soon realised that his skills lay on the production side and Wallace employed him to supervise his books' screen adaptations. This introduced Reed to the film world and in 1932 he joined the staff of Associated Talking Pictures as a dialogue director.

He quickly rose through the ranks and in 1934 he was assistant director of *Sing As We Go*, starring Gracie Fields. In the same year he directed his first film, *Midshipman Easy*. Seven films later in 1939 he directed *The Stars Look Down* which secured his reputation with the critics as an imaginative young talent to watch out for. This was followed by Launder and Gilliat's thriller, *Night Train To Munich* in 1940.

During the war he joined the Army Kinematograph service and directed *The Way Ahead* (1944), a semi-documentary account about the life of raw recruits which was a big hit with wartime audiences.

After the war he was hired by J. Arthur Rank and directed his first post-war film and box-office hit, *The Odd Man Out* (1946) about a wounded IRA man on the run. Shortly afterwards Reed left Rank to join Alexander Korda's London Films where he collaborated with the writer, Graham Greene. This resulted in *The Fallen Idol* (1948) and the film which was to be his greatest achievement, *The Third Man* (1949).

In the early fifties Reed's work sadly declined, but after a run of mediocre and forgettable films, such as *Our Man in Havana*

*The grave of **Carol Reed,** overgrown and obscured by trees in Kensington Cemetery.*

(1959) and *The Agony and the Ecstasy* (1965) he made a comeback in 1968 with his Oscar-winning musical, *Oliver*.
Twice married with one son, he died after a heart attack on 25 April 1976. His funeral was held in **Chelsea Old Church**. He had no desire to be buried in an idyllic country churchyard and so at his request he was laid to rest near the busy M4 at **Kensington Cemetery, Gunnersbury Avenue**, where two stones engraved with daisies mark his grave. The funeral was held in **Chelsea Old Church, Cheyne Walk, Chelsea Embankment.** All seemed to be going according to

plan until the pallbearers hoisted the coffin onto their shoulders. Suddenly, the unexpected sound of zither music drifted down from the balcony. Unknown to most of the mourners, Anton Karas, composer of the famous theme tune for *The Third Man*, had flown from Vienna to attend the funeral and slowly played his theme in the style of a funeral march as the coffin made its exit.

See also: Edgar Wallace, J. Arthur Rank, Sidney Gilliatt, *The Odd Man Out*, *The Stars Look Down*

Islington

THE
CRYING GAME
St Lukes

• 1992 112m c
Drama/Romance/Thriller Palace Pictures (UK)
• Stephen Rea (Fergus), Miranda Richardson (Jude), Forest Whitaker (Jody), Jim Broadbent (Col), Ralph Brown (Dave), Adrian Dunbar (Maguire), Jaye Davidson (Dil)
• p, Stephen Wooley; d, Neil Jordan; w, Neil Jordan; ph, Ian Wilson; ed, Kant Pan; m, Anne Dudley; prod d, Jim Clay; art d, Chris Seagers; cos, Sandy Powell
• AAN Best Picture; AAN Best Actor: Stephen Rea; AAN Best Supporting Actor: Jaye Davidson; AAN Best Director: Neil Jordan; AA Best Original Screenplay: Neil Jordan; AAN Best Editing: Kant Pan

Neil Jordan's acclaimed IRA thriller was filmed at various locations in England and Ireland. One of the main locations was the Metro pub where the enigmatic hairdresser and part-time singer, Dil, meets Fergus, the reformed terrorist responsible for Dil's boyfriend's death. The pub exterior was an empty building given the facade of a pub at **28-30 Coronet Street**

Stephen Rea and Jaye Davidson in **The Crying Game** *(1992, Palace Pictures)*

(Dil's flat was in nearby Hoxton Square), but the interior was shot in the **London Apprentice at 333 Old Street** (now The 333 Club). The hairdresser's where Dil was employed was also an empty building at **3 Fournier Street** and the building site where Fergus was employed was at **Dartmouth Terrace, Blackheath**. Fergus and fellow terrorist, Jude (Miranda Richardson), hatch their deadly plan in **The Lowndes Arms, 37 Chesham Street** and **Eaton Place**, where the attempted assassination took place, can be seen across the street from the pub.

The Lowndes Arms is a very cosmopolitan pub, frequented by nearby embassy staff, tourists and locals, offering lunches, evening meals, real ales and a beer garden.

Further information: The 333 Club has drastically changed its former pub interior. Opening hours: 10pm - 5am. Tel: 0171 739 5949.

See also: Neil Jordan, Burnham Beeches Walk

HUNTLEY FILM ARCHIVES
Highbury

Film and railway historian, John Huntley, started collecting 16mm and 35mm railway documentary films in 1939 and presenting

archive film-based live cinema shows. With more than forty thousand titles, Huntley Film Archives is now one of the largest film libraries in Europe.

Famous for uncovering rare unseen and unused footage, the collection now covers a wide range of subjects, including 14,000 documentaries, 3,000 feature films, 6,000 titles of news and current affairs and 8,000 films relating to science and education.

The archive also houses the Dalton-Nicholson Movie Stills Collection containing 250,000 pictures from the golden age of Hollywood. Posters, scripts and vintage projection and production equipment are also available for loan to museums or prop departments.

The archive also represents The London Film Archive, a charitable trust founded in 1996 to preserve and make available images of London from 1895 onwards.

Further information: Huntley Film Archives, 78 Mildmay Park, Newington Green, London, N1 4PR. Tel: 0171 923 0990 www.huntleyarchives.com

THE CORONET PUB
Holloway

Formerly the Coronet Cinema, it opened as a pub in 1996. A listed building, the exterior remains unchanged and the balcony is still intact but closed off to the public. Movie stills and posters decorate its walls, with an old cinema projector on a podium as a centre-piece.

Further information: The Coronet, 336 Holloway Road, London. Tel: 0171 609 5014.

Kensington & Chelsea

FORMER HOME OF JOSEPH LOSEY (1909-84)
Chelsea

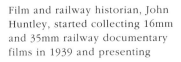

"... So much energy and so much time is taken up in struggle that you begin to wonder what the hell you're on the face of the earth for, because it doesn't make much difference."
Joeseph Losey *

Born in La Crosse, Wisconsin, he gave up a prospective career in medicine to work in the theatre as an extra, stage manager, director and critic. He studied under Sergei Eisenstein in 1935 and began working in films in the late thirties directing documentary shorts. 'Identified' as a communist in 1951, he refused to testify before the HUAC and was subsequently blacklisted. He worked in England under various pseudonyms where his radical politics and despondent outlook distanced him from popular audiences, but he gained a reputation as an experimental stylist which resulted in a cult following in France. Collaborations with the dramatist, Harold Pinter, produced his most successful films: *The Servant* (1963), *Accident* (1967) and *The Go-Between* (1971).

29 Royal Avenue - former home of **Joseph Losey**

Wendy Craig, Dirk Bogarde and James Fox in **The Servant** *(1963, Springbok)*

Mick Jagger and James Fox in **Performance** *(1970, Goodtime Performances)*

After filming *The Servant* in Royal Avenue he bought property on the other side of the square at **29 Royal Avenue** where he stayed for the rest of his life. He died there on 22 June 1984 and was cremated at Putney Vale Crematorium.

See also: *The Servant, The Go-Between*

THE SERVANT
Chelsea

• 1963 115m b/w Drama Springbok (UK)
• Dirk Bogarde (Hugo Barrett), Sarah Miles (Vera), Wendy Craig (Susan), James Fox (Tony)
• p, Joseph Losey, Norman Priggen; d, Joseph Losey; w, Harold Pinter (based on the novel by Robin Maugham); ph, Douglas Slocombe; ed, Reginald Mills; m, John Dankworth

Robin Maugham's novel of role-reversal, about a young aristocrat who is seduced and degraded by his manservant, was considered quite shocking when it was first published in 1949. A nephew of

Somerset Maugham and heir to a viscountcy, Maugham ignored pleas

from his family not to publish his semi-autobiographical novel. Joseph Losey procured the rights and began shooting during the freezing winter of 1962-3 in **Royal Avenue** with renowned Ealing cinematographer, Douglas Slocombe (*Kind Hearts and Coronets, The Lavender Hill Mob, The Man in the White Suit*).

Many people considered the film's homoerotic orgy scenes abhorrent, but *The Servant* was only the second British film to touch the subject of homosexuality at a time when it was still punishable by law (the first was *The Victim*, 1961, also starring Dirk Bogarde). After an initially apathetic reception from many critics *The Servant* was voted best British film of 1963.

See also: Joseph Losey, Dirk Bogarde

PERFORMANCE
Brompton

• 1970 105m c Drama Goodtime Enterprises (UK)
• James Fox (Chas Devlin), Mick Jagger (Turner), Anita Pallenberg (Pherber), Michele Breton (Lucy), Ann Sidney

(Dana), John Bindon (Moody), Stanley Meadows (Rosebloom), Allan Cuthbertson (The Lawyer), Anthony Morton (Dennis), Johnny Shannon (Harry Flowers)
• p, Sanford Lieberson; d, Nicolas Roeg, Donald Cammell; w, Donald Camell; ph, Nicolas Roeg; ed, Antony Gibbs, Brian Smedley-Aston; art d, John Clark

"The only performance that makes it, that really makes it, that makes it all the way, is the one that achieves madness..."
Turner (Mick Jagger)

Most of the interiors for this ingenious and disturbing movie were filmed at **23 Lowndes Square, Knightsbridge**, at the end of the 'swinging sixties'. Exteriors were shot at **Powis Square** in **Notting Hill Gate**. Co-directed by cinematographer Nic Roeg (*Far From The Madding Crowd, Farenheit 451*) and weird visionary, Donald Cammell, it tells the story of small-time hood, Chas Devlin (James Fox) who is on the run from the mob and hides out in the home of a 'has been' rock star (Jagger) who has alienated himself from the world since he lost his powers of incantation. Gradually Chas is sucked into a world of drugs, mysticism and bisexuality, which ends with the merging of two personalities.

Warner Brothers were disgusted by the film and many executives walked out of the preview, demanding a major re-edit. After major cuts and Nic Roeg threatening to remove his name from the credits, it was eventually released, but achieved little commercial success. It has since evolved into a cult classic, imaginatively recalling the more bizarre aspects of our psychedelic past.

See also: Donald Cammell

THE SCIENCE MUSEUM
South Kensington

Much of the Science Museum's Cinematography Collection was transferred to the National Museum of Photography, Film and Television in Bradford, but the museum still has a gallery of Photography and Cinematography, which includes magic lanterns, optical toys and apparatus belonging to pioneers Muybridge, Marey, Demeny, Friese-Greene, Paul, Prestwich, Acres and Newman. It also has examples of early Kinemacolor equipment and a Technicolor camera. All material relating to Le Prince was transferred to Bradford.

Further information: The Science Museum, Exhibition Rd., London, SW7 2DD. Tel: 0171 938 8000. Open: 10.00-5.50 seven days a week.

PEEPING TOM
Kensington

• 1960 109M C Thriller Anglo-Amalgamated (UK)

Karl Boehm in **Peeping Tom** *(1960, Anglo-Amalgamated)*

8 Melbury Road - scene of the home movie footage in **Peeping Tom**

• Karl Boehm (Mark Lewis), Moira Shearer (Vivian), Anna Massey (Helen Stephens), Maxine Audley (Mrs. Stephens), Esmond Knight (Arthur Baden), Bartlett Mullins (Mr. Peters), Shirley Ann Field (Diane Ashley)
• p, Michael Powell; d, Michael Powell; w, Leo Marks; ph, Otto Heller; ed, Noreen Ackland; m, Brian Easdale; art d, Arthur Lawrence; chor, Wally Stott

"The only really satisfactory way to dispose of Peeping Tom would be to shovel it up and flush it swiftly down the nearest sewer. Even then, the stench would remain."
Derek Hill, Tribune.

"I hated the piece and, together with a great many other British critics, said so. Today, I find I am convinced that it is a masterpiece. If in some afterlife conversation is

permitted, I shall think it my duty to seek out Michael Powell and apologise."
Dilys Powell, Sunday Times, 1994.

The subject of *Peeping Tom* is scoptophilia, the morbid urge to gaze voyeuristically. Tormented by his psychologist father (played by Michael Powell) who is researching fear in humans, Mark Lewis grows up with an overwhelming desire to kill. A focus puller at a film studio and a clandestine porn photographer, he lures his female victims to their death, while recording the event on film for posterity.

Much maligned on its release, *Peeping Tom* was viewed by the British critics at the time as little more than goulish pornography. Michael Powell never recovered from the censorious onslaught and never again regained his rightful position as a film maker of genius. Edited into oblivion by the studio, it took director Martin Scorsese's 1979 restoration of the film to make the world realize it had sunk a masterpiece.

Mark Lewis's house in the film was **no. 5 Melbury Road**, a tall red-bricked building which was once the home of Mr Bassett-Lowke, the designer of the famous model steam engines. At the time of filming, Michael Powell lived in a flat opposite at **no. 8**. (best viewed from the garden at the rear of Leighton House Museum, Holland Park Rd.), where the home movie footage of Mark as a child with his father (portrayed by Powell and his own young son) was shot in the garden. The opening shots of the film where Mark is filming a prostitute, who is soon to become a victim, were filmed in **Newman Passage**, which links Rathbone Street to Newman Street, near Goodge Street tube station.

See also: Michael Powell

CORONET CINEMA
Notting Hill

"Any theatre where Mrs Patrick Campbell slipped a live goldfish into Sarah Bernhardt's hand during a performance should definitely be preserved."
Ned Sherrin citing a 1905 production of *Pelleas and Melisande*

Built in 1898 in the style of the Italian Renaissance, the Coronet is the only surviving theatre designed by architect WGR Sprague. It was adapted for use as a cinema in 1916, becoming a full working cinema in 1923. From 1950 to 1979 it was known as the Gaumont. Live shows continued there until 1940, and included artists such as Henry Irving, Sybil Thorndike, Lewis Casson, Marie Lloyd and Lily Langtry. In the 1970s the Rank Organisation planned to convert the building into offices, shops and flats, but were defeated by a 10,000 name petition and a subsequent preservation order. A similar attempt in 1989 by Macdonalds to convert it into a hamburger joint

was also defeated. Today the Coronet, complete with its Louis XVI interior, but not quite its former glory, still survives.

See also: *Notting Hill*

Further information: Coronet, Notting Hill Gate, W11 A. Tel: 0171 727 6705. Seats: 388.

ELECTRIC CINEMA
Notting Hill

Built on the site of a former timber yard, the Electric Theatre at 191 Portobello Road opened in 1910 and is believed to be the second earliest purpose built cinema in London. It later became a music hall called the Imperial Playhouse, and after years of neglect it became the Electric Cinema. It went into receivership in 1922, and is now owned by Pullman Films, who may yet rescue it. The original interior still survives.

THE GATE CINEMA
Notting Hill

Formerly 'The North East and Harvey Dining Room' and the 'Golden Bell Coffee Palace', the lower half of the site became the Electric Theatre Palace in 1911,

with upper floors remaining in use as a hotel and restaurant until the late 1930s. It became a 'news and interest' cinema in the 1920s, and in 1931 it changed its name to The Embassy Cinema. It suffered bomb damage during WWII, and in 1957 the external facade was rebuilt.

In 1973 it was taken over by American couple, Barbara and David Stone, who converted it into an 'arts' cinema and re-named it The Gate. *"When we came to England we could not believe how few 'art' cinemas there were,"* explained David, *"Our aim is to show films that otherwise would just not get shown."*

After gutting the building of its threadbare seats, mouldy carpets, and local vermin, they succeeded in turning the former seedy Classic Cinema into one of London's most fashionable art-house venues. The Stones have since sold the cinema, but The Gate continues to prosper.

Further information: The Gate, Notting Hill Gate, London W11. Tel: 0171 727 4043. Seats: 240.

NOTTING HILL
Notting Hill

- 1999 123m c Comedy Working Title (UK)
- Hugh Grant (William Thacker), Julia Roberts (Anna Scott), Richard McCabe (Tony), Hugh Bonneville (Bernie), Rhys Ifans (Spike), James Dreyfus (Martin), Emma Chambers (Honey), Dylan Moran (Rufus the thief), Simon Callow (Restaurant lager lout)
- p, Tim Bevan; d, Roger Michell; w, Richard Curtis; ph, Michael Coulter; ed, Nicholas Moore; prod d, Stuart Craig

"People will just assume that because I am playing an actor in this movie that she is me, or that I understand everything about her life - I don't. Every actor's experience is different. We all have different personalities; we are not an assembly line breed."
Julia Roberts

'British Tommies rescuing a comrade under shell fire' - a frame from the film **The Battle of the Somme**, 1916 which has become one of the classic images of the First World War (Imperial War Museum).

Notting Hill bookshop owner, William Thacker (Hugh Grant) has his life changed forever when Anna Scott (Julia Roberts), 'the world's most famous movie star', enters his shop. As their relationship develops, the pressures of fame, and people's different perceptions of it, highlight what could happen when a famous actress falls in love with Mr Ordinary.

Notting Hill became the biggest-grossing British movie ever made in August 1999 when its box-office receipts totalled £168m around the world, taking it beyond the £164.5m total for *Four Weddings and a Funeral* which was produced by the same team.

Filmed on location in West London and at Shepperton Studios the filmmakers spent six weeks shooting in densely-populated Notting Hill capturing the atmosphere of this melting pot of cultures. The production team had considered building a huge exterior set as an alternative to location filming, but decided they would never be able to successfully create the atmosphere which makes Notting Hill unique.

Locations in the area included **Portobello Road, Westbourne Park Road, Golborne Road, Landsdowne Road** and the **Coronet Cinema, Notting Hill Gate**. Other London locations included the **Empire Leicester Square** (scene of the West End film premiere), the **Ritz Hotel**, the **Savoy Hotel** (scene of Anna's press conference), the **Nobu Restaurant in the Metropolitan Hotel**, the **Zen Garden of the Hempel Hotel** (scene of the wedding reception) and **Kenwood House** in North London (where William visits Anna on a film location). The interior scenes for William's house, the Travel Bookshop and Tony's Restaurant were filmed at Shepperton Studios.

See also: Coronet Cinema, Empire Leicester Square, *Four Weddings and a Funeral*

Lambeth

IMPERIAL WAR MUSEUM FILM AND VIDEO ARCHIVE
Lambeth

In 1920, the Museum took expert advice on how to ensure the preservation for posterity of the filmed record of the First World War. Today its Film and Video Archive holds some 120 million feet of film and 6,500 hours of videotape, ranging from the birth of the cinema to the present, detailing the military, political and social history of the 20th Century. Highlights of the collection include documentary accounts of battles from the original 1916 record of *The Battle of the Somme* ; *Germany Calling* (1941), *Target For Tonight* (Harry Watt, 1941), *I Was a Fireman* (Humphrey Jennings, 1943), *Mrs. John Bull Prepared* (1918), *Wales: Green*

Mountain, Black Mountain (1943, scripted by Dylan Thomas) and the Hi-8 videos shot by the official war artist John Keane during the Gulf War (1991).

The Archive also holds material from allies, neutrals and former enemies, including: The WWI French newsreel *Annales de la Guerre* ; Frank Capra's *Why We Fight* series and Nazi propaganda epics such as *Sieg im Westen* (1941) and *Triumph des Willens* (1936).

The Film and Video Archive has been used by researchers on behalf of film directors - and sometimes by the directors themselves - to help establish an authentic "feel" for features set in combat zones. Similarly, actors have paid visits to help them get "into" a particular mentality or period. Examples include Kubrick's *Paths of Glory*, Attenborough's *A Bridge Too Far*, Spielberg's *Empire of the Sun*, Boorman's *Hope and Glory*, Jarman's *War Requiem* and Peckinpah's *Cross of Iron*. The Public Services section provides non-commercial access to the collections for private, educational and service enquirers. A 180-seat cinema in the museum regularly screens programmes of films to the general public and to school parties. A smaller Preview Theatre in the All Saints Annexe may be booked for special screenings. The loan service offers film and video titles from the Archive to film theatres, festivals and societies and to educational and service users; 'one-off' video copies strictly for non-commercial private use may also be arranged. The Archive is also keen to extend its collections, and will be pleased to hear from amateur film makers and other owners of films and original videos.

All Saints is also just across the road from the site of the old Lambeth Hospital which, while derelict but not yet demolished, doubled for the streets of Brooklyn in one of the *Death Wish* sequels, and the local pub, 'The Two Eagles', has a signed photo of Charles Bronson on its wall. Peaceful and unspoiled West Square, and the junction of Brook Drive and Austral Street have been used frequently for location filming, notably in *The Krays* (1990) and *Scandal* (1989).

The main museum is in Lambeth Road where exhibits include some film props, including the model used in the filming of Ealing's *San Demetrio, London* (1943) and the eponymous *Wooden Horse* (1950). The museum was directly involved in the production of Stuart Cooper's *Overlord* (winner of the Silver Bear, Berlin Film Festival, 1975) providing archive footage, props, locations and staff members as extras. The museum has also been used as a site for previews and launches, including the opening night party for the Bond movie *Goldeneye*.

Further information: The Film and Video Archive is situated in the Museum's All Saints Annexe in Austral Street, London SE11 4SL. Tel: 0171 416 5290. Monday to Friday 10am to 5pm. An appointment is essential.

One week's notice for film viewing and 24 hours notice for other visits must be given. Cinema programmes are as announced. Ring 0171 416 5000.

BIRTHPLACE OF ROGER MOORE (1927-)
Lambeth

"Roger Moore modelled so many pullovers he was known as the Big Knit."
Michael Caine

Roger Moore as James Bond 007 in Live and Let Die (1973, UA/Eon)

16 Albert Square - childhood home of *Roger Moore*

Roger Moore was born at the **Annie McCall Maternity Hospital, Jeffreys Road**, on 14 October 1927 to Lily and George Moore, a police constable. The family lived half a mile away in three rented rooms on the first floor of **4 Aldebert Terrace**, between Lambeth and Clapham Road. Roger attended the nearby local school in **Hackford Road** (now Durand Junior School) and was evacuated to Amersham during the Blitz. He left school at fifteen, by which time the family had moved to a flat round the corner at **16 Albert Square**.

After he was sacked from his first job as a trainee illustrator he got a walk-on part at Denham Studios in Gabriel Pascal's *Caesar and Cleopatra* (1946). He trained at RADA in Gower Street for a year before doing his national service in 1945. A year later he married a cabbie's daughter, Doorn Van Steyn, and after his de-mob lived the life of a struggling actor, supplementing his actor's income with odd jobs including dishwashing, selling trinkets from a suitcase and modelling knitting patterns.

He became most successful for his TV series: *Ivanhoe* (1957), *Maverick* (1961) and *The Saint* (1963-68). None of his feature films could be called memorable, but he will be best remembered for his seven Bond movies in which he made his first appearance in *Live and Let Die* in 1973. His second marriage was to Dorothy Squires in 1952 and he met his third wife, Luisa Mattioli, while filming the *Rape of the Sabines* in Rome in 1961.

GRAVE OF CAPTAIN BLIGH (1754-1817)
Lambeth

The supposedly infamous captain of HMS Bounty who incited his crew to mutiny is buried in a replica of a 17th century 'Knot' Garden at the **Museum of Garden History** (formerly St Mary's Church), **Lambeth Palace Road**.

*The grave of **Captain Bligh** in the grounds of the Museum of Garden History, Lambeth*

*A replica of **HMS Bounty** used in Mutiny on the Bounty (1962, MGM/Arcola)*

George Cross first portrayed Bligh on the screen in an Australian silent in 1916, but he was immortalised by Charles Laughton in Frank Lloyd's 1935 adaptation of Charles Nordhoff's and James Hall's novels *Mutiny on the Bounty* and *Men Against the Sea*. It was probably Laughton's most accomplished film, which co-starred an initially reluctant Clark Gable in the role of Fletcher Christian. A lack-lustre remake was made in 1962, starring Trevor Howard as Bligh and a miscast Marlon Brando as Christian. Other attempts at the legend include Australian director, Charles Chauvel's *In the Wake of the Bounty* (1933) and Roger Donaldson's *The Bounty* (1984), with Anthony Hopkins, portraying the least caricatured Bligh to date.

William Bligh was born at Tinten, near the village of St. Tudy in Cornwall. His name is now inextricably linked with the Bounty, but his 3,600 mile voyage in an open boat after the mutiny was an incredible maritime feat which is often overshadowed by the mutineers' tales. Bligh eventually navigated his way to Timor and after two further mutinies and a governorship of New South Wales, he died a Vice Admiral.

Recent research by writer Dea Birkett portrays a man very different from his screen image: *"Bligh was a thoughtful, caring, if somewhat over-anxious man... He never keelhauled anyone... His fault was that he let the men have too good a time on Tahiti - sleeping with local women, drinking and having their bottoms tattooed. If he had been stricter perhaps they wouldn't have mutinied."* Fletcher Christian's great-great-great-great-great grand-daughter's response to Birkett's research was blunt: *"I'd like to see her hanged,"* she said.

See also: Fletcher Christian, Charles Laughton, Donald Crisp, Trevor Howard, Anthony Hopkins

Further information: The Museum of Garden History has a small display relating to Captain Bligh. Tel: 0171 261 1891.

Lambeth

PASSPORT TO PIMLICO
Lambeth

- 1949 84m b/w Comedy Ealing/Eagle-Lion (U.K.)
- Stanley Holloway (Arthur Pemberton), Hermione Baddeley (Eddie Randall), Margaret Rutherford (Prof. Hatton-Jones), Basil Radford (Gregg), Naunton Wayne (Straker)
- p, Michael Balcon; d, Henry Cornelius; w, T.E.B. Clarke; ph, Lionel Barnes, Cecil Cooney; ed, Michael Truman; art d, Roy Oxley
- AAN Best Original Screenplay

A WWII unexploded bomb goes off and exposes old catacombs containing an ancient charter which renounces British sovereignty of Pimlico, and cedes it to the Dukes of Burgundy. Pimlico duly declares its independence and sets up its own government.

Tibby Clarke was inspired to write the story after reading a newspaper article in which the Canadian government bestowed Dutch sovereignty on the room where the exiled Princess Juliana of the Netherlands was about to give birth. Although her daughter was born in Canada, the room was technically and legally on Dutch soil, making her daughter legal heir to the throne.

The film's location was not Pimlico, but on a bombed site in **Hercules Road, Lambeth**. All the exterior shots of streets, houses and the shells of bombed buildings were constructed on site by the studio.

See also: Stanley Holloway, Margaret Rutherford

BFI LONDON IMAX
Waterloo

IMAX stands for 'image maximum' and is a projection system which

The BFI London Imax Cinema

maximises an image on a massive screen. Developed by the Canadian-based IMAX Corporation, IMAX cinemas use horizontal projection systems to project 2D and 3D images, which makes for a unique and overwhelming cinema experience.

The BFI IMAX opened in May 1999 and is 482-seat, state-of-the-art cinema boasting the largest screen in the U.K. and the second largest in Europe. The screen is almost the height of five double decker buses and is over 26 metres wide. The sound is channelled through an 11, 600-watt digital surround-sound system, with 44 speakers positioned in seven clusters around the auditorium. Built in the middle of the concrete desert known as the 'Bullring', and housed in a seven storey glass enclosed cylinder, the BFI IMAX provides the ultimate cinema experience.

See also: Pictureville Cinema

Further information: The BFI London IMAX Cinema, 1 Charlie Chaplin Walk, South Bank, Waterloo, London SE1 8XR. Tel: 0171 902 1234 / 1200. Open seven days a week, the cinema is one minute's walk from Waterloo mainline and underground stations.

THE NATIONAL FILM THEATRE
Waterloo

The 1951 Festival of Britain site was on the South Bank, where one of its pavilions was the Telekinema, which demonstrated 3D film. This venue became the first home of the BFI's National Film Theatre. In 1957 the NFT moved to its present site near Waterloo Bridge, where it screens a wide range of film from all over the world, covering every genre and style, from the earliest silent films through to the latest releases, supported by background notes and lectures. More than two thousand films pass through its projectors annually, including features, shorts, animation and documentaries, and it has over 35,000 dedicated members. Its three cinemas, including one in the Museum of the Moving Image, screen Super 8 and 16mm to 70mm, and also video.

Further information: NFT, South Bank, Waterloo SE1. Tel: 0171 928 3232 / 3535.

The Museum of the Moving Image closed on 31 August 1999 and will be redeveloped as part of the South Bank redevelopment programme. It is expected that the new museum - which is to be nearly half as big again as the current one - will open around 2003. For information on South Bank redevelopment contact the BFI Corporate Press Office on 0171 957 8919.

BIRTHPLACE OF CLAUDE RAINS (1889-1967)
Stockwell

"...Claude Rains and Ingrid Bergman made a nice couple [in Notorious], but in the close shots the difference between them was so marked that if I wanted them both in frame, I had to stand Rains on a box."
Alfred Hitchcock

Hollywood may have considered him short and 'unattractive', and therefore not conforming to its perception of what constitutes star material, but Claude Rains' sophistication, style, and sheer presence more than compensated for his appearance.

He was born William Claude Rains on 10 November 1889, at **26 Tregothnan Road**, off Clapham Road, to Emily Cox and Fred Rains, an organ builder. He made his stage debut in August 1900 at the Haymarket Theatre, aged eleven, playing a child in *Sweet Nell of Old Drury*, later becoming a call-boy at His Majesty's Theatre, where he graduated to prompter and stage manager.

Claude Rains

He toured the world acting and working as a stage manager, before making his film debut at the late age of forty-four in the title role of James Whale's *The Invisible Man*. Despite his face being swathed in bandages, and not being seen by the audience until the final scene, the impact of his distinctive voice secured his screen career.

Frequently cast as a smooth villain or a venerable guru, he will be best remembered for his Oscar-nominated role as chief of police, Captain Louis Renault, in *Casablanca* (1943), whose line, *"I'm only a poor corrupt official"*, is now part of movie folklore. His other roles included Prince John in *The Adventures of Robin Hood* (1938), the underhanded Senator

26 Tregothnan Road - birthplace of **Claude Rains**

Paine in *Mr. Smith Goes To Washington* (1939), the heavenly Mr. Jordan in *Here Comes Mr. Jordan* (1941), the enigmatic Dr. Tower in *King's Row* (1942), the benign Dr. Jaquith in *Now Voyager* (1942), the long suffering Job in *Mr. Skeffington* (1944) and Nazi agent Alexander Sebastian in *Notorious* (1946).

In 1950 he returned to the stage after sixteen years, and worked on both the stage and screen for the next ten years. In 1962 he portrayed Mr. Dryden in David Lean's *Lawrence of Arabia*. He was married five times and died from an intestinal haemorrhage at Laconia, New Hampshire, on 30 May 1967.

See also: James Whale

THE CHARLIE CHAPLIN TRAIL
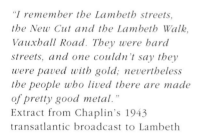
Lambeth

"I remember the Lambeth streets, the New Cut and the Lambeth Walk, Vauxhall Road. They were hard streets, and one couldn't say they were paved with gold; nevertheless the people who lived there are made of pretty good metal."
Extract from Chaplin's 1943 transatlantic broadcast to Lambeth

The story of Charlie Chaplin's childhood could easily have been penned by Dickens: his roots were in the grimy Victorian streets of Lambeth, where, against all odds, he rose above grinding poverty to become one of the world's greatest screen comedians.

His parents, Hannah Hill and Charles Chaplin, were talented entertainers who graduated from performing in local pubs to the professional music-hall. Charles's career prospered, but that of Hannah (who appeared under the name of Miss Lilly Harley) became

Hannah and Charles Chaplin Snr.

unpredictable. Charles was so successful that his portrait appeared on many popular song sheets of the day. They were married at **St John's Church, Larcom Street, Walworth**, on 22 June 1885. A few months previously, on 16 March 1885, Hannah had given birth to a boy named Sydney at **57 Brandon Street, Walworth**, whose father's identity is unknown.

Charles Spencer Chaplin (Charlie), was born in **East Street, Walworth** (plaque erected), on Tuesday 16 April 1889. No official record of his birth exists and most of the East Street (known locally as East Lane) of Chaplin's time, has since disappeared. All that remains is the **Mason's Arms pub** and the odd building.

Shortly after Charlie's birth, the family moved to the more salubrious surroundings of **West Square, Kennington**, where he recalled being *"lovingly tucked up in a comfortable bed"* by a housemaid. Many music-hall entertainers lived in Kennington, and the pubs in **Kennington Road**, such as **The Three Stags** and **The Tankard**, were popular haunts for performers.

In 1890, when Charles senior's career was at its height, he departed for a four month tour of America. Hannah and Charles's marriage began to deteriorate around this time, and by late 1891 Hannah was having an affair with music-hall singer, Leo Dryden, giving birth to his son, George

West Square

39 Methley Street

Dryden Wheeler, on 31 August 1892. Separated from her husband, Hannah was now a single mother with three boys to look after. Her affair with Dryden soon ended, culminating in his abduction of the child from her lodgings in the spring of 1893. George was never heard from again for thirty years. 1893 marked the beginning of Hannah's physical and mental decline. With no livelihood, and no support from her husband, she eked a living from dressmaking and nursing. Also at this time, her own parents separated and her mother was certified insane. Hannah was still performing erratically, and appeared before a rowdy army audience at the Canteen, Aldershot. Her performance was a disaster, but the manager, who had observed little Charlie's entertaining antics backstage, persuaded him to perform for the soldiers. So successful was he, that the audience tossed money onto the stage, at what was probably his earliest public appearance.

In 1895 Hannah became ill, and was admitted to Lambeth Infirmary for one month. Sydney was sent to West Norwood Schools for the Infant Poor of Lambeth, and Charlie was taken in by relations at **164 York Road** (off map). Their mother was later hospitalised again, and on this occasion, Sydney and Charlie, now aged eleven and seven, were taken into the care of the **Lambeth Workhouse, Renfrew Road**. The District Relief Committee traced Charles senior and authorised him to contribute fifteen shillings a week to their maintenance, which - despite earning good wages - he did reluctantly and irregularly.

In June 1896 Sydney and Charlie were placed in the Central London District Poor Law School at Hanwell. Here Charlie became infected with ringworm and his head was shaved, treated with iodine, and sheathed in a cloth. In November 1896 Sydney joined the Training Ship *Exmouth*, at Grays in Essex, where the children of the poor trained for a life at sea. In 1898, after eighteen months, Sydney and Charlie returned home.

By July, this time residing at **10 Farmer's Road (now Kennington Park Gardens)**, Hannah and her two children were again destitute,

*The old **Lambeth Workhouse**, off Renfrew Road. Parts of the workhouse are still standing, including the water tower and the Master's House (above), and the male and female receiving wards, and the day and night gate lodge (parts of which are pictured below).*

and placed themselves into the care of the parish authorities at the Lambeth Workhouse. Her sons were then separated from her and sent again to West Norwood Schools.

On Friday 12 August, missing her sons dreadfully, Hannah concocted a ploy to see them again. Pretending to discharge herself and her sons from the authorities care, she spent a glorious day with them in **Kennington Park**. After a day of eating cherries, drinking tea,

crocheting and playing games, they signed themselves back into the workhouse just in time for tea, much to the displeasure of those in charge.

On 15 September 1898 Hannah was transferred to Cane Hill Asylum from Lambeth Infirmary, and shortly afterwards Sydney and Charlie were discharged into the care of their father at **287 Kennington Road**, where Charles senior was living with a woman.

Lambeth

The Three Stags Pub (now Brendan O'Grady's) - where Charlie last saw his father.

Casey's Court Circus, 1906. Charlie - middle row wearing bowler

Hannah was discharged in November and moved with her sons to **39 Methley Street**, next door to Hayward's pickle factory and a slaughterhouse, the acrid smells of which lingered in Charlie's memory for the rest of his life. Hannah took up sewing again and Sydney was hired as a telegraph boy. In December 1898 Charles Snr convinced William Jackson, the founder of a clog dancing troupe called the Eight Lancashire Lads, to take on his son. Ten-year-old Charlie subsequently toured with the troupe from 1899 to 1900, and played one of the cats in the *Cinderella* pantomime at London's Hippodrome Theatre. Meanwhile, Sydney signed on as a steward with the steamship, *SS Norman*, bound for South Africa. Hannah and Charlie moved to two rooms at **24 Chester Street (now Chester Way)**, above a barber's shop off Kennington Road.

Music hall artists were actively encouraged by their management to mix and drink with the clientele and many subsequently died from drink-related illnesses. On the corner of Lambeth Road and Kennington Road is Brendan O'Grady's pub. In Chaplin's time it was known as The Three Stags and was a favourite haunt of music-hall performers, including Charles Chaplin Snr. It was here that young Charlie last saw his father alive, a few weeks before his death from cirrhosis of the liver and dropsy on 9 May 1901, aged only thirty-seven. This was the only time Charlie could remember his father giving him a kiss and a hug. The funeral was paid for by Charles senior's younger brother Albert, who had prospered in South Africa.

Around this time Hannah, Charlie, and Sydney (when not away at sea) were living at **3 Pownall Terrace, Kennington Road** (since demolished). It was this house that Charlie remembered more than any other from his childhood, making an emotional pilgrimage to it in 1921 during one of his visits to Britain. It also inspired the set for *The Kid* (1921). Charlie had numerous jobs during this period including those of barber's boy, chandler's boy, doctor's boy and page boy. He tried his hand at street trading, selling old clothes for a day at Newington Butts, and also made penny toys to survive. In the summer of 1903 Hannah was again admitted to the Cane Hill Asylum where she remained for eight months.

The same year, fourteen-year-old Charlie registered himself with H. Blackmore's Theatrical Agency in **Bedford Street, Strand** (off map), and was soon hired to play Billy the pageboy in a touring production of *Sherlock Holmes* which was to last two and a half years. In 1906, together with Sydney, he joined the Fred Regina comedy troupe, and later Casey's Court Circus Company.

*The gates of **St. Mark's Church** (left) - inspiration for the street corner set in **City Lights** (right)*

The Queen's Head - *Charlie's uncle Spencer was landlord here, c.1890-1900*

Sydney, now an entertainer in his own right, joined Fred Karno's Silent Comedians in 1907, who were based at **Karno's 'Fun Factory'**, at the top of **Harbour Road**, off **Coldharbour Lane, Brixton** (off map). Through Sidney's efforts, Karno reluctantly gave Charlie a two-week trial, describing him as, *"a pale, puny, sullen-looking youngster."* On 21 February 1908 Karno offered him a three-year contract, and with their new found fortune, the Chaplin brothers rented a flat a **15 Glenshaw Mansions, Brixton Road**.

In the summer of 1908, Charlie met and fell in love with Hetty Kelly, a fifteen year-old dancer with Bert Coutts's Yankee Doodle Girls who were performing on the same bill as Karno's troupe at the Streatham Empire. The romance lasted only eleven days, and was probably terminated as a consequence of Hetty's mother's concern for her daughter's uncertain future with a music-hall comedian. Charlie was devastated, and during his 1921 visit, he made a nostalgic stop at Kennington Gate, their first meeting place. Chaplin later had three successive marriages to teenage

brides, each of which were rumoured attempts to resurrect Hetty.

In the autumn of 1908 he appeared with Karno's troupe in Paris, where he first performed in the famous *Mumming Birds* sketch, and in September 1910 he embarked on his first tour of America. Also on the tour was young Stanley Jefferson, who would later achieve fame as Stan Laurel. After twenty-one months of touring, the troupe returned in June 1912. On his return, Charlie arranged for Hannah, who was still in Cane Hill Asylum, to be transferred to a private nursing home. By October the company had left England again for a second American tour.

After being spotted performing in Los Angeles, he left the Karno company in Kansas City on 28 November 1913 to join Mack Sennett at the Keystone Film Company for a $150 a week. He soon metamorphosed into the little tramp with toothbrush moustache, bowler hat and cane, an image which would eventually evolve into a universal icon of the twentieth century.

Glenshaw Mansions - *home of Charlie and Sydney in 1908*

Charlie brought his mother to the U.S.A. in 1921 where she lived in a seaside bungalow with housekeepers and a nurse. She died on 28 August 1928 at Glendale Hospital, California, where she was being treated for a gall-bladder infection, and is buried in the Hollywood Cemetery. Charlie was married four times, lastly to Oona, daughter of Eugene O'Neill. After being accused of Communist sympathies during the McCarthy era, he left the U.S.A. for

The Kid (1921) - produced, written and directed by Charlie Chaplin (Roy Export Co.)

The Goldrush (1925, Roy Export Co.)

Switzerland in 1952. Two years after receiving his knighthood, he died in his sleep at Manoir de Ban, Corsier sur Vevey, on Christmas Day 1977.

MAP KEY:

1: The Three Stags Pub (now Brendan O'Grady's) - where Charlie last saw his father.

2: Lambeth Walk - where Charlie gazed through the shop windows at the roasting meat.

3: The Tankard Pub - *"I often used to stand outside the Tankard watching those illustrious gentlemen alight... to enter the lounge bar, where the elite of vaudeville met."*

4: 39 West Square - where Charlie lived with his parents shortly after his birth.

5: Walcot Mansions - *"We would play at theatre at the back of Walcot Mansions. As the director I always gave myself the villain parts."*

6: Chester Way (formerly Chester Street) - Charlie lived here with his mother over a barber's shop, c.1901; he was also a barber's boy.

7: 3 Pownall Terrace (demolished in 1966, it stood close to the Ward Point tower block, on the west side of the road north of Black Prince Road) - Charlie lived here with his mother in 1903.

8: 287 Kennington Road - Charlie and Sydney lived here with Charles Snr, his mistress, Louise and their child, in late 1898. *"The family lived in two rooms, and, although the front room had large windows, the light filtered in as if from under water..."* Nearby, at **267 Kennington Road**, was the home of Andrew Jackson, founder of the Eight Lancashire Lads.

9: Queen's Head Pub (corner of Black Prince Road and Vauxhall Walk, just off map) - Charlie's uncle Spencer was landlord here, c.1890-1900. Here he saw the local tramp 'Rummy Binks' from whom he claimed to have copied his funny walk.

10: Kennington Cross - where Charlie often went to watch the world passing by. The Finca Tapas Bar was formerly the White Hart pub, where, sitting on the pavement, Charlie first discovered the joy of music. While living in Chester Street he attended school nearby in Sancroft Street.

11: 39 Methley Street - where Charlie lived with his mother from November 1898 - August 1899, next to the pickle factory and the slaughterhouse. Also the inspiration for the street set in *The Kid* (1921).

12: Kennington Park - where Hannah and her two sons 'escaped' the workhouse for a day in August 1898.

13: St Mark's Church (opp Oval tube) - the gates and railings on Clapham Road inspired the street corner set in *City Lights* (1931), where the blind girl (Virginia Cherrill) sells flowers .

14: Kennington Park Gardens (formerly Farmer's Road) - where Hannah and her sons lived in a room at 10 Farmer's Road in July 1898, and left here to enter the workhouse the following month.

15: Kennington Gate - where Charlie first met Hetty - *"Twas here, my first appointment with Hetty. How I was dolled up in my little tight-fitting frock coat, hat, and cane! I was quite the dude..."*

16: Site of the Electric Cinema (since demolished, now a butcher's shop) - where Charlie probably took Hetty to the movies.

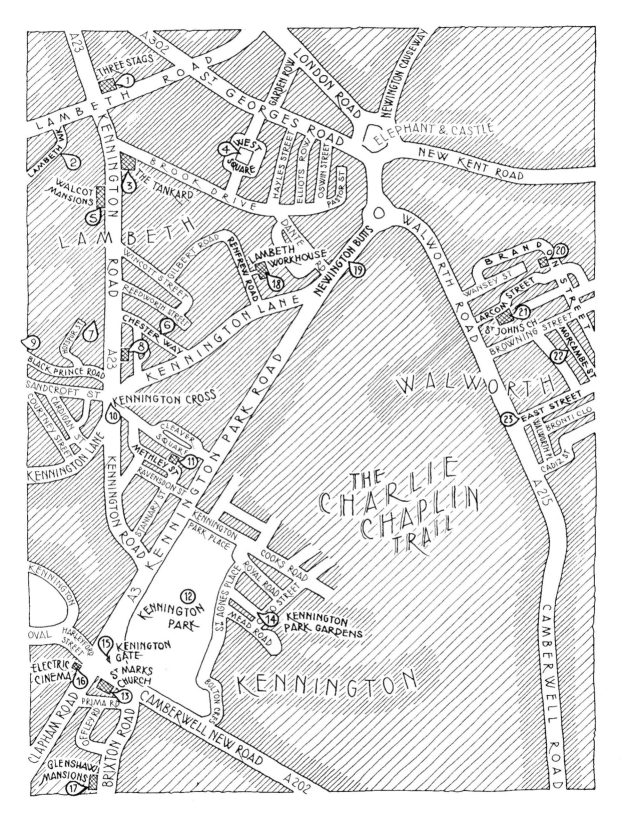

17: 15 Glenshaw Mansions, Brixton Road - where Charlie and Sydney lived in 1908. The flat was furnished from local second-hand shops, whose decor Charlie described as *"... a combination of a Moorish cigarette shop and a French whore-house. But we loved it."*

18: Lambeth Workhouse, off Renfrew Road - where Charlie, Sydney and Hannah were confined.

19: Newington Butts - where Charlie sold old clothes in the street.

20: 57 Brandon Street - where Charles senior and Hannah lived at the time of Sydney's birth on 16 March 1885, and also at the time of their marriage.

21: St John's Church, Larcom Street - where Charles and Hannah were married on 22 June 1885 and Sydney was baptised.

22: Morecambe Street (formerly Camden Street) - Hannah Chaplin was born at 11 Camden Street in 1865. Her parents also lived at 68 Camden Street.

23: East Street - Charlie was born here on 16 April 1889.

See also: Fred Karno, Stan Laurel, Newton Hotel, Chaplin Statue.

Further information: It is highly recommended that anyone interested in experiencing Chaplin's London to the full should join one of **Tony Merrick's Walking Tours of Lambeth**. A Chaplin authority and local historian, Tony brings to life the streets of Charlie's Victorian childhood, with stories, anecdotes, and above all, Cockney humour. A must for all Chaplin fans!
Tel: 0181 462 2464 or contact the **Vauxhall St Peter's Heritage Centre, Tyers Street. Tel: 0171 793 0263.**

RITZY CINEMA
Brixton

"The minute you start messing about showing films you can see in other cinemas, you are letting the audience down."
Peter Buckingham, Oasis cinema group

An early purpose-built cinema, it opened as the Electric Pavilion in 1911 and continued screening films until its closure in 1978. It was eventually rescued by a group of local enthusiasts who invested and borrowed money to buy a five-year lease from Lambeth Council, and in 1978, with its restored Edwardian decor, it reopened as the Little Bit Ritzy. In the early '80s it was renamed The Ritzy. Now with five screens and owned by the independent cinema group, Oasis, The Ritzy is Britain's largest art-house complex.

Further information: Ritzy, Brixton Oval, Coldharbour Lane, SW2. Tel: 0171 737 2121.

HOME OF BOB PENDER
Brixton

Fourteen-year-old Archie Leach was expelled from his Bristol school in 1918. Three days later he joined Bob Pender's Knockabout Comedians, a troupe of acrobatic dancers and stilt-walkers, with whom he quickly learned stage skills. His wages were ten shillings a week with board and lodgings at Pender's house. Pender at that time resided at **247 Brixton Road**. Archie toured the U.K. with the troupe and in 1920 they were hired to appear in New York. He never returned to England with the troupe, eventually making his way to Hollywood where he underwent a metamorphosis and became Cary Grant in 1931.

See also: Cary Grant

Merton

GRAVE OF WILL HAY (1888-1949)
Streatham

One of cinema's most gifted comedians, Will Hay was frequently teamed with 'Albert' and 'Harbottle' (Graham Moffatt and Moore Marriott) in comedy classics such as *Oh Mr. Porter!* (1937) and *Ask a Policeman* (1939). He died from a stroke on Easter Sunday, 1949, in his Chelsea flat while reading a book of Jewish proverbs.

The passage he had been reading at the time of his death is inscribed at the foot of his grave: *"For each one of us there comes a moment when death takes us by the hand and says 'It is time to rest; you are tired; lie down and sleep; sleep well'... the day is gone, and stars shine in the canopy of eternity."*

He is buried in the theatre corner of the **Garden of Remembrance** at **Streatham Park Cemetery, Rowan Road.**

See also: Will Hay (Stockton-on-Tees), *Oh, Mr. Porter!,*

Newham

FULL METAL JACKET
Beckton

Full Metal Jacket (1987, Warner/Stanley Kubrick)

- 1987 116m c War Natant (UK)
- Matthew Modine (Pvt. Joker), Adam Badwin (Animal Mother), Vincent D'Onofrio (Leonard Lawrence, Pvt. Gomer Pyle), Lee Ermey (Gunnery Sgt. Hartman), Dorian Harewood (Eightball), Arliss Howard (Pvt. Cowboy), Kevyn Major Howard (Rafterman)
- p, Stanley Kubrick; d, Stanley Kubrick; w, Stanley Kubrick, Michael Herr, Gustav Hasford (based on the novel 'The Shorttimers' by Gustav Hasford); ph, Douglas Milsome; ed, Martin Hunter; m, Abigail Mead; prod d, Anton Furst; art d, Rod Stratford, Leslie Tomkins, Keith Plain; fx, John Evans; cos, Keith Denny
- AAN Best Adapted Screenplay: Stanley Kubrick, Michael Herr, Gustav Hasford

Joker: *How can you shoot women and children?*
Cobra gunner: *Easy, you just don't lead 'em so much.*
Ain't war hell?

Kubrick's raw, brutal and technically brilliant depiction of a combat zone during Vietnam's Tet Offensive was recreated in the

Beckton Gas Works

London suburbs at Beckton. On the Thames marshes, owned by British Gas and centred around derelict **Beckton Gas Works**, earth-moving equipment smashed and sculpted the reinforced concrete buildings into the ruins of war. Palm trees from Spain and thousands of plastic plants from Hong Kong doubled for indigenous vegetation. Pyramids of old tyres burned continuously and before each scene teams with

Stanley Kubrick on the set of Full Metal Jacket

hammers and flame-throwers attacked the walls and scorched the earth. Surprisingly, military hardware consisted of only two tanks, two helicopters and a handful of trucks. Beckton Gas Works site is being redeveloped and is closed to the public.

See also: Stanley Kubrick, *Full Metal Jacket* (Cambs), *A Clockwork Orange*

BIRTHPLACE OF ANNA NEAGLE (1904-86)
Forest Gate

A young chorus girl transformed into one of Britain's best-loved actresses after a producer persuaded her to change her name to Anna Neagle in the ABC cafe on the corner of Wardour and Old Compton Streets on August 21, 1930. She was born Florence Marjorie Robertson, on October 20, 1904, at **3 Park Road**, Forest Gate, the youngest of three children of Florence Neagle and Herbert Robertson, a sea captain.

She made her first professional appearance in 1917 at the Ambassador's Theatre, Cambridge Circus, as one of eight child dancers in a production called *Wonder Tales*, based on the Nathaniel Hawthorne legends. After leaving school she toyed with the idea of becoming a missionary but eventually settled on a stage career. For many years she attended Miss Dillon's Dance School in Baker Street from where she was sent for various auditions, and it was through Miss Dillon that she secured her first professional part in the chorus of *Bubbly* at the Duke of York's Theatre in 1925.

Her stage career prospered and in 1929 she signed up for film-extra work at Cricklewood Studios. In 1932, producer / director Herbert Wilcox, whom she later married, cast her in her first important film as Jack Buchanan's leading lady in *Goodnight Vienna*. She became best known in the cinema for her portrayal of historical screen heroines, notably *Nell Gwyn* (1934), *Victoria the Great* (1937), *Nurse Edith Cavell* (1939), *Odette* (1950) and *The Lady with a Lamp* (1951). Her ability to immerse herself in the character she was playing resulted in many remarkable performances.

In 1974 she commented on her portrayal of the French Resistance heroine, Odette, who was tortured by the Gestapo: *"I lived through the making of the film in a dazed anguish. The atmosphere was so authentic I sometimes felt for the first time that although I was not Odette I was no longer truly myself. The fact that I wore the clothes Odette had worn during her imprisonment helped this illusion of stifling my own personality." *

*Anna Neagle and Cedric Hardwicke in **Nell Gwyn** (1934)*

In 1996 a plaque was unveiled in memory of Anna Neagle and Herbert Wilcox on the wall of their former home, **Aldford House in Park Lane** - the actual street where the opening scene of their 1948 film, *Spring in Park Lane* was shot.

See also: Edith Cavell

BIRTHPLACE OF GREER GARSON (1903-96)
Manor Park

Contrary to popular belief, Greer Garson was not born in Ireland. Like many Hollywood stars she chose the birthplace she thought would suit her American audience's perception of her, which was that of red-headed colleen from the romantic 'Emerald Isle'. She did in fact spend long holidays during her childhood with her grandparents in **Castlewellan, Co Down**, but she was born at **88 First Avenue, Manor Park**. Her father died when she was only one year old. Mother and daughter hated the dull little house they lived in and constantly suffered from homesickness for Ireland.

See also: Greer Garson (Co. Down), *Goodbye Mr Chips, Random Harvest*

Redbridge

BIRTHPLACE OF MAGGIE SMITH (1934-)
Ilford

Margaret Natalie Smith was born at **68 Northwood Gardens** in the **Clayhall** district, on 28 December 1934 to Nathaniel Smith, a medical laboratory technician and his wife Meg, who six years previously had given birth to twin boys. Her father was a Geordie and her mother a morose Glaswegian, daughter of an illiterate shipyard worker. To avoid German bombing raids at the outbreak of WWII the family moved

to safer surroundings at **55 Church Hill Road, Cowley**, on the outskirts of **Oxford.**

Maggie was a lonely child from a strict and religious background, but did not have an unhappy childhood, more a repressed and humourless one. Toys were in short supply. Her brothers were not allowed bicycles or roller skates and were forbidden from playing rugby. Rarely were relations made welcome and holidays were rare. Her mother wanted her to go to secretarial college after leaving school, but Maggie was determined to become an actress and joined the Oxford Playhouse Company in 1951, eventually progressing to the Old Vic and the National Theatre.

Maggie Smith has become synonymous with the character of Jean Brodie (*The Prime of Miss Jean Brodie*, 1969) which was the first X-rated film screened at a Royal Film Performance in 1969, her Oscar-winning performance being influenced by her mother's chilly and emotional character. Her film debut was in *Nowhere To Go* (1958). Other films include: *The VIPs* (1963), *California Suite* (AA

1978), *A Room with a View* (1985), *The Lonely Passion of Judith Hearne* (1987), *Hook* (1991), *The Secret Garden* (1993) and *Tea With Mussolini* (1999).

See also: Christina Kay

Richmond-upon-Thames

GRAVE OF R.D. BLACKMORE (1825-1900)
Teddington

Richard Doddridge Blackmore, author of the famous tale of love and intrigue on 17th Century Exmoor, *Lorna Doone* (1869), is buried in **Teddington Cemetery, Shacklegate Lane**. Three versions of *Lorna Doone* were adapted for the screen: 1935 (Basil Dean), 1951 (Phil Karlson), and 1990 (Andrew Grieve). Alas, none of his other novels have survived.

BIRTHPLACE OF NOEL COWARD (1899-1973)
Teddington

"Very flat, Norfolk"
Private Lives (1930) act 1

The Italian Job (1969, Paramount/Oakhurst)

Celebrated playwright, actor, songwriter, composer, producer and sparkling wit, Noel Coward, was born on 16 December 1899 at **131 Waldegrave Road, Teddington** (plaque erected), the second of three sons (Russell, the eldest, died a year before Noel was born, aged six) to Violet Agnes and Arthur Coward, a piano salesman.

The family lived in what Coward described as 'genteel poverty' and were always financially insecure. He attended ballet school when he was nine and received little formal education, but he was a voracious reader and educated himself, often in the local public library.

In 1908 the family moved to the top flat at **70 Prince of Wales Mansions, opposite Battersea Park** and in 1911 his mother responded on her son's behalf to an advertisement in the Daily Mirror for a *'talented boy of attractive appearance'* to appear in a production of Miss Lila Field's Children's Theatre. He passed the audition and made his first stage appearance as 'Prince Mussel' in *The Goldfish*. His success led him to be cast as a page boy in *The Rainbow Ends* by actor / manager, Charles Hawtrey, where he met and began writing songs, sketches and short stories with child actress, Esmé Wynne.

In the same year he made his screen debut in D.W. Griffiths' *Hearts of the World*, pushing a wheelbarrow beside Lilian Gish for £1 a day. He was invalided out of the army during WWI after inventing a 'nervous breakdown' and in 1921, after borrowing the cost of the fare from a friend, he tried his luck on Broadway - but to no avail.

In 1924 he wrote *The Vortex*, a scathing portrait of the upper middle-class which was nearly barred by the censor. The play launched his career and established him as a playwright and an actor. He bought his first Rolls Royce when he was twenty-six and by the age of twenty-seven he was the leading dramatist of the day and the highest paid writer in the world. From 1919 to 1930 he lived in **Ebury Street** where his mother ran a boarding house.

Many of his works were adapted for the screen, including *Private Lives* (1931), *Cavalcade* (1933), *Bitter Sweet* (1933 & '40), *Design For Living* (1934), *Blithe Spirit* (1945) and *This Happy Breed* (1945).

He also wrote, scored and produced the patriotic *In Which We Serve* (1941), based on the experiences of Lord Louis Mountbatten's naval exploits, for which he received a special Academy Award "for his outstanding production achievement".

In 1945 he co-wrote *Brief Encounter* with David Lean and Anthony Havelock-Allan, based on his play, *Still Life*. He also appeared as an actor in films such as *Around the World in Eighty Days* (1956), *Our Man in Havana* (1959), *Bunny Lake is Missing* (1964) and *The Italian Job* (1969).

See also: *Brief Encounter*

Ronald Colman in Beau Geste (1926, Paramount)

BIRTHPLACE OF RONALD COLMAN (1891-1958)
Kew

Hollywood screen idol and epitome of the English gentleman, Ronald Colman was born at **Woodville, Sandycombe Road (since renumbered 7 Broomfield Road), Richmond**, on 9 February 1891, the fourth of five chidren to Charles Colman, a silk merchant, and his wife Marjorie. Four years later, following the birth of their fifth child, the Colmans moved to a larger house in Ealing. Here Ronald attended a private school overlooking **Haven Green** and was later sent to boarding school in Sussex.

Hopes of a university education were quashed when his father died of pneumonia in 1907. With the family left without its breadwinner, sixteen-year-old Ronald was compelled to find a job. He started work as a clerk with the British Steamship Company and was soon promoted to junior accountant. As a contrast to the monotony of a shipping clerk's routine he joined the Bancroft Amateur Dramatic Society and became a member of the concert party 'The Mad Medicos'.

He joined the London Scottish Regionals, a territorial army regiment, in 1909, and volunteered to fight with them in France at the outbreak of WWI. After serving only two months at the front, his leg was injured by shellfire and he was medically discharged in May, 1915. In 1939 he spoke to *Photoplay Magazine* about his war experience: *"I loathe war... It certainly taught me to value the quiet life and strengthened my conviction that to keep as far out of range of vision as possible is to be as safe as possible. I am not one of those veterans who look back on the war with the happy comrade feeling. There may have been gay times behind the lines - I'm sure there were - but I can't remember them."* After his discharge he had considered joining the Foreign Office, but decided instead to try his luck as an actor.

His first walk-on part was in a sketch called *The Maharanee of Arakan* at the **London Coliseum**, in which he waved a flag and blew a trumpet. He was later introduced to Gladys Cooper, who thought him clumsy, but cast him in a small part in her new play, *The Misleading Lady* in 1916. His first film role was in a two-reeler by George Dewhurst in 1917, but the film was never released. In 1919 he appeared in Dewhurst's, *The Toilers,* and his name was subsequently lodged with the London Casting Bureau: *"Colman, Ronald. Height - 5ft 11in. Weight - 159. Remarks - does not screen well."* Brief film and stage parts followed, and in 1920 he married stage actress, Thelma Raye, at **Hanover Square Registry Office**.

A month later, promising Thelma he would send for her when he was settled, he bought a one-way steamer ticket to New York to seek out better prospects in the U.S. After a series of small parts in stage plays he was spotted by film director, Henry King, performing in *La Tendresse*, at the Thirty-ninth Street Theater. After a screen test King decided to cast him opposite Lillian Gish in *The White Sister* (1923).

The film launched his career as a romantic hero and was followed by other silent screen successes such as *Dark Angel* (1925) and *Beau Geste* (1926). His silky voice transferred to sound effortlessly and his best performances can be seen in *Bulldog Drummond* (1929, AAN), *Arrowsmith* (1931), *A Tale of Two Cities* (1935), *Lost Horizon* (1937), *The Prisoner of Zenda* (1937), *Random Harvest* (1942, AAN) and *A Double Life* (1947, AA Best Actor).

He divorced his first wife in the early twenties and later married actress Benita Hume with whom he had a daughter. He died in Santa Barbara in 1958.

See also: *Random Harvest,* Hepworth Studios, P.C. Wren, Sapper

Southwark

BIRTHPLACE OF LESLIE HOWARD (1893-1943)
Dulwich

Leslie Howard Steiner was born on 3 April 1893 at **31 Westbourne Road, Forest Hill** (since demolished), the eldest son of Ferdinand Steiner, a stockbroker's clerk and Lilian Blumberg. He was employed as a bank clerk after

Leslie Howard in Pimpernel Smith (1941, British National)

leaving school and enlisted in the Northamptonshire Yeomanry during WWI. He married Ruth Evelyn in 1916 and they had two children.

His first professional appearance as an actor was in *Peg o' My Heart* in 1917. In the 1920's he went to the U.S.A. and acted there until 1926 after which he regularly worked on both sides of the Atlantic. He made his film debut in 1930 when he co-starred with Douglas Fairbanks Jnr. in an adaptation of Sutton Vale's play, *Outward Bound*. He was frequently cast as a calm, scholarly romantic in films such as *The Scarlet Pimpernel* (1935), *The Petrified Forest* (1936), *Pygmalion* (1938 & co-d), *Gone With The Wind* (1939), *Intermezzo* (1939) and *49th Parallel* (1941).

He was killed on 1 June 1943 while returning from a trip to Spain and Portugal when his unescorted airliner was shot down by the Luftwaffe.

HUE AND CRY
Southwark

• 1947 82m b/w
Crime/Comedy Ealing (U.K.)
• Alastair Sim (Felix Wilkinson), Harry Fowler (Joe Kirby), Valerie White (Rhona), Jack Warner (Jim Nightingale), Alec Flinter (Detective Sgt. Fothergill), The Blood and Thunder Boys

• p, Michael Balcon, Henry Cornelius; d, Charles Crichton; w, T.E.B. Clarke; ed, Charles Hasse; ph, Douglas Slocombe

"Never turn down anything, because every time you appear on that screen it's an advert; to be a character actor at eighteen is worth being; stars come and go but as a character actor you'll work until you're ninety."
Jack Warner's advice to young Harry Fowler (Joe Kirby) on the set of *Hue and Cry.*

East End boy, Joe Kirby, stumbles on a fur smuggling racket in which the crooks receive their coded instructions through the ripping yarns of a weekly comic, written by oddball sleuth, Felix H. Wilkinson (Alaistair Sim).

The magic of this post-war Ealing comedy comes from its extensive use of London's bomb-sites for location shooting. The film's gripping climax where the kids ambush the thieves in 'The Battle of Ballard's Wharf', took place at the south end of **Southwark Bridge** on a bomb site now flanked by **Bankside, Emerson St.** and **Park Street**.

See also: Alaistair Sim, Ealing Studios

THE ELEPHANT MAN
Bermondsey

• 1980 125m b/w Biography Paramount (U.K.)
• Anthony Hopkins (Dr. Frederick Treves), John Hurt (John Merrick), John Gielgud (Carr Gomm), Anne Bancroft (Mrs. Kendall), Freddie Jones (Bytes), Michael Elphick (Night Porter)
• p, Jonathan Sanger; d, David Lynch; w, Christopher DeVore, Eric Bergren, David Lynch (based on The Elephant Man, A Study in Human Dignity by Ashley Montagu and The Elephant Man and Other Reminiscences by Sir Frederick Treves); ph, Freddie Francis; ed, Anne V. Coates
• AAN Best Picture, AAN Best Actor: John Hurt; AAN Best Director; AAN Best Adapted Screenplay, AAN Best Editing; AAN Best Score; AAN Best Art Direction; AAN Best Costume Design

"As a specimen of humanity, Merrick was ignoble and repulsive; but the spirit of Merrick, if it could be seen in the form of the living, would assume the figure of an upstanding and heroic man, smooth browed and clean of limb, and with eyes that flashed undaunted courage."
Sir Frederick Treves

The Elephant Man tells the true story of John Merrick, a grotesquely deformed man who was discovered at a Victorian freak-show in 1884 by Dr. Frederick Treves, who took him into care and was surprised to find that he was no imbecile, but a passionate and intelligent human being. His case attracted a lot of attention in the newspapers, which resulted in his being feted with many distinguished visitors, including the Princess of Wales, who visited him many times. He died suddenly in April, 1890, at his quarters in Bedstead Square after falling asleep *"like other people"* in a recumbent position, when his immense head probably caused a dislocation of his neck.

Treves first discovered Merrick in a vacant greengrocer's shop which was being used as a temporary freak show opposite the **London Hospital**, **Mile End Road**. In the film, however, Treves (Anthony Hopkins) discovers him in what

The Elephant Man *(John Hurt) takes ship for England after escaping from the clutches of the freak show owner in Belgium. (1980, EMI/Brooksfilms)*

appears to be an empty or abandoned East End warehouse with his 'owner', Bytes (Freddie Jones). **Shad Thames**, in Southwark, close to Tower Bridge, was used by David Lynch to re-create the film's dark and sinister nineteenth-century East End.

See also: Anthony Hopkins

CINEGRAFIX GALLERY
Bermondsey

Stockist of rare film posters.

Further information: Cinegrafix Gallery, 4 Copper Row, Shad Thames, Tower Bridge Piazza, London, SE1 2LH. Tel: 0171 234 0566 Open: Tues-Sat 11.00-7.00

CLASSIC LOCATION: BOROUGH MARKET
Borough

"It wouldn't be exaggerating to say Borough is used weekly."
Christabel Albery, London Film Commission

The area around **Borough Market**, near Southwark Bridge, is one of the last pockets of Dickensian London left for film makers. Any period from 1820 onwards can be shot here and the community is very much pro-film. Narrowly escaping demolition by Railtrack a few years ago, its atmospheric architecture still survives, and includes the **Borough Cafe on Park Street** which has fed many film crews over the years and was converted into a butcher's shop for *Keep the Aspidistra Flying* (1998), the 1787 **Wheatsheaf Pub** and the **Arches on Stoney Street**, the Georgian frontage of **Green Dragon Court**, **Southwark Cathedral**, and 11th century **Borough Market on Borough High Street**.

Films shot in the area include *Howard's End*, *101 Dalmatians*, *The French Lieutenant's Woman*, *Wilde*, *Keep the Aspidistra Flying* and *Entrapment*.

CHILDHOOD HOME OF MICHAEL CAINE (1933-)
Camberwell

"There were two routes out of the ghetto: sport or show business. Sport was out for me, so showbusiness was the only option, although I had very little practical experience."

Maurice Joseph Micklewhite was born in the charity wing of **St. Olave's Hospital, Rotherhithe** (now offices), on 14 March 1933. His mother was a charlady and his father a Billingsgate fish porter. Baby Maurice was born with rickets and an incurable eyelid swelling disease called blefora, to which he later attributed his 'sleepy' and 'sexy' looks. Shortly after his birth the family moved to a two-room top flat with one toilet shared between five families at **14 Urlwin Street, off Camberwell Road**. In 1936 his brother Stanley was born, cramping conditions even further. He attended his first infant school in nearby **John Ruskin Street**, where he was beaten by bullies because of his curly blond hair.

Michael Caine in Sleuth (1972, Palomar)

One day his mother arrived in the playground and asked him to point out the culprits. *"This I did"*, said Caine in his 1992 autobiography, *"and, much to my surprise, she beat the shit out of all of them."*

During WWII he was evacuated with his brother and mother to **North Runcton** in Norfolk where he won a scholarship place at an evacuated Jewish school called Hackney Down Grocers. In 1946 the family returned to London, where, due to bomb damage at Urlwin Street, they were rehoused in a prefab at Marshall Gardens at the Elephant and Castle in Southwark (now redeveloped), where they lived for eighteen years.

His interest in drama began accidentally at a youth club called Clubland in **Walworth Road**, when he was lustily eyeing up a class of girls through a window in a door against which he was leaning which suddenly flew open and pitched him into the room. The teacher duly enrolled him into the all girls drama class and his love affair with acting began. In his first

*14 Urlwin Street - childhood home of **Michael Caine***

role he had to portray a robot with an electronic voice. The review of his performance in the club magazine read, *"Maurice Micklewhite played the Robot who spoke in a dull mechanical monotonous voice to perfection."*

At Clubland he made friends with a boy called Jimmy Buckley who was a magnet to the opposite sex and had an endless supply of girlfriends. Many years later Jimmy would become the inspiration for Caine's portrayal of *Alfie*.

He left school aged sixteen and went to work first for Peak Films and then for the J. Arthur Rank Organisation as odd-job boy, both of which companies he was fired from. He served his national service with the Queen's Royal Regiment and fought in the Korean War where he caught a rare strain of Malaria which almost killed him.

After he was demobbed he bought a copy of *Stage* magazine and successfully applied for a vacancy

as an assistant stage manager at a theatre in Horsham in Sussex. While working in repertory in Lowestoft, he met and married actress Patricia Haines, with whom he had a daughter. The marriage ended in 1956, and after a succession of odd jobs, including those of laundry worker, dishwasher, plumber's mate and working in a Parisian café, he was offered a small part in his first film, *A Hill in Korea* (1956).

Shortly afterwards he changed his name to Michael Caine and after a period of theatre work, TV bit parts in shows such as *Dixon of Dock Green* , and forgettable films, he was cast as Lt. Gonville Bromhead in Cy Enfield's, *Zulu* (1964). After *Zulu*, the industry began to notice him and he was soon cast as the antihero, Harry Palmer in *The Ipcress File* (1965), which led in 1966 to his portrayal of the Cockney romeo *Alfie*, the film which established him as a star.

His career has had its share of failures but his best work includes *The Italian Job* (1969), *Get Carter* (1971), *Sleuth* (1972), *The Man Who Would Be King* (1976), *California Suite* (1978), *Educating Rita* (1983), *Hannah and Her Sisters* (AA Best Supporting Actor, 1985) and *Little Voice* (1998).

In 1973 he married Shakira Baksh, an Indian girl he had spotted dancing in a Maxwell House Coffee ad on TV. They have one daughter. He was awarded the CBE in 1992 and is partner in various London restaurants, including **The Canteen, Chelsea Harbour**.

After Michael Caine's mother died in 1989 he discovered that he had a half brother, David. Born in 1924 with epilepsy, David had spent most of his life in a psychiatric institution. His mother had visited her illegitimate son every Monday for sixty two years without anyone

knowing. Only the war and holidays had intervened, and she took her secret to the grave. David died in 1991.

See also: *Zulu, Sleuth, Little Voice, Get Carter, Educating Rita,* Metamorphosis of Maurice Micklewhite, Stage Debut of Michael Caine

Tower Hamlets

GRAVE OF ANNE BOLEYN (1507-36)

Queen of England, second wife of Henry VIII and mother of Elizabeth I, Ann Boleyn was accused of adultery and incest with her half-brother and was beheaded. Portrayed many times in the cinema, most notably by Merle Oberon in *The Private Life of Henry VIII* (1933), Genevieve Bujold in *Anne of the Thousand Days* (1969) and Charlotte Rampling in *Henry VIII and His Six Wives* (1973). She is buried on **Tower Hill**.

See also: Merle Oberon, Charles Laughton,

ORIGINS OF FU MANCHU
Limehouse

It was in **Three Colt Street, Limehouse**, in 1911, amid the warren of dark and dangerous streets of what was once London's Chinatown that thriller writer, Sax Rohmer, first saw the man who inspired him to create the mysterious and inscrutable master-criminal, Fu Manchu.

Chinatown, where much of the population was criminal and police patrols were double their normal strength, was not somewhere to

Christopher Lee in **The Brides of Fu Manchu**
(1966, Anglo Amalgamated)

venture into after dark. Here
Rohmer made contact with the
Chinese underworld of pigtailed
villains and opium-dens. One foggy
night he glimpsed a tall, dignified
Chinaman, wearing a fur-collared
overcoat and a fur cap, alighting
from a sleek limousine with a
young Arab girl wrapped in a cloak
and immediately his character was
born - *"I knew that I had seen Dr.
Fu Manchu! His face was the living
embodiment of Satan."*

See also: Sax Rohmer

Waltham Forest

BIRTHPLACE OF ALFRED HITCHCOCK (1899-1980)

Leytonstone

Alfred Joseph Hitchcock was born
on August 13, 1899, in living
quarters at the rear of his father's
grocery shop at **517 The High
Road**, Leytonstone (now site of
filling station - plaque erected). He
was the third child of William
Hitchcock and Emma Jane Whelan
who had inherited the grocer's
business from William's father. The
household was typically working-
class and staunch Catholic. Alfred,
or 'Cocky' as he was nicknamed at
school, was portly and virtually

William Hitchcock and young Alfred, outside the family shop (c.1906)

friendless throughout his
childhood, amusing himself with
his own games and reading. His
father was a strict disciplinarian
who once sent him to the local
police station, aged six, with a
note asking the police to lock him
up. This they duly did - for five
minutes - saying, *"This is what we
do to naughty boys."* He never
forgot the experience.

In 1910 he was enrolled as a pupil
at the Jesuit College of **Saint
Ignatius, Stamford Hill**, an
institution of puritanical strictness,
austerity and corporal punishment.
It was here he developed his love
of ritual acts and received citations
for his academic achievements.
He left college aged fourteen, and
in early 1915 secured an office job
with the Henley Telegraph and

Alfred Hitchcock and James Stewart on the set of Rear Window (1954)

notably *The Man Who Knew Too Much* (1934), *The Thirty-Nine Steps* (1935) and *The Lady Vanishes* (1938). The latter is considered by many to be his best English film.

He married script girl and assistant editor, Alma Reville, at **Brompton Oratory, Knightsbridge** in 1926, and they moved into a two-bedroomed flat at **153 Cromwell Road**, where they lived until their departure for Hollywood in 1939. Their only child, Patricia, was born in 1928. Hitchcock became an American citizen in 1955 and was knighted in 1980. He died in Los Angeles on 29 April 1980.

See also: Rebecca Trail, *Jamaica Inn*, Gainsborough Studios, Forth Bridge

Wandsworth

BIRTHPLACE OF MARGARET RUTHERFORD (1892-1972)
Balham

"I never intended to play for laughs. I am always surprised that the audience thinks me funny at all."

Margaret Rutherford's ill-fated parents, William Benn and Florence Nicholson, were married at All Saints, Wandsworth, in 1882. William's mental state started to deteriorate rapidly after the marriage, and in 1883 he was committed to the asylum for the criminally insane at Broadmoor for murdering his father by crushing his skull with a chamber pot. He was discharged after seven years and to avoid publicity changed his surname to Rutherford.

Margaret Rutherford was born on 11 May 1892 at **15 Dornton Road,**

Margaret Rutherford in Murder Ahoy (1964, MGM)

Balham. When she was only a few months old her parents took her to India where William pursued his occupation as a silk merchant. Sadly, their new life in India was also doomed and shortly afterwards, Florence, now pregnant again, hanged herself from a tree. William was eventually returned to Broadmoor in 1904 and remained there until the year of his death in 1921, aged sixty-six.

Margaret, now effectively orphaned, was brought up in Wimbledon by her mother's spinster sister, Bessie, who kept her father's fate a secret. At the age of thirteen, she discovered both that her father was still alive, and the circumstances surrounding his committal to Broadmoor. This instilled in her a life-long fear of hereditary insanity.

After leaving school she became a music teacher and did not take up professional acting until she was thirty-three when she joined the Old Vic as a student in 1925. Rejected from the Old Vic she later joined the Oxford Repertory Theatre where she met her future husband, the actor J.B. Stringer

Cable Company for fifteen shillings a week. During this period he became interested in art and attended a course in painting with aspirations to become an artist, soon graduating to the advertising department where he was able to sketch and design for a living.

In 1920 he left Henley's for a job designing the title-cards at Islington Studios for its American owners, Famous Players-Lasky, and later their successors, Gainsborough Pictures. Over the next five years he acquired expertise in most aspects of film production and in 1925 Michael Balcon asked him to direct his first film, *The Pleasure Garden*.

He made the first British talkie, *Blackmail*, in 1929 at Elstree and soon came to specialize in thrillers,

Davis who subsequently appeared in many of her films. She had a distinguished stage career in which her censorious voice, stocky physique and outspokenness assured her numerous comic roles.

She made many films but her notable successes were in David Lean's *Blithe Spirit* (1945), where she portrayed the spiritualist, Madame Arcati; *The Importance of Being Earnest* (1952) as Miss Prism; four films as Agatha Christie's tweeded sleuth Miss Marples including *Murder, She Said* (1962); and *The VIPs* (1964) which won her an Oscar for best supporting actress. She was appointed OBE in 1961 and DBE in 1967. She died on 22 May 1972.

See also: Margaret Rutherford (Bucks)

Westminster

FORMER HOME OF VIVIEN LEIGH

Belgravia

"A great actress for ever and ever... We vote you The Young at Heart and a True Beauty."
A tribute written in pencil by an unknown fan on the pillared doorway of Eaton Square shortly after her death.

At 11.30pm on 7 July 1967 Vivien Leigh was found dead in her bedroom at **54 Eaton Square** by her partner, Jack Merivale. He desperately tried to revive her with the kiss of life, but to no avail. She died of tuberculosis having had a delicate constitution all her life.

The next evening the lights of London's West End theatres were switched off for an hour. There was a Requiem Mass held at St Mary's, Cadogan Street on 12 July and later

Vivien Leigh as Scarlett O'Hara in Gone with the Wind (1939, MGM/Selznick International)

54 Eaton Square - former home of Vivien Leigh

that day she was cremated at Golders Green Crematorium. Her ashes were scattered on 'the lake' at Tickerage Mill, her luxurious, five-bedroomed Queen Anne house near the village of Blackboys in East Sussex.

Vivien Leigh was born into a strict Catholic household in Darjeeling on 5 November 1913 to Gertrude and Ernest Hartley, a junior partner in a brokerage business. Named Vivien Mary Hartley, she gave her first public performance at the age of three reciting 'Little Bo Peep' for a group of English memsahibs in the hill town of Ootacamund. When she was just six and a half years old Imperial tradition dictated she be sent to boarding school for her formal education and she was enrolled at the Convent School of the Sacred Heart in Roehampton, and later educated on the Continent.

At eighteen, she enrolled as a student at the Royal Academy of Dramatic Art. Shortly afterwards she married a young barrister named Herbert Leigh Holman, and in 1932 they had a daughter, Suzanne. In 1936 she met and fell in love with Laurence Olivier while filming *Fire Over England.* Four years later, following the collapse of her first marriage, she and Olivier were married, staying together for twenty years before divorcing in 1960.

She will be best remembered for her Oscar-winning portrayal of Scarlett O'Hara in *Gone With The Wind* (1939) and as Blanch Dubois in *A Streetcar Named Desire* (AA 1951). Her other films include *Waterloo Bridge* (1940), *Lady Hamilton* (1941), *Caesar and Cleopatra* (1945) and *Anna Karenina* (1948).

See also: Laurence Olivier

FLASHBACKS

Soho

One of London's leading stockists of vintage and modern movie posters, pressbooks and stills, with over sixteen thousand titles ranging from the silent days to the not-yet-released.

Further information: Flashbacks Film Memorabilia Specialists, 6 Silver Place, London W1R 3LJ. Tel / Fax: 0171 437 8562 email: Flashbacks@compuserve.com http://ourworld.compuserve.com/homepages/Flashbacks

LONDON TRANSPORT MUSEUM FILM COLLECTION

Strand

Since the early 1920s London Transport has used film to celebrate the virtues of public transport, train staff and give advice on safety. The London Transport Museum collects and manages an archive of these historic films which forms an important record of the capital's transport and social history. During the 1920s it operated a mobile open-air cinema. The cinema bus toured schools and church halls showing promotional films for free as a publicity device and in the 1930s a small cinema was built into the booking hall at Charing Cross (now Embankment) Underground.

In 1949, London Transport became part of the nationalised British Transport Commission and it was decided that this new authority should have a film unit to communicate its purpose and activities. Edgar Anstey, a protégé of John Grierson, was appointed as Producer-In-Charge of British Transport Films whose subsequent documentaries showed aspects of working life that would otherwise have gone unnoticed and unsung. The core of the museum's collection comes from BTF's documentary series of the 1950s and 1960s.

See also: John Grierson

Further information: The London Transport Museum, Covent Garden

Piazza, London, WC2E 7BB. The film collection is available for viewing on video in the Archives Office (by appointment only) or at the Museum Resource Centre during opening hours. Details of charges and available titles can be obtained from the Photograph and Film Archive and details of public screenings from the Resource Centre on 0171 379 6344.

BIRTHPLACE OF NORMAN WISDOM (1918-)

West Kilburn

"I've said it before and I mean it - I'm just a berk really..." *

Norman Joseph Wisdom, one of Britain's funniest slapstick comedians, was born on 4 February 1918 at **91 Fernhead Road, Paddington**, the second son of Maude and Frederick Wisdom, a chauffeur. His parents divorced when he was very young and his father, who was often violent and neglectful, was given custody of his two sons. Known as 'Wizzie' to his friends, Norman and his elder brother Fred frequently fended for themselves on the back streets of London by stealing food to avoid starvation and often went barefoot.

When he left school he was employed variously as a grocer's errand boy, apprentice waiter and cabin boy. He wandered the streets for a time as a vagrant before joining the army as a drummer boy, and during WWII he worked as a telephonist in the Strategic Command Room monitoring calls between Churchill and the military.

After the war he decided to try to get into showbusiness and made his first professional stage appearance on 17 December 1945 at Collins Music Hall in Islington. His success led to his first West End appearance in April 1948 when

Norman Wisdom *as the accident-prone window cleaner in* Up in the World *(1956, Rank)*

91 Fernhead Road - birthplace of **Norman Wisdom**

Bernard Delfont booked him to play at the London Casino. The Rank Organisation offered him a seven year contract in 1952 and he made his film debut as 'Norman' the stockroom assistant in *Trouble in Store* in 1953. It was this film which first featured the song which was to become his signature tune, *'Don't laugh at me, 'cos I'm a fool'*, which was written by himself and was such a hit in the film that it went to number one in the record charts and stayed in the Top Ten for nine months.

His other films include: *One Good Turn* (1954), *Man of the Moment* (1955), *The Square Peg* (1958) and *A Stitch in Time* (1963) which broke box-office records and took more money that year than *From Russia With Love*.

Twice married with two children, he was awarded the OBE in 1995 and now lives on the Isle of Man.

THE BARRETTS OF WIMPOLE STREET
Marylebone

"How do I love thee? Let me count the ways."
Elizabeth Barrett Browning (1806-61), *Sonnets from the Portugese* (1850) no. 43

Sidney Franklin directed both versions of MGM's adaptation of Rudolph Besier's famous stage play in 1934 (with Fredric March, Norma Shearer and Charles Laughton) and 1956 (with Bill Travers, Jennifer Jones and John Geilgud), which recounts the frustrated love affair of the celebrated Victorian poets, Elizabeth Barrett and Robert Browning. Confined to her sick - room in **Wimpole Street**, the infirm Elizabeth battles with her despotic father to free herself from his tyrannical and incestuous grip.

The Barretts, a family of eight sons and three daughters, moved to Wimpole Street from Sidmouth in 1835. Elizabeth was isolated from exercise and draughts - a procedure thought vital for her survival - in a room on the second floor where

she languished as an invalid, before eventually eloping with Browning to Italy.

A memorial monument to her parents, Edward and Mary Moulton-Barrett and their daughter Mary who died aged four, can be seen in the **Parish Church, Ledbury, Herefordshire.**

See also: Charles Laughton

BIRTHPLACE OF CHRISTOPHER LEE (1922-)
Belgravia

"As a rule by the age of thirty-five the men of my family had become Cardinals or Colonels, Chairman or Ambassadors."
Christopher Lee

Christopher Frank Carandini Lee was born on Saturday, May 27, 1922, at **51 Lower Belgrave Street**, the second child of the Contessa Estelle Marie Carandini and Lieutenant Colonel Geoffrey Lee, late of the King's Royal Rifle Corps. They later divorced in 1928. The origins of his mother's family, the Carandinis, can be traced to the Papal nobility in Italy and as far back as Imperial Rome.

Educated at Eton and Wellington College, he began his first job in 1939 working in the City as an errand boy for a shipping company in Leadenhall Street. During the war he joined the Home Guard and in 1941 volunteered for the RAF where he worked in Intelligence.

After the war, he decided more or less on a whim to become an actor and in 1947, armed with an introduction to Filippo del Guidice of the Rank Organisation from his cousin, the Italian Ambassador, he was given a seven-year contract, starting at ten pounds a week. Considered too tall by the studio to

51 Lower Belgrave Street - birthplace of **Christopher Lee**

make a success of acting, he made his first film appearance sitting down in Terence Young's *Corridor of Mirrors* (1948). After ten years in the cinema he was still an unknown.

Terence Fisher cast him in 1957 as The Creature, in Hammer's *The Curse of Frankenstein*, which marked the beginning of his long relationship with the horror genre, but it was his portrayal of *Dracula* (1958) and its many sequels, which eventually brought him success. This was a role he initially enjoyed, but he became increasingly dissatisfied with the deteriorating quality of its sequels. In his 1977 autobiography, *Tall, Dark And Gruesome*, he remarks: *"Hammer became complacent and careless, backed unimaginative scripts and tawdry production in the dangerously casual view that they had a captive audience who would take anything."* Another character he became associated with was Fu Manchu, whom he portrayed five times between 1965 and 1968.

His other films included *The Hound of the Baskervilles* (1959), *The Mummy* (1959), *Rasputin the Mad Monk* (1965), *The Devil Rides Out* (1968), *The Wicker Man* (1973) and *The Man with the Golden Gun* (1974).

See also: Hammer Studios, The Dracula Trail, Peter Cushing, *The Wicker Man*, *The Hound of the Baskervilles*, Sax Rohmer

A ZWEMMER
Holborn

Stockist in every aspect of cinema literature, its entire basement is devoted to film, which includes biographies, scripts, magazines, technical manuals and specialist American and European publications.

Further information: A Zwemmer, 80 Charing Cross Road, London, WC2H OBB. Tel: 0171 240

4157. Open 9.30-6.00 Mon-Fri, 10.00-6.00 Sat. Mail order service available.

BIRTHPLACE OF IAN FLEMING (1908-65)
Mayfair

*27 Green Street - birthplace of **Ian Fleming***

Ian Lancaster Fleming, author of escapist literature and creator of Secret Service agent No. 007 was born on 28 May 1908 at **27 Green Street, off Park Lane**, the second of four sons of Eve and Valentine Fleming. His second name was given to him because his mother believed she was descended from John of Gaunt, Duke of Lancaster the fourth son of Edward III; upper-class origins which were no doubt responsible for his Old Etonian creation, James Bond.

See also: Ian Fleming (Wilts)

FIRST CINEMA IN BRITAIN
Piccadilly

Cinematograph pioneer, Birt Acres (1854-1918) opened the first cinema

in Britain at **2 Piccadilly Mansions** at the junction of Piccadilly Circus and Shaftesbury Avenue on 21 March 1896.

Admission to the Kineopticon premiere was sixpence, where it screened: *A Visit to the Zoo, The Derby, Arrest of a Pickpocket, A Carpenter's Shop, Rough Seas at Dover, The Boxing Kangaroo* and *The German Emperor Reviewing his Troops*. Shortly after opening it was destroyed by fire.

See also: Birt Acres

AN AMERICAN WEREWOLF IN LONDON
Piccadilly

- 1981 97m c Comedy/Sci-Fi/Horror Universal (U.S.)
- David Naughton (David Kessler), Jenny Agutter (Alex Price), Griffin Dunne (Jack Goodman)
- p, George Folsey Jr; d, John Landis; w, John Landis; ph, Robert Paynter; art d, Leslie Dilley; fx, Rick Baker
- AA Best Makeup: Rick Baker

Piccadilly Circus is usually a no-go area for film makers, but director John Landis (*National Lampoon's Animal House, The Blues Brothers*) achieved the impossible when he persuaded the authorities to let him film his spectacular multiple car crash finale where werewolf David Naughton's frenzied jaywalking through the London traffic results in a nineteen vehicle pile-up.

Other London locations for the movie included: an escalator at **Aldwych Underground Station** (now closed), **Tottenham Court Road Underground Station, Regent's Park, Trafalgar Square** and a cage in **London Zoo**.

See also: The Black Swan

THE THEATRE MUSEUM & NATIONAL VIDEO ARCHIVE OF STAGE PERFORMANCE
Strand

The theatre, music-hall and vaudeville were traditionally the training grounds of movie actors before they were enticed to 'lower their dignity' and work in the cinema. Colossal salaries and instant stardom, however, soon made them appreciate the new medium.

The Theatre Museum, situated in the heart of Theatreland, houses the world's largest and most important collection of material relating to the British stage. Opened in April 1987, it contains an unrivalled collection of costumes, props, paintings, photographs and other theatrical memorabilia.

The video archive was created in 1992 to establish the best techniques and formats for recording live performances in front of an audience. The archive now holds 129 hours of live drama, opera, musical theatre and pantomime. The museum also possesses a unique research collection of programmes, presscuttings, publicity material, stage designs, photographic files containing over a million photographs, and a reference library of over 100,000 volumes.

Any member of the public can use the study room. It is fully booked every day, and it is normally necessary to make an appointment at least ten days before the date of your intended visit.

Further information: Theatre Museum, Russell Street, London, WC2E 7PA. Tel: 0171 836 7891

WEST END CINEMA THEATRE / RIALTO MERLE OBERON & THE CAFE de PARIS
Piccadilly

The West End Cinema Theatre at **3/4 Coventry Street** was the first cinema in the country, and the first building in the centre of London to use a neon sign in 1913, the year of its opening. The sign hung at right angles to the frontage advertising its name in red neon tubes with white tubes following the contours of its huge arched window.

Designed by architect, Hippolyte Blanc, with interior decor by Horace Gilbert, it originally seated 684. With its marble staircases and ornate plasterwork of cream and gold it had a grandeur to match any West End theatre. It was re-named the Rialto in 1924, and with the arrival of sound it screened mainly art house films. It escaped being converted into a shopping arcade in 1978 and held its final screening on Saturday 9 January, 1982. It acquired listed building status in 1989.

Underneath the cinema was the glamorous Café de Paris nightclub, whose entrance was beneath the cinema's canopy. It was here that actress Merle Oberon worked as a hostess in the early 1930s. She soon began mixing with the jet-set and had an affair with the famous singer and pianist, Leslie Hutchinson. 'Hutch' introduced her to many well-known society figures, including producer-director Alexander Korda, whom she later married.

Estelle Merle O'Brien Thompson was born in Bombay to a Eurasian mother and an English father, but she kept her Eurasian origins hidden all her life knowing it would have hampered her early film career. Beautiful and

The West End Cinema Theatre

ambitious, she arrived in England in 1929 and registered her details with Film Casting, the central casting office in Wardour Street.

While waiting for film work to come along she worked as a dance hostess at Hammersmith's Palais de Danse and shortly afterwards graduated to the Café de Paris.

Her first notable film role was Anne Boleyn in the *Private Life of Henry VIII* (1933) with Charles Laughton and Robert Donat. In 1934 she starred with Leslie Howard, with whom she had a long-running affair, in *The Scarlet Pimpernel*.

She will, however, be best remembered for her portrayal of Cathy in William Wyler's *Wuthering Heights* (1939), a film fraught with difficulties, which neither Merle Oberon nor Laurence Olivier enjoyed making. Married four times, she died in Malibu aged sixty-eight.

See also: Grave of Merle Oberon's Mother

Westminster

PLANET HOLLYWOOD
Piccadilly

Launched in London on 17 May 1993, Planet Hollywood is one of a chain of restaurants themed around movies and movie memorabilia owned by Arnold Schwarzenegger, Sylvester Stallone, Bruce Willis, Demi Moore and restaurateur Robert Earl. The London branch is on three floors, covering 25,000 square feet with 400 seats and is situated in the **Trocadero** on the corner of **Coventry Street** and **Rupert Street**, near Piccadilly Circus.

The main restaurant is on the first floor and contains memorabilia such as Marilyn Monroe's dress from *The Seven Year Itch* and the dress Elizabeth Taylor wore in *Cleopatra*. James Bond memorabilia can be seen in 'The Bond Room', and 'The Sci-Fi Room' includes the pod from *Alien*. Its merchandise store stocks a selection of speciality items, including that essential accessory for the British film tourist - the umbrella!

See also: Planet Hollywood (West Sussex & Dublin)

Further information: Planet Hollywood, 13 Coventry Street, London W1V 7FE. Tel: 0171 287 1000.

FRASER'S AUTOGRAPHS
Strand

Realizing the investment value of autographed memorabilia, some stars have stopped giving them, or will restrict their autographs to one per collector. Despite a few difficult stars, there is still, however, a huge memorabilia market for the collector and Fraser's in the Strand have over 60,000 items in stock, all

*Proprietors of **Planet Hollywood** - Sylvester Stallone, Bruce Willis, Demi Moore and Arnold Schwarzenegger.*

guaranteed authentic. Reputedly the largest selection of autographs to view and buy in Europe, Fraser's is part of the Stanley Gibbons group and deals in signed photographs, letters, documents, clothing and memorabilia.

It also offers an appraisal and valuation service, investment portfolios and bar and restaurant decor packages. Some investment recommendations from Fraser's have included: a black and white, head and shoulders length photograph of James Dean in a white T-shirt and a dark zip-up jacket, dedicated and signed in black ink for £9500, and a signed photograph of a reclining Marilyn Monroe, probably the most sought after piece in autograph collecting, also for £9500. A signed photo of Tom Hanks, however, who is still alive and a long way from screen icon status can be had for a mere £125.

Further information: Fraser's, 399 Strand, London WC2R OLX. Tel: 0171 836 8444.
http://www.stangib.com/frasers/ Free catalogue available.

BRITISH DEBUT OF THE LUMIÈRES' CINEMATOGRAPH
Soho

The first public demonstration of Auguste and Louis Lumière's 'Cinematographe' and films was in the Indian Salon of the Grand Café, Boulevard des Capucine, Paris, on 28 December 1895. On 20 February 1896 they exhibited their scientific curiosity to an astonished British press in an evening hosted by the magician, Felicien Trewey, at the **Marlborough Hall of the London Polytechnic Institute** (now Westminster University), **309 Regent Street**. The public were admitted the following day. The first provincial demonstration is believed to have taken place in Bradford.

FIRST EDISON KINETOSCOPE PARLOUR
Mayfair

The Kinetoscope was a peepshow machine for observing moving pictures through a single viewer and could be described as the forerunner of modern cinema. Invented by Thomas Edison, the first Kinetoscope parlour was opened on 17 October 1894 at **70 Oxford Street**, and run by Americans Frank Z. Maguire and Joseph D. Baucus. Its short films were on a continuous loop with titles such as: *A Cock Fight, Scenes in a Bar Room, A Blacksmith's and a Barber's Shop,* and *The Serpentine Dancer Annabelle.* All the films were made in Edison's Black Maria studio at West Orange, New Jersey. The Kinetoscope's popularity ended when it was replaced by projected films in 1896.

See also: Robert Paul

FLICKER ALLEY
Strand

In the early years of the British film industry movies were first exhibited in music halls and theatres. Most production and distribution companies therefore, were based near the hub of the major halls and their management, mostly in **Cecil Street** (a narrow passage linking **Charing Cross Road** with **St Martin's Lane**), which became known as 'Flicker Alley'. By the late 1920s the majority of the industry had moved to Soho, and predominantly to Wardour Street.

STAGE DOOR PRINTS
Strand

Founded in the early 1980s by the former principal soprano of The Sadler's Wells Opera Company, Barbara Reynold, as a retail shop devoted to the performing arts. It recently branched into cinema and now half the shop concentrates on film related merchandise, including a large selection of autographs, sheet music, posters, lobby cards,

vintage film stills and film biographies.

Further information: Stage Door Prints, 9 Cecil Court, London, WC2N 4EZ. Tel: 0171 240 1683. Open: 11.00-6.00 Mon-Fri, 11.30-6.00 Sat.

THE BLUE LAMP
Paddington

• 1949 82M B/W Mystery General Films (U.K.)
• Jack Warner (George Dixon), Jimmy Hanley (Andy Mitchell), Dirk Bogarde (Tom Riley),
Robert Flemying (Sgt. Roberts), Bernard Lee (Inspector Cherry), Peggy Evans (Diana Lewis)
• p, Michael Balcon; d, Basil Dearden; w, T.E.B. Clarke; ph, Gordon Dines; ed, Peter Tanner; m, Ernest Irving

After the murder of P.C. Dixon by a small time crook, a city-wide manhunt is set in motion to track down the killer.

Shot largely in and around **Paddington Green** whose landmarks have all but vanished, the film vividly portrays a period in London's past when bobbies still patrolled the beat. *The Blue Lamp* was a landmark post-war British film, instrumental in launching the career of 28 year-old Dirk Bogarde and the inspiration for the long-running TV series, *Dixon of Dock Green.* The Police Station in the film was old Paddington Green Police Station, now demolished and engulfed by the **Westway Flyover**. **St. Augustine's Church**, in nearby **Kilburn Park Road** appears in the film, and is still standing, although the adjacent terraced housing was replaced by council houses in the sixties.

See also: Dirk Bogarde, Ealing Studios

VINTAGE MAGAZINE CO. LTD.
Soho

The VinMagCo was established in 1975 and was the first shop of its kind trading exclusively in back issues of magazines and comics. It now has six shops selling 20th Century collectables and memorabilia with the emphasis on entertainment. Stock includes thousands of vintage magazines, original cinema posters, programmes, lobby sets and collectors' ephemera. During the early 1980s Vintage developed

along two divergent lines. To the retail of original memorabilia was added the sale of reproduction posters, postcards and photographs - much of which was published under licence by the company itself. Simultaneously service to commercial interests was enhanced by setting up an archive and picture library which is now reputedly the largest distributor of movie stills and posters in Europe.

Further information: VinMagCo, 39-43 Brewer Street, London, W1R 3FD. Tel: 0171 439 8525.

Other locations: London - 247 Camden High St., 55 Charing Cross Rd., 7-8 Greenland Place (Collector's Emporium). Essex - 417 Lakeside Shopping Centre, 3rd Floor, Thurrock. Brighton - 37 Kensington Gdns.

Commercial Services / Wholesale UK & Export - 203-213 Mare St., London E8 3QE. Tel: 0181 533 7588.
email: vintage.soho@ndirect.co.uk
www.vinmag.com

THE CINEMA STORE
Strand

Founded by cinephiles Paul McEvoy and Neil Palmer in 1993, The Cinema Store stocks a huge range of movie merchandise, including soundtracks, videos, DVD, posters, magazines, trading cards, press kits and autographs. Regular celebrity signing sessions take place at the store and past guests have included William Friedkin and Terry Gilliam.

Further information: The Cinema Store, Unit 4B, Orion House, Upper Saint Martin's Lane, London, WC2H 9EJ. Tel: 0171 379 7838. Website: http//www.thecinemastore.com Open: 10.00-6.00 Mon-Wed, Sat, 10.00-7.00 Thu-Fri.

LET IT BE
Mayfair

" I'd like to say thank you on behalf of the group and ourselves, and I hope we passed the audition!"
John Lennon's rooftop farewell

The Beatles final film, originally titled, *Get Back*, was intended to portray the unpredictable road from raw rehearsal to flawless studio performance. It was recorded in 1969 at Twickenham Studios, the Apple studio and on the rooftop of Apple's headquarters at **3 Saville Row**. Filmed by Lindsay-Hogg on 30 January, the live rooftop session seemed to briefly rekindle the magic of the Beatles at a time when they were drifting apart. As they sang versions of *Get Back, I've Got a Feeling, Dig a Pony, Don't Let Me Down* and *One After 909*, it was clear one was watching the end of an era and one of their last live performances.

The film was finished in January 1969, but was not released until May 1970. Neglected by critics at the time and rarely seen on television, the film has never been officially released on video.

COLLECTORS' FILM CONVENTIONS
Westminster

Ed Mason began organising his Collectors' Film Conventions for the dedicated movie fan in 1991. There are now six a year held at **Westminster Central Hall** (opposite Westminster Abbey) dealing mostly in paper memorabilia, including stills, lobby cards, posters, programmes, autographs, postcards, records, CDs, videos, laser discs, magazines, press books, cuttings and books. Dealers' collections are unpredictable. There's no telling what you can turn up.

Further information: Ed Mason, Room 301, 3rd Floor, River Bank House Business Centre, 1 Putney Bridge Approach, London, SW6 3JD. Tel: 0171 736 8511.

METAMORPHOSIS OF MAURICE MICKLEWHITE
Strand

"I always tell people that I changed my name from Maurice Micklewhite because there was already another Maurice Micklewhite who was a star. That shuts them up."

In the late fifties, struggling actor Maurice Micklewhite changed his name to Michael Scott. Every evening at six o'clock he would phone his agent from **Leicester Square tube station** to see if any offers of work had arrived that day. The usual answer was *"Nothing today."* One evening he was informed that he had been offered a small part on television in a play called *The Lark* by Jean Anouilh, but in order to get this part he had to join the British actors' trade union, Equity. As there was already a member of Equity called Michael Scott, he would have to change his name - and within the next half hour.

*Plaque of **Michael Caine's** handprints near the entrance to the Odeon Leicester Square*

Sitting in Leicester Square he struggled to come up with a suitable name. One of the cinemas in the square was advertising the new Humphrey Bogart movie, *The Caine Mutiny*. Michael Mutiny was definitely out, so he settled for Michael Caine.

See also: *Zulu, Sleuth, Little Voice, Get Carter, Educating Rita,* Michael Caine (Southwark & Norfolk)

ODEON LEICESTER SQUARE
Strand

Built on the site of the Alhambra Music Hall, the Odeon Leicester Square opened its doors on 2 November 1937. A flagship cinema for the Oscar Deutsch chain, it had 2,116 seats and cost £232,755, five times the cost of the average Odeon. Its imposing exterior and decorative and luxurious interior, which included leopard-skin pattern seating and naked figures leaping up the walls, was marvelled at by its patrons. During WWII a landmine badly damaged the building and it closed for a month for repairs. On 14 May 1953 Britain's first wide screen was installed here for the film *Tonight We Sing.* The same year Cinemascope premiered here with a screening of *The Robe* on 19 November. In 1967 the Odeon was 'modernised' with disastrous results which destroyed most of its uniqe character. In 1990 five new screens

were added called the Odeon Mezzanine.

Further information: Odeon Leicester Square, London WC2. Tel: 0181 315 4215

CHARLIE CHAPLIN STATUE
Strand

This bronze statue by John Doubleday in **Leicester Square** was unveiled by Sir Ralph Richardson in April 1981, and depicts Chaplin in his tramp costume with bowler hat and cane. The plinth legend reads: *"The comic genius who gave pleasure to so many."*

See also: The Charlie Chaplin Trail (Lambeth)

EMPIRE LEICESTER SQUARE
Strand

Cinema architect, George Coles, restored and modernised this 1920s cinema (pictured above) in 1962. It reopened the same year with the Doris Day musical, *Jumbo,* but failed to pull in the punters until

the management decided to risk screening a revival of old Garbo classics. Their gamble paid off and 18,000 fans passed through their doors for a week's run of *Queen Christina.* The Cinema International Corporation took over ownership of the Empire from MGM in 1973, and in 1989 the cinema described itself as 'The World's Most Spectacular Movie Venue' after £2 million worth of improvements. The Empire was also the location of the 'film premiere' in Roger Michell's 1999 romantic comedy, *Notting Hill.*

See also: *Notting Hill*

Further information: Empire, Leicester Square. Tel: 0171 437 1234.

THE SHERLOCK HOLMES COLLECTION
Marylebone

If you have ever wondered why cinema's greatest detective smoked opium, or what happened to Professor Moriarty, and who the deerstalker hat really did belong to, then The Sherlock Holmes Collection will answer all your questions.

Included in the collection are books, journals, magazines, photographs, cuttings, reviews, film scripts, Conan Doyle biographies, Bradshaw's Railway Guide and a complete set of the Strand Magazines up to 1930.

Viewing the collection is by prior arrangement and it can only be consulted at weekends.

See also: Sir Arthur Conan Doyle, Sherlock Holmes Festival, *The Hound of the Baskervilles.*

Further information: Sherlock Holmes Collection, Marylebone Library, Marylebone Rd., London NW1 5PS. Tel: 0171 641 1037.

SCOTLAND

Aberdeenshire

BIRTHPLACE OF *DRACULA*
Cruden Bay

A research trip for a production of *Macbeth* at London's Lyceum Theatre first brought Bram Stoker to Cruden Bay in the late 1880s. Historical accuracy was required if they were to build convincing sets, and a research group toured the Scottish Highlands to observe its moors and castles.

While journeying to Inverness they came across Cruden Bay and the cliff-top **Slains Castle**. Stoker loved the setting and returned alone in 1893 for a walking tour, taking lodgings at the **Kilmarnock Arms Hotel**. He returned in the summer of 1894 to introduce his family to his romantic idyll, and it was during an August holiday here in 1895 that he was inspired to write the immortal classic, *Dracula*. The early chapters of the book, in which Jonathan Harker journeys to the Castle Dracula, were written at the Kilmarnock Arms, and the final

Slains Castle

pages were written here the following summer.

There is no evidence that Slains Castle was the original inspiration for Castle Dracula, but most visitors to this desolate place will agree that it could easily double for Transylvania and could well have influenced Stoker. However, when he first saw Slains in the late 1880s it was still inhabited and was not

the crumbling and foreboding ruin it is today - a result of the roof having been removed in the 1920s to avoid paying taxes. Built at the end of the 16th century it was the home of the Earls of Erroll, chiefs of the clan Hay, and its distinguished guests have included Dr. Samuel Johnson, who wrote, *"The walls of one of the towers seem only the continuation of a perpendicular rock, the foot of*

The Kilmarnock Arms Hotel

which is beaten by the waves... I would not for my amusement wish for a storm, but as storms, whether wished or not, will sometimes happen, I may say without violation of humanity, that I would willingly look out upon them from Slains Castle."

Great care should be taken when visiting Slains Castle which is situated perilously close to the cliff edge on the grassy headland known as the **Bow**.

In 1895 Stoker published *The Watter's Mou'* about smuggling in Cruden Bay and mentions the Kilmarnock Arms. In 1902 he rented **'The Crookit Lum'**, a house still standing in nearby **Whinnyfold** overlooking the sea, which became his summer retreat until his death in 1912.

See also: Bram Stoker, Christopher Lee, Hammer Studios, Peter Cushing, The Dracula Trail

Further information: The Kilmarnock Arms Hotel, Bridge Street. Tel: 01779 812213. Slains Castle can be reached by footpath from the Main Street car park, Cruden Bay.

BIRTHPLACE OF LORNA MOON (1886-1930)
Strichen

"Lorna wouldn't have made much of a mother for anyone, but she was an admirable artist."
Richard De Mille

Hollywood screenwriter, Lorna Moon, was born Nora Helen Wilson Low at the **Temperance Hotel, Strichen** in 1886 to Charlie and Margaret Low. When she was nineteen she eloped and emigrated to Canada with William Hebditch, by whom she had one son. She later met a travelling salesman named Walter Moon by whom she had a daughter. While working as a journalist she wrote to Cecil B De Mille criticising one of his films; he replied, *"If you think you can do better, come to Hollywood and try."*

This she did, and so began her new life as a successful Hollywood scenario writer, her work including *Don't Tell Everything* (1921), *After Midnight* (1927), *Min and Bill* (1930, adapted from her novel *Dark Star*), *Love* (1927) with Greta Garbo and *Mr Wu* (1927) starring Lon Chaney.

Lorna had an affair with Cecil B De Mille's brother William, by whom she had a son. William was already married, and to avoid a scandal Cecil B De Mille adopted his brother's son, an arrangement Lorna was happy to accept; she had already given up her two elder children. During the pregnancy she developed tuberculosis and was bedridden for ten years both at home and in T.B. sanatoriums. She died in a sanatorium at Albuquerque, New Mexico, on 1st May 1930, aged forty four. Her ashes were returned to Strichen at her own request and scattered on **Mormond Hill.** Her son, Richard De Mille, never discovered who his natural mother was until he was

thirty-three. In researching his mother's past he discovered his half-brother and half-sister and in 1999 wrote about Lorna's life in his book, *My Secret Mother*, where he states: *"... Lorna was not cut out to be a mother. Her temperament was not suited to it and she had a rough childhood with a mother who was herself not very loving. The conspiracy provided me with a good home and a loving mother and I would have met Lorna eventually if she hadn't died so young."*

Lorna Moon

Further information: Her two books, *Dark Star* and *Doorways to Drumorty* , were republished by Gourdas House in Aberdeenshire in 1980, but are now out of print. In 1998 local playwright, Greg Dawson Allen, wrote *Lorna*, a one-woman play based on her life.

CLASSIC LOCATION: DUNNOTTAR CASTLE
Stonehaven

This impressive and ominous edifice, perched on the cliffs near Stonehaven, doubled as one of the locations for Elsinore in Franco Zeffirelli's acclaimed 1990 production of *Hamlet,* starring Mel Gibson. With a bloody history that stretches back to the 9th century, Dunnottar has been the scene of

Aberdeenshire

many notable events, including the burning alive of its English Plantagenet garrison by William Wallace and the imprisoning of 167 Covenanters in atrocious conditions in 1685.

Further information: Dunnottar Castle can be reached via the A92 road about one and a half miles south of Stonehaven. Due to steep access paths it is not suitable for the disabled. Open all year. Closed Sat. & Sun. during winter. Tel: 01569 762173.
Zeffirelli also used Dover Castle and Blackness, in West Lothian, for additional Elsinore locations.

Pennan

LOCAL HERO
Pennan

• 1983 111m c Comedy
Enigma / Goldcrest (UK)
• Burt Lancaster (Happer), Peter Riegert (Mac), Fulton Mackay (Ben), Denis Lawson (Urquhart), Victor (Christopher Rozycki), Norman Chancer (Moritz), Peter Capaldi (Oldsen), Rikki Fulton (Geddes), Alex Norton (Watt), Jenny Seagrove (Marina), Jennifer Black (Stella)
• p, David Putnam; d, Bill Forsyth; w,

Bill Forsyth; ph, Chris Menges; ed, Michael Bradsell; m, Mark Knopfler; prod d, Roger Murray-Leach; art d, Richard James, Adrienne Atkinson, Frank Walsh, Ian Watson; fx, Wally Veevers

"Excuse me, do you have an adaptor? I have to charge my briefcase."
Macintyre

A Texas oil tycoon (Burt Lancaster), with a passion for astronomy, decides to build a refinery in Scotland and sends young troubleshooting executive, Macintyre (Peter Riegert), to negotiate the purchase of an entire Highland community. Gradually Mac's materialistic perspective on life is eroded, and he begins to appreciate the simpler pleasures, like clean air, beachcombing, idyllic scenery, and a good malt whisky.

No doubt influenced by Mackendrick's *Whisky Galore* and *The Maggie*, and Powell and Pressburger's *I Know Where I'm Going*, Bill Forsyth's masterpiece ranks alongside the great Ealing comedies. Set in almost mystical locations, with a host of eccentric characters and wry Scots humour.

The village of Ferness was shot at two different locations. **Pennan** in Aberdeenshire served as the village and **Camusdarrach Beach**, near **Morar** on the west coast, was the beach location. Pennan is a small fishing community strung along the base of rugged cliffs which shield it from much of the sunlight in winter. An extremely steep road descends into the village from the cliff tops, and leads almost to the door of the Pennan Inn (01346 561201) where the cast stayed while making the film. Burt Lancaster, however, never came to Pennan. For the exterior of the hotel in the film, a hoarding was hung on two houses along the seafront, and the hotel interiors were shot at the **Lochailort Hotel**, near Morar. The Pennan Inn displays photographs on its walls connected to the making of the film, and is a popular port of call for movie fans. Mark Knopfler unveiled a plaque outside the inn commemorating the film and shortly after the film was released, locals had difficulty getting into their own local because of the influx of tourists. Many visitors like to pose for a photograph in front of the famous phone box opposite, but the actual phone box used in the film was only a prop, located at the harbour. This fact doesn't seem to bother tourists, and fans still call the phone box on 01346 561210 from around the world, just to say hello.

The ceilidh scenes couldn't be shot in Pennan Village Hall, because the ceiling was too low for the cameras and their tracking, so a set was built at **Burnside**, above the harbour. Nearby **Hilton Community Hall**, near **Boyndie**, was where the ceilidh actually took place. The village shop was located at **Pole of Itlaw** (plaque erected) and a Fraserburgh herring boat doubled for the Russian trawler. The road Mac and Oldsen travelled along on their way to Pennan, and where they hit the rabbit, was the **B862, near Fort Augustus, south of Loch Ness.**

The Houston scenes were all shot on location in Texas, except for the scene where Felix Happer demonstrates his Planetarium to junior executive Mackay. This set was built inside a disused warehouse at the **Ben Nevis Distillery** just outside Fort William. The warehouses at the distillery are often used by film companies to create sets or for storage and most recently were used by the *Rob Roy* and *Braveheart* production units.

See also: *Local Hero* (Morar)

Angus

THE MYTH OF DAVID NIVEN'S BIRTH (1910-83)
Kirriemuir

"Kirriemuir may not know it, but a young man who crashed Hollywood little more than a year ago, and is making his way in films, was born in Kirriemuir twenty-seven years

David Niven *as the suave butler in My Man Godfrey (1936, Universal)*

ago - so the newspapers say..." The Kirriemuir Free Press and Angus Advertiser, 21st May, 1936.

Many visitors have arrived in Kirriemuir over the years searching in vain for the birthplace of David Niven. As well as being a prolific actor, Niven was a great storyteller, but in his best-selling autobiographies, *The Moon's a Balloon* (1971) and *Bring on the Empty Horses* (1975), he never reveals his place of birth. Most movie reference books list his birthplace as Kirriemuir, but he was in fact born on 1 March 1910 at **Belgrave Mansions, London**.

Even in death his birthplace was an enigma, with the Times obituary still claiming he was born in Kirriemuir. In 1957 Niven said: *"You can trace the decline in the family fortunes by the lowering in tone of our different addresses. We went from* **Craig House** *in Kirriemuir to Fairford Park, Gloucestershire; Golden Farm, Cirencester to 47 Cadogan Place, London; 110 Sloane Street to 11 Cheyne Walk; and finally to Rose Cottage, Bembridge on the Isle of Wight."* The Forfar Assessor's Office could find no trace of a Craig House in the Kirriemuir district at the time Niven was born.

There is a Craig Lodge in Glen Prosen, but no locals can recall the Nivens having lived there. It's difficult to believe that he wasn't aware of his real birthplace, but to a spinner of tales like Niven, combined with the Hollywood publicity machine, Bonnie Scotland was probably a more desirable origin than city centre London.

He was the youngest of four children of William Niven, a landowner, and Henrietta Degacher. His father was killed at Gallipoli in 1915 and in 1917 his mother remarried businessman, Thomas Platt. Much of his childhood was spent unhappily at a succession of boarding schools - one of which he was expelled from for stealing. His final school report read, *"Not clever, but useful to have around. He will be popular wherever he goes unless he gets into bad company which ought to be avoided because he does get on with everybody."* In 1928 he entered the Royal Military College at Sandhurst and later joined the Highland Light Infantry in Malta. He resigned his commission in 1933 and sailed for Canada. He worked in New York as a whisky salesman and then with a horse-racing syndicate in Atlantic City before drifting to Hollywood where he became a film extra.

He quickly graduated to minor roles, and a love-affair with Merle Oberon was instrumental in kick-starting his career. Soon he was starring in a string of successful films, including *The Charge of the Light Brigade* (1936), *The Prisoner of Zenda* (1937) and *Wuthering Heights* (1939). During WWII he joined the Rifle Brigade and made three films in England: *The First of the Few* (1942), *The Way Ahead* (1944) and *A Matter of Life and Death* (1945). In 1940 he married Primula Susan, who later died tragically in California when she fell down a flight of cellar stairs. Niven won an Oscar for *Separate*

Tables in 1958, but with the exception of *The Guns of Navarone* (1961), *Paper Tiger* (1974) and *Murder By Death* (1976), his post-war films never equalled his early work.

In 1948 he married Swedish model, Hjordis Paulina Tersmeden, and they later adopted two children. Apart from his bestselling memoirs he also wrote two novels, and it was during a literary tour in 1981 that he became afflicted with motor-neurone disease. On 27 July 1983 he died at his home in Chateau d'Oex in Switzerland where he is buried. Five thousand people attended his memorial service at St Martin-in-the-Fields in London.

See also: David Niven (Wilts), *A Matter of Life and Death*

BIRTHPLACE & GRAVE OF J.M. BARRIE (1860-1937)
Kirriemuir

Sir James Matthew Barrie, creator of Peter Pan, was born on May 9th., 1860, at **9 Brechin Road**. The house now forms an interesting museum run by the National Trust for Scotland containing manuscripts, diaries, photographs, period furnishings and Barrie's own writing desk. At the top of **Bellies Brae** is **Strathview**, the house where J.M. Barrie's family lived for a time, and in which he married the actress Mary Ansell. Across the road is the white cottage described by Barrie in his novel, *A Window in Thrums*. Outside the offices of the Hamlyn Angus Mill in the **Glengate** stands a statuette of Peter Pan, modelled on the original statue in London's Kensington Gardens.

Many of J.M. Barrie's novels and plays became feature films,

Peter Pan (1953, Walt Disney Productions)

including: *Peter Pan* (1924, 1953), *The Admirable Crichton* (1957), *The Little Minister* (1934), *What Every Woman Knows* (1934), *Quality Street* (1937) and *Hook* (1991).

In **St. Mary's Episcopal Church, off Hillbank**, J.M. Barrie's burial service took place in 1937. His grave, which is signposted, is in the town cemetery, **off Brechin Rd.**

See also: Peter Pan

Argyll & Bute

BIRTHPLACE OF ERIC CAMPBELL (c1878-1917)
Dunoon

Everyone knew his face, but few people knew his name. A hulking 6ft 5ins tall, weighing around 20 stones, with his piercing eyes and bushy black beard, Eric Campbell was one of the silent screen's great

Eric Campbell

villains, endlessly bullying little Charlie Chaplin in films such as *The Vagabond* (1916), *The Floorwalker* (1916) and *The Cure* (1917).

He was born in Dunoon, although the exact house and date of his birth (possibly 1878) is not known. A talented singer, he toured with the D'Oyly Carte Opera Company performing Gilbert and Sullivan from 1907-1914 and he also wrote for the London Film Company. He became a member of Fred Karno's celebrated music-hall troupe, which included Stan Laurel and Charlie Chaplin, and in Hollywood D.W. Griffith cast him in his 1915 epic, *The Birth of a Nation.*

He died aged only thirty-seven shortly after completion of the Chaplin comedy, *The Adventurer* in 1917 when the car he was driving - allegedly speeding on the wrong side of the road, drunk - was in a head-on crash with another vehicle at the corner of Wilshire Boulevard and Vermont Avenue, Hollywood. He was killed outright.

In June, 1996, his granddaughter unveiled a plaque in the **Castle Gardens** (opposite the pier) commemorating his time in Dunoon.

See also: Charlie Chaplin, Fred Karno

BIRTHPLACE OF JACK BUCHANAN (1890-1957)
Helensburgh

"He wasn't a subject for muck-raking because there wasn't any muck."
Wifred Hyde White

Actor, director, producer and dapper song-and-dance man, Walter John Buchanan, better known as Jack, was born on 2 April 1890 at **'Fairy Knowe', 30 Lomond Street, Helensburgh**, the second child of Patricia McWatt and Walter Buchanan, an auctioneer. Shortly after Jack's birth the family moved house to **'Westwood'** (renamed **'Garthland')** at **38 Argyll Street**, where his best friend and close neighbour was the local rector's son, John Logie Baird, who was also destined to make a name for himself.

Jack Buchanan

*38 Argyll Street, Helensburgh (pictured in 1978) - childhood home of **Jack Buchanan***

He attended **Larchfield School** (now part of Lomond School) at **37 Colquhoun Street**, which at the time of writing is under threat of demolition.

When he was twelve his father died leaving considerable gambling debts. His mother was forced to sell their house and move to rented premises in Glasgow where she took in boarders. In Glasgow he attended Glasgow Academy and his first job on leaving school was in the Glasgow auctioneering house in which his father had also worked.

Aware that he could make people laugh, his ambition was to become a comedian and he made his first professional appearance in 1911 at the **Pickard's Panoptican**, a rough and ready Glasgow music hall where he was booed off the stage. Undeterred, he left for London and appeared in many theatrical productions, until, by the mid 1920s he had risen from the chorus to become Britain's top musical comedy star.

He made his film debut as an extra for the Neptune Film Company in 1913 when he was in the chorus of the Leicester Square Empire, and from 1917 to 1939 he made twenty five British films. His first notable success was when he played the title role in *Bulldog Drummond's Third Round* in 1925.

The title song to *Goodnight Vienna* gave him a hit song in 1932 and he continued to make musical comedies throughout the 1930's, including *Brewster's Millions* (1933), *This'll Make You Whistle* (1937) and *The Gang's All Here* (1939). His career dipped in the 1940s until he was cast with Fred Astaire and Cyd Charisse in 1953 in the classic musical *Bandwagon.*

He died of cancer on 21 October 1957 and according to his wishes his ashes were taken on board the *Queen Mary* and scattered at sea in Southampton Water. A plaque was unveiled in the **Templeton Library, John Street**, in 1996, celebrating his achievments in the cinema.

CHILDHOOD HOME OF DEBORAH KERR (1921-)
Helensburgh

"A plump little dumpling who was obviously going places."
Michael Powell

Contrary to popular belief, Deborah Kerr Trimmer was not born in Helensburgh, but in a private nursing home at **7 St James Terrace, Hillhead, Glasgow**, in the early hours of 30 September 1921, to Kathleen Rose and Arthur (Jack) Trimmer, a civil engineer.

The Trimmers lived in Helensburgh for three years. For most of this time they stayed with Arthur's parents at **'Nithsdale', 96 West King Street**, and from 1923 to 1924 they lived at nearby **48 Ardencaple Quadrant**. Deborah Kerr's only memory of Helensburgh

is of travelling with her grandmother in a horse-drawn cab and suffering the heartbreaking experience of losing a penny between its seats.

Her grandparents moved to **Alfold in Surrey**, to start up a timber haulage business, and Deborah's parents followed shortly afterwards. Jack Trimmer opened a small filling station in Alfold and in May, 1925, Deborah's brother Edmund was born. Many Trimmers are buried in the local **St Nicholas' Parish Church**, including her father, who died in 1937, who had suffered from poor health after being gassed and losing a leg in the Battle of the Somme. Her grandfather, Arthur Kerr Trimmer, who died aged sixty-one in 1926, is also buried in the same grave. In 1930 the Trimmer family went to stay with Jack's widowed mother at **Pound Cottage**, halfway between the main Horsham-Guildford Road and Alfold, where Jack converted his father's sawmill behind the house into a small engineering workshop.

Deborah attended **St Martha's Kindergarten at Bramley** in September 1928, and in 1933 she was enrolled at **Northumberland House Private School, Bristol**, where her Aunt Jane (who acted under the stage name of Phyllis Smale) taught drama. Jane later set up her own drama school, taking Deborah with her, which eventually led to her being accepted as a ballet student at Sadler's Wells. Shortly afterwards she made her professional stage debut in *Prometheus*, on 29 March 1938. Too tall at five feet six and three-quarter inches to become a professional ballerina, she began acting in small roles with the Open Air Theatre at Regents Park, where she was spotted and signed up by London agent, John Gliddon.

While dining with Gliddon at the Mayfair Hotel, she met Hungarian

producer-director, Gabriel Pascal, who said to her: *"Sweet virgin, are you an actress?"* Pascal subsequently cast her as Jenny, in *Major Barbara* (1941). Within two years she had become a major star in films such as *The Life and Death of Colonel Blimp* (1943) and *Black Narcissus* (1947). She became adept at portraying refined ladies, nuns and governesses, but was cast against type, her "sweet virgin" image laid to rest, when she played nymphomaniac, Karen Holmes, in *From Here to Eternity* in 1953.

Her other films include *The Hucksters* (1947), *Edward My Son* (1949), *The King and I* (1956), *Heaven Knows Mr Allison* (1957), *Separate Tables* (1958), *The Sundowners* (1960), *The Innocents* (1961) and *Casino Royal* (1967). She retired from film making in 1969, but continued performing on stage, and received an honorary Oscar in 1994.

See also: *Black Narcissus*, Bluebell Railway

THE MAGGIE
Islay

• 1954 93m b/w Comedy (U.K.) aka High and Dry
• Paul Douglas (Marshall), Alex Mackenzie (Skipper), James Copeland (Mate), Abe Barker (Engineer), Tommy Kearins (Wee Boy), Hubert Gregg (Pusey), Geoffrey Keen (Campbell)
• p, Michael Truman; d, Alexander Mackendrick; w, William Rose

"A piece of American folklore—the innocent American vanquishing the wicked, experienced Europeans—is set bottomside up."
Pauline Kael

The canny Scots crew of a condemned Glasgow 'puffer' boat runs circles round a tyrannical American millionaire (Paul Douglas) while transporting a cargo of bathroom fittings to his privately owned Western Isle. Seething with frustration after a series of mishaps and delays, he eventually accedes defeat and rescues their old hulk from sinking by throwing his precious cargo overboard. End result: a born again millionaire, inclined towards benevolence and a better understanding of his fellow man.

Shot mainly around **Bowmore** and **Port Askaig** on the Isle of Islay, this Ealing-style gem wonderfully evokes the pace and tranquillity of the Western Isles. The pheasant poaching scene was shot on the **Crinan Canal** near **Lochgilphead**. The coastline around Crinan was also the location for the exciting sea chase in *From Russia with Love* (1963).

See also: Ealing Studios

THE EMPIRE TRAVEL LODGE
Lochgilphead

This was built originally as the Empire Cinema for the Empire Exhibition at Ballahouston in 1938. Records show that Queen Mary visited the cinema on more than one occasion when she toured the exhibition. Films screened included *The Champion* with Charlie Chaplin and *Sixty Glorious Years* starring Anna Neagle. After the Exhibition closed, the Empire Cinema was taken apart and rebuilt in Lochgilphead.

It survived as a cinema until 1984, and was briefly used as a snooker

hall before its conversion to a travel lodge in 1991. In the 1960s the cinema was hired for six weeks by Shepperton Studios during the making of *From Russia With Love* (1963). Many of the film's locations were shot in this part of Argyll and the rushes were shown each day to the crew and cast, including Sean Connery.

Further information: Eric & Mavis Haysom, Empire Travel Lodge, Union Street, Lochgilphead, Argyll, PA31 8JS. Tel: 01546 602381.

I KNOW WHERE I'M GOING
Isle of Mull

"The film's lilting look at the Scottish landscape and people presaged Local Hero by forty years."
Carrie Rickey

- 1945 91m bw Romance/Comedy Archers (UK)
- Roger Livesey (Torquil MacNeil), Wendy Hiller (Joan Webster), Pamela Brown (Catriona Potts), Nancy Price (Mrs. Crozier), Finlay Currie (Ruairidh Mur), John Laurie (John Campbell), George Carney (Mr. Webster), Walter Hudd (Hunter), Murdo Morrison (Kenny), Margot Fitzsimmons (Bridie)
- p, Michael Powell, Emeric Pressburger; d, Michael Powell, Emeric Pressburger; w, Michael Powell, Emeric Pressburger; ph, Erwin Hillier; ed, John Seabourne; m, Allan Gray; art d, Alfred Junge

Bank manager's daughter, Joan Webster (Wendy Hiller), always knows where she's going and is convinced only money will secure her future happiness. Determined to marry her ageing millionaire employer, she travels to his remote Scottish island retreat for the wedding. A storm prevents her crossing from the mainland and she is forced to shelter with the locals. Here she meets Torquil MacNeil (Roger Livesey), the true laird of

the Isle of Kiloran, and assorted eccentric natives. Attracted to MacNeil, she feels her wealthy future slipping away and foolishly risks her own and other people's lives to cross the treacherous seas. Suitably repentent, she slowly falls under the spell of this simple community, allowing her love for MacNeil to surface and her destiny to be transformed.

Location filming took six weeks on the Isle of Mull and studio scenes were shot at Denham Studios. Erraig, the house owned by Catriona Potts (Pamela Brown) in which Joan waits for the storm to clear, is **Carsaig House** at the south end of the island. The film crew also used this area as their base. Torquil MacNeil's cursed castle was **Moy Castle** at nearby **Lochbuie** and the castle where Joan stayed with friends of her future husband was **Torosay, near Craignure**. The ceilidh scenes were shot close by at **Duart Castle**. **Colonsay** doubled as the Isle of Kiloran and the perilous **Corrievrechan Whirlpool** played itself and is located in the **Gulf of Corrievrechan** between the islands of **Jura and Scarba**.

See also: Michael Powell, Emeric Pressburger, Finlay Currie

Further information: Tobermory Tourist Information 01688 302182

BIRTHPLACE OF A.J. CRONIN (1896-81)
Cardross

Archibald Joseph Cronin was born on 19 July 1896 at **Rosebank Cottage, Murray's Road**, the only child of Patrick Cronin, a clerk and commercial traveller, and Jessie Montgomerie. He was educated at Dumbarton Academy and Glasgow University, where he studied medicine. His first practice was in a

mining area in Wales which was the inspiration for his semi-auto-biographical novel, *The Citadel*, filmed by King Vidor in 1938, starring Robert Donat. It was the success of his first novel, *Hatter's Castle* (1931), which enabled him to give up medicine and concentrate on writing. A master story-teller, most of his works have an autobiographical streak, with Dumbarton portrayed as the fictitious Levenford.

Many of his books were made into successful films, including: *Hatter's Castle* (1941), *The Keys of the Kingdom* (1944), *The Green Years* (1946) and *The Spanish Gardener* (1956). He will probably be best remembered for the popular radio and TV series, Dr Finlay's Casebook, based on his experiences as a doctor. He married Agnes Gibson in 1921 and had three sons. He died in 1981 at Glion, near Montreux, Switzerland.

See also: Robert Donat, *The Citadel*

KIDNAPPED
Ballachulish

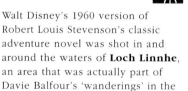

Walt Disney's 1960 version of Robert Louis Stevenson's classic adventure novel was shot in and around the waters of **Loch Linnhe**, an area that was actually part of Davie Balfour's 'wanderings' in the original story. The production company was based in Oban, and filmed extensively in **Ballachulish, Ardgour** and **Glen Nevis**. Directed by Robert Stevenson, Peter Finch starred as Alan Breck and James MacArthur as Davie Balfour.

Stevenson's tale of the aftermath of the Jacobite rising in 1745 has been frequently adapted for the screen over the years, the earliest version being filmed in 1938, with Warner Baxter as Alan Breck and Freddie Bartholomew as Balfour. 'The Hawes Inn', where Davie Balfour

James MacArthur and Peter Finch in
***Kidnapped** (1960, Walt Disney)*

was 'kidnapped' in the novel, is a real place and still a working inn, situated beneath the Forth Rail Bridge at South Queensferry.

See also: Robert Louis Stevenson

THE PICTURE HOUSE
Campbeltown

"Stand up there till I see where you're sittin'!"
Lizzie Speed, usherette in the 1930s

Affectionately known as the 'Wee Pictures' by locals, the Picture House Cinema is one of the earliest purpose-built cinemas in Scotland, and the oldest retaining its original name. Designed by architect, Albert V. Gardner, it opened on 26 May 1913 screening films on a white painted wall. In 1931 it introduced sound to its audience with a performance of *The Desert Song*, which the local *Courier* newspaper reviewed as follows: *"It was pleasing to note that Campbeltown audiences, which were inclined to be rather noisy at the silent shows, were completely silent, and in sympathy with the production of the film."*

The cinema closed in 1986, but after substantial fund-raising efforts by the community in 1989 it reopened, and at the time of writing is still screening films.

Further information: Picture House, Hall Street, Campbeltown. Tel: 01825 553899.

Borders

NEW PALACE CENTRE
Greenlaw

The New Palace Centre is the home of the Scottish Theatre Organ Preservation Society (STOPS) which preserves old cinema organs and furthers the appreciation of organ music. Its intimate theatre hosts occasional silent film screenings with live organ accompaniment, successfully recreating the vanished atmosphere of early cinema. Its purpose built headquarters in Greenlaw houses a giant Hilsdon Orchestral Organ formerly owned by The Playhouse Cinema in Edinburgh, which was taken out of use in 1985 and donated to the society. To sit and watch the silent classics of Lon Chaney or Buster Keaton in this fascinating little venue, accompanied by the mighty Hilsdon's wall of sound, is an experience never to be forgotten.

Further information: STOPS, New Palace Centre, Todholes, Greenlaw, Berwickshire, TD10 6XA. Tel: 01361 810759.

THE ROXY
Kelso

Formerly Edenside United Free Church, the building was converted to a cinema in 1932. Now the oldest working cinema in the Scottish Borders, its dilapidated state is more than compensated for by its unique interior, which includes wooden booth-style seating downstairs and a licensed bar in the auditorium. Two Polish soldiers reputedly entered the Roxy with fixed bayonets during WWII and were later arrested. The reason for their gripe has since been forgotten, but it surely couldn't have been over ticket prices: cheap day on Sundays is a bargain!

Further information: The Roxy, Horsemarket, Kelso. Tel: 01573 224609. Seats: 260

GREYSTOKE: THE LEGEND OF TARZAN, LORD OF THE APES

Kelso

• 1984 129m c Adventure Warner Bros. (U.K.)
• Ralph Richardson (6th Lord of Greystoke), Ian Holm (Capt. Phillipe D'Arnot), Christopher Lambert (John Clayton/Tarzan), Andie MacDowell (Jane Porter), James Fox (Lord Esker), Ian Charleson (Jefferson Brown), Nigel Davenport (Maj. Jack Downing), Paul Geoffrey (Lord Jack Clayton), Cheryl Campbell (Lady Alice Clayton)
• p, Hugh Hudson, Stanley S. Canter; d, Hugh Hudson; w, Robert Towne, Michael Austin
(based on the novel *Tarzan of the Apes* by Edgar Rice Burroughs); ph, John Alcott; ed, Anne V. Coates; m, John Scott; prod d, Stuart Craig; art d, Simon Holland, Norman Dorme; fx, Albert Whitlock
• AAN Best Supporting Actor: Ralph Richardson; AAN Best Adapted Screenplay: P.H. Vazak, Michael Austin; AAN Best Makeup: Rick Baker, Paul Engelen

This is the most enlightened Tarzan movie to date, which closely follows the original Edgar Rice Burroughs (1875-1950) yarn of 1914 about an aristocratic child, missing, presumed dead, in the African jungle. Reared by apes after his parents' death, he is accidentally

Baby Tarzan with his surrogate mother in **Greystoke** *(1984, Warner Bros)*

Lord Greystoke (Ralph Richardson) conducts Tarzan around his stately pile

Floors Castle

found by an explorer and safely returned to his family's ancestral seat at Greystoke Manor. Unable to comprehend and appreciate the joys of 'civilisation', Tarzan eventually returns to his primitive, but uncomplicated jungle home.

The main U.K. location was **Floors Castle**, which was used as the setting for Tarzan's ancestral home. Some interior scenes were also shot here, including the banquet scene and Lord Greystoke's fatal tea-tray escapade on the stairs. Studio scenes were shot at Elstree and the African locations were filmed in Cameroon. Other locations included **Hatfield House** in Hertfordshire, London's **Natural History Museum** and **Kensington Gardens** around the Albert Memorial.

One of the scriptwriters, Robert Towne, had his name removed from the credits because he was unhappy with many of the changes made by the director. He substituted the name of P.H. Vazak, his pet dog, who was nominated for an Oscar.

See also: Ralph Richardson, Ian Charleson, Maureen O'Sullivan

Further information: Floors Castle, home to the Duke and Duchess of Roxburghe, is open daily to the public from April until October. Tel: 01573 223333.

GRAVE OF SIR WALTER SCOTT (1771-1832)
Dryburgh

Poet, novelist, critic and antiquarian, Sir Walter Scott is now chiefly remembered for his historical fiction. His classic novels, *Ivanhoe* (1819) and *Rob Roy* (1817) have both been adapted for the screen. MGM's lavish 1952 production of *Ivanhoe* starred Robert Taylor in the title role and was the most expensive epic produced in England at that time. In 1955 Robert Taylor also portrayed Scott's *Quentin Durward*, set in 15th-century France, and Scottish folk-hero, Rob Roy, was portrayed by Richard Todd in Disney's wearisome *Rob Roy, the Highland Rogue* (1954). A more realistic account of *Rob Roy* was made by Michael Caton-Jones in 1995.

In 1812 Scott purchased Cartley Hall farmhouse on the banks of the River Tweed which he renamed **Abbotsford**. He later demolished the old house and replaced it with the building which stands on the site today. Abbotsford is open to the public and it houses Scott's collection of historic relics, including Rob Roy's gun, Montrose's sword and over 9,000 rare books in his library. Towards the end of his life Scott wrote at a hectic pace to pay off his debts after the bankruptcy of his publishing company. He is buried in the north transept of **Dryburgh Abbey, near St. Boswells.**

See also: Richard Todd, Liam Neeson, Michael Caton-Jones, *Rob Roy*

Further information: Dryburgh Abbey, Tel: 01835 822381. Abbotsford, near Melrose, is open daily from March to October. Tel: 01896 752043.

*Cinefantastique Magazine, volume 6, no.3, dedicated to **The Wicker Man***

Dumfries & Galloway

THE WICKER MAN TRAIL
Burrow Head

• 1973 102m c Horror/Mystery British Lion (UK)
• Edward Woodward *(Sgt. Neil Howie)*, Christopher Lee *(Lord Summerisle)*, Diane Cilento *(Miss Rose)*, Britt Ekland *(Willow MacGregor)*, Lindsay Kemp *(Alder MacGregor)*, Ingrid Pitt *(Librarian-Clerk)*
• p, Peter Snell; d, Robin Hardy; w, Anthony Shaffer; ph, Harry Waxman; ed, Eric Boyd Perkins; m, Paul Giovanni

"Celtic beliefs, I have never really seen treated properly. There is so much there in Celtic mythology that no one has ever laid a glove on, and I thought it was about time someone did."
Anthony Shaffer *

When devout Christian policeman and sexually repressed virgin, Sergeant Howie (Edward Woodward), arrives on the remote Summerisle to investigate the disappearance of a schoolgirl, he discovers a community of promiscuous heathens who still believe in the virgin sacrifice. Only a bedroom wall and a stiff prayer prevents him losing his virginity to Willow (Britt Ekland), the seductive landlord's daughter. Had he succumbed, he would probably have lived. His destiny now sealed, it is only in the final scene that he realizes his fate was predetermined by the islanders - a human sacrifice in the Wicker Man.

Made for $750,000, and entirely on location in Scotland, *The Wicker Man* is a tale of opposing religions

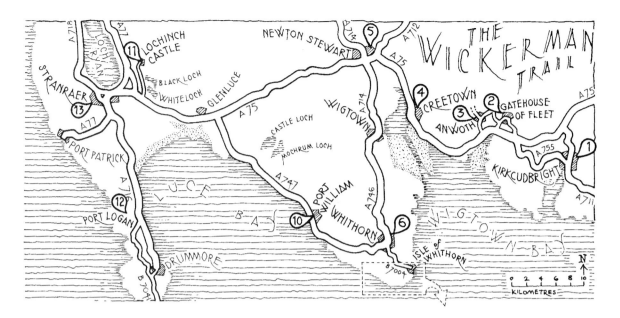

The Ellangowan Hotel, Creetown - location for the interior of The Green Man.

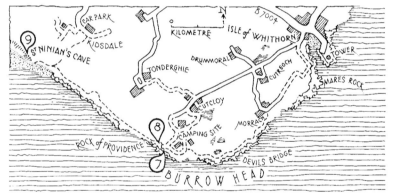

and beliefs, and the conflict between Christianity and Paganism.

The film was butchered by its distributors (who regarded it as one of the ten worst films ever made), from 102 minutes to 84 minutes. Whatever happened to the missing footage remains a mystery. The film almost disappeared into 'B' movie limbo until the 1977 Winter issue of the American movie magazine, 'Cinefantastique', devoted an entire issue to it, describing it as *"the Citizen Kane of Horror films"*. The subsequent publicity brought about

a major revival, and the same year two entrepreneurs decided to buy up the rights, re-releasing the film in 1977-78.

Now regarded as a cult classic, Christopher Lee still maintains it's the best film he ever made. In 1998 he claimed, *"The Wicker Man is one of the most remarkable films I think probably ever made, let alone made in this country... I have no proof whatsoever, but I am convinced, and I will always be convinced, that the negative of The Wicker Man still exists. I believe it is somewhere in this country. I believe that there are one or two or three people who know exactly where it is and have been sworn to silence."*

The film was set in spring, but was actually shot in freezing conditions during October and November 1972. The nude dancing was done wearing body stockings, and fake apple trees with plastic blossom were used in the background. Many different locations were used, over a seven week shooting schedule.

MAP KEY:

1. Kirkcudbright: An empty shop next to Police Close on the High Street was the location of 'May Morrison's Post Office', mother of Rowan, the missing girl.

'May Morrison's Post Office',
Kirkudbright

The Old Kirk ruins, Anwoth

The Old Schoolhouse, Anwoth

The alleyways of the town were also used for the hobby-horse and masked carnival scenes.

2. Gatehouse of Fleet: Cally Estates Office in Ann Street, opposite the Masonic Arms, was the exterior of 'The Green Man Inn' where Sergeant Howie stayed on Summerisle. The chemist shop in Gatehouse also put in an appearance.

3. Anwoth: The Old Schoolhouse (now a self-catering cottage Tel: 01557 814444), was used for the classroom scenes, and the grass opposite for the Maypole scenes. The Old Kirk ruins, where many of the tombstones are fashioned with skulls and crossbones, were also used.

4. Creetown: The interiors for 'The Green Man', where the locals made merry and Howie met the seductive Willow (Britt Ekland), the landlord's daughter, were filmed in the Ellangowan Hotel, St John Street. Tel: 01671 820201.

5. Newton Stewart: The Sports shop at 29A Victoria Street was used as the photographic dark room, and the Kirroughtree Hotel was where the cast and crew stayed during filming.

6. Whithorn: The library scenes, where Howie researched Paganism, were shot at the local library in St John Street.

7. Burrow Head: Site of the sacrifice scene. Substantial stumps were still remaining of the Wicker Man until they were used as the foundations for a bonfire. At the time of writing, remains are still visible in the earth. **8. Cave Exit Hole:** The shallow hollow which was used as the cave roof exit where Howie is confronted with the Wicker Man, is close to the sacrifice site.
Chalets, holiday homes and

camping are available at Burrow Head. Tel: 01988 500252.

9. St Ninian's Cave: Where Howie sees the missing girl, Rowan Morrison, and is enticed into the cave. The cave was reputedly the retreat of St. Ninian, who brought Christianity to Scotland in the fifth century. Walking distance from the car park to the cave is three miles.

10. Port William: Graveyard scenes.

11. Lochinch Castle: The interior scenes of Lord Summerisle's castle were shot here, and the grounds were used for the Mayday procession. The castle is not open to the public but the grounds are. Known as Castle Kennedy Gardens, they are located at Castle Kennedy village, 2mls east of Stranraer on the A75.

12. Port Logan: The nearby Logan Botanical Gardens were the location of Lord Summerisle's gardens, where Howie was given a 'tour' of the estate by Lord Summerisle.

13. Stranraer: The West Pier was used for the aircraft's take-off at the beginning of the film.

Ballantrae, on the A77 north of Stranraer, was the location of the cave interior used in the chase sequence. **Culzean Castle** (01655 760274), near Maybole in Ayrshire, was used for the exterior shots of Lord Summerisle's castle. **Plockton**, in the West Highlands, was the harbour location used for the seaplane's arrival at Summerisle.

The Wicker Man in the film stood 60ft high, and incredible as it may seem, such structures did exist and were used by Druids to burn their sacrificial victims. Julius Caesar mentions British tribes burning Roman prisoners of war in them in his *Diaries*, in 55 BC.

Cally Estates Office, Gatehouse of Fleet - the exterior of The Green Man

St. Ninian's Cave

The cave exit hole, Burrow Head

Edward Woodward had not memorised his lines properly when they shot the final scene and the script had to be written on giant boards off camera. As goats pee on him from above, he screams the immortal words, *"Hear ye the words of the Lord - Awake ye heathens..."*, but they fall on deaf ears as the sun sets on Burrow Head.

See also: Christopher Lee, *Wicker Man* (Cornwall)

Further information: Copies of 'Nuada', *The Wicker Man* Fanzine, can be obtained from Gail Ashurst, 15 Moor Road, Northern Moor, Manchester M23 9BQ.

The film's soundtrack was released for the first time in 1998 and is available from: Trunk Records, P.O. Box 56, Aldershot, Hampshire GU11 3YN.

Copies of the Cinefantastique magazine, volume 6, no.3, dedicated to *The Wicker Man* can be purchased from Cinefantastique, PO Box 270, Oak Park, Illinois 60303, U.S.A.

BIRTHPLACE OF JOHN PAUL JONES (1748-92)
Kirkbean

Robert Stack portrayed the Scottish-born 'Father of the American Navy' in John Farrow's 1959 biopic, *John Paul Jones*, in which the director's daughter, Mia Farrow, made her film debut.

Jones was born in a two-roomed cottage on 6 July 1747 at the **Abrigland Estate, near Kirkbean** (13 miles SW of Dumfries), where his father was head gardener. After a career as trader and slaver, he became a naval officer fighting for both America and Russia. In his flagship, *Bonhomme Richard*, he

plundered British shipping during the American Revolution, capturing the British warship, *Serapis*, off Scarborough in 1779. He later became an admiral in the Russian Navy. Jones died in Paris in 1792 soon after his forty fifth birthday and is buried in the US Naval Academy in Annapolis, Maryland. His birthplace has been restored and in an adjacent room the cabin of his flagship has been recreated.

Further information: Abrigland House & Gardens, Kirkbean, Dumfries, DG2 8BQ . Tel: 01387 880283. Open Easter to September.

THE CINEMA
Newton Stewart

Local entrepreneur, George Gouldson, was responsible for introducing Newton Stewart to the moving image in 1916 when he built the town's first cinema, a wood and corrugated iron hall in Jubilee Road. In 1933 he opened the town's first 'proper' cinema, an art-deco structure in Victoria Street, seating 490 people complete with a screen framed with hanging tapestries and marble statues in the foyer, including a six foot 'Nubian Slave' by Rosetti.

The Cinema survived better than most, but falling audiences and dwindling profits resulted in Gouldson selling the cinema in 1968 to a property investment company whose intention was to convert it into a supermarket. After a series of public meetings the local community led a successful campaign to buy back the cinema and it survived for another fourteen years until it was forced to close its doors in December, 1982. In 1983, a group of local film enthusiasts formed the Save The Cinema Committee and secured the running of the premises, but in 1991 Wigtown District's licensing authority refused to renew its cinema licence without major expenditure on the building and the cinema was closed down. In 1994 the committee was able to purchase the building and succeeded with an application to the National Lottery Board and Scottish Arts Council for funding to rebuild and refurbish it as a film theatre. The local community also raised the considerable sum of £100,000 and the new cinema officially opened on 20th February 1997. With seating (identical to the Paris Opera House) for 240 and additional facilities for drama, concerts and opera, The Cinema is now one of the most comfortable and well designed film theatres in the country. And strangely enough, it runs at a profit!

Further information: The Cinema, Newton Stewart. Tel: 01671 403333.

BIRTHPLACE OF MURDOCH OF THE TITANIC
Dalbeattie

William McMaster Murdoch was born on 28 February 1873 at **3 'Sunnyside', Barr Hill,** Dalbeattie, the fourth son of Captain Samuel Murdoch and Jane Muirhead. The family later moved to **'Oakland Cottage'** in the **High Street**. He was educated at **Dalbeattie Primary School** in the **High Street** (now a private house with its former playground occupied by the 'Ship' pub) and at the **High School** in **Alpine Street**. His father was a sea captain and it was inevitable that William would follow in his footsteps.

He joined The White Star Line in 1901 and served on successive ships until being transferred to the *Titanic*. His role during the final hours of the sinking is well documented. There are accounts from survivors of how he struggled to save as many passengers as he

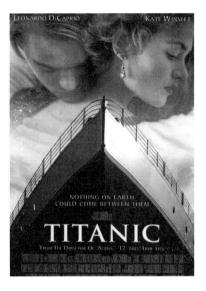

could before he was washed overboard while battling to free a lifeboat. His last words to a seaman were: *"Goodbye and good luck."*

In 1912, after his death, the people of Dalbeattie set up a memorial bursary for the schoolchildren of the town in his memory and a memorial monument to him can be seen on the wall of the **Town Hall**.

Accurate historical revisionism, however, has never been one of Hollywood's strong points and James Cameron's 1997 epic, *Titanic*, was no exception. In the film Murdoch is depicted as a bribe-taking coward who panicked and shot a passenger before taking his own life. Outraged by the slur on their town hero's character, the people of Dalbeattie, like David before them, took on Goliath and demanded an apology from 20th Century Fox. It was slow in coming and initially they received no response, but as the town's campaign gathered momentum, reaching its peak at publicity-sensitive Oscar time, Hollywood eventually admitted it had got it wrong.

On 15 April 1998 an executive of 20th Century Fox arrived in

Dalbeattie to formally apologise and to donate £5,000 to the Murdoch Memorial Prize Fund of Dalbeattie High School. A small price to pay for a brave man's defamed reputation.

See also: *A Night to Remember,* Wallace Hartley

Dundee

DUNDEE CONTEMPORARY ARTS

Situated down by the banks of the River Tay, Dundee's new £9m centre for contemporary art and film opened on 20 March 1999. Supported by a grant of £5.4m from the Scottish Arts Council National Lottery Fund, the building was designed by the award-winning architect Richard Murphy. As well as art galleries, a print studio, a visual research centre and a cafe-bar, DCA has two cinemas each equipped with Dolby and DTS Digital sound. An unusual feature in the larger cinema is a shuttered window with a view across the Tay, which is opened between film screenings.

Further information: Dundee Contemporary Arts, 152 Nethergate, Dundee DD1 4DY. Tel: 01382 432000 / 432290. Open seven days a week - 10am-11pm.

East Dunbarton-shire

SHALLOW GRAVE
Milngavie

"But, Juliet—you're a doctor! You kill people every day!"

Kerry Fox, Ewan McGregor and Chris Eccleston portray three flatmates: a doctor, a journalist and an accountant. When their latest flatmate, a complete stranger, dies in his room from an overdose and leaves a suitcase of money, they decide to dispose of his body and pocket the loot. After dismembering the corpse and burying and incinerating the remains, they begin to mistrust each other and their persecution complexes result in tragic consequences.

Set in Edinburgh, but filmed almost entirely in Glasgow, Danny Boyle's movie is a visually stylish, irreverent, shocking and blood spattering thriller, often compared to the Coen Brothers' *Blood Simple*.

Interiors were filmed in a warehouse in Anniesland, Glasgow. Location shots featured the interior of the **Glasgow Evening Times** offices, the **Townhouse Hotel, West George Street, Glasgow** (now closed) where the country dancing scene was shot and **Rouken Glen Park, Rouken Glen Road, Giffnock, East Renfrewshire**, where the body was buried.

Mugdock Country Park was the location of the quarry where the vehicle was dumped. Unfortunately the flotation collar failed to work and it still lies submerged in the shallow water of the quarry along with several other vehicles which have been dumped there over the years.

See also: *Shallow Grave* (Edinburgh), Ewan McGregor

Further information: Mugdock Country Park, Craigallan Road, near Milngavie, Glasgow, G62 8EL. Tel: 0141 956 6100.

Edinburgh

BIRTHPLACE OF ROBERT LOUIS STEVENSON (1850-94)

*"Fifteen men on a dead man's chest
Yo-ho-ho, and a bottle of rum!
Drink and the devil had done for the rest -
Yo-ho-ho, and a bottle of rum!
Treasure Island*

Robert Louis Stevenson's historical adventure stories have always inspired film makers, and his work, which has never gone out of fashion, seems to translate effortlessly to the screen. Fortunately for humanity young Louis decided not to pursue a career as harbour and lighthouse engineer as his father had intended, but determined to become a writer instead.

He was born on 13 November 1850 at **8 Howard Place** to Thomas Stevenson, a civil engineer, and Margaret Balfour. At the age of seven his parents moved to **17 Heriot Row** nearby in Edinburgh's New Town. Dogged by ill health throughout his life, he studied law and regularly explored the brothels and taverns of the city.

He began his literary career by contributing essays to the *Cornhill Magazine* and the *London Magazine*. The model for *Jekyll and Hyde* was based on the double life of Deacon William Brodie, a cabinetmaker and civic dignitary by day and a burglar by night, who is now immortalised by a tavern which bears his name in **The Royal Mile**.

In 1880, RLS married an American woman, Fanny Osbourne, and in 1888 his ill health forced them to search for a more congenial climate

*Bobby Driscoll as Jim Hawkins and John Laurie as Pew in **Treasure Island** (1960, RKO/Walt Disney)*

*8 Howard Place - birthplace of **Robert Louis Stevenson***

to live in. This he eventually found in Upolu, Samoa, his home until his early death on 3 December 1894. An accomplished essayist, novelist, poet and travel writer, he will be best remembered for his colourful adventure stories. A memorial to RLS was erected in West Princes Street Gardens, Edinburgh, by the RLS Club in 1989.

Edinburgh

Works adapted for the screen include: *Dr. Jekyll and Mr. Hyde* (many versions), *The Body Snatcher* (1945), *Treasure Island* (many versions), *The Master of Ballantrae* (1953), *Ebb Tide* (1937), *Kidnapped* (many versions) and *The Wrong Box* (1966).

See also: *Treasure Island, Kidnapped*

Further information: The Writer's Museum (Lady Stair's House, Lady Stairs Close, Lawnmarket, Edinburgh Tel: 0131 529 4901) holds one of the most significant Stevenson collections anywhere, including personal belongings, paintings, photographs and early editions. The Robert Louis Stevenson Club, 5 Albyn Place, Edinburgh, EH2 4NJ. Deacon Brodie's Tavern, 435 Lawnmarket. Tel: 0131 225 6531.

THE CLAREMONT BAR

Affectionately known by its regulars as 'The USS Claremont', this pub boldly goes where few pubs have gone before. Over the past few years it has become a regular meeting place for sci-fi aficionados and members of the Star Wars, Star Trek and Dr. Who Appreciation Societies. Sci-fi posters and photographs of visiting celebrities adorn its walls; these include Walter Koenig (Star Trek's 'Chekov') and Gareth Thomas (Blake of Blake's Seven). Highly recommended for its friendly atmosphere and interesting characters - like Martin - who denies dressing like a flamboyant 'Time Lord' but admits to building a full-size 'Tardis' in the middle of his living room.

Further information: The Claremont Bar, 133 East Claremont Street. Tel: 0131 556 5662.

BIRTHPLACE OF CHRISTINA KAY (1878-1951) THE 'ORIGINAL' JEAN BRODIE

Christina Kay

"Little girls, I am in the business of putting old heads on young shoulders, and all my pupils are the crème de la crème. Give me a girl at an impressionable age, and she is mine for life."

Ronald Neame's *The Prime of Miss Jean Brodie* (1969) starring Maggie Smith in her AA-winning role, and

Celia Johnson as the austere Miss MacKay was based on Muriel Spark's 1961 novel about her schooldays in the twenties and thirties at **James Gillespie's School**, where she was taught by the unorthodox Miss Christina Kay, the inspiration for Jean Brodie. Like many other pupils before her, Muriel was fascinated by Miss Kay and fell quickly under her spell. Miss Kay did not, however, have love affairs with the art master and the singing teacher, and was not dismissed for teaching treason and sedition to her students as is Jean Brodie; however, the two share many similar characteristics such as a love of music, Renaissance painters, exotic travel and admiration for Mussolini's Fascisti. Like Brodie's sweetheart Hugh, who fell on Flanders Field *'like an autumn leaf'*, Miss Kay also lost a lover in the Great War.

She was born at **4 Grindlay Street**, off Lothian Road, on 11 June 1878, the only child of Mary McDonald and Alexander Kay, a cabinet maker. She was enrolled at

*Jean Brodie (Maggie Smith) enjoying a picnic with her 'gels' in **The Prime of Miss Jean Brodie** (1969, TCF)*

*4 Grindlay Street - birthplace of **Christina Kay***

Gillespie's School at the age of five, and, except for two years at training college, here she remained, teaching her *'crème de la crème'* until her retiral in 1943.

An article in the school magazine recalls her career the same year: *"Many a child has delighted in her vivid descriptions of Italian towns and their picture galleries. From her love of ancient Greece she pushed home the lesson of the value and beauty of perfection in minute and hidden things, 'for the gods see everywhere'. Through many changes and great progress, Gillespie's ever remained her well-loved 'alma mater'. Her colleagues and pupils take this opportunity of saying how greatly they appreciated her faithful and inspired work here, and of wishing her many happy days of freedom to devote herself to her many interests."*

She lived at Grindlay Street for most of her life, where she often entertained her pupils to tea. She never married, and died on 23 May 1951 at **Midhope, Hopetoun,**

South Queensferry, of chronic bronchitis and chronic myocarditis, aged seventy-two, unaware of the legend she would become.

Most of the locations for the film were shot in Edinburgh. The exterior shots for the school were filmed at the junior department of **Donaldson's School for the Deaf** in **Henderson Row, Stockbridge**, and **Barnbougle Castle** (Gordon Lowther's country home), on Lord Rosebery's **Dalmeny Estate**. Other locations included **Greyfriar's Churchyard, Candlemaker Row; Edinburgh Castle, The Royal Scottish Museum** and **The Vennel** in the **Grassmarket**. The studio scenes were shot at Pinewood.

Muriel Spark (nee Camberg) was born into a Jewish family at **160 Bruntsfield Place, Morningside**, in 1918 to Sarah and Bernard Camberg, an engineer. She was enrolled at **James Gillespie's School** on **Bruntsfield Links** (now Edinburgh University student accommodation) in 1922 where she remained for twelve years. When she was eleven, the young Muriel encountered Miss Kay whose eccentric teaching and idealism formed the basis for the fictional character in her 1961 novel.

After leaving school Muriel attended Heriot Watt College (now Heriot Watt University) in Chambers Street, and at eighteen took a job in the office of William Small & Sons' department store at 106 Princes Street. In 1937, aged nineteen, she married Sydney Spark in Salisbury, Southern Rhodesia, and their son Robin was born in Bulawayo a year later. Her husband became increasingly mentally unstable, and following Muriel's return to Britain in 1944, the couple were divorced.

She joined the political department of the Foreign Office secret intelligence service, MI6, during

WWII. After the war she became a celebrated novelist who also published plays, poems and short stories. She now lives in Italy.

See also: Maggie Smith, Celia Johnson

Further information: All the city locations are within easy walking distance of the city centre. The Dalmeny Estate (0131 333 1331) is a few miles along the coast, close to the Forth Bridges. James Gillespie's School is now situated in Lauderdale St., Bruntsfield.

CHILDHOOD HOME OF IAN CHARLESON (1949-1990)

"For me, his voice always symbolized a special spirit he had. I don't know how you define special spirits: you just know them when you meet them."
Alan Bates

Ian Charleson, who died tragically of AIDS on 6 January 1990, will be chiefly remembered in the cinema for his outstanding portrayal of the Scottish missionary and athelete, Eric Liddell, in *Chariots of Fire* (1981).

He was born on 11 August 1949 at the **Eastern General Hospital, Seafield**, the second of three children of John Charleson, a printer. The family lived in a tenement flat in **Piershill** and later at nearby **14 Britwell Crescent, Craigentinny**. A quiet boy who disliked sports, he made his stage debut in a Sunday School play, *Princess Chrysanthemum*, cast as a cat. He attended the local **Parsons Green Primary School** in **Meadowfield Road** and at the age of eleven he won a scholarship to the **Royal High School, Regent Road**.

Edinburgh

In 1967 he was accepted by Edinburgh University to study architecture where he became involved with the university dramatic society.

He quit university in his second year and gained a place at LAMDA. Having no student grant he supported himself by singing in the restaurant Food For Thought in Covent Garden, and clearing tables at the Hard Rock Cafe. He joined the Young Vic where he played Jimmy Porter in *Look Back In Anger* and Hamlet in *Rosencrantz and Guildenstern Are Dead*. As his career progressed he had seasons in the West End, the National Theatre and the RSC and made his film debut in Derek Jarman's *Jubilee* in 1977. His other film roles include: Charlie Andrews in *Gandhi* (1982), the depraved Jefferson Brown in *Greystoke* (1984) and Gerald the prat in *Car Trouble* (1985).

Ian Charleson discovered he was HIV positive in 1986 but continued working up until just a few weeks before his death, giving his last performance playing *Hamlet* at the National Theatre on 13 November 1989. He died of septicaemia on the evening of Saturday 6 January 1990.

See also: *Chariots of Fire, Greystoke*

BIRTHPLACE OF ALISTAIR SIM (1900-76)

"In my opinion your performances never fail to deteriorate"
A line from Alistair Sim's favourite fan letter.

Alistair Sim was born above his father's shop on 9 October 1900 at **96-98 Lothian Road**, near Edinburgh's West End, the youngest of four children of Isabella

Alistair Sim in The Happiest Days of Your Life (1950, British Lion)

*96 - 98 Lothian Road - **Alistair Sim's father's shop** (now an optician's)*

McIntyre and Alexander Sim, tailor and clothier. When he was six the family moved to a larger house nearby at **'Craigmount', 73 Viewforth, Bruntsfield.** He attended **Bruntsfield Primary School, Montpelier** and later went to **Gillespie's School** in **Gillespie Crescent** where his father was a school governor. He remembered his father telling the staff not to hold back beating his son just because he was a governor.

When he left school at fourteen he went to work as a messenger boy at his father's shop where he was eventually deemed unsuitable and fired. He often recalled his father lamenting, *'Mark my words, that boy will end on the gallows.'* His father found him a job at Gieves,

the men's outfitters, in Princes Street, ·but they also soon parted company with him and he later worked in the borough assessor's office. In 1918 while studying analytical chemistry at Edinburgh University he was called up, but fortunately the Armistice came before he was sent to the front.

After the war he worked in the Highlands as a migrant farm-hand sleeping in bothies and barns. In the early 1920s he was accepted for the post of Fulton Lecturer of elocution at **New College** Edinburgh and later ran his own 'School of Drama and Speech Training' on the second floor at **5 Manor Place**.

He was by now becoming very involved in amateur dramatics and hoped to become a professional director in London. When he was twenty-nine, poet and playwright John Drinkwater gave him an introduction to director Maurice Browne who was staging a production of Othello at the Savoy Theatre with Paul Robeson. Here Sim was cast in the part of the Messenger at £5 a week. His stage career blossomed and he later joined the Old Vic, making his screen debut in 1935 as a Scottish police sergeant in *Riverside Murder* at Wembley Studios.

He went on to make a great many films, but was at his best in droll comedy roles such as Inspector Cockerill in *Green For Danger* (1946), *Scrooge* (1951), Inspector Poole in *An Inspector Calls* (1954) and as Millicent and Clarence Fritton in *The Belles of St Trinian's* (1954).

In 1932 he married drama student Naomi Plaskitt. They had one daughter, Merlith. He was diagnosed as having cancer in 1975 and died the same year.

See also: St. Trinians

BIRTHPLACE OF FINLAY CURRIE (1878-1968)

"I shall go on working till I drop. Working is fun."

The craggy-featured Scottish character actor, Finlay Currie, was born on 20 January 1878, at **35 Cumberland Street, Stockbridge**, to Annie Currie, a post office clerk, and William Finlay Currie, a professional soldier. He attended George Watson's College and Edinburgh University as a music student. Intending to be a musician, he became an assistant church organist and was introduced to the stage while playing the organ in the wings for a production of *Henry IV* at Edinburgh's Theatre Royal.

His stage debut was as a courtier in *Cramond Brig* at the Pavilion Theatre, Grove Street, in May 1898, and he later became known as *'the boy with the double voice'*, because he could sing both soprano and baritone. He married an American musical comedy star, Maude Courtenay, and they formed a musical duo touring the U.S.A., Australia and South Africa. Their

marriage lasted over fifty years until Maude's death in 1959. During WWI he joined the Seaforth Highlanders on active service in France but was wounded and invalided out in 1916. Returning to the stage after the war he made his debut on the London stage, appearing in a series of Edgar Wallace productions.

After a successful stage career he made his film debut in *Criminal at Large* (1932) but will be best remembered on the screen as the escaped convict 'Magwitch' in David Lean's *Great Expectations* (1946). His other films include *The Edge of the World* (1938), *History of Mr Polly* (1949), *The Mudlark* (1951), *Ben Hur* (1959), *Kidnapped* (1960), *Billy Liar* (1963) and *The Fall of the Roman Empire* (1964).

Actor, Laurence Payne, who portrayed Joseph in *Ben Hur*, recalls an amusing incident during the filming of the nativity scene with Finlay Currie: *"Finlay was one of the three kings, and was in the centre of the trio as they entered the stable. The king in front of Finlay tripped up, and his turban and frankincense went flying. As he fell to the ground, he screeched, 'Jesus Christ!' Finlay quickly turned towards Joseph and Mary, saying, 'Now there's a good name to call the bairn!'"*

See also: *Great Expectations, The Edge of the World, Billy Liar. Kidnapped*

FIRST RECORDED FILM SHOW IN SCOTLAND

Film first arrived in Scotland with Edison's Kinetoscope peep-shows which had their earliest recorded appearance at H.E. Moss's Christmas Carnival at the **Waverley Market, Princes Street** (now a shopping centre) on 24 December

1894. Moving pictures were first projected in a Scottish theatre alongside music hall acts on 13 April 1896 at Moss's **Empire Palace** (now The Festival Theatre) , **Clerk St., Edinburgh.**

A review of the week-long event in *The Scotsman*, 13 April 1896, suggests the evening was not particularly memorable: *"The great advertised attraction for this week at the Empire is an exhibition of the 'Cinematographe'....... Mr. T. Howard, who showed the scenes, apologised for the hitches which had occurred, but claimed at the same time the indulgence of the audience on the ground that the cinematograph was only in its infancy, and that it would take several months yet to perfect ...There was a large audience."*

BIRTHPLACE OF SEAN CONNERY (1930 -)

'Big Tam' portrays James Bond 007

Thomas Connery was born on the 25th August, 1930, in a 'room and kitchen' tenement flat at **176 Fountainbridge** (now demolished) to Effie Connery, a cleaner, and Joe

Connery, an unskilled labourer. His brother Neil was born in 1938. He attended **Bruntsfield Primary School**, Montpelier and nearby **Darroch Secondary** (now St. Thomas of Aquin's High School) 7 Gillespie St., which he left at the age of thirteen. Tommy had numerous jobs, including milkman, furniture remover, French polisher, stage hand, bouncer and lifeguard.

Known locally as 'Big Tam', he enjoyed weight-lifting and developing his muscular physique. In 1953 he travelled to London by motorbike to enter a 'Mr. Universe' contest. He didn't win, but by chance he heard there was to be auditioning for the chorus of the stage musical, *South Pacific*, the only talent required being muscular good looks. He got the part and embarked on his chance career as an actor.

He struggled for ten years in obscure and indifferent roles until he was cast as James Bond in the 1962 film, *Dr No*. The public loved the film's implausible sex, violence, voyeurism and thrills which

transformed 'Big Tam' from a struggling actor into a star. In later years he successfully disentangled himself from his Bond image and established himself as an actor in his own right.

His films include: *The Hill* (1965), *The Man Who Would Be King* (1975), *The Name of The Rose* (1986), *Highlander* (1986), *The Untouchables* (1987, AA) and *The Russia House* (1990).

See also: *Goldfinger, Highlander,* Ian Fleming, Desmond Llewelyn

BIRTHPLACE OF DONALD CAMMELL (1934-96)

Donald Cammell, scriptwriter and nonconformist director of stylish and often extremist films, was born in the **Outlook Tower,** under the **Camera Obscura**, in the **Royal Mile**. He achieved notoriety with his first film, *Performance* (1970), about the blending of sexual identities, which he co-directed with Nicolas Roeg.

He began his career as a painter of prodigious talent but dropped it when he discovered a new art form in film. Unwilling to direct anything he had not written, he turned away many offers and directed only three other films, including *Demon Seed* (1977) and *White of the Eye* (1986).

An outsider who always had a strange fascination with suicide and death, he died from a self-inflicted gunshot wound to the head in his Los Angeles home on 24 April 1996.

See also: *Performance*

EDINBURGH UNIVERSITY FILM SOCIETY

"Our trademark double-bills operate in a Hagelian dialect of thesis, antithesis and synthesis to provide a greater understanding of the totality of cinema. In other words we come up with links that you hadn't noticed before."

Founded over thirty years ago by a small group of enthusiasts, the award-winning EUFS has progressed from showing films in a small back room to becoming a society of over 1500 members, screening films at two venues: **George Square Theatre** (35mm), next to the University Main Library, George Square, and the **Pleasance Theatre** (16mm), upstairs in the **Societies' Centre, 60 The Pleasance**.

Voted 'Best Film Society in the U.K.' in 1997, its innovative and broad programming tackles all genres and tastes, from *My Fair Lady* to *Yojimbo*.

Further information: Season: Oct - March. Membership is open to anyone, whether or not you study at Edinburgh University. Guest tickets can be purchased from most

*Mark Bauer and Neil Chue Hong of **Edinburgh University Film Society** proudly display their 'Film Society of the Year Award*

Union shops, Teviot Row House Front Desk and other outlets. Tel: 0131 557 0436 email: filmsoc@ed.ac.uk.

CAMEO CINEMA

The Cameo Cinema at **38 Home Street, Tollcross** (0131 228 2800/4141), first opened its door to the public on January 8th 1914. Originally The King's Cinema, its single screen 673-seat auditorium had the only mirrored screen in Scotland and musical accompaniment was provided by Madame Egger's Ladies' Costume Orchestra. It screened its first talkies, *Married in Hollywood* and *Dance Away the Night* in 1930, and in 1947, suffering from neglect, it passed into the hands of the Poole family.

Jim Poole, whose family had been involved with film exhibition since 1905, was a film officer during WWII who organised mobile cinemas for the troops in the Middle East. After the war, he was keen to screen European films to a wider audience and on March 25th 1949 he reopened The Cameo as a specialist continental cinema.

Over the years The Cameo has established a successful affiliation with the Edinburgh Film Festival and in 1953 Orson Welles gave the first 'Festival Celebrity Lecture' there to a packed house. It became

Edinburgh's first cinema to obtain a drinks licence in 1963 despite objections from locals that there were already thirteen pubs within three hundred yards of its front door! The Cameo closed in 1982 when Jim Poole retired, but after considerable restoration it reopened in 1986, and in 1991 two extra screens were added.

Cary Grant, Orson Welles and Quentin Tarantino have all visited The Cameo - and 007 sipped a vodka martini there when he opened the bar in 1963. The cinema celebrated its 50th anniversary in March 1999 and among those who sent congratulatory telegrams were Woody Allen, Omar Sharif, Elizabeth Taylor, Alec Guinness and Ken Loach. Fifty years on, The Cameo shows no signs of fatigue and is still arguably Edinburgh's most enlightened cinema.

THE LUMIÈRE

Located within the Royal Museum, The Lumière was officially opened by director Bill Forsyth on 4 December 1998. Its Honorary Patron is actor John Gordon-Sinclair, star of *Gregory's Girl*. Utilising the museum's old lecture theatre, The Lumière screens mostly non-mainstream films.

Further information: The Lumière, Chambers Street, Edinburgh, EH1 1JF. Tel: 0131 247 4219. Open: Fridays, Saturdays and Sundays throughout the year. Entrance is via Lothian Street at the back of the Museum. Wheelchair access.

THE EDINBURGH FILM GUILD & FILMHOUSE

The Film Society movement was only five years old when the

Edinburgh Film Guild, reputedly the oldest film society in the world, was founded in 1930 by Norman Wilson (the title 'Guild' was originally used to distinguish it from the Edinburgh Workers' Film Society which had propagandist predilections). The first film to be screened was *The Blue Angel* (1929) and in the 1930s, Guild founding fathers, Forsyth Hardy and Norman Wilson, launched *Cinema Quarterly*, Britain's first serious film magazine.

In 1947, with no financial subsidies, the Film Guild founded the Edinburgh International Film Festival, now the oldest continuously running film festival in the world.

The Guild was also instrumental in establishing Edinburgh's Filmhouse, a former church in Lothian Road. Renovation began in 1978 to convert it to a film theatre and it is now a successful three-screen venue with bar and restaurant, screening mainly non-mainstream films.

Further information: The Edinburgh Film Guild & Filmhouse, 88 Lothian Road, Edinburgh, EH3 9BZ. Tel: 0131 228 6382/2688.

Edinburgh

*The former **St. Trinneans School** - Palmerston Road*

*Flash Harry (George Cole) and Millicent Fritton (Alistair Sim) in **The Belles of St Trinians** (1954, British Lion/London Films)*

THE ORIGINAL ST TRINIANS

"There was a big rumpus when all that came out and we all felt the films desecrated our school. Our headmistress, Miss Lee, stood up and told the school 'After 20 years at St. Trinneans, I am broken-hearted'."
Yvonne Macleod, ex-pupil

The disreputable establishment of schoolgirls portrayed in *The Belles of St Trinians* (1955) was inspired by headmistress, Catherine Fraser Lee's St. Trinneans School at **10 Palmerston Road, Marchmont**, and later at nearby **St Leonard's**, Edinburgh.

Miss Lee's extremist educational methods included making pupils exercise and dance on the lawn while memorizing facts and figures and making them eat their meals in reverse order, starting with dessert and finishing off with soup.

Her pupils were first portrayed by the cartoonist, Ronald Searle, who

heard about them when he was stationed as a soldier at Kirkudbright in 1941. The subsequent films made them famous throughout the world. School reunion organiser, Joan Campbell, said the girls had *"no complaints at all"* about the films. *"In fact, it was great to be known as the girls from St. Trinneans."* *

The film generated many sequels, but none can match the original with Alistair Sim as headmistress, Millicent Fritton, Joyce Grenfell as Sgt. Ruby Gates and George Cole as Flash Harry. St. Trinneans closed in 1946.

See also: Alistair Sim, Sidney Gilliat

SHALLOW GRAVE

Although Danny Boyle's 1994 black comedy is set in Edinburgh, the majority of the film was shot in Glasgow with the exception of the opening scenes where the car

speeds over the New Town cobbled streets of **Heriot Row, Great King Street, Drummond Place** and **St. Vincent Street** to **North East Circus Place**, the location of the flat. The tenement stair interior was shot in **Scotland Street**.

See also: *Shallow Grave* (E. Dunbartonshire), Ewan McGregor

THE 39 STEPS GUEST HOUSE

This Victorian guest house, which is quietly situated close to the city centre, was named by its first owner, a Mr. Hannay. Like the Gideon Bible, a copy of Buchan's thriller can be found in every room, and stills from the movie decorate their walls.

Further information: Douglas Morton, The 39 Steps Guest House, 62 South Trinity Road, Edinburgh. Tel: 0131 552 1349.

GRAVE OF JOSEPH BELL: THE 'ORIGINAL' SHERLOCK HOLMES

"Doyle was always making notes. He seemed to want to copy down every word I said. Many times after the patient had departed my office, he would ask me to repeat my observations so that he would be certain he had them correctly." Joseph Bell

When Arthur Conan Doyle was a young unknown medical student at Edinburgh his most memorable clinical teacher was Dr. Joseph Bell, whose talent for making lightning diagnoses, combined with his acute powers of observation, inspired Doyle in later life to use him as the model for Sherlock Holmes. Doyle later wrote in a letter to Bell: *"It is most certainly to you that I owe Sherlock Holmes although, in the stories, I have the advantage of being able to place him in all sorts of dramatic situations."*

Born in Edinburgh in 1837, Joseph Bell was the eldest of nine children, and was born into a medical family which spanned four generations. Educated at Edinburgh Academy and Edinburgh University, he began his surgical career as a House Surgeon at the **Royal Infirmary, Lauriston Place**, Edinburgh. In 1887 he became the first chief surgeon at the fledgling Department of Surgery in the **Royal Hospital for Sick Children, Sciennes Road**. A popular and approachable man, he was strict about cleanliness, informing his nursing staff, *"I hold that hospital gangrene is in nearly every case caused by dirt, and dirt communicated to the patient by his doctor or his nurses."* His attitude towards nursing was enlightened for his day; in 1868 he established classes for nurses at the Infirmary and began taking them with him on his ward rounds. Sir James Affleck commented after his death: *"It may be truly said that the development of modern nursing among us owes much to Dr. Bell - more indeed than he has ever received credit for."* In 1863 he became a fellow of the **Royal College of Surgeons of Edinburgh**, becoming its President in 1887.

In 1865 he married Edith Murray with whom he had three children. When Edith died of puerperal peritonitis in 1874 Dr. Bell's black hair is said to have turned white almost overnight. He died on 4 October 1911 and the crowds at his funeral were staggering, with thousands of people lining the streets. He is buried in **Dean Cemetery, Ravelston Terrace**.

Sir Arthur Conan Doyle (1859-1930) was born in **Picardy Place** near the east end of Princes Street. His birthplace has since been demolished, but a statue of Sherlock Holmes stands near the site. Also nearby is the Conan Doyle Pub at 71-73 York Place.

See also: Sir Arthur Conan Doyle, *The Hound of the Baskervilles*, Peter Cushing, Hammer Studios,

The Royal College of Surgeons

Sherlock Holmes Festival, Frensham Common

Further Information: The Joseph Bell archive can be viewed at the library of The Royal College of Surgeons of Edinburgh, 18 Nicolson Street, Edinburgh EH8 9DW. Tel: 0131 527 1600. Fax: 0131 557 6406. Normally, visits are confined to the hours between 10am and 3pm. Closed on public holidays, Saturdays and Sundays.

ST BRIDE'S CENTRE

Cinema is a regular feature of St Bride's with weekly Friday afternoon screenings. The St Bride's annual film festival takes place in April involving schools and local community groups. A perennial favourite at the festival is their own production of *The Magic Umbrella*. Directed by Edinburgh film-maker, Ian Rintoul, the film won an international prize as one of the 'Ten Best' independent short films of 1999, along with an award for 'Best Film Editing'. Inspired by the French classic, *The Red Balloon*, it was produced as a project for Cinema 100 in co-operation with local schoolchildren.

The Magic Umbrella (Ian Rintoul)

See also: Forth Bridge

Further information: St Bride's Centre, 10 Orwell Terrace, Edinburgh EH11 2DY. Tel: 0131 346 1405 / 552 2939. Bar and snacks available.

CLASSIC LOCATION: FORTH RAIL BRIDGE
South Queensferry

"We forgot about the steps. I did think of having thirty-nine spies in the film and showing them all coming to a meeting, each with his own step, but it was too complicated."
Alfred Hitchcock

Built in 1882-90 and spanning the Firth of Forth between **North and South Queensferry** this Victorian wonder of the world will always be associated with Richard Hannay's daring escape among its girders in *The 39 Steps* (1935 & 1959). Filmed at Shepherd's Bush Studios, Hitchock's adaptation of John

Buchan's thriller used only ten percent of the novel. In 1943 Buchan sold the film rights for *The Thirty-Nine Steps* to the Gaumont British company for a meagre sum, regarding film-making and his own 'shocker' writing as a rather eccentric amusement. While he had ambivalent feelings regarding the liberties Hitchcock took with the original text, many people objected at the time.

Hitchcock kept the nucleus of the plot but gave it a contemporary setting and a romance. Mr Memory, who reveals the truth about the thirty-nine steps, was based on a real music-hall performer called Datas. The enemy in the film is never identified because Hitler had just become Chancellor of Germany and the Foreign Office had warned film-makers that hostile representation of Germany was undesirable.

When John Buchan attended the film's premiere at the New Gallery Cinema in Regent Street, he thought it a great improvement on the original. Robert Donat remains the definitive Hannay, with Kenneth More a distant second. A Centenary Plaque at North Queensferry viewpoint celebrates the bridge in the film.

Ian Rintoul, Scotland's award-winning short film maker - known for his meticulous reconstructions of historic events - used the Forth Rail Bridge as a location in his film, *The Hour of the Eagle* (1975), based on a Luftwaffe raid on the Rosyth naval base in 1939. In 1940, Harry Watt of the GPO film unit directed *Squadron 992*, which told the story of a barrage balloon squadron's defence of the bridge against Luftwaffe dive-bombers.

See also: John Buchan, Alfred Hitchcock, Robert Donat, Madeleine Carroll, Severn Valley Railway, St. Bride's Centre

Further information: The 1978 version, starring Robert Powell, used the Victoria Bridge on the Severn Valley Railway.

Falkirk

CHILDHOOD HOME OF JIMMY FINLAYSON (1887-1953)
Larbert

"Jimmy was a born comedian. Even as a schoolboy, he was forever making us all laugh. One of his favourite cracks was to ask the question: 'Who's stolen the steam-roller out of my money-box?'"
John Ferguson, boyhood friend

Jimmy Finlayson, the bald, prune-faced, squinty and pop-eyed comedian with a walrus moustache, will be best remembered for his supporting roles with Laurel and Hardy. He was born James Henderson Finlayson on 27 August 1887, one of eight children of Isabella and Alexander Finlayson, a blacksmith. The exact location of his birth in Larbert cannot be established, but the family did live at **87 Main Street** (since demolished) and moved to **215 Dundas Street, Grangemouth** in the early 1900s.

A budding comedian from an early age, young Jimmy and his pals gave many an impromtu concert in his back yard at **North Broomage** where admission was a 'jeelly jar', exchangeable at the local grocer's for a halfpenny. Jimmy attended the local school in Larbert and was later sent to **George Watson's College** in Edinburgh during which time his friendship with actor John Clyde instilled in him an interest in the stage.

After leaving school he became an apprentice tinsmith at **Jones and Campbell's Torwood Foundry** in Larbert, before joining a repertory company in a production of *Bunty Pulls the Strings*.

In 1916 the production toured the United States where he decided to remain. After several years on the American stage he made his screen debut in the L-KO and Mack Sennett comedies.

He first appeared with Laurel and Hardy in Hal Roach's comedies in 1923, making a total of 33 films with them, including *Big Business*, *Way Out West* and *Saps at Sea*.

His other films include *The Dawn Patrol* (1930) with Douglas Fairbanks Jr. and Michael Powell's *Oh, No, Doctor!* He was married three times and died in Hollywood in 1953.

See also: Laurel and Hardy

Further information: A plaque was erected to Jimmy Finlayson's memory in the foyer of the Falkirk Town Hall Cinema in 1996.

BARONY FILM SOCIETY
Bo'ness

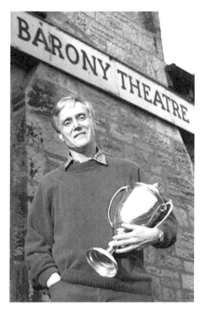

Ian Kerr clutching the Roebuck Cup

A former primary school, the Barony was converted into a community theatre in 1964, and the film society was founded in 1984. With no cinema in the town, the Barony is the only big screen venue in Bo'ness. In its early days equipment was begged and borrowed from wherever it could be found and most of the 124 seats came from the old Poole's Synod Hall in Edinburgh.

Its opening film was *Paint Your Wagon*, and apart from screening the second reel of *Local Hero* in reverse, it has run almost trouble-free ever since, converting from 16mm to 35mm in 1988. The Society has established a good relationship with local primary schools, screening films as part of the curriculum, and, consequently, was awarded the first British Federation of Film Societies' 'Community Development Award' in 1994. In 1999 Barony member and film society pioneer, Ian Kerr, was awarded the Roebuck Cup at the

BFFS annual awards ceremony at the National Film Theatre for his outstanding work for the wider film society community.

Further information: Barony Film Society, Maureen Maciver, 1 Lower Granton Road, Edinburgh EH5 2RX.

Fife

CHARIOTS OF FIRE
St. Andrews

"Gosh, aren't the British remarkable? They win Olympic races despite running in slow motion..."
Geoff Andrews, Time Out.

• 1981 123m c Biography/Sports Enigma (UK)
• Ian Charleson (Eric Liddell), Ben Cross (Harold Abrahams), Nigel Havers (Lord Andrew Lindsay), Nicholas Farrell (Aubrey Montague), Ian Holm (Sam Mussabini), John Gielgud (Master of Trinity), Lindsay Anderson (Master of Caius), Nigel Davenport (Lord Birkenhead), Cheryl Campbell (Jennie Liddell), Alice Krige (Sybil Gordon)
• p, David Putnam; d, Hugh Hudson; w, Colin Welland; ph, David Watkin; ed, Terry Rawlings; m, Vangelis

Chariots of Fire was based on the true story of two British atheletes, Eric Liddell, a devout Scottish missionary, and Harold Abrahams, an English Jew, both of whom won gold medals at the 1924 Paris Olympics. The film conveniently overlooks British athelete, Douglas Lowe, who also won a gold medal for winning the 800 metres and repeated his win in 1928. The film received mixed reviews from the critics, and scriptwriter Colin Welland cockily informed Hollywood at the Oscars that *"the British were coming!"* The film's title is taken from *"Bring me my chariots of fire!"*, in William Blake's *Jerusalem*.

The almost poetic opening and closing scenes of the atheletes running barefoot along Broadstairs beach to the sound of Vangelis' haunting theme was actually filmed at **West Sands**, St. Andrews, and the atheletes can be seen running by the **Royal and Ancient Golf Club.** A plaque was erected in 1996 near the British Golf Museum commemorating the West Sands location.

See also: Ian Charleson, *Chariots of Fire* (Wirral)

BIRTHPLACE OF THE ORIGINAL 'ROBINSON CRUSOE': ALEXANDER SELKIRK
Lower Largo

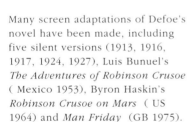

Many screen adaptations of Defoe's novel have been made, including five silent versions (1913, 1916, 1917, 1924, 1927), Luis Bunuel's *The Adventures of Robinson Crusoe* (Mexico 1953), Byron Haskin's *Robinson Crusoe on Mars* (US 1964) and *Man Friday* (GB 1975).

The Scottish sailor who was the inspiration for Daniel Defoe's, *Robinson Crusoe* (1719), was born in the small fishing village of Lower Largo, at **97-99 Main Street**. At the age of eighteen he ran away to sea and spent several years as a buccaneer. In 1703 he joined Dampier's privateering expedition to the South Seas aboard the frigate *Cinque Ports*. In the autumn of 1704 Selkirk quarrelled with the ship's tyrannical Captain Stradling and demanded to be put ashore on the uninhabited island of Juan Fernandez where he remained marooned for more than four years.

After his eventual rescue he returned to Lower Largo where he made a cave in his father's garden to remind himself of his days of solitude on the island. He died aboard ship off the coast of West Africa from yellow fever in 1721. The house now on the site of his birthplace is not open to the public, but the Crusoe memorial statue can be seen above the doorway.

Further information: The Crusoe Hotel (01333 320759) by Lower Largo harbour has a permanent Alexander Selkirk exhibiton.

CHILDHOOD HOME OF JOHN BUCHAN (1875-1940)
Kirkcaldy

John Buchan, father of the modern espionage novel, has been generally disregarded by filmmakers, with only *The 39 Steps* (1935, 1959, 1978) and a silent version of *Huntingtower* (1927) adapted for the screen to date.

He was born at **20 York Place** in Perth on 20 August 1875 to Helen Masterton and the Reverend John Buchan, minister of Knox Free Church, South St. (now demolished). Soon after his birth the family moved to **Kirkcaldy** where his father was appointed minister of Pathhead Free Church (now demolished), and the church manse in **Smeaton Road** was the home of the Buchans for more than thirteen years.

The thirty-nine steps are reputed by locals to be the steps on the west side of **Ravenscraig Castle** leading down to **Pathhead Beach**, and the opening chapter of *Prester John* was supposedly set on **Pathhead Sands** after young John heard an African minister preaching there. When Buchan was thirteen his father became minister of John

Kenneth More and Taina Elg in **The Thirty-Nine Steps** *(1959, Rank)*

Buchan's original thirty-nine steps? - *on the west side of Ravenscraig Castle.*

Knox Church in Glasgow, and from Kirkcaldy High School he was sent to Hutcheson's Grammar School, Glasgow, and later to Glasgow University. He won a scholarship to Braesnose College, Oxford and in 1901 became assistant private secretary to the High Commissioner for South Africa. In S.A. he became involved in the running of concentration camps and the repatriation of prisoners following the end of the Boer War. Buchan returned to England and the Bar in 1903 and in 1907 married Susan Grosvenor.

A prolific writer from his youth, he wrote seven volumes of prose and poetry while still at Oxford. In 1914 he went to France as correspondent for 'The Times' before being commissioned in the Intelligence Corps. In 1915 *The Thirty-Nine Steps* first appeared anonymously in *Blackwood's Magazine* which began the first of the Richard Hannay novels and established him as a popular novelist.

He was created a Baron in the mid-thirties, choosing the title Lord Tweedsmuir of Elsfield and in 1935 he was appointed Governor-General of Cananda, where he died on Sunday, 11th February, 1940 after an injury to his head after a fall. His ashes are buried in **St. Thomas of Canterbury Churchyard, Elsfield, Oxfordshire.**

See also: Alfred Hitchcock, Robert Donat, Madeleine Carroll, Forth Bridge

Stan Laurel in 1919

Glasgow

STAGE DEBUT OF STAN LAUREL

"The act was bloody awful. But I finished strong. And what's more, the applause was very big. I didn't realize that this was because the audience felt sorry for me. I figured that out for myself later on. At any rate, it was my first time before a live audience, and I felt good." Stan Laurel

Sixteen year old Lancashire lad, Arthur Stanley Jefferson, launched his career in 1906 on the miniature stage of **Pickard's Museum, 115 Trongate, Glasgow Cross**. It was a mixture of peep show parlour, side show museum and seatless theatre, run by Cockney show business impresario, Arthur E. Pickard. In an act which Stan later admitted was 'bloody awful', he was accompanied by the resident three-piece ladies' orchestra while he went through a routine mostly stolen from the popular music hall acts of the day.

His father was Arthur "A.J." Jefferson: actor, playwright, producer and at that time manager of the Metropole Theatre in George Cross (now demolished). A.J. wanted to train his son in theatre management, but realising Stan's yearning to perform on stage found him a job with a touring pantomime company who were performing *Sleeping Beauty*. Stan later joined Fred Karno's music hall troupe, where he understudied Charlie Chaplin, and did two tours of the U.S.A. After the company closed he stayed in the U.S.A. performing in vaudeville theatres and made his first film, *Nuts in May*, in 1917. In 1920 he signed a contract with Hal Roach Studios who were ultimately to team him with Oliver Hardy.

See also: Stan Laurel (Lancs, Durham, N. Tyneside), Laurel & Hardy Museum, Fred Karno.

Further information: Stan Laurel lived at Buchanan Drive, Rutherglen, and was a pupil at Stonelaw School, Melrose Avenue, Rutherglen and Queens Park School, Grange Road, opp. Victoria Infirmary in the Battlefield area of Glasgow, from 1905-1906.

BIRTHPLACE OF BILLY CONNOLLY (1942-)

"I always knew I could get to the top. I've known it since I was a

small boy. I knew I was a wee bit special." *

Glaswegian comedian, Billy Connolly, has to date made no lasting impact on the silver screen, appearing mostly in forgettable productions like *Absolution* (1978) and *Water* (1984), but he does have considerable screen presence as he proved in his portrayal of Queen Victoria's Highland servant, John Brown, in *Mrs Brown* (1997).

Connolly was born on 24 November 1942 at **65 Dover Street, Anderston** (now demolished), the second child of Mary MacLean and William Connolly, an optical instrument technician. His parents separated when he was five years old and he and his sister, Florence, were brought up by his father and his two aunts in their two-roomed flat in **White Street, Partick**. He endured a miserable and violent childhood, and attended **St. Peter's Primary School** and **St. Gerard's Secondary School** in Govan. His first job on leaving school, aged fifteen, in 1957, was with John Smith's Bookshop in St. Vincent Street, Glasgow, delivering books on a bicycle. In 1960 he began a five-year welder's apprenticeship in Stephen's shipyard at Lindhouse, Govan, and in 1965 after returning from a welding job in Biafra, he formed *The Humblebums* folk group, which later included singer/songwriter, Gerry Rafferty. The group was a great success, but Connolly's comic antics began to overshadow the group's music content, exasperating the purist Rafferty and in 1971 the band broke up. In 1973 Connolly decided to devote his career to comedy and the following year teamed with Glasgow promoter, Frank Lynch, who was responsible for launching him to comic stardom.

See also: *Mrs Brown*

SCOTTISH FILM & TELEVISION ARCHIVE

***Out For Value** (1931, SFTA)*

***Eriskay - A Poem of Remote Lives** (1935, SFTA)*

The Scottish Film & Television Archive was established in 1976 and holds material from 1896 to the present day on Scottish social, cultural and industrial history. Within the collection, emphasis is on local cinema newsreels, advertising, industrial and promotional films, educational, documentary and amateur footage.

Special collections include: *Upper Clyde Shipbuilders 1926-71* - official records of launches and trials of vessels built by constituent companies; *Films of Scotland* - documentary and sponsored film about Scotland in all aspects; *James S. Nairn* - cinema manager and local topicals made for various cinemas, 1929 - 1959.
The archive also has a collection of scripts, stills, production files, press cuttings, souvenir programmes, oral history and memorabilia.

Further information: Scottish Film Archive, Scottish Screen, 74 Victoria Crescent Road, Glasgow, G12 9JN. Tel: 0141 302 1700. e-mail: info@Scottish screen.demon.co.uk http://www.Scottish screen.demon.co.uk

LAUREL & HARDY'S GLASWEGIAN WELCOME

"Honestly, we escaped with our lives only by a miracle." Stan Laurel

During their first British tour in 1932, the organisers of Laurel & Hardy's visit to Glasgow were concerned that few fans would bother to turn out to greet them because of their late arrival at Glasgow's **Central Station** at 10.47pm on the evening of Friday 29 July.

They needn't have worried. Eight thousand people surrounded the station, the largest reception committee Glasgow has ever witnessed, all whistling Laurel and Hardy's theme tune, 'The Cuckoo Song' in eager anticipation. Extra police were drafted in and Stan and Ollie were surrounded by seven policemen as they alighted from the train.

Suddenly the crowd pushed forward, crushing those against the security barriers. Many people screamed and fainted. Prevented from leaving through the main thoroughfare the duo were filtered into a narrow side street. Now unable to move forward or back, the police, seriously undermanned, struggled to keep order as the crowd surged and screamed in panic. Some fans collapsed and were lifted out over the heads of the crowd. Stan later commented: *"I was so tightly wedged in the crowd, I thought my last hour had come. I couldn't breathe, my clothes were torn, and I almost lost a shoe."*

As they slowly moved towards the nearby **Central Hotel, Gordon Street**, the stone balustrade in front of the building disintegrated from crowd pressure and crumbling masonry fell into the melee. Ambulances and extra police speeded to the area.

When Laurel and Hardy eventually reached the safety of their hotel they were shocked and horrified. Their clothes were in shreds and their pockets had been picked, including Stan's fifty-guinea watch. Stan later remarked: *"I've never seen anything like it... Nothing that has happened in the States or elsewhere can compare with our experiences last night."* They later waved to the crowds who filled Hope Street, from the window on the staircase leading to the lobby.

The following morning Ollie headed for the **Western Gailes Golf Course**, and both appeared at the **La Scala Cinema, Sauchiehall Street** in the afternoon. On Sunday Ollie played at **Gleneagles Golf Course** and both departed for Blackpool on August 1, Bank Holiday Monday.

See also: Laurel and Hardy Museum, Stan Laurel

Further information: When Roy Rogers and his wife, Dale Evans stayed at the Central, a room was also reserved for his horse Trigger!

It was also from the Central that John Logie Baird transmitted the first television pictures down a telephone line from a fourth floor bedroom on the 26th May 1927, to London.

MUSEUM OF TRANSPORT

As well as telling the wide-ranging story of transport in Scotland, Glasgow's transport museum has also created a replica of a typical cobbled side street such as could have been found in the city fifty years ago. The time and date for fictitious Kelvin Street has been set as late afternoon on Friday 9 December 1938. A collection of shops can be seen, including a post office, a pub, an Art Deco style Continental Cafe, Lipton's grocery store and the ornate frontage of the Regal Cinema.

The entrance to the cinema features advertisements for two 1938 films, *The Drum* and *Little Miss Broadway*. Behind the entrance is a small exhibition area and a purpose-built miniature cinema. In the 1930s Glasgow was known as 'cinema city', with more cinemas per head of population than any other city in the country, and boasted 98 cinemas in 1937!

*The **Regal Cinema** frontage - Museum of Transport*

Further information: Museum of Transport, 1 Bunhouse Road, Glasgow, G3 8DP. Tel: 0141 287 2720. Open: 10.00-5.00 Sunday: 11.00-5.00

GLASGOW FILM THEATRE

The origins of the Glasgow Film Theatre go back to the Cosmo Cinema. Opened in 1939 by the Singleton family who owned a chain of cinemas, the Cosmo was Scotland's first (and Britain's second) arts continental cinema. The cinema was custom built and with its European Modernist exterior and post art deco style interior, the Cosmo was different from any other cinema in Scotland at that time. It offered a much wider range of films than the Hollywood mainstream and brought foreign language films to Glasgow for the first time.

Pioneering entrepreneur, George Singleton's philosophy that "films should help improve things in the world", established the Cosmo's reputation as a unique haven for international cinema.

George and Vincent Singleton brought Charles Oakley on board as programme advisor and publicist. Oakley, one of the founder members of the British Film Institute and the Scottish Film Council, designed the Mr Cosmo character with his bowler hat who became a successful publicity gimmick for the cinema. Oakley had met Hitchcock in the 1930s who revealed that he had named the 'Merry Widow' murderer (Joseph Cotten) in *Shadow of a Doubt* (1943) after Mr. Oakley!

The Cosmo was sold to the Scottish Film Council which opened as the GFT on 1 May 1974. The large auditorium was converted to a smaller 404 seater auditorium and a large conference space was created where the cinema's stalls area had previously been.

In 1988 it launched a long-term plan to refurbish and develop the premises and in 1991 it opened its 144 seat second screen. Throughout the developments Mr. Cosmo was slowly brought back to life again by naming the bar, Cafe Cosmo, and reinstating his welcoming face above the box office, emblazoned with GFT's motto, 'Cinema For All'.

Further information: GFT, 12 Rose Street, Glasgow, G3 6RE. Tel: 0141 332 6535.

Highland

GRAVES OF MACBETH & DUNCAN
Iona

*Judith Anderson and Maurice Evans in George Schaefer's production of **Macbeth** (1959, British Lion)*

In 563AD the Irish monk Columba landed on Iona and founded a monastery which resulted in the spread of Christianity throughout Britain. In the 12th century Benedictines established an abbey where Duncan and his murderer, Macbeth, are said to be interred in the hallowed burial ground of the medieval Kings of Scotland, Ireland and Norway, close to the grave of the late Labour leader, John Smith.

Shakespeare's tragedy has had a long and difficult relationship with the movies. An early silent version starring Sir Herbert Beerbohm-Tree in 1916, was a box-office catastrophe. Slightly more successful was Orson Welles' 1948 production which was shot in only twenty-three days. Akira Kurosawa directed his Japanese interpretation, *Throne of Blood*, in 1957, and Roman Polanski, with help from Playboy publisher, Hugh Hefner, shot his controversial version (complete with Lady Macbeth nude scene) in 1971.

See also: Maurice Evans

BREAKING THE WAVES
Lochailort

• 1995 135m c Drama UK/Swe/Den/Fin/Nor/Neth
• Emily Watson (Bess), Stellan Skarsgard (Jan), Katrin Cartlidge (Dodo McNeill), Jean-Marc Barr (Terry), Adrian Rawlins (Dr. Richardson), Jonathan Hackett (Clergyman), Sandra Voe (Mother)
• p, Vibeke Windlov, Peter Aalbak Jensen; d & w, Lars Von Trier; ph, Robby Muller; art d, Karl Juliusson; ed, Anders Refn
• Jury Prize for Best Film, 1996 Cannes Film Festival

A profoundly moving film about an ingenuous and religious young girl, whom many would describe as 'simple'. Set in the early seventies in a remote Scottish community, Bess (Emily Watson) marries roughneck oil-rig worker, Jan (Stellan Skarsgard) regardless of local opposition. Following an accident on the rig which paralyses Jan, he agonises that Bess too will cease to live a 'normal' life caring for a bedridden husband. Frustrated and impotent, he persuades her that his road to recovery lies in her taking a lover and relating their sexual acts to him. Bess's subsequent sexual mission to keep

*The Lochailort Church in **Breaking the Waves***

her husband alive ostracises her from the community and the church, but not from God, with whom she regularly converses.

The film was shot in **Mallaig** and on the **Isle of Skye** around **Glendale** and **Uig**. The austere church where Bess is 'cast out' is just outside **Lochailort**, going towards Morar.

LOCAL HERO
Morar

"Would you give me a pound note for every grain of sand I hold in my hand? Now you can buy the beach for that."
Ben Knox (Fulton Mackay)

*Bill Forsyth and David Putnam on **Camusdarrach Beach**.*

The most idyllic setting in Bill Forsyth's 1983 comedy was Ferness's beautiful sand duned beach, home to the hermit, Ben Knox . Its real location was at **Camusdarrach Beach**, just south of the village of Morar, on the road to Mallaig. Ben's beach has a house at its northern edge, which was dressed as a church for the film. He also had a long walk to Ferness village, as it was located on the East coast of Scotland, about one hundred and fifty miles away, at Pennan in Aberdeenshire.

The **Morar Hotel** (01687 462346) was used to shoot the film's bedroom scenes. On the day of filming, its expansive car park was filled with trucks and equipment, including a generator. A well known local left the hotel having had one too many, and tripped over the main power cable, ripping it out of its socket, causing a complete power failure. The entire film crew glared at him as he lay on the ground in a drunken stupor. Bringing up his rear was the landlord, who, pointing at his motionless body, exclaimed, *"That's our Local Hero!"*

About twelve miles south of Morar on the A830 is Lochailort. The **Lochailort Hotel**, where the interior hotel scenes were shot, was subsequently destroyed by fire, and a new hotel has since been built on the site.

Just outside Lochailort, on the main road to Morar, is the church which was used as a model for the mock-up on Camusdarrach beach (this church also appears in the 1995 film, *Breaking the Waves*). The church interiors were shot nearby at **Our Lady of the Braes Church** in **Polnish.**

See also: *Local Hero* (Aberdeenshire), Fulton Mackay, *Breaking the Waves*

Further information: Glennan Cross B&B (opposite beach) 01687 450294. Camusdarrach Camp Site 01687 450221. Mallaig Tourist Information 01687 462170.

Brian Davenport with a replica of Mel Gibson's Lowland two-handed sword

BRAVEHEART
Glen Nevis

Mel Gibson's 1995 film of Scottish patriot, William Wallace, was only partly shot in Scotland. The bulk of the film was shot in Ireland which offered the film-makers its army, studio space and tax incentives. Despite this, the film became a great boon for the Scottish tourist industry, trebling the visitors to the National Wallace Monument in 1996.

The medieval village and fort were located in **Glen Nevis**, near **Fort William**. No sets from the film remain, but the parking area used by the film crew is now called **Braveheart Car Park**.

The second armourer on the film was Brian Davenport, who made most of the weapons, including Mel Gibson's Lowland two-handed sword, often mistaken for a Claymore. Most of the weapons in the film were made from moulded rubber, cast from a metal original. Only weapons used in close-up were made of metal.

Brian and his wife decided to opt out of their 'rat-race' existence in

Derbyshire nearly thirty years ago and moved to the Highlands for a slower pace of life. Brian now manufactures medieval weaponry for collectors and film-makers alike and welcomes the curious visitor to his workshop in Fort William (please phone beforehand).

See also: *Braveheart* (Meath)

Further information: Brian Davenport, 1 Zetland Avenue, Fort William. Tel: 01397 705292. National Wallace Monument, Abbey Craig, Stirling.

HIGHLANDER
Dornie

Occasionally a dull film is worth watching solely for its breathtaking locations and one such, arguably, is Russell Mulcahey's, *Highlander* . Forgettable in content, it is nonetheless stitched around unforgettable settings, in which time travellers Sean Connery and Christopher Lambert duel their way from 16th-century Scotland to 1980s New York. Lambert sets out on his quest from **Eilean Donan Castle** situated on an island in **Loch Duich, near Kyle of Lochalsh.**

*Ramirez (Sean Connery) trains Connor MacLeod (Christopher Lambert) for the final battle with his ultimate enemy, The Kurgan in **Highlander** (1986, EMI)*

A castle was first built on this site in the 13th-century, but the present building dates from the early 1900s. Other locations included **'The Study' near Glencoe village, Loch Shiel at Glenfinnan, Refuge Bay at Cuartaig near Morar**, and the **Cioch** rock pinnacle in the **Cuillin Hills, Isle of Skye.**

See also: Sean Connery

Further information: Eilean Donan Castle is open Easter to October. Visitors' Centre open all year. Tel: 01599 555202. Kyle of Lochalsh T.I. : 01599 534276

CHILDHOOD HOME OF ALISTAIR MACLEAN (1922-87)
Daviot

"I'm an extraordinarily ordinary man. Basically I'm a person who tells stories - and what does that mean? How much is it worth?"
Alistair MacLean

Popular and prolific adventure novelist, Alistair MacLean, was born in **Shettleston, Glasgow**, on 21 April 1922, the third of four sons of Mary Lamont and the Reverend Alistair MacLean. The same year his family moved from the city to the idyllic village of **Daviot**, near Inverness, where he was raised at **Torguish House**, an old three-

storey manse of red sandstone close to the Reverend's new kirk. Alistair was educated at Daviot school and Inverness Academy.

After his father's sudden death in 1934 from a cerebral haemorrhage the family moved back to Glasgow to a tenement flat at **Carrington Street, off the Great Western Road** and lived off Mrs. MacLean's meagre kirk pension. Alistair won a bursary for Hillhead High School and his first job on leaving school was in a Glasgow shipping office before joining the navy during WWII. After the war he studied for an English Language and Literature degree at Glasgow University and in 1954, while teaching at **Gallowflat School** (now an annexe of Stonelaw High) in **Reid Street, Rutherglen**, he entered a short-story competition in the *Glasgow Herald* newspaper, winning the first prize of £100.

In October 1955 he published his first novel, *HMS Ulysses*, a drama of the WWII Russian convoys written in only three months. By the end of

*Torguish House, Daviot - birthplace of **Alistair MacLean***

the year it had sold over a quarter of a million copies. MacLean's second book - and the first to be filmed - was *The Guns of Navarone*, the success of which enabled him to give up teaching forever.

From then on he wrote a book almost every year for the next thirty years, many of which were adapted for the screen, including *The Satan Bug* (1965), *Ice Station Zebra* (1968), *Where Eagles Dare* (1969), *When Eight Bells Toll*

*Anthony Quinn, Anthony Quayle and Gregory Peck in **The Guns of Navarone** (1961, Columbia)*

(1970), *Puppet on a Chain* (1971), *Fear is the Key* (1972), *Caravan to Vaccares* (1975), *Breakheart Pass* (1976), *Force Ten from Navarone* (1978) and *Bear Island* (1979).

A complex man who preferred anonymity to the glare of publicity, he was twice married and had three sons. He died in Munich in 1987 and was buried at a private funeral in Celigny, Switzerland, where he had lived in tax exile.

Further information: Torguish House, Daviot, Inverness. Tel: 01463 772208. Now a B&B it is situated approximately 4 miles south of Inverness. The entrance is directly off the south bound carriageway of the A9.

THE NEWTON HOTEL
Nairn

The secluded building and grounds of the Newton Hotel was a favourite holiday destination of Charlie Chaplin for several consecutive years during the seventies, who, for two or three weeks each summer, would occupy the second floor with his large family and staff. Set in 21 acres with views of the Moray Firth and Ross-shire hills, Chaplin's peace and relaxation was guaranteed here during the last decade of his life.

The hotel's 'Chaplin Suite' celebrates his time there, displaying on its walls local photographs of Chaplin and his family, and replica bowler hat and cane.

Other screen guests at the hotel have included Burt Lancaster and Christopher Lee.

See also: Charlie Chaplin Trail

Further information: The Newton Hotel, Nairn, Scotland IV12 46X. Tel: 01667 453144.

The Newton Hotel, Nairn

SAVING PRIVATE RYAN
Corpach

Five of the landing craft used in Steven Spielberg's epic 1998 war film are owned by the Corpach Boat Company. Four craft lie in the boatyard and a larger, ex-Russian tank-carrying craft is used to ferry cargo up and down the west coast. The boatyard welcomes visitors, and ardent fans of the movie can purchase a landing craft, as lying, for £10,000.

*Landing craft from **Saving Private Ryan** at the Corpach Boatyard*

See also: *Saving Private Ryan* (Wexford, Herts)

Further information: Corpach Boat Co., Corpach, Nr. Fort William, PH33 7NN. Tel: 01397 772861.

CLASSIC LOCATION: GLENCOE

Synonymous with the massacre of 1692, and home to cattle-rustlers and clan conflict for over a thousand years, Glencoe possesses some of the most dramatic mountain scenery in Scotland. Its breathtaking locations have been used in films such as Hitchcock's *The Thirty Nine Steps* (1935), *Monty Python and the Holy Grail* (1975), *Highlander* (1986) and *Rob Roy* (1995) in which its foreboding back-drop dominates and dwarfs the action.

Glencoe is also home to mountaineer and travel writer Hamish MacInnes. A world authority on mountain rescue, and founder of Glencoe Mountain Rescue, Hamish advises on all aspects of filming in hazardous terrain such as locations, safety and camera positions. As advisor to the BBC on live outside broadcasts he did pioneering work and shooting on such programmes as the award-winning *Ascent of The Old Man of Hoy*. His feature film work has included Fred Zinneman's *Five Days One Summer* (1983), *The Eiger Sanction* (1975), *The Living Daylights* (1987), *The Mission* (1986) and most films shot in Glencoe. He now runs his own film company, **Glencoe Productions Ltd** (01855 811258).

The mountains of Glencoe should be avoided by the novice climber and walker. There are, however, many pleasurable walks on the lower slopes in the areas around An Torr and Signal Rock, Loch Achtriochtan, Lairig Eilde and the Devil's Staircase.

The **River Coe Restaurant** is a recommended port of call for all film tourists, run by Jack-of-all-trades proprietor, Peter Weir, a former member of Glen Coe Mountain Rescue. Peter has also been involved in filming, and worked on both *Highlander* and *Rob Roy*. Location stills shot in the area adorn his restaurant walls and he will always find time for a chat with movie fans. The food is good (Hamish MacInnes often has his breakfast here) and the atmosphere one of typical Highland hospitality. Also - guys 'n' gals - you never know who might be dishing up the all-day breakfast or his delicious home-baked scones...

Peter Weir with one of his local kitchen staff.

See also: *Highlander, Rob Roy, Monty Python and the Holy Grail*, Forth Bridge

Further information: River Coe Restaurant, Glencoe Village, Highland PA39 8LA. Tel: 01855 811248. Open all year. National Trust Visitors' Centre 01855 811307. Ballachulish Tourist Information 01855 811296.

CASTAWAY
Achiltibuie

Nicolas Roeg's 1986 south sea saga, *Castaway*, starring Oliver Reed and Amanda Donohoe, about a girl who answers an advertisement which reads '*Writer seeks "wife" for a year on tropical island*', was based on Lucy Irvine's autobiographical narrative *Castaway*. Shot in the Seychelles the film recounts the couple's unpredictable adventures on the island of Tuin off the north coast of Australia.

Lucy Irvine grew up at her father's remote **Summer Isles Hotel** in the **Western Highlands**, near **Ullapool**, and it was here that she wrote *Castaway* in the early 1980s. The hotel is now run by her brother Mark, and sister-in-law Geraldine Irvine. A line from their current brochure reads, *"There is a marvellous amount of nothing to do in Achiltibuie..."*

See also: Oliver Reed

Further information: Summer Isles Hotel, Achiltibuie, Highland IV26 2YG. Tel: 01854 622282.

CULLODEN
Culloden
Moor

On 16 April 1746, the last battle on British soil was fought at Culloden Moor, near Inverness, when the Jacobite army of Bonnie Prince Charlie faced the Duke of Cumberland's forces, during the Rising of 1745. Cumberland's defeat of the 'Young Pretender' led to his exile and the birth of a romantic legend. Peter Watkin's 1964 black and white film turns this legend on its head, and questions Charlie's dubious reputation as a strategist and leader of men.

Culloden was not a clear cut, Scots versus English, or Highlander versus Lowlander conflict. It was about religious and political beliefs, and many Scots fought alongside the English.

The battle scenes were shot on Culloden Moor, using extras whose

forefathers had fought and died in the actual battle. Shot in the innovative style of a newsreel, with jerky camera movements and on the spot interviews, the film graphically conveys the true horror of the battle and its bloody aftermath. Originally made for television, the film received a limited cinema release.

Further information: The National Trust Centre at Culloden, Tel: 01463 790607. Open all year except January. Located app. 5 miles from Inverness on the B9006.

North Lanarkshire

GREGORY'S GIRL
Cumbernauld

• 1981 91m c Romance/Comedy Lake (UK)
• Gordon John Sinclair (Gregory), Dee Hepburn (Dorothy), Jake D'Arcy (Phil Menzies), Clare Grogan (Susan), Robert Buchanan (Andy), Billy Greenlees (Steve), Alan Love (Eric), Caroline Guthrie (Carol), Carol Macartney (Margo), Douglas Sannachan (Billy), Chic Murray (Headmaster)

• p, Clive Parsons, Davina Belling; d, Bill Forsyth; w, Bill Forsyth; ph, Michael Coulter; ed, John Gow; m, Colin Tully

After his successful screen debut with *That Sinking Feeling* (1979), Bill Forsyth cast the Glasgow Youth Theatre for a second time in *Gregory's Girl* . This simple and tender film, bursting with teenage hormones, ranks among the very best of Scottish cinema and matches anything Ealing could have produced in its heyday without trundling out the usual Scots stereotypes.

Filmed on location in the **Abronhill** district of **Cumbernauld**, a Scottish new town whose soporific architecture dominates the film. **Abronhill High School, Larch Road**, was the main location and **Cumbernauld Town Centre** was where Gregory waited beside the huge clock for Dorothy.

Perth & Kinross

CHILDHOOD HOME OF EWAN McGREGOR (1971-)
Crieff

"Working on films back to back, I began to find I was losing myself..."

Since he was cast as the arrogant Edinburgh journalist, Alex, in Danny Boyle's *Shallow Grave* in 1994, Ewan McGregor has hardly paused for breath, pouring out a prolific body of work which includes: *Trainspotting* (1995), *Emma* (1996), *Brassed Off* (1996) *A Life Less Ordinary* (1997),*Velvet Goldmine* (1998), *Little Voice* (1998), *Rogue Trader* (1999) and *Star Wars, The Phantom Menace* (1999).

Born 31 March 1971 at **Perth Royal Infirmary**, to schoolteachers Jim McGregor and Carol Lawson. At the time of his birth the family resided at **'Edgemont', Sauchie Terrace, Crieff**. He has one brother, Colin, an RAF pilot. He attended **Morrison's Academy, Crieff**, a private school where his tempestuous behaviour frequently found him on the carpet in the headmaster's office. He left school at sixteen, and after many years of being influenced by old movies and his actor/uncle, Denis Lawson (best known as the lawyer-innkeeper, Urquhart, in *Local Hero*), he joined the Perth Repertory Theatre. Following a drama course at **Kirkcaldy College of Technology** he left for London, aged seventeen, and attended the Guildhall School of Speech and Drama.

His first film role was as an extra in *A Passage to India* (1984) but in his final year at Guildhall he was offered the role of the daydreaming clerk who fantasises about rock'n'roll in Dennis Potter's *Lipstick on your Collar*, which launched his career. In 1995 he married French set designer, Eve Mavrakis. They have one daughter.

See also: *Brassed Off, Little Voice, Shallow Grave*

THE MYTH OF DONALD CRISP'S BIRTHPLACE (1880-1974)
Aberfeldy

At the time of writing, a Cinema 100 Commemorative Plaque in the **Main Square** proclaims Aberfeldy as the birthplace of actor and director, Donald Crisp. Recent research, however, by the staff of the A.K. Bell Library in Perth - and confirmed by Crisp's relatives - has proved this claim to be false. The library unearthed his birth

Donald Crisp in Greyfriars Bobby (1960, Walt Disney)

certificate which states clearly that George William Crisp was born at **3 Clayhall Road, Bow,** London (now demolished) on 27 July 1882 to James Crisp, a groom, and Elizabeth Christy. Crisp's nephew in California confirms that he changed his Christian name to Donald when he arrived in the U.S.A. Crisp's sister is said to have lived in Aberfeldy and he is purported to have visited the town in 1950, but little else connects Donald Crisp to Scotland. He once claimed his father was physician to King Edward VII, when in fact the 1881 census describes his father as a 'cowman' and in 1891 as a 'labourer at the chemical works'.

After returning from the Boer War he left for the US in the early 1900s where he worked as an actor and stage manager. He joined D.W. Griffith's stock company and later became an assistant director on many of his films, including *The Birth of a Nation* (1915) where he was responsible for the vast army of extras, and *Broken Blossoms* (1919) with Lilian Gish. When the talkies arrived he concentrated on acting.

His many films included *Mutiny on the Bounty* (1935), *The Life of Emile Zola* (1937), *Wuthering Heights* (1939) and *The Man From Laramie* (1955). After his portrayal as the father of the Morgan family in *How Green Was My Valley* (1941), for which he won a Best Supporting Actor Oscar, he became typecast as the benign patriarch in films such as, *Lassie Come Home* (1943) and *National Velvet* (1944).

While his credits as actor and director exceed four hundred, he also had a keen financial brain, acting as an advisor to film companies for the Bank of Italy (later the Bank of America). He married screenwriter, Jane Murfin, and died in Van Nuys, California, in 1974. He had no children.

See also: *How Green Was My Valley*

ORIGINS OF WILLIAM CAMERON MENZIES (1896-1957)
Aberfeldy

Charles Menzies, the father of Hollywood production designer, William Cameron Menzies, was born at his family's house and plumbing yard at **Bridgend, Aberfeldy** (now Country Fare Coffee Shop). With three brothers already involved in the family business, Charles saw no future for himself as an Aberfeldy plumber and emigrated to America with his wife in the 1890s where their Connecticut-born son became one of Hollywood's great production designers.

Menzies' work included: *The Thief of Baghdad* (1924), *The Dove* (1928 AA), *Gone with the Wind* (1939), *Foreign Correspondent* (1940), *Our Town* (1940) and *Kings Row* (1942). He was best known as an influential designer, but also directed films, the most notable being: *Things to Come* (1936), and the cult sci-fi film, *Invaders From Mars* (1953), for which he was both director and production designer.

ROB ROY
Muthill

• 1995 139m c Drama / Action (Scotland/US)
• Liam Neeson (Rob Roy), Jessica Lange (Mary), John Hurt (Montrose), Tim Roth (Cunningham), Eric Stoltz (McDonald)
• p, Richard Jackson, Peter Brougham; d, Michael Caton-Jones; w, Alan Sharp (based on the novel by Sir Walter Scott).

"I can think of no higher compliment to the movie than that it awakened in me a desire to read Scott's novel, although when I failed to find it on my shelves, I was able to live with the disappointment."
Roger Ebert

*John Hurt as the Marquis of Montrose in **Rob Roy** (1995, UIP/UA)*

Hollywood originally intended to shoot this biopic about the legendary Scottish outlaw in New Zealand, but Michael Caton-Jones refused to direct the film unless it was shot in his native Scotland. He claims *"It was very satisfying for me to be able to come back to a place I*

knew instinctively and to make a picture here."

Drummond Castle, two miles south of **Crieff** on the Muthill Road (A822), was the seat of the Marquis of Montrose in the film and was chosen primarily for its stunning gardens which were first laid out in the early 17th century and redesigned and terraced in the early 19th century. The gardens on view today were replanted during the 1950's, preserving features such as the ancient yew hedges and the copper beech trees planted by Queen Victoria to commemorate her visit in 1842.

The original location of the MacGregor village was in **Glen Nevis, near Fort William**, but torrential rain turned the site into a quagmire and it was relocated indoors at the Perth Equestrian Centre. This was also the location for the memorable duel between Rob Roy and Cunningham.

Other locations included the hills above **Kinlochleven in the Highlands** where the opening shots were filmed; the Gothic courtyard of 15th century **Megginch Castle**, 10 miles east of Perth, near Errol, where the village square was constructed; **Crichton Castle**, near Pathhead, Midlothian, was the gambling den exterior; **Bracorina on Loch Morar** was the site of Rob and Mary's cottage and **Glencoe** was the location for the cattle-rustling scene.

See also: Michael Caton-Jones, Liam Neeson, Sir Walter Scott, Rob Roy's Grave

Further information: Megginch Castle grounds and Crichton Castle are open to the public. Drummond Castle Gardens (01764 681257) are open to the public Easter Weekend, then daily from May to October. The castle is not open to the public.

Renfrewshire

THE GLEN CINEMA DISASTER
Paisley

The worst cinema disaster in British history occurred on the afternoon of Tuesday, 31st December, 1929. The Glen Cinema was screening a children's matinee performance of the exciting western, *Desperado Dude*. Being Hogmanay, more children were in attendance than usual, possibly because their parents wanted them out of the house to prepare for the New Year celebrations. There are no official figures for the audience size that day, but the hall was packed and overcrowded, with children seated on wooden benches and in the gangways. The official estimate was 700 children, but there could have been many more.

The Glen staff consisted of the manager, an operator, an assistant operator, a woman taking the entrance money, a girl selling chocolates, and a male attendant. After the first reel of the film had been shown, it was taken by the assistant operator, fifteen-year-old James McVey, to the small rewinding room. After rewinding the film he placed it in its can, secured the lid and left it in a corner of the room. While reaching for another reel he heard a hissing sound which he thought might be a gas radiator leaking outside the room. He opened the door and looked out, but saw nothing wrong. It was then he noticed smoke issuing from the film can in the corner. Fearful of a fire breaking out he realized he would have to get the smouldering can outside the building. He quickly carried it to an exit door opposite the rewinding room, but unfortunately it was either locked or jammed. He set the film can down in the passageway

The Glen Cinema c.1928-29 screening King Vidor's The Crowd. (SFTA).

and ran to inform the projectionist who told him to fetch the manager. Hurriedly he waded down the gangway through the sea of children to the manager's office. When he and the manager returned the smouldering can was giving off dense fumes. The manager opened the door and kicked the film outside down some steps.

By now the smoke had seeped into the main hall. The children, no doubt worried by the fumes and

Renfrewshire

alarmed by McVey and the manager running up the gangway, rushed in a panic for the exits on either side of the stage. These exits led down a short flight of steps to a double exit door with 'push' bars. On the other side of this door was a locked gate. The children piled up in a heap at the bottom of the steps, and back up the steps into the passages, and - it is said - practically into the hall. Most of those who escaped did so through the front entrance. The fire brigade arrived promptly but their work was hampered by the semi-darkness of the hall.

The injured children were rushed to the Royal Alexandra Infirmary in commandeered trams, buses and cars. The final death toll was seventy-one, ranging in age from eighteen months to thirteen years and between thirty and forty children were injured. Of the seventy-one fatalities most had been crushed to death at the exit as a result of children at the back throwing themselves over the top of the ones in front. No one was burned as there was no fire.

Betty Staples, who was five years old at the time of the tragedy, attended the Glen Cinema on the fatal afternoon accompanied by her two brothers. She described the chaotic scenes inside the cinema to the *Paisley Daily Express* in 1996: " *I remember the hall was just full of smoke and someone shouted fire. Then everyone started to head for the door to try and get out... there were even people jumping from the balcony.*" Betty was saved by her elder brother's school fire drill training; he told her to remain where she was. *"There were people all around me, climbing over me and screaming but I was so young I just trusted my brother and did exactly what he said."* The three waited until the hall was nearly empty then headed towards the exit, but were forced to turn back

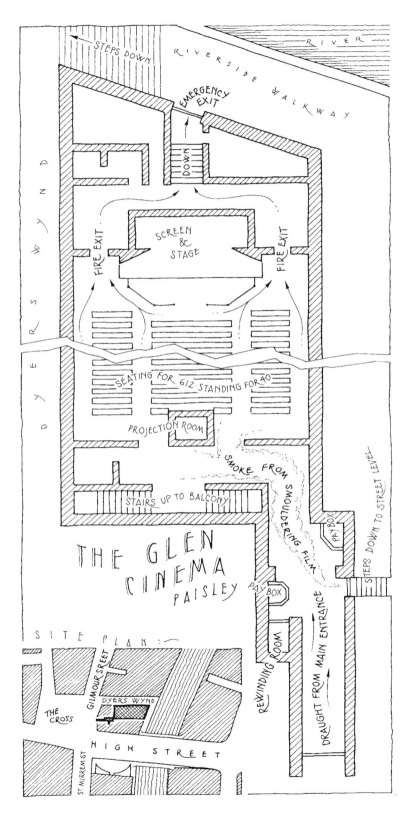

because so many were crushed against the outside gate. Separated from her brothers in the crowd, Betty was found by a fireman and led outside. She remembers her father describing how some of the dead were laid out in the street while heartbroken parents hunted for their children. Both her brothers had fortunately managed to escape.

A report on the 'Circumstances attending the Loss of Life at the Glen Cinema' was submitted to the Secretary of State for Scotland in May, 1930. The cause of the ignition of the film was ascertained by questioning assistant operator, James McVey. *"...we came to the conclusion that his account was truthful and that smoking could be dismissed. Further questions elicited the fact that when he put the tin box down in the corner there was a 6-volt accumulator there. This was used for an instrument in the orchestra named a 'panatrope', and had been sent back for recharging... This accumulator shows signs of tinning on one of the terminals and there were marks on the box. There is no doubt, whatever, that the boy, McVey, put the tin box down on the accumulator and caused a short circuit across the terminals."* Experiments were witnessed at the London Fire Brigade H.Q. shortly after the tragedy when a can of nitrate film was placed across an accumulator and was ignited in four seconds, emitting extremely dense fumes containing a high percentage of carbon monoxide and other poisonous and inflammable gasses (nitrate-based film stock was gradually withdrawn from use in the 1950s). The report, amongst other things, seriously criticised the cinema's exit system, the insufficiency of attendants and laxity in management. The tragedy led to the introduction of stricter safety regulations for cinemas throughout the country and to this day the phrase, *"Remember*

The **Glen Cinema** building today with Dyers Wynd in the foreground and the steps leading to Riverside Walkway on the left.

The Glen memorial, Hawkhead Cemetery, Paisley

Paisley", is still used in the trade to reproach staff who jeopardise a cinema's safety.

The Glen is situated in the centre of Paisley at the junction between **Gilmour Street** and **High Street**. The main entrance was in **Gilmour Street** opposite **The Cross**. It was never used as a cinema again after the tragedy, but it still stands intact today. The Glen once formed part of the Good Templar Halls, which is now partly occupied by a furniture shop. Its auditorium and ornate ceiling are concealed behind a false wall in the shop, but at the time of writing these could be seen by torchlight from a partition on the shop staircase.

A memorial was erected to the children's memory in 1930 at **Hawkhead Cemetery, Hawkhead Road**, Paisley. A plaque honouring the children who died was erected in 1996 and can be seen on the wall close to the furniture store.

See also: Barnsley Public Hall Disaster, Scala Picture House Tragedy

BIRTHPLACE OF FULTON MACKAY (1922-87)
Paisley

The son of a grocer, Fulton Mackay was born on August 12th 1922 at **10 Underwood Lane**, off Well Street, in Paisley's West End. He moved in early childhood to Arderseir, near Fort George in the Highlands, where his father worked in the local NAAFI. When he was three and a half years old his mother died of diabetes and he was brought up by an aunt in Clydebank, who took in theatrical lodgers.

He trained for the stage at the Royal Academy of Dramatic Art and from 1949 to 1958 he was a leading member of the Citizens' Theatre, Glasgow. He was also a talented writer, and under the pseudonym Aeneas McBride wrote four television plays for BBC Scotland. Television brought him national fame as prison officer, Mr Mackay, in the comedy series *Porridge*, but he will be best remembered in the movies for his portrayal of Ben Knox, the eccentric skywatching beachcomber, in Bill Forsyth's, *Local Hero* (1983).

His other films include: *The Brave Don't Cry* (1952), *Laxdale Hall* (1953), *Gumshoe* (1971), *Nothing but the Night* (1973), *Porridge* (1979), *Brittania Hospital* (1982), *Ill Fares the Land* (1983) and *Water* (1985).

See also: *Local Hero*

Shetland

THE EDGE OF THE WORLD
Foula

- 1937 81m bw Drama (UK)
- Finlay Currie (James Gray), Niall MacGinnis (Andrew Gray), John Laurie (Peter Manson), Belle Chrystall (Ruth Manson), Eric Berry (Robbie Manson), Grant Sutherland (Cathechist)
- p, Joe Rock; d, Michael Powell; w, Michael Powell; ed, Derek Twist; ph, Ernest Palmer, Skeets Kelly, Monty Berman; m, Cyril Ray

In this, Michael Powell's story of an island community desperately trying to eke a living from a harsh and desolate landscape, some of the crofters are content to live just as their forefathers did, but some think it a pointless struggle and dream of a comfortable life on the mainland. With such a small population, any person who deserts the island risks endangering the existence of the community. The

island's destiny is eventually decided by a race up the cliffs, with fatal results.

Inspired by the depopulation of St. Kilda in 1930, this was Michael Powell's first opportunity to direct something original and imaginative after cutting his teeth on a succession of low-budget quota-quickies. Using St. Kilda as a location was impossible because of its status as a nature reserve, so the remote Shetland Island of Foula was used instead.

Foula is the most westerly island in the Shetlands, and lying about fourteen miles west of the Mainland, was a Norse kingdom until the 17th century. One of the main locations on the island was Britain's second highest cliff, **The Kame**, on the western side of the island. The population of Foula in 1985 was forty-six, one third being children. The main sources of livelihood are sheep and crofting, lobster and crab fishing, spinning and weaving, tourism and the sale of knoitweat, sheepskin rugs and craftwork.

Michael Powell returned to Foula in the 1970s with some of the original cast and crew to shoot his documentary, *Return to the Edge of the World*.

See also: Michael Powell, Finlay Currie

Further information: The ferry crossing from the Walls on the Shetland Mainland is in a thirty-five foot ex-lifeboat, the maximum size which can be winched out of the sea. The eighteen mile crossing takes about two hours. Booking is essential as the ferry can only carry six passengers. Tel: 01595 3232.

Loganair run flights to Foula from Tingwall, mid-May to early September. Tel: 01595 84246. Lerwick Tourist Info 01595 693434.

SHETLAND FILM CLUB
Lerwick

"The waves are brisk and have tell-tale white tops; our suspicions increase as the crew cheerfully rope our Land Rover onto the deck, telling us that the one and a half hour journey is likely to be 'a bit choppy' The waves break across the deck..."

Kathy Hubbard describing an SFC 'community film tour' to the Isles of Out Skerries, 1992.

*Kathy Hubbard of the **Shetland Film Club***

Eight hundred miles north of the National Film Theatre, the Shetland Islands can be likened to a cinematic desert, with no commercial cinema in any of its communities. This gap is admirably filled by the Shetland Film Club whose season runs on a fortnightly basis in Lerwick, the island's capital. Supported by the Shetland Arts Trust, membership is small in this sparse and widely strewn community, consisting of sixty-odd faithful members. In 1992, a community tour to some of the more remote islands on island-hopping planes and ferries screened films to a total of 2,800 people - 12% of the islands' population.

Further information: Stuart Hubbard, Nethaburn, Wester Quarff, Shetland, ZE2 9EZ. Tel: 01950 477235. Guests welcome.

Stirling

GRAVE OF ROB ROY (1671-1734)
Balquhidder

Highland folk hero, Rob Roy, who lost his estates and lived by cattle theft and extortion, was first portrayed on the screen by Richard Todd in Disney's dreary *Rob Roy, the Highland Rogue* in 1954. Michael Caton-Jones breathed life into the brigand with his 1995 version, *Rob Roy*, with Liam Neeson in the title role. Rob Roy, his wife Mary and their two sons, are buried in the local churchyard.
See also: Sir Walter Scott, *Rob Roy*, Michael Caton-Jones

Further information: Rob Roy & Trossachs Visitor Centre, Ancaster Square, Callander, The Trossachs. Tel: 01877 330342.

CHILDHOOD HOME OF JOHN GRIERSON (1898-1972)
Cambusbarron

"The penalty of realism is that it is about reality, and has to bother forever, not about being beautiful but about being right." John Grierson

Founding father of the British documentary movement, John Grierson was born on 26 April 1898, at **the Old Schoolhouse** (now demolished), **Deanston, near Dunblane**, the fourth of eight

The Schoolhouse, Cambusbarron - childhood home of John Grierson

children of Jane Anthony and Robert Grierson, the village headmaster. In 1900 they moved to **The Schoolhouse** in **Main Street, Cambusbarron** (next to Bruce Memorial Church, plaque erected), where his father became headmaster of the local school. In September 1908 he attended **Stirling High School**, which he reached by walking from his home which lay on the edge of town, up the steep **Back Walk.** He left school in July 1915 having been awarded a bursary for Glasgow University, but the war interrupted his studies and on 7 January 1916 he joined the R.N.V.R. as an telegraphist. He was posted to **Aultbea**, on Loch Ewe in the Highlands and a year later joined the minesweeper H.M.S. Surf for the remainder of the war.

In 1923 he graduated with a philosophy degree and won a Rockefeller fellowship to study the American media in Chicago where he was encouraged to study the social significance of the cinema. In 1927 he became assistant film officer of the newly-formed Empire Marketing Board and made his first documentary film, *Drifters* (1929). He formed a talented team under his leadership that included Edgar Anstey, Basil Wright, Paul Rotha and Arthur Elton. After the EMB was wound up in 1933 he moved

to its successor, the General Post Office and formed the GPO film unit, where he worked with W.H. Auden, Benjamin Britten, Robert Flaherty and Alberto Cavalcanti at **21 Soho Square, London**.

The new and pioneering documentary film movement, inspired and led by Grierson, was by now gaining in momentum, with many film-makers beginning to experiment with the genre in which Grierson set standards for others to follow. The GPO unit made many prestigious documentaries about the importance of ordinary people and their everyday lives, such as *Industrial Britain* (1933), *Coal Face* (1935) and *Nightmail* (1936).

He became head of the National Film Board of Canada from 1939 to 1945 during which time he made many memorable films. He later worked for Unesco and the British Central Office of Information until producing his weekly TV programme, *This Wonderful World* from 1957 to 1963.

In 1930 he married Margaret Taylor. They had no children. John Grierson died of cancer on Saturday 19 February 1972.

See also: Ashes of John Grierson

Further information: The school at which Grierson's father was headmaster in Cambusbarron is now demolished. John Grierson opened the new Cambusbarron Primary School in Thomson Place in 1967 and his visit is commemorated by a plaque. One of the school houses is named after him and there is also a Grierson Crescent in the village.

A plaque was erected at the MacRoberts Arts Centre, Stirling, in 1996 celebrating Grierson's contribution to cinema.

Stirling

TUNES OF GLORY
Stirling Castle

- 1960 106m c Drama/War Hi Mark (UK)
- Alec Guinness (Lt. Col. Jock Sinclair), John Mills (Lt. col. Basil Barrow), Dennis Price (Maj. Charlie Scott), Susannah York (Morag Sinclair), John Fraser (Cpl. Piper Fraser), Allan Cuthbertson (Capt Eric Simpson), Kay Walsh (Mary), John Mackenzie (Pony Major), Gordon Jackson (Capt. Jimmy Cairns), Duncan Macrae (Pipe Maj. Maclean)
- p, Colin Lesslie; d, Ronald Neame; w, James Kennaway (based on his novel); ph, Arthur Ibbetson; ed, Anne V. Coates; m, Malcolm Arnold
- AAN Best Adapted Screenplay: James Kennaway

Tunes of Glory is based on James Kennaway's tale of two colonels at loggerheads with one another in a Highland regiment. When Lt. Colonel Jock Sinclair (Alec Guinness), an El Alamein veteran, and Lt. Colonel Basil Barrow (John Mills), a 'by the book' officer, are sent to knock the regiment into shape, their antagonism for each other ends in one going insane and the other committing suicide.

The Argyll and Sutherland Highlanders were initially willing to allow **Stirling Castle** to be used as a location for the film, but refused permission once they read the script on the grounds that the film would disgrace the regiment. The film was eventually shot at Shepperton Studios and at locations around Windsor Castle, but the film makers did get permission to use Stirling Castle as a back-drop so long as they made it unrecognizable. This was done using a 'matte' shot which completely distorted its appearance.

After the film was released and became successful, with an AAN for James Kennaway and a Best Actor Award at the 1960 Venice Film Festival for John Mills, the Argyll and Sutherland Highlanders requested permission to use it in their recruiting drive.

MONTY PYTHON AND THE HOLY GRAIL
Doune

- 1975 89m c Historical/Comedy Python (UK)
- Graham Chapman (King Arthur/Hiccoughing/Three-Headed Knight), John Cleese (Second Soldier with a Keen Interest in Birds/Large Man with Dead Body/Black Knight/Mr. Newt, a village Blacksmith Interested in Burning Witches/A Quite Extraordinarily Rude Frenchman/Tim the Wizard/Sir Lancelot), Terry Gilliam (Patsy, Arthur's Trusty Steed/The Green Knight/Soothsayer/Bridgekeeper/Sir Gawain, the First to be Killed by the Rabbit), Eric Idle (The Dead

*Arthur Jones of the Callander Pipe Band beneath the ramparts of **Doune Castle** at 'The Doune and Dunblane Fling', 1999*

Collector/Mr. Blint, a Village Ne'er-Do-Well Very Keen on Burning Witches/Sir Robin/The Guard Who Doesn't Hiccough but Tries to Get Things Straight/Concorde, Sir Lancelot's Trusty Steed/Roger the Shrubber, a shrubber/Broth), Neil Innes (The First Self Destructive Monk/Robin's Least Favourite Minstrel/The Page Crushed by a Rabbit/The Owner of a Duck), Terry Jones (Dennis's Mother/Sir Bedevere/Three-Headed Knight/Prince Herbert), Michael Palin (1st Soldier with a Keen Interest in Birds/Mr. Duck, a Village Carpenter Who is Almost Keener Than Anyone Else to Burn Witches/Three-Headed Knight/Sir Galahad/King of Swamp Castle/Brother Maynard's Roommate), Connie Booth (The Witch), Carol Cleveland (Zoot and Dingo), Bee Duffell (Old Crone to Whom King Arthur Said "Ni–")
p, Mark Forstater; d, Terry Gilliam, Terry Jones; w, Graham Chapman, John Cleese, Terry Gilliam, Eric Idle, Terry Jones, Michael Palin; ph, Terry Bedford; ed, John Hackney; m, Neil Innes, De Wolfe; prod d, Roy Smith

Guard 1: *What - a swallow carrying a coconut?*
Arthur: *It could grip it by the husk!*
Guard 1: *It's not a question of where he grips it! It's a simple question of weight ratios! A five ounce bird could not carry a one pound coconut.*

Any attempt to write a plot synopsis of a Monty Python movie would be futile. It must therefore suffice to say that the film is loosely based on the Arthurian legend of the Knights of the Round Table and their quest to find the cup of Christ - the Holy Grail.

Much of the film was shot on location in Scotland. The opening scenes where the horseless King Arthur (Graham Chapman) approaches a medieval fortress with his servant, Patsy (Terry Gilliam, who mimics the hooves of their pretend horses by clattering coconut shells together), was shot

at **Doune Castle**. Owned by Historic Scotland, this 14th-century courtyard castle was built for the Regent Albany, and includes a keep-gatehouse, the Lord's Hall and a musicians' gallery. It receives around 20,000 visitors a year. Approximately one fifth are Python fans, many of whom arrive with their own coconut shells and gallop around the Castle, while the staff smile politely, and try to look busy. Some fans have actually arrived at Doune straight from the airport, still with their luggage in tow. Video copies of the movie can be bought in the castle gift shop, but its distinct lack of customised coconut shells and stuffed swallows is tantamount to commercial suicide.

Other locations included **Sheriffmuir near Bridge of Allan, Arnhall Castle near Killin, Bracklinn Falls near Callander**, and the **Meeting of the Three Waters in Glencoe**, scene of the Bridge of Death. The final scenes were shot on and near the island fortress of **Castle Stalker, near Appin** (viewing by appointment only, Tel: 01631 730234).

See also: Michael Palin

Further information: Doune Castle is 8 miles south of Callander on the edge of Doune village, just off the A84. Open all year (Winter: closed Thursday afternoons, Fridays and Sunday mornings). Tel: 01786 841742.

Doune Castle was also used as a film location for the 1996 BBC production of *Ivanhoe*, starring Christopher Lee.

'The Doune & Dunblane Fling' takes place every May during Spring Bank Holiday weekend, combining activities such as music, song, dance, drama, crafts and storytelling at the castle.

West Dunbarton-shire

REGENERATION
Milton

- 105m c War Canada/UK
- Jonathan Pryce (Dr. William Rivers), James Wilby (Siegfried Sassoon), Jonny Lee Miller (Billy Prior), Stuart Bunce (Wilfred Owen)
p, Eric Coulter; d, Gillies MacKinnon; ph, Glen MacPherson; ed, Pia Di Ciaula, art d, John Frankish

Regeneration is based on Pat Barker's 1995 Booker Prize-winning novel about a real-life encounter between writer, Siegfried Sassoon, and army psychologist, W.H.R. Rivers, at Craiglockhart Hospital, Edinburgh, in 1917.

Overton House in the village of Milton, near Dumbarton, doubled for Craiglockhart and was built in 1859 by local businessman, James White. Formerly a maternity hospital and convalescence home, Overton was gifted to Dumbarton in 1939. Its grounds are open to the public. The original Craiglockhart Hospital is now part of **Napier University** at **219 Colinton Rd., Edinburgh**, and has changed considerably since WWI. The battlefield scenes were recreated at Airdrie in North Lanarkshire.

West Lothian

CHILDHOOD HOME OF MICHAEL CATON-JONES (1957-)
Broxburn

"It's a place about the size of Bellshill. Everyone works in the same industry. They all go to the same parties, the same restaurants and they all read about one another in the industry papers. Once you realize that, once you're there in the middle of it, you realize it's really no different from living in Broxburn."

Michael Caton-Jones on the similarities between Broxburn and Hollywood.

42 Aitken Orr Drive, Broxburn - childhood home of Michael Caton-Jones

Michael Jones, the son of a miner, was born in nearby **Uphall Station**, to Margaret and Aubrey Jones. His family moved to a council house at **42 Aitken Orr Drive**, **Broxburn** where he attended **St. Nicholas' Primary School** in **Power Station Road**, **Broxburn**, and **Bathgate's St. Mary's Academy** (now demolished). As a youngster, he delivered movie posters to the shops in Broxburn every week in exchange for free tickets to the local **Regal Cinema** (now a bingo hall) in **Greendykes Road**, but at that time had no inclination to work in the film industry. His only ambition as a boy was to play football for Celtic, but just as his talent was emerging an ankle injury dashed his hopes and he had to be contented with the local Grangemouth International Boys Club team.

He left school aged fifteen with no particular direction in life and after a period of dead-end jobs, including loading lorries and digging ditches, he ended up on the dole. When he was eighteen he moved to London where he lived in a squat. More odd jobs followed before he found work as a stage hand which eventually led him into the National Film and Television School at Beaconsfield.

He went on to win the European Film Students Awards for Best Film with his debut movie, *Liebe Mütter*. Now with a wife and child to support (Caton is his wife's maiden name), he was given the chance to direct the TV mini-series, *Brond*, adapted from Frederic Lindsay's psychological thriller. The success of *Brond* got him noticed and other projects were soon offered to him, including: *Scandal* (1989), *Memphis Belle* (1990), *Doc Hollywood* (1991), *This Boy's Life* (1993) and *Rob Roy* (1995). All were box-office successes and he now lives and works in Hollywood.

He refuses to be pigeon-holed as a Scottish director and when asked if he thought Scotland could ever sustain an independent film industry he commented: *"It's like expecting Scotland to win the World Cup. It's not going to happen."*

See also: *Memphis Belle*, *Rob Roy*

LINLITHGOW FILM SOCIETY
Linlithgow

"...the percentage of the population which could be be classified as cineaste/film buff is probably about 0.2 to 0.4%... given a large enough catchment you could probably get a society devoted exclusively to 'Underground Politically Correct Guatamalan Cinema Noir'.
Bob Henderson

Since the closure of the town's Regal Cinema in 1973, Linlithgow

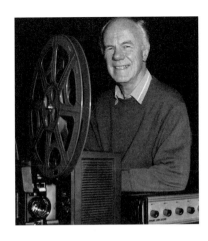

Bob Henderson

Film Society has screened the latest releases (with a sprinkling of art house) at the town's Burgh Halls. With membership at between 150 and 200, it also serves the surrounding community organising screenings at Day Centres, Sheltered Housing, Nursing Homes and schools. It has twice won the British Federation of Film Societies' national 'Community Development Award' and was recently awarded West Lothian Council's 'Art Organisation of the Year' award.

LFS's chairman of 25 years, Bob Henderson, recalls: *"What really causes ulcers is the audiences' reaction to your carefully chosen selection of films. We have to book well in advance and generally without having seen them, mainly on the strength of reviews, awards and Barry Norman's reactions. Our audiences can quite cheerfully disagree with all three!*

Mix-ups over reels are at the heart of most of our clangers. In 'Jeremiah Johnson' reel one ended with Robert Redford creeping through the woods to ambush sleeping Indians. Reel two started with bright sunshine, a desert and Peter Cushing being attacked by Kung-Fu warriors in 'The Legend of the Seven Golden Vampires'. Then there was the society's own version of 'Frankie and Johnny', a love story featuring Al Pacino and Michelle Pfeiffer, which came to a premature end after the final reel was put on mid-way through. The only comment came from a couple who had seen it before and said we had improved the film as the 'uncut' version had dragged in the middle. The highs however far outnumber the lows, giving us all a sense of achievement and satisfaction."

Further information: Linlithgow Film Society, Jenny Gilford, 81 Belsyde Court, Linlithgow, West Lothian EH49 7RL. Films are screened fortnightly from September to March.

Western Isles

WHISKY GALORE
Barra

• 1948 82m b/w Comedy Ealing Studios (UK)
• The English: Basil Radford (Capt. Waggett), Catherine Lacey (Mrs. Waggett), Bruce Seton (Sgt. Odd) The Islanders: Joan Greenwood (Peggy Macroon), Wylie Watson (Joseph Macroon), Gabrielle Blunt (Catriona Macroon), Gordon Jackson (George Campbell), James Robertson Justice (Dr. Maclaren), Duncan Macrae (Angus MacCormack), Compton Mackenzie (Capt. Buncher)
• p, Michael Balcon, Monja Danischewsky; d, Alexander Mackendrick; ph, Gerald Gibbs; w, Compton Mackenzie & Angus Mcphail; ed, Joseph Sterling; m, Ernest Irving

Whisky Galore is based on Compton Mackenzie's 1946 novel which in turn was inspired by actual events which occurred in 1941 when the 8,000 ton cargo ship, SS Politician, ran aground in treacherous seas in the Sound of

Eriskay, off the coast of Barra. Part of her cargo was a quarter of a million bottles of whisky.

Ealing bought the film rights and in the summer of 1948 the eighty strong location unit, the largest ever to leave a British studio, landed on the Hebridean Island of Barra. The film took fourteen weeks to shoot in foul weather and constant gales. The crew lived with local families who had no electricity and a generator had to be installed to power lights and cameras. The church in **Northbay** was turned into a studio and **Castlebay** hall was used to project the daily rushes. Compton Mackenzie, who suffered from sciatica, never went anywhere without an inflated car inner-tube, known as 'Compton's bum-ring', while his secretary (later his second wife), Chrissie Macsween, coached the cast with their island accents.

*Concealing the evidence - **Whisky Galore** (1948 Ealing)*

Although *Whisky Galore* is now considered a classic, it did not make much impact on its release after its West End premier at the Haymarket Gaumont on 16 June 1949. Unfortunately it entered the arena during the same week that *Kind Hearts and Coronets* was released and at the time that *Passport to Pimlico* was breaking box-office records. It is now,

however, regarded as one of the great Ealing comedies.

See also: Ealing Studios

Further information: Barra Tourist Information: 01871 810336. Castlebay Hotel: 01871 810223. There is no Youth Hostel and neither are there campsite facilities on Barra, but wild camping is allowed. Ferry crossings from Oban and Mallaig are app. 5hrs. in duration.

BENBECULA FILM CLUB
Sgoil Lionacleit

Situated in the Uists on the edge of the Atlantic with a population of around 6,000 people, Benbecula has never had a commercial cinema, but since 1998 it has been home to Britain's most westerly film society. One is tempted to imagine the traditional and idealised image of shawled Hebridean islanders sitting on their lobster creels watching films in a tin hut on a windswept beach. Nothing, however, could be further from the truth. In 1989 a new community secondary school opened at Sgoil Lionacleit, which includes a public library, swimming pool, sports facilities and a small theatre with a 16mm projection room and screen. Films are screened monthly during the summer and fortnightly in the winter by the Uist Arts Association. In the 1970's, 'Cinema Sgire' was a project run on the islands which involved documenting island life on video, and which led to the inaugural Celtic Film Festival being held in Benbecula.

Further information: Sgoil Lionacleit Community School, Benbecula, Western Isles HS7 5PJ. Contact: Helen McDonald 01870 602039.
www.taighchearsabhagh.org

WALES

Blaenau Gwent

THE PICTURE HOUSE PUB
Ebbw Vale

The original Picture House Cinema was demolished and a supermarket built on the site, which was subsequently converted into a pub in 1998. Movie stills, posters and photos of the old Picture House decorate its walls.

Further information: The Picture House, Market Street, Ebbw Vale. Tel: 01495 352382.

Bridgend

HOW GREEN WAS MY VALLEY
Gilfach Goch

John Ford's 1941 Oscar-winning masterpiece about a Welsh mining valley at the turn of the century was adapted from the 1939 best-selling novel by Richard Llewellyn.

How Green Was My Valley (1941, Twentieth Century Fox)

The film was a Hollywood studio production but the book's setting was based on **Gilfach Goch** in the **Rhonnda Valley**. Llewellyn was introduced to Gilfach Goch by the Griff brothers, natives of the village, who kept a Welsh bookshop in London and told him tales about the mining industry in their father's day. Gwilyn Morgan, the head of the family whose fortunes the novel depicts, was based on Joseph Griffiths.

The script was written by Philip Dunne, who was of Irish descent, but had never been to Wales, and was doubtful about undertaking the script. John Ford, a strong Irish nationalist, dispelled his doubts with the remark, *"Remember the Welsh are really Irishmen, only Protestants."* The award-winning script was written in fifteen weeks.

Richard Llewellyn's birth was not officially registered. His birth details were written in the family Bible which, together with members of his family, was destroyed by a V2 in 1944. He was reputedly born in **St. David's, Pembrokeshire** in 1905 or 1906 to William Llewellyn Lloyd, a hotelier, and Sarah Anne. His childhood details are sketchy as his father's job involved frequent moves around the country.

He enlisted in the army in 1926 and was posted to India and Hong Kong. He became a film reporter for 'Cinema Express' and later wrote a celebrated play, *Poison Pen*, which encouraged him to write his first novel, *How Green Was My Valley* (originally entitled *Slag*). The book was a tremendous success and was translated into twenty-one different languages, selling over ten million copies. He was married twice and died of a heart attack in Dublin in 1983.

See also: John Ford, Donald Crisp, Maureen O'Hara

Carmarthen-shire

MERLIN'S HILL
Carmarthen

The folklore connected to the Merlin legend is vast and sites linked to him can be found all over Britain. He was usually portrayed on screen as counsellor to King Arthur, but his name first appeared in *The History of the Kings of Britain* by Geoffrey of Monmouth in 1136 which places him in the middle of the fifth century when Vortgern was King of Britain.

Carmarthen is reputed to be his birthplace and the remnants of an old oak tree, known as Merlin's Oak, can be seen in **Carmarthen Musem, Abergwili**.

Three miles east of Carmarthen on the A40 is **Merlin's Hill** where he is said to have prophesied and was also the site of *The Crystal Cave* in Mary Stewart's Arthurian tale. **Merlin's Stone** stands in a field opposite the hill at **Tyllwyd Farm** and he prophesied that one day a raven would drink a man's blood from it.

The prophecy came true when a treasure-hunter digging beneath it was crushed to death when the stone collapsed on top of him.

Llyn y Fan Fach, a remote lake on the **Black Mountain** (now a reservoir) near **Myddfai** is the home of the Lady of the Lake in Welsh legend and the rock outcrop, **Craig-y-Ddinas**, near Pontneddfechan, Powys, is reputed to be the spot where Arthur drew *Excalibur* from the rock.

William V. Mong portrayed Merlin in a silent version of *A Connecticut Yankee In King Arthur's Court* in 1921 and Brandon Hurst and Murvyn Vye were cast as the wizard in subsequent remakes in 1931 and 1949. Other portrayals included John Laurie in *Siege of the Saxons* (1963), Mark Dignam in *Lancelot and Guinevere* (1963), Laurence Naismith in *Camelot* (1967), Ron Moody in *The Spaceman and King Arthur* (1979), Nicol Williamson in *Excalibur* (1981) and Karl Swenson was the voice of Merlin in Disney's animated feature, *The Sword in the Stone* (1963).

See also: King Arthur

Further information: Carmarthen TI: 01267 231557. Brecon TI: 01874 622485

Ceredigion

NATIONAL LIBRARY OF WALES SOUND AND MOVING IMAGE COLLECTION
Aberystwyth

The National Library of Wales started collecting audiovisual material relating to Wales in 1979 and now has available sound recordings, audio and video tapes, and films for library users.

The Library's film collection is administered by the Wales Film Archive. Printed catalogue and price list are availble on request.

Further information: National Library of Wales, Aberystwyth, Dyfed, SY24 5AE. Tel: 01970 623816. email: nlw@aber.ac.uk http://nlsvmss.aber.ac.uk/nlwhome.html

Flintshire

CHILDHOOD HOME OF EMLYN WILLIAMS (1905-87)
Glan-yr-Afon

*The White Lion Inn, Glan-yr-Afon - childhood home of **Emlyn Williams***

"...once, sitting with my father in the trap on his way down to Mostyn for beer, I asked him what that place was over the water, with all that sand? He said it was another country, where Welsh was not spoken and the public-houses were open on Sunday."
George, Emlyn Williams

Actor, playwright, screenwriter and director, George Emlyn Williams was born in **Mostyn**, on 26 November 1905, the eldest of three sons of Mary and Richard Williams. Shortly afterwards the family moved to **Glan-yr-Afon**, where his father became the new licensee of **The White Lion Inn**, known as Pen-y-Maes, which he describes in his 1961 autobiography as, *"A large slate-roofed white-washed box perched on a hillock, not picturesque, not ugly, it dominated Glanrafon..."* With his father working long hours and a mother who was emotionally distant, he was cared for by a live-in nurse and household help called Annie, who became a mother-figure to him. He started school at the age of four, where he was taught by nuns at the nearby **Talacre Convent**. In 1914 he moved to the new **Picton Council School** in **Trelogan**, and in 1916 he won a scholarship to **Holywell County School**. Here he met Miss Cooke, a teacher who recognised his academic potential, and was instrumental in encouraging him to study at Christ Church College, Oxford in 1923.

In 1927 he joined J.B. Fagan's repertory company and began writing and acting for the stage. He achieved success as a playwright with *A Murder Has Been Arranged* in 1930, and other works such as *Night Must Fall* (1935) and *The Corn is Green* (1938). He appeared in the West End and on Broadway, and made his film debut in *The Case of the Frightened Lady* (1932). His other film appearances included *The Citadel* (1938), *The*

Stars Look Down (1939), *Major Barbara* (1941), *Hatter's Castle* (1941), *The Last Days of Dolwyn* (1949), *The Deep Blue Sea* (1956), *The L-Shaped Room* (1962) and *David Copperfield* (1969).

See also: *The Citadel, The Stars Look Down*

Further information: The White Lion Inn is still a traditional country inn, serving meals and real ale, with photos of Emlyn hanging above the piano. It also has a beer garden, aviary and a sheltered garden leading down to the river. Tel: 01745 560280.

Gwynedd

THE INN OF THE SIXTH HAPPINESS
Nantmor

• 1958 158m c Drama
Twentieth Century Fox (US)
• Ingrid Bergman (Gladys Aylward), Kurt Jurgens (Eurasian Colonel), Robert Donat (Mandarin), Athene Sayler (Jenny Lawson)
• p, Buddy Adler; d, Mark Lawson; ph, Freddie A. Young; ed, Ernest Walter; w, Isobel Lennart; m, Malcolm Arnold

"In China there are five happinesses - wealth, longevity, good health, virtue and a perfect death in old age, but the sixth happiness you must find in your own heart."

Based on the book *The Small Woman*, by Alan Burgess, the film recounts the true story of missionary Gladys Aylward (1902-70) in Northern China during the Sino-Japanese war of the late 1920s. When working as a parlour maid, Gladys (Ingrid Bergman) becomes convinced that God wants to send her to China to become a missionary. Rejected by the

"This old man, he played one, he played knick knack on my drum ... " - Northern Wales doubles for the mountains of Northern China in **The Inn of the Sixth Happiness** *(1958, Twentieth Century Fox)*

See also: Gladys Aylward, Robert Donat

Further information: Gladys Aylward died in T'ai-pei, Taiwan in 1970, she is buried in a marble tomb in the garden of Christ's College, Tamshui, overlooking the sea and facing China. Porthmadog Tourist Information 01766 512981.

THE DRUM
Rhinog Fawr

• 1938 96m c Adventure/War Korda/London Films (UK)

• Sabu (Prince Azim), Raymond Massey (Prince Ghul), Valerie Hobson (Mrs. Carruthers), Roger Livesey (Capt. Carruthers), Desmond Tester (Bill Holder)

• p, Alexander Korda; d, Zoltan Korda; w, Arthur Wimperis, Patrick Kirwan, Hugh Gray (based on Lajos Biro's adaptation of the novel by A.E.W. Mason); ph, Georges Perinal, Osmond Borradaile, Robert Krasker, Christopher Challis, Geoffrey Unsworth; ed, William Hornbeck, Henry Cornelius; m, John Greenwood; prod d, Vincent Korda; fx, Edward Cohen

missionary society she makes her own way to Wangcheng where she aids Jenny Lawson (Athene Sayler) in running the 'Inn of the Sixth Happiness'. When the inn is bombed, Gladys leads over a hundred refugee children on a perilous journey to safety.

Political problems or unsatisfactory terrain excluded China or Formosa as a location but, by chance, photographs of North Wales were spotted which looked identical to the mountains of Northern China.

It was filmed in **Nantmor**, near **Beddgelert**, and close by in the **Ogwen Valley**. The hill behind Nantmor, **Cwm Bychan**, was the site of the walled city of Wangcheng which was constructed of great sheets of plaster casting from the studios at Boreham Wood, with a steep road made from railway sleepers up to its gates. A Chinese village was built on the terraces of the old copper mine just outside of Beddgelert and a

graveyard was created in the village of **Llanfrothen**. Locals were hired as extras for two guineas a day, and the children were bussed in from the Chinese community in Liverpool.

Gladys Aylward accused the film of shamefully glamourizing her life and referred to Ingrid Bergman as *"that wicked woman"*, a reference to Bergman's affair with Roberto Rosselini with whom she had a child out of wedlock. She also objected to the invented romance with the Eurasian Colonel (Kurt Jurgens), commenting, *"I never had a love affair in my life".*

Robert Donat was very ill during filming and had difficulty remembering his lines. A nurse with oxygen was always on call in his dressing room. It was later discovered that he had a brain tumour the size of a duck egg and cerebral thrombosis was certified as the primary cause of death on 9 June 1958.

Prince Azim (Sabu) in **The Drum** *(1938, Korda/London Films)*

Following Sabu's successful film debut in *The Elephant Boy* (1937), Alexander Korda searched around for another movie in which to cast his former stable boy star. *"It shall be a film for Sabu,"* said Korda. *"A film about India - and there must be a drum in it... I can see Sabu beating a drum..."* *

Adventure novelist, A.E.W. Mason was approached to write the story and was inspired by the legend of the Yudeni Drum in Durand's *The Making of a Frontier* in which a fairy drum brings good fortune as long as nobody looks at it when it beats from a high tower. Mason set his 'film-story' of treachery and murder on India's North-West frontier in the days of the Raj and shooting began at Denham Studios during the summer of 1937.

For the scenes depicting the arrival at Tokot, the battle after the attack on the Agency and the final parade, **Cwm Bychan**, up in the Snowdonia hills between **Harlech** and **Dolgelly** where the **Roman Steps** climb up to **Llyn Morwynion** were the chosen locations, selected by the Army as closely resembling the North-West Frontier.

See also: A.E.W. Mason, Valerie Hobson

Further information: Harlech Tourist Information 01766 780658

BIRTHPLACE OF T.E. LAWRENCE

Tremadog

Thomas Edward Lawrence, who achieved fame as the mystical guerrilla leader, Lawrence of Arabia, (better known to his family as 'Ned'), was born on the morning of 16th August 1888 at **'Gorsswysfa'**, a rented house on Tremadog's main street. The Lawrences moved to Kirkcudbright

Anthony Hopkins as the original Zorro, Don Diego de la Vega in The Mask of Zorro (1998, TriStar)

in Dumfries & Galloway thirteen months after he was born and young Thomas had no recollection of his birthplace. A plaque to the left of the front door marks his birthplace, which is the first house on the right coming from Porthmadog.

See also: Lawrence of Arabia Trail

Neath Port Talbot

BIRTHPLACE OF ANTHONY HOPKINS
Margam

77 Wern Road, Margam - birthplace of
Anthony Hopkins

Phillip Anthony Hopkins was born on New Year's Eve 1937, at his parents' three-bedroomed semi-detached house at **77 Wern Road, Margam**, near **Port Talbot**, the only child of Dick Hopkins, who was employed in his father's bakery business, and his wife, Muriel Frederick. He was a loner at school and never excelled. Packed off to boarding school aged twelve in an attempt to improve his academic performance, he surfaced five years later with only one O-level.

After appearing in the local YMCA Easter play he discovered his vocation and enrolled at Cardiff College of Music and Drama. Following his demob. from National Service in the Royal Artillery, he was accepted for RADA and later

auditioned successfully for the National Theatre.

He made his film debut in 1968 when he was cast as Richard the Lionheart in *The Lion in Winter*. His career however, was being constantly threatened by his addiction to alcohol and by frequent drinking bouts. In the mid-seventies after 'divine inspiration' he turned to Alcoholics Anonymous and made a fresh start. Since then his career has gone from strength to strength with films such as: *The Elephant Man* (1980), *The Bounty* (1984), *84 Charing Cross Road* (1986), *Silence of the Lambs* (1991 AA), *Howards End* (1992), *The Remains of the Day* (1993, AAN) and *Nixon* (1995, AAN).

The M4 gouged its way through the Vale of Glamorgan in the late sixties and the countryside around Margam now bears little resemblance to the unspoiled landscape of Anthony Hopkins' childhood, but 77 Wern Road still remains unscathed.

See also: *Howards End, Remains of the Day, The Elephant Man*

BIRTHPLACE OF RAY MILLAND (1905-86)
Neath

"I was born on a mountain called Cymla, above the town of Neath on the west coast of Wales..."
Ray Milland's romanticised description of his birthplace in his 1974 autobiography, *Wide-Eyed in Babylon*.

Reginald Alfred John Truscott-Jones, known as Reggie Jones, was born on 3 January 1908 at **66 Coronation Road** (changed to **Dalton Rd** in the 1980's) into a family of four children. He was educated at Gnoll Hall School, Neath and Cardiff's King School

66 Dalton Road (formerly Coronation Road) - birthplace of **Ray Milland**

(University College Cardiff). He worked in the local steel mills and later as a clerk for a shipping company in Tiger Bay.

When he was nineteen he joined the Household Cavalry before drifting into stage acting in the late 1920's. After a few minor roles in British films he left for Hollywood in 1930 and appeared in many B features before Columbia cast him as the male lead opposite Loretta Young in *The Doctor Takes a Wife* (1940). His greatest acting achievement was his Oscar-winning role as the compulsive alcoholic in *The Lost Weekend* (1945). Altogether he appeared in over 200 films, including, *Beau Geste* (1939), *Arise My Love* (1941), and *Dial M for Murder* (1954).

His name was taken from a plot of land close to his home called 'Mill Land'. For many years there was doubt about his original place of birth and, because of this doubt, a plaque is dedicated to him in the **Melincryddan Community Centre**, Neath. Recently, however, his eighty five year old sister, Enid Lewis, was found living in Surrey and revealed that he was born and raised at 66 Coronation Road. Married with one daughter and one son, he died of cancer in 1986, aged eighty one, in Torrance, California.

BIRTHPLACE OF RICHARD BURTON (1925-1984)
Pontrhydyfen

Richard Walter Jenkins was born on 10 November, 1925, the twelfth of thirteen children of Richard Jenkins, a miner, and Edith Thomas, at **No 2 Dan-y-bont**, **The Bends**. When he was only two years old his mother died and he was raised by his eldest sister, Cecilia, and her husband. He was educated at Eastern Primary School, Port Talbot, and Port Talbot Secondary School (now Dyffryn Comprehensive). He left school at fifteen, but rather than follow his father down the pit as was

Richard Burton *and Clint Eastwood in* Where Eagles Dare *(1969, MGM/Winkast)*

traditionally expected, he worked in the men's outfitting department at the local Co-op. He first experienced amateur dramatics at his local youth club and later joined the Air Training Corps where he met English teacher, theatre-lover and mentor, Philip Burton, who convinced him that education was his only escape route from the Welsh valleys. He returned to school in 1941 and after matriculating in 1943, changed his name legally to Burton.

He made his first professional stage appearance in 1944 as Glan in Emlyn William's play, *The Druids' Rest.*, and had many successes on the West End stage before making his film debut in *The Last Days of Dolwyn* in 1949. His first Hollywood film was Henry Koster's *My Cousin Rachel* (1952) and in 1958 he gave what is often considered to be his finest performance on screen as Jimmy Porter in *Look Back in Anger.* His portrayal of Mark Anthony in *Cleopatra* (1963) established him as a star, and his subsequent marriage to Elizabeth Taylor began a long and turbulent relationship which often overshadowed his career.

Critics had hailed him as a successor to Olivier and Gielgud

but he preferred the lure of Hollywood and a lavish lifestyle which, in the end, destroyed his promising career. He made many films, but with the exceptions of *Becket* (1964), *The Spy Who Came In From The Cold* (1965) and *Who's Afraid of Virginia Woolf?* (1966), most of them were forgettable.

Married five times, he died of a cerebral haemorrhage in Geneva on 5 August 1984, aged fifty-eight, and is buried in the graveyard of the Protestant Church in Celigny.

See also: Elizabeth Taylor, *The Spy Who Came in from the Cold*

Further information: Actor Ivor Emmanuel, best remembered for his portrayal of 'Private Owen' in *Zulu* (1964) was also born in Pontrhydyfen.

Newport

CHILDHOOD HOME OF DESMOND LLEWELYN (1914-)
Newport

"I hardly ever meet any Bond girls because I do all my scenes with

*No 2 Dan-y-bont, The Bends - birthplace of **Richard Burton***

Bond. It's very sad."
Desmond Llewelyn

Desmond Llewelyn will be best remembered in the cinema as "Q", the crotchety old boffin who designs James Bond's lethal gadgets, from folding sniper rifles to his specially adapted Aston Martin DB5.

He grew up in the **Malpas** district of Newport at **Blaen-y-Pant House, 76 Blaen-y-Pant Crescent**. After a typical upper middle-class childhood - *"I was more or less brought up by my nanny..."* - he was sent to boarding school in 1922, aged nine, and from there to Radley public school in Oxfordshire.

He joined the Royal Welsh Fusiliers during WWII and was taken prisoner just before Dunkirk. Interned in a PoW camp in Germany, he attempted to escape but was caught in a tunnel.

He began acting in rep. in 1936 and continued his acting career after the war. His first appearance as "Q" was in *From Russia With Love* (1963), and he has since appeared in 17 Bond films.

See also: Sean Connery

Pembrokeshire

UNDER MILK WOOD
Fishguard

"I don't know how you make a film of it. It's, as Dylan said, 'a play for voices'"
David Berry

Lower Town, the old harbour area of Fishguard, doubled for the fictional fishing village of Llareggub in Andrew Sinclair's 1972 adaptation of Dylan Thomas's radio play. Richard Burton played First Voice and Guide; Peter O'Toole the blind Captain Cat and Elizabeth Taylor the Captain's lost love, Rosie Probert.

Captain Cat's house was constructed on the quay and **Bear's Cave Cottage** doubled as the Sailors' Arms. The budget for the film was only £300,000 and was shot in just five days.

Llareggub (sounds funnier if read backwards) is often said to be inspired by **Laugharne** in **Dyfed**, where Dylan Thomas lived in the **Boat House, Cliff Walk**, but he always denied this. After a

turbulent life of wine, women and chronic alcoholism brought him an early death in New York, his body was returned to Laugharne Churchyard where his grave is marked by a wooden cross.

See also: Richard Burton, Elizabeth Taylor, Peter O'Toole

Powys

ZULU
Brecon

On 22 January 1879 the 24th Regiment (later the South Wales Borderers) fought two of the British Army's bloodiest colonial battles against South Africa's Zulu nation. The first was at Isandhlwana, which turned out to be Britain's worst defeat in the history of the colonial wars. 1,500 British and colonial troops, along with their African allies faced 24,000 Zulu warriors. In the open and vastly outnumbered, the Zulus outflanked the imperial forces on both sides with their lethal 'horns of the buffalo' tactic, killing 600 members of the 24th and six companies of the 2nd Warwickshire Regiment.

The defence of the nearby mission station at Rorke's Drift by 110 British troops, mostly from B Company, 2/24th, against 4,000 Zulus, resulted in the awarding of 11 Victoria Crosses, the highest number for any single engagement. The original buildings at Rorke's Drift have been reconstructed and include a museum. Close by are the graves of the 17 soldiers who fell.

The incident was immortalised in Cy Enfield's *Zulu* (1964), which took three months to film in the Drakensburg Mountains in Natal. Four thousand descendants of the original Zulu warriors were used

*Michael Caine as Lt. Gonville Bromhead in **Zulu** (1964, Paramount/Diamond)*

them that the actor would be along later. And Michael would show up, I'd introduce him and as he started to speak I could see them thinking, 'Oh God, I thought he was one of us!'"

The Regimental Museum in Brecon, formerly the old militia armoury, has been the Regiment's home for over 120 years. The Zulu War Room contains a fascinating display of memorabilia. **Brecon Cathedral** contains the Regimental Chapel. Here hangs the Colour, saved at Isandhlwana by Lts Mevill and Coghill, both posthumously awarded the Victoria Cross, and the Wreath of Immortelles which was placed by Queen Victoria in memory of the battle of Rorke's Drift.

See also: Michael Caine, Stanley Baker

Further information: The South Wales Borderers & Monmouthshire Regimental Museum of The Royal Regiment of Wales (24th / 41st Foot), The Barracks, Brecon, Powys, LD3 7EB. Tel: 01874 613275. Open: April - September 9.00am-5.00pm, Monday to Friday.

THE WINDSWEPT FILM SOCIETY
Elan Valley

Founded in 1997 by Bell Crewe and Daniel Butler, Windswept screens a programme of films during the winter months for the people of Rhayader at the **Elan Valley Hotel** (01597 810448) in the remote Cambrian Mountains. Weather conditions can be unbelievebly appalling - hence the name 'Windswept'. Their prime objective is to screen features which would otherwise be inaccessible for local people as the nearest commercial cinema is about an hour's drive away. Past programmes have included a mix of mainstream,

as extras and were led by the now prominent South African politician, Chief Mangosuthu Buthelezi. Unfamiliar with warfare and action movies, Cy Enfield had great difficulty trying to make the Zulus understand what was required of them on the battlefield. After they were shown an old Gene Autry western, however, they soon got the hang of it.

Michael Caine was originally intended to portray Private Hook but was later given the part of the gentleman officer, Lt Gonville Bromhead. Caine researched his part by lunching frequently with Guards officers in London and based much of his character on the Duke of Edinburgh. Cy Enfield recalls, *"After Zulu, Stanley Baker and I were courted by the upper-class military, and invited to the Army and Navy Club and to all sorts of soirees. They all liked the character of Bromhead and thought the actor who played him was 'marvellous, absolutely marvellous'. I got great pleasure from telling* classic, foreign and Welsh language features, including *On the Black Hill* which was based on Bruce Chatwin's Booker prize-winning novel and shot locally around Hay-on-Wye and in the Black Mountains.

Further information: The Windswept Film Society, Tan-y-Cefn, Nr Rhayader, Powys LD6 5PD. Tel: 01597 811168. http://www.butcrewe.demon.co.uk/windswept

Rhondda Cynon Taff

BIRTHPLACE OF STANLEY BAKER (1927-76)
Ferndale

Stanley Baker was born at **32 Albany Street** (plaque erected) in the mining town of Ferndale in the Rhondda valley. The son of a miner, his movie career stretches over 33 years and he appeared in over fifty films. As a child at **Ferndale Senior School for Boys, North Road** (now an infants' school), he was encouraged to take part in school productions and

32 Albany Street, Ferndale - birthplace of **Stanley Baker**

local dramas in churches and workingmen's halls.

The first review of his work was in the South Wales Echo when he was cast in his school play, *The Light,* aged thirteen. It reads: *"Stanley Baker gave a study that would have done credit to a far more mature actor and his name should be heard in the dramatic world."*

He made his screen debut at the early age of fourteen, when he successfully auditioned for the part of a boy patriot in Ealing Studios' 1943 drama, *Undercover,* about the Yugoslav resistance movement during WWII. In his early films he was often typecast as a working-class hard man and anti-hero, but he will be best remembered for his portrayal of officer Bennett in *The Cruel Sea* (1953), CPO Brown in *The Guns of Navarone* (1961) and in his greatest triumph, as engineer Lt. John Chard in *Zulu* (1964), which he also co-produced.

He died of lung cancer six weeks after receiving his knighthood, aged

forty-eight, at his home in Malaga. His ashes were scattered on top of Ferndale's **Llanwono Mountain** in a ceremony attended by 2,000 people, including his wife, former actress, Ellen Baker and his three children.

A plaque celebrating his contribution to the cinema was unveiled in the middle of parkland across the road from his birthplace in 1996.

See also: *The Cruel Sea, Zulu*

THE CITADEL
Treherbert

The Citadel is based on A.J. Cronin's semi-autobiographical novel of a young idealistic doctor's struggle in the Welsh mining valleys. He is slowly losing faith in his work because of the prejudice of the people he is trying to help; treating wealthy hypochondriacs in Harley Street seems easier and much more profitable. However, tragic circumstances propel him back to those who need him most.

Like many American directors - John Ford included - King Vidor interpreted the Welsh mining communities as a romantic, choir-singing fairy land, without really understanding or connecting with their culture. Vidor was 'astonished' when he saw miners returning to their homes after a day's work with black faces, *"not a particle of white skin could be seen."* *

Most of the film was shot at Denham Studios, including the mines, which were created on an immense sound stage. The opening scenes in the film were shot on location at **Treherbert**.

See also: A.J. Cronin, Robert Donat

NORTHERN IRELAND

Antrim

ORIGINS OF JOHN WAYNE

Randalstown

Robert Morrison, the great great grandfather of Marion Michael Morrison (John Wayne) hailed from Randalstown in County Antrim. Young Robert was a weaver by trade who was forced to flee Ulster in 1801 because of his involvement with the United Irishmen and their plotting against the British Crown. He emigrated to America where he became an elder of the Presbyterian Church and a Brigadier General in the Ohio Militia during the war of 1812.

John Wayne was born on 26 May 1907, at 224 South Second St., Winterset, Iowa, the first child of Mary and Clyde Morrison. His name was duly registered as Robert Michael. Shortly afterwards, his mother remembered that her only chance of inheriting money would be from a wealthy relative called Marion. In an attempt to curry favour, she renamed baby Robert,

Marion Michael Morrison - a name he was to hate for the rest of his life.

See also: John Ford, *The Quiet Man*

BIRTHPLACE OF VALERIE HOBSON (1917-98)

Larne

Valerie Babette Louise Hobson was born on 14 April 1917 in **Chain Memorial Road**, Larne, the daughter of a Royal Navy Commander who was serving on a minesweeper.

She was educated at St Augustine's Priory, London, and was taught ballet by Espinosa: *"These lessons were intended to 'give me grace', but were precious training for the stage, which I'd been heading for ever since I grabbed a bath towel and pretended to be the Queen of Sheba..."*

She was accepted for RADA, and made her stage debut at the age of fifteen, in *Orders Are Orders*, in which she was spotted by Oscar Hammerstein II who subsequently

Valerie Hobson in Kind Hearts and Coronets (1949, Ealing)

cast her in his production, *Ball at the Savoy*, at Drury Lane.

During this show she made her film debut in the thriller *Eyes of Fate* (1933). It was her performance in the screen adaptation of R.C. Sherriff's play, *Badger's Green* (1934), which led to a contract from Universal Pictures. In 1935, aged only seventeen, she left for Hollywood with her mother, but soon grew weary of her roles: *"I'd been there 18 months and learnt a great deal, but I was getting tired of horror pictures and doing nothing but scream and faint... In The Bride of Frankenstein, I was carried by Boris Karloff over almost every artificial hill in Hollywood."*

She returned to England in 1936 where she began to develop a reputation as a leading lady with a flair for comedy who personified dignity and class, most notably as Estella in David Lean's *Great Expectations* (1946) and as Edith D'Ascoyne in *Kind Hearts and Coronets* (1949). Her other films included *This Man is News* (1938), *The Drum* (1938), *This Man in Paris* (1939), *The Spy in Black* (1939), *Contraband* (1940), *Blanche Fury* (1947) and *Train of Events* (1949).

She married producer Anthony Havelock-Allan in 1939, with whom she had two sons. Their marriage was dissolved in 1952, and in 1954 she retired from the screen when she married MP John Profumo. She stood stoically behind her husband after he resigned from his post as Secretary of State for War following his involvement in the Christine Keeler sex scandal. She died in London on 15 November 1998.

See also: *Great Expectations, Kind Hearts and Coronets, The Drum,* Anthony Havelock-Allan.

Further information: Another interesting Larne connection is the actor Whitford Kane, who was born here in 1881. The son of a local doctor, he was educated at Larne Grammar School and the RBAI in Belfast, where he made his stage debut in 1900. He co-founded the Ulster Literary Theatre before emigrating to America and establishing himself as one of the great Shakesperian actors. He became great friends with Orson Welles, who, in 1940, was working on a script with Herman Mankiewicz. Mankiewicz wanted to

Citizen Kane (1941, RKO)

call the film *Citizen Craig*, but Welles disagreed. Kane had a better ring to it, suggested Welles, and named the film after his old friend from Larne. In Welles' next film, *The Magnificent Ambersons* (1942), he cast Kane as the newspaper editor, his first major Hollywood role.

Ards

TUDOR CINEMA
Comber

When Noel Spence's local cinema, the Tudor in nearby Bangor, closed down in 1962, he was heartbroken

and a void entered his world. Determined to recapture his lost dream-palace, he managed to salvage many of the original fittings and in 1974 he opened his own small cinema in a converted hen-house next to his home. The Tudor, named after its Bangor namesake, has red velvet and gold braid seats, 1930s doors, original double poster boards, carpets and curtains, and is reminiscent of a cinema museum. It seats 66, screening only sci-fi and horror movies from the fifties, Noel's favourite period.

For the past six years, a regular visitor has been Boris Karloff's only daughter Sara, who, surprisingly, saw most of her father's films for the first time at the Tudor.

In the cinema's early days Noel screened *The Sound of Music,* and was complimented on his wonderful stereo sound system by one lady in the audience: *"It felt like the sheep were all around me"*, she said. *"They were"*, replied Noel, *"I don't have a stereo system. They were real sheep in the field next door!"*

Further information: The Tudor Cinema, Drumhirk Rd, Comber, Co. Down BT23 5LY Tel: 01247 878589.

*Sara Karloff outside the **Tudor Cinema***

Ballymena

CHILDHOOD HOME OF LIAM NEESON (1952-)
Ballymena

"I've always found [it] particularly hard to comprehend this purported sexual magnetism... For donkey's years, Liam Neeson would walk down the High Street in Ballymena and no girl would bat an eyelid at him. He had all the allure of your average lamppost." *
Gerry McKeown, Neeson's former schoolteacher

William John Neeson was born on 7 June 1952, the third of four children and only son of school cook and janitor, Kitty and Barney Neeson, at the **Waveney Hospital, Cushendall Road** (since demolished). They lived in a small three-bedroom terraced house at **10 Corlea Gardens**, on the **Demesne Council Estate**. He was a sheepish, introverted child, who never rebelled, and became an altar boy at **All Saints Roman Catholic Church**. He attended boxing classes at the local All Saints Youth Club, in the Parochial Hall (since destroyed by fire) and eventually became Ulster Youth Heavyweight Champion for three successive years. He attended **All Saints' Boys' Primary School, Hugomount**, and in 1963, in his first year at **St. Patrick's High School, Broughshane Road**, he met English teacher, Gerry McKeown, who introduced him to drama.

In 1969 he joined McKeown's newly formed drama group called the Slemish Players, and in 1970 they competed at the Larne Drama Festival, where Liam carried off the Best Actor award. After finishing at school he attended **Ballymena Technical College, Trostan**

Liam Neeson *in the title role of Rob Roy (1995)*

Avenue (now know as the North-East Institute of Further & Higher Education), where he had ambitions to become a naval architect, and later moved on to **Queen's University, Belfast** (an experience he hated), to study maths and computer science.

His local pub in Ballymena was **Johnny Joe's (McCollam's Bar, Cushendall)**, named after the grandson of Nancy Joe who was the publican in 1908 and was reputed to have weighed 18 stone. Neeson soon dropped out of university and worked at various jobs, including those of fork-lift driver, truck driver and repro assistant in an architect's office. He attended teacher training college for a short time, before auditioning in 1975 for a production being staged at **Belfast's Lyric Theatre**. He got the job and stayed at the Lyric for two years before joining Dublin's prestigious **Abbey Theatre**. Here he was spotted by director John Boorman, who cast him in his first film role as Sir Gawain, in *Excalibur* (1981). During the filming he met Helen Mirren who persuaded him to leave the Abbey and concentrate on a film career.

Over the next few years his films included *The Bounty* (1984), *Lamb* (1985), *The Mission* (1986), *Darkman* (1990), *Shining Through* (1992) and Woody Allen's *Husbands and Wives* (1992).

In 1992, Steven Spielberg was impressed by his performance in a Broadway production of *Anna Christie*, and offered him the title role in *Schindler's List* (1993). His other films include *Nell* (1994), *Rob Roy* (1995), *Before and After* (1996), *Michael Collins* (1996) and *Les Misérables* (1998).

See also: *Rob Roy*, *Michael Collins*

Belfast

CHILDHOOD HOME OF KENNETH BRANAGH (1960-)

"Lacking the matinee idol looks of the young Olivier, his somewhat plebeian features (pug nose, weak chin, and slightly jowly countenance) brought an earthy reality to his roles..."
Baseline

Kenneth Branagh *as Iago in Othello*

Kenneth Charles Branagh was born on 10 December 1960, in Belfast, the second son of Frances Harper, a textile mill worker, and William

Branagh, a joiner. Shortly after his birth his family moved from Downview prefab estate to a three-up, three-down terraced house at **96 Mountcollyer Street**. In his 1989 autobiography, *Beginning*, he recalls his first visit to the street in eleven years: " *I was astonished at how small the houses seemed... The streets were tightly packed together... when it was time for our tea, my mum would simply stand on the front step and yell "Ken!", 'Bill!' - I could hear her streets away. I wish I'd inherited her projection.*"

In 1970 the 'troubles' prompted his family to leave Ireland and move to **Berkeley Avenue** in **Reading**, where he attended **Whiteknights County Primary School** and later, **Meadway Comprehensive**. He became stagestruck when he was sixteen years old after he was persuaded to take part in a school production of *Oh! What a Lovely War*. He soon joined an amateur drama group called the Progress Theatre and in 1979 was accepted for RADA. Theatre and TV work followed, and in 1983 he joined the Royal Shakespeare Company. In 1987 he co-founded the Renaissance Theatre Company. By the age of thirty he had become adept at acting, directing, producing and writing.

His first leading film role was in *A Month in the Country* (1987). Other films include *Henry V* (1989, director, adaptor, performer), *Dead Again* (1991, director, performer), *Peter's Friends* (1992, producer, director, performer), *Much Ado About Nothing* (1993, producer, director, screenwriter, performer), *Mary Shelley's Frankenstein* (1994, co-producer, performer) and *Othello* (1995, performer). He was married to actress Emma Thompson from 1989 to 1995.

See also: Mary Shelley

ODD MAN OUT

"Makes Hollywood chatter ridiculous and lifts our art and industry to a pinnacle. At the end there was silence. No clapping. No talking... A thousand people got up and walked out... Like zombies..."
Paul Holt, Daily Express

- 1947 116m bw Drama Two Cities (UK)
- James Mason (Johnny McQueen), Robert Newton (Lukey), Kathleen Ryan (Kathleen), Robert Beatty (Dennis), William Hartnell (Barman), F.J. McCormick (Shell), Cyril Cusack (Pat), Dan O'Herlihy (Nolan)
- p, Carol Reed; d, Carol Reed; w, F.L. Green, R.C. Sherriff (based on the novel by F.L. Green); ph, Robert Krasker; ed, Fergus McDonell
- AAN Best Film Editing

An IRA leader escapes from prison and masterminds an armed raid at a mill to fund his underground activities. During the robbery he is fatally wounded by a cashier whom he shoots dead. Alone, and bleeding to death, he staggers semi-conscious through the Belfast streets, and is given refuge by various characters along the way.

Inevitably his luck runs out, and he and his girlfriend are shot dead on the waterfront.

Odd Man Out was a landmark film of the British cinema. Director Carol Reed rarely equalled it again, and James Mason gave one of the best performances of his career as the wounded IRA rebel. Robert Krasker's graphic cinematography drenched the film in a poetic despair which passionately evoked the bleak and shadowy world of a dying fugitive.

Studio scenes took twenty weeks to shoot at Denham, finishing in January 1946. Shortly afterwards, location shooting started in Belfast and included **Shaftesbury Square, Boomer Street, Cupar Street** and **Queen's Square** - with the **Albert Clock** very prominent in the film. Although the exterior of **The Crown pub in Great Victoria Street** appears in the film (where Johnny McQueen found shelter in a booth and Lukey the artist brawled with the obsequious Shell), the interior was a studio set, faithfully reconstructed from original plans at Denham Studios. Location filming was also done in Shoreditch and Islington, where the Georgian

Johnny McQueen (James Mason) and Shell (F.J. McCormick) in **Odd Man Out** *(1947, Two Cities)*

and Victorian terraced houses resembled those of Belfast.

Six months after the film was completed, F.J. McCormick (real name Peter Judge) died aged fifty-six. His daughter, Marie, is convinced that his sudden death was linked to the scene in which Robert Newton tries to force him to reveal the hiding place of the fugitive by throttling him with his muffler. After the sixth take McCormick collapsed and was taken to hospital. Two weeks later, when it was thought he had recovered, he returned to the studio to finish the film. On his return to Dublin he was forced to withdraw from film and stage committments. His daughter is reported to have been advised by doctors that the damage sustained by her father on the film set had caused injuries to his neck and throat and had also created a pressure on the brain which increased during the ensuing months. He died on 24 April 1947.

See also: James Mason, Carol Reed, F.L. Green

HOME OF ERROL FLYNN'S FATHER

Professor Theodore Flynn lived on the **Stranmillis Road**, Belfast. Errol often visited his father who was an eminent Australian marine biologist and zoologist. He held a zoology seat at Queen's University from 1931 till 1948, and was a leading expert on the sex of whales. During WWII he acted as chief casualty officer for the Civil Defence Service in Belfast and was awarded the MBE in 1945. It was at the house in Stranmillis Road that Errol Flynn received a telegram from Jack Warner offering him the title role in *Captain Blood* (1935) - the film which would establish him as a star.

Down

CHILDHOOD HOME OF GREER GARSON (1903-96)
Castlewellan

"The Key to her career was that she was in the right place at the right time. If she was lucky, then so was MGM."
David Shipman

Eileen Evelyn Greer Garson always claimed she was born in Co. Down, in 1908, but researchers from Ulster University recently discovered she was born at **88 First Avenue,**

Manor Park, Essex, in 1903. *"I think she knew that American audiences would find Ireland more romantic than Essex, and some of her family did live there,"* said Michelle Morgan, a former research fellow at the university.

Her mother, Nina Greer, was a civil servant from Downpatrick who married George Garson, a newspaper foreign correspondent who died when his only child was one year old. Greer Garson's maternal grandparents lived in Castlewellan where her grandfather, David, was the local police sergeant. They lived in a large house called **The Rowans** (now Clarmont House) in **Clarmont Avenue**, where Garson and her mother returned frequently during her childhood for lengthy summer visits. A plaque to the Garson family was erected in the local Presbyterian Church and the family burial ground is at Drumee. *"I remember playing under blue skies in Co. Down and even today when I hear Irish music tears well up in my eyes,"* she once said.

After graduating from the University of London she worked with a London advertising company. In 1932 she joined the Birmingham Repertory Theatre. Two years later she was playing opposite Laurence Olivier in a West End production

*The Rowans, Castlewellan - childhood home of **Greer Garson***

called *The Golden Arrow*. The play flopped but led to other productions and, in 1937, she was spotted by the head of MGM, Louis B. Mayer, in a play called *Old Music*. He offered her a contract and Garson left for Hollywood where she languished for a year doing nothing because the studio did not know what to do with her. *"It was the most difficult and unhappiest year of my life,"* she said. *"I decided that once I was fortunate enough to get away from Hollywood, it would take wild horses to drag me back."*

Director Sam Wood offered her the part of Mrs Chipping in *Goodbye Mr Chips* (1939), which was to be filmed in England. Initially she refused the part thinking the role insubstantial. The film's success, however, introduced her to American audiences and secured her an Academy Award Nomination, the first of seven she would receive during her career. Returning to Hollywood she was cast opposite Robert Taylor in the lacklustre, *Remember?* (1939) and was reunited with Laurence Olivier for *Pride and Prejudice* (1940). When Norma Shearer refused to play the mother of a grown-up son in the title role of *Mrs Miniver* (1942), Garson was offered the part. This simple, if unrealistic story of an 'ordinary' family enduring Dunkirk and the Blitz, turned Garson into a top box office star and won her a Best Actress Oscar. Her acceptance speech lasted 45 minutes and new rules were later introduced to prevent it happening in the future. Winston Churchill commented that the film had done more for the British war effort than a flotilla of destroyers.

Her other films included: *Random Harvest* (1942), *Madame Curie* (1943), *Mrs Parkington* (1943), *The Valley of Indecision* (1945), *The Miniver Story* (1950) and *Julius Caesar* (1953). She virtually retired in 1955 and afterwards made only

Greer Garson as a child with her mother, Nina

occasional films, including: *The Singing Nun* (1966) and *The Happiest Millionaire* (1967).

She was married three times - to Abbot Slenson, actor Richard Ney, who played her son in Mrs Miniver, and finally, in 1949 to Texas oil millionaire, Buddy Fogelson, who died in 1987. Garson had a

pacemaker implanted after a heart attack in 1980. She died in a Dallas hospital where she had been for three years on 6 April 1996, aged ninety-two.

See also: Greer Garson (Newham), *Random Harvest*, *Goodbye Mr Chips*, James Hilton

REPUBLIC OF IRELAND

Clare

HEAR MY SONG
Doolin

• 1991 113m c Comedy/Drama
Limelight Ltd/Film Four
International/Windmill Lane
Productions/Vision Investments
(U.K./Ireland)
• Ned Beatty (Josef Locke), Adrian
Dunbar (Mickey O'Neill), Shirley Anne
Field (Cathleen Doyle), Tara Fitzgerald
(Nancy Doyle), William Hootkins (Mr.
X), Harold Berens (Benny Rose), David
McCallum (Jim Abbott), John Dair
(Derek), Stephen Marcus (Gordon),
Britta Smith (Kitty Ryan)
• p, Alison Owen; d, Peter Chelsom; w,
Peter Chelsom, Adrian Dunbar (from a
story by Chelsom); ph, Sue Gibson; ed,
Martin Walsh; m, John Altman; prod d,
Caroline Hanania; art d, Katharine
Naylor; cos, Lindy Hemming

Hear My Song is a gem of a
shaggy dog story inspired by the
life of Irish tenor, Josef Locke, who
was a fugitive from the Inland
Revenue for nine years until he
finally cleared his name of alleged

tax evasion. Liverpool nightclub
impresario, Mickey O'Neill (Adrian
Dunbar), always on the lookout for
'names' that will pull in the crowds,
books several imposters, including
Franc Cinatra (Joe Cuddy) and Mr.
X (William Hootkins), a Josef Locke
impersonator. Mickey's continual
conning of the public eventually
forces Heartly's to close and his
girlfriend to desert him. Down on
his luck, he resolves to track down
the real Joseph Locke, still in
hiding in Ireland, to persuade him
to return to Liverpool for a one-
night-stand.

The exterior scenes where Mickey
stumbles upon Locke and his
cronies drinking in an old tower
were shot at **O'Briens Tower** on
the **Cliffs of Moher**. This was also
the spot where Mickey was dangled
over the cliff edge on suspicion of
being a spy for the tax authorities.
The farm where Mickey unearths
Locke was at **Howth**, near Dublin.
Heartly's, the Liverpool nightclub,
run by the trickster impresario,
Mickey O'Neill (Adrian Dunbar) in
the film, was really Dublin's
Merrion Hall in Merrion Square.
Destroyed by fire six months after
the film was completed, only the

frontage remains, and it has since
been incorporated into the
Davenport Hotel.

The real Josef Locke was born Josef
McLaughlin at **Creggan Street**
(now redeveloped) opposite **St.
Eugene's Cathedral, Derry**, in
1917. His dad was a Bogside
butcher and cattle dealer with a
family of ten musical children.
Little Jo first sang in public aged
seven.

He eventually grew to six feet two
inches and joined the police force
where his singing was constantly in
demand at police functions and he
soon became known as 'The
Singing Bobby'. During WWII he
joined the Irish Guards and was
posted to North Africa and sang for
the troops at camp concerts.

After the war he decided to turn
professional and considered a
career in opera, but on the advice
of the famous Irish singer, John
McCormack (1884-1948), he
pursued a career in light
entertainment, changing his name
on the way. He became enormously
successful and performed at an
unprecedented nineteen summer

Shirley Anne Field as Cathleen Doyle with Ned Beatty as Josef Locke in **Hear My Song** *(photo Tom Collins)*

seasons at Blackpool. EMI signed him to their Columbia label and he released his first record in August, 1947. In the 1940s and 50s his earnings were £100,000 a year, with sell-out concerts around the world.

For nine years he was a fugitive from the British Inland Revenue until finally clearing his name. After his disappearance many impersonators toured the halls, including the mysterious 'Mr. X' whose role appears in the film. Josef Locke and his second wife, Carmel, lived in Co. Kildare, where he died in a nursing home in 1999.

Further information: The Cliffs of Moher are a favourite location for film-makers. John Ford shot scenes for *The Quiet Man* here in 1952, but they were later abandoned. Cliffs of Moher Visitors' Centre is app. 5 miles from Doolin. Tel: (353 65) 708 1565.

Cork

ASHES OF JOHN GRIERSON (1898-1972)
Kinsale

*And none will hear the postman's knock
Without a quickening of the heart,
For who can bear to feel himself forgotten?*
An extract from *Night Mail*, by W.H. Auden

John Grierson, founder of the British documentary movement, died of cancer on Saturday 19 February 1972, at the Forbes Fraser Hospital in Bath. He left very definite instructions for his funeral. He wished to be cremated with no one in attendance but the undertaker, no reading of the burial service, no musak, no memorial service and a delay in the announcement of his death for a few days.

Grierson had a soft spot for Cork and made frequent fishing trips on his boat, *Able Seaman,* which was moored in Kinsale harbour. His ashes, along with those of his brother, were taken out to sea aboard the *Able Seaman,* accompanied by a flotilla of Kinsale boats, and lowered into the ocean off the **Old Head of Kinsale**.

See also: John Grierson (Stirling)

MOBY DICK
Youghal

"Call me Ishmael"

Scenes for John Huston's 1956 version of Herman Melville's monumental and arduous 1851 novel about whaling in the early 1800s were shot in this small Cork fishing port. Youghal doubled as the whaling port of New Bedford, Massachusetts, and the frontage of the harbour houses were made to resemble New England. Gregory Peck portrayed the obsessed Captain Ahab and the often treacherous sea filming was shot off the north Pembrokeshire coast.

Dublin

GRAVE OF ERSKINE CHILDERS (1870-1922)

Erskine Childers was court-martialled and executed by firing squad for taking up arms against the Irish Free State. Before he became embroiled in Irish politics he wrote the classic spy novel, *The Riddle of the Sands* (1903). It was adapted for the screen in 1979 by Tony Maylam, who cast Simon

MacCorkindale and Michael York as the intrepid yachtsmen who unravel the Hun's invasion plans while sailing in the Frisian Islands. Childers actually wrote the book to alert Britain to the growing German menace and greatly influenced the father of the modern thriller, John Buchan. He is buried in **Glasnevin Cemetery, Finglas Road**, Dublin.

BIRTHPLACE OF RICHARD TODD (1919-)

Richard Andrew Palethorpe Todd was born on 11 June 1919, the only child of Marvilla Rose Agar-Daly and Andrew William Palethorpe Todd, an army surgeon, at **89 Lower Baggott Street**, Dublin. Born into a world of landowning farmers and landed gentry, he spent the first three years of his life in India when his father was posted there. On their return the family lived at the family's **Brecart Estate,** near the village of **Toome** in **County Antrim** and three years later moved to **Holsworthy, West Devon**, where his father ran a practice from their house at **The Elms**, opposite the local church. When he was twelve years of age he developed pericarditis, a serious

heart condition, which restricted his lifestyle for many years.

He first became interested in drama at school and in 1936 he joined the Italia Conti Stage School in Lambs Conduit St., Bloomsbury. He made his screen debut in 1937 in a half-hour cinema commercial for Cadbury's chocolate and in 1939 he became a founder member of the Dundee Repertory Theatre. During WWII he was one of the first men to parachute into Normandy with the 6th Airborne Division on D-Day. In 1948 he made his first film, *For Them That Trespass*, after signing a seven-year contract with the Associated British Pictures Corporation.

Often criticised for being wooden and predictable, he will be chiefly remembered for his Oscar-nominated performance as the doomed Scottish soldier in *The Hasty Heart* (1949), Walt Disney's *Robin Hood* (1952) and as Wing Cmdr. Guy Gibson - whom he closely resembled - in *The Dambusters* (1955). In 1993 he was a special guest at the 50th anniversary of the Dambuster raid, when 85,000 people attended the event in the Derwent Valley in Derbyshire.

See also: *The Dambusters*

GRAVE OF MICHAEL COLLINS (1890-1922)

The life and political career of this controversial Irish revolutionary was filmed by Neil Jordan in *Michael Collins* (1997), starring Liam Neeson in the title role. Collins fought in the Easter Rising in Dublin and was the founder and director of intelligence for the Irish Republican Army. He played a crucial part in the Anglo-Irish treaty of 1921 which established the Irish Free State. In the civil war that

*Liam Neeson in the title role of **Michael Collins** (1996, Evergreen/Geffen)*

Michael Collins

George Brent - *former dispatch rider for Michael Collins*

followed he was shot dead in an ambush, aged thirty-two, and is buried in **Glasnevin Cemetery**.

Locations for the film included **Dublin Castle** and **Grangegorman Hospital**, where the film-makers built a replica of the General Post Office and O'Connell Street, the largest set ever built in Ireland. The Collins address was shot in the village of **Rathdrum** in County Wicklow and the scenes at the Gaelic football match at the Carlisle ground in **Bray**.

Hollywood star, George Brent (1904-79), was born in **Shannonsbridge**, Ireland, and rode as a dispatch rider for Michael Collins. He was forced to flee the country because of his political activities during the 'troubles', and was smuggled aboard a ship bound for North America, where he became a leading man of the thirties and forties in films such as *Jezebel* (1938), *Dark Victory* (1939), *The Great Lie* (1941) and *The Spiral Staircase* (1946).

See also: Liam Neeson, Neil Jordan

MY LEFT FOOT

Locks in **Windsor Terrace, Portobello** (00353-1-4543391), was where director Jim Sheridan shot the disturbing restaurant scene in *My Left Foot* (1989) in which Doctor Eileen Cole (Fiona Shaw) informs a drunken Christy Brown (Daniel Day-Lewis) that she is soon to be married. Christy, whose love for her is returned only platonically, throws a tantrum on hearing this news and hauls the tablecloth from the table with his teeth. Threatened with having his whisky removed he responds: *'Touch it and I'll kick you in the only part of your anatomy that's animated.'*

***Locks Restaurant**, Windsor Terrace*

The final scene in the film where Christy and his future wife, nurse Mary Carr (Ruth McCabe) are on a hill overlooking Dublin, was shot on top of **Victoria Hill, Killiney**, Dublin.

See also: *My Left Foot* (Wicklow), Daniel Day Lewis, Christy Brown

THE COMMITMENTS

• 1991 120m c Drama/Musical Beacon Communications/First Film Co./Dirty Hands Productions/Sovereign Pictures (U.S./U.K.)
• Robert Arkins (Jimmy Rabbitte),

Michael Aherne (Steven Clifford), Angeline Ball (Imelda Quirke), Maria Doyle (Natalie Murphy), Dave Finnegan (Mickah Wallace), Bronagh Gallagher (Bernie McGloghlin), Felim Gormley (Dean Fay), Glen Hansard (Outspan Foster), Dick Massey (Billy Mooney), Johnny Murphy (Joey "The Lips" Fagan) • p, Roger Randall-Cutler, Lynda Myles; d, Alan Parker; w, Ian La-Frenais, Dick Clement, Roddy Doyle (from his novel); ph, Gale Tattersall; ed, Gerry Hambling • AAN Best Editing: Gerry Hambling

"The Irish are the blacks of Europe; Dubliners are the blacks of Ireland; and the Northsiders are the blacks of Dublin. So say it out loud: I'm black and I'm proud."

The Commitments is Alan Parker's tale about a motley crew of musicians and singers struggling to bring soul music to Dublin. Asked to manage a dire wedding band, maverick manager and philosopher Jimmy Rabbitte has other plans and places an ad in the local paper: *"Have you got soul? If so, the World's Hardest Working Band is looking for you."* After a series of hilarious auditions his vision of a

Director Alan Parker (fourth from left) directs members of the Commitments, (left to right) Bernie (Bronagh Gallagher), Imelda (Angeline Ball), Natalie (Maria Doyle), Outspan (Glen Hansard) and Deco (Andrew Strong, seated). Photo David Appleby.

Dublin

classic soul band begins to take shape. In reality Parker auditioned over 3,000 hopefuls before deciding on his final 12. All band members had to be able to play their own instruments and sing. No miming actors were used.

Roddy Doyle's original story was set in the imaginary Barrytown, based on Dublin's Kilbarrack estate where he once worked as a teacher. Parker used over forty different locations to create the book's working-class ghetto and in doing so produced the antithesis of picture-postcard Ireland.

The exterior of Joey "The Lips" Fagan's mother's house was shot in **Pembroke Road, Ballsbridge**, and the interiors and garden scenes were in **Gardiner Street**, opposite **St. Francis Xavier Church**. The market scenes where Jimmy Rabbitte sells his tapes and T-shirts were shot in **Sheriff Street**, near the docks.The room above **Ricardo's Snooker Hall**, a former cinema in **Lower Camden Street**, was used in the film as the rehearsal venue for the band and the hall downstairs was also used for a few scenes. The band's venues included the **Guide Hall, Synge Street** and the **Waterfront Rock Cafe** at **Sir John Rogerson's Quay** which was also the location for the Wilson Pickett limo scene. **The Olympic Ballroom, off Camden Street**, was where the band fall out in their dressing room after their successful gig, supposed to have been attended by Pickett.

Trinity College, Dublin

The Stag's Head, Dame Court, Dublin

*Julie Walters and Michael Caine in **Educating Rita** (1983, Acorn)*

EDUCATING RITA

• 1983 110m c Drama Acorn (UK)
• Michael Caine (Dr. Frank Bryant), Julie Walters (Rita), Michael Williams (Brian), Maureen Lipman (Trish), Jeananne Crowley (Julia), Malcolm Douglas (Denny), Godfrey Quigley (Rita's Father), Dearbhla Molloy (Elaine), Pat Daly (Bursar), Kim Fortune (Collins)
• p, Lewis Gilbert; d, Lewis Gilbert; w, Willy Russell (based on his play); ph, Frank Watts; ed, Garth Craven; m. David Hentschel; art d, Maurice Fowler
• AAN Best Actor: Michael Caine; AAN Best Actress: Julie Walters; AAN Best Adapted Screenplay: Willy Russell

'Life is such a rich and frantic form that I need drink to help me step delicately through it'
Dr. Frank Bryant (Michael Caine)

Twenty-six year old hairdresser, Rita, wants to escape her

predictable working-class existence and discover her real self. She enrolls at college for an open university literature course where she encounters drunken academic, Dr. Frank Bryant. Here her disillusioned tutor introduces her to the great works of literature and gradually her metamorphosis begins. Soon she is discoursing on the classics, attending summer school, dressing tastefully, going to the theatre and challenging Frank's philosophy on life. Rita not only passes her exams but restores Frank's faith in life.

Much of the filming took place in the grounds of **Trinity College**, including the **Exam Hall** and the **Graduates' Memorial Building** where Frank's study was located. Trinity College is open to the public and guided tours are available. Close to Trinity College is **The Stag's Head pub** (679 3701) in **Dame Court**, where Rita's mother wept during the sing-song, lamenting that there must be better songs to sing (the Dame Tavern opp. was used for the exterior). With its friendly banter and original period fittings, The Stag's Head has been used as a location in many feature films, including *December Bride* and scenes from *Michael Collins* which were eventually cut. With a mixed clientele of city people, students and detectives, cheerful repartee is guaranteed.

Other locations included **Dobbin's, 15 Stephen's Lane, off Mount Street** (676 4679), where Trish (Maureen Lipman) and Rita worked as waitresses; **Belfield campus of University College Dublin** which became Rita's summer school; Frank Bryant's house was in **Burlington Road**; Rita's sister's wedding was at the **Church of the Holy Family in Aughrim Street**; Trish and Rita shared a flat in **Crothwaite Park**; the disco where Frank searches for Rita was at the **Stillorgan Park Hotel**; the park

Christy Brown (Hugh O'Conor) makes his first successful attempt to communicate in My Left Foot (1989, Palace Pictures)

where Frank and Rita deliberate over William Blake was the **People's Gardens** in **Phoenix Park** and Frank departed for Australia from **Dublin Airport**.

See also: Michael Caine

BIRTHPLACE OF CHRISTY BROWN (1932 - 1981)

Christy Brown was born a victim of cerebral palsy. Unable to use his hands or to express himself he was diagnosed mentally defective at the age of five. His mother refused to accept the diagnosis and her belief in him was confirmed when one day he picked up a piece of chalk with his foot and copied the letter 'A' which she had drawn on the floor. In his autobiography, *My Left Foot*, he writes: *'That one letter...was my road to a new world, my key to mental freedom.'*

Daniel Day-Lewis won the best actor's Oscar for his portrayal of Christy Brown and Brenda Fricker won a 'Best Supporting Actress' Oscar for her portrayal of his mother in director Jim Sheridan's *My Left Foot* (1989) which was shot in and around Dublin.

In 1970 Christy Brown published his bestselling autobiographical novel, *Down All the Days*, recalling his frustrated Dublin childhood when the Brown family resided at **54 Stannaway Road, Crumlin.** The book was translated into fourteen languages. His other books include two volumes of poetry, *Of Snails and Skylarks* and *Background Music*. In 1972 he married his nurse, Mary Carr, and they lived together until his death in 1981.

See also: *My Left Foot*, Daniel Day-Lewis

BIRTHPLACE OF BARRY FITZGERALD (1888-1961) & ARTHUR SHIELDS (1896-1970)

Brothers William and Arthur Shields were born at **1 Walworth Road, Portobello.** The family soon moved to **12 Vernon Avenue, Clontarf**, where the brothers began their schooling at Green Lane National School and later at the Merchant Tailor's School. Arthur, whose nickname was 'Boss', joined the Abbey Theatre in 1914 eventually leaving for Hollywood in 1939 where his many credits

Barry Fitzgerald

*1 Walworth Road, Dublin - birthplace of **Barry Fitzgerald and Arthur Shields***

Barry Fitzgerald, a name he was to keep throughout his career.

In 1926 Sean O'Casey wrote the part of Fluther Good in *The Plough and the Stars* especially for him. The play caused riots in the theatre and Fitzgerald's home was besieged by armed men. Fortunately he did not return home that night. He toured America with the Abbey Players in the late 1920s and made his film debut in Alfred Hitchcock's British production of O'Casey's *Juno and the Paycock* (1930).

He was invited to the US in 1936 by John Ford to recreate his stage role in *The Plough and the Stars* (1936) and stayed on to become one of Hollywood's finest character actors, portraying likable Irish stereotypes, from rogues to priests, in roles such as Cocky in *The Long Voyage Home* (1940), in his Oscar-winning performance as Father Fitzgibbon in *Going My Way* (1944), as Judge Quincannon in *And Then There Were None* (1945) and as match-maker Michaeleen Flynn in *The Quiet Man* (1952).

Both brothers are buried beside each other in **Deans Grange Cemetery.**

See also: *The Quiet Man*

BIRTHPLACE OF REX INGRAM (1892-1950)

The son of a clergyman, Reginald Ingram Montgomery Hitchcock was born at **58 Grosvenor Square, Rathmines, 6** (plaque erected). He was educated at St. Columba's College, Rathfarnham, and studied for a law degree at Trinity College, Dublin, before cutting his studies short and emigrating to the U.S.A. in 1911. There he studied sculpture at the Yale School of Fine Arts while working as a clerk in the railroad depot at New Haven.

Rex Ingram

*58 Grosvenor Square, Dublin - birthplace of **Rex Ingram***

He later worked as an actor, set designer and writer with various studios, including the Edison company, Vitagraph and Fox before joining Universal as a director-writer-producer where his productions included: *Black Orchids* (1916), *Broken Fetters* (1916) and *The Flower of Doom* (1917).

During WWI he served as a second lieutenant with the Canadian Royal Flying Corps. After the war he joined Metro Pictures Corporation and won international recognition

included: *Drums Along the Mohawk* (1939), *The Long Voyage Home* (1940) and *The Keys of the Kingdom* (1944).

His brother Will also joined the Abbey Players as a part-time actor while keeping on his day job as a civil servant which he held on to until he was over forty, even when he was being billed as Ireland's greatest character actor. In order to keep his thespian pursuits a secret from his employers he adopted the stage name, Barry Fitzpatrick, but a printer's error reproduced it as directing screenwriter June Mathis' adaptation of the best-selling anti-war novel, *The Four Horsemen of the Apocalypse* (1921). The film's immense success not only established Ingram's reputation as one of the world's leading directors but was also instrumental in launching the unknown lead, Rodolfo Alfonzo Raffaele Pierre Philibert Guglielmi, better known as Rudolph Valentino, to stardom.

Ingram's other films included: *The Prisoner of Zenda* (1922), *Scaramouche* (1923), *The Arab* (1924) and *The Garden of Allah* (1927).

In 1925 he moved to France with his wife, actress Alice Terry, where they continued to make films from their own small studio in Nice. He retired in the early 1930s to Morocco for a time where he became a practising Mohammedan, finally returning to the US where he died in 1950.

See also: Michael Powell

BIRTHPLACE OF BRAM STOKER (1847-1912)

"...the master of a particularly lurid and creepy kind of fiction..." Extract from The London Times Obituary, 1912.

Abraham Stoker was born on November 8, 1847, at **15 Marino Crescent, Clontarf, 3**, (known as The Crescent) the third of seven children of Abraham Stoker, a Dublin Castle civil servant, and Charlotte Thornley. Born into a Protestant middle-class family, he was a sickly child who was not expected to live long, and remained bed-ridden until he was seven years old. Apart from admitting that his illness had passed, leaving him in good health, Stoker was strangely reluctant to elaborate on its cause. He was educated by his mother until he was twelve when he attended the Rev. Wood's school in Dublin's **Rutland Square (now Parnell Sq.).** In 1863 he attended **Trinity College** and later entered the civil service. He then studied law and was called to the Bar.

Fascinated by the theatre he became an unpaid theatre critic for the Dublin Evening Mail and during this time he lived at **39 Kildare Street** and later at **16 Harcourt Street**. His writing came to the notice of actor-manager, Sir Henry Irving in 1876 which led to Stoker becoming his secretary and managing London's Lyceum Theatre. He lived in Irving's shadow for rest of his life, an association which was to last thirty years.

In 1878 he married Florence Balcombe, his neighbour at **1 The Crescent** and former sweetheart of the young Oscar Wilde. They had one son, Noel, born in 1879.

Stoker wrote eighteen novels during his lifetime, including *Under the Sunset* (1881), *The Mystery of the Sea* (1902) and *The Lair of the White Worm* (1909), but he will be best remembered for *Dracula* (1897), his gothic horror story which inspired countless vampire movies and gave the cinema one of its greatest icons.

15 Marino Crescent, Dublin - birthplace of Bram Stoker

He died in London, fifteen years after Dracula was published, on an April evening in 1912, aged sixty-four, unaware of the world sensation *Dracula* would become. His death certificate lists the primary cause of death as 'locomotor ataxia', a tactful medical term for tertiary syphilis, which, according to his great nephew and biographer, Daniel Farson, he probably contracted from prostitutes after his wife spurned sex following the birth of her child.

The funeral took place at **Golders Green Crematorium** where his ashes lie in the **Eastern Columbarium**. In his will he left only £4,723.

See also: *Dracula*, The Dracula Trail, Christopher Lee, Hammer Studios, Peter Cushing

Further information: The Dublin Writers' Museum, 18 Parnell Square, Dublin 1. Tel: (353 1) 872 2077. In 1988 the Bram Stoker Archives were established in the Graduates' Memorial Building at Trinity College.

Dublin

FIRST PUBLIC FILM SHOW IN IRELAND

Films were first screened to the paying public in Ireland at **The Star of Erin Music Hall, Crampton Street** (off Dame Street, now site of Olympia Theatre), on 20 April 1896. The evening was not a great success, with only the pale images of prize-fighters and acrobats appearing faintly on the screen. Six months were to pass before the public would enjoy the thrill of a professional moving image when superior projection equipment was installed in October and a Lumière programme was screened which included the now legendary, *L'Arrivée d'un Train en Gare de la Ciotat.*

The Star of Erin Music Hall was owned by Dan Lowrey, an illiterate entertainer, showman and entrepreneur who was born in Roscrea, Co. Tipperary, in 1823. When he was six his family emigrated to Leeds, where his father found work in the textile mills. After a career as a music hall entertainer, and running a tavern in Liverpool, Dan returned to Ireland in the 1870s when he bought The Alhambra Music Hall in North Street, Belfast and in 1879 he opened The Star of Erin. Lowrey's other theatres included The Empire Theatre in Victoria Street, Belfast, and The Palace Theatre of Varieties in King Street, Cork. The Star of Erin Music Hall closed in 1897. Ireland's first Edison Kinetoscope Parlour opened in Dame Street in April, 1895.

THE VOLTA: IRELAND'S FIRST CINEMA

It comes as a surprise to many people to discover that Irish novelist, James Joyce, who revolutionised literature with his massive experimental novel, *Ulysses*, was also responsible for Ireland's first cinema, the Volta.

In 1909 Joyce was living in Trieste in Italy. One day a casual observation by his sister about Ireland's lack of cinemas set him thinking. Shortly afterwards he set up a meeting with four Trieste businessmen who had links with cinemas in the town and convinced them that Ireland was a land of cinematic opportunity, just waiting for its first cinema, and that Dublin was the place to build it. After signing a contract that would net him ten per cent of profits, Joyce set off for Dublin to track down a location. He found it in **Mary Street, off Sackville Street** (now O'Connell Street).

One of the Trieste businessmen, bicycle-shop retailer Francesco Novak, was chosen to run the cinema, together with an Italian projectionist and assorted Irish staff. The Volta opened on 20 December 1909 with a programme which included *Bewitched Castle*, *The First Paris Orphanage* and *The Tragic Story of Beatrice Cenci.* Admission was 6d, 4d and 2d with a continuous performance from 5pm to 10pm.

It soon became apparent, however, that Francesco Novak's bicycle-shop background did not qualify him to run a cinema and after seven months of screening mostly Italian films the Volta closed down and was sold to the Provincial Theatre Company.

See also: James Joyce, *Ulysses*

BIRTHPLACE OF JAMES JOYCE (1882-1941)

"History, Stephen said, is a nightmare from which I am trying to awake."
Ulysses

James Joyce was born on 2 February 1882, the eldest of eight children at **41 Brighton Square, Rathgar.** He was educated by Jesuits, and in 1904 he exiled himself from Ireland, eloping with

The Volta Cinema, *Mary Street, off Sackville Street (now O'Connell Street), Dublin*

Nora Barnacle. He lived with Nora for the rest of his life in various European cities, including Trieste, Paris and Zurich. In 1909 he returned to Dublin to establish Ireland's first cinema, the Volta, in **Mary Street**. He died in Zurich in 1941 and is buried beside Nora in Fluntern Cemetery above Zurich.

Adapting the works of James Joyce to the screen has always attracted more than the usual criticism for film-makers; much of his work could be described as unfilmable because of his experimental linguistic innovations and 'stream of consciousness' technique. However, undaunted film-makers and their films have included: Joseph Strick's *Ulysses* (1967) and *Portrait of the Artist as a Young Man* (1977), and Mary Ellen Bute's *Passages from James Joyce's Finnegans Wake* (1965).

See also: The Volta Cinema, *Ulysses*

Further information: The James Joyce Museum, Joyce Tower, Sandycove, Co Dublin. Tel: (353 1) 280 9265. Open April to October.

ULYSSES

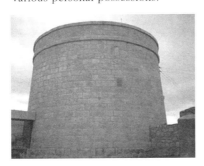

"Solemnly [Buck Mulligan] came forward and mounted the round gunrest. He faced about and blessed gravely thrice the tower, the surrounding country and the awaking mountains."
Ulysses

"Twenty-four hours in Dublin with a young poet and a Jewish newspaper man."
Leslie Halliwell

Any film maker who has the guts to tackle adapting James Joyce's *Ulysses* for the cinema deserves a medal for their pluck, no matter what the end product turns out to be. Joseph Strick's 1967 version, with Milo O'Shea and Barbara

Jefford portraying Leopold and Molly Bloom, was a creditable attempt to interpret Joyce's masterpiece in 140 minutes.

Filmed on location in Dublin, the opening scenes in the book and film take place at the top of the **Martello Tower** at **Sandycove** with *"stately, plump Buck Mulligan"* coming from the stairhead. Shaving in the open air, Mulligan is joined by Stephen Dedalus, whom he derides about his protracted mourning for his mother.

The Martello Tower was one of a series built in 1804 by the British Army for defence against a threatened invasion by Napoleon. Joyce stayed at the Tower in 1904, when it was the residence of his friend, Oliver St. John Gogarty. In 1962 it was opened by Sylvia Beach, publisher of *Ulysses*, as a James Joyce Museum. The Round Room, depicted in the opening chapter, has been reconstructed as it is described in the book. Other exhibits include first editions of Joyce's work, a deluxe copy of *Ulysses* illustrated by Matisse, and various personal possessions.

The Martello Tower, Sandycove

See also: James Joyce, Volta Cinema

Further information: The James Joyce Tower, Sandycove, Co. Dublin. Tel: (3531) 280 9265. Open: April to October

BIRTHPLACE OF MAUREEN O'HARA (1920-)

Maureen O'Hara in Malaga (1954)

"I was never petite, tiny, or cute, so there was never anything about me that would go out of style."

Irish redhead, Maureen Fitzsimons, was born on 17 August, 1920, at **32 Upper Beechwood Avenue**, one of six children of Marguerita Lilburn and Charlie Fitzsimons. Her father was a retail hatter, actor and singer who also owned 25% of the soccer team, Shamrock Rovers. Her mother was a former actress and operatic soprano. Their upper middle-class Catholic family was comfortably off, and able to afford acting, singing, dancing and elocution lessons for all the children. Maureen attended the Guild School of Music in London and joined the Abbey Theatre School in Dublin when she was fourteen.

In 1938 she went reluctantly to London with her mother for what turned out to be a disastrous screen test at Elstree Studios. *"They put me in this gold lamé gown with huge accordion pleats dangling from my arms, and they covered me with*

*32 Upper Beechwood Avenue, Dublin - birthplace of **Maureen O'Hara***

Mata Hari makeup...I thought, 'My God, get me back to the Abbey!'" Before leaving England an agent arranged an appointment with Charles Laughton, who was searching for an unknown to play opposite him in a forthcoming production. Laughton thought the screen test was terrible but was fascinated by her eyes. He changed her surname to O'Hara and signed her up for *Jamaica Inn* (1939) and *The Hunchback of Notre Dame* (1939). Before starting work on *Jamaica Inn*, she made her screen debut in *My Irish Molly* (1938) supporting child star, Binkie Stuart, followed by *Kicking the Moon Around* (1938).

She married George Hanley Brown, her dialogue director on *Jamaica Inn*, prior to sailing to America to make *The Hunchback of Notre Dame*, but the marriage was annulled shortly afterwards. In 1941 she married film director, Will Price, with whom she had a daughter, Bronwyn (named after the character played by Anna Lee

in *How Green Was My Valley*) in 1944.

She ultimately became one of Hollywood's leading ladies and became known as the 'Queen of Technicolour'. She made over fifty films, but will be best remembered for the classics: *How Green Was My Valley* (1941), *Miracle on 34th Street* (1947), *Sitting Pretty* (1948), *Rio Grande* (1950) and her favourite film, *The Quiet Man* (1952).

John Wayne became a lifelong friend of hers. *"We met through Ford,"* she said, *"and we hit it right off. I adored him, and he loved me. But we were never sweethearts. Never, ever."* She divorced Will Price in 1952 and in 1968 she married the aviator, Charlie Blair. After her retirement she became involved in her husband's Caribbean airline, Antilles Air Boats. Blair died in a plane crash in 1978, aged sixty-nine.

She won several awards for her charitable deeds, including the John F. Kennedy Memorial Award (1982) and the Variety Club 'Heart of Show Business Award'. In 1991 she successfully returned to the screen as John Candy's mother in *Only the Lonely*.

See also: *The Quiet Man, Jamaica Inn, How Green Was My Valley*

BIRTHPLACE OF GEORGE BERNARD SHAW (1856-1950)

"I don't want to talk grammar, I want to talk like a lady." Pygmalion

Shaw was initially reluctant to allow film adaptations of his plays after some turkeys over which he had no control, notably *How He Lied to Her Husband* (1930) and

Arms and the Man (1931). Hungarian producer-director, Gabriel Pascal eventually persuaded him to allow *Pygmalion* (1938) to be filmed, assuring him that no dialogue would be changed without consulting him, and Shaw insisted Wendy Hiller should portray Eliza Doolittle. The film was a great success and Shaw, plus screenwriters, Ian Dalrymple, Cecil Lewis and W.P. Lipscomb, were awarded an Oscar. Shaw was so convinced he had found the right man to produce film versions of his work, he gave Pascal permission to film all his plays and in the late 1940s they even considered setting up an Irish film studio. Pascal, however, only succeeded in filming three versions of Shaw plays before he died in 1954: *Major Barbara* (1941), *Caesar and Cleopatra* (1946) and *Androcles and the Lion* (1952).

*Leslie Howard and Wendy Hiller in **Pygmalion** (1938)*

Other film adaptations of Shaw's work included: *Saint Joan* (1957), *The Devil's Disciple* (1959) and the musical remake of *Pygmalion* - *My Fair Lady* (1964).

Shaw was born at **33 Synge Street** and described it as follows: *"It had in the basement, kitchen, servants'* *bedroom and pantry; the rez de chaussée, parlour (dining room), nursery and return room (my bedroom and my father's dressing room, over the pantry) and on the first (top) floor, drawing-room and best bedroom. . My sisters slept in the nursery when we grew out of it. We moved into* **1 Hatch Street**, *and after my mother went to London, I lived in lodgings with my father at* **61 Harcourt Street. Torca Cottage**, on **Dalkey Hill** *was our country house."*

Further information: The Shaw Birthplace: (353 1) 475 0854

BIRTHPLACE OF OSCAR WILDE (1854-1900)

"Anybody can be good in the country."
The Picture of Dorian Gray

Oscar Wilde's contribution to the cinema is profuse and many of his brilliantly witty comedies were adapted for the screen. He is perhaps more famous as a cause célèbre and for his homosexual affair with Lord Alfred Douglas, which resulted in a notorious trial in which he was charged with sodomy and perversion, resulting in two years' imprisonment.

Screen portrayals of Wilde have included: Robert Morley in *Oscar Wilde* (1960), Peter Finch in *The Trials of Oscar Wilde* (1960), John De Marco in *The Best House in London* (1969) and Stephen Fry in *Wilde* (1997). Other films of his work include: *The Canterville Ghost* (1944), *The Picture of Dorian Gray* (1945), *An Ideal Husband* (1948, 1999) and *The Importance of Being Earnest* (1952).

Oscar Fingal O'Flahertie Wills Wilde was born at **21 Westland Row**, one of three children of poetess Jane Francesca Elgee and

Peter Finch in **The Trials of Oscar Wilde** *(1960, Warwick/Viceroy)*

Sir William Wilde, an aural surgeon. A year later his family moved to **1 Merrion Square**. He attended school at Portora Royal School, Enniskillen and won a scholarship to **Trinity College** (he shared rooms with his brother Willie on the first floor of No.18 in the Botany Bay quadrangle). At Trinity he won a scholarship to Magdalen College, Oxford, where he was the leader of the *aesthetic* movement. Exiled to Europe after his imprisonment, he died in Paris in 1900.

THE SPY WHO CAME IN FROM THE COLD

"By this stage in Burton's life, masquerading as a seedy drunk was not exactly difficult; it was a lot harder for him to masquerade as anything else."
Christopher Tookey

John Le Carré's acclaimed spy novel, which explores the psychology of espionage, was filmed in 1965 by Martin Ritt at Shepperton and Ardmore Studios, Bray. Shot in semi-documentary style, Richard Burton gave one of

his rare memorable screen roles portraying Alec, an agent on his last mission, who is set up by his bosses. Claire Bloom portrayed Nan, whose love affair with Alec ends tragically when they are both gunned down escaping over the Berlin Wall.

Checkpoint Charlie, the infamous Cold War gateway in the wall, was reconstructed at **Smithfield Market**.

See also: Richard Burton

CINE MANIA

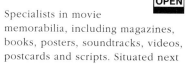

Specialists in movie memorabilia, including magazines, books, posters, soundtracks, videos, postcards and scripts. Situated next to the Irish Film Centre.

Further information: Cinemania, Eustace Street, Temple Bar, Dublin 2. Tel: (353 1) 670 3665

PLANET HOLLYWOOD

This Irish outpost of the American movie theme bar and restaurant chain opened in 1997 with seating for 350. Its three rooms contain a total of 20 large video screens showing trailers and music videos. The rooms are adorned with movie memorabilia such as James Bond's *Octopussy* rocket, Freddy Krueger's mask from *A Nightmare on Elm Street*, the suits from *Men in Black*, an anchor from *Speed 2*, Steven Segal's uniform from *Under Siege*, baskets and suitcases from *Titanic* and weaponry from *Braveheart*. 'Die Hard Daiquiris' and a cocktail called 'The Terminator' (Cointreau, Kalua, vodka, rum & gin) can be ordered at the bar.

See also: Planet Hollywood (Westminster & West Sussex)

Further information: Opening hours: Noon till midnight Monday to Thursday. Weekends noon until 1am. Planet Hollywood, 128-134 St. Stephen's Green, Dublin 2. Tel: (353 1) 478 7827.

IRISH FILM CENTRE

The Irish Film Centre opened in 1992 and is owned and managed by The Film Institute of Ireland. Housed in a restored 17th century Quaker Meeting House with a glass-roofed courtyard, the IFC is a popular meeting place for film fans, incorporating two cinemas, a bar and restaurant, a specialist film bookshop and library, and the Irish Film Archive.

The Archive has been based in the Centre since 1992, and contains collections of Irish and Irish-related material which can be freely accessed by members of the public. The collection dates from 1908 to the present day and includes advertising material, amateur films, documentaries, feature films, news and current affairs, science and educational films, shorts and travelogues. The archive also has a collection of stills, posters, scripts and correspondence relating to Irish film production.

Further information: Irish Film Centre, 6 Eustace Street, Temple Bar, Dublin 2, Republic of Ireland. Tel: (353 1) 679 5744.

Galway

BIRTHPLACE OF JOHN FEENEY: FATHER OF JOHN FORD
Spiddal

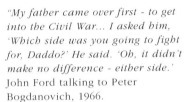

"My father came over first - to get into the Civil War... I asked him, 'Which side was you going to fight for, Daddo?' He said. 'Oh, it didn't make no difference - either side.'
John Ford talking to Peter Bogdanovich, 1966.

John Ford, the Irish-American director who gave the Western genre respectability and elevated it to the realm of the masterpiece, was born Sean Aloysius O'Fearna, in Cape Elizabeth, near Portland, Maine, USA, on 1 February 1895 to Irish immigrants, Barbara Curran and John Feeney. His father was born in a cottage on the Morris family's estate in the village of Spiddal, County Galway, in 1856. In 1872 he sailed for America where he worked as a saloon-keeper at his uncle's boarding house in Portland. Shortly afterwards he ran a saloon called Feeney's, an illegal speakeasy on the town's waterfront. The business prospered and in 1878 he met and married Barbara Curran. They had eleven children together of which John Ford was the tenth.

John Ford took his surname from his older thespian brother Francis, who adopted it after substituting for an actor billed as Ford who was too drunk to go on stage. His brother became a writer-director at Universal Studios in Hollywood where John joined him in 1913, serving his apprenticeship as a prop boy, stuntman, and bit part player. He eventually became assistant director to his brother and directed his first Western, *The Tornado*, in 1917.

In a career which lasted over fifty years John Ford never labelled himself as an artist, and once commented: *"Anybody can direct a picture once they know the fundamentals. Directing is not a mystery, it's not an art."*

He will be best remembered for his Westerns, including *The Iron Horse* (1924), *Stagecoach* (1939), *My Darling Clementine* (1946), *Fort Apache* (1948), *She Wore A Yellow Ribbon* (1949), *Rio Grande* (1950), *The Searchers* (1956), *The Horse Soldiers* (1959), and *The Man Who Shot Liberty Valance* (1962).

Many of his Westerns featured John Wayne with whom he remained associated throughout his life. He will also be remembered for exploring his Irish roots and was often accused of perpetuating the Irish stereotype in classics such as *The Quiet Man* (AA, 1952) and *The Informer* (AA, 1935) which is believed to hold the record for the most cuts made to any film by the British Board of Film Censors (129 in all) for its references to the Troubles.

Other classics included *The Grapes of Wrath* (AA, 1940) and *How Green Was My Valley* (AA, 1941). He co-directed *How the West Was Won* in 1962, the first film shot in Cinerama, and in 1973 he received the American Film Institute Life Achievement award. He visited Ireland several times during his life and shot *The Quiet Man* on location there in 1951. He died of cancer in 1973.

See also: *The Quiet Man, How Green Was My Valley,* John Wayne, *Man of Aran*

MAN OF ARAN
Aran Islands

Robert Flaherty's 1934 documentary masterpiece, *Man of Aran,* about a remote fishing community, was shot on location in The Aran Islands off the coast of Galway. Filmed over 18 months, 37 hours of film was shot for the final 76 minute film. Flaherty's depiction of man's struggle against nature, most notably in the storm and shark hunting scenes, won him the Grand Prix award at the 1934 Venice Film Festival.

Flaherty was born in Iron Mountain, Michigan on 16 February 1884 of Irish Protestant stock. His other work included *Nanook of the North* (1922), *Moana* (1926) and *Industrial Britain* (1933).

The Aran Islands were also the home of the ancestors of director John Ford's mother, Barbara Curran.

CHARLIE BYRNE'S BOOKSHOP
Galway

This bookshop houses a very large selection of second-hand film books, including hundreds of cinema-related US imports, in a comfortable atmosphere for browsing.

Further information: Charlie Byrne's Bookshop, The Cornerstore, Middle Street, Galway, Ireland. Tel: (353 9) 156 1766.

Kerry

RYAN'S DAUGHTER
Dingle Peninsula

- 1970 192m c Romance / War Faraway (UK)
- Robert Mitchum (Charles Shaughnessy), Sarah Miles (Rosy Ryan), Trevor Howard (Father Collins), Christopher Jones (Randolph Doryan), John Mills (Michael), Leo McKern (Tom Ryan), Barry Foster (Tim O'Leary)
- p, Anthony Havelock-Allan; d, David Lean; w, Robert Bolt; ph, Freddie Young; ed, Norman Savage; m, Maurice Jarre; prod d, Stephen Grimes; art d, Roy Walker; fx, Robert MacDonald; cos, Jocelyn Rickards
- AAN Best Actress: Sarah Miles; AA Best Supporting Actor: John Mills; AA Best Cinematography: Freddie Young; AAN Best Sound: Gordon K. McCallum, John Bramall

"They were great days in Dingle when there were beautiful film stars walking up and down the street

when I went to put out my bins." Landlady of the 'Kirrary' bed and breakfast *

Inspired by Gustave Flaubert's *Madame Bovary,* David Lean's Irish epic tells the story of publican's daughter Rosy Ryan's impotent marriage to a schoolteacher many years her senior, and her subsequent affair with a British officer in 1916. Much criticised on its release for being too long, overly romantic, and thin on plot, the critics could nonetheless not fault Freddie Young's breathtaking photography, which contains one of the greatest storm sequences ever filmed, and which rightly won him an Oscar.

Location filming took a year to complete because of the appalling weather on County Kerry's isolated **Dingle peninsula**. The village of Kirray was constructed on **Maoilinn na Ceathrun**, a hill near **Dunquin**. Little remains of Kirray today, other than a patch of cobbled street and some foundations, but the shell of the

*The village of Kirray - custom-built for **Ryan's Daughter***

schoolhouse still stands on the cliffs, about a mile from the site of the village. Two beaches were used on the peninsula - **Inch Strand**, on the south eastern coast of the peninsula, and **Coumeenoole Strand**, near Dunquin, which featured the road where the villagers salvaged the arms shipment and the rowing boat scene in which John Mills and Trevor Howard were almost drowned in rough seas. Other locations included **Barrow Strand**, near Tralee, and the **Bridges of Ross** near Ennis in County Clare where much of the storm scenes were shot over four to five months.

Robert Mitchum and his family lived exclusively at **Milltown House**, Dingle, for over a year during the filming. Mitchum, who drank heavily during the making of the film and didn't hit it off with Lean, once commented, *"Working for David Lean is like being made to build the Taj Mahal out of toothpicks."* He frequented many of the local watering holes in the area, including **O'Flaherty's, The Skellig Hotel, Ashe's Bar**, and **Kruger's Bar** at **Slea Head**, the most westerly bar in Europe. On one occasion he received a black eye in a fight with locals, making close-up shots impossible for weeks.

Ryan's Daughter brought considerable financial benefits to the Dingle community, employing locals and renting their houses at wages and rents far in excess of the going rate; so much so, that the film is often criticised for upsetting the local economy and increasing emigration. Over seventy percent of Dingle's population is now made up of incomers.

See also: David Lean, Anthony Havelock-Allan, Trevor Howard

Further information: Milltown House is now an Irish Tourist

Rosy Ryan (Sarah Miles) with her shell-shocked lover, Randolph Doryan (Christopher Jones) in **Ryan's Daughter**

Father Collins (Trevor Howard) and Michael (John Mills), the village idiot, in **Ryan's Daughter**

Milltown House

Board approved 4-star guest house, situated about 3km from Dingle, overlooking Dingle Harbour.
Tel: (353 66) 915 1372.
email: milltown@indigo.ie
http://indigo.ie/~milltown/
In March 1999 Dingle Peninsula Tourism hosted the 'Ryan's

Daughter Revisited Festival', a ten day event which included daily activities and tours connected to the film. Those interested in any future festivals should contact the Dingle Tourist Office, The Quay, Dingle, Co. Kerry. Tel: (353 66) 915 1188.

Limerick

KILMALLOCK FILM ARCHIVE
Kilmallock

John O'Leary has been collecting film and video material relating to Limerick since the early 1980s and his collection includes documentaries, newsreels, travelogues, trailers and feature films. Production notes, newspaper cuttings and stills can also be supplied. A catalogue is available on request.

Further information: Cullamus, Kilmallock, County Limerick, Republic of Ireland.
Tel: (353) 63-98910.

LIMERICK FILM ARCHIVE
Limerick City

The film archive at the Belltable Arts Centre was set up in 1992 by the centre's film officer, Declan McLoughlin. It contains film and video material of Irish interest with emphasis on Limerick and Clare counties. Recent acquisitions include the 1933 version of *The Lily of Killarney*, British Gaumont Newsreel of the *Shannon Airport Crash* in April 1948, and a very young Maureen O'Hara in her second film, *My Irish Molly* (1938). The archive also has a large collection of posters, stills, press packs, production notes and photographs, and memorabilia relating to Irish cinemas. It also houses a large reference library on Irish cinema. Run by a small dedicated group of volunteers, it welcomes film makers, researchers, students, and film buffs to access the collection. Viewing is by appointment only.

Further information: Limerick Film Archive, c/o Belltable Arts Centre, 69 O'Connell Street, Limerick City, Republic of Ireland. Tel: (353) 61-341435.

Mayo

THE QUIET MAN
Cong

• 1952 129m c Romance / Comedy
Argosy (U.S.)
• John Wayne (Sean Thornton), Maureen O'Hara (Mary Kate Danaher), Barry Fitzgerald (Michaeleen Flynn), Ward Bond (Father Peter Lonergan), Victor McLaglen (Red Will Danaher), Mildred Natwick (Mrs. Sarah Tillane), Francis Ford (Dan Tobin), Eileen Crowe (Mrs. Elizabeth Playfair), Arthur Shields (Rev. Cyril Playfair)
• p, Merian C. Cooper, John Ford, Michael Killanin (uncredited); d, John Ford; w, Frank S. Nugent, Richard Llewellyn (based on a story by Maurice Walsh); ph, Winton C. Hoch, Archie Stout (Technicolour); ed, Jack Murray; m, Victor Young; art d, Frank Hotaling; cos, Adele Palmer
• AAN Best Picture; AAN Best Supporting Actor: Victor McLaglen; AA Best Director: John Ford; AAN Best Screenplay: Frank S. Nugent; AA Best Color Cinematography; Winton Hoch, Archie Stout; AAN Best Art Direction-Set Decoration (Colour): Frank Hotaling, John McCarthy Jr., Charles Thompson; AAN Best Sound Recording: Daniel J. Bloomberg

"The Quiet Man he sate him down, and to himself did say,

Matchmaker Michaeleen Flynn (Barry Fitzgerald) and Mary Kate Danaher (Maureen O'Hara) in **The Quiet Man**

"I'll sit and look at Shannon's Mouth until my dying day: For Shannon Mouth and Ocean-blue are pleasant things to see, But Woman's mouth and sky-blue eye! - to hell with them!"
said he.
Maurice Walsh

Set in the 1920s, American boxer, Sean Thornton (John Wayne), turns his back on his harsh past after accidentally killing an opponent, and returns to his native Ireland to buy his birthplace - White O' Morn' cottage. Almost immediately he sees and falls in love with beautiful red-headed colleen, Mary Kate Danaher (Maureen O'Hara). The road to the altar, however, is a complicated one. Local custom requires the services of matchmaker, Michaeleen Flynn (Barry Fitzgerald), but Mary Kate's brother, Red Will (Victor McLaglen), is against the match and furious at a "dirty Yank" buying land he feels should be his by

right. They eventually marry, but Danaher refuses to hand over Mary Kate's dowry, and as a consequence their marriage hits the rocks. The inevitable showdown between Danaher and Thornton results in one of the greatest punch-ups ever recorded on film.

The 'Oirish' blarney in this movie is so thick you can cut it with a knife. In lesser hands this film could have become just another sentimental pot-boiler, but John Ford's Irish western is magical and eternal, and audiences never tire of watching it. The research for this book took me to many out of the way places, but I have never come across anywhere like Cong, the film's location base. After almost fifty years, it is still making a living from the spin-offs connected with this film. Besides visiting the film's locations, you can stay at The Quiet Man Tourist Hostel or The Quiet Man Holiday Cottages, visit The Quiet Man Heritage Cottage, have a snack in

Left to right: Francis Ford (John Ford's brother), John Wayne, Victor McLaglen, John Ford and Barry Fitzgerald

Shooting the scene where Maureen O'Hara is tending sheep at the start of the film

John Wayne and Maureen O'Hara with local extras

Sean Thornton and Mary Kate Danaher's marriage hits the rocks

The Quiet Man Coffee Shop, and purchase Quiet Man souvenirs from Pat Cohan's Bar. It sounds over the top, but it isn't, as Cong's enthusiasm is very laid back, and the village has changed little since the film was shot there.

Location filming took place during the summer of 1951, and it was John Ford's friend, Lord Killanin, who tracked down most of the locations, settling on the area around Cong because the nearby **Ashford Castle Hotel** (00353 9246003) could accommodate the cast in relative luxury. Victor McLaglen, however, was driven every night to the **Imperial Hotel** (00353 9324188) in **Tuam**, because it was the only place he could get a decent steak. Cong doubled for both Innisfree and Castletown.

MAP KEY:

1. Pat Cohan's Bar: Originally a grocery store, it was given the outward appearance of a bar for the movie. The interiors were shot in the studio. The bar appears frequently in the film, most memorably during the fight scenes, when Thornton and Danaher break off for a drink.

Today it is a gift shop selling Quiet Man souvenirs, run by Jack Murphy, who was a driver and extra in the film's fight scene. The Market Cross opposite also appeared in the film.

2. Rev. Playfair's House: Where Sean and Mary Kate took the tandem to escape matchmaker Michaeleen, and it also appears in scenes with the Bishop. Interiors were shot in the studio. Not open to the public.

3. The Riverside Fight Scene: Where Danaher fights Thornton and ends up in the river. Shot on the banks of the River Cong in the grounds of Cong Abbey.

Ballyglunin Railway Station

The ruins of 'White of Morn' Cottage

The humpback bridge near the village of Oughterard from where Sean first saw 'White of Morn' Cottage

A confrontation at Pat Cohan's Bar between Sean Thornton and Red Will Danaher

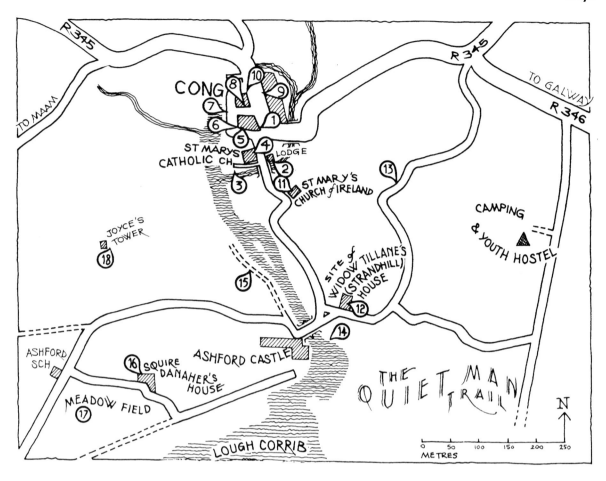

4. St. Mary's Catholic Church:
Now horrendously modernised, the interior of the church was used in the film, mainly because of its beautiful Harry Clarke window, which has since been moved from its original location. During filming the church's water font was removed and left at the Protestant church by mistake, causing a local outcry.

5. The Quiet Man Holiday Cottages: For reservations Tel: 00353 9246089 Fax: 00353 9246448. These are also the contact numbers for The Quiet Man Tourist Hostel.

6. The Quiet Man Heritage Cottage: A replica of White O' Morn' cottage, this visitors' centre comes complete with four poster bed, thatched roof, emerald green

half door and a whitewashed exterior. Souvenirs on sale.

7. Courting & Cheering Bishop Scenes: Circular Road was the street where Danaher and the Widow Tillane began their official courting, accompanied by Michaeleen who warns, *"No patty fingers if you please, hold onto your hats."* It was also the location where Father Lonbergan (Ward Bond) asks his congregation to *"cheer like Protestants"* at the Bishop's passing car.

8. Dying Man's House: The third house on the left in Riverview Street, going towards Ryan's Hotel, was the house where Dan Tobin is given the last rites, and miraculously revives when he hears the fight scene going by outside.

9. Curran's Pub: Now Ryan's Hotel, this was the scene of Danaher's sheep sale at Castletown.

10. Emily O'Connor's: Mary Kate and Sean quarrel about money outside this craft shop on the day of the Castletown Fair, and Sean ends up walking home.

11. St. Mary's Church of Ireland: Situated inside the grounds of Ashford Castle, St. Mary's was used for the exteriors of Innisfree Catholic Church. The pillar to the left of the entrance gates, leaving the church, was the one Mary Kate peered round to stare at Sean Thornton before taking off on her bicycle down the path on the left.

12. Site of The Widow Tillane's House: The two storey

whitewashed house that belonged to the richest woman in Innisfree, Widow Tillane (Mildred Natwick), has since been demolished. The site is now á car park.

13. Where Sean Thornton First Sees Mary Kate: There was no golf course here at the time of filming and this area was just a wooded field. The site where Mary Kate herded her sheep through the trees would have been on the third fairway.

14. Opening Titles: Stand on Ashford Castle pier and look downstream. The two concrete pillars was the camera location for the opening credits, with Ashford Castle in the background.

15. Fishing Scenes: This was where Father Lonergan fished, and where the curate informed him of Danaher and Thornton's fight. Sean and Mary Kate also walked along this path during the courting scenes with Michaeleen bringing up the rear.

16. Squire Danaher's House: Ashford Estate farmhouse was the home of Mary Kate and Will Danaher, and where Sean requests Mary Kate's hand in marriage. Not open to the public.

17. The Big Fight: Meadow Field was where the epic fight started, when Sean drags Mary Kate across the field, and throws her at Danaher's feet.

18. Joyce's Tower: Sean rode his black hunter past this tower in the days following Danaher's refusal to sanction his marriage to Mary Kate.

Other locations included: **Ross Errilly Friary**, Headford, which was used in the courting scenes during the storm; **Ballyglunin Station**, between Athenry and Tuam, doubled for Castletown Station, where Sean first arrives and

Pat Cohan's - the bar that never was

where he later drags Mary Kate from the train; **Thoor Ballylee**, near Ardrahan, was where Mary Kate removed her stockings to cross the river during the courting scene; **White O' Morn' Cottage**, Sean's birthplace, was Teernakill, near Maam Bridge, and is now a ruin. To get there turn left at Keanes Bar in Maam Bridge, heading for Maam Cross. Soon you'll come to a bridge over the Failmore River. The cottage is 100 metres on your right; the humpback bridge from where Sean first saw the cottage is near the village of **Oughterard**; **Lettergesh Beach**, near Tully Cross, was where the race meeting was held. Turn right at Tully Cross, go through Gowlaun, and the beach is beside the camping and caravan park; **Clifden** doubled for parts of Castletown in the scene in which Mary Kate journeys to the fair, passing an Ivy Lodge and Clifden Jail; **The Red Bridge**, Kylemore Abbey, near Letterfrack, was crossed by Sean and Mary Kate on their way to the fair.

See also: Maureen O'Hara, Barry Fitzgerald, Arthur Shields, John Ford, Origins of John Wayne

Further information: Cong Tourist Information (353) 92-46542.

Meath

BRAVEHEART
Trim

*James Cosmo as Campbell in **Braveheart** (1995, Icon/Ladd Co/Marquis Films)*

• 1995 177m c Historical/Drama Icon Productions/The Ladd Co./Marquis film/Paramount (U.S.)

• Mel Gibson (William Wallace), Sophie Marceau (Princess Isabelle), Patrick McGoohan (Longshanks - King Edward I), Catherine McCormack (Murron), Angus McFadyen (Robert the Bruce)

• p, Mel Gibson, Alan Ladd, Jr., Bruce Davey; d, Mel Gibson; w, Randall Wallace; ph, John Toll; ed, Steven Rosenblum; m, James Horner; art d, Dan Dorrance; cos, Charles Knode

• AA Best Picture; AA Best Director; AA Best Cinematography; AA Best Makeup; AA Best Sound Effects

Scottish nationalist, William Wallace, led his revolt against the English in 1297 and fought his greatest battles near the Scottish towns of Stirling and Falkirk. In the 1990s, tax incentives and the offer of the Irish army to the film-makers guaranteed these battles would be restaged in Ireland. Only the early medieval village and fort scenes were shot in Scotland.

Trim Castle on the banks of the River Boyne doubled as York and London. The York scenes were shot from one side, and London from the other. The largest Anglo-Norman castle in Ireland, Trim Castle was first built as a wooden structure in 1172. Swift justice was carried out here in the past and in 1971 ten headless skeletons were unearthed. Its ruined stone towers and walls were recently used as the setting for a *Braveheart* pilot TV series. The ruins of twelfth century **Bective Abbey**, near the village of Bective, seven miles north-east of Trim, was also used as a location. **Dunsoghly Castle**, near Dublin, doubled as Edinburgh Castle. The **Curragh Plains, near Kildare, Co. Kildare**, was the location for the Battle of Stirling Bridge and nearby **Ballymore Eustace** the setting for the Battle of Falkirk.

See also: *Braveheart* (Highland)

Jane (**Maureen O'Sullivan**) and Tarzan (Johnny Weissmuller)

Roscommon

BIRTHPLACE OF MAUREEN O'SULLIVAN (1911-98)
Boyle

"I have lived in a great many places but the best part of me I owe to Boyle. Its influence, Lough Key, the countryside, has given me whatever poetry is in my soul, whatever love I have of God. Whatever it is, it comes from here."
Maureen O'Sullivan

Maureen O'Sullivan was born in **Main Street**, Boyle on 17 May 1911, in a house which is now **Brendan Sheerin's Bicycle Shop**. Her father was an officer in the Connacht Rangers, who were stationed in Boyle, just a few yards from her birthplace. Her mother

was a member of the Frazer family who lived nearby and were of Scottish descent.

During WWI her father was wounded and invalided out of the army. The family then moved to **Riversdale House** in **Knockvicar, Boyle**. At the age of seven or eight her family moved to Dublin. She was educated at the Convent of the Sacred Heart in Roehampton (where one of her classmates was Vivien Leigh) and a finishing school in Paris, returning to Dublin in the late 1920s.

She was discovered by Hollywood director, Frank Borzage at a dinner-dance at Dublin's International Horse Show. Borzage asked a waiter to pass her a note: *"If you are interested in being in a film, come to my office tomorrow at 11am."*

*Brendan Sheerin's Bicycle Shop, Main Street, Boyle - birthplace of **Maureen O'Sullivan***

She made her screen debut, aged nineteen, with Irish tenor John McCormack, in *Song O' My Heart* (1930) and in 1932 MGM cast her in the role for which she will be best remembered - Jane, in *Tarzan the Ape Man* (1932) with co-star and ex-Olympic swimming champion, Johnny Weissmuller. She made five more *Tarzan* films, culminating in *Tarzan's New York Adventure* (1942). The second film, *Tarzan and His Mate* (1934) was of a higher calibre than the rest of the series but caused an uproar with thousands of women complaining to the studio about Jane's scanty garments. A nude swimming scene was cut from the film, but was later restored on the video version. *"Everyone cared about the Tarzan pictures,"* said O'Sullivan, *"and we all gave of our best. They weren't quickies - it often took a year took make one."*

During the filming of *Tarzan Escapes* (1936), often considered the most violent Tarzan movie, she met her future husband, director John Farrow. Their marriage lasted twenty-seven years until Farrow's death in 1963. They had seven children, including their eldest daughter Maria, who became the actress Mia Farrow. Her son Michael died in a plane crash in the fifties, aged nineteen.

Maureen O'Sullivan was cast in over forty films by MGM including: *The Barretts of Wimpole Street* (1934),

David Copperfield (1935), *Anna Karenina* (1935), *Devil Doll* (1936), *A Day at the Races* (1937), *A Yank at Oxford* (1938) and *Pride and Prejudice* (1940). After her last *Tarzan* film in 1942 she raised her family for six years before returning to the screen in 1948 in John Farrow's, *The Big Clock.*

After her husband died in 1963 she became more involved with theatre and television work. She later appeared in a few feature roles, including that of Hannah's drunken mother in Woody Allen's *Hannah and Her Sisters* (1986) and as Elisabeth Alvorg in Francis Coppola's *Peggy Sue Got Married* (1986).

In the late sixties she fell in love with actor Robert Ryan, but he died in 1973 before they could be married. In 1983 she married building contractor, James Cushing, and on 7 August 1988, Maureen O'Sullivan returned to Boyle with Cushing where she unveiled a plaque outside her birthplace. She died on 22 June 1998, at Scottsdale Memorial Hospital near Phoenix, Arizona, aged eighty-seven, but will always be remembered as the definitive Jane.

Further information: Riversdale House is now a guest house (open April - September), 4km off N4 between Carrick and Boyle. Tel: (353) 79-67012 / Fax: (353) 79-67288.

Cheeta the chimpanzee, comic relief and veteran of seventeen Tarzan movies, including the early O'Sullivan and Weissmuller classics, was still alive and enjoying the occasional cigar, aged sixty-one in 1998 and living with his owner, Dan Westfall at Casa de Cheeta, Palm Springs, California. His body will be freeze-dried and donated to a museum when he dies.

Sligo

BIRTHPLACE OF NEIL JORDAN (1951-)
Rosses Point

*Melrose Cottage, Rosses Point - birthplace of **Neil Jordan***

"I think art is a dangerous activity, and once you begin to toy with it you get into an area and you don't know where it'll lead you."
Neil Jordan, *In Dublin*, 29.4.1982

The son of a schoolteacher, writer-director, Neil Jordan was born at **Melrose Cottage** on the seafront at **Rosses Point**, near Sligo. He became obsessed with the movies when he saw *The Seventh Seal* and *La Strada*, at college in the sixties. He later studied English and History at Dublin University, where he became involved in experimental theatre, and began writing, directing and acting with the Slot Players at Jim and Peter Sheridan's theatre in Sheriff Street. After his finals he worked briefly in Chicago, staging *Becket* and Sean O'Casey productions for Irish-Americans.

On his return he worked as a labourer in England, where he lived in a squat and began writing his first story called *Last Rites*. Other works followed, including *A Night in Tunisia* and a radio play called *Miracles and Miss Langan* which was broadcast on RTE. He became interested in writing for film and television, and in the early seventies considered going to film school. In 1978 he wrote a script called *Travellers*, which he sent to director John Boorman, which was filmed by Joe Comerford in 1981. Boorman liked his work and asked him to act as creative consultant on the script of *Excalibur* (1981).

Shortly afterwards he made his directorial debut with *Angel* (1982), starring Chris Rea. He followed this with *The Company of Wolves* (1984), an adult rendering

of the tale of *Little Red Riding Hood*, but his international breakthrough as a director and screenwriter came in 1986 when he made the urban thriller, *Mona Lisa*. His other notable films include *We're No Angels* (1989), *The Miracle* (1991, from his original story *A Night in Tunisia*), *The Crying Game* (1992), which earned six Oscar nominations (winning for Jordan's screenplay), *Interview with the Vampire* (1994) and *Michael Collins* (1996).

See also: *The Crying Game, Michael Collins*

Wexford

SAVING PRIVATE RYAN
Curracloe Beach

"But it was toughest for Frederick. I think he always felt guilty because he was brought home. He and his brothers had shared two bedrooms as boys. From the day Frederick

came home from France he never again set foot upstairs in his mother's house. He had his bed brought downstairs and refused to go into those bedrooms. It was just too heartbreaking."
Joe Niland talking about his cousin Frederick Niland.

Steven Spielberg's 1998 film is based on the true story of the Niland family whose three out of four boys were reported killed in action during WWII. When news reached the US War Department that three brothers from one family had been killed it instigated its "sole survivor policy", which stated that for any family who had lost more than two sons their remaining sons would be returned home. *Saving Private Ryan* tells the true story of Frederick Niland's rescue. Matt Damon was cast in the title role and Tom Hanks portrayed Captain John Miller, leader of the rescue squad.

The harrowing opening scenes depicting the carnage of the Normandy landings were shot on **Curracloe Beach**, near Wexford. The beach landings were co-ordinated by Square Sail Marine of Charlestown in Cornwall, who also supplied and refurbished all twelve landing craft used in the film. Eight original WWII landing craft, veterans of Vietnam, were found in a scrap yard in Palm Springs and refurbished by Square Sail. The scrap yard also owned an original copy of a landing craft driver's manual for the Normandy invasion and these instructions they followed.

Around a thousand Irish Marines and part-time soldiers were used as extras and a portable pontoon jetty was built to access the landing craft. The shoot lasted six weeks and used five cameras. Only half a day was lost through bad weather and the shoot finished a day ahead of schedule.

*D-Day on Curracloe Beach in **Saving Private Ryan***

When the war ended, Frederick Niland trained as a dentist, married and raised a family. He died in 1988. His brother Edward was found alive in a Japanese PoW camp in 1945 and spent the rest of his life living in the same neighbourhood as his brother. After the film was released the Normandy American Cemetery, where 9,386 soldiers who died in the invasion are buried, reported a marked increase in visitors, with many searching for the grave of Captain John Miller, the character played by Tom Hanks. *"We have to tell them that it is a fictitious name,"* the superintendent said.

See also: *Saving Private Ryan* (Herts & Highland)

GRAVE OF OLIVER REED (1938-99)
Churchtown

Amanda Donohue and **Oliver Reed** *in Castaway (1986, Cannon/United British Artists)*

"Gone, all gone. Flynn, Burton, Bogart. Richard Harris doesn't anymore. Who's going to captain the 2nd XI if I fall down?"
Oliver Reed lamenting his ilk

More famous for his off-screen hell-raising and heavy drinking than for his acting career, Oliver Reed began his life in sleepy Wimbledon on 13 February 1938.

He was grandson of the actor-manager Herbert Beerbohm Tree and nephew of director Carol Reed. Reputedly expelled from thirteen schools, he ran away from home when he was seventeen and became a bouncer at a Soho strip club. Other jobs included Boxer, mini-cab driver and mortuary attendant. After national service in the Army Medical Corps, he decided to become an actor, and began working as an extra and playing bit parts in movies such as *Beat Girl* (1959) and *The League of Gentlemen* (1960).

His first starring role was in Hammer's *Curse of the Werewolf* (1961) which typecast him as a sullen villain. During his career he made a great many pot-boilers, but he will be best remembered for *The Trap* (1966), *The Jokers* (1967), *Oliver!* (1968), *Hannibal Brooks* (1968), *Women in Love* (1970), *The Devils* (1971) and *Tommy* (1975).

His notoriety made him a familiar face on the chat show circuit, where he would frequently discuss his "mighty mallet" on which were tattooed a pair of bird's talons. When asked once how he would like to die, he commented,: *"Somewhere near Cork, after having a heart attack, due to laughing too much at a bad joke."*

He eventually did die of a heart attack, nowhere near Cork, but in Valletta, Malta, after collapsing during a drinking session in a local bar, during a break from filming Stephen Spielberg's *Gladiator*. He was married three times, and had two children. His funeral service was at **St James's Church** in **Mallow, County Cork**, and he is buried under a beech tree in **Churchtown cemetery**, close to **O'Brien's Bar**, one of his favourite watering holes.

See also: D.H. Lawrence, *Castaway*

Wicklow

MY LEFT FOOT
Bray

Dr. Eileen Cole (Fiona Shaw) painstakingly trains Christy (Daniel Day Lewis) to control his speech in **My Left Foot** *(1989, Grananda)*

"As time went on I began to depend more and more on my left foot for everything. It was my main means of communication, of making myself understood to the family. Very slowly it became indispensable to me."
Christy Brown *

• 1989 98m c Biography Granada (Ireland)
• Daniel Day-Lewis (Christy Brown), Ray McAnally (Mr. Brown), Brenda Fricker (Mrs. Brown), Ruth McCabe (Mary Carr), Fiona Shaw (Dr. Eileen Cole), Eanna Macliam (Old Benny), Alison Whelan (Old Sheila), Declan Croughan (Old Tom), Hugh O'Conor (Young Christy), Cyril Cusack (Lord Castlewelland)
• p, Noel Pearson; d, Jim Sheridan; w, Shane Connaughton, Jim Sheridan (based on the book by Christy Brown); ph, Jack Conroy; ed, J. Patrick Duffner; m, Elmer Bernstein; prod d, Austin Spriggs; cos, Joan Bergin
• AAN Best Picture; AA Best Actor: Daniel Day-Lewis; AA Best Supporting Actress: Brenda Fricker; AAN Best Director: Jim Sheridan; AAN Best Adapted Screenplay: Jim Sheridan, Shane Connaughton

My Left Foot is based on the 1954 autobiography of cerebral palsy victim Christy Brown (1932-81).

Severely handicapped, he could neither walk, talk, nor co-ordinate his limbs. The tenth of thirteen children, he was unable to communicate until he was five, when he suddenly grasped a piece of chalk in his left foot and drew the letter 'A' on his sister's slate. His mother then taught him the alphabet.and gradually he acquired the ability to paint, read and write using the toes of his left foot.

During the six weeks of filming Daniel Day-Lewis confined himself to a wheelchair and experienced at first hand the humiliation of being dressed, washed and fed by another person. He learned to write and paint with his left foot and his characterisation in the end was so convincing it won him a well deserved Best Actor Oscar.

The opening scene in which the nurse reads Christy's autobiography at a charity event was filmed at **Kilruddery House, near Bray.** The exterior of Christy's childhood home was shot at **St. Kevin's Square, Bray**, and the interiors at Ardmore Studios, Bray.

See also: Christy Brown, Daniel Day-Lewis, *My Left Foot* (Dublin)

Further information: Kilruddery House and gardens is approximately one and a half miles south of Bray and is open to the public. Tel: (353) 12-863405.

HENRY V
Enniskerry

"...perhaps the first true work of art that had ever been put on film." Kenneth Tynann

• 1944 127m c Drama/War Two Cities (UK)
• Laurence Olivier (King Henry V), Robert Newton (Ancient Pistol), Leslie Banks (Chorus), Renee Asherson (Princess Katherine), Esmond Knight (Fluellen), Leo Genn (Constable of France), Felix Aylmer (Archbishop of Canterbury), Ralph Truman (Mountjoy), Harcourt Williams (King Charles VI of France)
• p, Laurence Olivier, Filippo Del Giudice; d, Laurence Olivier, Reginald Beck; w, Alan Dent, Laurence Olivier (based on the play by William Shakespeare); ph, Robert Krasker; ed, Reginald Beck; m, William Walton; art d, Paul sheriff; cos, Roger Furse
• AAN Best Picture; AAN Best Actor: Laurence Olivier; AAN Best Score: William Walton; AAN Best Art Direction: Paul Sheriff, Carmen Dillon

Made during WWII when Britain had its back to the wall, this celluloid adaptation of Henry's victory against colossal odds at Agincourt was just the morale booster Britain needed. Turned down by Carol Reed, William Wyler and Terence Young, Laurence Olivier decided to direct the film himself. The making of Henry V took nearly a year, from the summer of 1943 to the spring of 1944.

The film opens on the stage of the Globe Theatre and the stylised sets of Denham Studios, and slowly evolves into the reality of Agincourt, shot on location at the **Powerscourt Estate**, Eniskerry. Filming the Battle of Agincourt at Powerscourt took six weeks, cost £80,000 and represented 15 minutes of the most memorable battle scenes ever filmed. Since Ireland was not at war with Germany, extras were in plentiful supply; 200 mounted and 500 footsoldiers were used. Olivier was badly injured when a rider smashed into the camera and gashed his lip, leaving him with a scar he would cover in future with a moustache.

Powerscourt waterfall (5km from the gardens) has been used in various films, including John Boorman's *Excalibur* (1981). Powerscourt was also the location for the battle scenes in the 1953 production of *Knights of the Round Table*, which starred Robert Taylor and Ava Gardner. Situated 12 miles south of Dublin in the foothills of the Wicklow mountains, the house and its 47 acres of gardens are open to the public.

See also: Laurence Olivier

Further information: Powerscourt Estate, Enniskerry.
Tel: (353) 1 2046000.

The Battle of Agincourt re-enacted on the Powerscourt Estate, in **Henry V** *(1944, Two Cities)*

FILM FESTIVAL CALENDAR UK & IRELAND

(Film Festival dates often fluctuate. For precise dates and venues contact the festival organisers)

JANUARY

International Film and Video Festival
24c West Street, Epsom, Surrey KT18 7RJ

FEBRUARY

The Comedy Film Festival
Harbour Lights Cinema, Ocean Village, Southampton SO15 2RZ. Tel: 01703 635335 Fax: 01703 234444

Green Screen
45 Shelton Street, Covent Garden, London WC2H 9JH. Tel: 0171 3797390 Fax: 0171 3797197

Viva 8
London Filmmakers Co-op, 12-18 Hoxton Street, London N1 6NG. Tel: 0171 739 7132
E-mail: 101563.332@compuserve.com

Southampton Film Festival
Harbour Lights Cinema, Ocean Village, Southampton SO15 2RZ. Tel: 01703 635 335 Fax:
01703 234 444

MARCH

Dublin Film Festival
1 Suffolk Street, Dublin 2, Ireland. Tel: (00) 353 1 679 2937 Fax: 00353 1 679 2939

Bradford Film Festival
National Museum of Photography, Film and Television, Cinema Dept., Bradford BD1 1NQ. Tel: 01274 203308. Web: http://www.nmsi.ac.uk/nmpft/

London Lesbian and Gay Film Festival
South Bank, Waterloo, London SE1 8XT. Tel: 0171 815 1322 Fax: 0171 633 0786

Celtic Film and Television Festival
1 Bowmont Gardens, Glasgow G12 9LR. Tel: 0141 342 4947 Fax: 0141 342 4948
E-mail: mail@celticfilm.co.uk
Web: http://www.celticfilm.co.uk

APRIL

Italian Film Festival
32 Nicolson Street, Edinburgh EH8 9EW. Tel: 0131 243 3601 Fax: 0131 220 2443

Limerick Irish Film Festival
3 Upper Hartstonye Street, Limerick, Ireland. Tel: 00353 61 318 150 Fax: 00353 61 318 152
E-mail: bmadden.rsl@rtc-limerick.ie

MAY

Brighton Arts Film Festival
21-22 Old Steine, Brighton BN1 1EL. Tel: 01273 713875 Fax: 01273 622453

JUNE

BAF!
Bradford Animation Festival
National Museum of Photography, Film and Television, Cinema Dept., Bradford BD1 1NQ. Tel: 01274 203308. Web: http://www.nmsi.ac.uk/nmpft/

London Jewish Film Festival
South Bank, Waterloo, London SE1 8XT. Tel: 0171 815 1322 Fax: 0171 633 0786
E-mail: jane.ivey@bfi.org.uk

North Devon Film Festival
The Plough, Fore Street, Torrington, North Devon EX38 8HQ.

Nottingham Shots in the Dark Mystery and Thriller Film Festival
Broadway Media Centre, 14 Broad Street, Nottingham NG1 3AL. Tel: 0115

962 6600 Fax: 0115 952 6622
E-mail:
broadway@bwymedia.demon.co.uk

JULY

Galway Film Festival
Seaport House, New Dock Street, Galway, Ireland. Tel: 00353 91 583 800 Fax: 00353 91 587 169
E-mail: gaf@id.ie

AUGUST

Dublin Lesbian and Gay Film Festival
Film Institute of Ireland, 6 Eustace Street, Temple Bar, Dublin 2, Ireland. Tel: 00353 1 679 5744 Fax: (00) 353 1 677 8755
E-mail: sexton@iol.ie
Web: http://www.iftn.ie/dublingayfilm/

Edinburgh International Film Festival
88 Lothian Road, Edinburgh EH3 9BZ. Tel: 0131 228 4051 Fax: 0131 229 5501
E-mail: info@edfilmfest.org.uk

SEPTEMBER

Bite the Mango: Black and Asian Film Festival
National Museum of Photography, Film and Television, Cinema Dept., Bradford BD1 1NQ. Tel: 01274 203308. Web: http://www.nmsi.ac.uk/nmpft/

British Short Film Festival
Room 313, Threshold House, 65-69 Shepherd's Bush Green, London W12 7RK. Tel: 0181 743 8000 Fax: 0181 740 8549

Festival of Fantastic Films & Southport North West Film Festival
33 Barrington Road, Altrincham WA14 1H. Tel: 0161 929 1423 Fax: 0161 929 1067

OCTOBER

Cork International Film Festival
Hatfield House, Tobin Street, Cork,

Ireland. Tel: 00353 21 271711 Fax: (00) 353 21 275945 E-mail: ciff@indigo.ie Web: http://www.corkfilmfest.r

Leeds International Film Festival
The Town Hall, The Headrow, Leeds LS1 3AD.
Web: http://www.sensei.co.uk/films/

Kinofilm Manchester International Short Film and Video Festival
48 Princess Street, M16HR. Tel: 0161 288 2494 Fax: 0161 281 1374
E-mail: john.kino@good.co.uk
Web: http://www.kinofilm.org.uk

London Raindance Film Showcase
81 Berwick Street, London W1V 3PF.
Tel: 0171 287 3833 Fax: 0171 439 2243
Web: http://www.ftech.net/n.ind

Sheffield International Documentary Festival
The Workstation, 15 Paternoster Row, Sheffield. Tel: 0114 276 5141 Fax: 0114 272 1849
E-mail: shefdoc@fdgroup.co.uk

NOVEMBER

Birmingham International Film & TV Festival
Central Television, Broad Street, Birmingham B1 2JP. Tel: 0121 634 4213 Fax: 0121 634 4392 Web: http://www.centralcyberco.uk/filmfest

Cinewomen Film Festival
Cinema City, St. Andrews Street, Norwich NR2 4AD. E-mail: j.h.morgan@uea.ac.uk

European Student Film Festival
11 Holbein House, Holbein Place, London SW1 W8NH. Tel / Fax: 0171 259 9278
E-mail: kohle@mail.bogo.co.uk
Web: http://www.bogo.co.uk.kohle/pearl.htm

London Film Festival
South Bank, Waterloo, Lon. SE1 8XT.
Tel: 0171 928 3535 Fax: 0171 633 0786.
E-mail: jane.ivey@bfi.org.uk

Welsh International Film Festival
Tel: 01222 406220
E-mail: wiff@pcw-aber.co.uk

Brynmawr Film Festival
Blaenau Gwent Arts Development Office, Beaufort Theatre, Beaufort, Ebbw Vale, Blaenau Gwent, South Wales NP3 5QQ. Tel / Fax: 01495 308996

French Film Festival
French Institute, 13 Randolph Crescent, Edinburgh EH3 8TX. Tel: 0131 243 3601 Fax: 0131 220 2443

The Mavericks Film Festival
Filthy McNastys, 68 Amwell Street,

Finsbury, London, EC1. Tel: 0171 8376067

Foyle Film Festival
The Nerve Centre, Magazine Street, Derry. Tel: 01504 267 432 / 260 562
E-mail: f.kelpie@nerve-centre.org.uk
Web: http://www. nerve-centre.org.uk

DECEMBER

Cinemagic International Film Festival for Young People
4th floor, 38 Dublin Road, Belfast BT2 7HN. Tel: 01232 311900 Fax: 01232 319709

Tom & Jerry at the Bradford Animation Festival (BAF!)

SONS OF THE DESERT TENTS

'The Sons of the Desert' is the official Laurel and Hardy appreciation society. Divided into various 'tents', they have regular meetings throughout the country to which anyone is welcome. Contact the local 'Grand Sheik' for details.

"Busy Bodies" of Stourbridge
Grand Sheik: Tony Bagley
118 Orchard Street
Brockmoor
Brierley Hill
West Midlands DY5 1HN

"Laughing Gravy" of Birmingham
Grand Sheik: John Ullah
164 Gravelly Hill
Erdington
Birmingham B23 7PF

"County Hospital" of Bradford
Grand Sheik: Dave Thackray
16 Westwood Avenue
Eccleshill
Bradford BD2 1NJ

"Laughing Gravy" of Tingley
Grand Sheik: Graham McKenna
5 Ryedale Way
Tingley
Wakefield WF3 1AP

"One Good Turn" of Huddersfield
Grand Sheik: David Barker
52 Tom Lane
Crosland Moor
Huddersfield
Kirklees HD4 5PP

"Fraternally Yours" of Bristol
Grand Sheik: Peter Andrews
50 Clare Road
Kingswood
Bristol BS15 1PJ

"Come Clean" of Widnes
Grand Sheik: Eric Woods
Laurel House
102 Hough Green Road
Widnes
Cheshire WA8 9PF

"Berth Marks" of Ulverston
Grand Sheik: Marion Grave
Crake Valley House
Greenodd
Near Ulverston
Cumbria LA12 7RA

"Them Thar Hills" of Carlisle
Grand Sheik: Stephen Neale
Blue Mill House
Lamonby
Penrith
Cumbria CA11 9SS

"Early to Bed" of Chesterfield
Grand Sheik: Grahame Morris
Appleton Lodge
87 Shuttlewood Road
Bolsover
Derbyshire S44 6NX

"Hog Wild" of Bishop Auckland
Grand Sheik: Stan Paterson
2 Compton Grove
Bishop Auckland
Co. Durham

"Men o' War" of Colchester
Grand Sheik: Paul Harding
38 Kingsman Drive
Clacton-on-Sea
Essex CO16 8UR

"Saps at Sea" of Leigh on Sea
Grand Sheik: Roger Robinson
115 Neil Armstrong Way
Leigh on Sea
Essex SS9 5UE

"Helpmates" of Kent
Grand Sheik: Rob Lewis
63 Wollaston Close
Parkwood
Gillingham
Kent ME8 9SH

"Chickens Come Home" of Lancaster
Grand Sheik: David Wilkinson
37 Seaview
Hest Bank
Nr. Lancaster
Lancs LA2 6BY

"Bacon Grabbers" of St Helens, Wigan and Manchester Central
Grand Sheik: Chris Coffey
64 Dale Crescent
Sutton Leach
St. Helens
Merseyside WA9 4YE

"Leave 'Em Laughing" of Merseyside
Grand Sheik: Bob Spiller
169 Higher Road
Halewood
Liverpool L26 1UN

"Be Big" of Tameside
Grand Sheik: Bob Hickson
69 Bucklow Drive
Northenden
Manchester M22

"Blotto" of Tameside
Grand Sheik: Peter Brodie
4 Wilson Crescent
Ashton-under-Lyne
Tameside OL6 9SA

"Double Whoopee" of Salford
Grand Sheik: Wesley Butters
43 Enville Road
Salford
Manchester M6 7JX

"Night Owls" of North Shields
Grand Sheik: Robbie Crawford
76 Purley Road
Plains Farm
Sunderland
Tyne & Wear SR3 1RF

"Fixer Uppers" of Norfolk
Grand Sheik: Mike Brand
9 Cawstons Meadow
Poringland
Norwich
Norfolk NR14 7SX

"You're Darn Tootin'" of Stillington
Grand Sheik: Tony Gears
1A South Street
Stillington
Stockton-on-Tees TS21 1JN

"A Chump at Oxford" of Oxford
Grand Sheik: Alan Kitchen
102 Lime Walk
Headington
Oxford OX3 7AF

"Brats" of Sheffield
Grand Sheik: John Burton
337 Handsworth Road
Handsworth
Sheffield S13 9BP

"Hats Off" of Derby
Grand Sheik: Howard Parker
138 Smithfield Road
Uttoxeter
Staffs ST14 7LB

"Midnight Patrol" of Staffordshire
Grand Sheik: Anthony Waite
3 Oakdene Avenue
Porthill
Newcastle-under-Lyme
Staffs ST5 8HQ

"A Spot of Trouble" of Stockport
Grand Sheik: Laurence Reardon
8 Powderham Close
Packmoor

Stoke-on-Trent
Staffs ST6 6XN

"Live Ghost" of London
Grand Sheik: Del Kempster
112 Tudor Drive
Morden
Surrey SM4 4PF

"Their Purple Moment" of Stranraer
Grand Sheik: Dougie Brown
The Mill House
Seabank Road
Stranraer DG9 0EF

"Blockheads" of Edinburgh
Grand Sheik: Charlie Lewis
70 Silverknowes Gardens
Edinburgh EH4 5NG

"Our Relations" of Fife & Tayside
Grand Sheik: Trevor McCrindle

25 Upper Wellheads
Limekilns
Fife KY11 3JQ

"Bonnie Scotland" of Glasgow
Grand Sheik: Fred Terris
29/7 Howdenhall Court
Edinburgh EH16 6UZ

"Call of the Cuckoos" of the Clyde Coast
Grand Sheik: Willie McIntyre
39 Bankhouse Avenue
Largs
North Ayrshire KA30 9PF

"Perfect Day" of Mold
Grand Sheik: Shelley Moore
10 Cae Berwyn
Sychdyn
Nr. Mold CH7 6AJ

SOURCE NOTES

Devon
A Touch of the Memoirs, p.190, Donald Sinden (Futura Publications 1983)

East Sussex
A Postillion Struck by Lightning, p.62, p.60, Dirk Bogarde (Triad 1978)

Hertfordshire
Jacques Tourneur, p.54, Interview - Bernard Tavernier (Edinburgh Film Festival 1975)

Lancashire
David Lean, p.199, Kevin Brownlow (Faber & Faber 1997)

Leicestershire
Laurel & Hardy: The British Tours, p.180. A.J. Marriot (A.J. Marriot, 1993, Blackpool)

Norfolk
Candidly Caine, p.5, Elaine Gallagher (Guild Publishing, 1990, London)

North Tyneside
Laurel & Hardy: The British Tours, p.180. A.J. Marriot (A.J. Marriot, 1993, Blackpool)

Portsmouth
P.S. I Love You, page 95 Michael Sellers (Fontana/Collins 1981)

Sandwell
A new copy of Madeleine Carroll's birth certificate was obtained by Verna Hale-Gibbons, Madeleine Carroll's biographer.

Somerset
Forever Ealing, p.138, George Perry (Pavilion Books, 1981, London)

Trafford
Robert Bolt, Scenes From Two Lives, p.181, Adrian Turner (Vintage, London, 1999)

Windsor & Maidenhead
The Hammer Story, p.94. Marcus Hearne & Alan Barnes (Titan Books, 1997, London)

Wirral
Glenda Jackson, p.22. Ian Woodward (George Weidenfeld & Nicolson Ltd., 1985, London)

Warrington
George Formby, p.96, John Fisher (Woburn-Futura, 1975)

Bexley
A.E.W. Mason, p.91, Roger Lancelyn Green (Max Parrish 1952)

Kensington & Chelsea
Joseph Losey, p.286, Edith de Rham (Andre Deutsch, 1991, London)

Westminster
Cos I'm A Fool, p.8, Norman Wisdom with Bernard Bale (Breedon Books, 1996)

Croydon
David Lean, p.4, Kevin Brownlow (Faber & Faber 1997)

Newham
Anna Neagle, An Autobiography, p.152 (Futura, 1979, London)

Edinburgh
Stephen Goodwin, p.7, The Independent, (23 October, 1998)

Dumfries & Galloway
Cinefantastique, p.18, volume 6 no 3, David Bartholomew (Frederick S. Clarke, Oak Park, Illinois)

Glasgow
Billy Connolly, talking to the Daily Mail, 6 May 1976.

Gwynedd
A.E.W. Mason, p.220, Roger Lancelyn Green (Max Parrish & Co. Ltd., 1952, London)

Rhondda Cynon Taff
Wales and Cinema, p.151. David Berry (University of Wales Press, 1994, Cardiff)

Ballymena
Liam Neeson, p.30-31, Ingrid Millar (St Martin's Press, New York, 1996)

Kerry
David Lean, p.567, Kevin Brownlow (Faber & Faber 1997)

Wicklow
My Left Foot, p.21, Christy Brown (Minerva, 1990, London)

BIBLIOGRAPHY

Allister, Ray. Friese-Greene, Close-up of an Inventor (Marsland Publications, London, 1948)

Barber, C. & Fitzgerald, D. *Made in Devon* (Obelisk Publications, Exeter, 1988)

Baxter, John . *Stanley Kubrick* (Harper Collins, London, 1997)

Baxter, John. *Stanley Kubrick* (Harper Collins, London, 1997)

Begg, Ean and Rich, Deike. *On The Merlin Trail* (The Aquarian Press, London, 1991)

Belford, Barbara. *Bram Stoker* (Weidenfeld & Nicolson, London, 1996)

Belford, Barbara. *Bram Stoker* (Weidenfeld & Nicolson, London, 1996)

Berry, David. *Wales & Cinema* (University of Wales Press, Cardiff, 1994)

Bogarde, Dirk . *A Postillion Struck By Lightning* (Triad/Granada, London, 1983)

Branagh, Kenneth . *Beginning* (Chatto &

Windus, London, 1989)

Braun, Eric . *Deborah Kerr* (W.H. Allen, London, 1977)

Briggs, Julia. *A Woman of Passion, The Life of E.Nesbit 1858-1924* (Hutchinson, London, 1987)

Brownlow, Kevin . *David Lean* (Faber and Faber, London, 1997)

Brownlow, Kevin, *David Lean* (Richard Cohen Books, London, 1996)

Bruce, David. *Scotland the Movie* (Polygon, Edinburgh, 1996)

Burgess, Anthony . *Little Wilson and Big God* (Heinemann, London, 1987)

Caine, Michael . *What's It All About?* (Turtle Bay Books, New York, 1992)

Chaplin, Charles. *My Autobiography* (Penguin Books, Harmondsworth, 1966)

Christie, Ian. *Arrows of Desire* (Faber & Faber, London, 1994)

Coveney, Michael. *Maggie Smith, A Bright Particular Star* (Victor Gollancz Ltd, London, 1992)

Crozier, Major T.H. *Report to the Right Honourable the Secretary of State for Scotland on the Circumstances attending the Loss of Life at the Glen Cinema, Paisley, on the 31st December, 1929* (HM Stationery Office, 1930)

Curtis, James . *James Whale* (The Scarecrow Press, Metuchen, New Jersey, 1982)

Derek Jarman: A Portrait (Thames and Hudson, London, 1996),

Donovan, Paul. *Roger Moore* (Whallen 1983)

Dyja, Eddie. *BFI Film and Television Handbook* (BFI, London, 1998)

Eyles. A. & Skone. K. *London's West End Cinemas* (Keytone Publications, Sutton, 1991)

Faith, William Robert. *Bob Hope, A Life in Comedy* (Granada Publishing, London, 1983).

Falk, Quentin. *Albert Finney in Character* (Robson Books, London, 1992)

Finler, Joel W. *The Movie Directors Story* (Octopus Books, London, 1985)

Fisher, John. *George Formby* (Woburn-Futura, London, 1975)

Flory, Joan and Wlane, Damien. *Diana Dors: Only a Whisper Away* (1987).

Ford, John. *Pappy, The Life of John Ford* (Da Capo Press, New York, 1998)

Fox. K., Grant. E., Imeson. J. *The Virgin Film Guide* (Virgin Publishing Ltd., London, 1998)

Freedland, Michael . *Peter O'Toole* (W.H. Allen. London, 1983)

French, John. *Robert Shaw, The Price of Success* (Nick Hern Books, London, 1993)

Gallagher, Elaine. *Candidly Caine* (Guild Publishing, London, 1990)

Grant, Sally. *Edith Cavell* (Larks Press, Dereham, 1995)

Hallam, Vic. *Lest We Forget, The Dambusters in The Derwent Valley* (Vic Hallam).

Halliwell, Leslie. *Halliwell's Filmgoer's and Video Companion* (Paladin Grafton Books, London, 1989)

Hardwicke, Sir Cedric. *A Victorian in Orbit* (Methuen, London, 1961)

Hardy, Forsyth. *John Grierson, A Documentary Biography* (Faber & Faber, London, 1979)

Hearn, M. & Barnes, A. *The Hammer Story* (Titan Books, London, 1997)

Hearn, Marcus and Barnes, Alan. *The Hammer Story* (Titan Books, London, 1997)

Herbert. S. & McKernan. L. *Who's Who of Victorian Cinema* (BFI, London, 1996)

Higham, Charles and Mosley, Roy. *Merle* (New English Library, Sevenoaks, 1983).

Hordern, Sir Michael and England, Patricia. *A World Elsewhere* (Michael O'Mara Books Ltd.,London, 1993)

Houston, Penelope. *Went The Day Well?* (BFI Publishing, London, 1992)

Hoving, Thomas. *Tutankhamun, The Untold Story* (Hamish Hamilton, London, 1979)

Jacobs, Gerald. *Judi Dench* (George Weidenfeld & Nicolson Ltd, London 1985).

Jenkins, Garry . *Daniel Day-Lewis, The Fire Within* (St. Martins Press, New York, 1995)

Karney, Robyn, *The Movie Stars Story* (Guild Publishing, London, 1984)

Kelly, Richards & Pepper. *Filming T.E. Lawrence* (I.B. Tauris Publishers, New York, 1997)

Kerrigan, Michael, *Who Lies Where* (Fourth Estate, London,1995)

Kirchner, Daniela. *The Researcher's Guide To British Film & Television Collections* (British Universities Film & Video Council, London, 1997)

Lee, Christopher. *Tall, Dark and Gruesome* (W.H. Allen, London, 1977)

Ludlam, Harry. *A Biography of Dracula* (W. Foulsham & Co. Ltd., Slough, 1962)

Maltin, Leonard. *Movie and Video Guide* (Signet, London, 1993)

Margolis, Jonathan . *Michael Palin* (Orion Media, London, 1997)

Margolis, Jonathan. *The Big Yin* (Orion, London, 1994)

A.J. Marriot. *Laurel & Hardy: The British Tours* (A.J. Marriot, 1993, Blackpool)

McAlee, Neil . *Odyssey* (Victor Gollancz Ltd., London, 1992)

McCabe, John. *Mr Laurel & Mr Hardy* (Robson Books, London, 1976).

McCann, Graham. *Cary Grant* (Fourth Estate, London, 1996)

McIlroy, Brian. *World Cinema 4: Ireland* (Flicks Books, Trowbridge, 1989)

Mellor, G.J. *Movie Makers and Picture Palaces* (Bradford Libraries, 1996)

Mellor, G.J.. *Picture Pioneers* (Frank Graham, Newcastle-upon-Tyne, 1971)

Milland, Ray. *Wide-Eyed In Babylon* (Bodley Head, London, 1974).

Millar, Ingrid . *Liam Neeson* (St Martin's Press, New York, 1996)

Milne, Tom. *The Time Out Film Guide* (Penguin, Harmondsworth, 1989)

More, Kenneth. *More or Less* (Hodder and Stoughton, London, 1978)

Morley, Sheridan. *Dirk Bogarde, Rank Outsider* (Bloomsbury Publishing, London, 1996)

Morley, Sheridan. *Robert, My Father* (Weidenfeld & Nicolson, London, 1993)

Moseley, Roy. *Rex Harrison* (New English Library, London, 1987)

Moules, Joan. *Our Gracie* (Robert Hale Ltd, London, 1983)

Munn, Michael. *Trevor Howard* (Robson Books, London, 1989)

Neagle, Anna. *There's Always Tomorrow* (Futura Publications, London, 1979)

Neaverson, Bob, *The Beatles Movies* (Cassell, London, 1997)

Niven, David. *The Moon's a Balloon* (Coronet, London, 1974)

Pendreigh, Brian. *On Location* (Mainstream Publishing Co., Edinburgh, 1995)

Perry, George. *Forever Ealing* (Pavilion Books Ltd., London, 1981)

Powell, Michael. *A Life in Movies* (Heinemann, London, 1986)

Powell, Michael. *Million-Dollar Movie* (Mandarin, London, 1993)

Rawlence, Christopher, *The Missing Reel* (Atheneum, New York, 1990)

Robertson, Patrick. *The Guinness Book of Movie Facts & Feats* (1997)

Robinson, David. *Chaplin, His Life and Art* (Grafton, London, 1992)

Rutherford, Margaret . *An Autobiography* (W.H. Allen, London, 1972)

Seaton, Ray and Martin, Roy. *Good Morning Boys, Will Hay, Master of Comedy* (Barrie and Jenkins Ltd, London, 1978).

Sellers, Peter. *P.S. I Love You* (Fontana, London, 1982)

Silverman, Stephen M., *David Lean* (Andre Deutsch, London, 1989)

Simmons, Dawn L, *Margaret Rutherford, A Blithe Spirit.* (Arthur Barker Ltd, London, 1983)

Sinden, Donald. *A Touch of the Memoirs* (Futura, London, 1983)

Spoto, Donald, *Elizabeth Taylor* (Warner Books, London, 1995)

The K&WVR Railway Experience (K&WVR Preservation Soc. 1990)

Thompson, Douglas. *Dudley Moore* (Little, Brown & Co, London, 1996)

Tookey, Christopher. *The Critics' Film Guide* (Boxtree, London, 1994)

Trewin, J.C. *Robert Donat* (Heinemann, London, 1968)

Turner, Hugh. *Fletcher Christian* (The Printing House, Cockermouth).

Underwood, Peter. *Horror Man* (Leslie Frewin Publishers Ltd., London, 1972)

Van Nash, Cay and Rohmer, Elizabeth Sax. *Master of Villainy* (Tom Stacey Ltd, London, 1972).

Virgin Film Guide (Virgin Books, London, 1998)

Wakelin, Michael. *J. Arthur Rank* (Lion Publishing, Oxford, 1996)

Walker, Alexander. *Vivien* (Weidenfeld and Nicolson, London, 1987)

Warren, Patricia. *British Film Studios* (B.T. Batsford Ltd., London, 1995)

Warren, Patricia. *British Film Studios* (Batsford, London, 1995)

Williams, Emlyn, *George* (Penguin Books, Harmondsworth, 1976)

Williams, Kenneth. *Just Williams* (J.M. Dent & Sons Ltd, London, 1985)

Wilson, Anthony, *You've Had Your Time* (Heinemann, London, 1990)

Wisdom, Norman and Bale, Bernard. *'Cos I'm A Fool* (Breedon Books, Derby, 1996)

INDEX

2001: A Space Odyssey, 130
333 Club, 167
39 Steps Guest House , 224
Abbotsbury, 63
Abbotsford, 212
ABC Magdalen Street, Oxford, 120
Aberfeldy, 237, 238
Aberystwyth, 249
Abronhill High School, 237
Achiltibuie, 236
Acres, Birt, 156, 169, 196
Agutter, Jenny, 16
Alice in Wonderland, 77
Alien 3, 114
Allerton Park, 87
Allestree, 51
Alnsdale, 125
Alnwick Castle, 114
Alpha Picture Palace, 80
Alresford, 78
Amberley, 74
Ambleside, 49
American Werewolf in London, An, 135, 196
Amersham, 37
Anne of the Thousand Days, 87
Anwoth, 214
Apocalypse Now, 72
Aran Islands, 277
Armley Palace Picture Hall, 97
Arnhall Castle, 245
Ashford Castle Hotel, 280
Aspall, 132
Athelhampton, 62
Avening, 74
Aylward, Gladys, **158**, 250
Backbeat, 102
Bader, Douglas, 122
Badminton House, 12
Bagnold, Edith, 68
Baird, John Logie, 207, 231
Baker, Hylda, **13**, 115
Baker, Stanley, 57, 256, **257**
Balcon, Michael, 76
Balgarnie, W.H., 38
Balham, 192
Ballachulish, 210
Ballantrae, 214
Ballymena, 260
Balquidder, 243
Bamburgh Castle, 114
Banbury, 119
Barnes Bridge, 120
Barnsley Public Hall Disaster, 11

Barony Film Society, 227
Barra, 247
Barretts of Wimpole Street, The, 195
Barrie, J.M., 81, **206**
Barry, John, 149
Basingstoke, 76
Bassingbourne, 38
Bates, Alan, **51**, 62, 86, 96, 107
Baxter, Cecil William, 22
Beachy Head, 24
Beaconsfield, 29
Beanos, 157
Beaton, Cecil, 143
Beau Geste, 74, 186
Beaulieu, 119
Beckton Gas Works, 183
Bekesbourne, 89
Belgravia, 193, 195
Bell, Joseph, 225
Belles of St Trinians, The, 224
Ben Nevis Distillery, 205
Benbecula Film Club, 247
Berkhamstead, 80, 81
Bermondsey, 189
Berwick-upon-Tweed, 113
Bewdley Station, 118
Bewdley, 149
BFI London Imax, 174
Bhowani Junction, 77
Bill Douglas Centre for the History of Cinema & Popular Culture, 59
Billy Liar, 20
Binbrook, 100
Birkenhead, 146
Bishop Auckland, 67
Black Beauty, 107
Black Narcissus, 69, **140**
Black Park, 34
Blackbeard the Pirate, 27
Blackbushe Airport, 78
Blackhall Beach, 106
Blackmore, R.D., 185
Bligh, Captain, 47, **173**
Bloomsbury, 156
Blow-up, 162
Blue Lamp, The, 71, **199**
Blue Max Movie Aircraft Collection, 30
Bluebell Railway, 70
Blyth, 114
Bo'ness, 227
Bodinnick-by-Fowey, 42
Bodmin, 42
Bogarde, Dirk, 61, **70**, 168, 199
Bognor Regis, 141
Bolebroke Mill, 71
Boleyn, Anne, 87, **190**

Bolt, Robert, 119, **138**, 277
Bolventor, 44
Booker, 30
Borough Market, 189
Boston, 101
Bottesford, 99
Bovington, 60
Boy, a Girl and a Bike, A, 22
Boyle, 283
Boyndie, 205
Bracklinn Falls, 245
Bracorina, 238
Branagh, Kenneth, 260
Brassed Off, 10
Braveheart, 233, 282
Bray, Windsor & Maidenhead, 145
Bray, Wicklow, 286
Breaking the Waves, 232
Brent, George, 266
Brentford, 152
Bricket Wood, 79
Brief Encounter, 84, **94**
Brighton Rock, 23
British Film Institute, 157
British Photographic Museum, 57
Brixton, 182
Broad Chalke, 143
Brompton, 168
Brontë, Charlotte, 19
Brontë, Emily, 19
Broughton Castle, 120
Brown, Christy, 267, **269**, 286
Browning Version, The, 63
Broxburn, 245
Brunel University, 165
Buchan, John, 118, 226, **228**
Buchanan, Jack, 207
Bull Inn, The, 99
Burnham Beeches, **31**, 114
Burnley, 96
Burrow Head, 212, 214
Burton, Richard, 87, 118, **254**, 255, 275
Burwash, 68
Byrne's Bookshop, Charlie, 277
Byron, Lord, 116
Cafe de Paris, 197
Caine, Michael, 62, 105, 107, 112, **189**, 200, 256, 268
Camber Sands, 133
Camberley, 78
Camberwell, 189
Cambridge, 38
Cambusbarron, 243
Camden Town, 155, 156
Cameo Cinema, 223
Cammell, Donald, 168, **222**

Campbell, Eric, 206
Camusdarrach Beach, 232
Canterbury Tale, A, 88
Captain Kettle Film Company, 22
Cardross, 209
Carmarthen, 249
Carnarvon, Lord, 76
Carnegie Library, West Bromwich, 124
Carnforth Railway Station, 94
Carrington, 71
Carroll, Lewis, 77
Carroll, Madeleine, **124**, 226
Carry on Sergeant, 133
Cars of the Stars Museum, 48
Castaway, **236**, 286
Castle Combe, 143
Castle Stalker, 245
Castle, Roy, 93
Castlewellan, 262
Caton-Jones, Michael, 100, 238, **245**
Cavell, Edith, **106**, 184
Central Hall Cinema, 96
Central Hotel, Glasgow, 231
Central Station, Glasgow, 231
Chaplin Charlie, 58, **176**, 235, 201, 206
Charing, 86
Chariots of Fire, 146, 148, **227**
Charleson, Ian, 211, **219**, 227
Charlestown Harbour, 45
Cheeta the chimpanzee, 284
Cheltenham Film Society, 75
Cheltenham, 73
Cheney Road, 153
Chester, 41
Chesterton, G.K., 29
Chiddingstone, 90
Childers, Erskine, 265
Christ Church College, 117
Christ Church Meadow, 119
Christian, Fletcher, **47**, 173
Churchtown, 286
Cinegrafix Gallery, 189
Cinema Bookshop, 156
Cinema Store, The, 200
Cinema, The, 215
Cinemania, 275
Citadel, The, 257
Citizen Kane, 259
Claremont Bar, 218
Clark, Petula, 63, **135**
Clarke, Arthur C., 129
Cliddesden, 75
Cliffs of Moher, 264
Clifton Pub, 66
Clockwork Orange, A, 165
Cockermouth, 47

Coliseum Pub, 152
Collectors' Film Conventions, 200
Collins, Michael, 266
Colman, Ronald, 42, 49, 74, 137, **186**
Colne, 96
Comber, 259
Commitments, The, 267
Comrades, 63
Cong, 279
Connery, Sean, 30, 144, 149, 209, **221**, 233, 254
Connolly, Billy, 82, **229**
Conrad, Joseph, 72
Cooper, Gladys, 154
Coronation Hall Pub, 135
Coronet Cinema, 170, 171
Coronet Pub, 167
Corpach, 235
Corsham Court, 12
Cosmo Cinema, 231
Coward, Noel, 94, **185**
Creetown, 214
Crichton Castle, 238
Crieff, 237
Crinan Canal, 209
Crisp, Donald, **237**, 248
Cronin, A.J., 49, **209**, 257
Crow Cragg, 50
Crowborough, 69
Crowcombe Heathfield Station, 129
Crown Pub, Belfast, 261
Cruden Bay, 202
Cruel Sea, The, **57**, 257
Crusoe Hotel, 228
Crusoe, Robinson, 228
Crying Game, The, 32, **166**, 285
Culloden, 236
Culzean Castle, 214
Cumbernauld, 236
Curracloe Beach, 285
Currie, Finlay, 85, 209, **221**, 242
Cushing, Peter, 76, 84, **85**, 146
Dalbeattie, 216
Dambusters, The, **52**, 100, 102, 266
Darlington, 51
Dartmoor, 54
Davenport, Brian, 233
Daviot, 234
Day-Lewis, Daniel, 90, **161**, 267, 286
De Mille, Cecil B., 203
Deanston, 243
Dench, Judi, 82, 90, 119, **149**
Derry, 264
Derwent Valley, 52
Devonport, 57
Dickens, Charles, 86

Didcot Railway Centre, 120
Dingle Peninsula, 277
Disney, Walt, 101
Ditchingham, 106
Dobbin's Restaurant, 269
Doctor Dolittle, 143
Dome Cinema, 141, 142
Donat, Robert, 38, **103**, 226, 251, 257
Doolin, 264
Dorchester, 64
Dorchester-on-Thames, 118
Dorking, 136
Dornie, 233
Dors, Diana, 22, **138**, 146
Douglas, Bill, **59**, 63
Doune Castle, 244
Dower House, 144
Down Place, 145
Downham, 96
Doyle, Sir Arthur Conan, 54, 69, **78**, 225
Dr. Syn, Alias the Scarecrow, 84
Dracula, 42, **109**, 146, 202, 271
Dreamland Cinema, 84
Driscoll, Bobby, 41
Drum, The, 251, 259
Drummond Castle, 238
Dryburgh Abbey, 212
du Maurier, Daphne, 43, 44
Dublin Castle, 267
Dudley, 64, 65
Duke Humphrey's Library, 119
Duke of York's Cinema, 22
Dulwich, 187
Dundee Contemporary Arts, 216
Dunnottar Castle, 203
Dunoon, 206
Duns Castle, 83
Dunston Staithes, 106
Durham, 106
Duxford, 38
Dyrham Park, 11
Ealing Studios, 29, 57, 87, 128, 155, **158**, 174, 187, 199, 208, 247
East Anglian Film Archive, 107
East Cowes, 82
East Preston, 140
Eastbourne, 69
Eastwood, 116
Ebbw Vale, 248
Edge of the World, The, 242
Edinburgh Film Guild, 223
Edinburgh University Film Society, 222
Edison Kinetoscope Parlour, 198
Edison, Thomas, 97
Educating Rita, 268

Index

Edwards, Henry, 137
Eilean Donan Castle, 233
Elan Valley, 256
Electric Cinema, 170
Electric Palace Cinema, 73
Elephant Man, The, **188**, 253
Ellangowan Hotel, 213
Elmbridge Film Heritage Centre, 135
Elsfield, 118
Eltham, 160
Elvis's Palace, 131
Empire Leicester Sq., 171, **201**
Empire Travel Lodge, 209
Epsom, 135
Eton College, 120, **146**
Evans, Maurice, **64**, 232
Ewell, 135
Excalibur, 287
Exeter, 58, 59
Fal, River, 41
Falkirk, 227
Falmouth Arts Centre, 45
Falmouth, 41
Far From the Madding Crowd, 62
Farnham Common, 31
Farnworth, 13
Father Brown, 29
Feeney, John, 276
Ferndale, 256
Fields, Gracie, 122
Film Collection, The, 113
Filmhouse, Edinburgh, 223
Films on Art, 132
Finlayson, Jimmy, 226
Finney, Albert, 63, 115, **124**, 129
First Cinema in Britain, 196
First Public Film Show in Ireland, 272
First Recorded Film Show in Scotland, 221
Fishguard, 255
Fitzgerald, Barry, **269**, 279
Flaherty, Robert, 277
Flashbacks, 193
Fleming, Ian, **144**, 196
Flicker Alley, 199
Floors Castle, 211
Flynn, Errol, 262
Ford, John, 68, 248, 258, **276**, 279
Fordwich, 89
Forest Gate, 184
Formby, George, 139
Forth Rail Bridge, 226
Foula, 242
Four Feathers, The, 22, 151
Four Weddings and a Funeral, 37
Fowey, 43

Foxwold, 90
Frankenstein, 14, **64**, 145
Fraser's Autographs, 198
French Lieutenant's Woman, The, 63
Frensham Common, 134
Friese-Greene, William, **25**, 154, 169
Fu Manchu, 12, 190
Full Metal Jacket, 38, **183**
Full Monty, The, 126
Gainsborough Film Studios, 163
Galway, 277
Garden History, Museum of, 173
Garner, Clive, 147
Garner, James, 113
Garson, Greer, 49, 184, **262**
Gate Cinema, 170
Gatehouse of Fleet, 214
Gatwick Airport, 141
Genevieve, **31**, 72
Gerrard's Cross, 29
Get Carter, 105
Gilfach Goch, 248
Gilliat, Sidney, 131
Girl on a Motorcycle, 78
Glan-yr-Afon, 250
Glasgow Film Theatre, 231
Glasgow Museum of Transport, 231
Glastonbury, 128
Glen Cinema Disaster, 239
Glen Nevis, 233
Glencoe, **235**, 245
Gloucester, 74
Go-Between, The, 107
Godden, Rumer, **69**, 141
Gods and Monsters, 65
Goldeneye, 121
Golders Green Crematorium, 271
Goldfinger, **30**, 149
Goodbye Mr. Chips, **38**, **53**, 63, 143, 163, 263
Grade, Lew, 152
Grangegorman Hospital, 267
Grangemouth, 227
Granger, Stewart, **14**, 68, 106, 134
Grant, Cary, **27**, 182
Gravesend, 83
Great Central Railway, 99
Great Escape, The, 113
Great Expectations, **85**, 259
Great Lever, 13
Great Maytham Hall, 87
Green, F.L., **78**, 261
Greenlaw, 210
Gregory's Girl, 236
Greystoke, 73, **211**
Grierson, John, **243**, 265

Grimethorpe, 10
Grizedale Forest Park, 48
Guildford, 133
Guinness, Alec, 87
Gunnersbury, 165
Hadrian's Wall, 114
Haggard, Henry Rider, 106
Halifax, 37
Hall, Willis, 96, **98**
Halliwell, Leslie, 13
Hammer Studios, 145
Hampstead, 150, 154
Hancock, Tony, **14**, 141
Hard Day's Night, A, 129
Hardwicke, Cedric, **66**, 135
Harlesden, 152
Harpenden, 80
Harrison, Rex, **93**, 143
Hartfield, 71
Hartley, Wallace, 95
Harwich, 73
Hatfield House, 211
Hatfield, 81
Hathersage, 52
Havelock-Allan, Anthony, **51**, 85, 94, 259, 277
Haverthwaite, 48
Hawkins, Jack, 57, **163**
Haworth, 16, 19
Hay, Will, 58, 75, **131**, 182
Haywards Heath, 70
Headington Quarry, 117
Hear My Song, 264
Heathfield Hospital, 133
Heaven's Gate, 117
Helensburgh, 207, 208
Hempel Hotel, 171
Henderson, Bob, 246
Henry V, 287
Hepworth Studios, 137
Hepworth, Cecil, 137
Heroes of the Telemark, The, 121
Hertford College Bridge, 117
Hever, 87
Highbury, 167
Highclere, 76
Highgate Cemetery, 154
Highlander, **233**, 235
Hilton, James, 38, 49, **142**
Hitchcock, Alfred, 44, 49, 163, **191**, 226
Hobson, Valerie, 85, 87, 252, **258**
Holborn, 155, 196
Holkam Estate, 120
Holloway, 167
Holloway, Stanley, 94, 128, **140**, 174
Holsworthy, 266

Hope, Anthony, 134
Hope, Bob, 160
Hopetoun, 219
Hopkins, Anthony, 11, 79, 118, 188, **253**
Hordern, Michael, **80**, 87
Horrocks, Jane, 112
Horton-cum-Studley, 119
Hound of the Baskervilles, The, **54**, 134
Hour of the Eagle, The, 226
How Green Was My Valley, 238, **248**, 274, 276
Howard, Leslie, **187**, 274
Howard, Trevor, **84**, 94, 277
Howards End, **118**, 149, 253
Hoxton, 162, 163
Hucknall, 116
Huddersfield, 92
Hue and Cry, 187
Hughes, Thomas, **118**, 140
Huish, 144
Hull, Edith Maude, 52
Huntley Film Archives, 167
Huyton, 93
I Know Where I'm Going, 209
Idehill, 90
If, 73
Ilford, 184
Ilkeston, 53
Imperial War Museum Film & Video Archive, 171
Ingram, Rex, 61, 89, **270**
Inn of the Sixth Happiness, The, 77, 104, 158, **250**
Innes, Hammond, 132
Innocents, The, 70
Institute of Cinematographers, 135
Iona, 232
Ipswich, 132
Irish Film Centre, 276
Irvine, Lucy, **236**, 286
Islay, 208
Isle of Skye, 232
It's A Wonderful Life, 113
Jackson, Glenda, 146
Jamaica Inn, **44**, 274
James Bond, 30, 120, 144, 149, 172, 221, 254
Jarman, Derek, 88
Jeffries, Lionel, 15
Jennings, Humphrey, 132
Johnson, Celia, 94, **116**, 134, 218
Joint, The, 24
Jones, John Paul, 215
Jordan, Neil, 284
Josef Locke, 264

Joyce, James, 272
Jump the Gun, 24
Kane, Whitford, 259
Karas, Anton, 166
Karloff, Boris, 65, **133**
Karno, Fred, **58**, 207
Kay, Christina, 185, **218**
Keighley and Worth Valley Railway, 15
Kelso, 210, 211
Kendall, Kay, 31, **72**
Kensal Green, 163
Kensington Gardens, 211
Kenwood House, 171
Kerr, Deborah, 70, 106, 134, 141, **208**
Kerr, Ian, 227
Kersey, 132
Keswick, 48
Kew, 186
Kidnapped, 210
Kilmallock Film Archive, 278
Kilmarnock Arms Hotel, 202
Kilruddery House, 287
Kind Hearts and Coronets, **87**, 259
Kinema in the Woods, 102
King Arthur's Castle Hotel, 43
King Arthur, 128, 249
King Kong, 30
King's Cross, 153
Kingston Museum, 26
Kinlochleven, 238
Kinsale, 265
Kipling, Rudyard, **68**, 74
Kirkbean, 215
Kirkcaldy, 228
Kirkcudbright, 213
Kirriemuir, 205, 206
Knebworth House, 82
Knights of the Round Table, 287
Krays, The, 160
Kubrick, Stanley, **81**, 130, 165, 183
Lady Vanishes, The, 77, 163
Ladykillers, The, 153, **155**
Lakeside & Haverthwaite Railway, 48
Lamas, 107
Lambeth Workhouse, 177
Larbert, 226
Larne, 258
Lasham, 76
Laugharne, 255
Laughton, Charles, **108**, 195
Laurel & Hardy Museum, 45
Laurel & Hardy, 59, 98, 99, 227, 230
Laurel, Stan, **45**, 58, 67, 108, 229
Lawrence of Arabia, **60**, 252
Lawrence, D.H., 116
Le Prince, Louis, 97

Lean, David, 61, 85, 94, 139, **157**, 277
Leatherhead, 134
Lee, Christopher, 76, 111, **195**, 212
Leeds Castle, 88
Leigh, Mike, 123
Leigh, Vivien, 193
Lerwick, 242
Let it Be, 200
Lewis, C.S., 79, **117**
Leys School, The, 39
Leytonstone, 191
Liddel, Alice, 77
Limehouse, 190
Limelight Cinema, 65
Limerick Film Archive, 278
Lincoln, 102
Linlithgow Film Society, 246
Lion, **103**, 128
Little John, 52
Little Marlow, 30
Little Voice, 112
Llanfrothen, 251
Llewellyn, Richard, **248**, 279
Llewelyn, Desmond, 254
Local Hero, **204**, **232**, 242
Lochailort, 232
Lochgilphead, 209
Lochinch Castle, 214
Locks Restaurant, 267
London Hospital, 188
London Polytechnic Institute, 198
London Transport Museum Film Collection, 194
London Video Art Archive, 155
Longmoor Military Railway, 77
Loot, 23
Losey, Joseph, 107, **167**
Lost Horizon, 143
Loughborough, 99
Lower Beeding, 140
Lower Edmonton, 158
Lower Largo, 228
Lowndes Arms, The, 167
Lucan, Arthur, 91, 101
Lullington, 70
Lulworth, 63
Lumière's 'Cinematographe', 198
Luton Hoo, 87
Lux Centre, 162
Lye, 66
Lyme Regis, 63
Lyndhurst, 77
Macbeth & Duncan, 232
MacInnes, Hamish, 235
Mackay, Fulton, 204, **241**
MacLean, Alistair, 234

Index

Magdalen College, 119
Maggie, The, 208
Magic Umbrella, The, 225
Maidenhead Town Hall, 133
Maidstone, 87
Mallaig, 232
Man for all Seasons, A, 12, 119
Man of Aran, 277
Manor Park, 184
Mansfield College, 117
Marble Hill House, 120
Margam, 253
Margate, 84
Mark Ash, 114
Marriott, Moore, 75
Martello Tower, Dublin, 273
Marylebone Crematorium, 105
Marylebone, 195
Mason's Arms, 176
Mason, A.E.W., **151**, 252
Mason, James, **92**, 261
Matter of Life and Death, A, 60
Mayfair, 196, 200
McCormick, F.J., 262
McGregor, Ewan, 10, 217, **237**
McKellen, Ian, 65
Megginch Castle, 238
Melbourne-Cooper, Arthur, 80
Melton Constable, 107
Memphis Belle, **100**, 246
Menzies, William Cameron, 42, **238**
Merlin, 249
Merrion Hall, 264
Metropolitan Hotel, 171
Michael Collins, 260, **266**, 285
Midford, 128
Milland, Ray, 74, **253**
Mills, Hayley, 96
Milltown House, 278
Milngavie, 216
Milton Abbas, 63
Minehead, 129
Mitchum, Robert, 278
Moby Dick, 265
Moffat, Graham, 75
Mompesson House, 145
Monkton Combe, 128
Monty Python and the Holy Grail, 235, **244**
Moon Under the Water Pub, 103
Moon, Lorna, 203
Moore, Dudley, 150
Moore, Roger, `120, **172**
Morar Hotel, 233
More, Kenneth, 122, 226
Morecambe, Eric, 80

Moreton, 60
Morley, Robert, 148
Morpeth, 113
Morrison's Academy, 237
Mrs. Brown, 82
Mrs. Miniver, **143**, 263
Mugdock Country Park, 217
Mull, 209
Murdoch, William, 216
Mutiny on the Bounty, 47, 173
Muybridge, Eadweard, **91**, 169
My Left Foot, 267, 269, **286**
Nairn, 235
Nantmor, 250
Napier University, 245
National Film Theatre, 174
National Library of Wales Sound & Moving Image Collection, 249
National Motorcycle Museum, 139
National Museum of Photography, Film & Television, 19
National Velvet, 68
National Video Archive of Stage *Performance,* 197
Natural History Museum, 211
Neagle, Anna, 107, **184**
Neath, 253
Neeson, Liam, 238, **260**, 266
Nene Valley Railway, 120
Nesbit, Edith, 15, **83**
Nettlebed, 116
Nettlecombe Court, 129
Nettlefold Studios, 138
New Palace Centre, 210
Newport, 254
Newton Hotel, 235
Newton Stewart, 214, 215
Newton, Robert, 41, 140, 262, 287
Night of the Demon, 79
Night to Remember, A, 164
Niven, David, 60, 68, 144, **205**
No Highway in the Sky, 78
North Runcton, 107
North Shields, 108
North West Film Archive, 103
Norton Disney, 101
Norwich, 107
Notting Hill, 170, 171
Notting Hill, 171
O'Hara, Maureen, 248, **273**, 279
O'Sullivan, Maureen, 283
O'Toole, Peter, 61, 63, **98**, 255
Oakley Court, 145
Obby Oss Festival, 41
Oberon, Merle, 78, **197**
Ockham, 135

Octopussy, 120
Odd Man Out, 78, **261**
Odeon Leicester Sq., 201
Odeon, Muswell Hill, 164
Odeon, Salisbury, 144
Odeon, Weston-super-Mare, 108
Odette, 184
Offstage Theatre & Film Bookshop, 156
Oh! What a Lovely War, 23
Oh, Mr. Porter!, 75, 163
Old Ferry Inn, The, 42
Old Flying Machine Company, The, 38
Old Mother Riley, 91, **101**
Old Romney, 88
Old Wardour Castle, 114
Oldest Building to Screen Films, 41
Olivier, Laurence, 62, **136**, 287
One That Got Away, The, 48
Orwell, George, 117
Osborne House, 83
Overton House, 245
Oxford, 117, 118, 120
Paddington, 199
Padstow, 41
Paignton, 59
Paisley, 239, 241
Palin, Michael, **127**, 245
Paradine Case, The, 49
Parker, Alan, 64
Passport to Pimlico, 174
Pat Cohan's Bar, 280
Pathead Beach, 228
Paul, Robert, **155**, 169
Payne, Laurence, 221
Peeping Tom, 169
Pender, Bob, 27, **182**
Pennan, 204
Penshurst Place, 87
Performance, 168
Peter Pan, 81, 206
Petwood Hotel, 100
Phoenix Park, 269
Pickard's Museum, 229
Picture House Pub, Ebbw Vale, 248
Picture House Pub, Stafford, 130
Picture House, Stratford-on-Avon, 140
Picture House, Campbeltown, 210
Pictureville Cinema, 20
Pirbright, 135
Planet Hollywood, 141, 198, 275
Planet of the Apes, 64
Playhouse Cinema, Beverley, 72
Plaza Pub, 131
Plockton, 214
Plymouth, 59
Pocahontas, 83

Polnish, 233
Pontrhydyfen, 254
Port Logan, 214
Port William, 214
Portman & Pickles Pub, 37
Potter, Beatrix, 48
Powderham Castle, 12
Powell, Michael, 42, 60, 63, 69, **74**, 88, **89**, 132, 138, 141, 169, 209, 242
Powerscourt Estate, 287
Presley, Elvis, 131
Pressburger, Emeric, 60, 63, 88, 89, **132**, 141, 209
Prime of Miss Jean Brodie, The, 185, **218**
Prisoner of Zenda, The, 134
Private Function, A, 22
Punch and Judy Man, The, 14, **141**
Quadrophenia, 24
Quayle, Anthony, 87, **125**
Queen Victoria's Diamond Jubilee Screening, 20
Queen's Head Pub, 180
Quiet Man, The, 258, 270, 274, 276, **279**
Radcliffe Camera, 119
Railway Children, The, **15**, 83
Rains, Claude, 175
Randalstown, 258
Randolph Hotel, 119
Random Harvest, **49**, 263
Rank, J. Arthur, **90**, 113, 163
Rare Discs, 156
Rathdrum, 267
Rattigan, Terence, 61, 63, **163**
Reach for the Sky, 122
Rebecca, 43
Reed, Carol, 49, **165**, 261
Reed, Oliver, 116, 236, **286**
Regal Moon Pub, 123
Regal Pub, 74
Regeneration, 245
Regent Pub, 134
Remains of the Day, The, **11**, 253
Rennie, Michael, 18
Repton, 53
Rhinog Fawr, 251
Ricardo's Snooker Hall, 268
Richardson, Ralph, **73**, 151, 154, 211
Richmond, 134
Riddle of the Sands, The, 265
Rintoul, Ian, 225, 226
Ritz Hotel, 171
Ritz Pub, 102
Ritzy Cinema, 182
River Coe Restaurant, 235
Rob Roy, 212, 235, **238**, 243, 246, 260

Robin Hood's Bay, 113
Robin Hood, 92
Robin Hood: Prince of Thieves, 114
Rogers, Roy, 231
Rohmer, Sax, **12**, 190
Rolvenden, 87
Romney Marsh, 84
Room at the Top, 21
Room with a View, A, 90
Rosses Point, 284
Rotherfield Peppard, 118
Rottingdean, 68
Roxy, 210
Royal College of Surgeons of Edinburgh, 225
Rugby, 140
Rugeley, 131
Ruislip, 164
Rustington, 142
Rutherford, Margaret, 29, 174, **192**
Ryan's Daughter, 277
Sabu, 69, 251
Sale, 138
Salford, 123, 124
Samuelson, G,B., 125
Samuelson, Sir Sydney, 125
Sapper, 42
Saturday Night and Sunday Morning, 115
Saunton, 60
Saving Private Ryan, 45, **81**, 235, **285**
Scala Cinema, 53
Scala Picture House Tragedy, 21
Scarborough, 108, 112
Scene From Leeds Bridge, A, 97
Schilling, Paul, 64
Scholes, 93
Science Museum, 169
Scott, Sir Walter, **211**, 238, 243
Scottish Film & Television Archive, 230
Seaford, 70
Secret Garden, The, 87
Sedgley, 66
Selkirk, Alexander, 228
Sellers, Peter, **121**, 155
Selling, 89
Sennen, 42
Servant, The, 71, **168**
Seven Sisters Cliffs, 114
Sevenhampton, 144
Severn Valley Railway, 149
Sewell, Anna, 107
Shadowlands, **79**, 100, 118
Shaffer, Anthony, 62, 212
Shaftesbury Arts Centre Film Society, 64
Shaftesbury, 62

Shakespeare in Love, 119
Shallow Grave, 216, 224
Shannonsbridge, 267
Shap, 50
Shaw, George Bernard, 274
Shaw, Robert, 12, 119
Sheldonian Theatre, 117, 119
Shelley, Mary, 14
Sherborne School, 63
Sheriffmuir, 245
Sherlock Holmes, 54, 69, 78, 134, 201, 225
Shetland Film Club, 242
Shields, Arthur, **269**, 278
Shottenden, 89
Sillitoe, Alan, 115
Sim, Alistair, **220**, 224
Slains Castle, 202
Sleddale Hall, 50
Sleuth, 62
Small Back Room, The, 63
Smith, C. Aubrey, **22**, 151
Smith, Maggie, 87, 90, **184**, 218
Soho, 193, 199
South East Film & Video Archive, 25
South Queensferry, 226
Southport, 125
Southsea, 121
Spark, Muriel, 219
Spence, Noel, 259
Spiddal, 276
Spread Eagle Bookshop, 161
Spy Who Came In from the Cold, The, 254, **275**
Squadron 992, 226
St. Albans, 80, 81
St. Andrews, 227
St. Bride's Centre, 225
St. Buryan, 44
St. George's Hall Pub, 27
St. Lukes, 166
St. Mark's Church, 179
St. Mary's in the Marsh, 83
St. Mary's Marshes, 85
St. Ninian's Cave, 214
St. Pancras, 153
St. Trinneans School, 224
Stafford, 130
Stag's Head Pub, 269
Stage Door Prints, 199
Stan Laurel Inn, 46
Stanford-Le-Hope, 72
Stanley and Livingstone, 66
Stanley, Henry Morton, 135
Stars Look Down, The, 49
Steeton, 22

Index

Stevenage, 82
Stevenson, Robert Louis, 210, **217**
Stillorgan Park Hotel, 269
Stirling Castle, 244
Stockwell, 175
Stoke Poges Golf Club, 30
Stoker, Bram, 109, 202, **271**
Stonehaven, 203
Stoughton, 133
Strand, 194, 197, 198, 199, 200, 201
Stranraer, 214
Stratford-on-Avon, 140
Straw Dogs, 44
Streatham, 182
Strichen, 203
Studley Priory, 119
Summer Isles Hotel, 236
Sunningdale, 146
Surbiton, 135
Sutton Courtenay, 91, 117
Swardeston, 106
Symond's Yat Rock, 79
Syon Park, 152
Talacre Beach, 102
Tankard, The, 176
Taylor, Alma, 137
Taylor, Elizabeth, 68, **150**, 254, 255
Teddington, 185
The Lumière, 223
Theatre Museum, 197
Thief of Baghdad, The, 42
Third Man, The, 84
Thirty-Nine Steps, The, 149, **226**, 228, 235
Thompson, J. Lee, 26
Thomsett, Sally, 16
Three Stags, The, 176
Tintagel, 42
Titanic, 216
Titfield Thunderbolt, The, 103, **128**
Todd, Richard, 52, **266**
Tolkien, J.R.R., 117
Tom Brown's Schooldays, 66, 118, **140**
Tom Jones, 129
Toome, 266
Torbay Cinema, 59
Torguish House, 234
Totnes, 57
Tourneur, Jacques, 80
Travers, Henry, 49, **113**, 135
Treasure Island, 41
Treherbert, 257
Trim Castle, 282
Trinity College, Dublin, **269**, 275
Tudor Cinema, 259
Tunes of Glory, 244

Turn of the Tide, 113
Turnerspuddle, 60
Turville, 29
Tutankhamen, 76
Tyneside Cinema, 105
Uffington, 118
Ultimate Picture Palace, 120
Ulverston, 45
Ulysses, 273
Under Milk Wood, 255
Uphall Station, 246
Uxbridge, 165
Valentino, Rudolph, 53
Vintage Magazine Co. Ltd., 199
Volta Cinema, 272
Walberswick, 132
Wallace, Edgar, 30
Walton-on-Thames, 134, 137
War of the Worlds, 133
Wareham, 60
Wargrave, 148
Warren, Gary, 16
Water Oakley, 145
Watercress Line, The, 78
Waterhouse, Keith, 96, **98**
Waterloo Station, 24
Waterloo, 174
Watkins, Peter, 236
Watt, Harry, 226
Wayne, John, **258**, 274, 276, 279
Weir, Peter, 235
Welles, Orson, 259
Wells, H.G., 133
Went The Day Well?, 29
West Bromwich, 124
West End Cinema, 197
West Heath, 151
West Kilburn, 194
West Somerset Railway, 129
Westhoughton, 12
Westminster, 200
Weston-super-Mare, 12
Wexham, 34
Weybridge, 135
Whale, James, 64, 109
Whisky Galore, 247
Whistle Down the Wind, 96
Whitby, 109
Whitchurch, 79
White Lion Inn, 250
White, Chrissie, 137
Whithorn, 214
Whitstable, 85
Wicker Man, The, 41, **212**
Wickhambreaux, 88
Wigan Pier, 143

Wilde, Oscar, 275
Willesden, 152
Williams, Emlyn, 250
Williams, Kenneth, 153
Williton, 129
Wilton House, 83, 144
Windswept Film Society, 256
Wingham, 89
Wisdom, Norman, 194
Wish You Were Here, 141, 142
Withernsea, 72
Withnail and I, 49
Woking, 133
Wolvercote Cemetery, 117
Wood Green, 163
Woodhall Spa, 100, 102
Woodley, 122
Woolmer Forest, 77
Woolton Picture House, 102
Woolwich, 162
Workington, 49
Worston, 96
Worthing, 141, 142
Wray, Cecil, 22
Wrecker, The, 76
Wren, P.C., 74
Wuthering Heights, 19
Wyler, William, 100
Yanks, 22
Youghal, 265
Young Winston, 77
Zeffirelli's, 49
Zillessen, Marcel, 113
Zulu, 149, **254**, 257
Zwemmers, 196